천랑열전 4

天狼熱戰

Chun Rhang Yhur Jhun

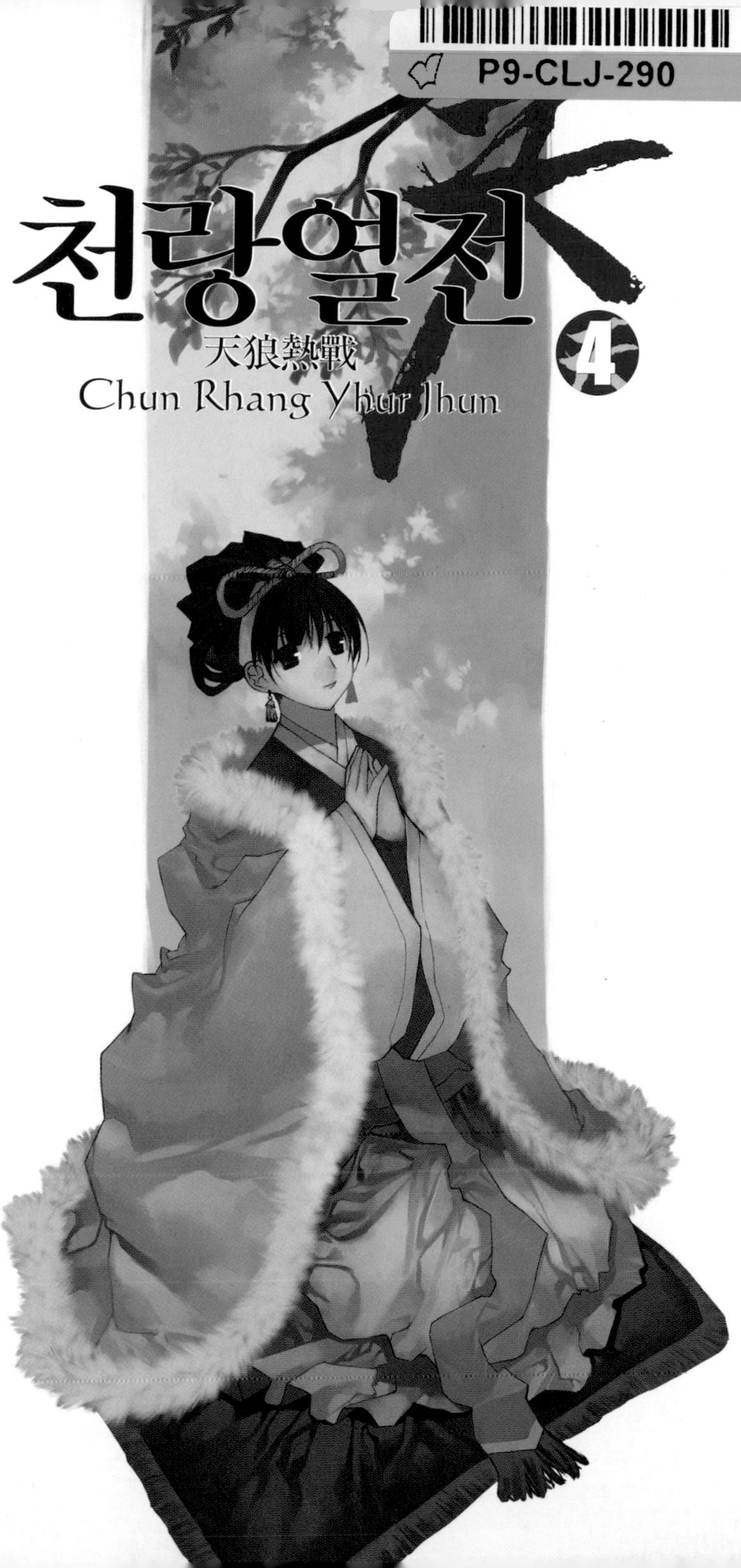

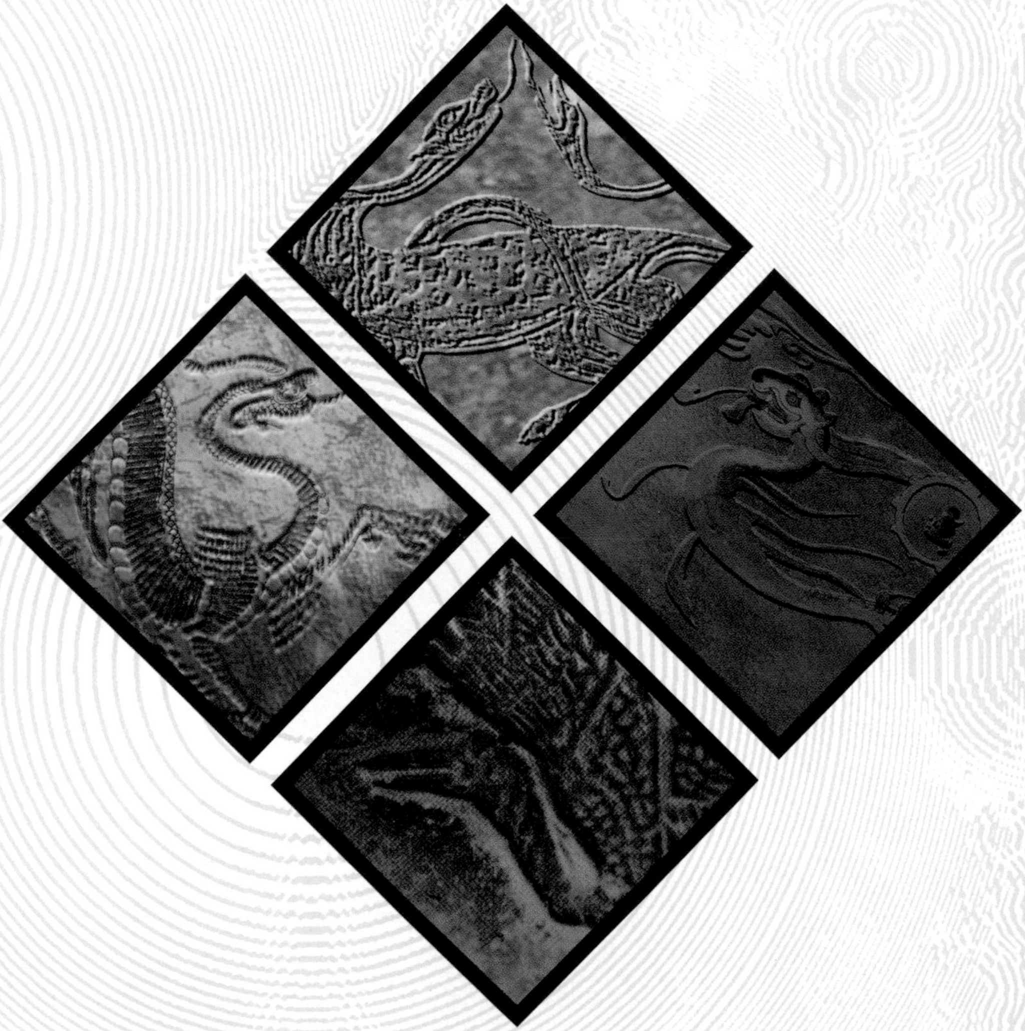

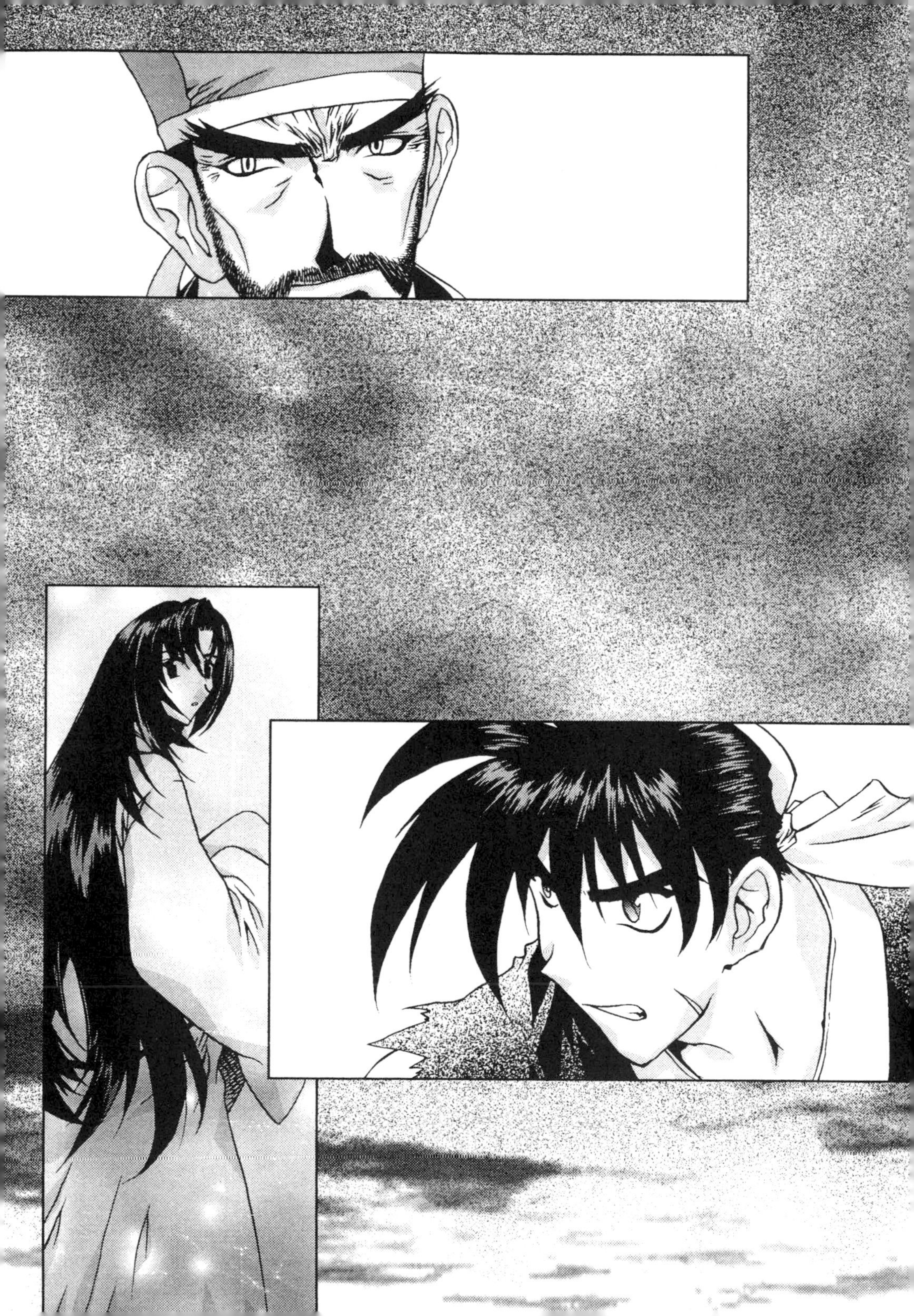

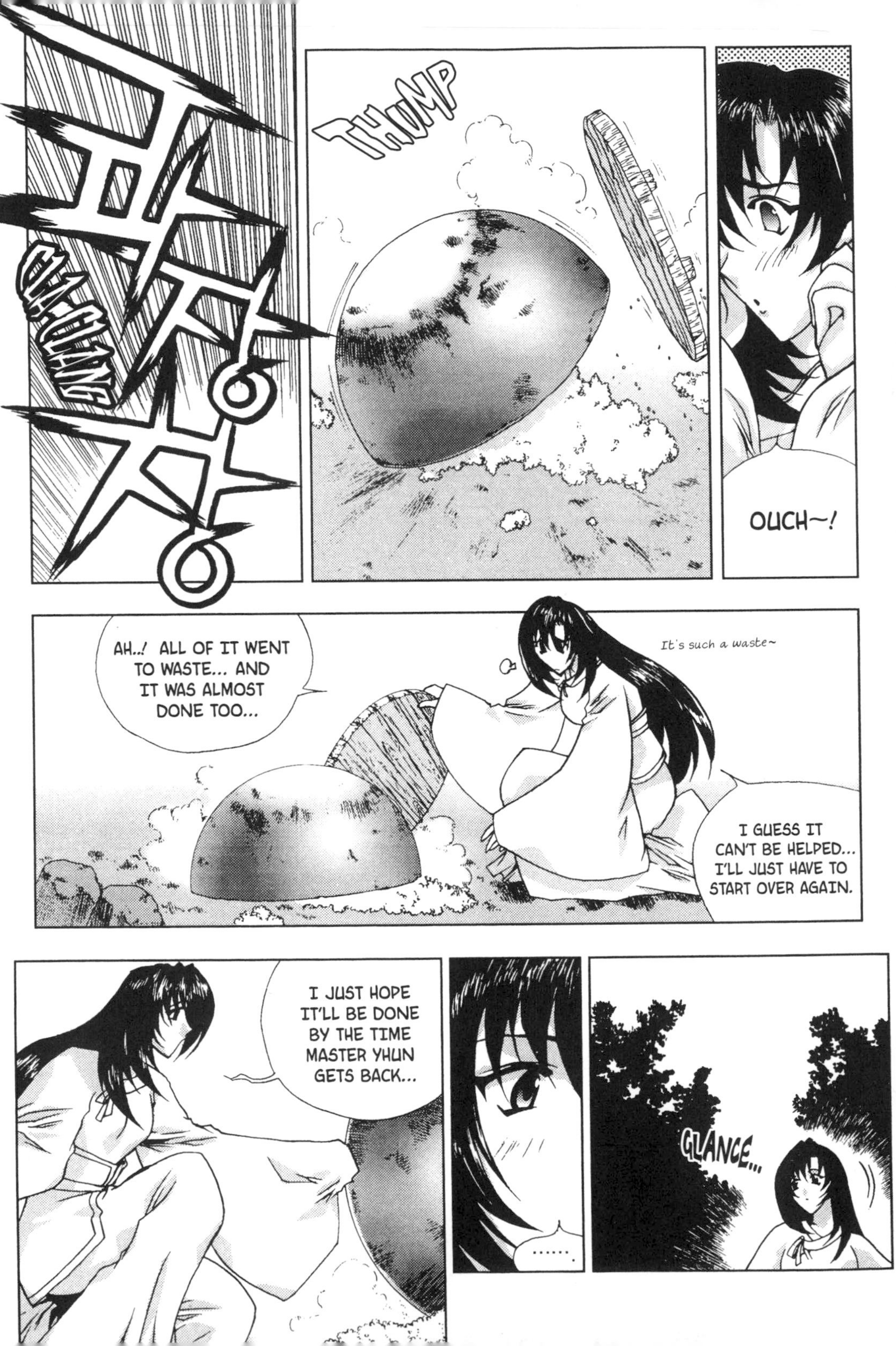
THUMP
OUCH~!
AH..! ALL OF IT WENT TO WASTE... AND IT WAS ALMOST DONE TOO...
It's such a waste~
I GUESS IT CAN'T BE HELPED... I'LL JUST HAVE TO START OVER AGAIN.
I JUST HOPE IT'LL BE DONE BY THE TIME MASTER YHUN GETS BACK...
......
GLANCE...

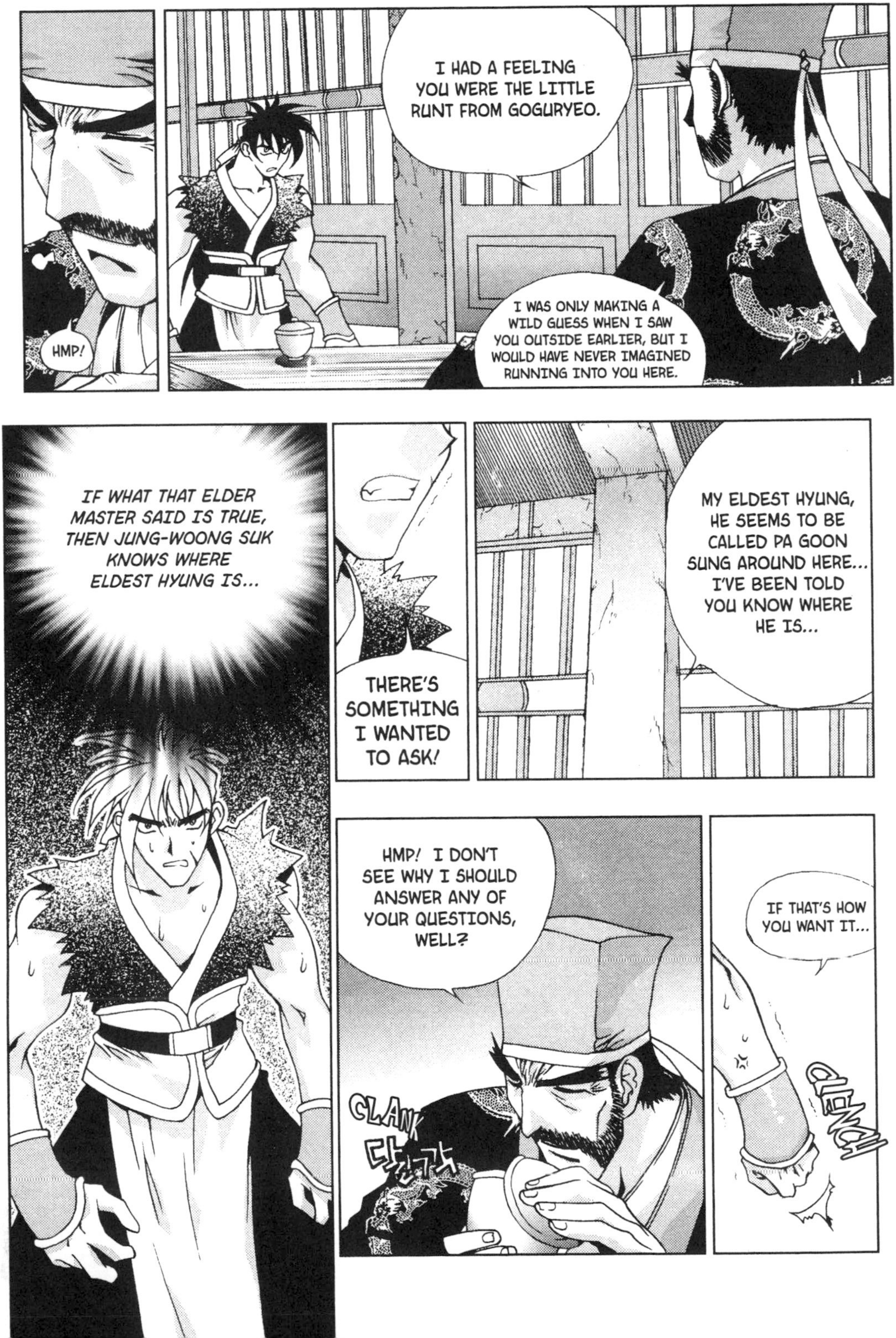
HMP!
I HAD A FEELING YOU WERE THE LITTLE RUNT FROM GOGURYEO.
I WAS ONLY MAKING A WILD GUESS WHEN I SAW YOU OUTSIDE EARLIER, BUT I WOULD HAVE NEVER IMAGINED RUNNING INTO YOU HERE.
IF WHAT THAT ELDER MASTER SAID IS TRUE, THEN JUNG-WOONG SUK KNOWS WHERE ELDEST HYUNG IS...
THERE'S SOMETHING I WANTED TO ASK!
MY ELDEST HYUNG, HE SEEMS TO BE CALLED PA GOON SUNG AROUND HERE... I'VE BEEN TOLD YOU KNOW WHERE HE IS...
HMP! I DON'T SEE WHY I SHOULD ANSWER ANY OF YOUR QUESTIONS, WELL?
CLANK
IF THAT'S HOW YOU WANT IT...
CLENCH

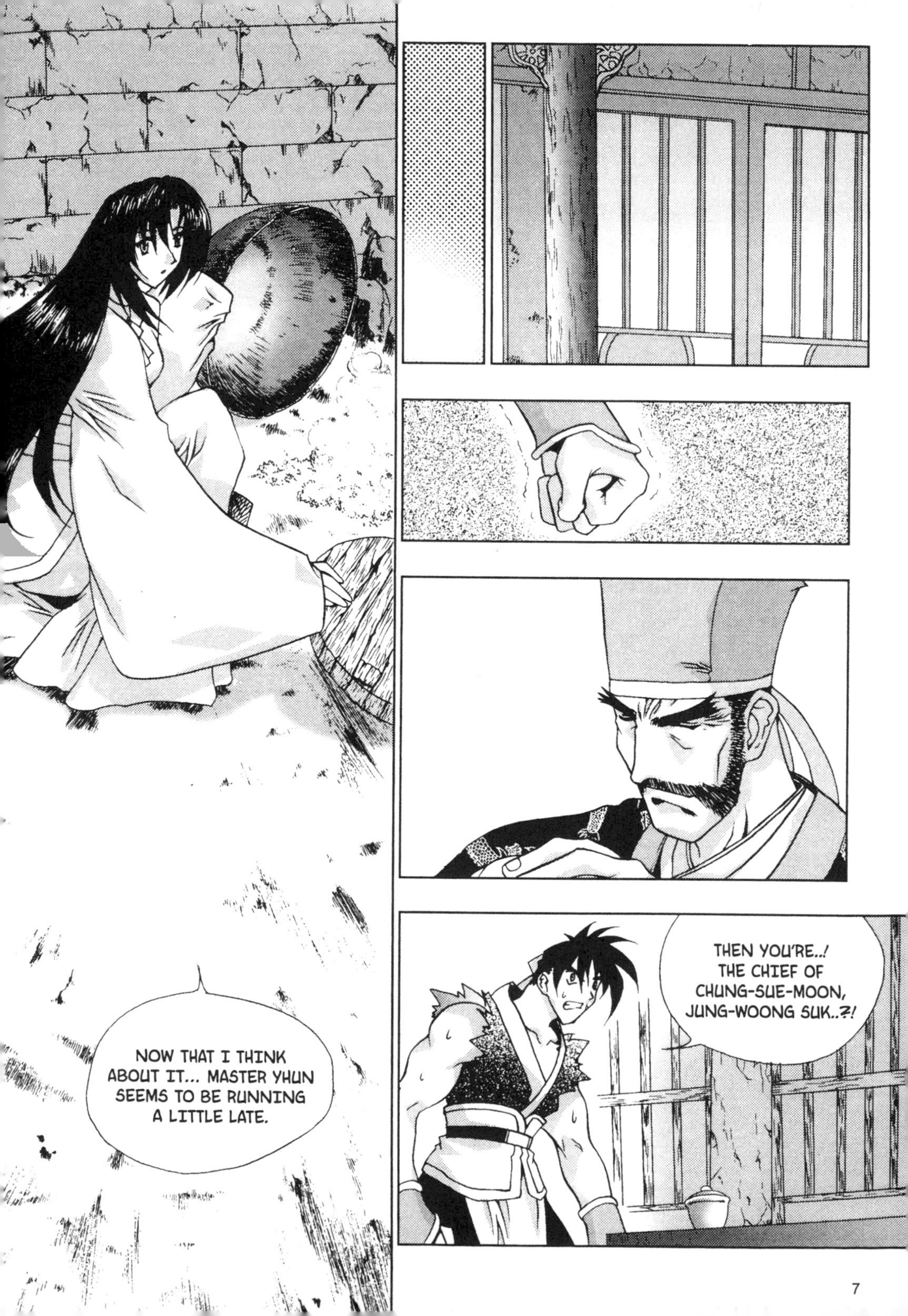
NOW THAT I THINK ABOUT IT... MASTER YHUN SEEMS TO BE RUNNING A LITTLE LATE.
THEN YOU'RE..! THE CHIEF OF CHUNG-SUE-MOON, JUNG-WOONG SUK..?!

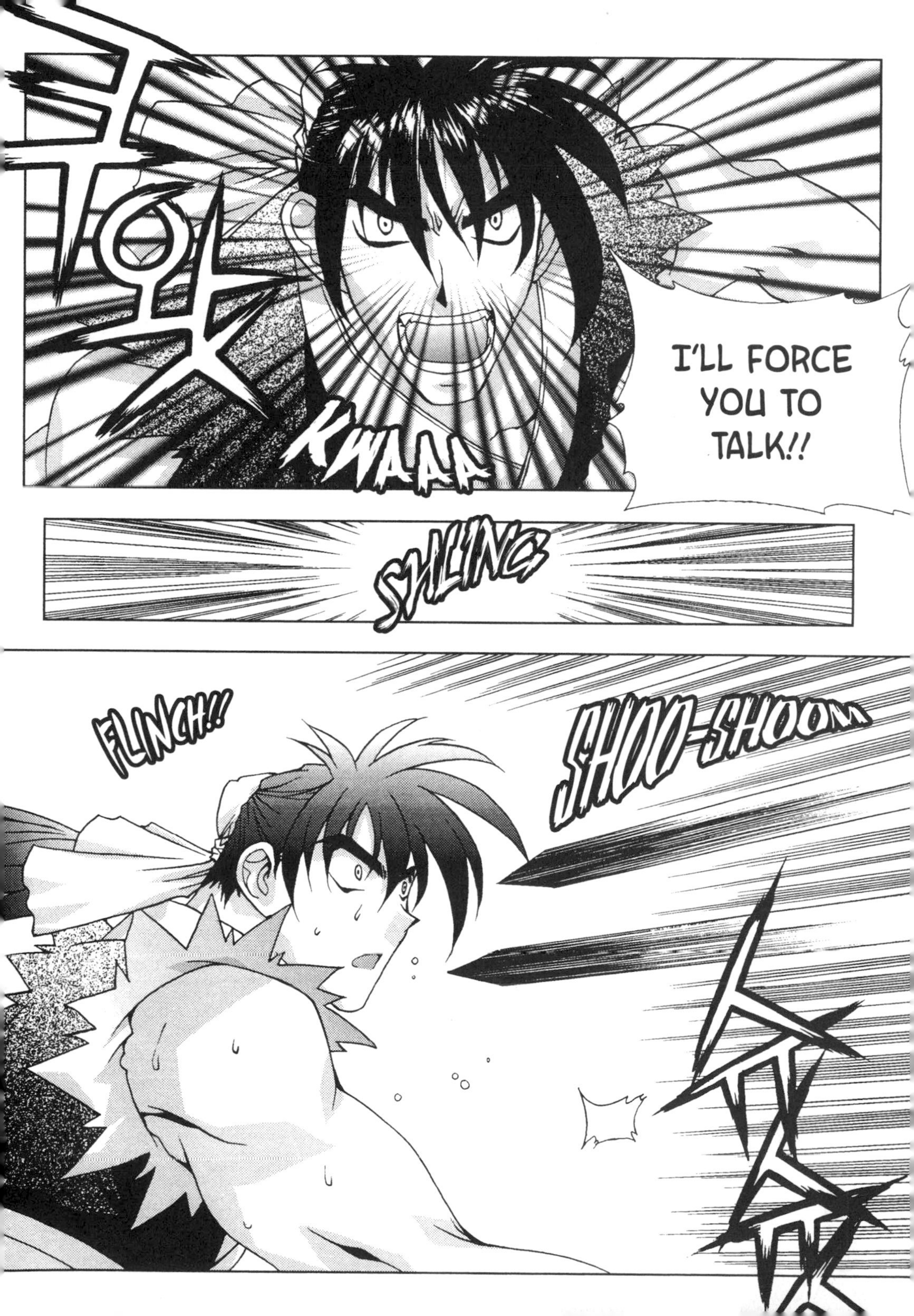

KWAAA
I'LL FORCE YOU TO TALK!!
SHLING
SHOO-SHOOM
FLINCH!!

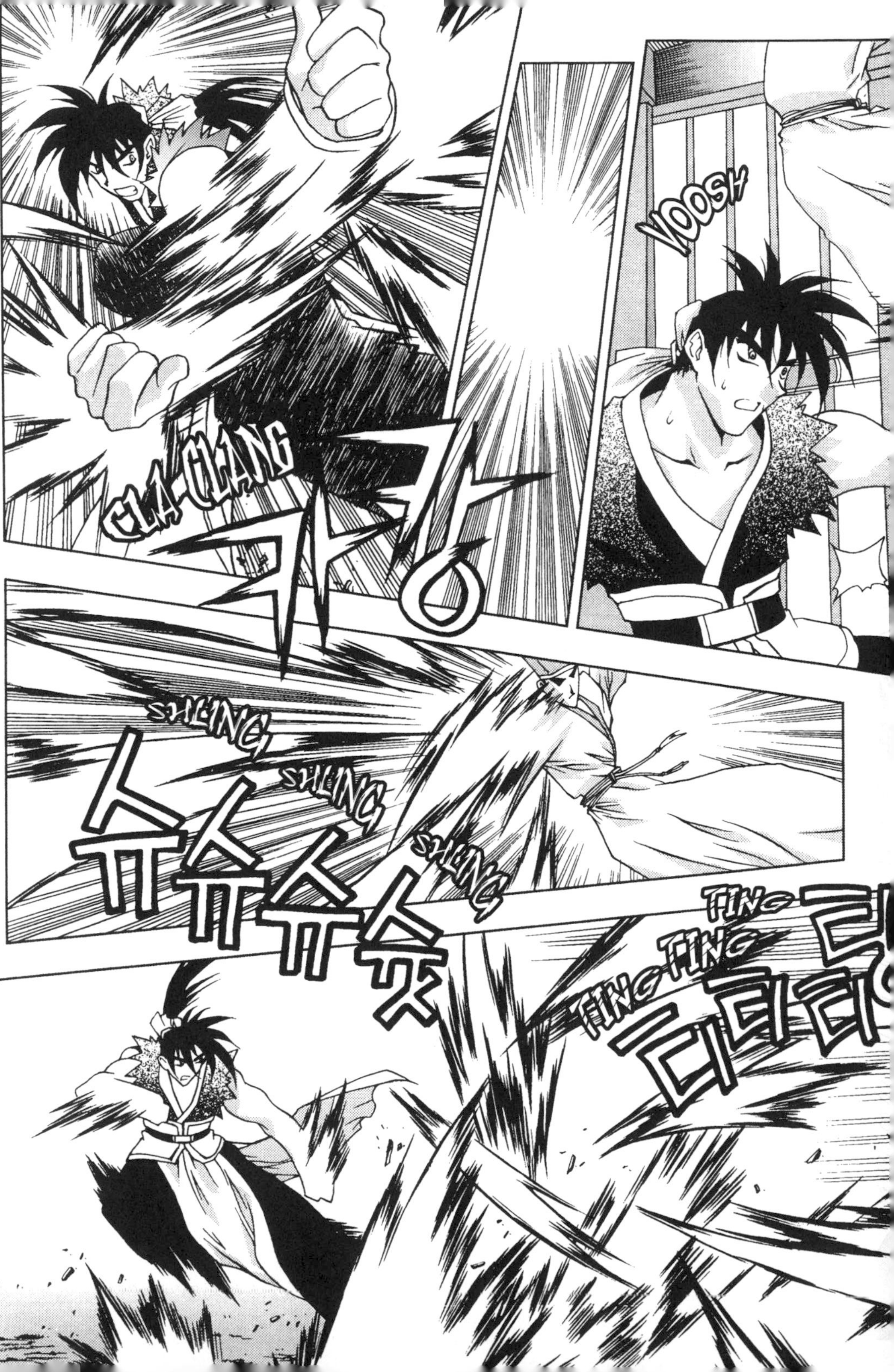
CLA-CLANG
VOOSH
SHLING,
SHLING,
SHLING
TING-TING
TING

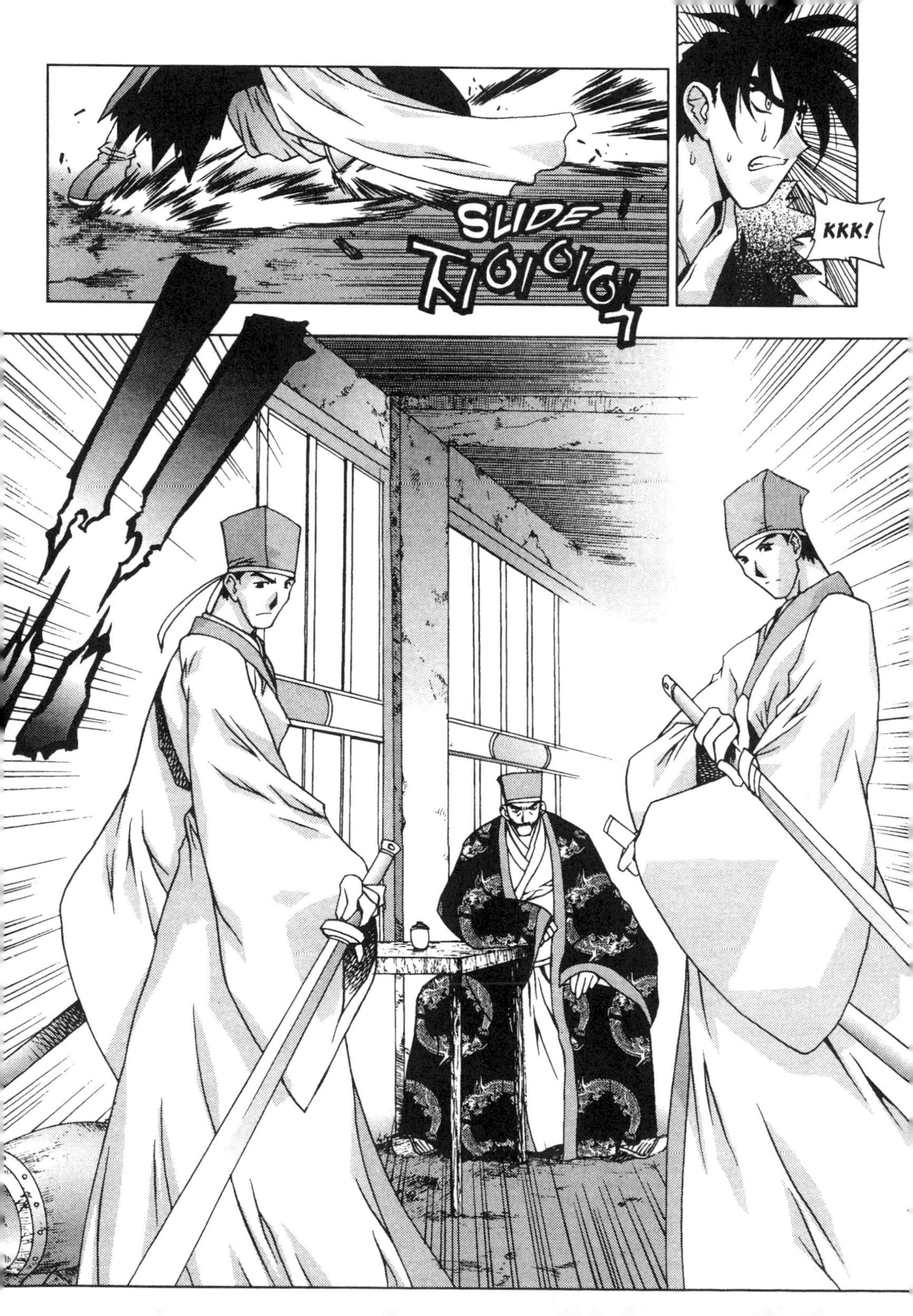
KKK!
SLIDE
지이이익

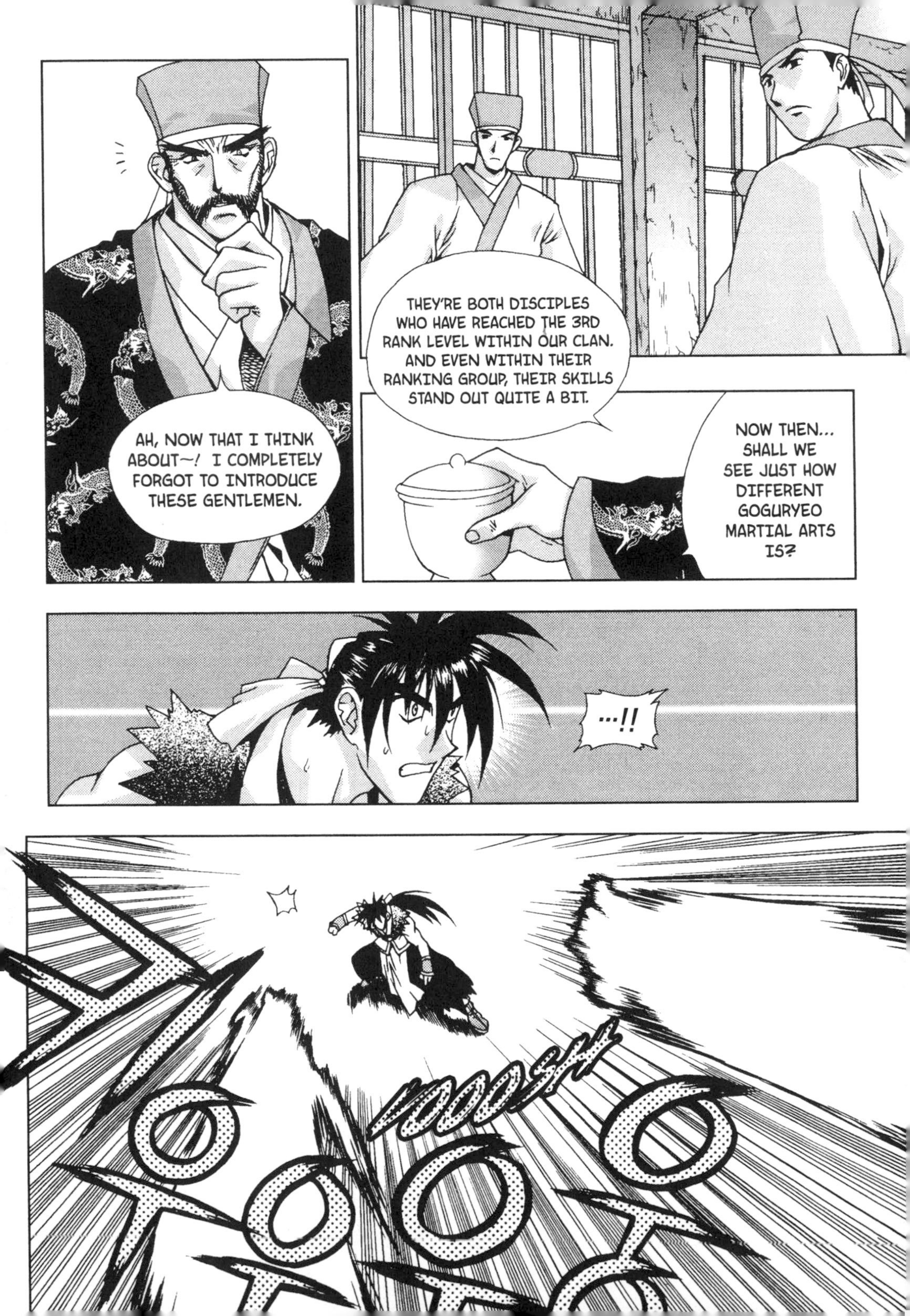
AH, NOW THAT I THINK ABOUT~! I COMPLETELY FORGOT TO INTRODUCE THESE GENTLEMEN.
THEY'RE BOTH DISCIPLES WHO HAVE REACHED THE 3RD RANK LEVEL WITHIN OUR CLAN. AND EVEN WITHIN THEIR RANKING GROUP, THEIR SKILLS STAND OUT QUITE A BIT.
NOW THEN... SHALL WE SEE JUST HOW DIFFERENT GOGURYEO MARTIAL ARTS IS?
...!!
WOOOSH

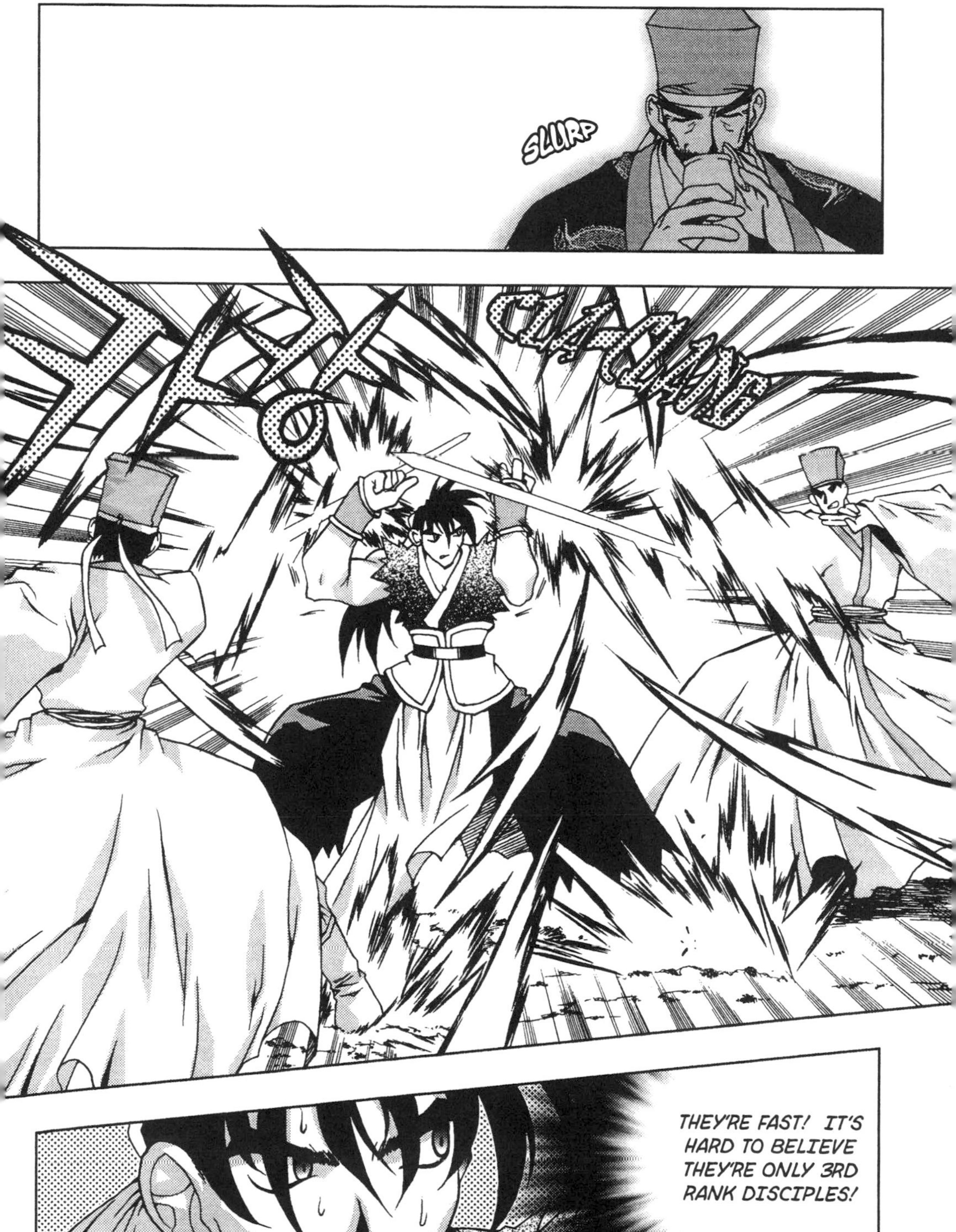
SLURP
THEY'RE FAST! IT'S HARD TO BELIEVE THEY'RE ONLY 3RD RANK DISCIPLES!

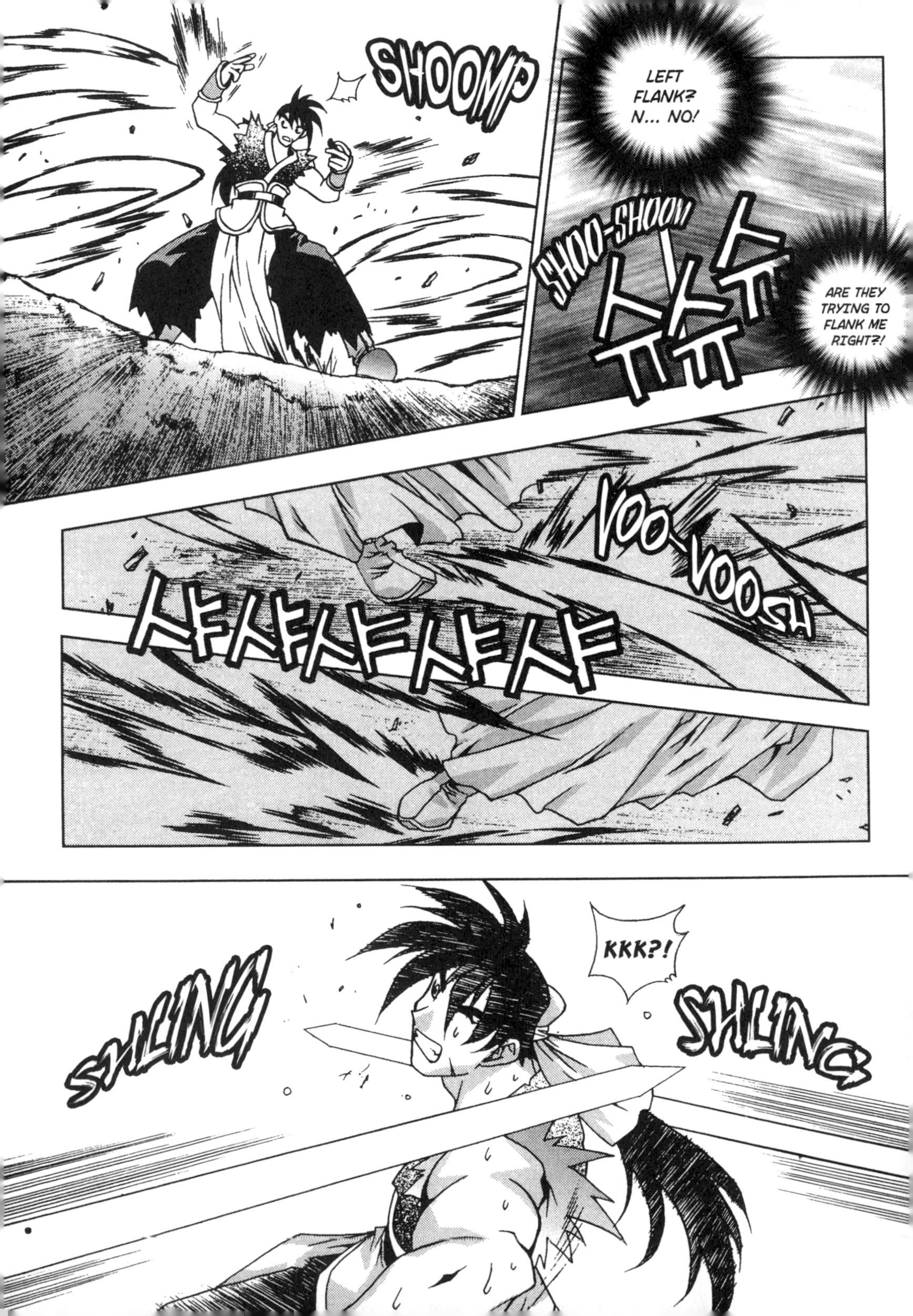
LEFT FLANK? N... NO!
SHOO-SHOOM
ARE THEY TRYING TO FLANK ME RIGHT?!
SHOOMP
VOO-VOOSH
KKK?!
SHLING
SHLING

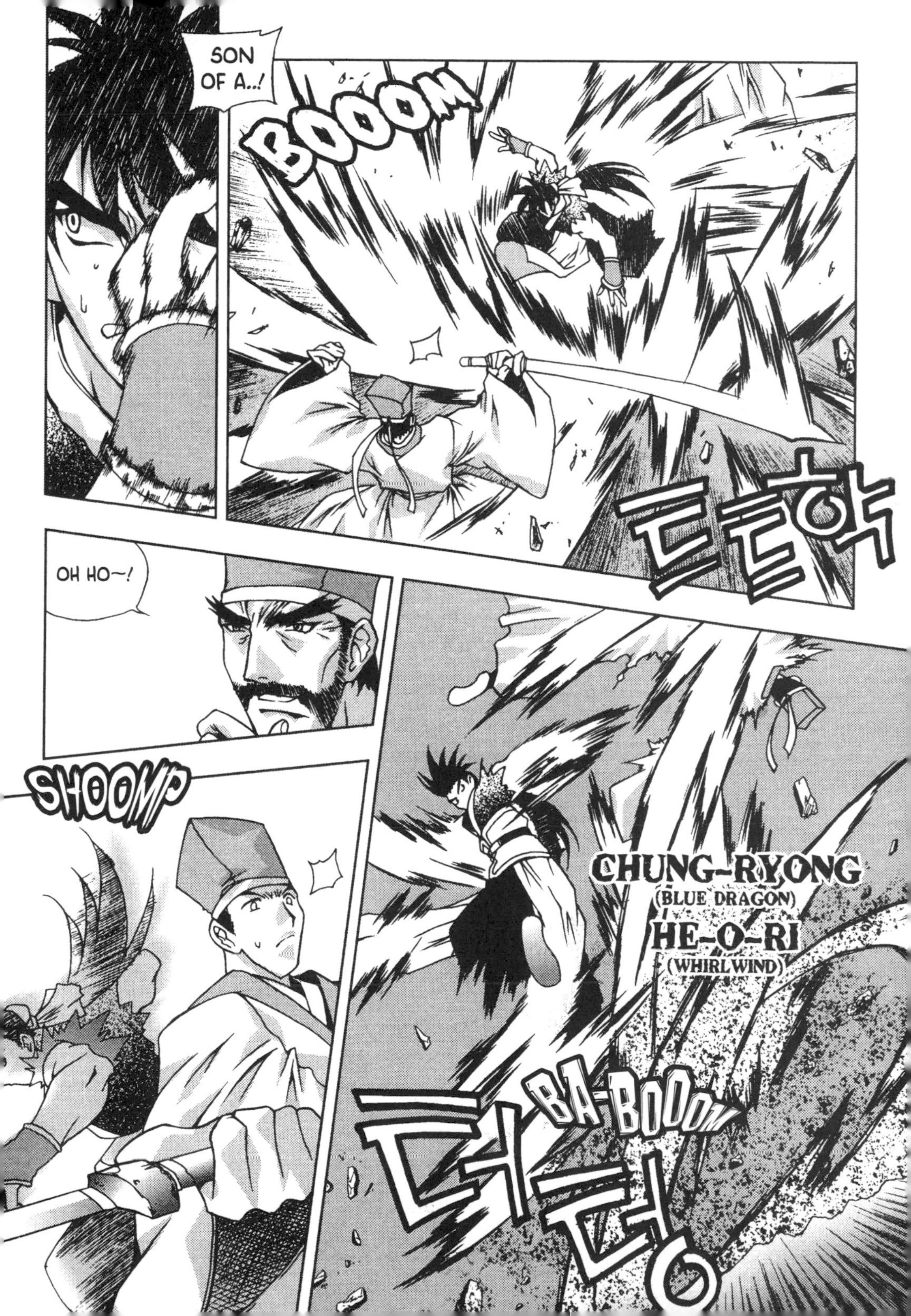
SON OF A..!
BOOOM
OH HO~!
SHOOMP
CHUNG-RYONG
(BLUE DRAGON)
HE-O-RI
(WHIRLWIND)
BA-BOOOM

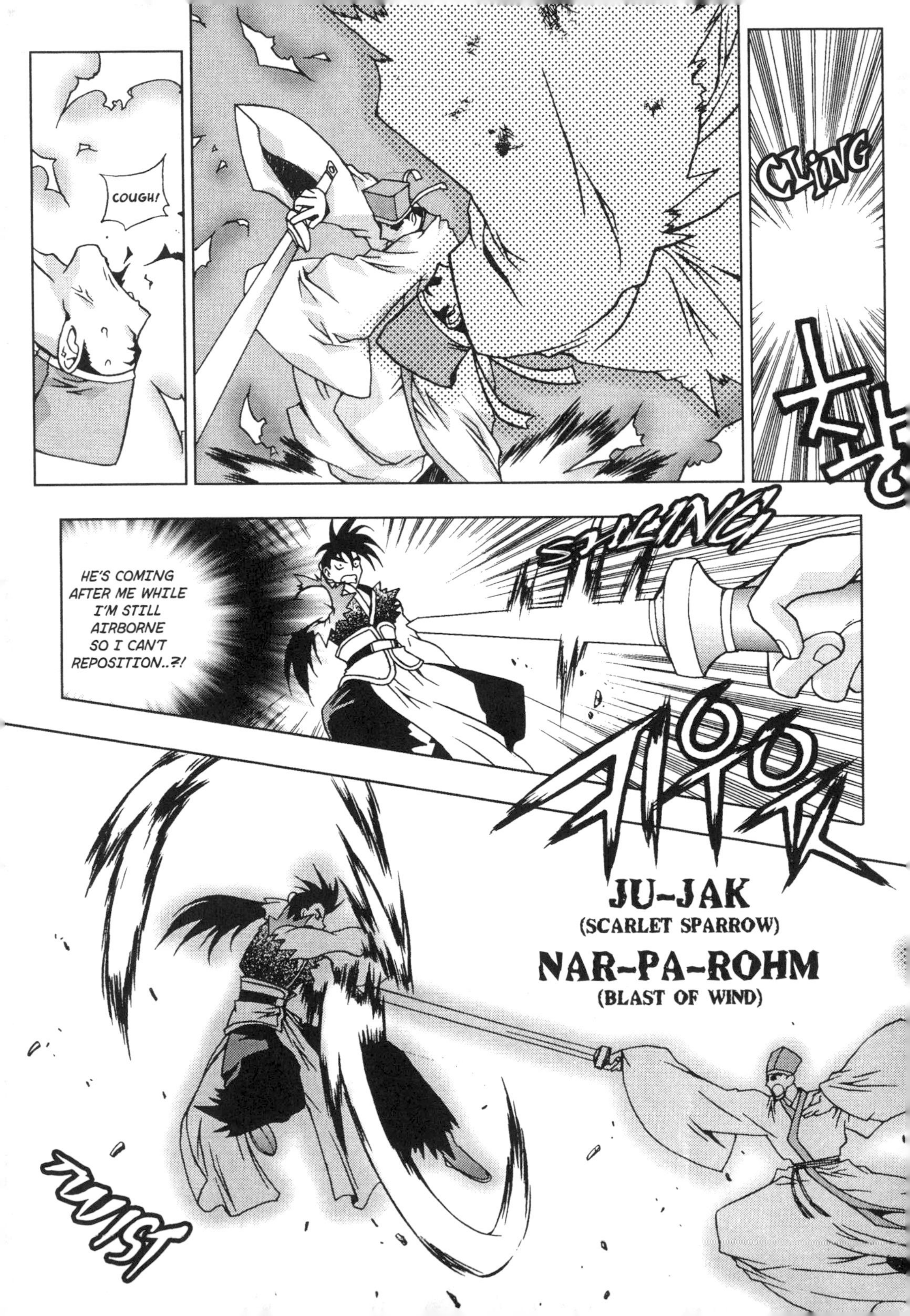
CLING
COUGH!
SPLING
HE'S COMING AFTER ME WHILE I'M STILL AIRBORNE SO I CAN'T REPOSITION..?!
JU-JAK
(SCARLET SPARROW)
NAR-PA-ROHM
(BLAST OF WIND)
TWIST

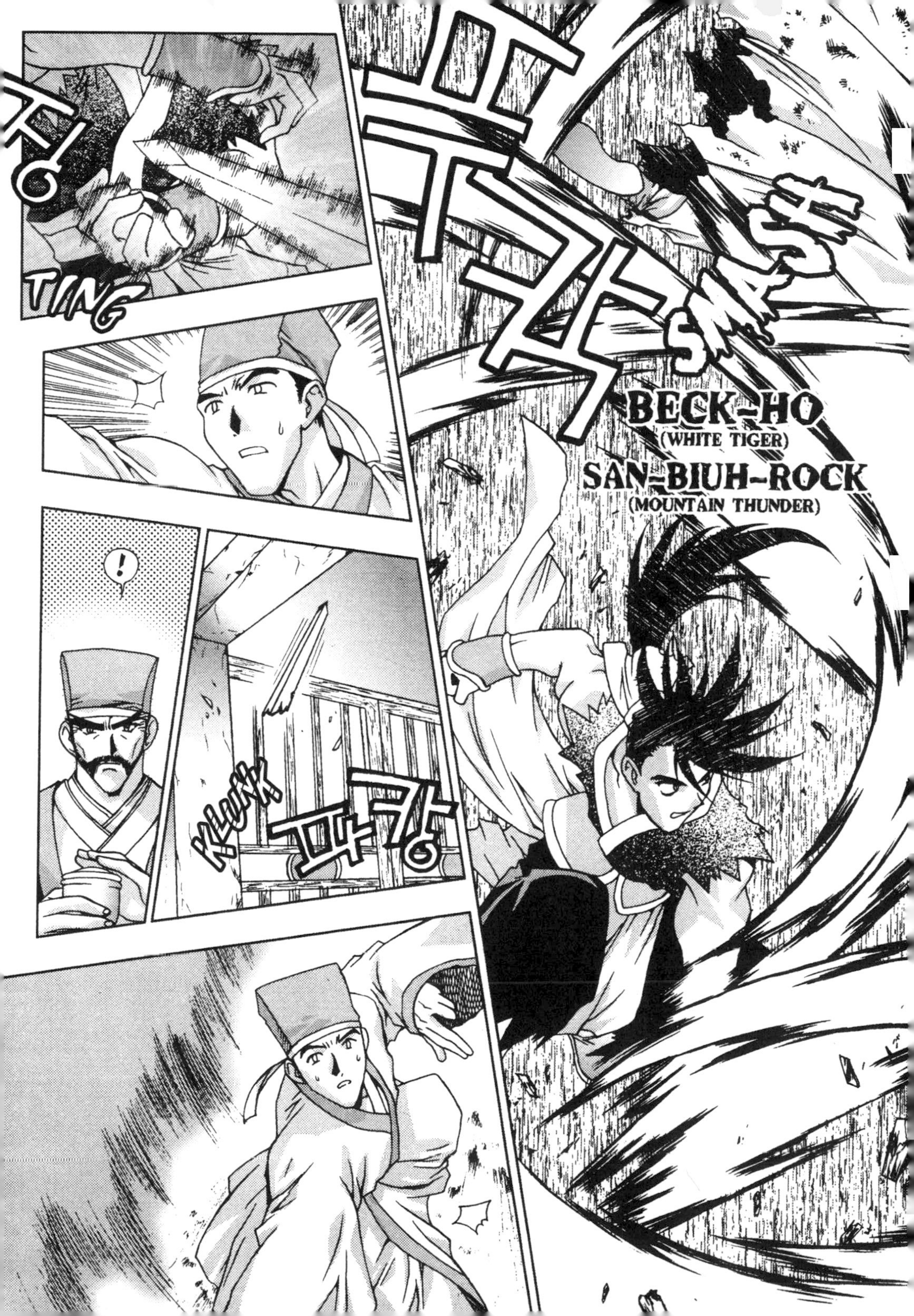
TING
!
KLUNK
SMASH
BECK-HO
(WHITE TIGER)
SAN-BIUH-ROCK
(MOUNTAIN THUNDER)

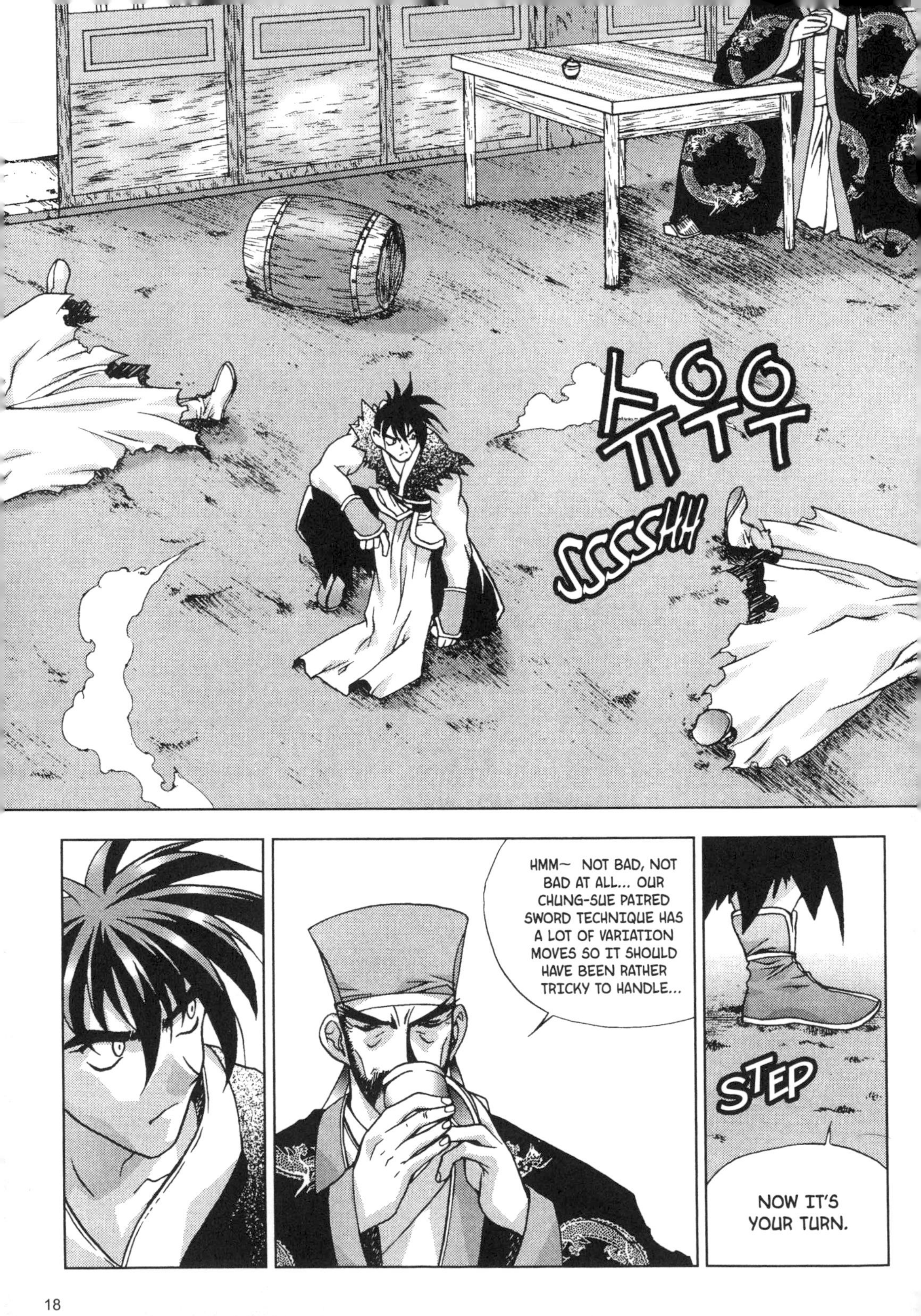
SSSSHH
HMM~ NOT BAD, NOT BAD AT ALL... OUR CHUNG-SUE PAIRED SWORD TECHNIQUE HAS A LOT OF VARIATION MOVES SO IT SHOULD HAVE BEEN RATHER TRICKY TO HANDLE...
STEP
NOW IT'S YOUR TURN.

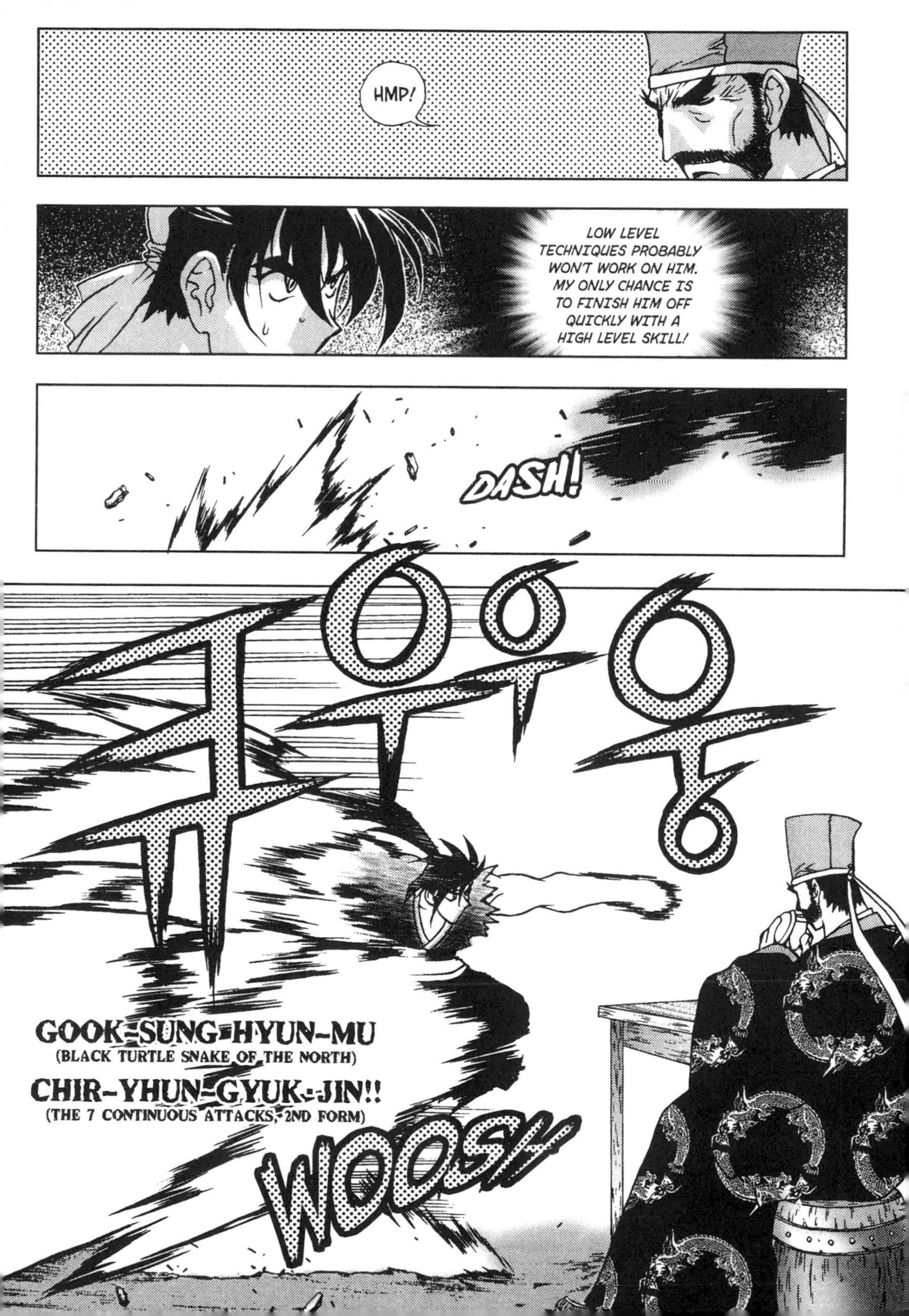
HMP!
LOW LEVEL TECHNIQUES PROBABLY WON'T WORK ON HIM. MY ONLY CHANCE IS TO FINISH HIM OFF QUICKLY WITH A HIGH LEVEL SKILL!
DASH!
GOOK-SUNG-HYUN-MU
(BLACK TURTLE SNAKE OF THE NORTH)
CHIR-YHUN-GYUK-JIN!!
(THE 7 CONTINUOUS ATTACKS, 2ND FORM)
WOOSH

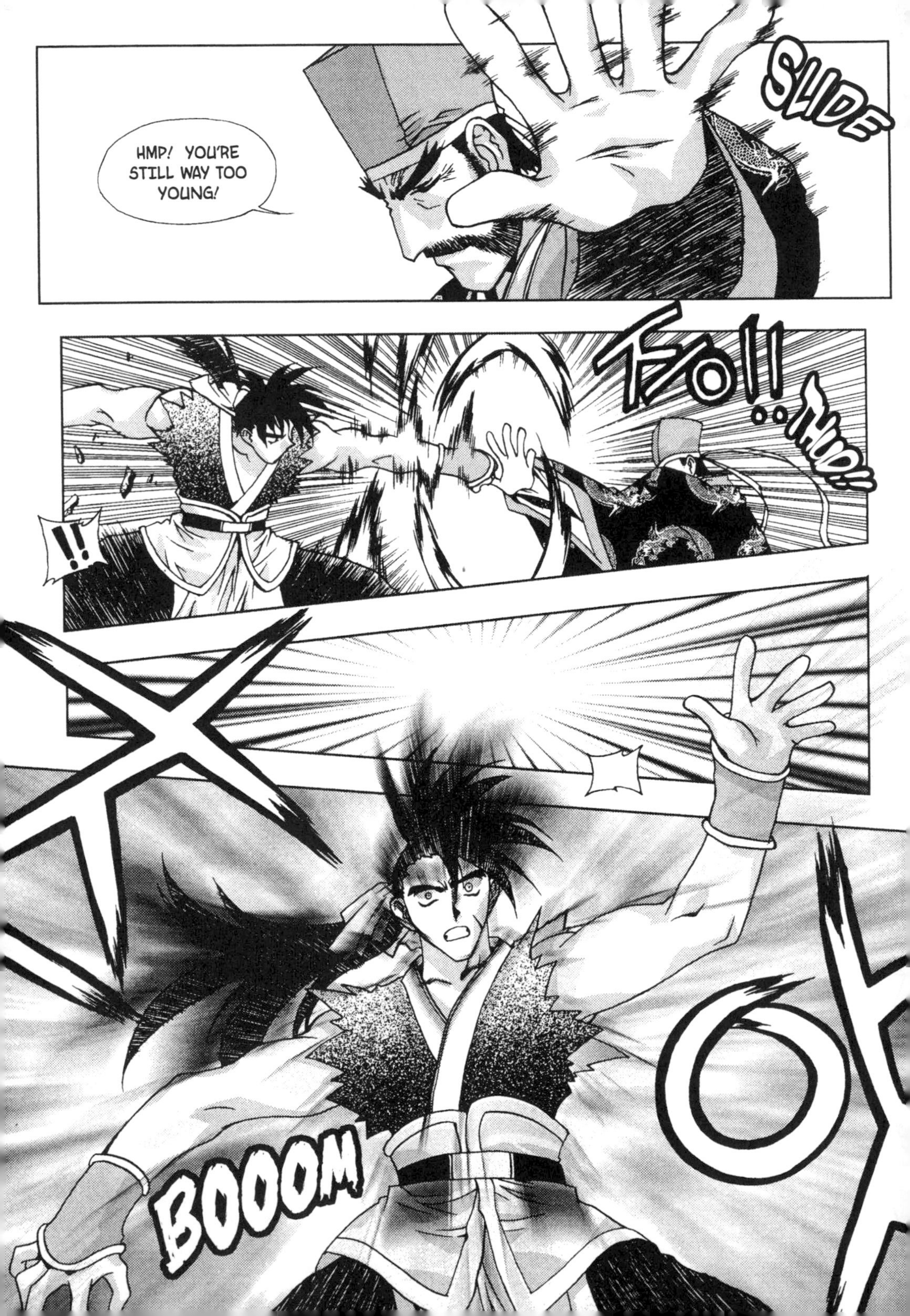
SLIDE
HMP! YOU'RE STILL WAY TOO YOUNG!
!!
THUD!!
BOOOM

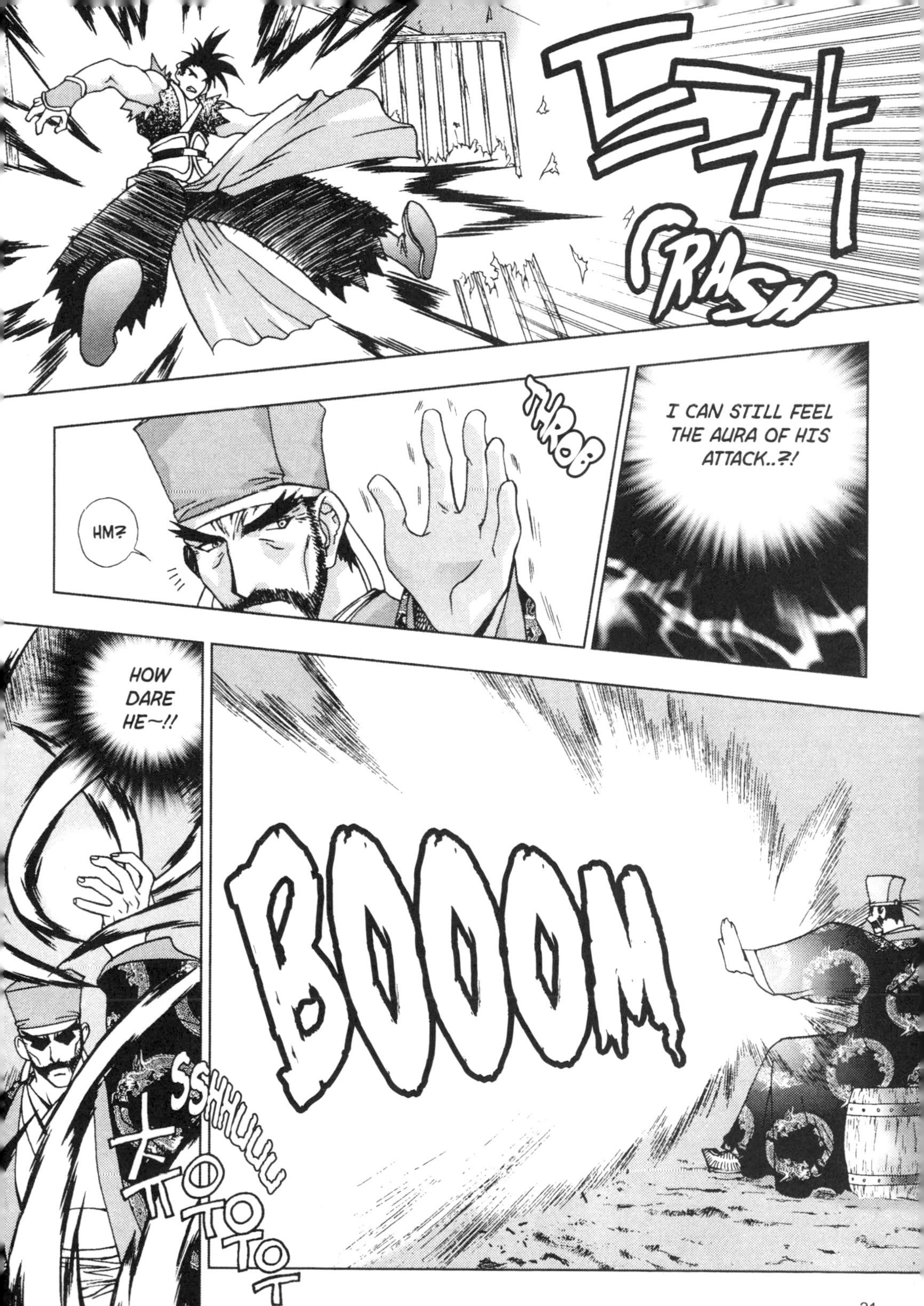
CRASH
THROB
HM?
I CAN STILL FEEL THE AURA OF HIS ATTACK..?!
HOW DARE HE~!!
BOOOM
SSHUUUU

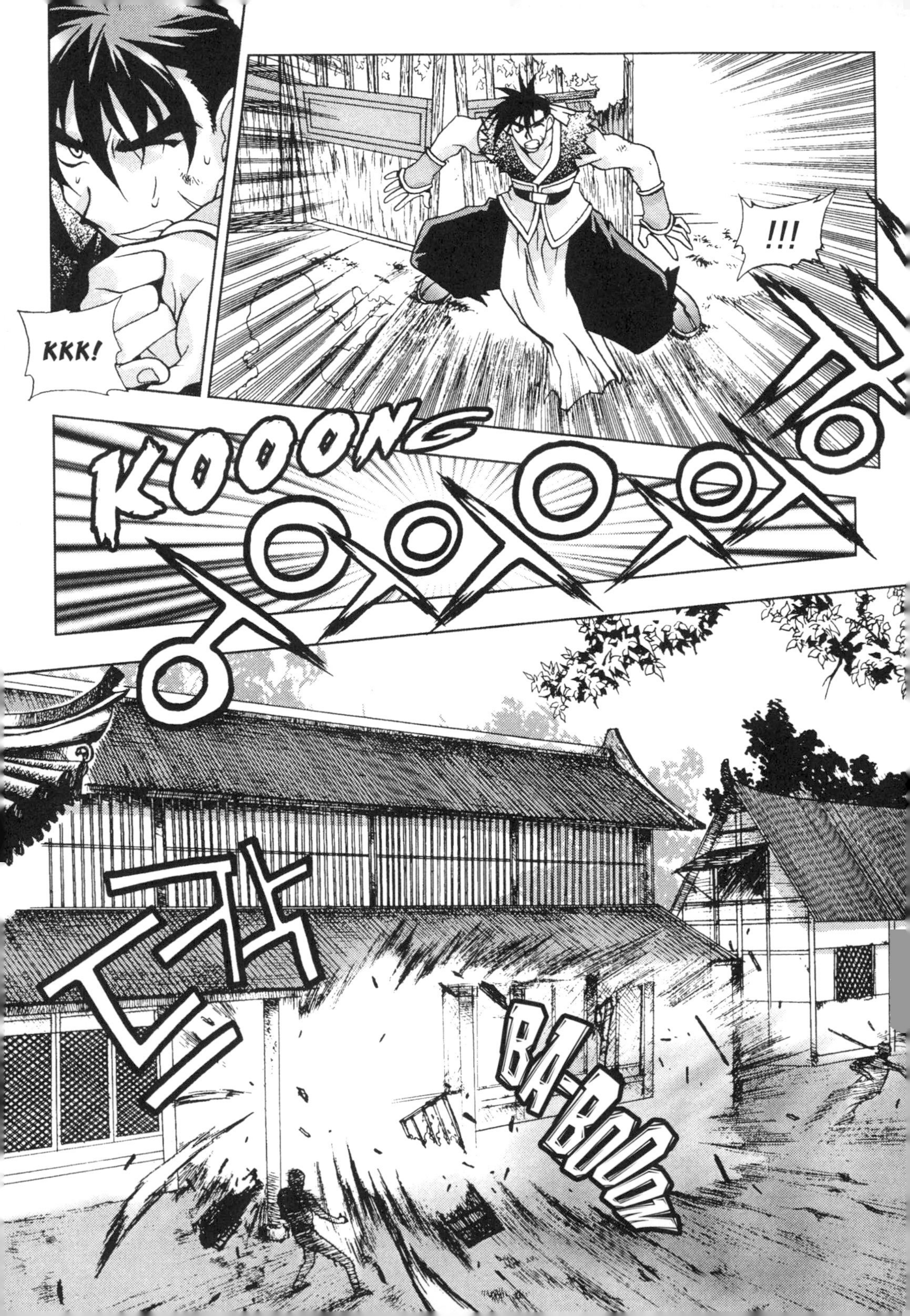
KKK!
!!!
KOOONG
TOOOOOOOO
BA-BOOM

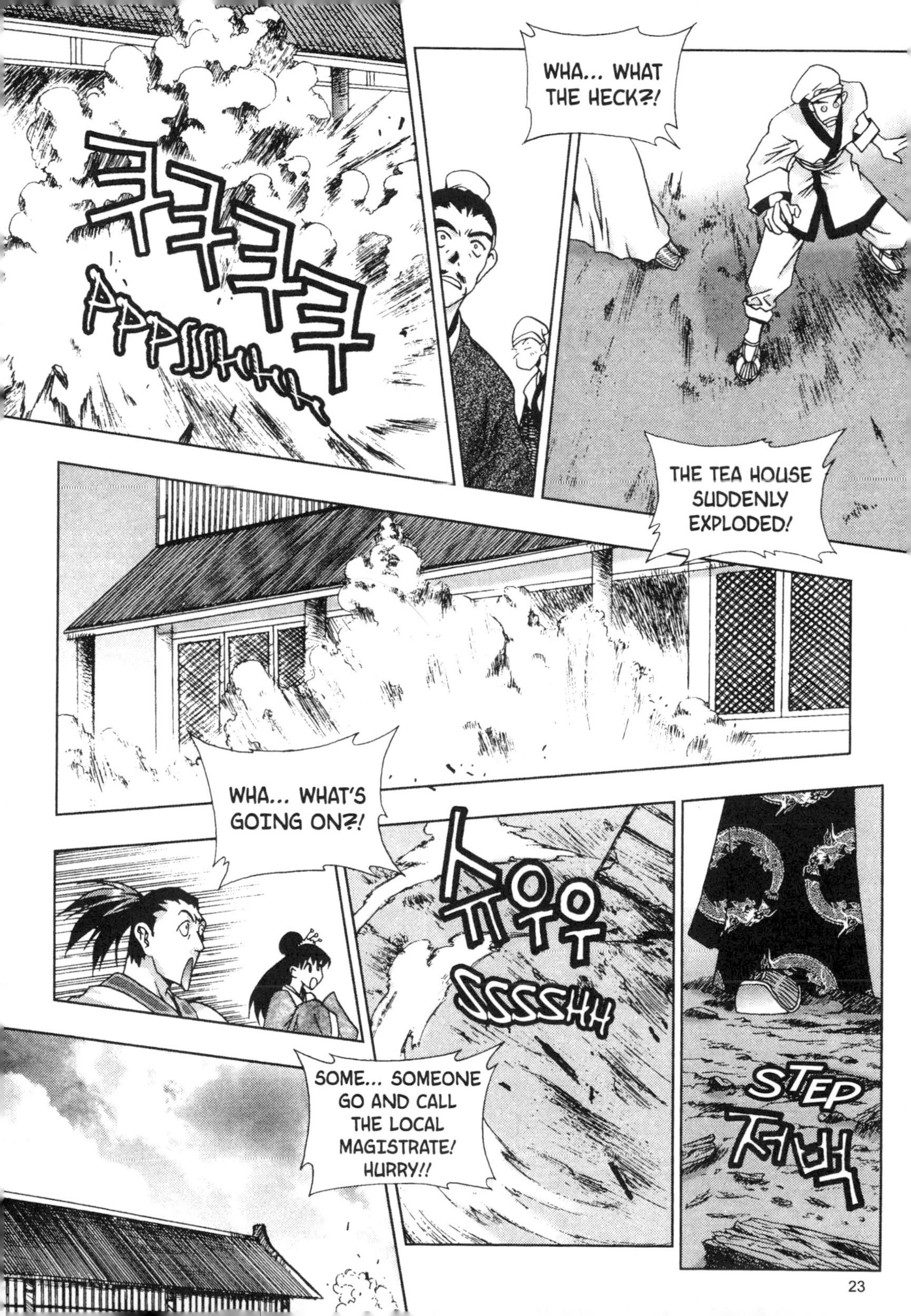
PPPSSHHHH
WHA... WHAT THE HECK?!
THE TEA HOUSE SUDDENLY EXPLODED!
WHA... WHAT'S GOING ON?!
SSSSHH
STEP
SOME... SOMEONE GO AND CALL THE LOCAL MAGISTRATE! HURRY!!

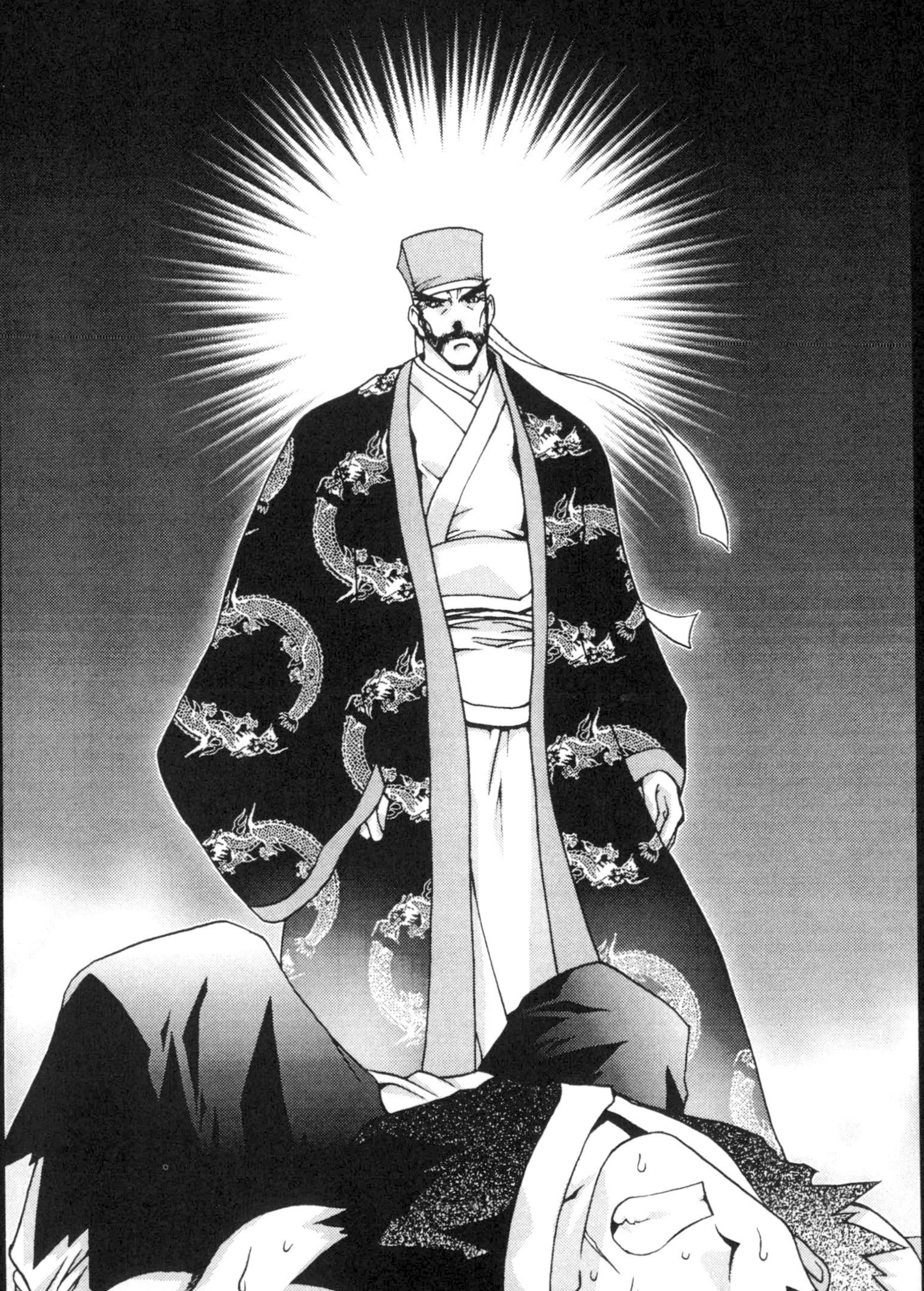

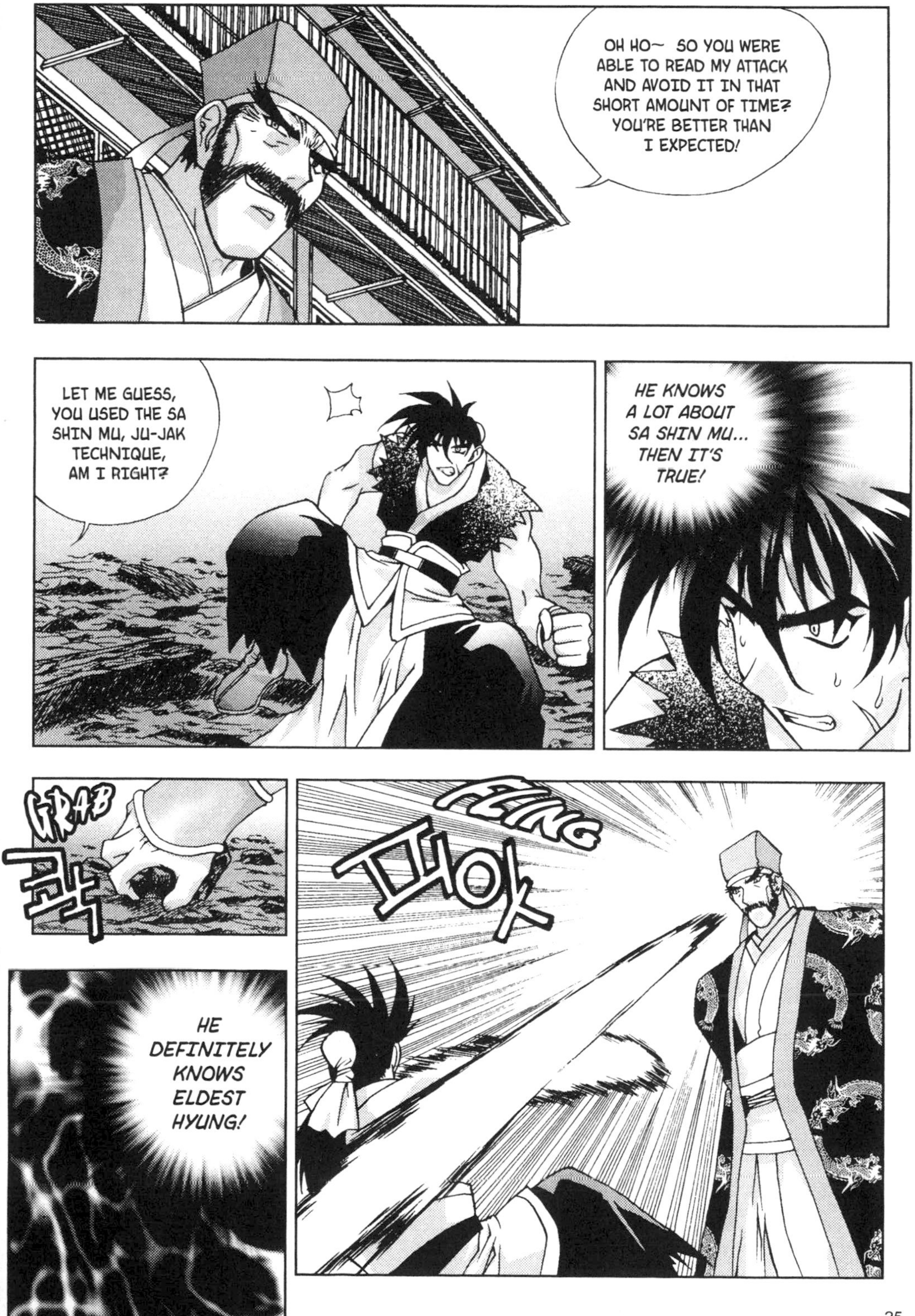
OH HO~ SO YOU WERE ABLE TO READ MY ATTACK AND AVOID IT IN THAT SHORT AMOUNT OF TIME? YOU'RE BETTER THAN I EXPECTED!
LET ME GUESS, YOU USED THE SA SHIN MU, JU-JAK TECHNIQUE, AM I RIGHT?
HE KNOWS A LOT ABOUT SA SHIN MU... THEN IT'S TRUE!
GRAB
FLING
HE DEFINITELY KNOWS ELDEST HYUNG!

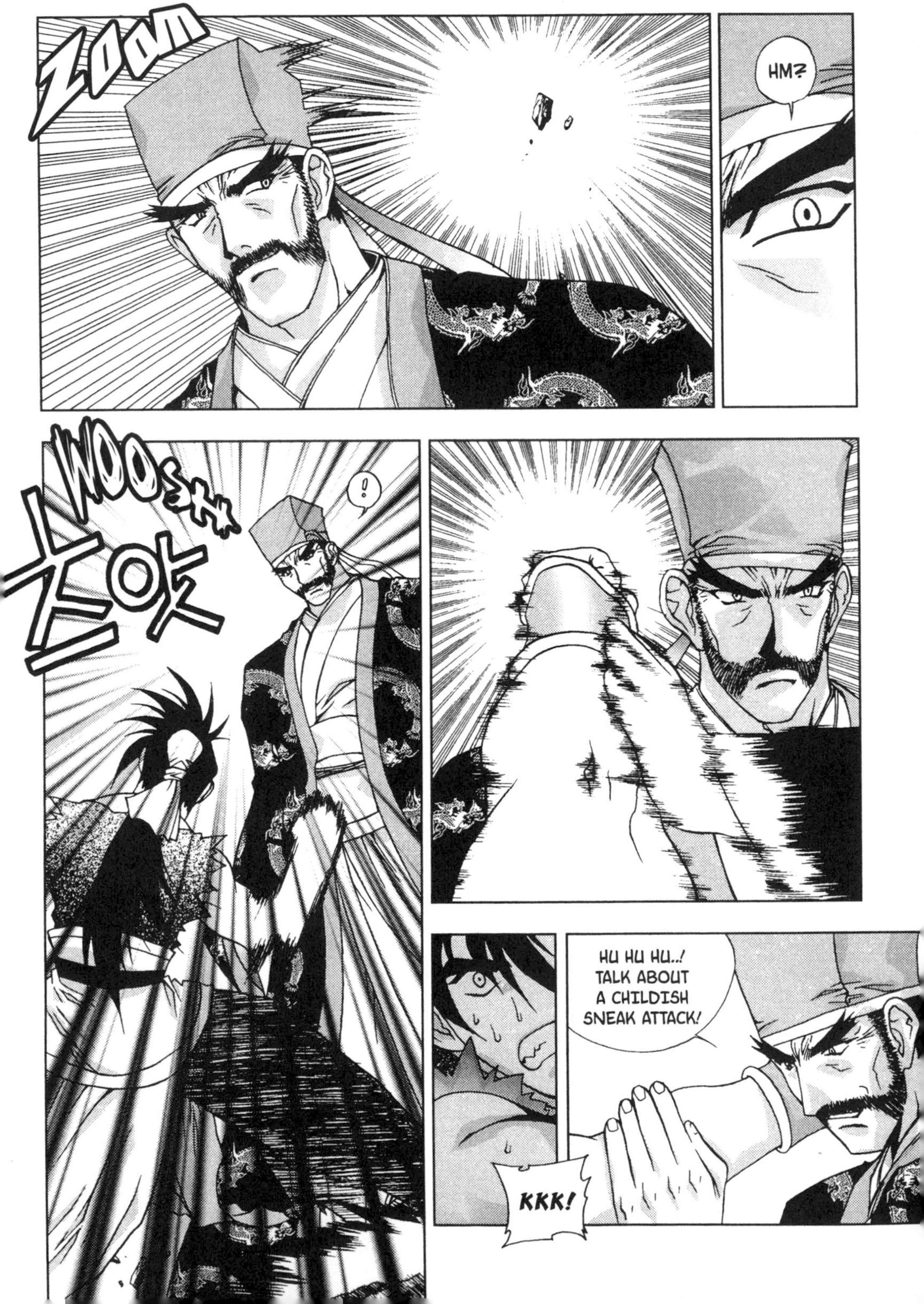
ZOOM
HM?
WOOSH
!
HU HU HU..! TALK ABOUT A CHILDISH SNEAK ATTACK!
KKK!

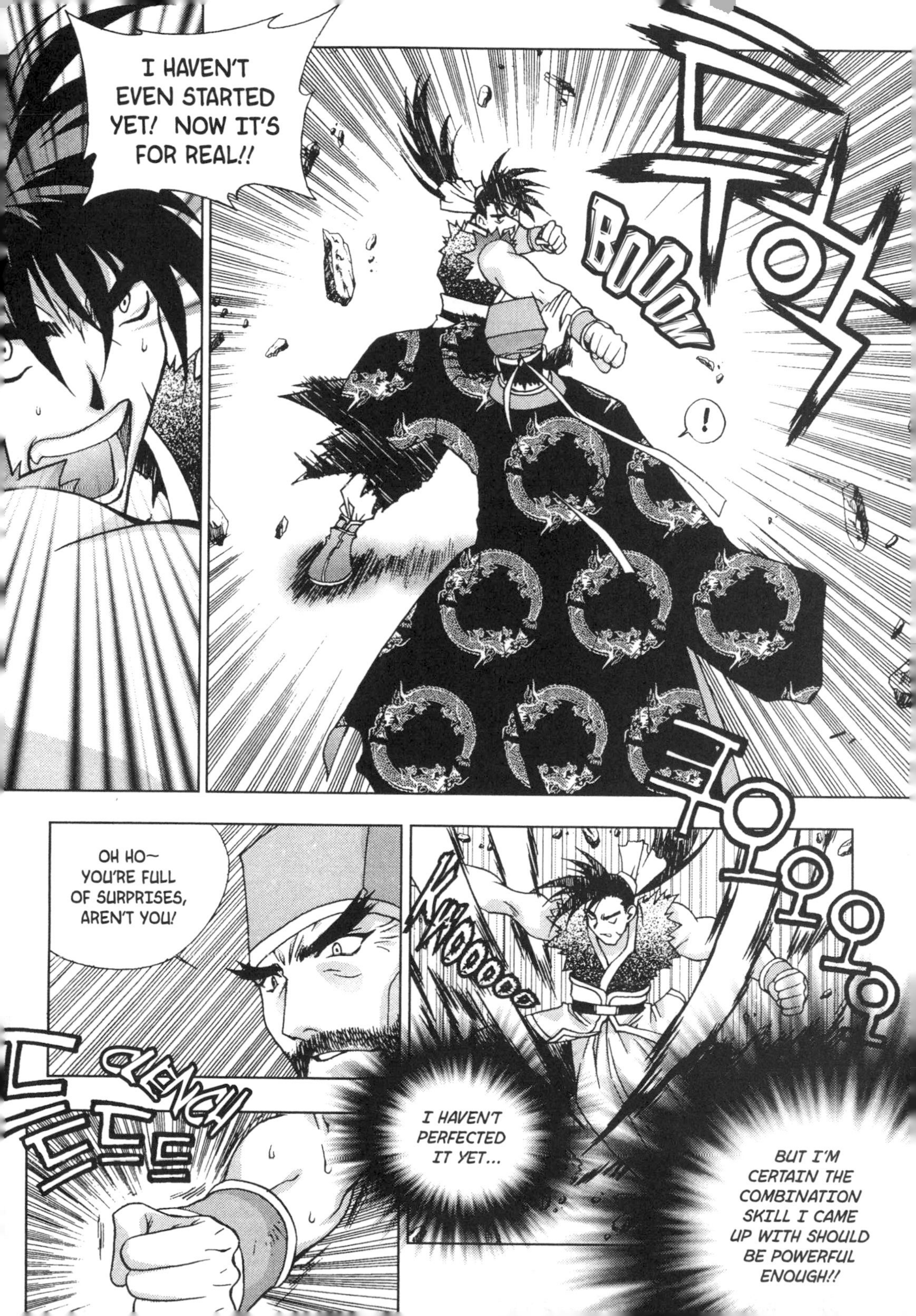
I HAVEN'T EVEN STARTED YET! NOW IT'S FOR REAL!!
BOOOM
!
OH HO~ YOU'RE FULL OF SURPRISES, AREN'T YOU!
CLENCH
I HAVEN'T PERFECTED IT YET...
BUT I'M CERTAIN THE COMBINATION SKILL I CAME UP WITH SHOULD BE POWERFUL ENOUGH!!

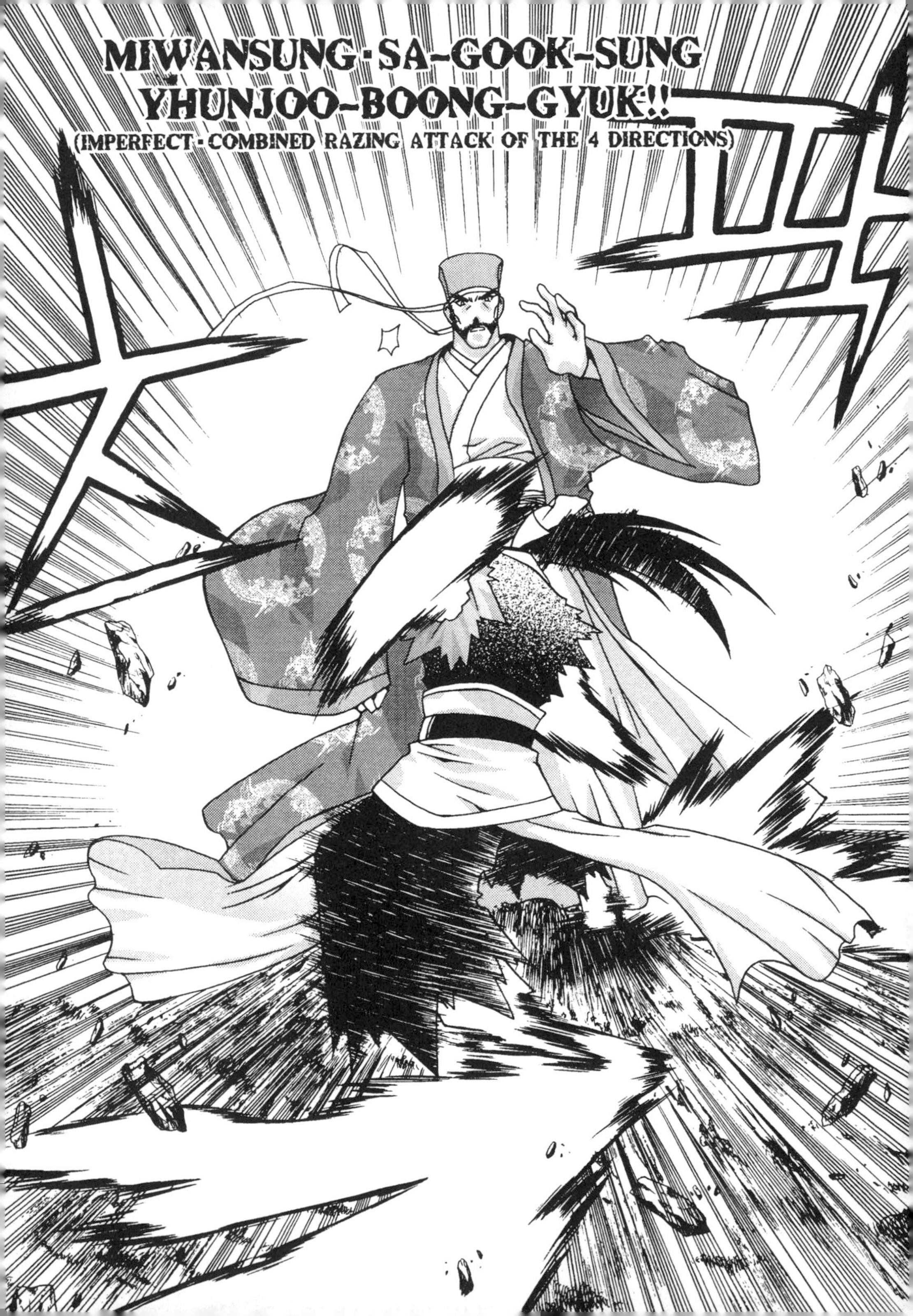
MIWANSUNG-SA-GOOK-SUNG
YHUNJOO-BOONG-GYUK!!
(IMPERFECT-COMBINED RAZING ATTACK OF THE 4 DIRECTIONS)

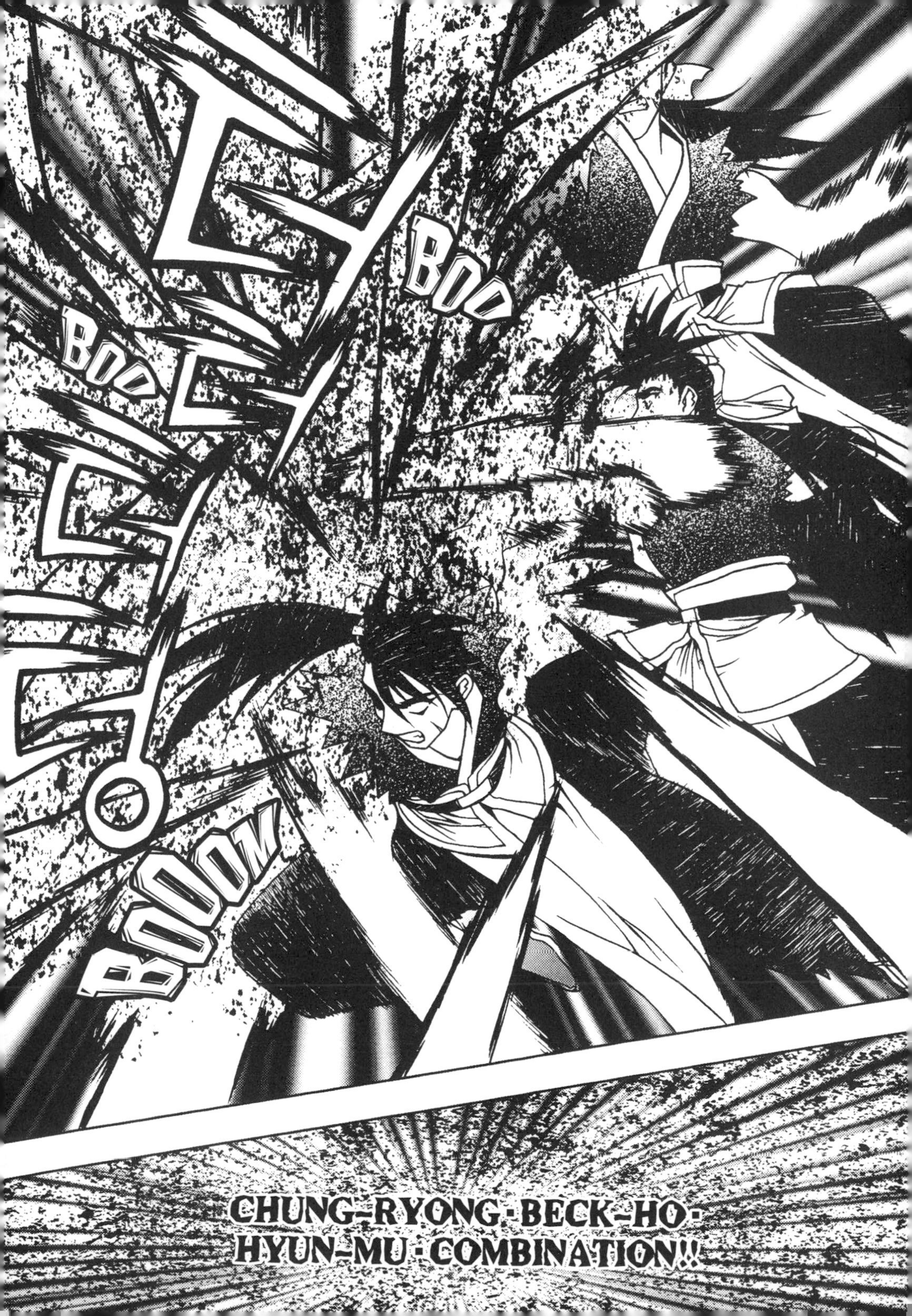

BOO
BOO
BOOOM
CHUNG-RYONG · BECK-HO · HYUN-MU · COMBINATION!!

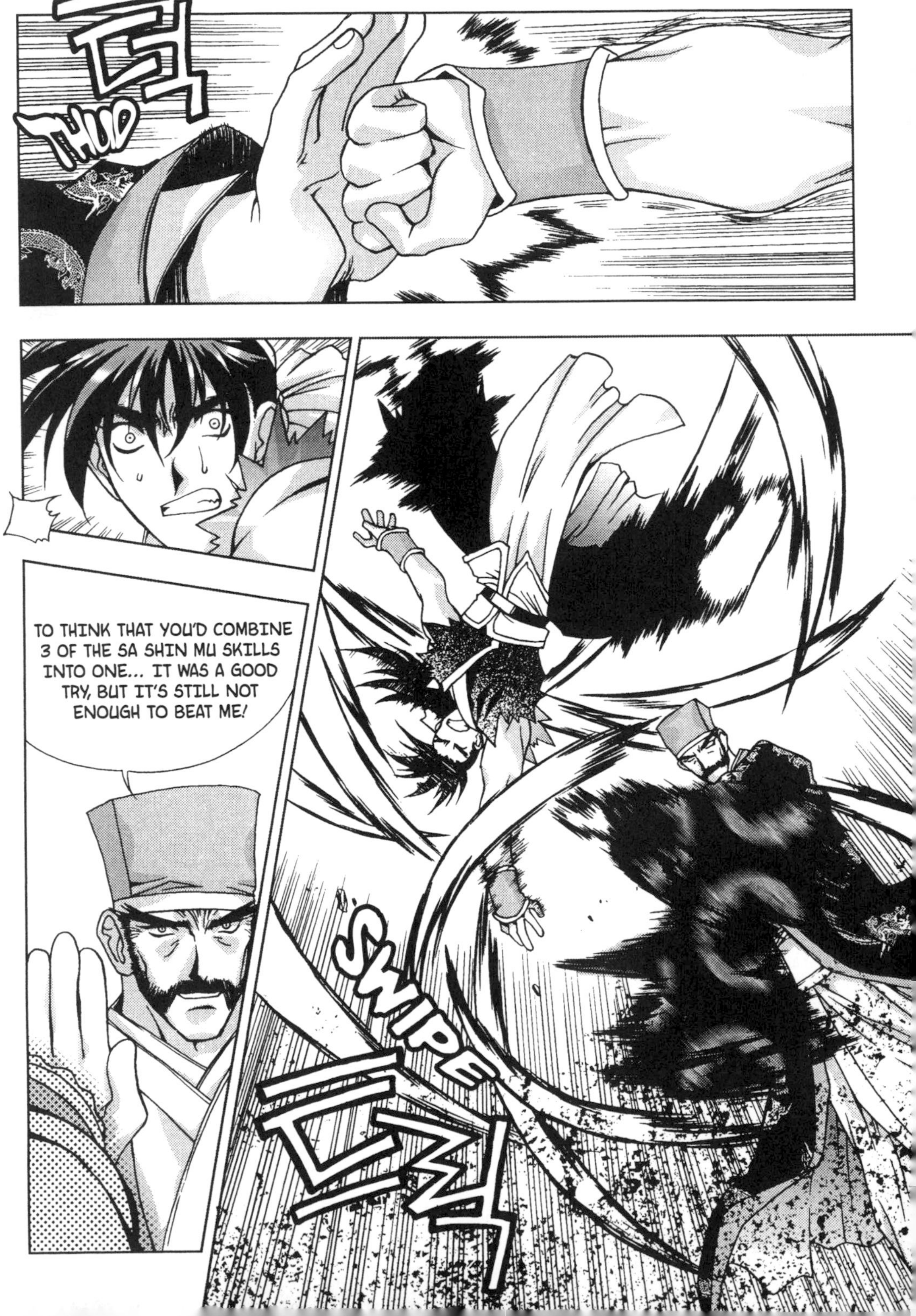
THUD
TO THINK THAT YOU'D COMBINE 3 OF THE SA SHIN MU SKILLS INTO ONE... IT WAS A GOOD TRY, BUT IT'S STILL NOT ENOUGH TO BEAT ME!
SWIPE

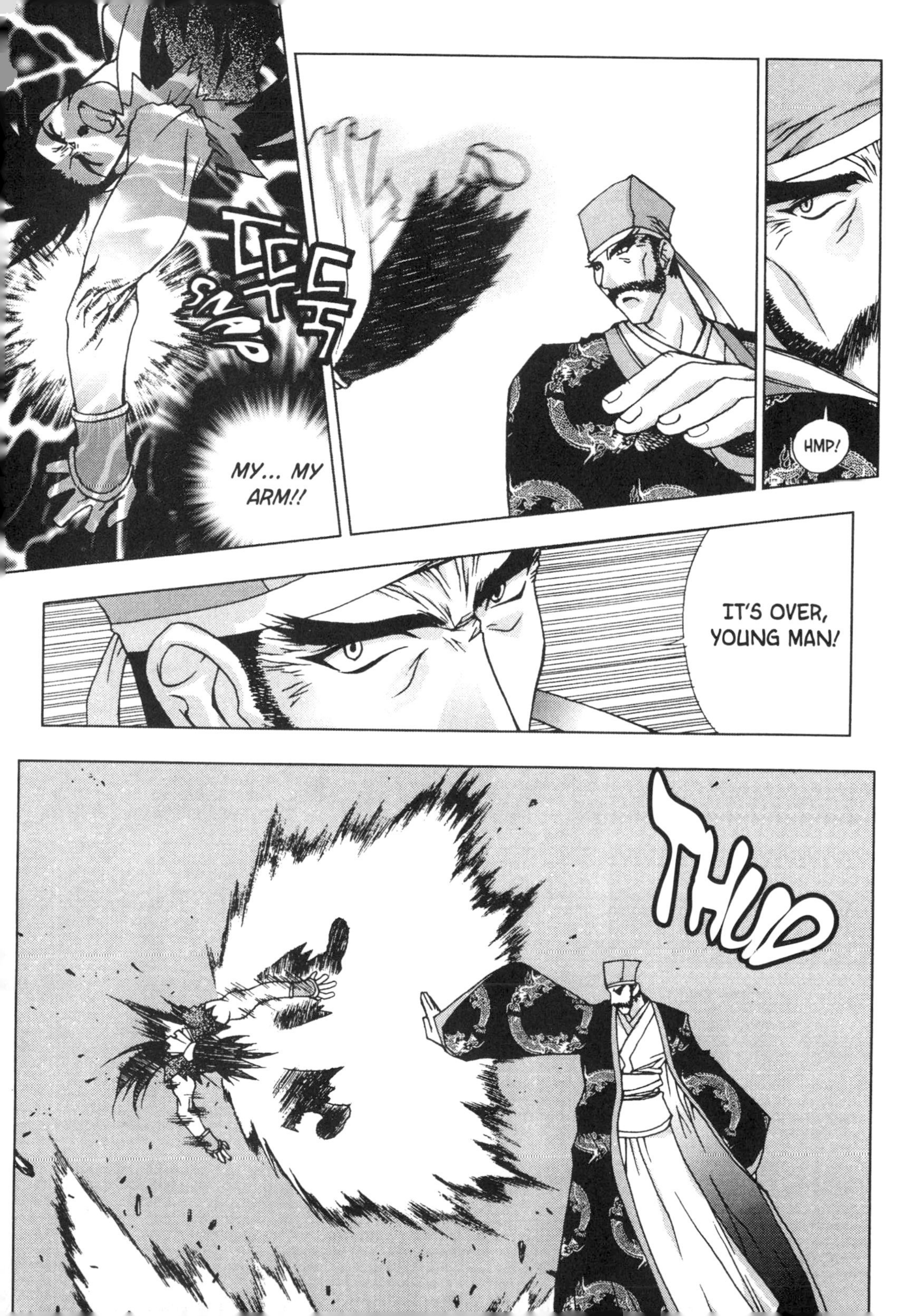
SNAP
MY... MY ARM!!
HMP!
IT'S OVER, YOUNG MAN!
THUD

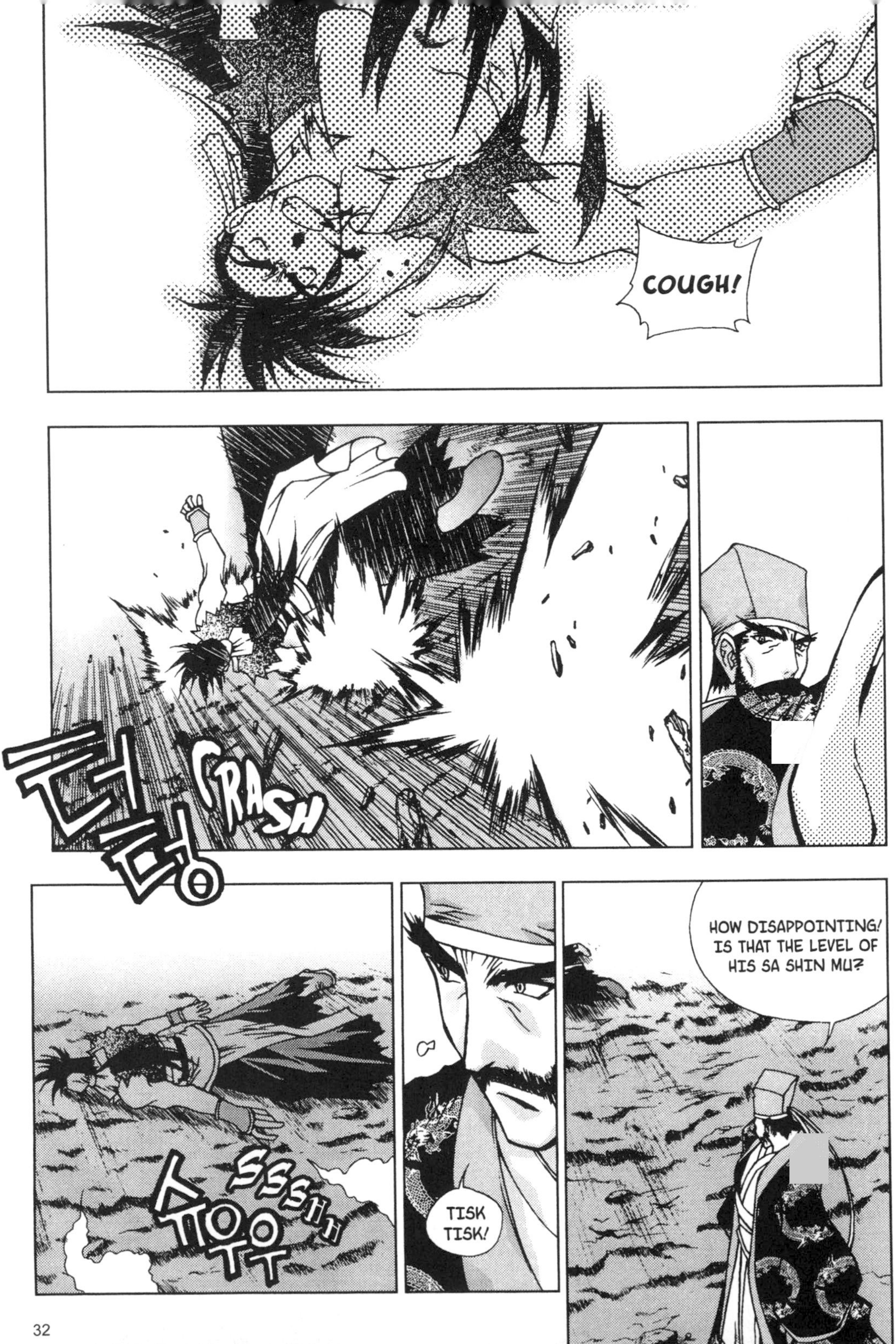
COUGH!
CRASH
SSSHH
TISK TISK!
HOW DISAPPOINTING! IS THAT THE LEVEL OF HIS SA SHIN MU?

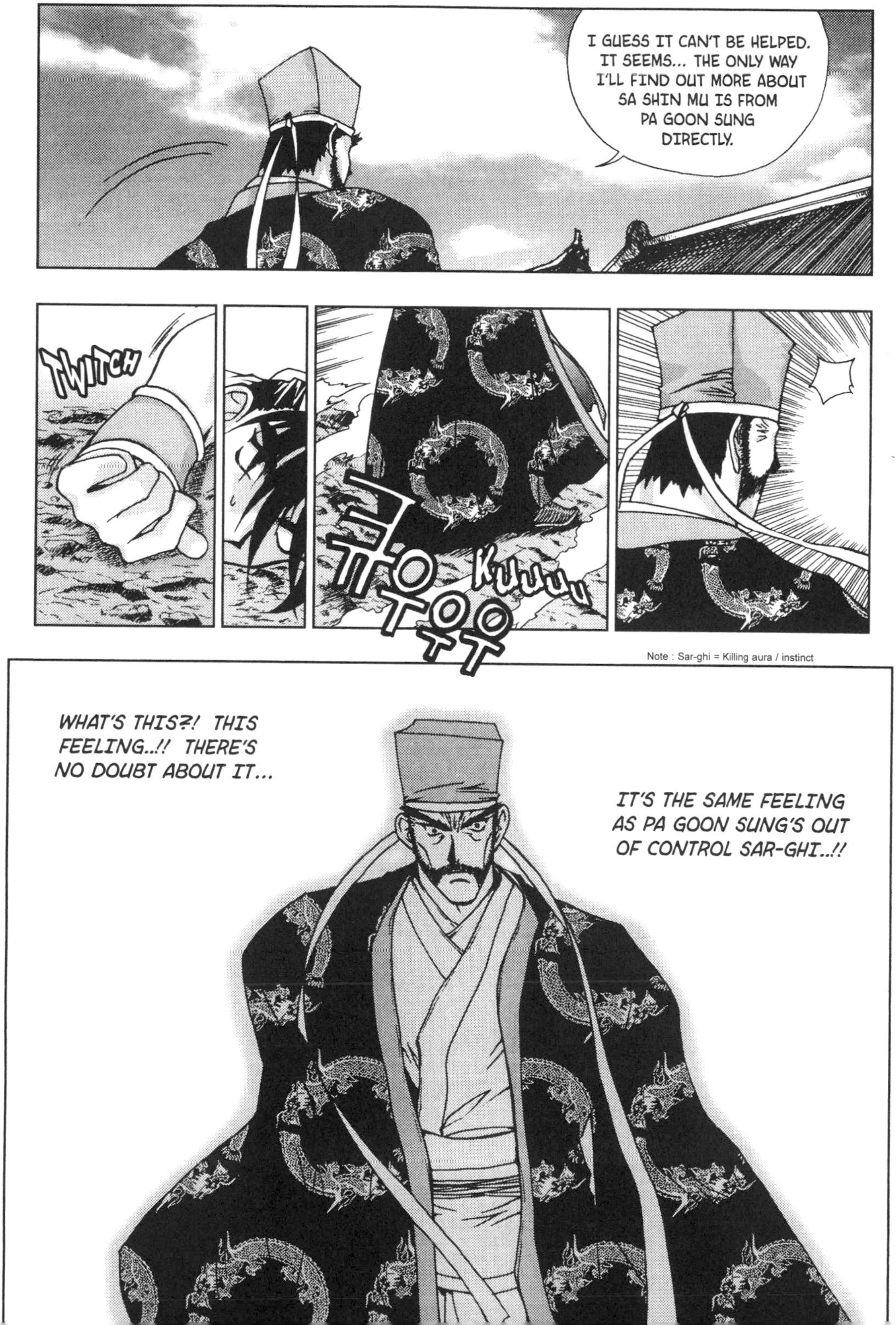
I GUESS IT CAN'T BE HELPED. IT SEEMS... THE ONLY WAY I'LL FIND OUT MORE ABOUT SA SHIN MU IS FROM PA GOON SUNG DIRECTLY.
TWITCH
쿠우우우
KUUUUU
Note : Sar-ghi = Killing aura / instinct
WHAT'S THIS?! THIS FEELING..!! THERE'S NO DOUBT ABOUT IT...
IT'S THE SAME FEELING AS PA GOON SUNG'S OUT OF CONTROL SAR-GHI..!!

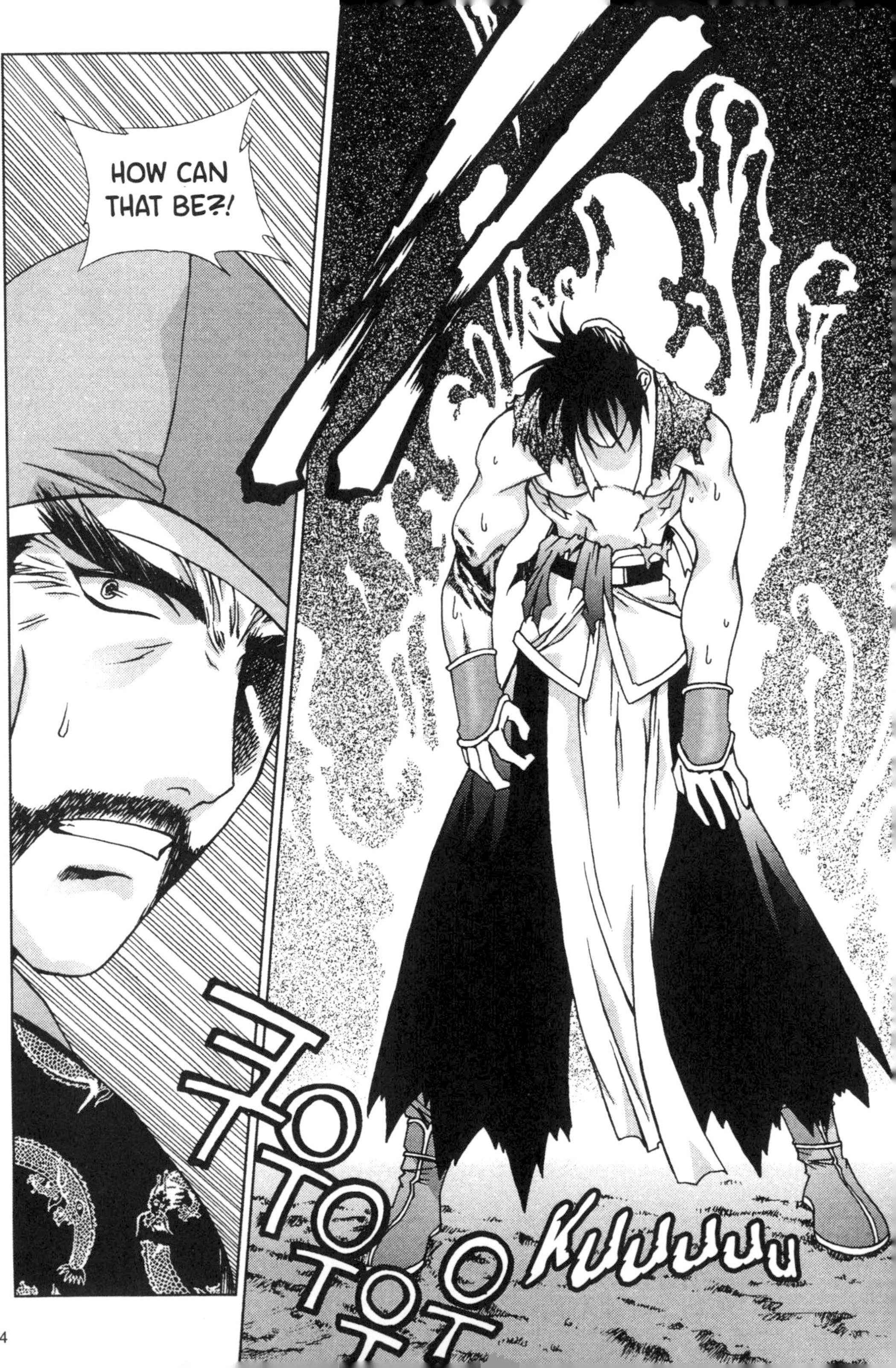
HOW CAN THAT BE?!
ZOTOTOTO
KUUUUUU

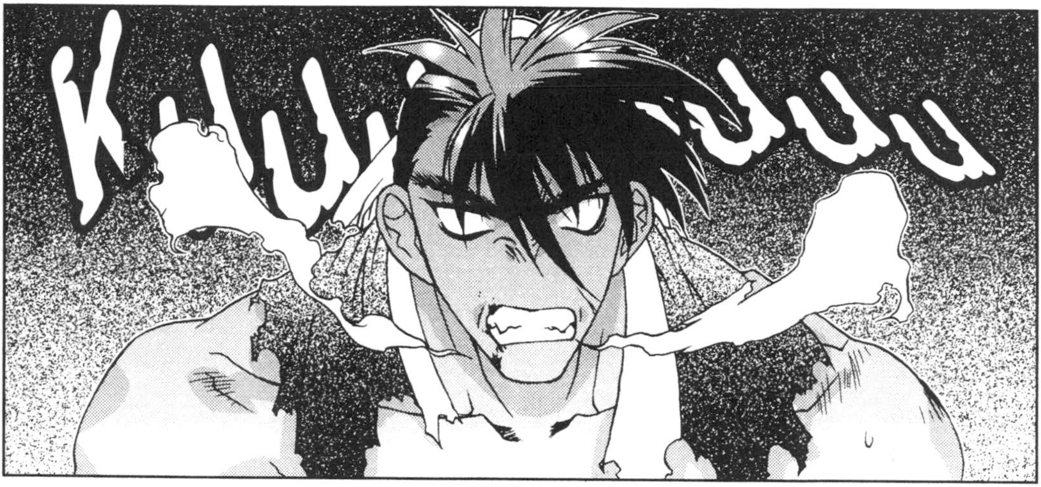

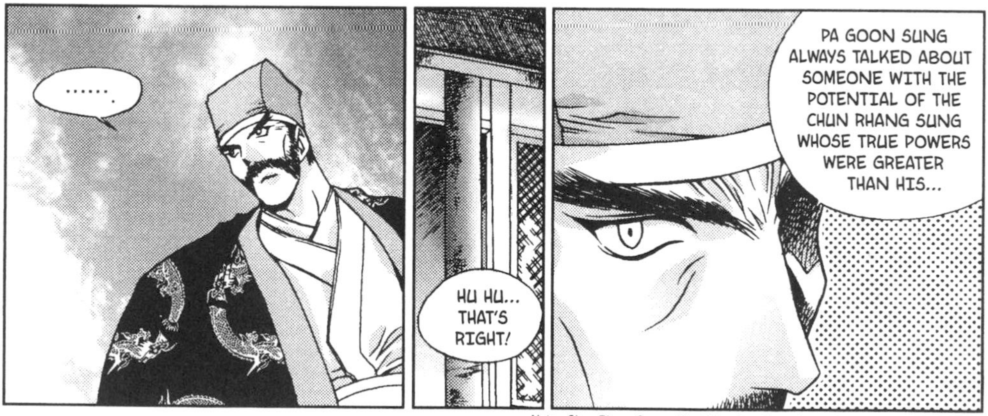

....
PA GOON SUNG ALWAYS TALKED ABOUT SOMEONE WITH THE POTENTIAL OF THE CHUN RHANG SUNG WHOSE TRUE POWERS WERE GREATER THAN HIS...
HU HU... THAT'S RIGHT!

Note : Chun Rhang Sung = The Sirius Star (the only star brighter than the North Star)

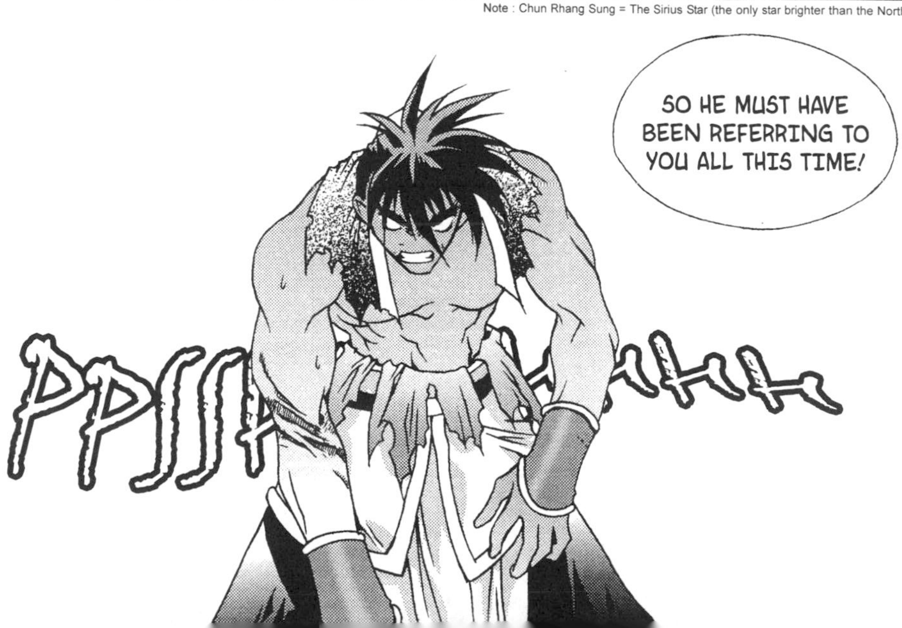

SO HE MUST HAVE BEEN REFERRING TO YOU ALL THIS TIME!

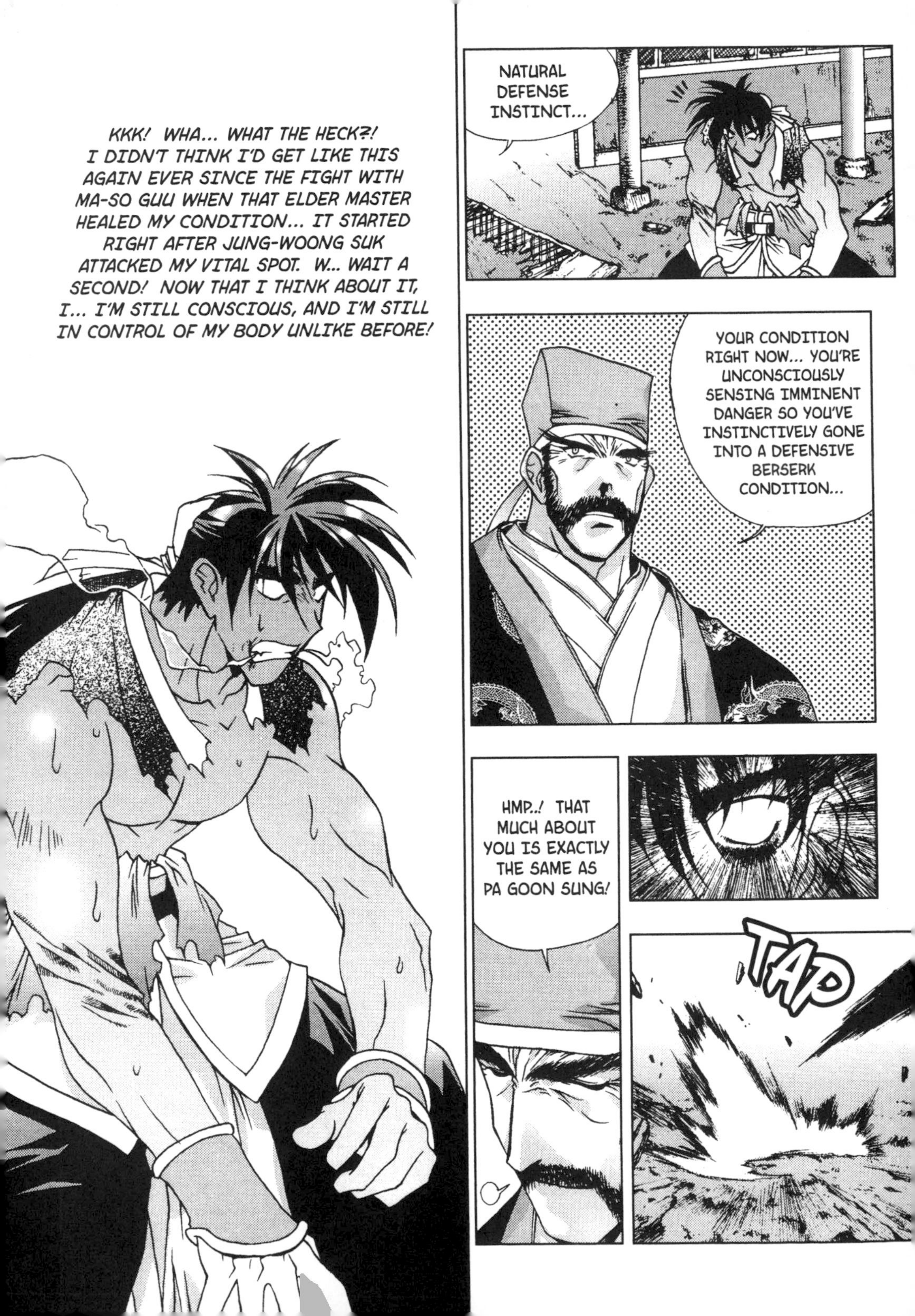
KKK! WHA... WHAT THE HECK?! I DIDN'T THINK I'D GET LIKE THIS AGAIN EVER SINCE THE FIGHT WITH MA-SO GUU WHEN THAT ELDER MASTER HEALED MY CONDITION... IT STARTED RIGHT AFTER JUNG-WOONG SUK ATTACKED MY VITAL SPOT. W... WAIT A SECOND! NOW THAT I THINK ABOUT IT, I... I'M STILL CONSCIOUS, AND I'M STILL IN CONTROL OF MY BODY UNLIKE BEFORE!
NATURAL DEFENSE INSTINCT...
YOUR CONDITION RIGHT NOW... YOU'RE UNCONSCIOUSLY SENSING IMMINENT DANGER SO YOU'VE INSTINCTIVELY GONE INTO A DEFENSIVE BERSERK CONDITION...
HMP..! THAT MUCH ABOUT YOU IS EXACTLY THE SAME AS PA GOON SUNG!
TAP

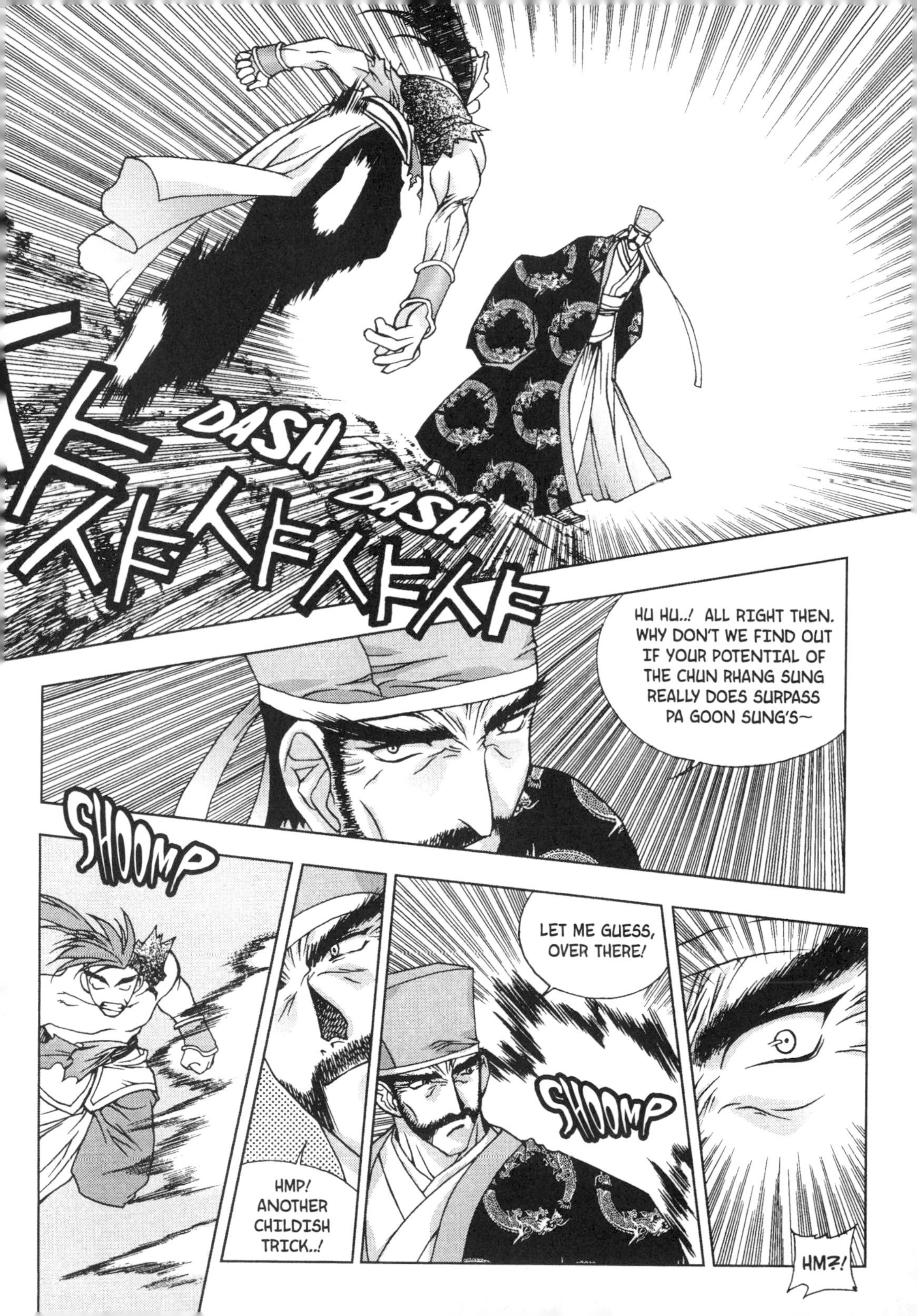
DASH
DASH
HU HU..! ALL RIGHT THEN. WHY DON'T WE FIND OUT IF YOUR POTENTIAL OF THE CHUN RHANG SUNG REALLY DOES SURPASS PA GOON SUNG'S~
SHOOMP
HMP! ANOTHER CHILDISH TRICK..!
LET ME GUESS, OVER THERE!
SHOOMP
HM?!

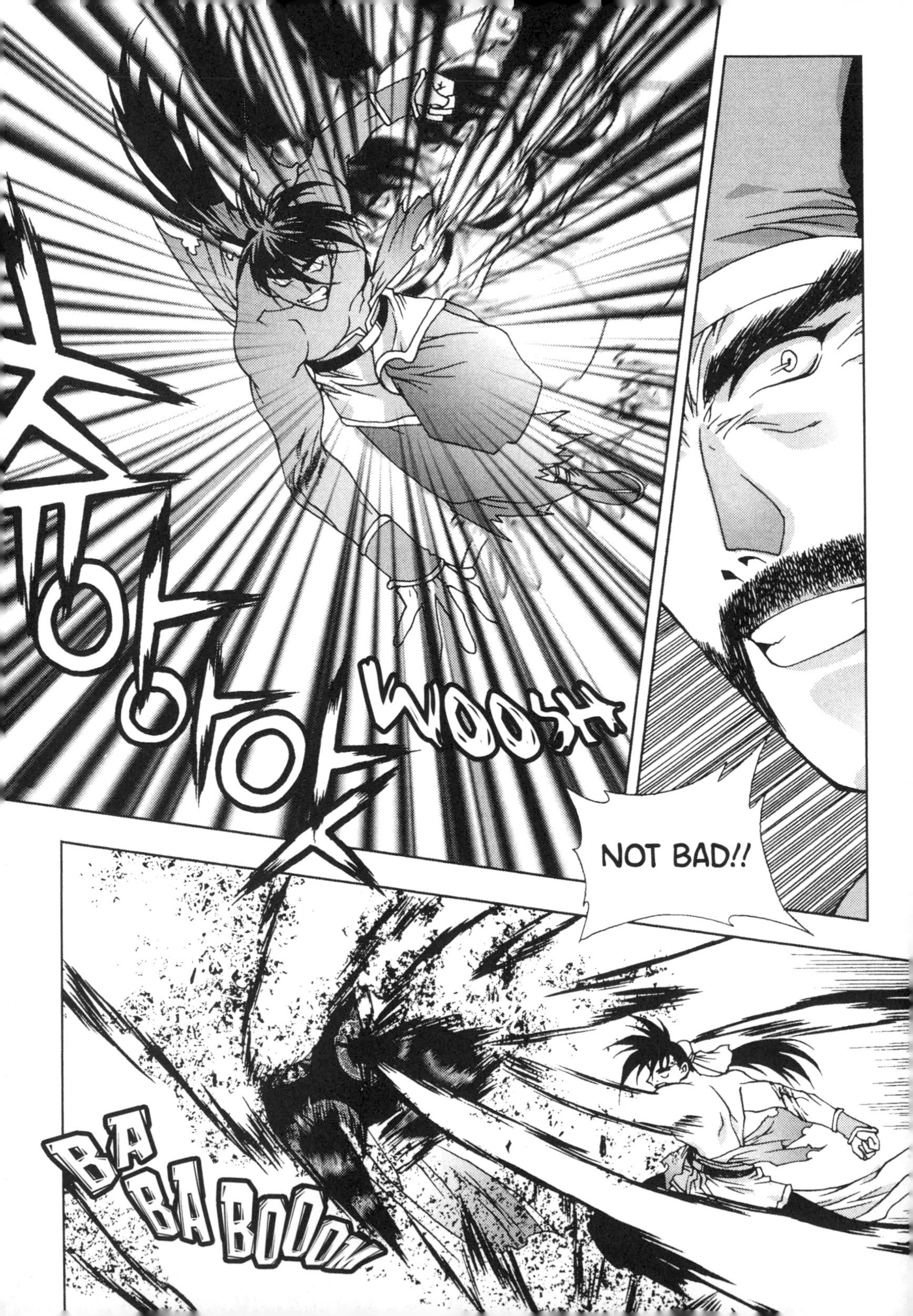

WOOSH
NOT BAD!!
BA BA BOOOM

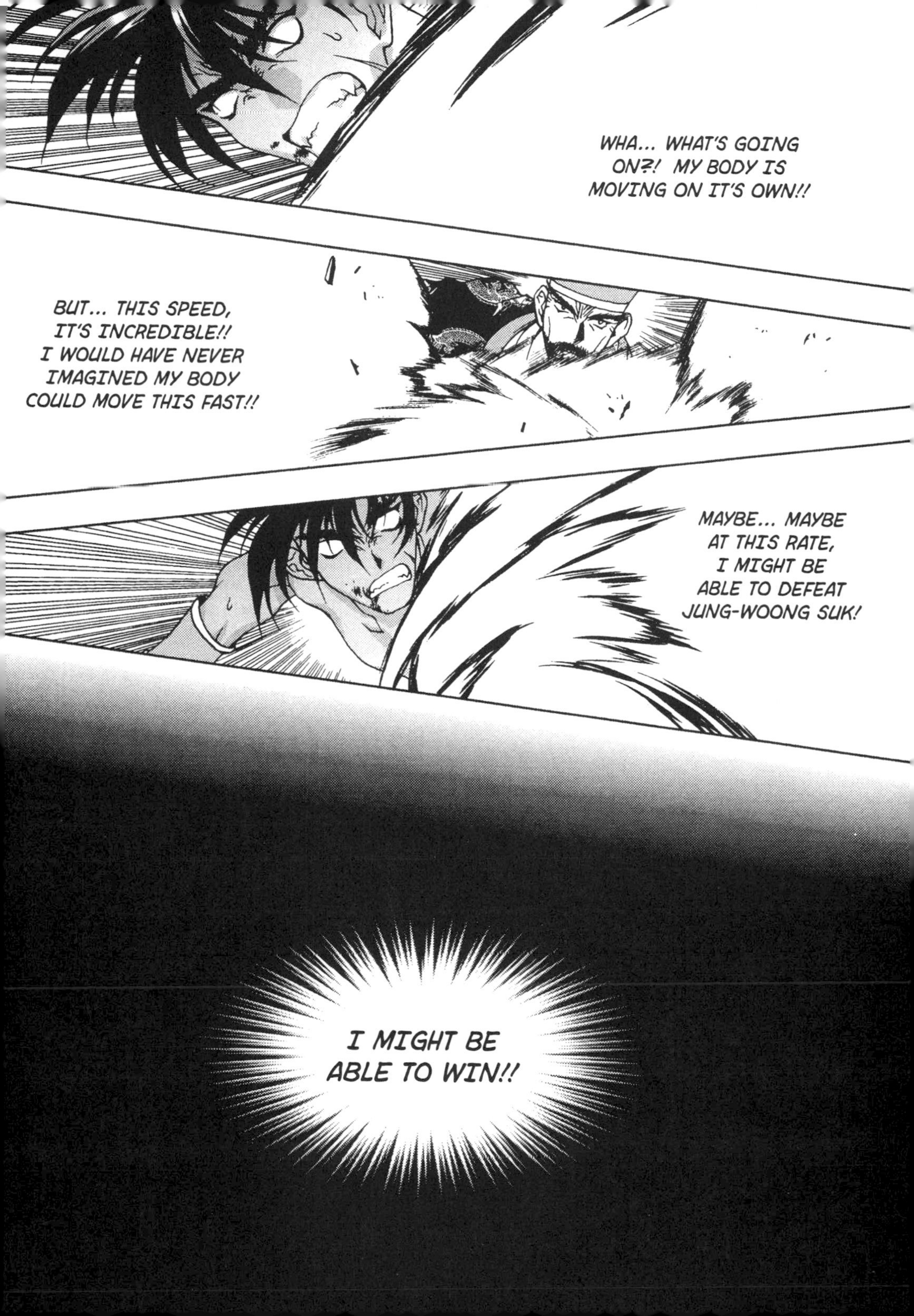
WHA... WHAT'S GOING ON?! MY BODY IS MOVING ON IT'S OWN!!
BUT... THIS SPEED, IT'S INCREDIBLE!! I WOULD HAVE NEVER IMAGINED MY BODY COULD MOVE THIS FAST!!
MAYBE... MAYBE AT THIS RATE, I MIGHT BE ABLE TO DEFEAT JUNG-WOONG SUK!
I MIGHT BE ABLE TO WIN!!

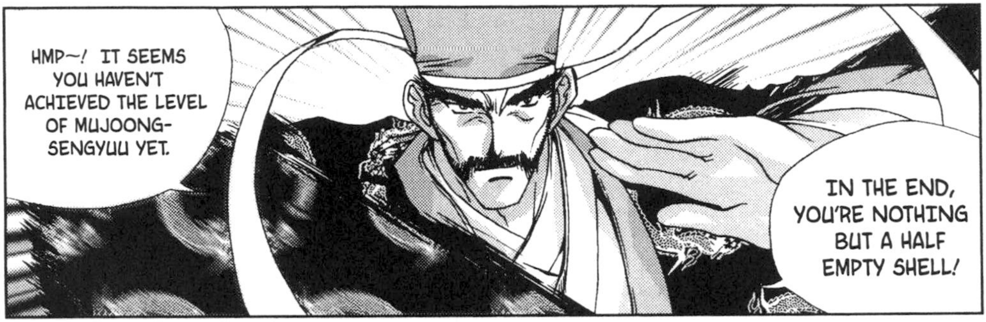
HMP~! IT SEEMS YOU HAVEN'T ACHIEVED THE LEVEL OF MUJOONG-SENGYUU YET.
IN THE END, YOU'RE NOTHING BUT A HALF EMPTY SHELL!

Note : Mujoong-Sengyuu = Existence within emptiness

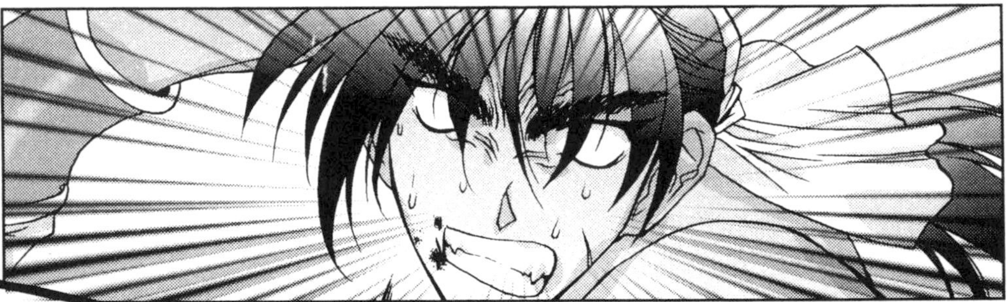

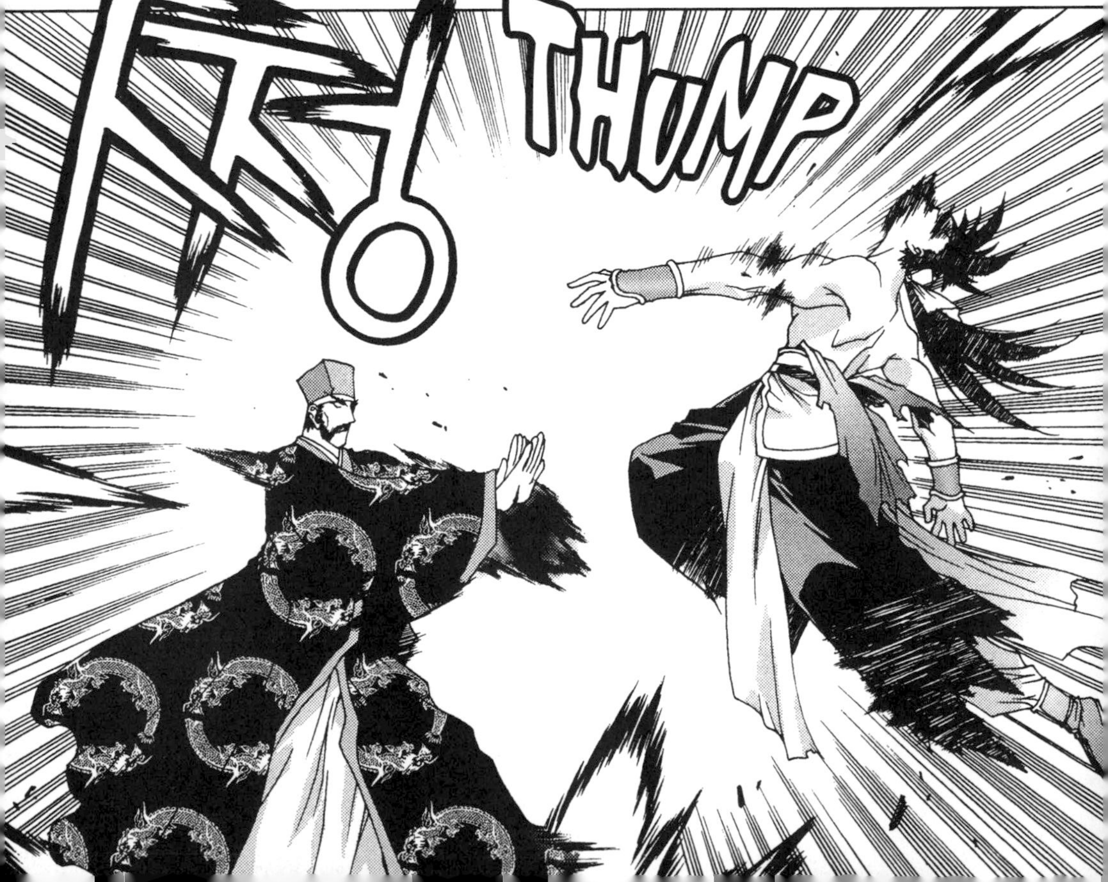
THUMP

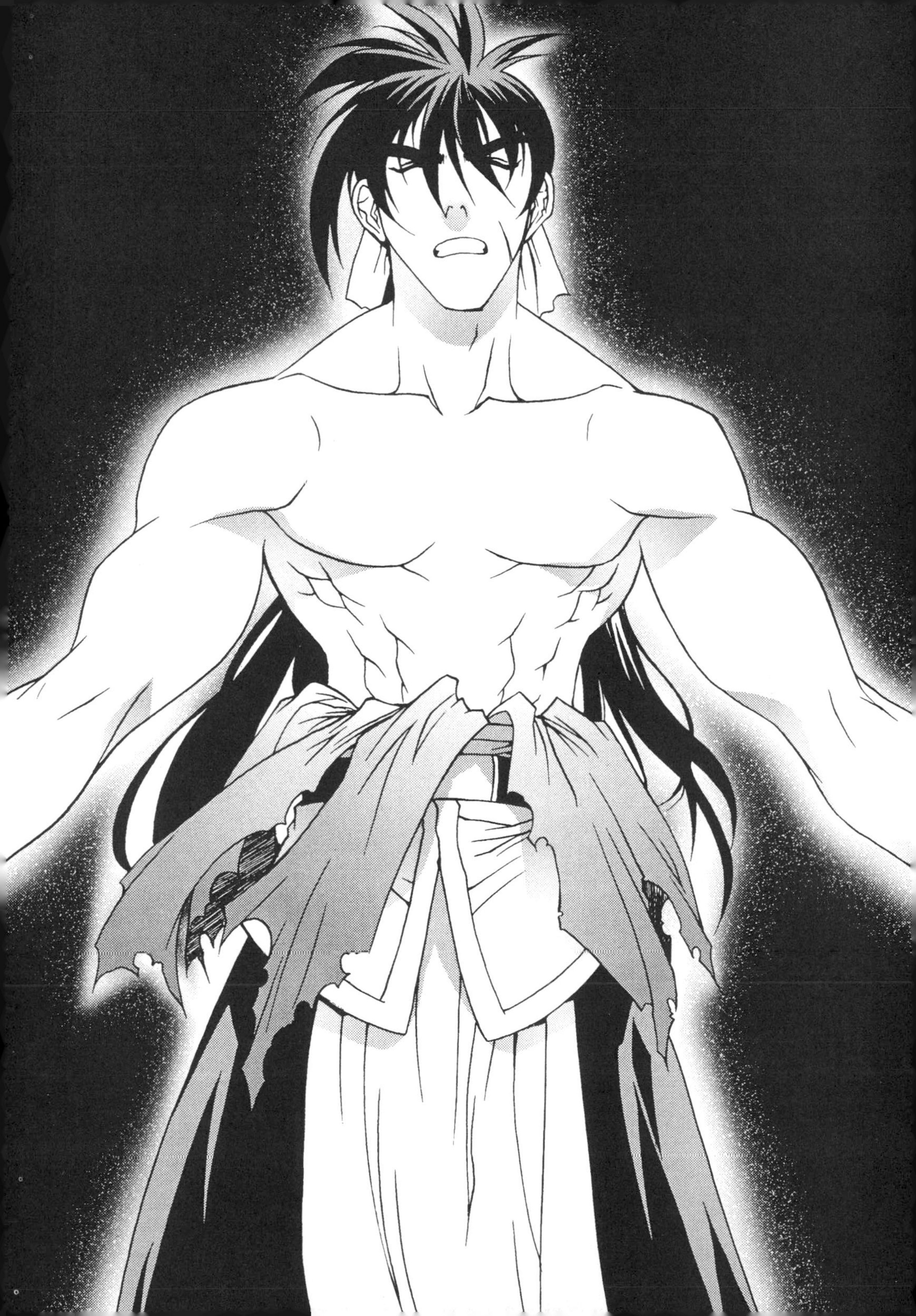

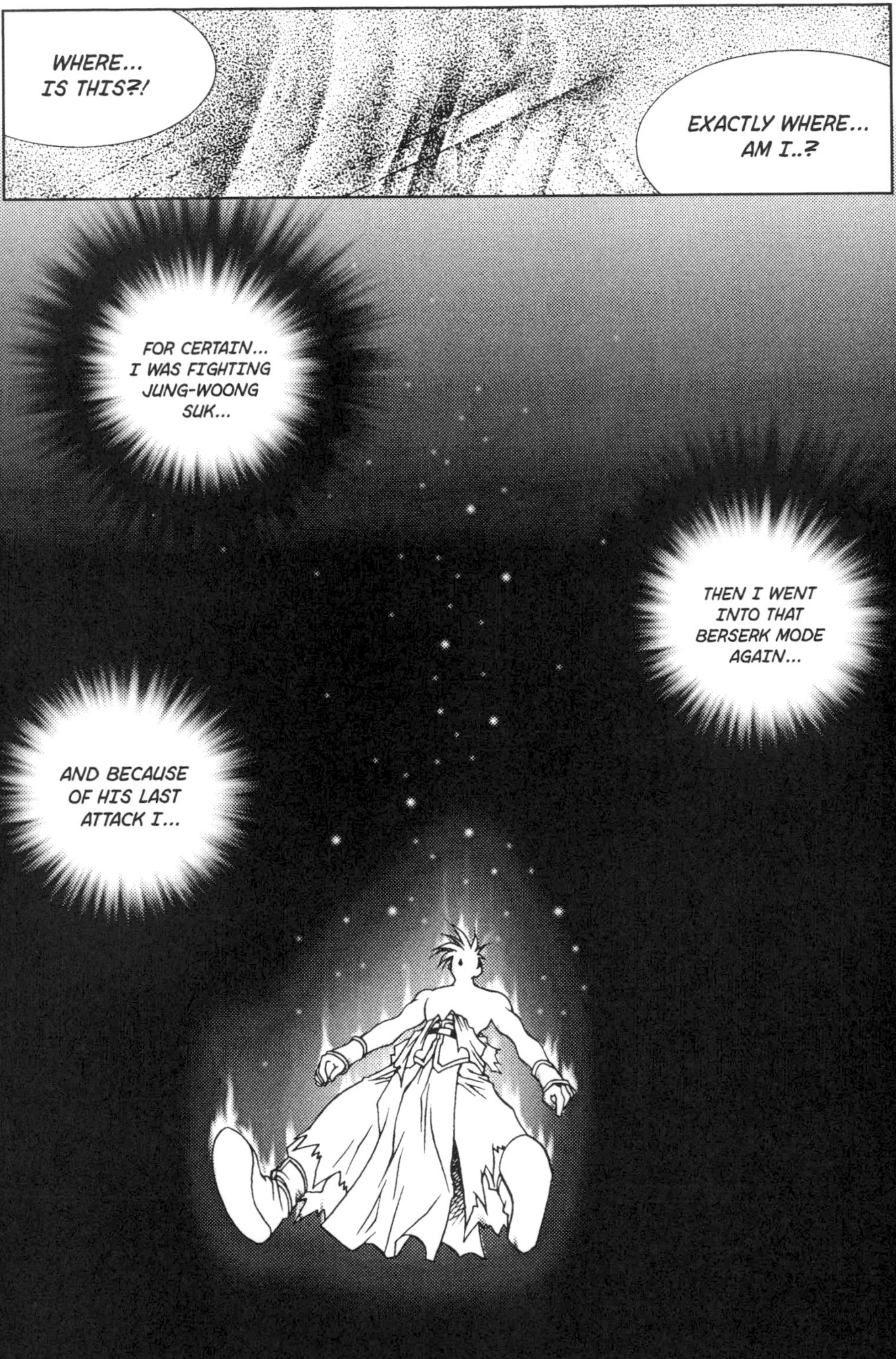
WHERE... IS THIS?!
EXACTLY WHERE... AM I..?
FOR CERTAIN... I WAS FIGHTING JUNG-WOONG SUK...
THEN I WENT INTO THAT BERSERK MODE AGAIN...
AND BECAUSE OF HIS LAST ATTACK I...

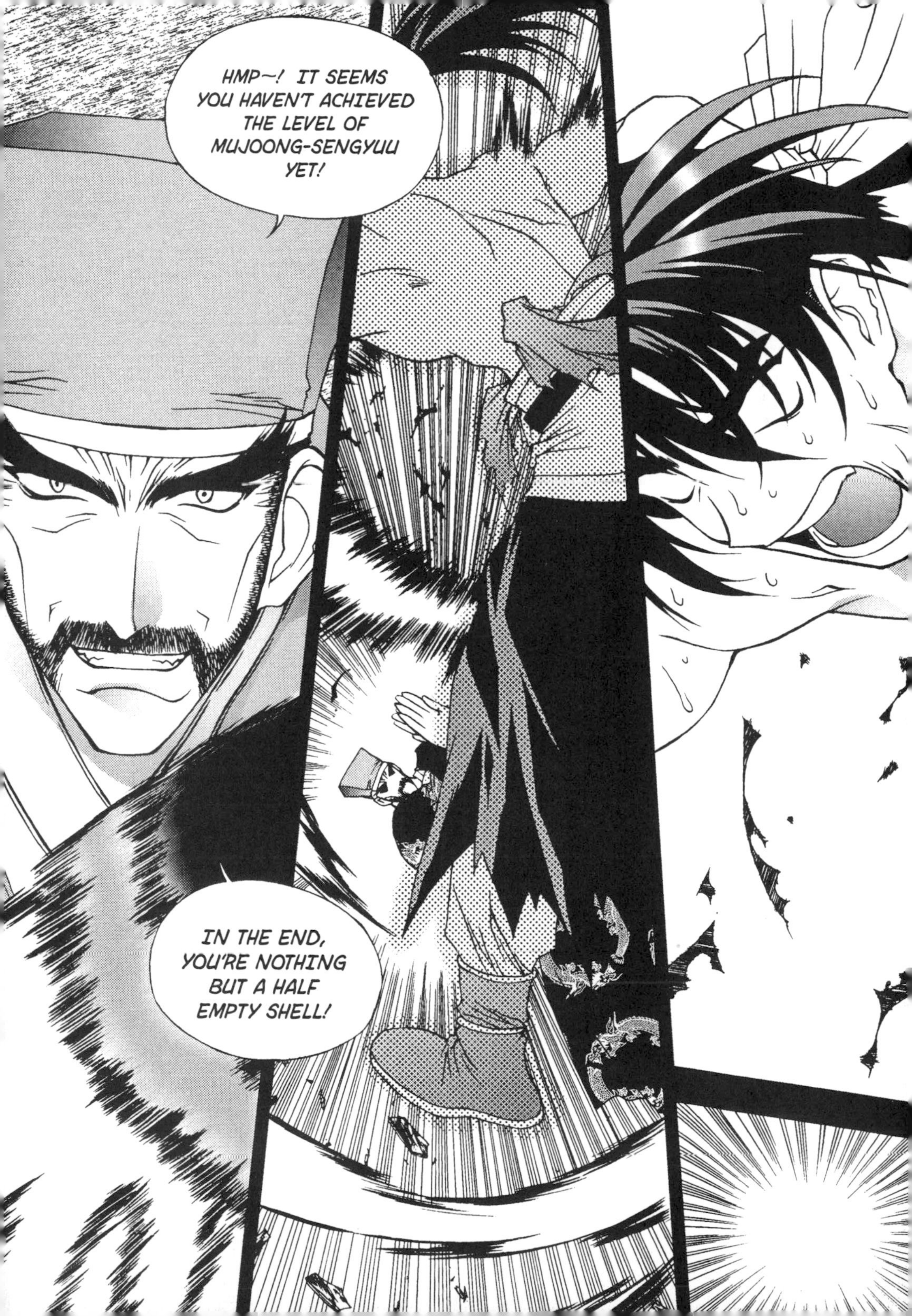
HMP~! IT SEEMS YOU HAVEN'T ACHIEVED THE LEVEL OF MUJOONG-SENGYUU YET!
IN THE END, YOU'RE NOTHING BUT A HALF EMPTY SHELL!

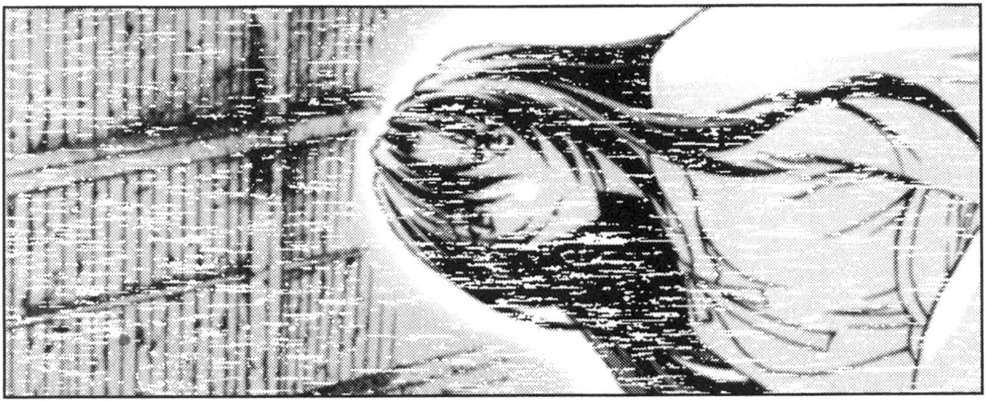
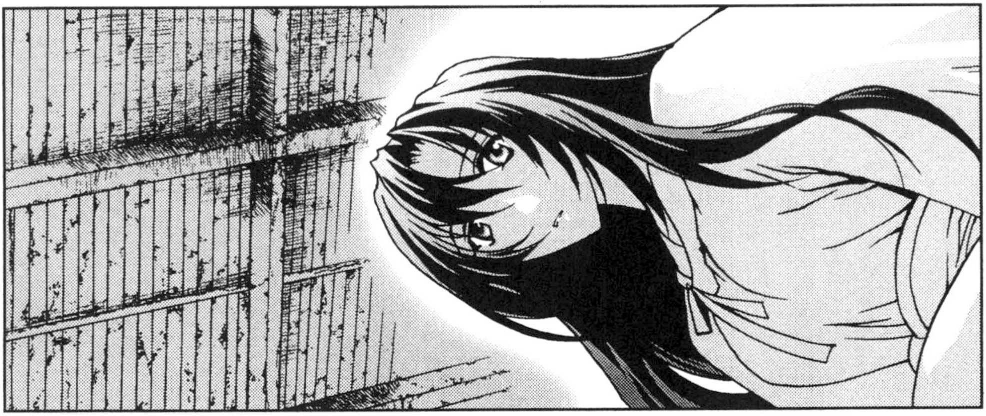
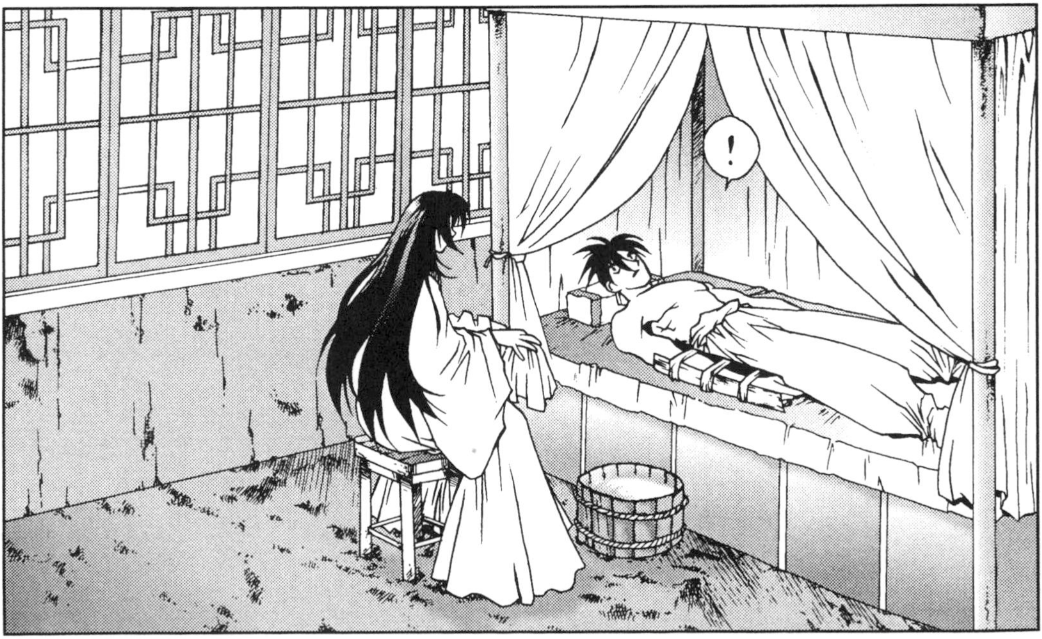
!

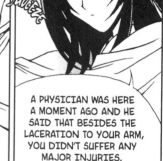

WE'RE AT AN INN NEARBY TOWN RIGHT NOW. I THOUGHT SOMETHING MIGHT HAVE HAPPENED BECAUSE YOU WERE LATE, MASTER YHUN. WHEN I CAME INTO TOWN, I FOUND YOU UNCONSCIOUS SO I BROUGHT YOU HERE.

A PHYSICIAN WAS HERE A MOMENT AGO AND HE SAID THAT BESIDES THE LACERATION TO YOUR ARM, YOU DIDN'T SUFFER ANY MAJOR INJURIES.

......

BUT...

......

IT'S DIFFICULT TO IMAGINE THAT THERE ARE MANY PEOPLE OUT THERE WHO ARE STILL CAPABLE OF PUTTING YOU IN THIS CONDITION, MASTER YHUN...

......

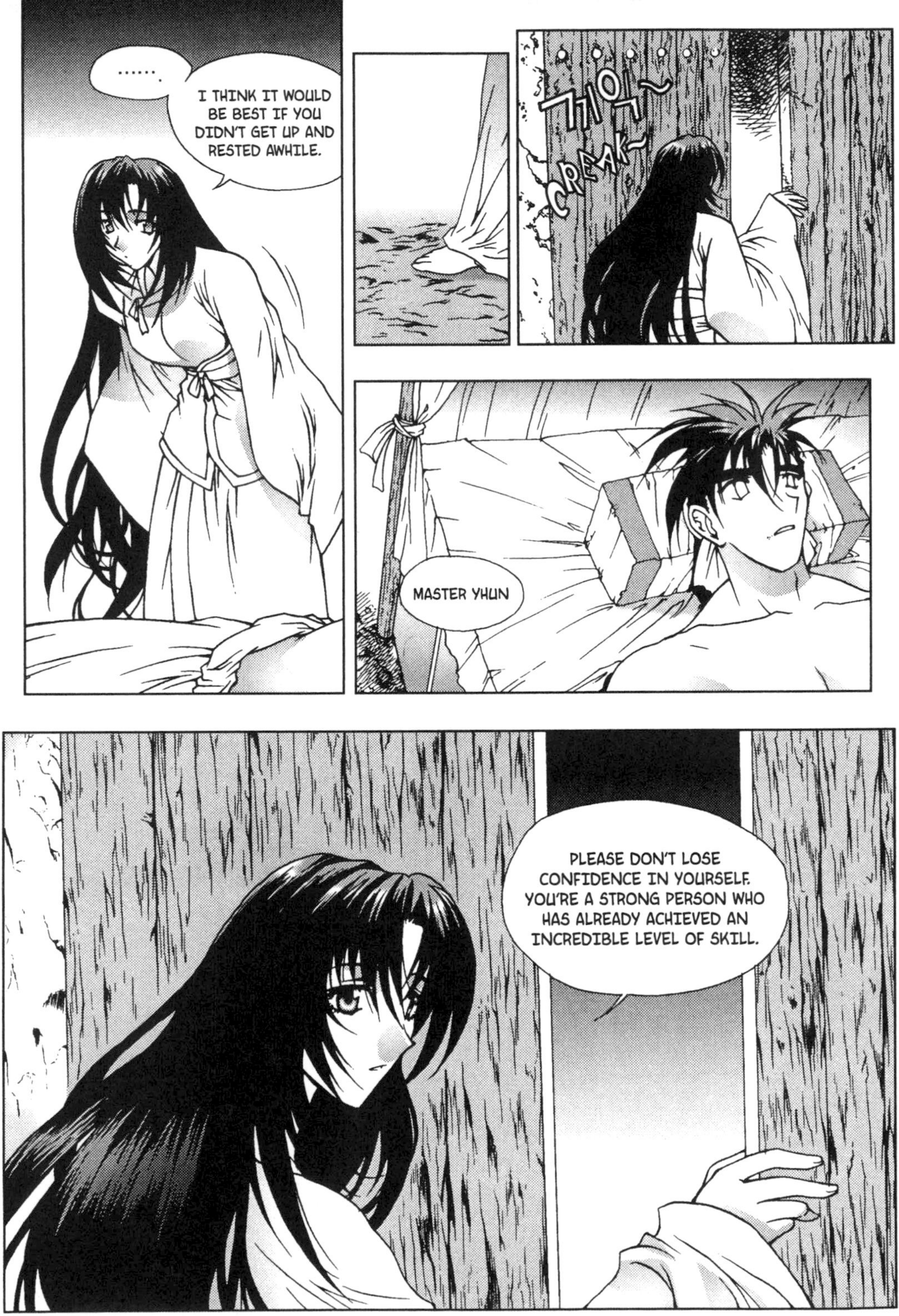
....
I THINK IT WOULD BE BEST IF YOU DIDN'T GET UP AND RESTED AWHILE.
끼익~
CREAK~
MASTER YHUN
PLEASE DON'T LOSE CONFIDENCE IN YOURSELF. YOU'RE A STRONG PERSON WHO HAS ALREADY ACHIEVED AN INCREDIBLE LEVEL OF SKILL.

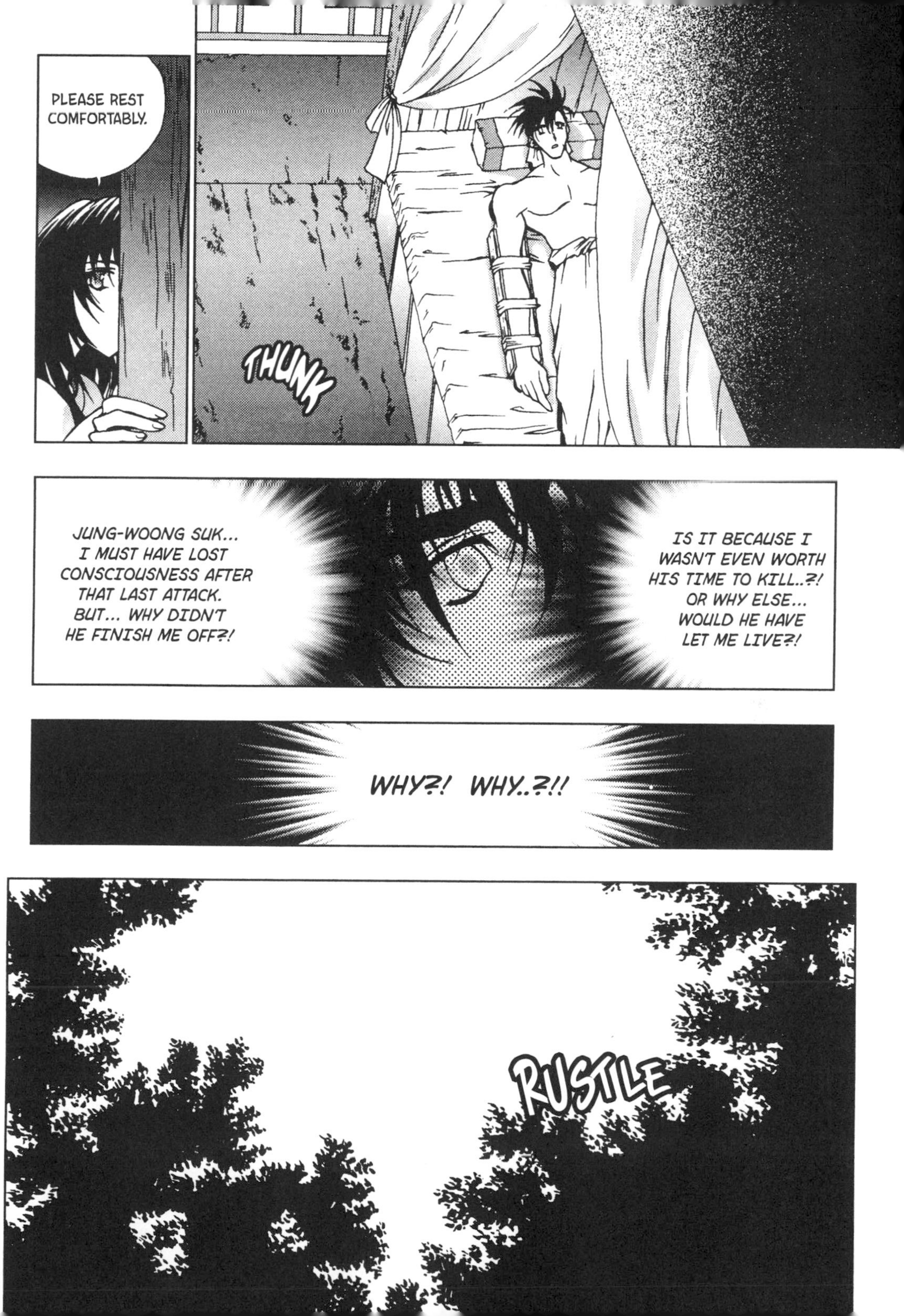
PLEASE REST COMFORTABLY.
THUNK
JUNG-WOONG SUK... I MUST HAVE LOST CONSCIOUSNESS AFTER THAT LAST ATTACK. BUT... WHY DIDN'T HE FINISH ME OFF?!
IS IT BECAUSE I WASN'T EVEN WORTH HIS TIME TO KILL..?! OR WHY ELSE... WOULD HE HAVE LET ME LIVE?!
WHY?! WHY..?!!
RUSTLE

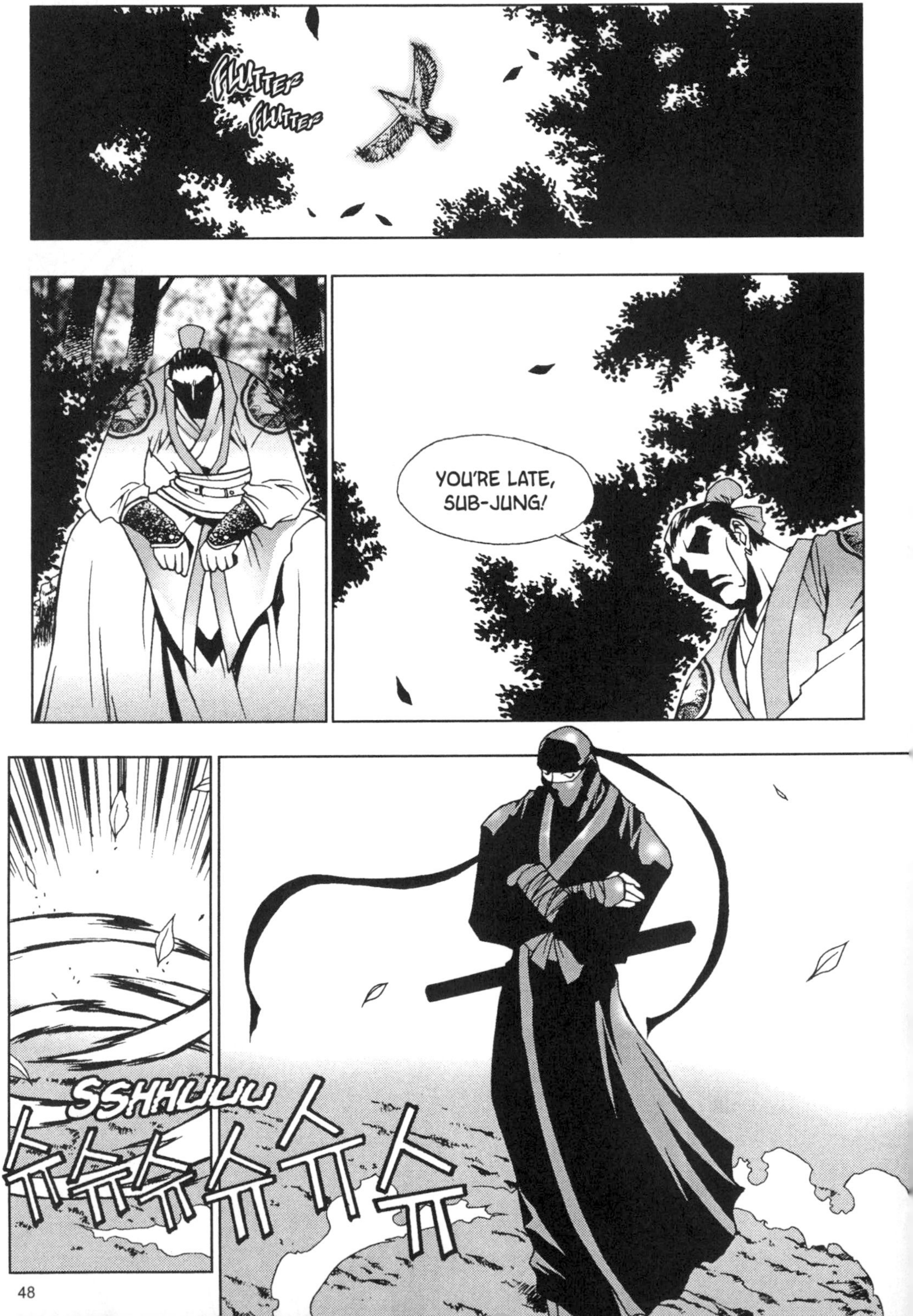
FLUTTER
FLUTTER
YOU'RE LATE, SUB-JUNG!
SSHUUU

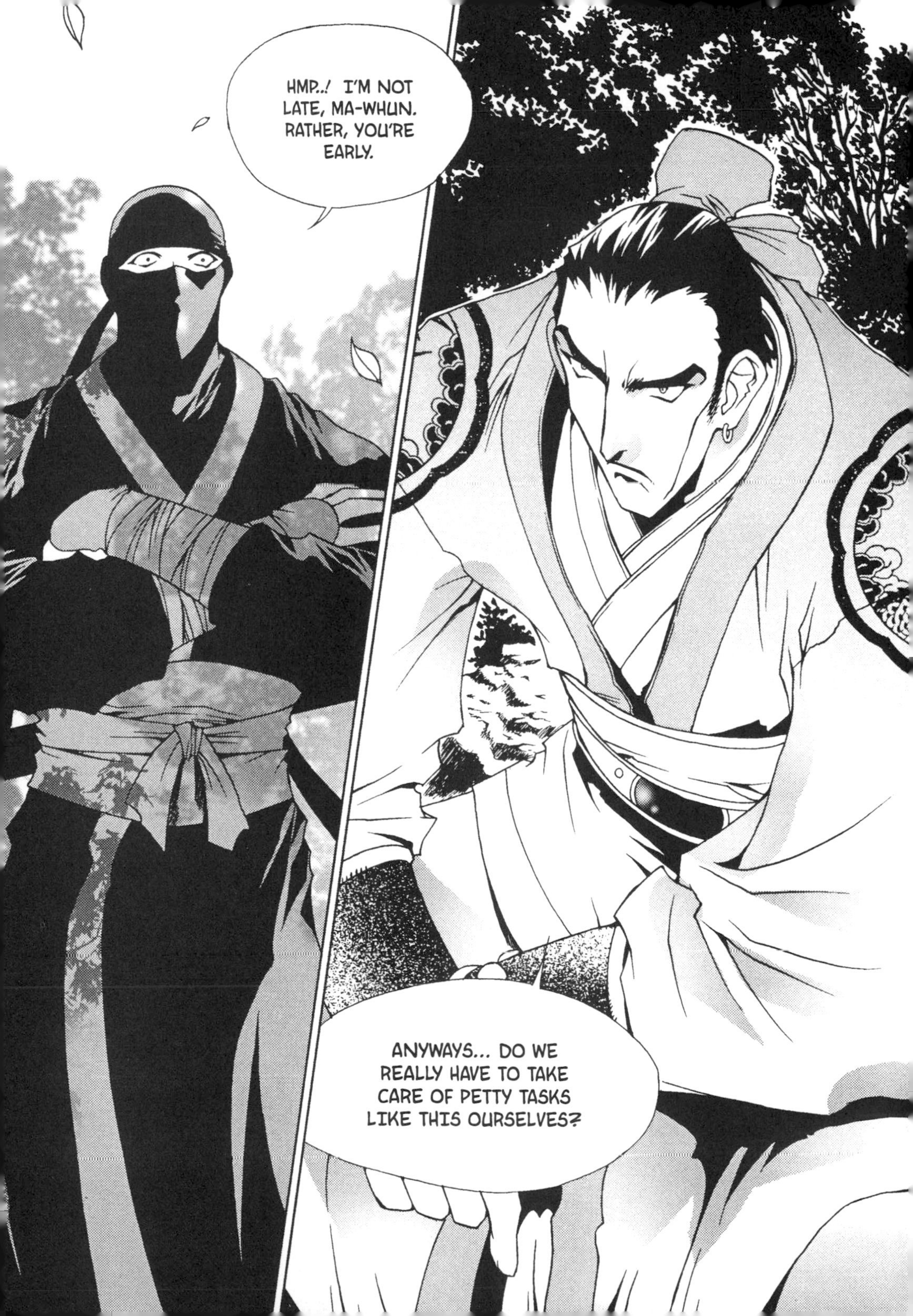
HMP..! I'M NOT LATE, MA-WHUN. RATHER, YOU'RE EARLY.
ANYWAYS... DO WE REALLY HAVE TO TAKE CARE OF PETTY TASKS LIKE THIS OURSELVES?

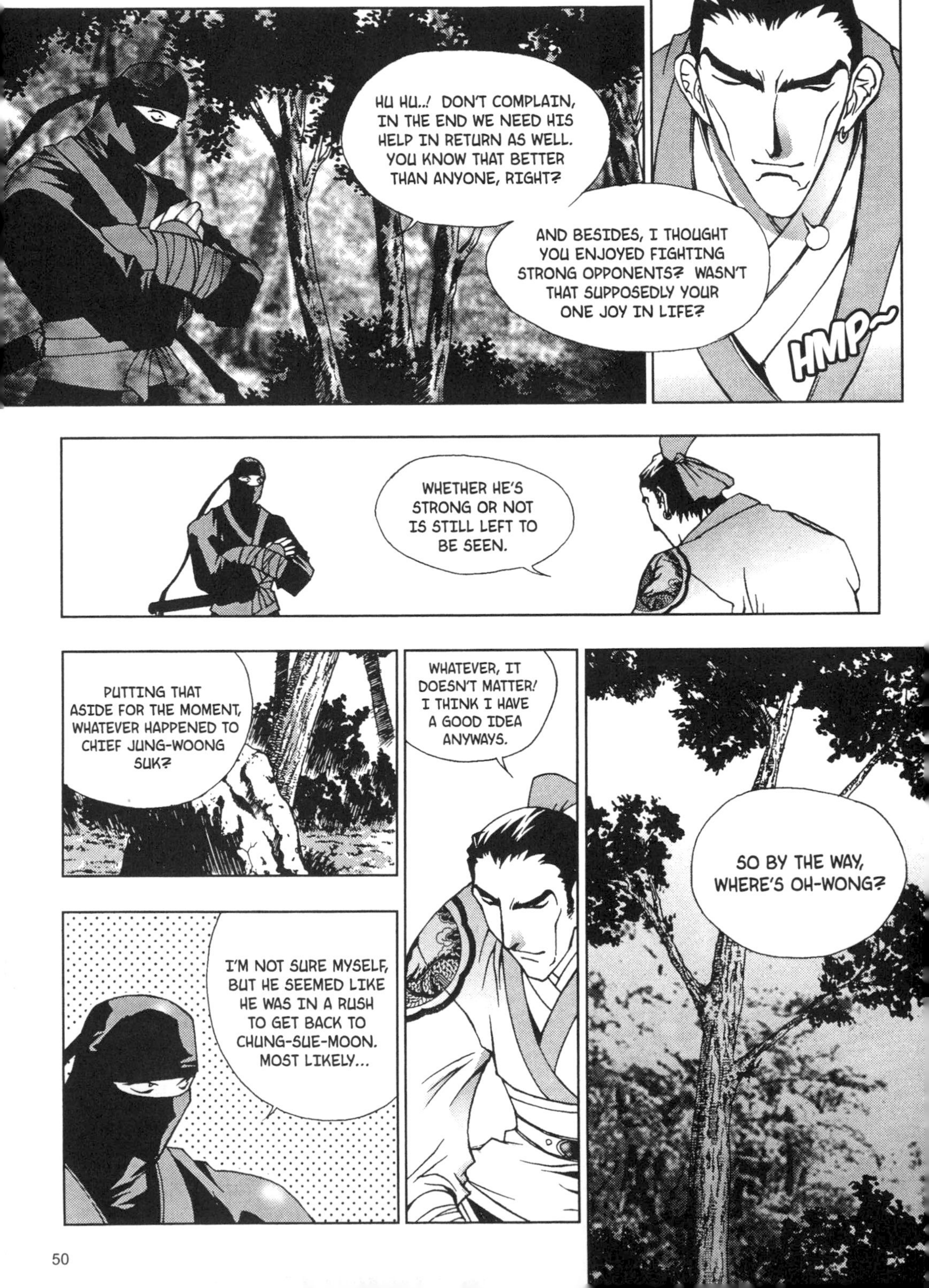
HU HU..! DON'T COMPLAIN, IN THE END WE NEED HIS HELP IN RETURN AS WELL. YOU KNOW THAT BETTER THAN ANYONE, RIGHT?
AND BESIDES, I THOUGHT YOU ENJOYED FIGHTING STRONG OPPONENTS? WASN'T THAT SUPPOSEDLY YOUR ONE JOY IN LIFE?
HMP~
WHETHER HE'S STRONG OR NOT IS STILL LEFT TO BE SEEN.
PUTTING THAT ASIDE FOR THE MOMENT, WHATEVER HAPPENED TO CHIEF JUNG-WOONG SUK?
WHATEVER, IT DOESN'T MATTER! I THINK I HAVE A GOOD IDEA ANYWAYS.
SO BY THE WAY, WHERE'S OH-WONG?
I'M NOT SURE MYSELF, BUT HE SEEMED LIKE HE WAS IN A RUSH TO GET BACK TO CHUNG-SUE-MOON. MOST LIKELY...

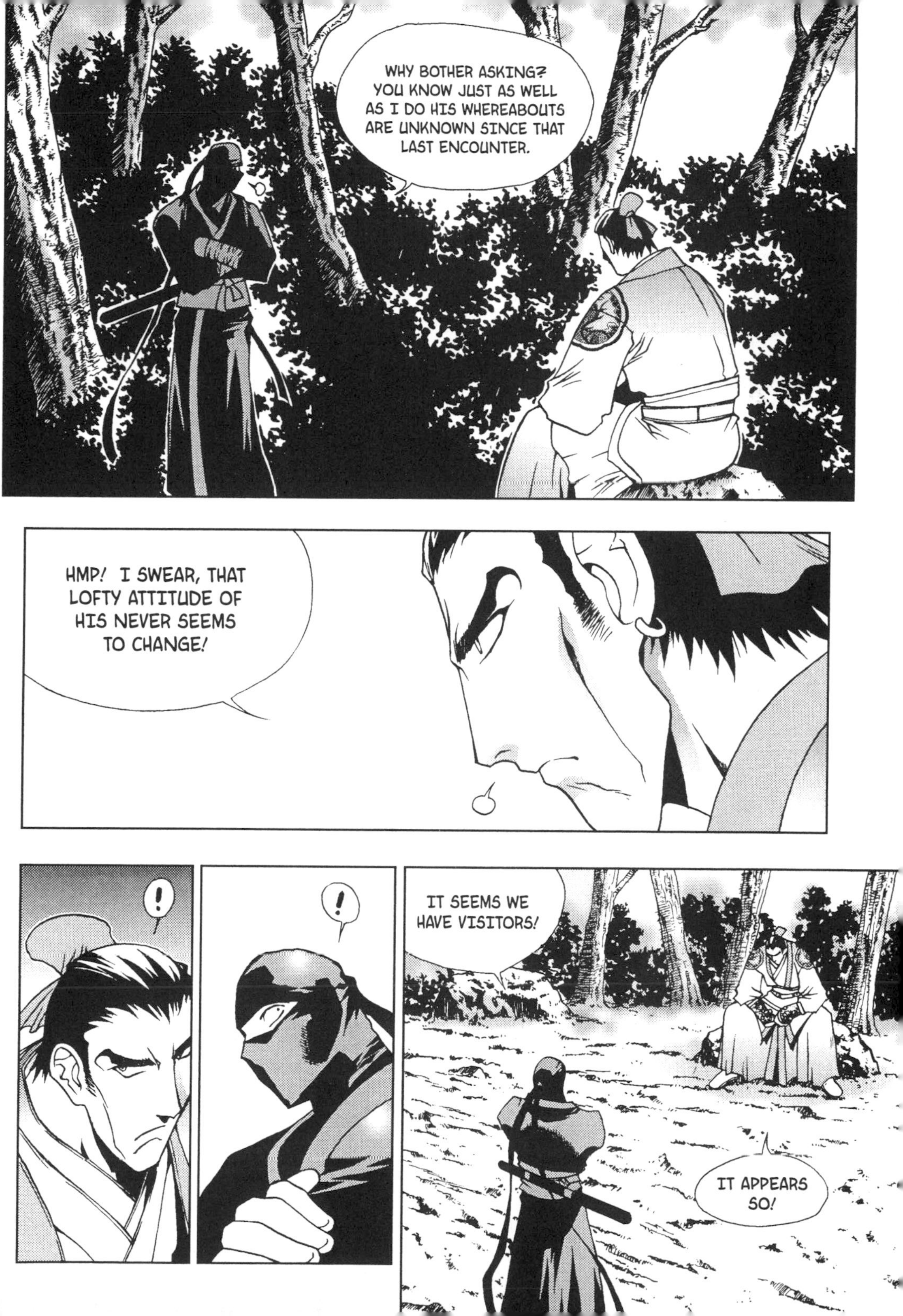
WHY BOTHER ASKING? YOU KNOW JUST AS WELL AS I DO HIS WHEREABOUTS ARE UNKNOWN SINCE THAT LAST ENCOUNTER.
HMP! I SWEAR, THAT LOFTY ATTITUDE OF HIS NEVER SEEMS TO CHANGE!
!
!
IT SEEMS WE HAVE VISITORS!
IT APPEARS SO!

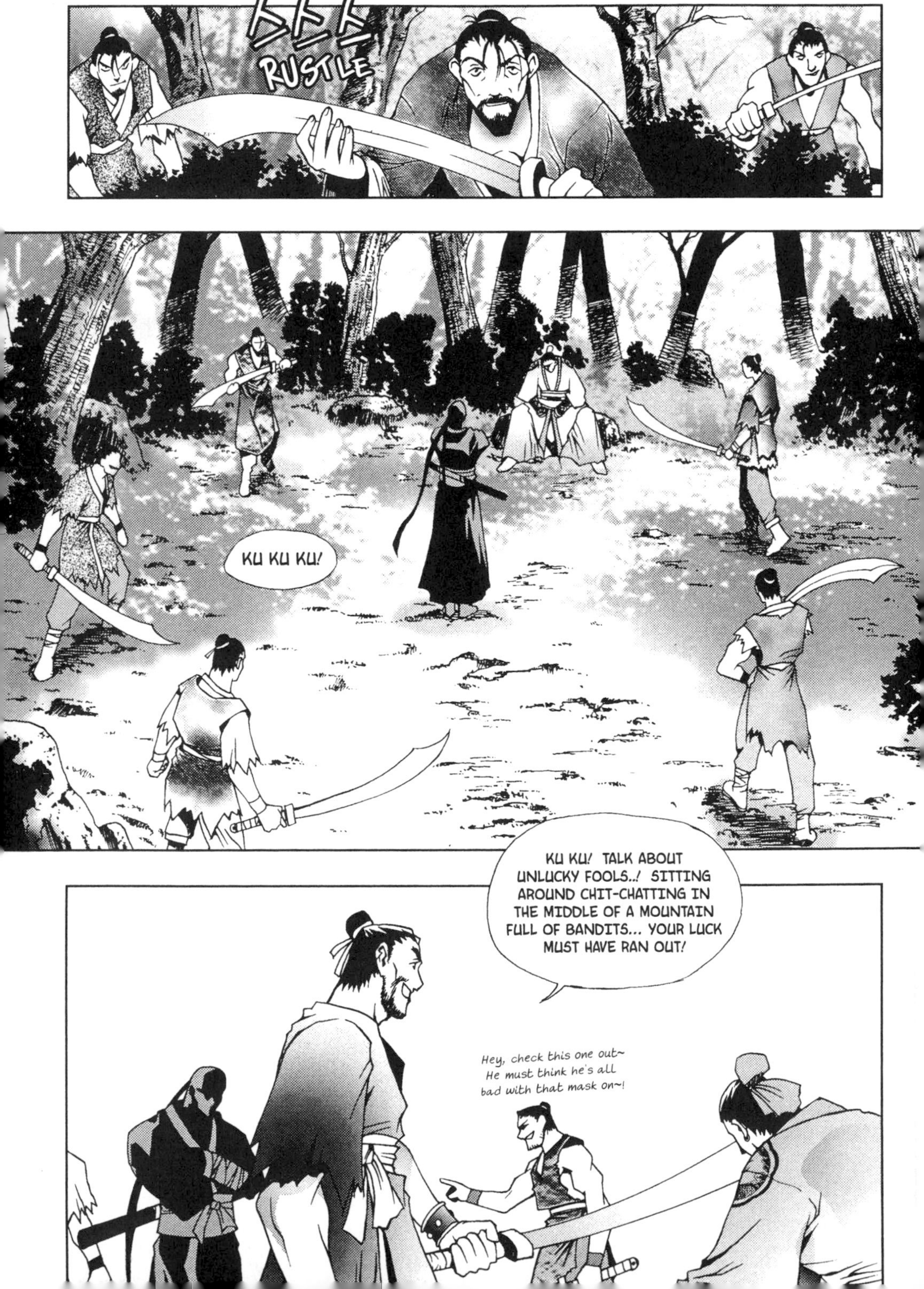
스스스
RUSTLE
KU KU KU!
KU KU! TALK ABOUT UNLUCKY FOOLS..! SITTING AROUND CHIT-CHATTING IN THE MIDDLE OF A MOUNTAIN FULL OF BANDITS... YOUR LUCK MUST HAVE RAN OUT!
Hey, check this one out~ He must think he's all bad with that mask on~!

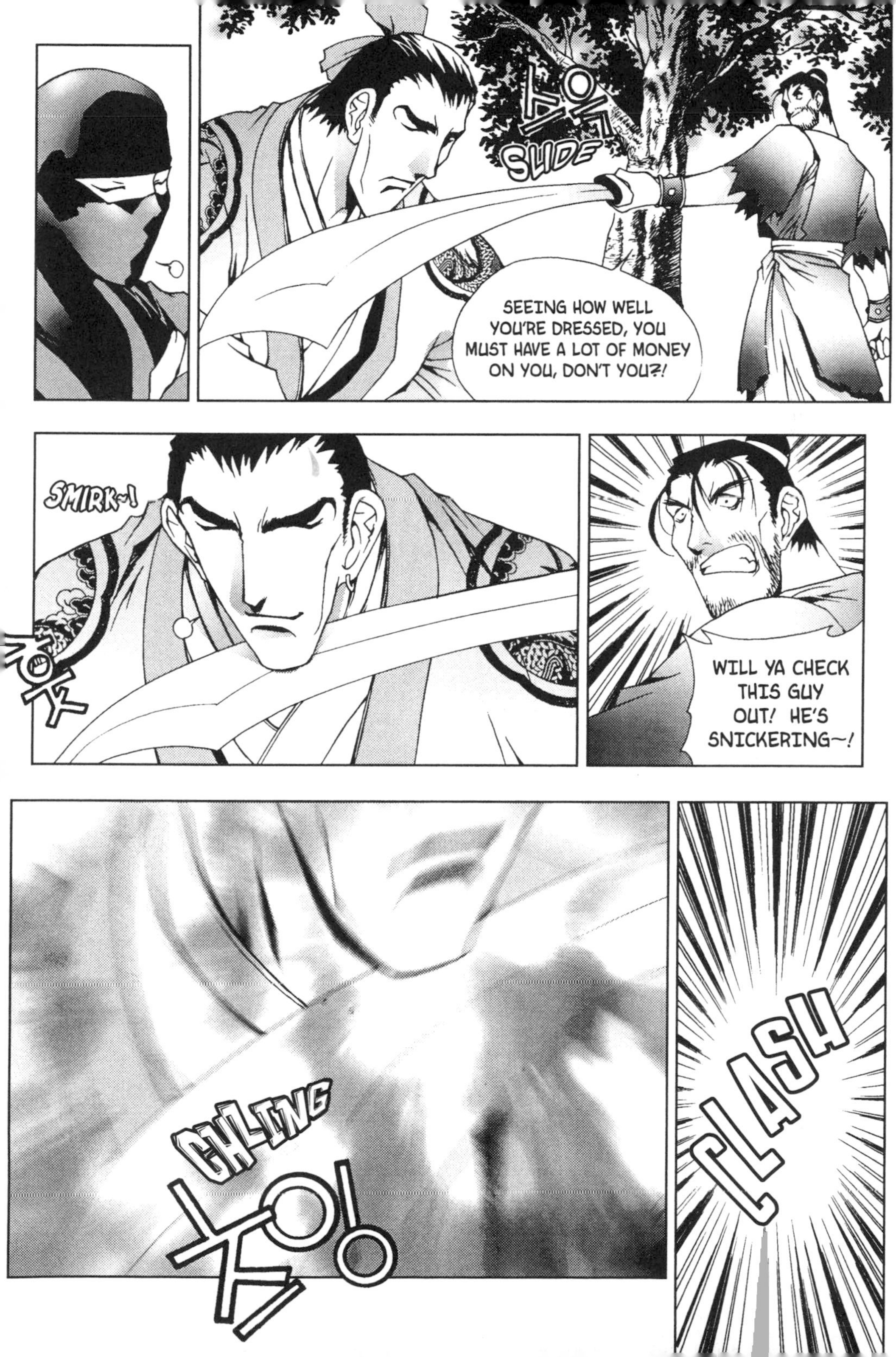
SLIDE
SEEING HOW WELL YOU'RE DRESSED, YOU MUST HAVE A LOT OF MONEY ON YOU, DON'T YOU?!
SMIRK~!
WILL YA CHECK THIS GUY OUT! HE'S SNICKERING~!
CHLING
CLASH

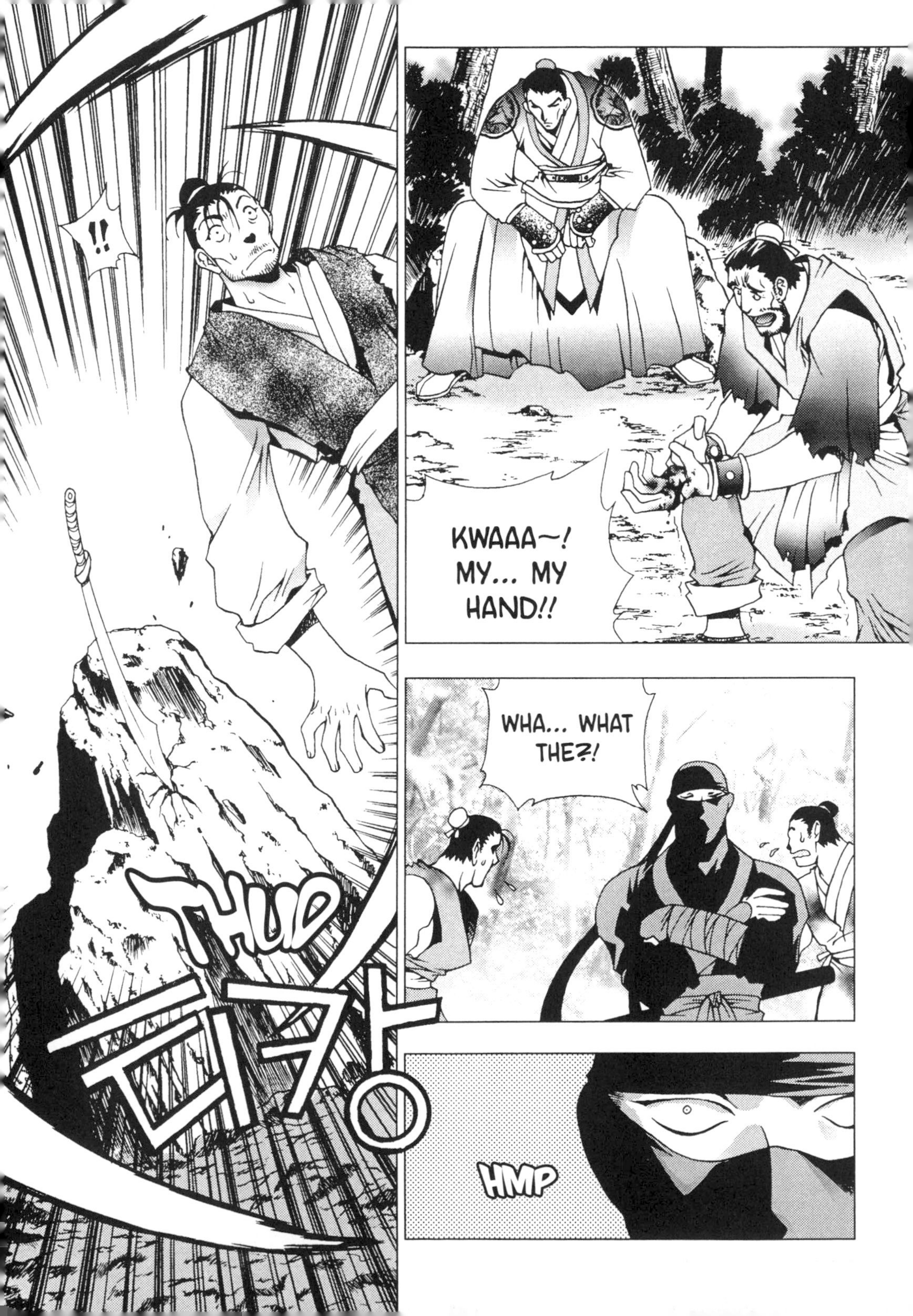
!!
THUD
KWAAA~! MY... MY HAND!!
WHA... WHAT THE?!
HMP

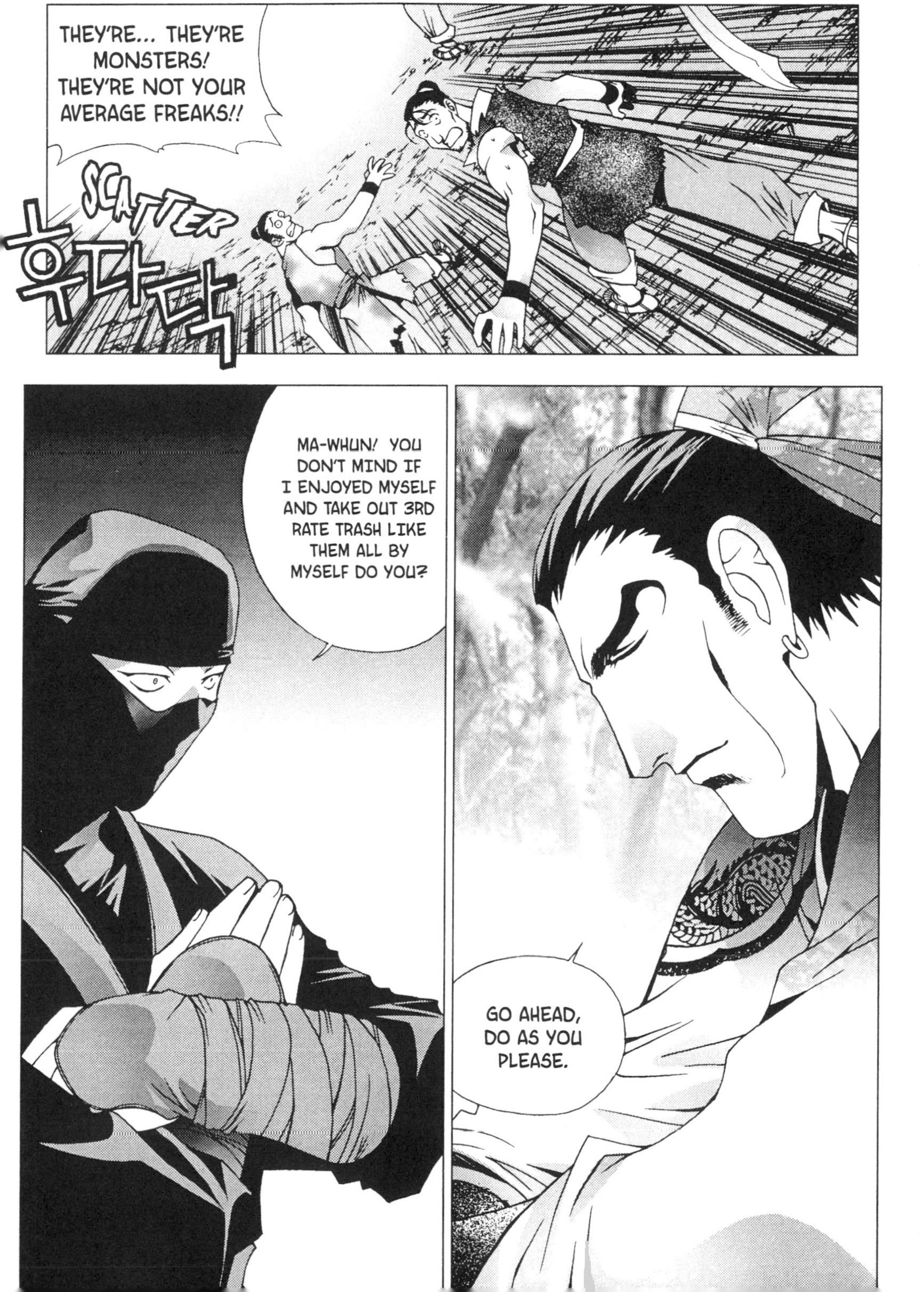
THEY'RE... THEY'RE MONSTERS! THEY'RE NOT YOUR AVERAGE FREAKS!!
SCATTER
후다닥
MA-WHUN! YOU DON'T MIND IF I ENJOYED MYSELF AND TAKE OUT 3RD RATE TRASH LIKE THEM ALL BY MYSELF DO YOU?
GO AHEAD, DO AS YOU PLEASE.

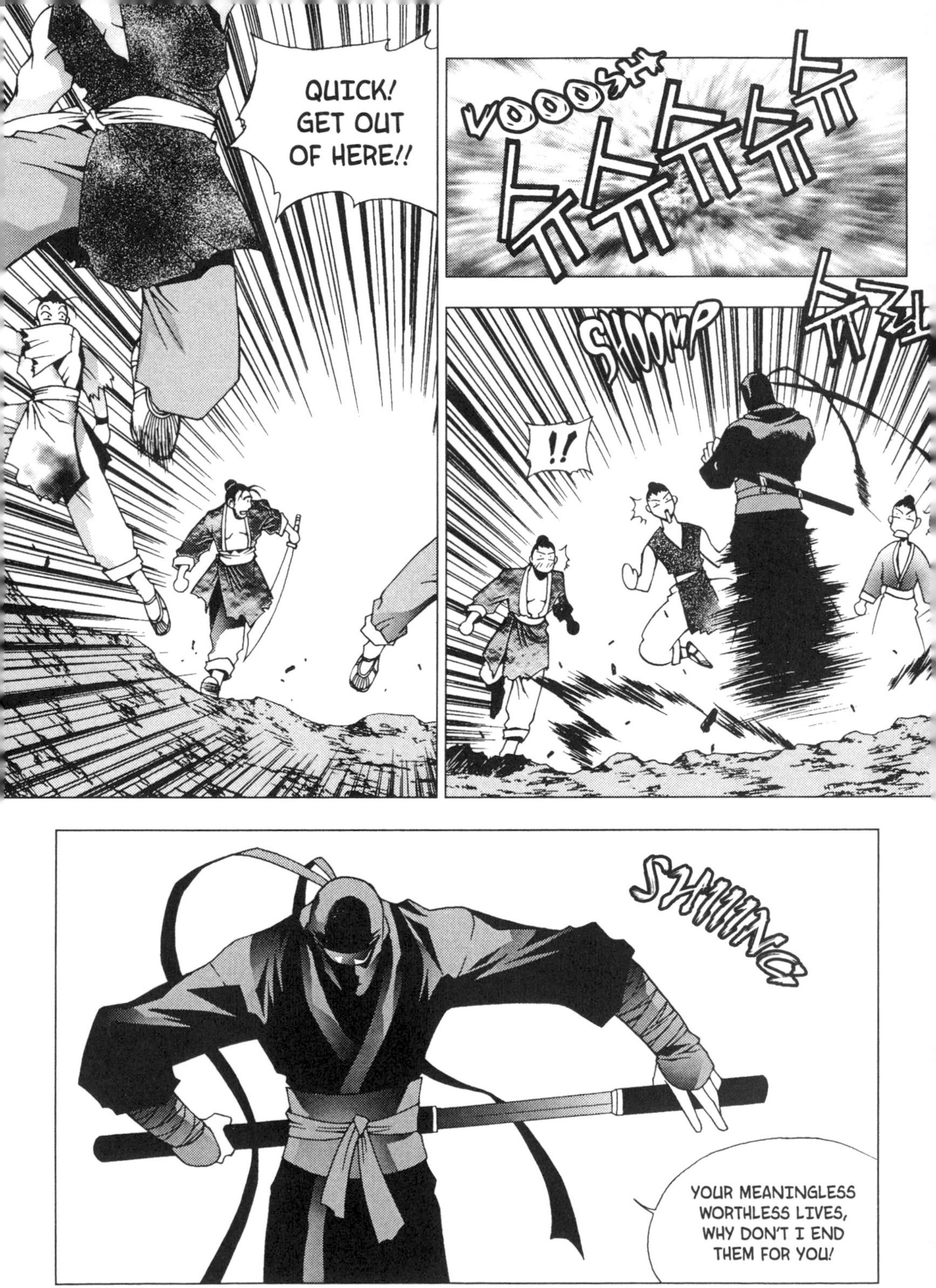

QUICK! GET OUT OF HERE!!
VOOOSH
SHOOMP
!!
SHHING
YOUR MEANINGLESS WORTHLESS LIVES, WHY DON'T I END THEM FOR YOU!

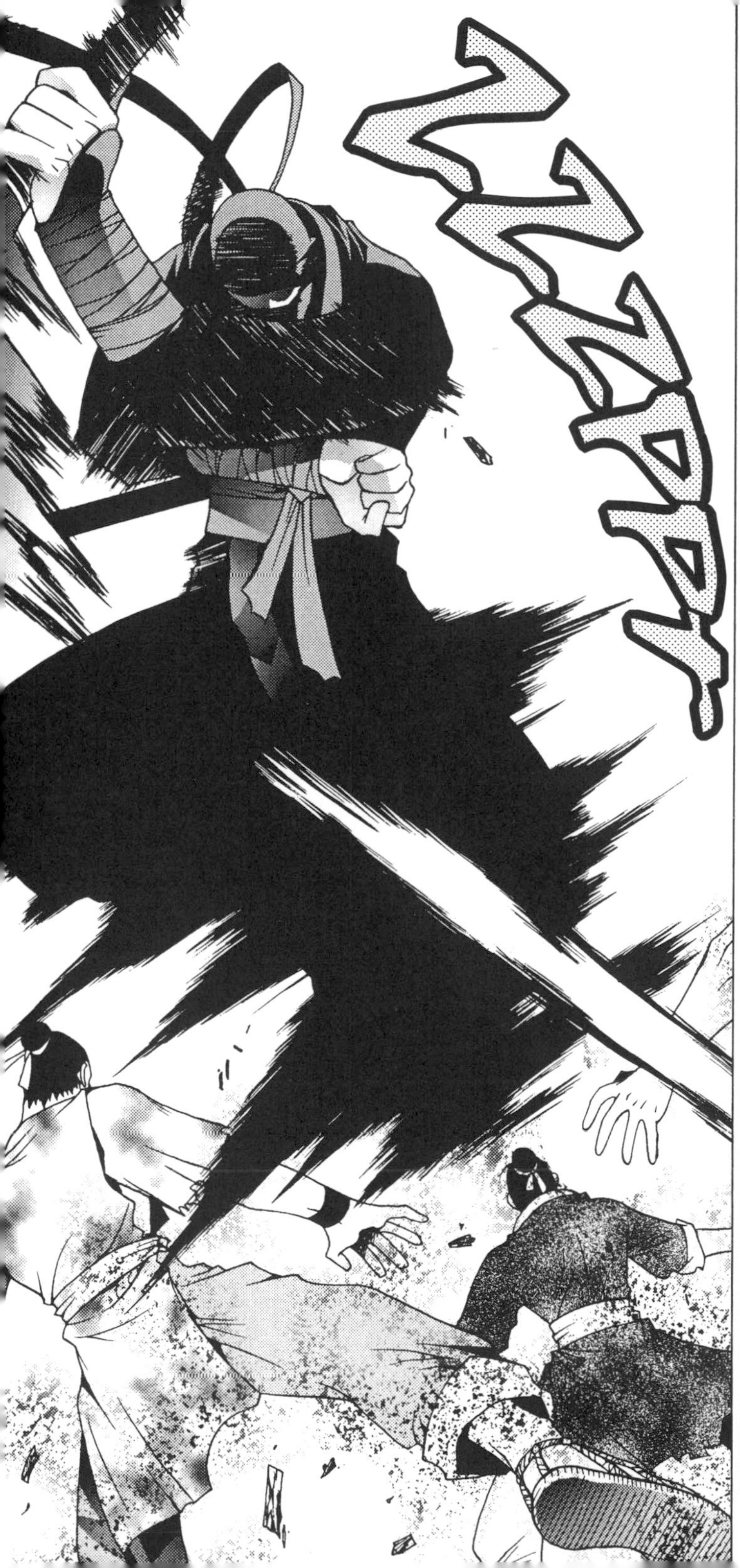

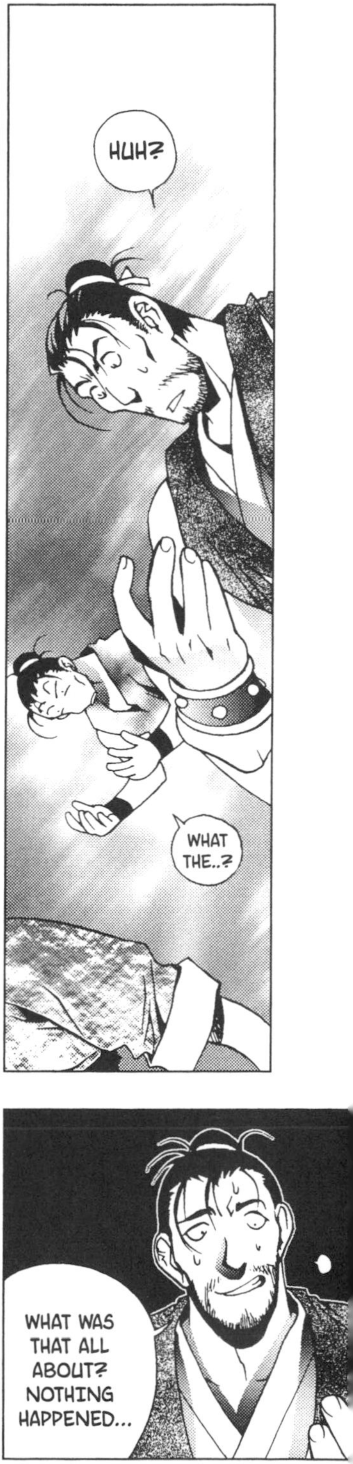
HUH?
WHAT THE..?
WHAT WAS THAT ALL ABOUT? NOTHING HAPPENED...

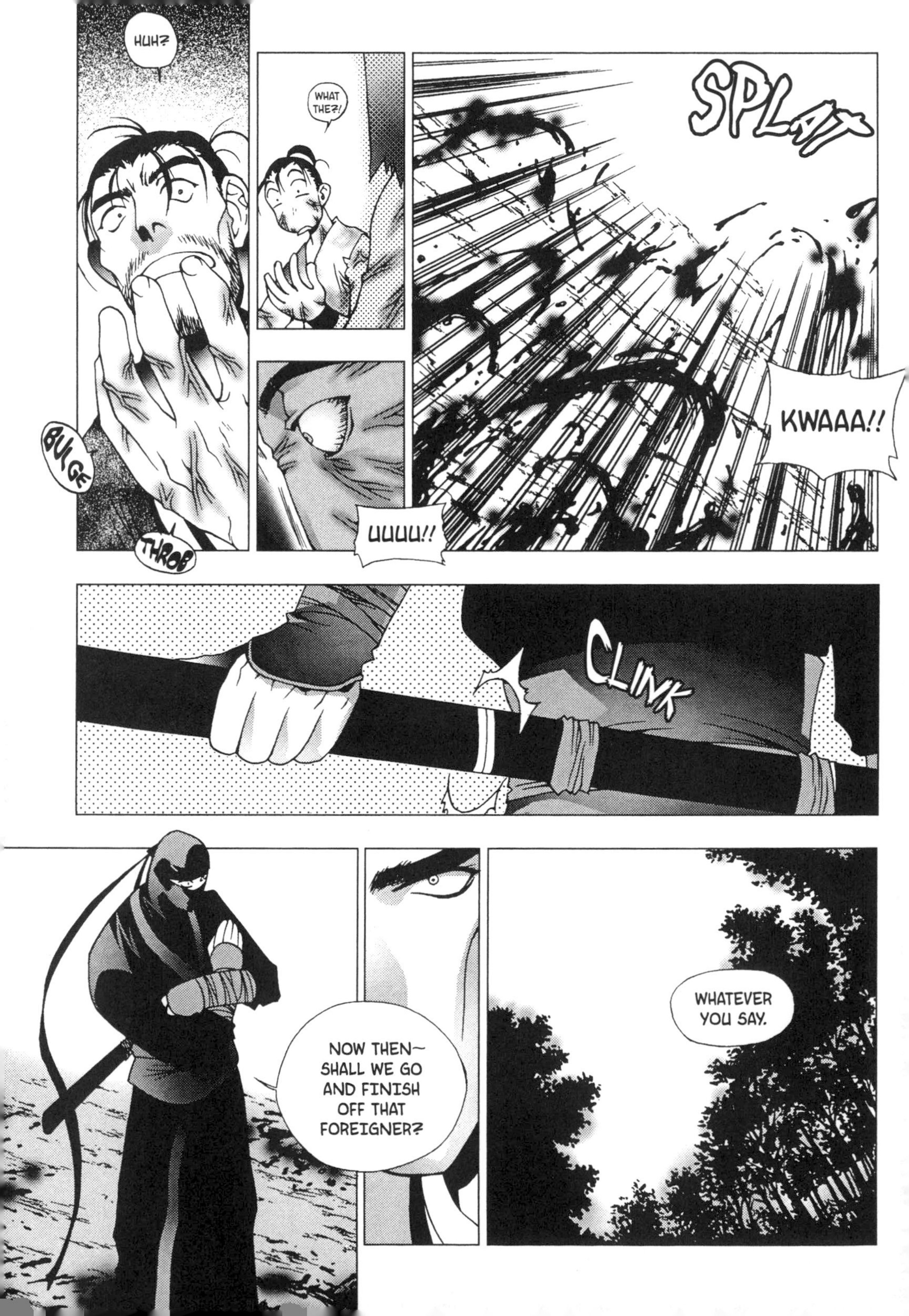
HUH?
WHAT THE?!
SPLAT
BULGE
THROB
UUUU!!
KWAAA!!
CLINK
NOW THEN~ SHALL WE GO AND FINISH OFF THAT FOREIGNER?
WHATEVER YOU SAY.

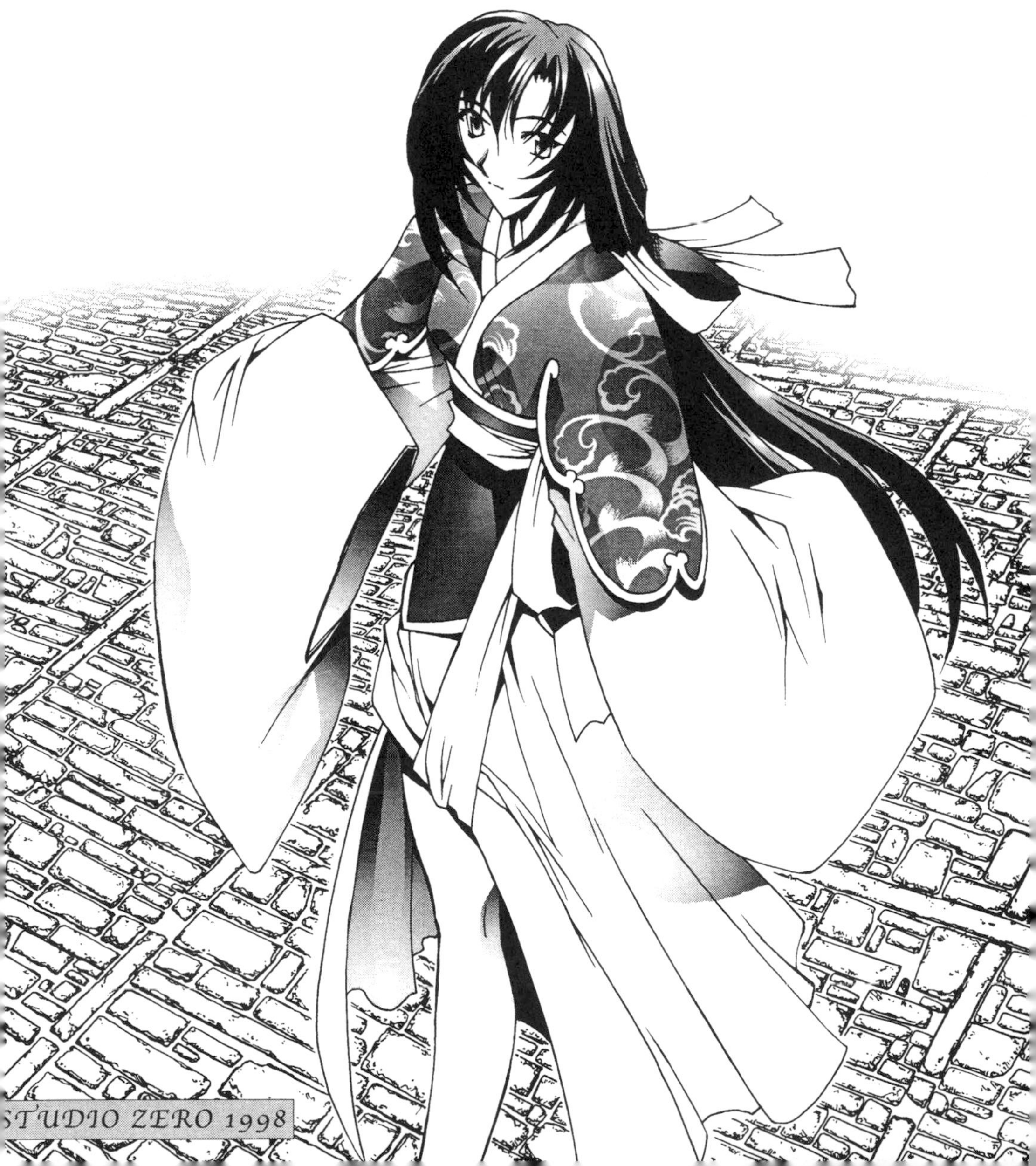
STUDIO ZERO 1998

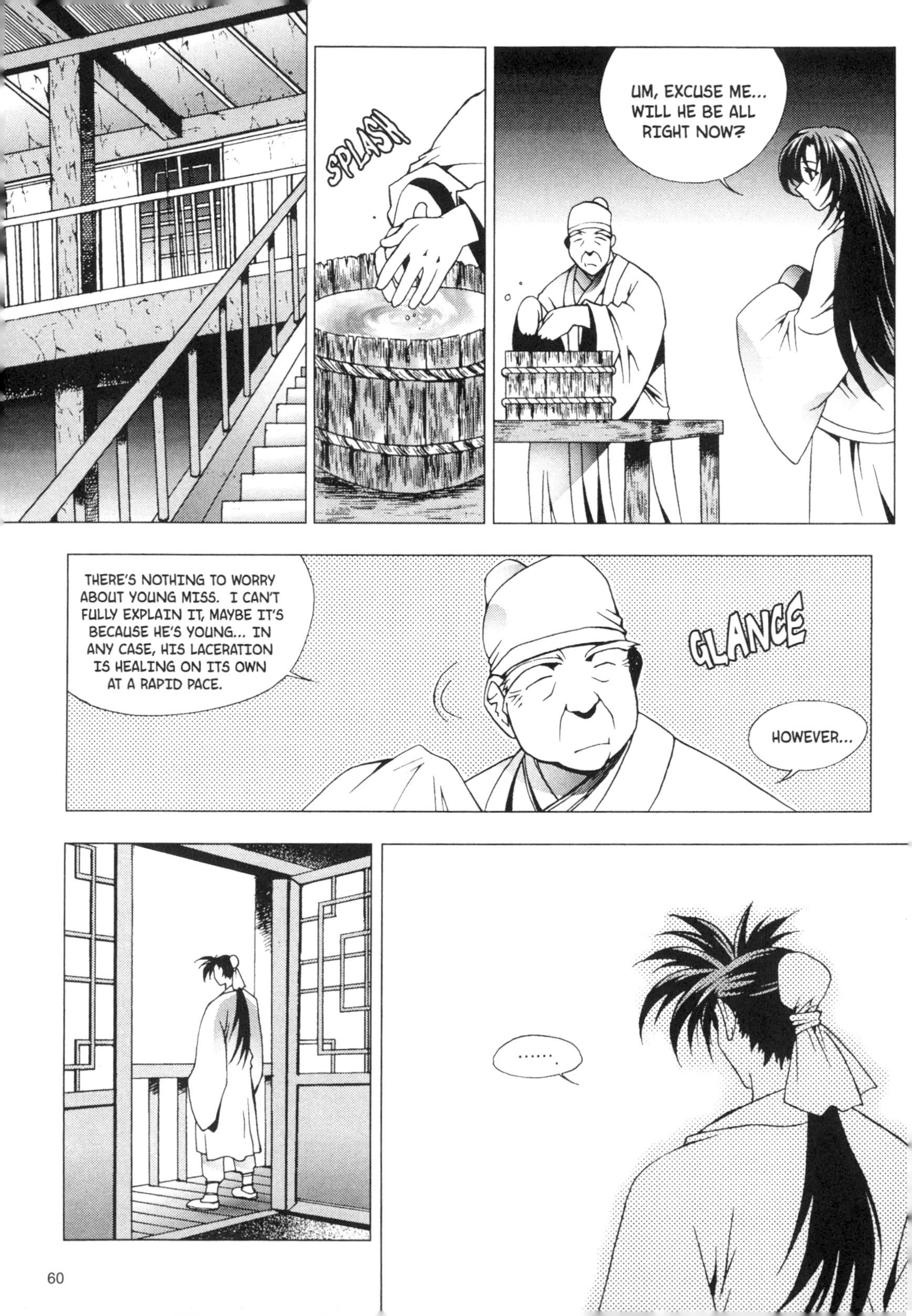
SPLASH
UM, EXCUSE ME... WILL HE BE ALL RIGHT NOW?
THERE'S NOTHING TO WORRY ABOUT YOUNG MISS. I CAN'T FULLY EXPLAIN IT, MAYBE IT'S BECAUSE HE'S YOUNG... IN ANY CASE, HIS LACERATION IS HEALING ON ITS OWN AT A RAPID PACE.
GLANCE
HOWEVER...
....

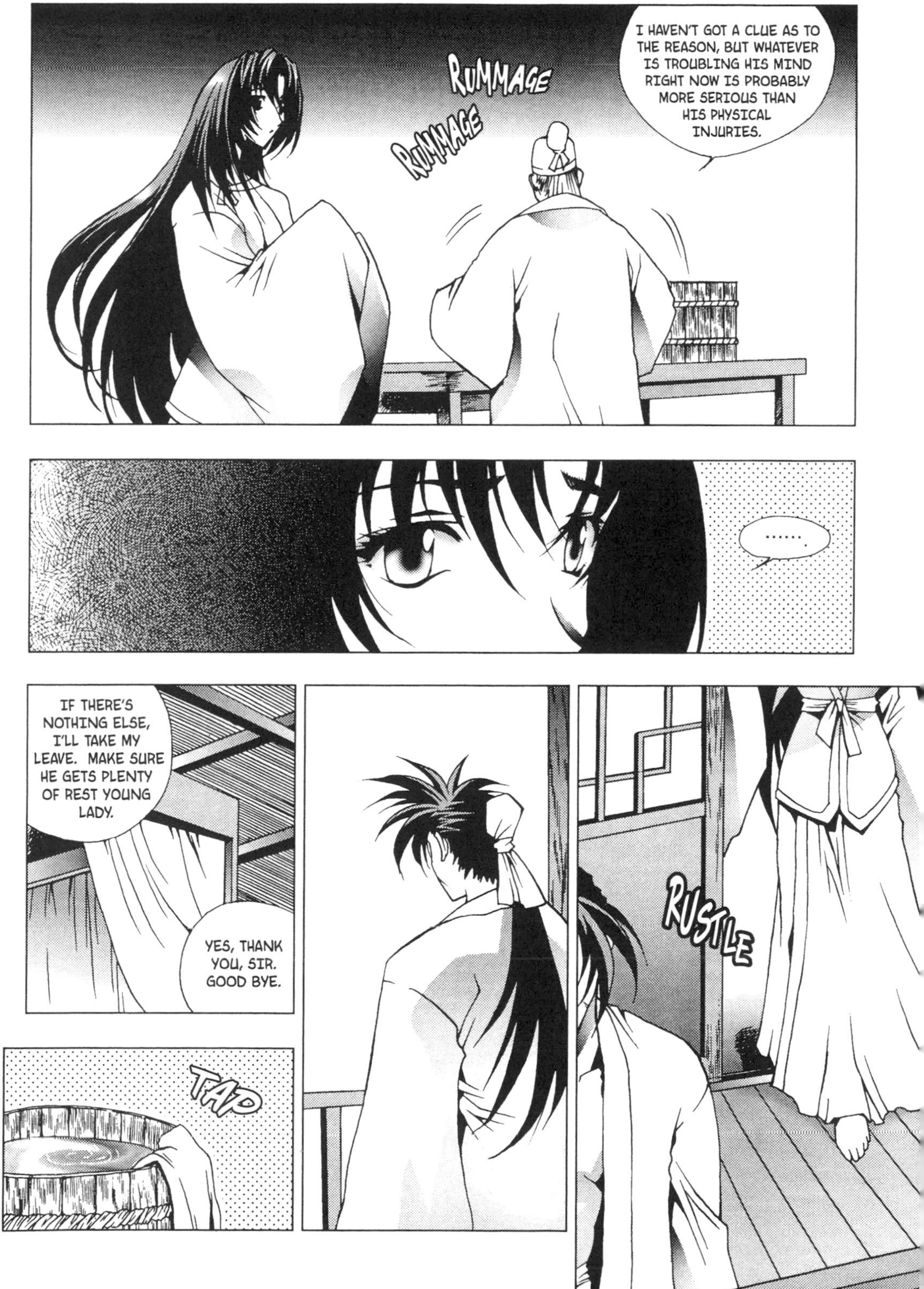
I HAVEN'T GOT A CLUE AS TO THE REASON, BUT WHATEVER IS TROUBLING HIS MIND RIGHT NOW IS PROBABLY MORE SERIOUS THAN HIS PHYSICAL INJURIES.
RUMMAGE
RUMMAGE
......
IF THERE'S NOTHING ELSE, I'LL TAKE MY LEAVE. MAKE SURE HE GETS PLENTY OF REST YOUNG LADY.
YES, THANK YOU, SIR. GOOD BYE.
TAP
RUSTLE

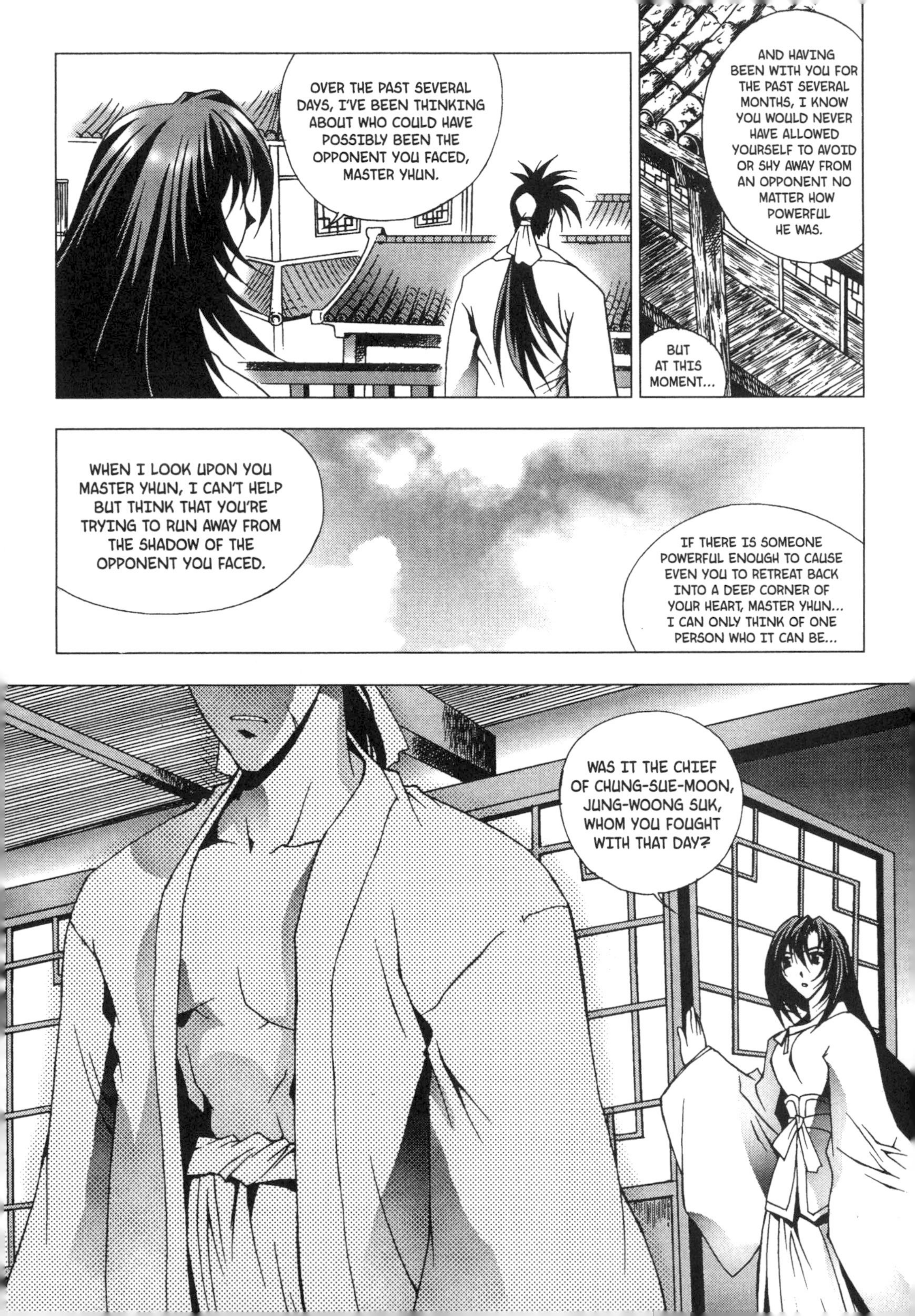
OVER THE PAST SEVERAL DAYS, I'VE BEEN THINKING ABOUT WHO COULD HAVE POSSIBLY BEEN THE OPPONENT YOU FACED, MASTER YHUN.
AND HAVING BEEN WITH YOU FOR THE PAST SEVERAL MONTHS, I KNOW YOU WOULD NEVER HAVE ALLOWED YOURSELF TO AVOID OR SHY AWAY FROM AN OPPONENT NO MATTER HOW POWERFUL HE WAS.
BUT AT THIS MOMENT...
WHEN I LOOK UPON YOU MASTER YHUN, I CAN'T HELP BUT THINK THAT YOU'RE TRYING TO RUN AWAY FROM THE SHADOW OF THE OPPONENT YOU FACED.
IF THERE IS SOMEONE POWERFUL ENOUGH TO CAUSE EVEN YOU TO RETREAT BACK INTO A DEEP CORNER OF YOUR HEART, MASTER YHUN... I CAN ONLY THINK OF ONE PERSON WHO IT CAN BE...
WAS IT THE CHIEF OF CHUNG-SUE-MOON, JUNG-WOONG SUK, WHOM YOU FOUGHT WITH THAT DAY?

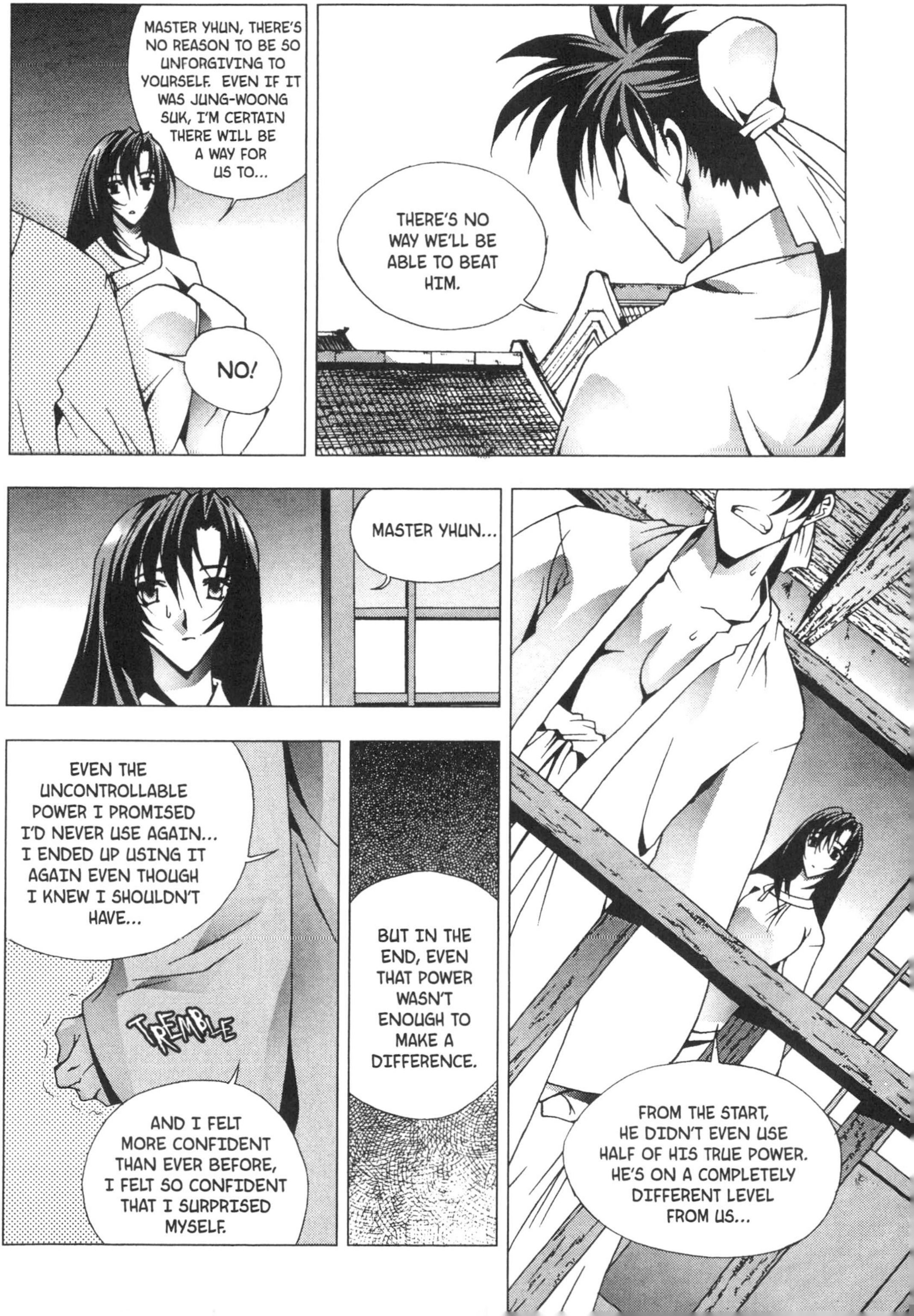
MASTER YHUN, THERE'S NO REASON TO BE SO UNFORGIVING TO YOURSELF. EVEN IF IT WAS JUNG-WOONG SUK, I'M CERTAIN THERE WILL BE A WAY FOR US TO...
THERE'S NO WAY WE'LL BE ABLE TO BEAT HIM.
NO!
MASTER YHUN...
EVEN THE UNCONTROLLABLE POWER I PROMISED I'D NEVER USE AGAIN... I ENDED UP USING IT AGAIN EVEN THOUGH I KNEW I SHOULDN'T HAVE...
TREMBLE
AND I FELT MORE CONFIDENT THAN EVER BEFORE, I FELT SO CONFIDENT THAT I SURPRISED MYSELF.
BUT IN THE END, EVEN THAT POWER WASN'T ENOUGH TO MAKE A DIFFERENCE.
FROM THE START, HE DIDN'T EVEN USE HALF OF HIS TRUE POWER. HE'S ON A COMPLETELY DIFFERENT LEVEL FROM US...

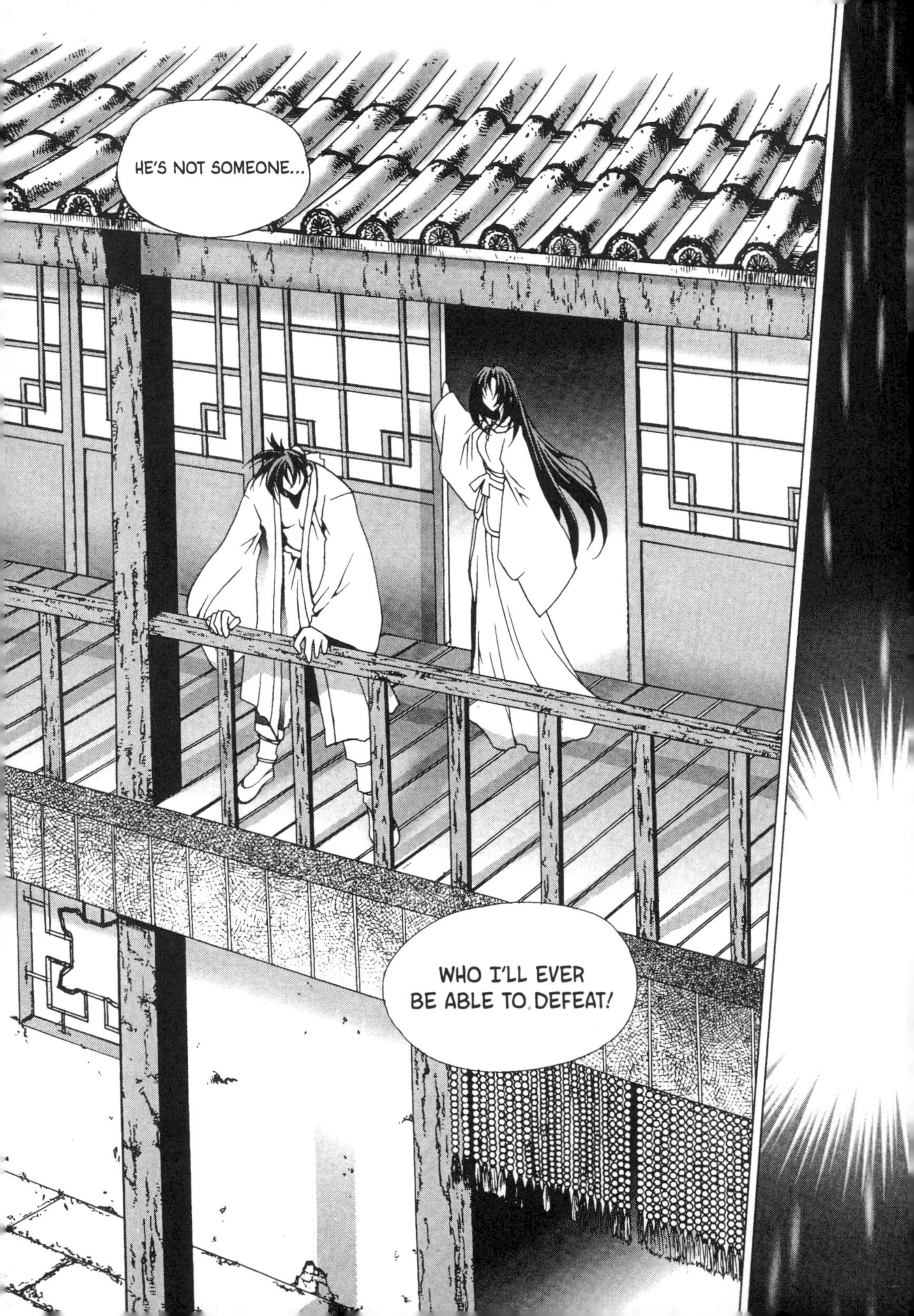
HE'S NOT SOMEONE...
WHO I'LL EVER BE ABLE TO DEFEAT!

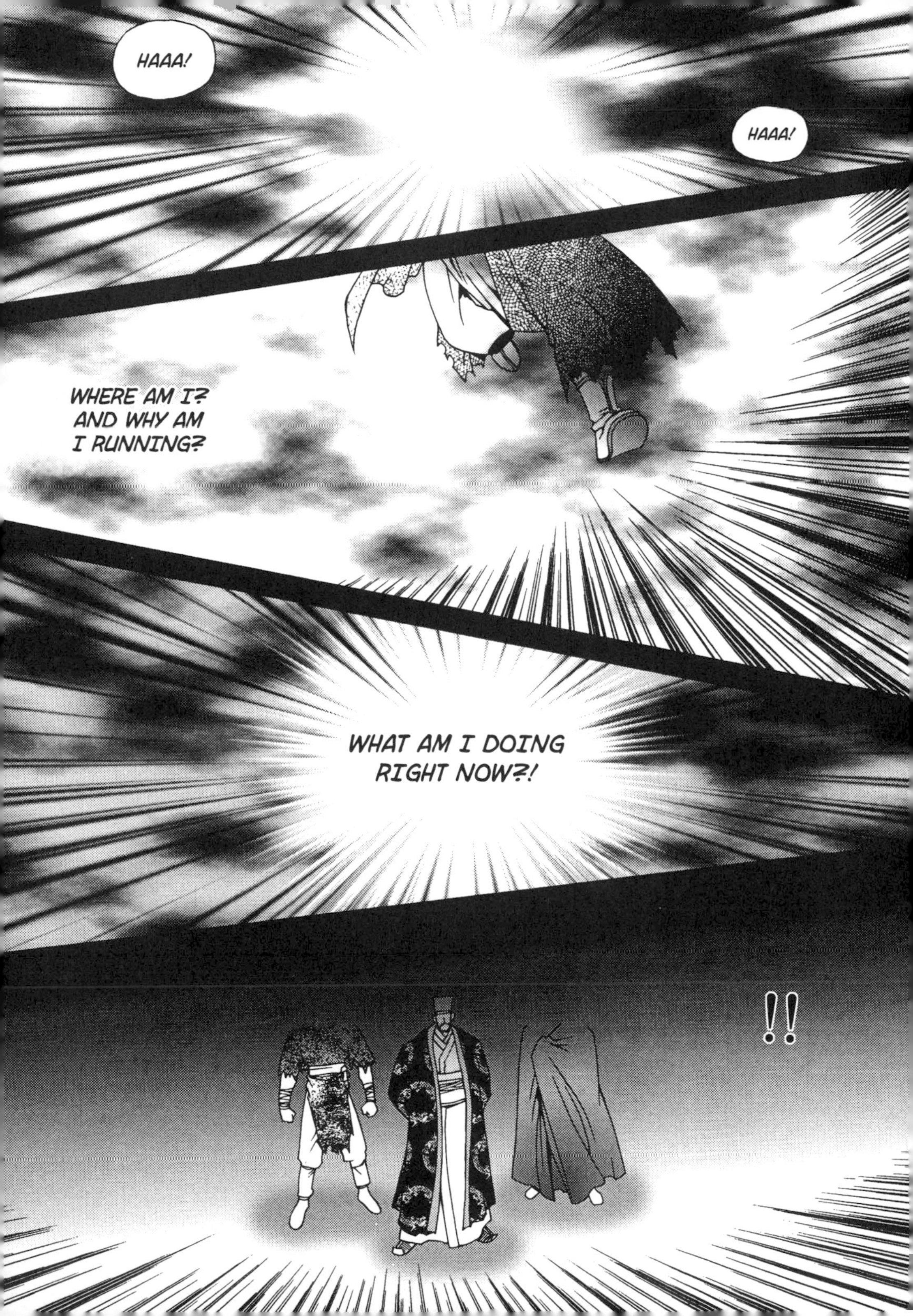
HAAA!
HAAA!
WHERE AM I? AND WHY AM I RUNNING?
WHAT AM I DOING RIGHT NOW?!
!!

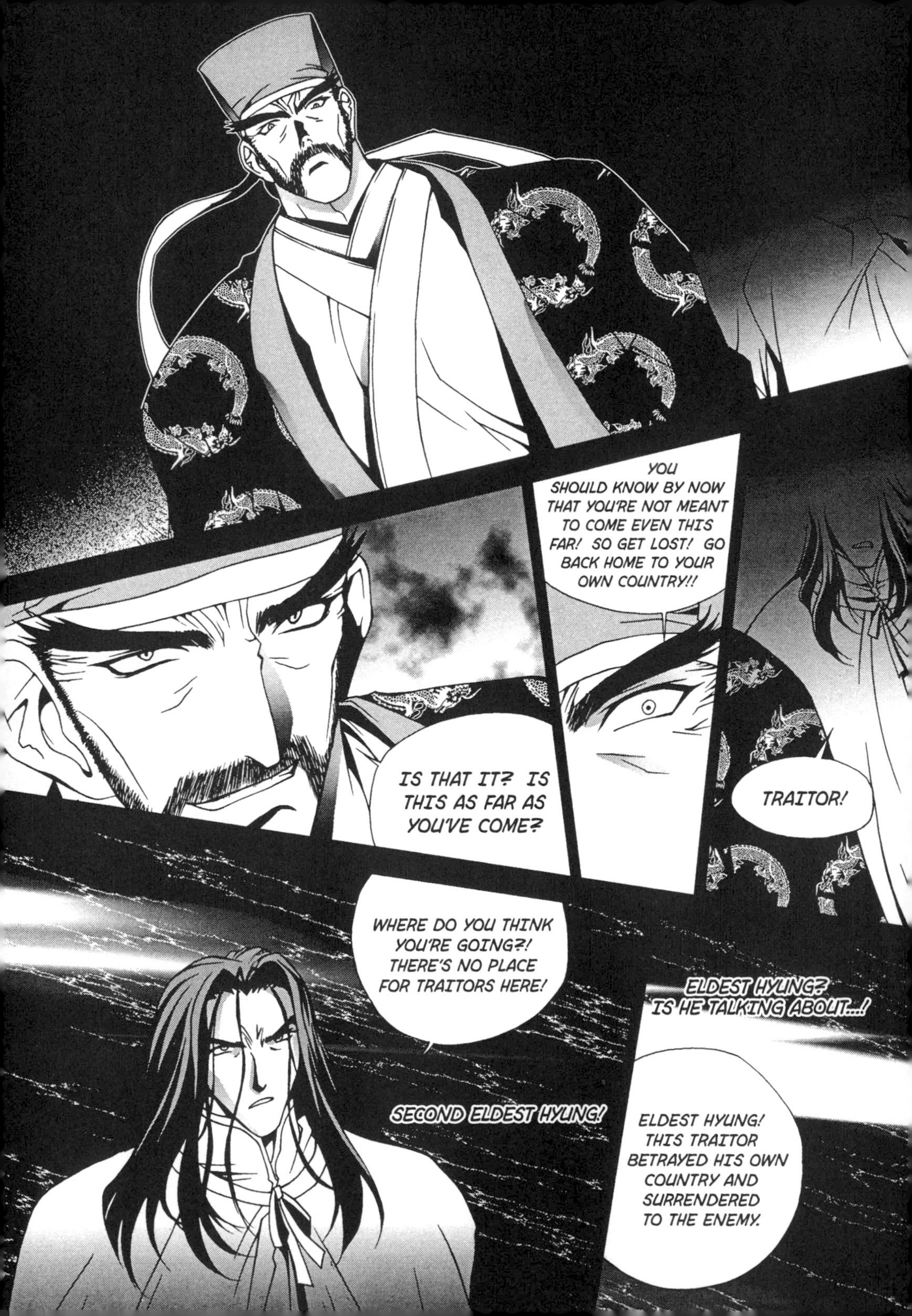
YOU SHOULD KNOW BY NOW THAT YOU'RE NOT MEANT TO COME EVEN THIS FAR! SO GET LOST! GO BACK HOME TO YOUR OWN COUNTRY!!
IS THAT IT? IS THIS AS FAR AS YOU'VE COME?
TRAITOR!
WHERE DO YOU THINK YOU'RE GOING?! THERE'S NO PLACE FOR TRAITORS HERE!
ELDEST HYUNG? IS HE TALKING ABOUT...!
SECOND ELDEST HYUNG!
ELDEST HYUNG! THIS TRAITOR BETRAYED HIS OWN COUNTRY AND SURRENDERED TO THE ENEMY.

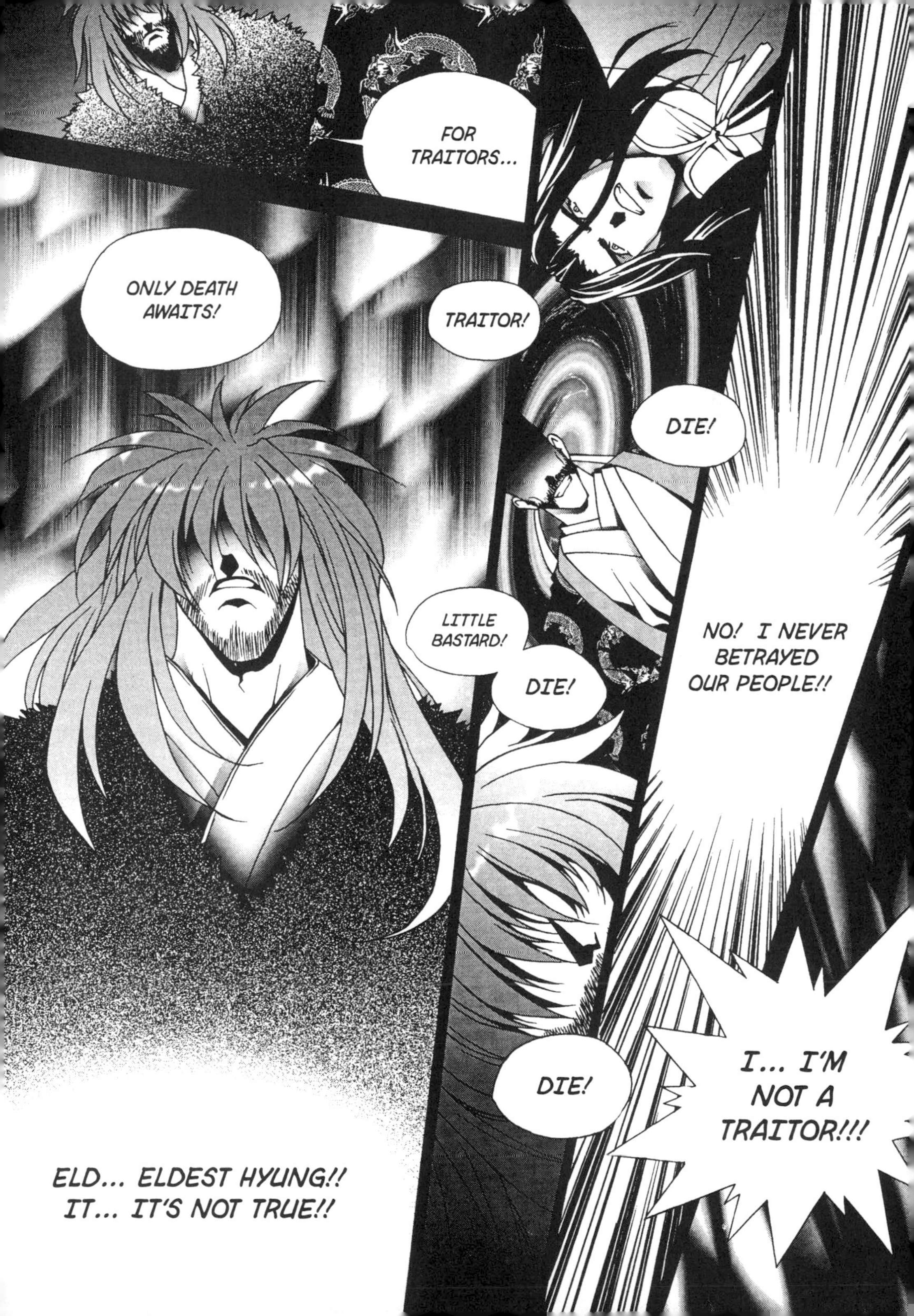
FOR TRAITORS...
ONLY DEATH AWAITS!
TRAITOR!
DIE!
LITTLE BASTARD!
DIE!
NO! I NEVER BETRAYED OUR PEOPLE!!
DIE!
I... I'M NOT A TRAITOR!!!
ELD... ELDEST HYUNG!! IT... IT'S NOT TRUE!!

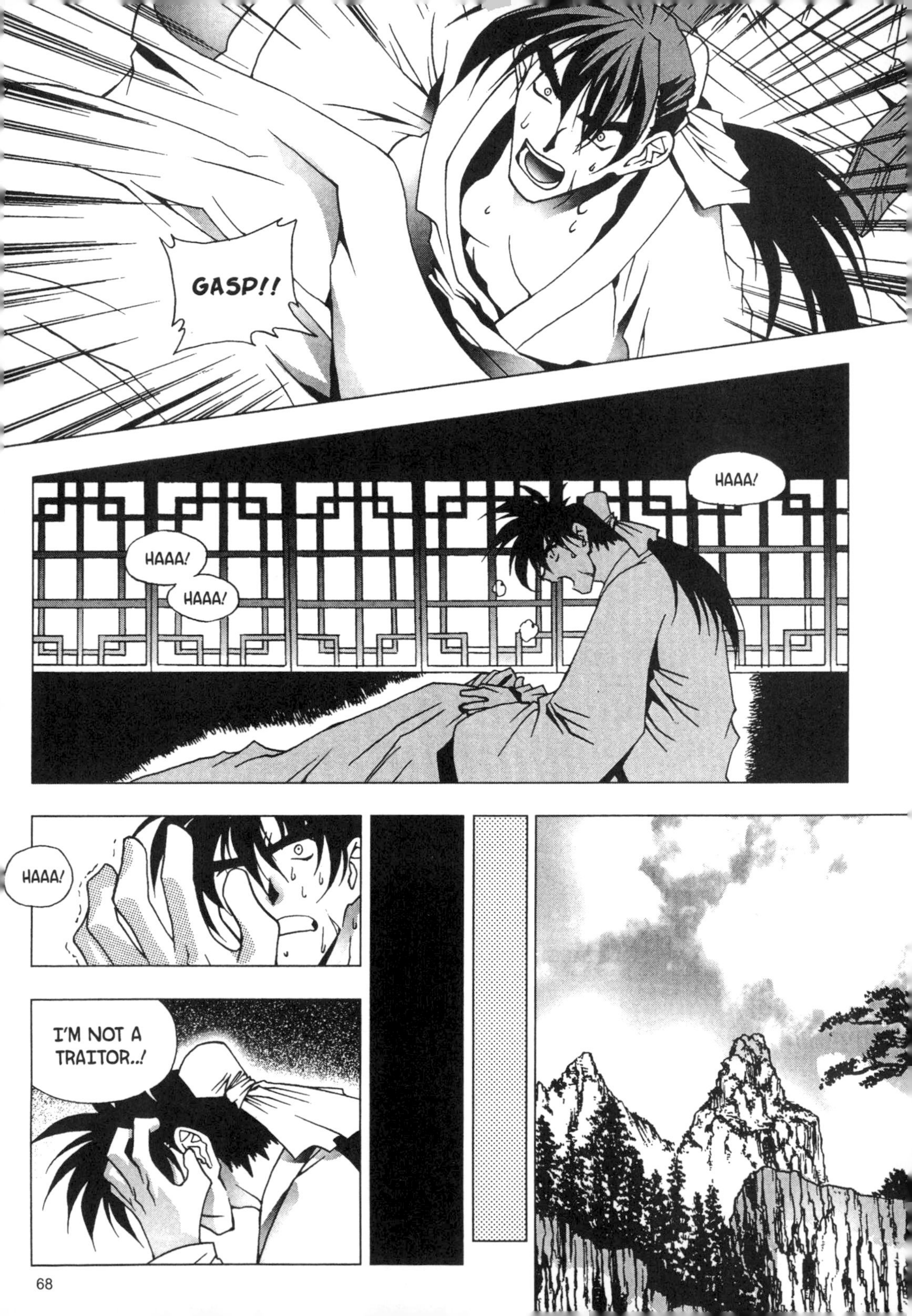
GASP!!
HAAA!
HAAA!
HAAA!
HAAA!
I'M NOT A TRAITOR..!

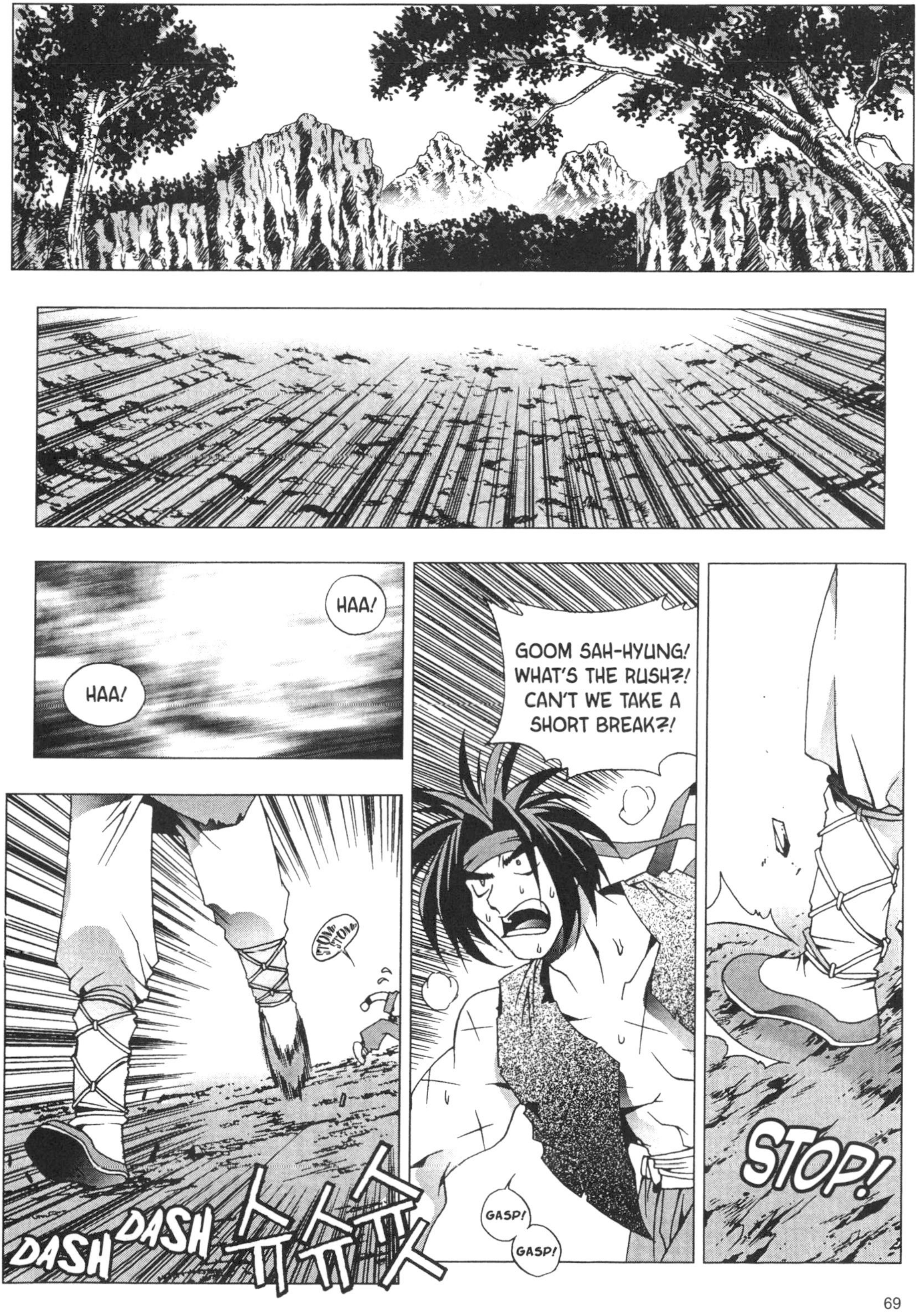
HAA!
HAA!
GOOM SAH-HYUNG! WHAT'S THE RUSH?! CAN'T WE TAKE A SHORT BREAK?!
STOMP STOMP
DASH DASH
GASP!
GASP!
STOP!

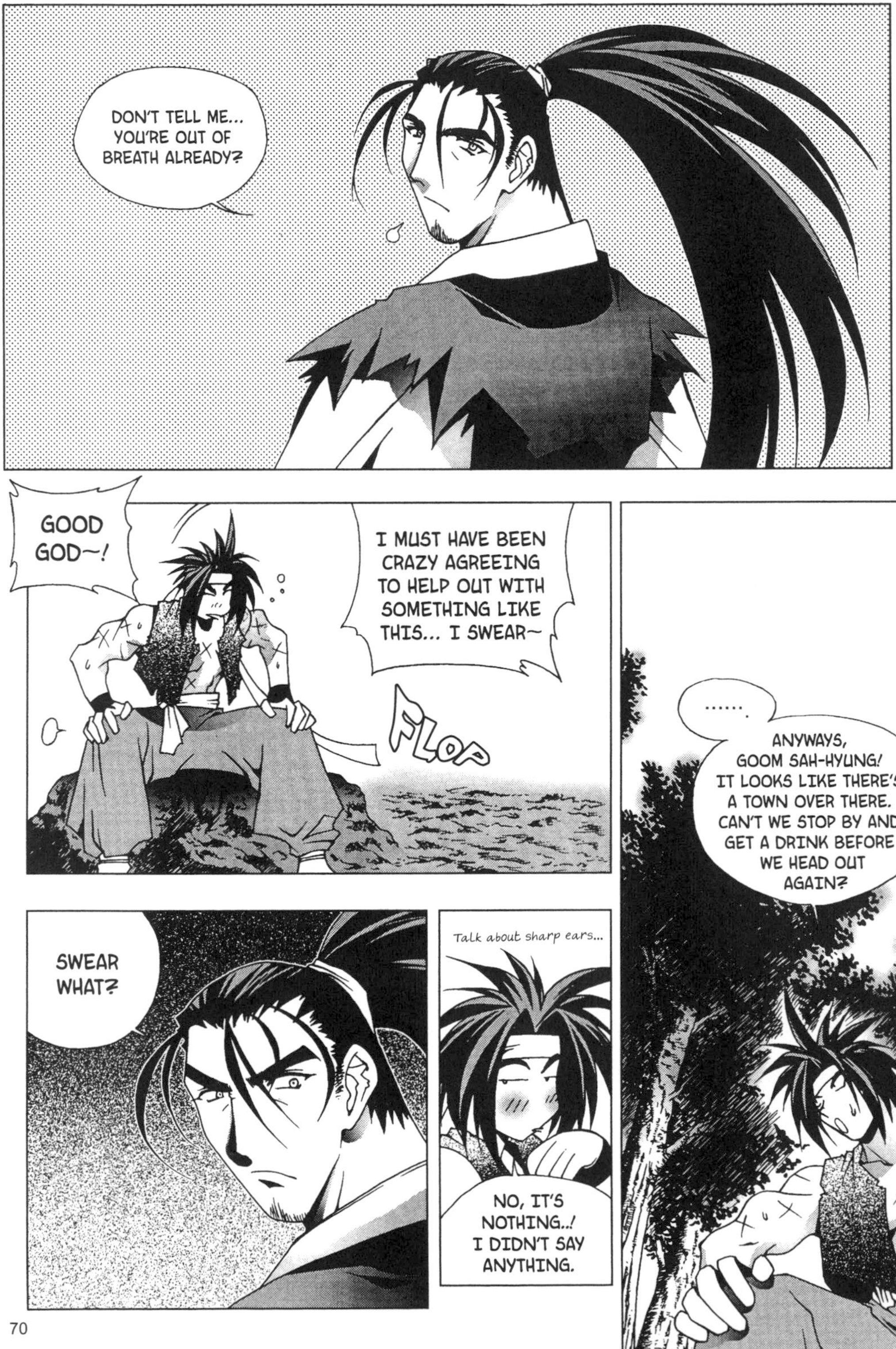
DON'T TELL ME... YOU'RE OUT OF BREATH ALREADY?
GOOD GOD~!
I MUST HAVE BEEN CRAZY AGREEING TO HELP OUT WITH SOMETHING LIKE THIS... I SWEAR~
FLOP
SWEAR WHAT?
Talk about sharp ears...
NO, IT'S NOTHING..! I DIDN'T SAY ANYTHING.
....
ANYWAYS, GOOM SAH-HYUNG! IT LOOKS LIKE THERE'S A TOWN OVER THERE. CAN'T WE STOP BY AND GET A DRINK BEFORE WE HEAD OUT AGAIN?

Note : Gwun-Shin = Fighting God

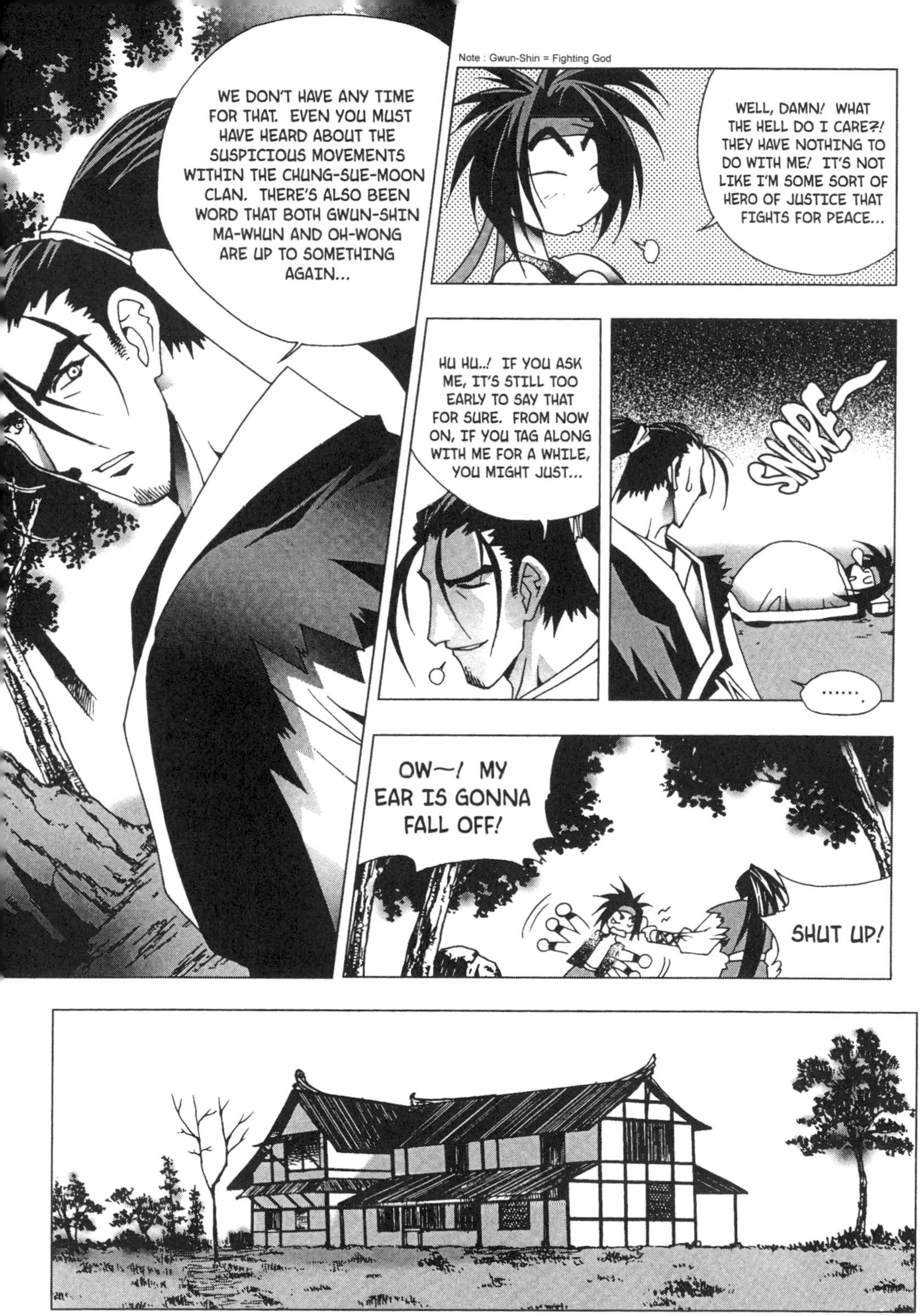
WE DON'T HAVE ANY TIME FOR THAT. EVEN YOU MUST HAVE HEARD ABOUT THE SUSPICIOUS MOVEMENTS WITHIN THE CHUNG-SUE-MOON CLAN. THERE'S ALSO BEEN WORD THAT BOTH GWUN-SHIN MA-WHUN AND OH-WONG ARE UP TO SOMETHING AGAIN...
WELL, DAMN! WHAT THE HELL DO I CARE?! THEY HAVE NOTHING TO DO WITH ME! IT'S NOT LIKE I'M SOME SORT OF HERO OF JUSTICE THAT FIGHTS FOR PEACE...
HU HU..! IF YOU ASK ME, IT'S STILL TOO EARLY TO SAY THAT FOR SURE. FROM NOW ON, IF YOU TAG ALONG WITH ME FOR A WHILE, YOU MIGHT JUST...
SNORE~~
....
OW~! MY EAR IS GONNA FALL OFF!
SHUT UP!

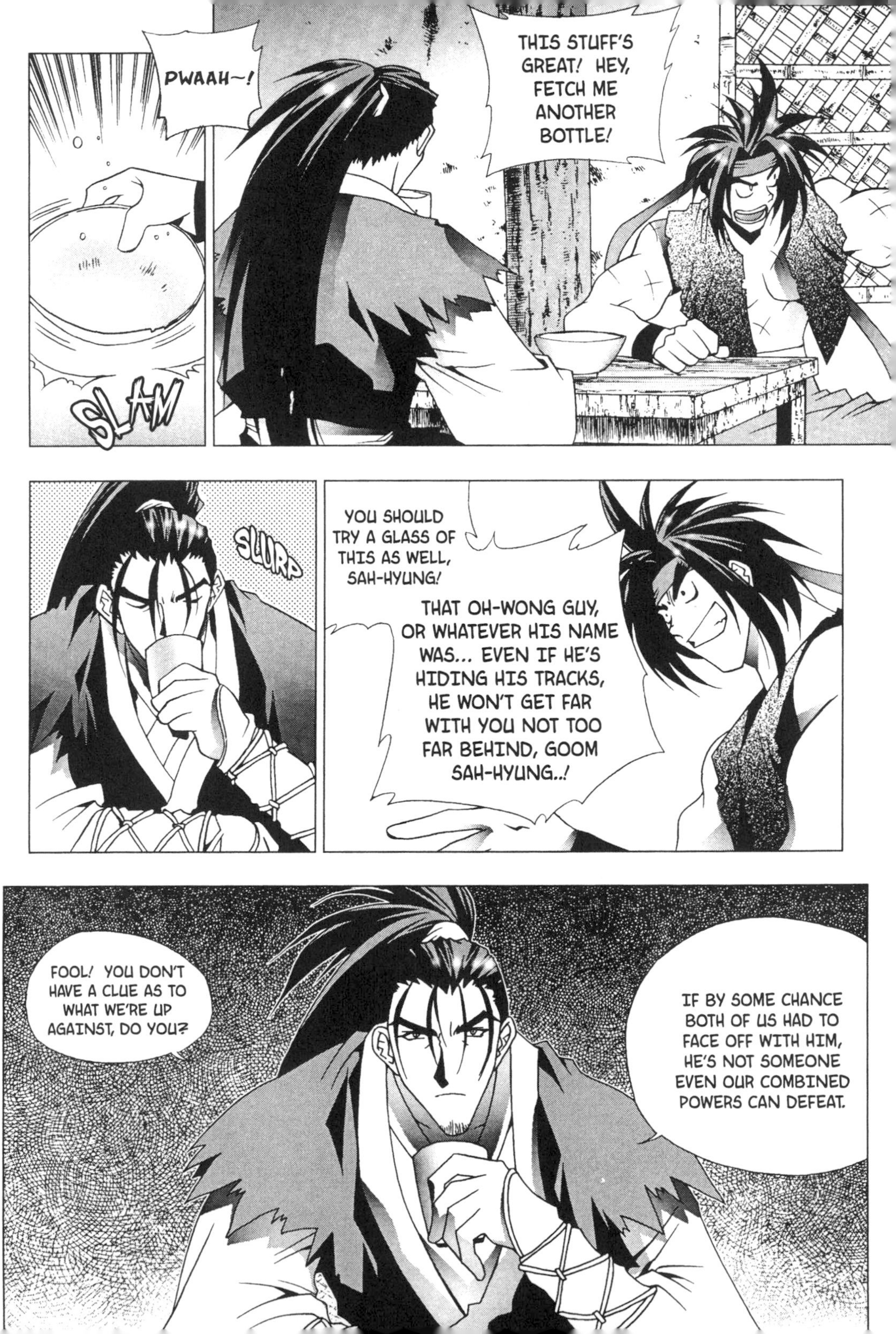
PWAAH~!
SLAM
THIS STUFF'S GREAT! HEY, FETCH ME ANOTHER BOTTLE!
SLURP
YOU SHOULD TRY A GLASS OF THIS AS WELL, SAH-HYUNG!
THAT OH-WONG GUY, OR WHATEVER HIS NAME WAS... EVEN IF HE'S HIDING HIS TRACKS, HE WON'T GET FAR WITH YOU NOT TOO FAR BEHIND, GOOM SAH-HYUNG..!
FOOL! YOU DON'T HAVE A CLUE AS TO WHAT WE'RE UP AGAINST, DO YOU?
IF BY SOME CHANCE BOTH OF US HAD TO FACE OFF WITH HIM, HE'S NOT SOMEONE EVEN OUR COMBINED POWERS CAN DEFEAT.

IF WE'RE LUCKY...

WE MIGHT BARELY BE ABLE TO ESCAPE WITH OUR LIVES...

......

DAMMIT! THIS STUFF DOESN'T TASTE SO GREAT ANYMORE!

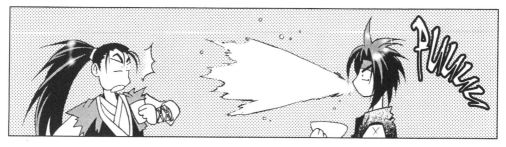

PUUUU

WHAT THE..?! IS... ISN'T THAT..!!

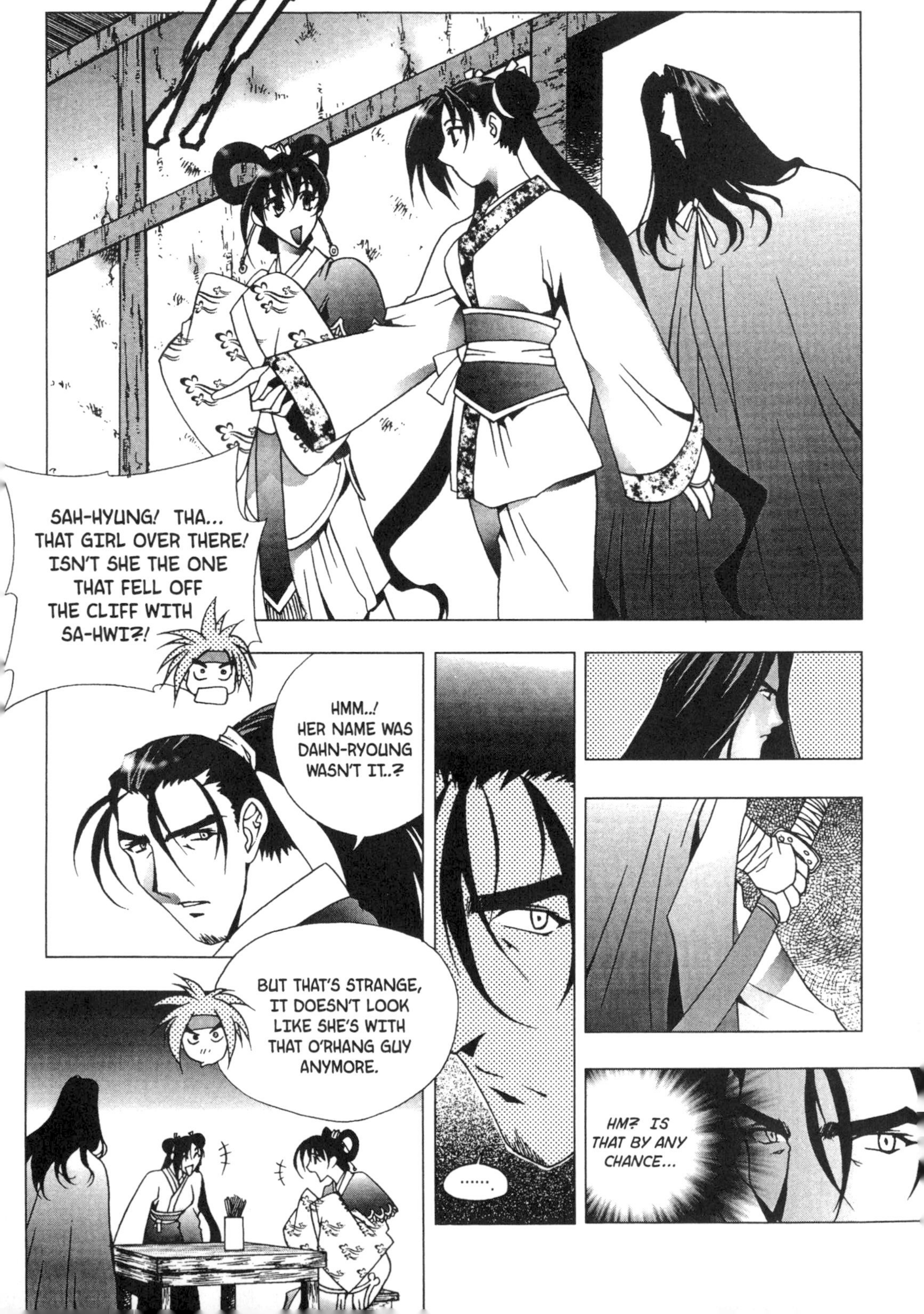
SAH-HYUNG! THA... THAT GIRL OVER THERE! ISN'T SHE THE ONE THAT FELL OFF THE CLIFF WITH SA-HWI?!
HMM..! HER NAME WAS DAHN-RYOUNG WASN'T IT..?
BUT THAT'S STRANGE, IT DOESN'T LOOK LIKE SHE'S WITH THAT O'RHANG GUY ANYMORE.
......
HM? IS THAT BY ANY CHANCE...

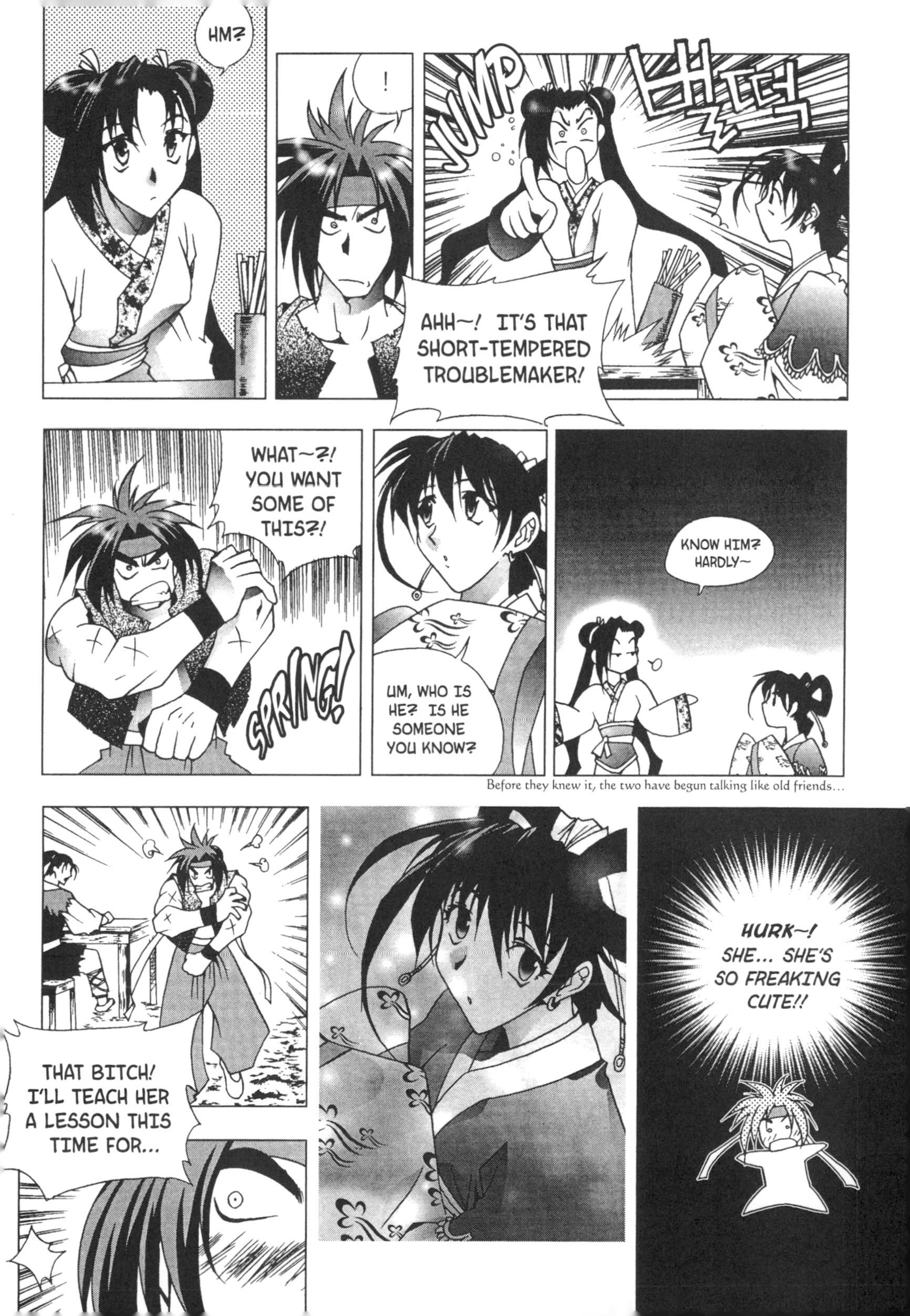
HM?
!
JUMP
AHH~! IT'S THAT SHORT-TEMPERED TROUBLEMAKER!
WHAT~?! YOU WANT SOME OF THIS?!
SPRING!
UM, WHO IS HE? IS HE SOMEONE YOU KNOW?
KNOW HIM? HARDLY~
Before they knew it, the two have begun talking like old friends...
THAT BITCH! I'LL TEACH HER A LESSON THIS TIME FOR...
HURK~! SHE... SHE'S SO FREAKING CUTE!!

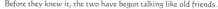

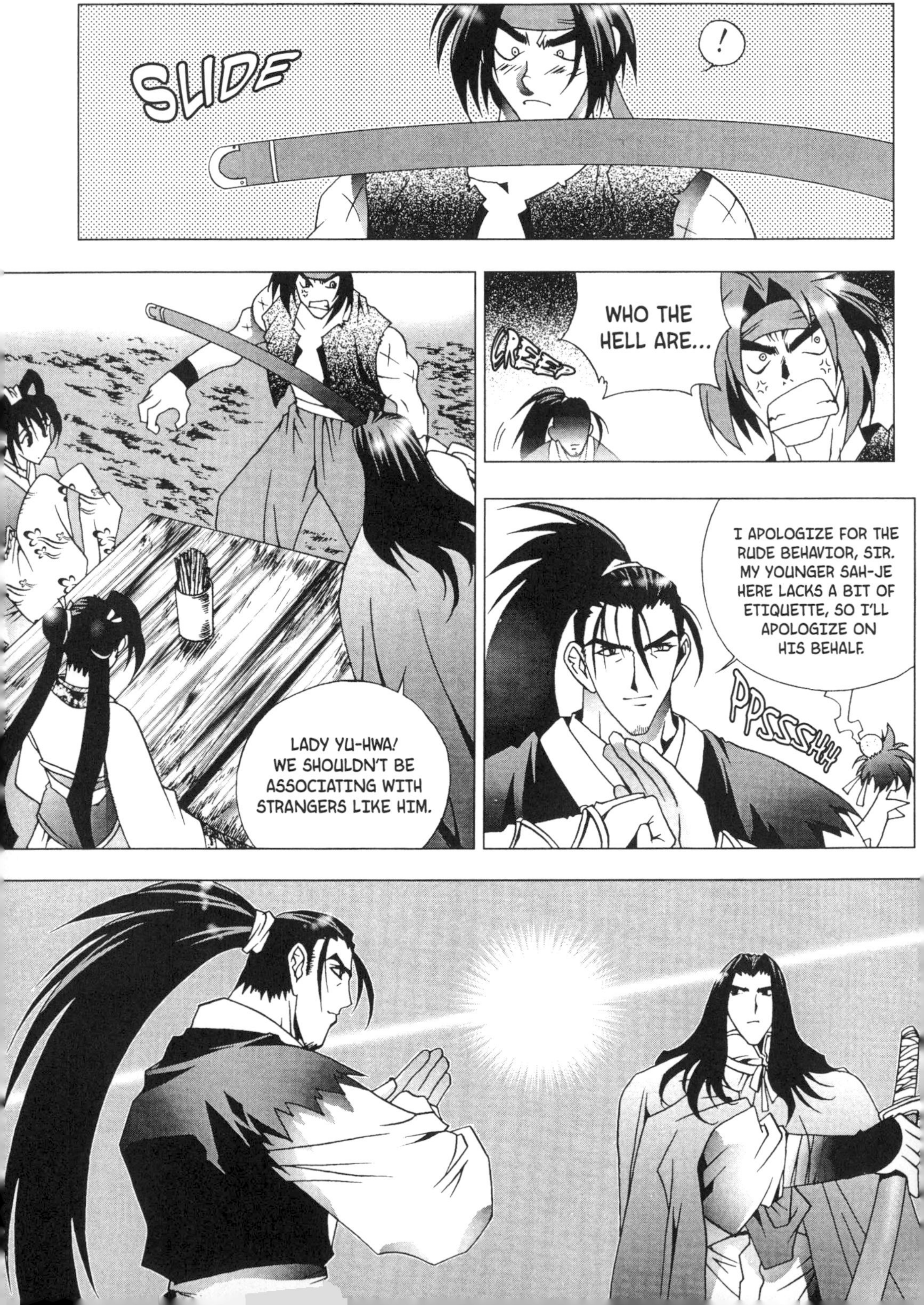
SLIDE
!
LADY YU-HWA! WE SHOULDN'T BE ASSOCIATING WITH STRANGERS LIKE HIM.
WHO THE HELL ARE...
I APOLOGIZE FOR THE RUDE BEHAVIOR, SIR. MY YOUNGER SAH-JE HERE LACKS A BIT OF ETIQUETTE, SO I'LL APOLOGIZE ON HIS BEHALF.
PPSSSHH

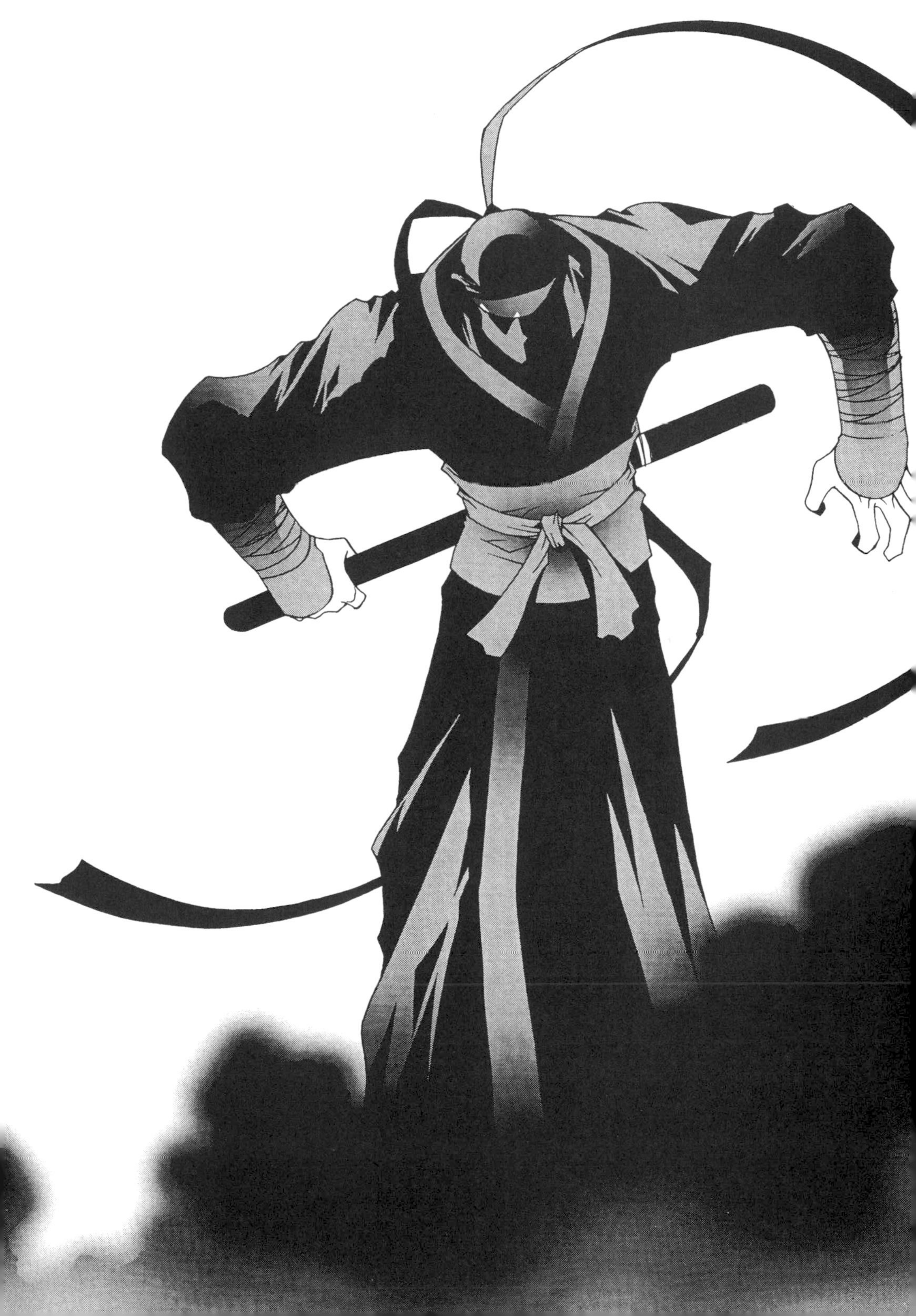

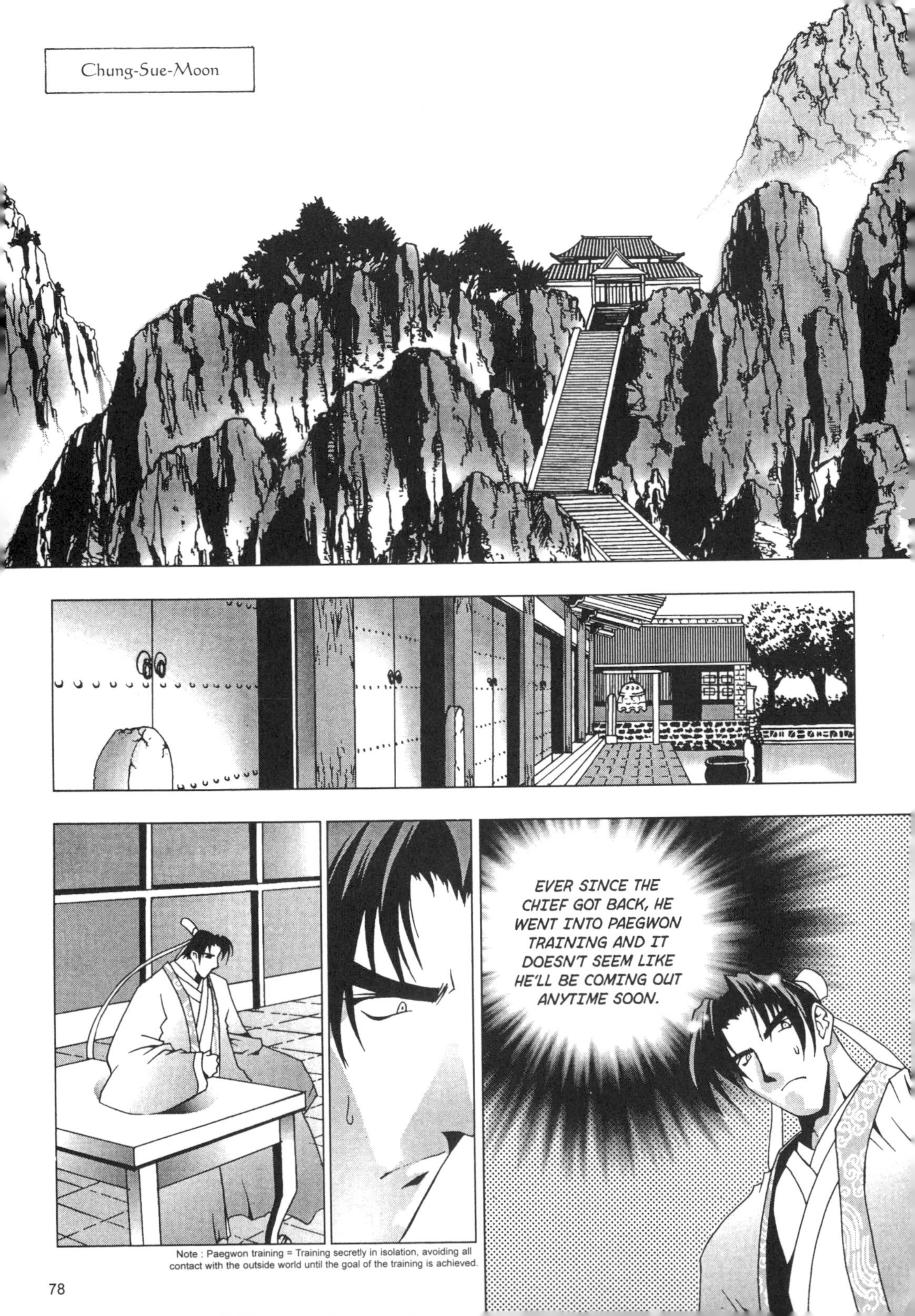
Chung-Sue-Moon
EVER SINCE THE CHIEF GOT BACK, HE WENT INTO PAEGWON TRAINING AND IT DOESN'T SEEM LIKE HE'LL BE COMING OUT ANYTIME SOON.

Note : Paegwon training = Training secretly in isolation, avoiding all contact with the outside world until the goal of the training is achieved.

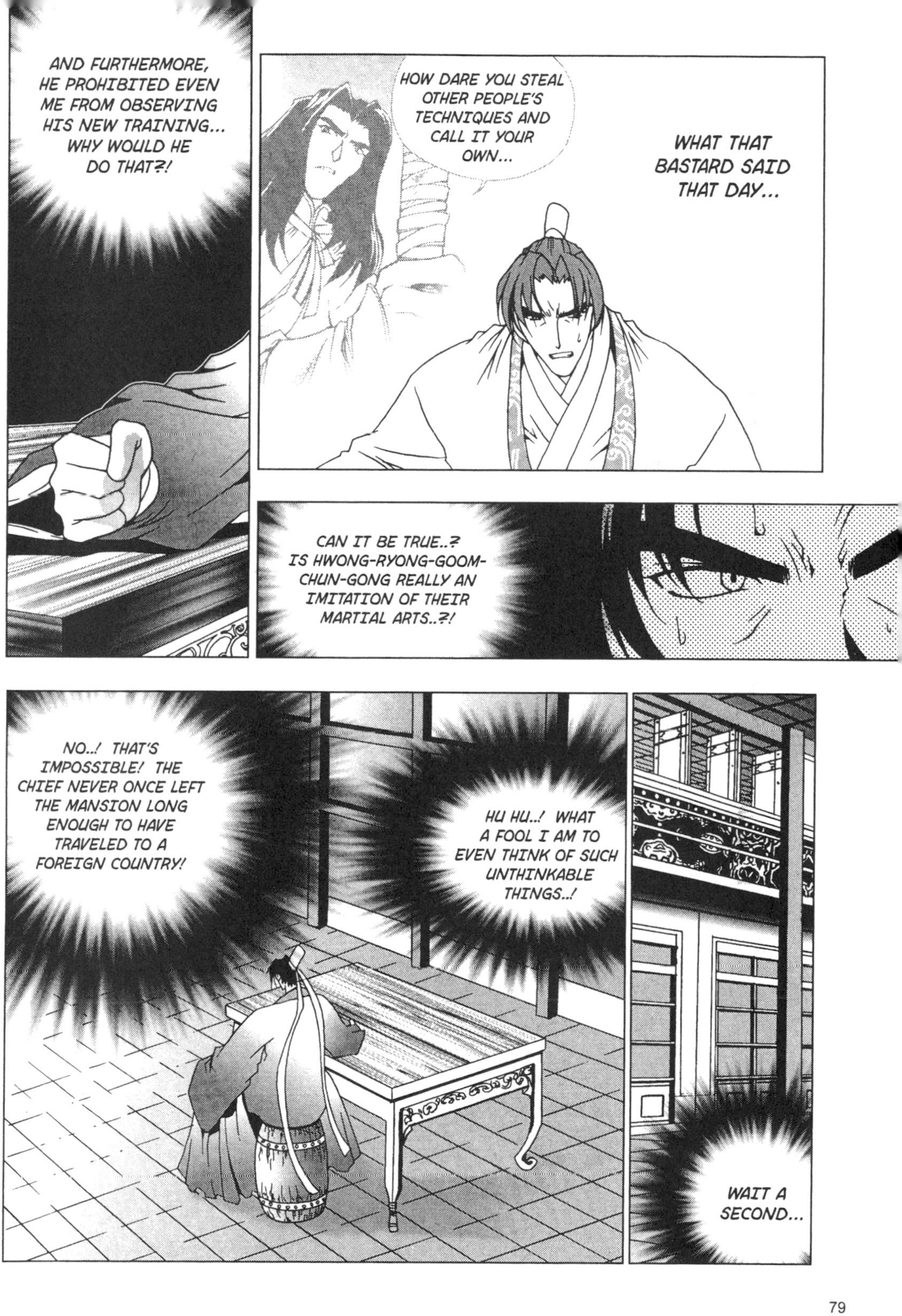
AND FURTHERMORE, HE PROHIBITED EVEN ME FROM OBSERVING HIS NEW TRAINING... WHY WOULD HE DO THAT?!
HOW DARE YOU STEAL OTHER PEOPLE'S TECHNIQUES AND CALL IT YOUR OWN...
WHAT THAT BASTARD SAID THAT DAY...
CAN IT BE TRUE..? IS HWONG-RYONG-GOOM-CHUN-GONG REALLY AN IMITATION OF THEIR MARTIAL ARTS..?!
NO..! THAT'S IMPOSSIBLE! THE CHIEF NEVER ONCE LEFT THE MANSION LONG ENOUGH TO HAVE TRAVELED TO A FOREIGN COUNTRY!
HU HU..! WHAT A FOOL I AM TO EVEN THINK OF SUCH UNTHINKABLE THINGS..!
WAIT A SECOND...

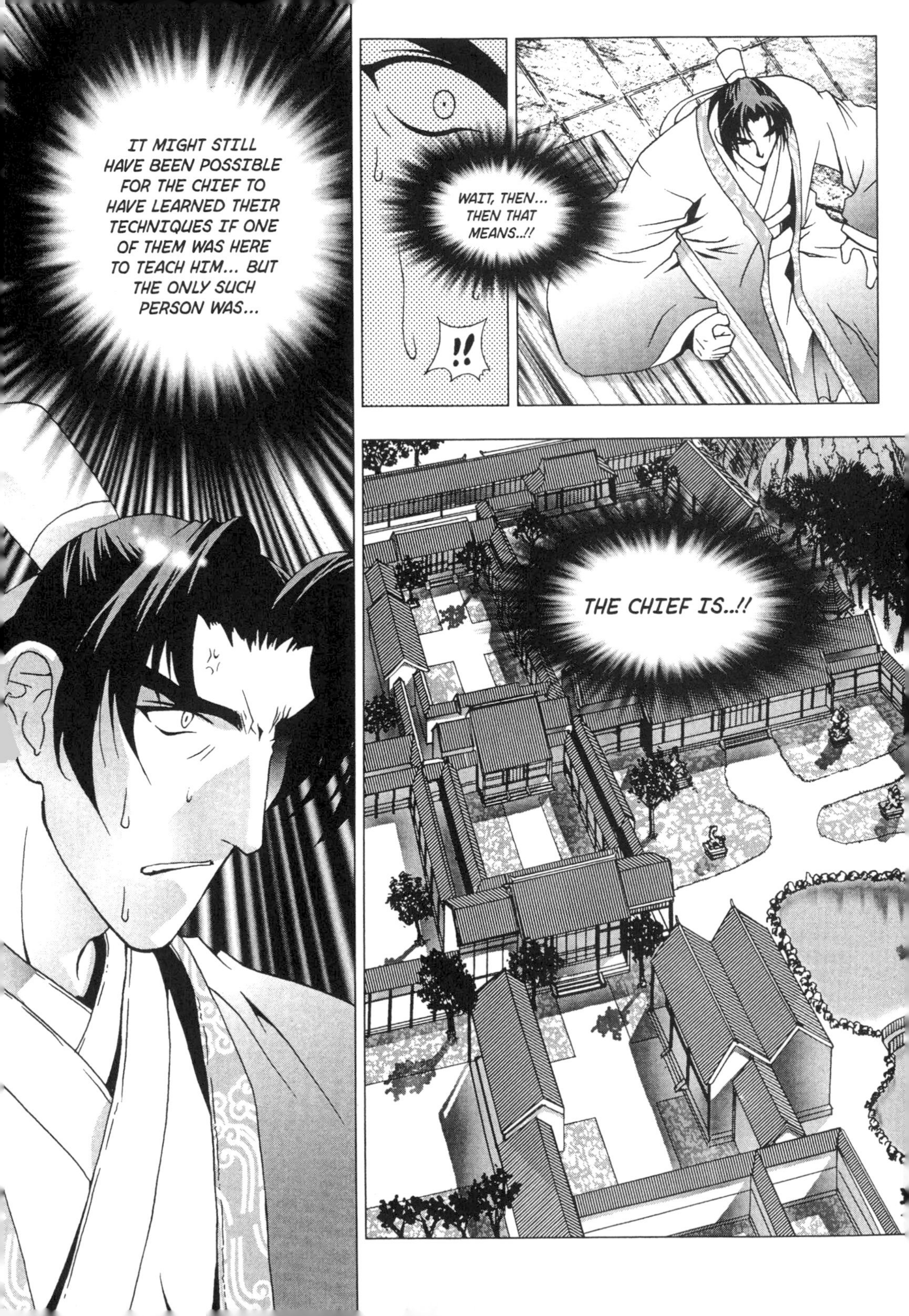
WAIT, THEN... THEN THAT MEANS..!!
!!
IT MIGHT STILL HAVE BEEN POSSIBLE FOR THE CHIEF TO HAVE LEARNED THEIR TECHNIQUES IF ONE OF THEM WAS HERE TO TEACH HIM... BUT THE ONLY SUCH PERSON WAS...
THE CHIEF IS..!!

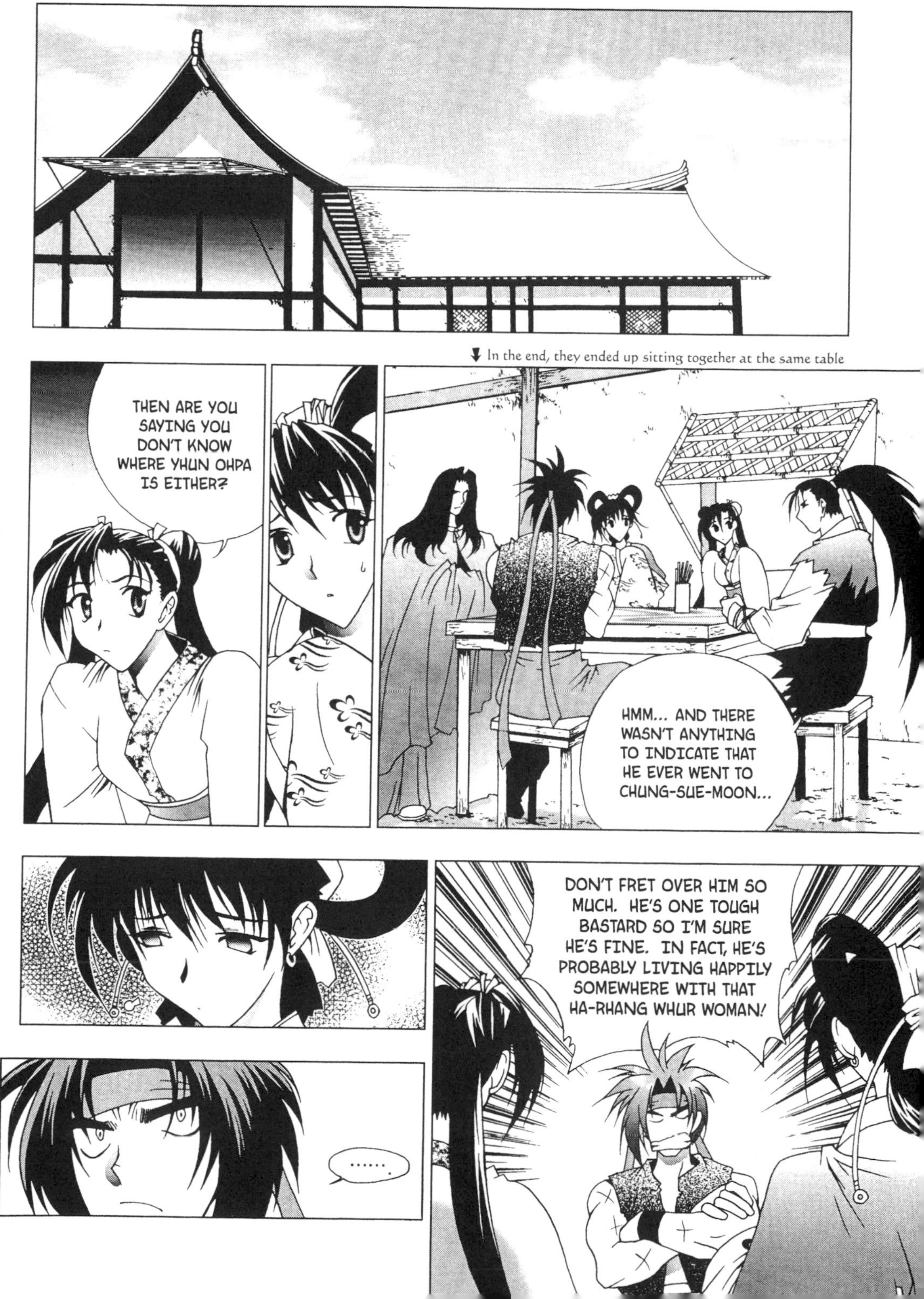

In the end, they ended up sitting together at the same table
THEN ARE YOU SAYING YOU DON'T KNOW WHERE YHUN OHPA IS EITHER?
HMM... AND THERE WASN'T ANYTHING TO INDICATE THAT HE EVER WENT TO CHUNG-SUE-MOON...
DON'T FRET OVER HIM SO MUCH. HE'S ONE TOUGH BASTARD SO I'M SURE HE'S FINE. IN FACT, HE'S PROBABLY LIVING HAPPILY SOMEWHERE WITH THAT HA-RHANG WHUR WOMAN!
....

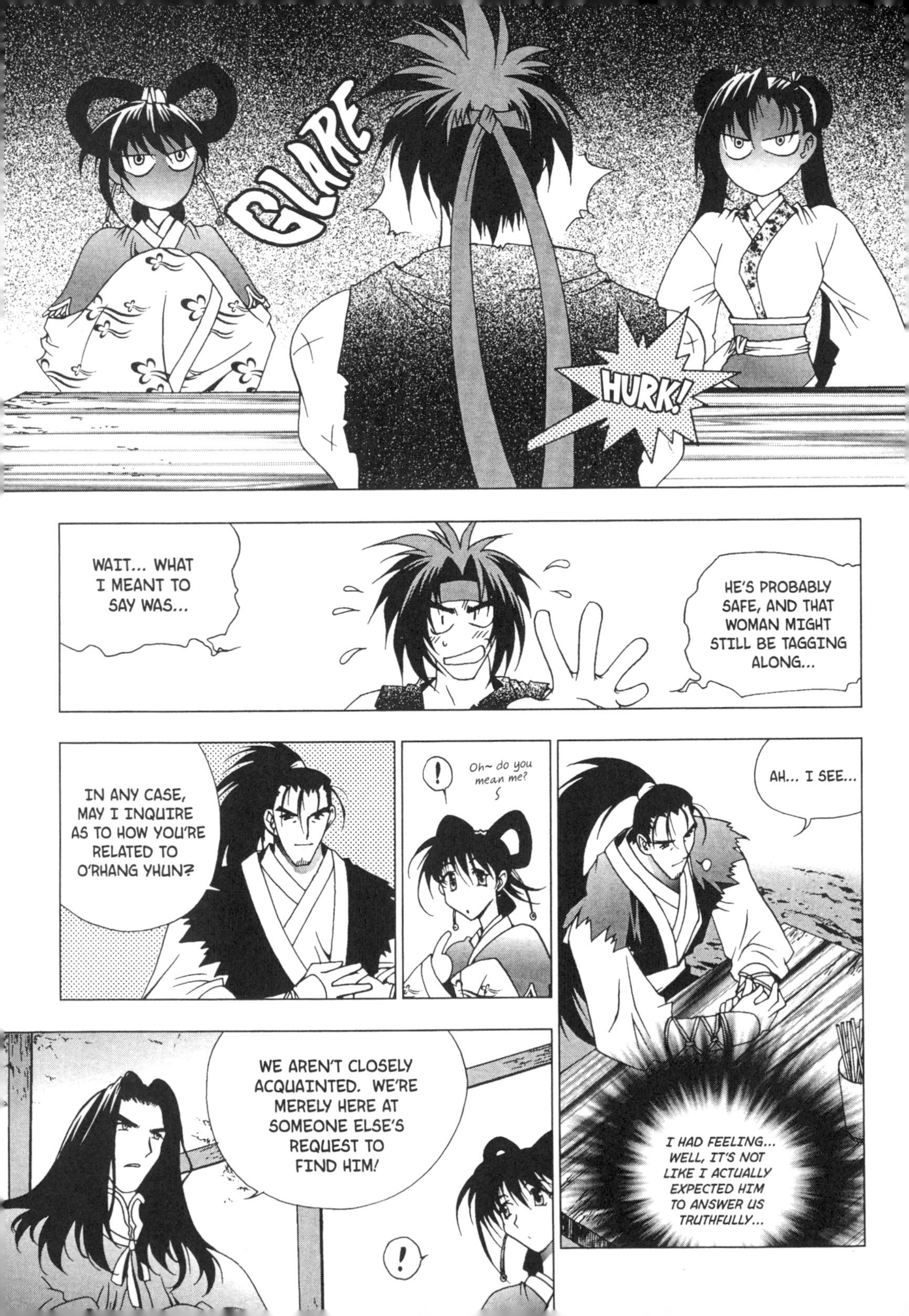
GLARE
HURK!
HE'S PROBABLY SAFE, AND THAT WOMAN MIGHT STILL BE TAGGING ALONG...
WAIT... WHAT I MEANT TO SAY WAS...
AH... I SEE...
!
Oh~ do you mean me?
IN ANY CASE, MAY I INQUIRE AS TO HOW YOU'RE RELATED TO O'RHANG YHUN?
I HAD FEELING... WELL, IT'S NOT LIKE I ACTUALLY EXPECTED HIM TO ANSWER US TRUTHFULLY...
WE AREN'T CLOSELY ACQUAINTED. WE'RE MERELY HERE AT SOMEONE ELSE'S REQUEST TO FIND HIM!
!

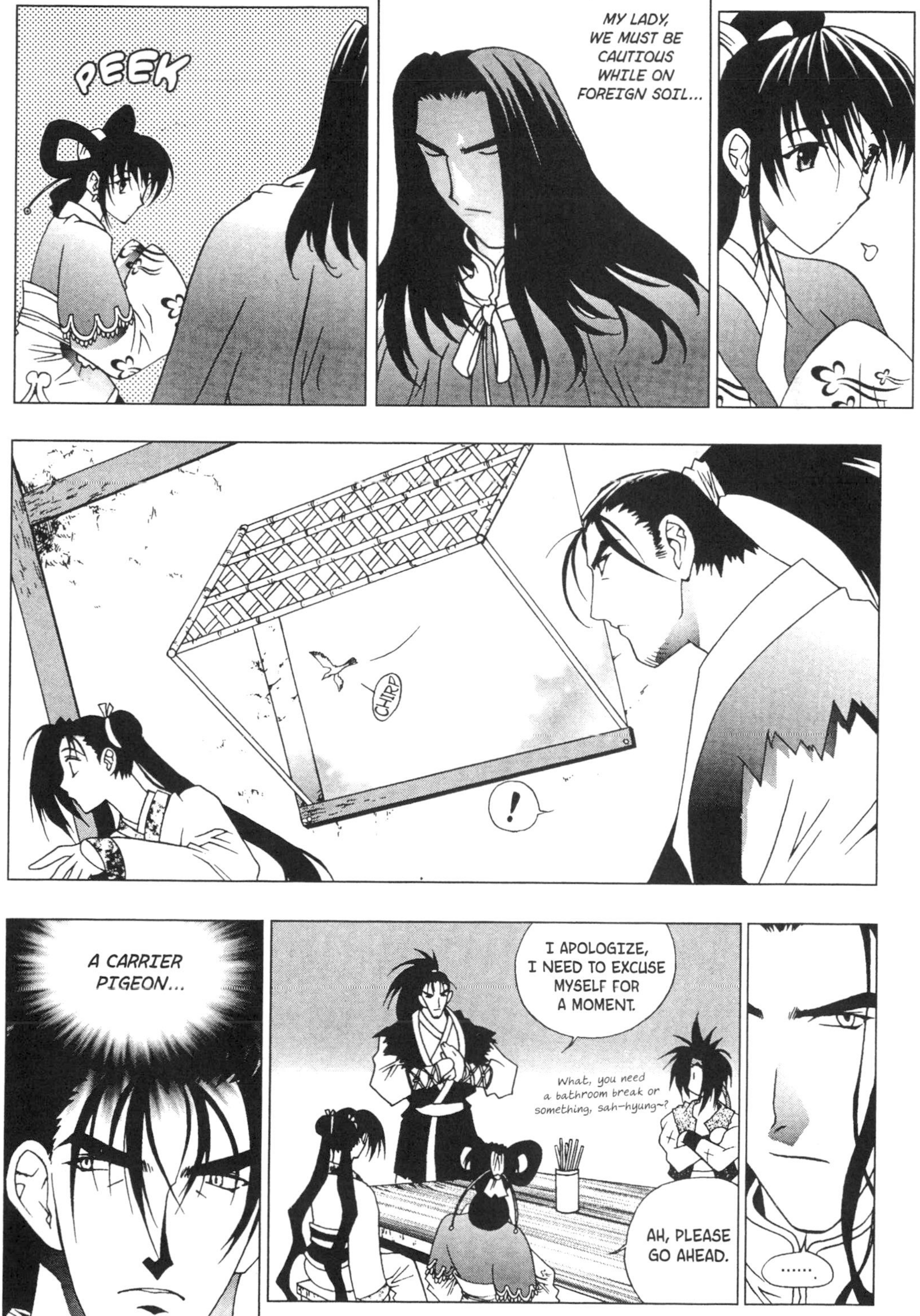
PEEK
MY LADY, WE MUST BE CAUTIOUS WHILE ON FOREIGN SOIL...
CHIRP
!
A CARRIER PIGEON...
I APOLOGIZE, I NEED TO EXCUSE MYSELF FOR A MOMENT.
What, you need a bathroom break or something, sah-hyung~?
AH, PLEASE GO AHEAD.
....

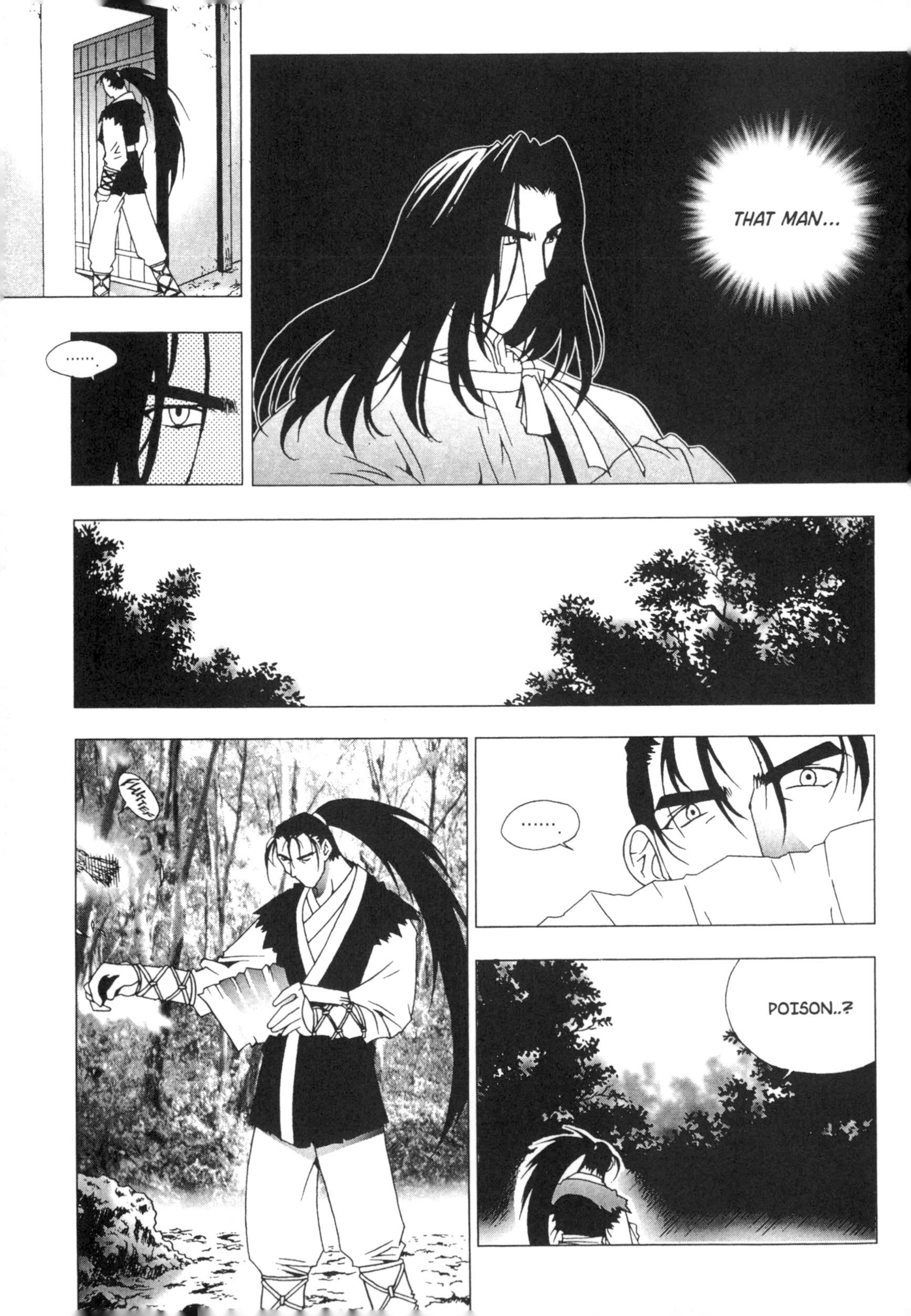
THAT MAN...
....
FLUTTER
....
POISON..?

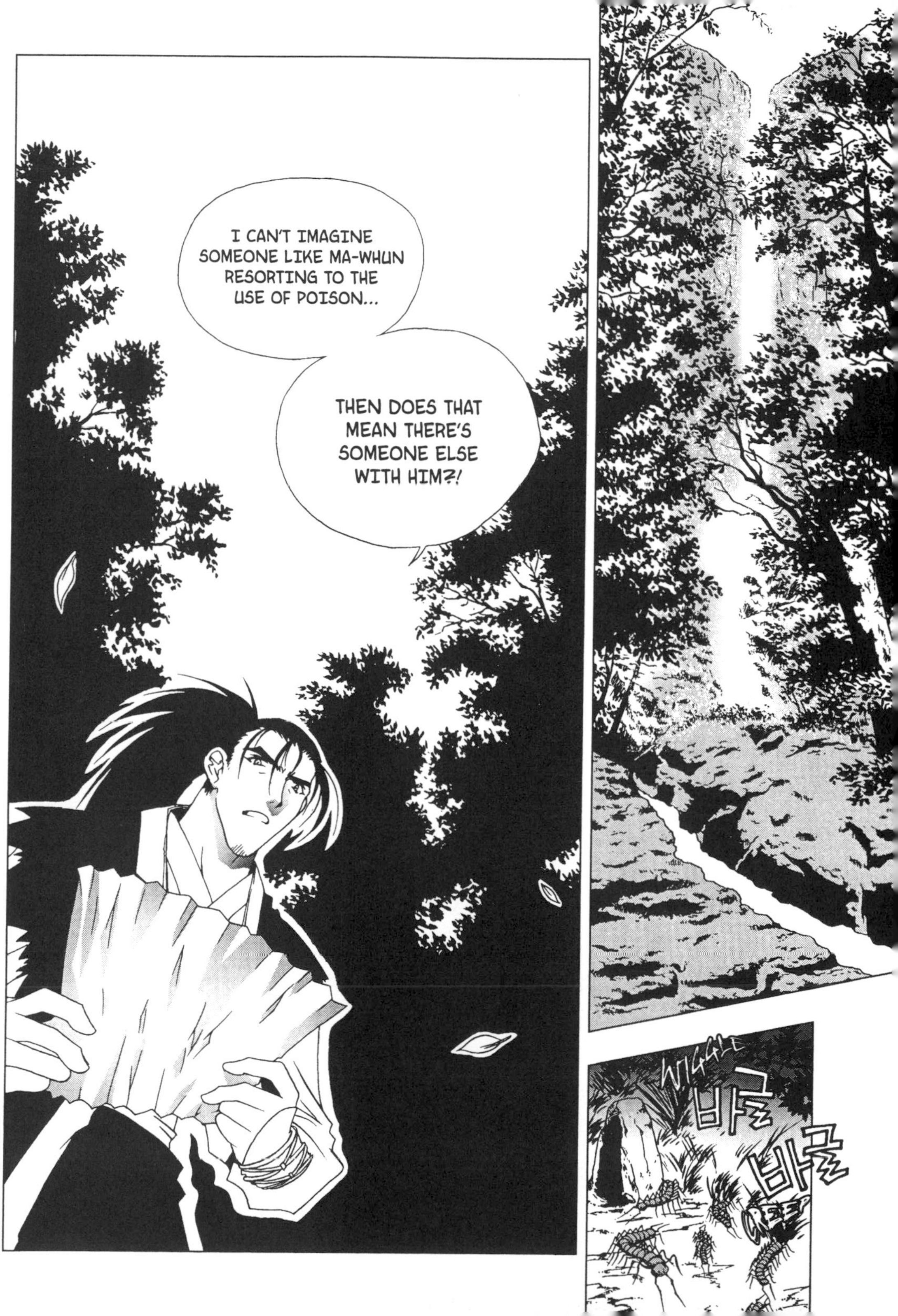
I CAN'T IMAGINE SOMEONE LIKE MA-WHUN RESORTING TO THE USE OF POISON...
THEN DOES THAT MEAN THERE'S SOMEONE ELSE WITH HIM?!
WIGGLE
바글
바글

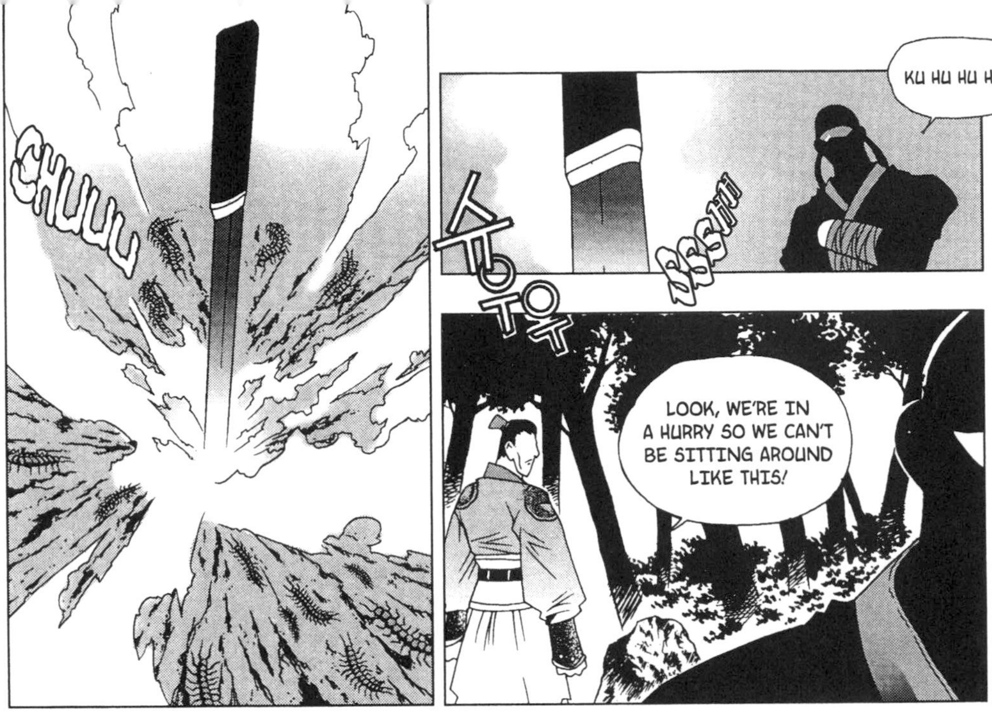
CHUUL
KU HU HU HU..!
LOOK, WE'RE IN A HURRY SO WE CAN'T BE SITTING AROUND LIKE THIS!

Note : Gu-Roh-Ja Sword = Black Earthly Moxa Cautery Sword

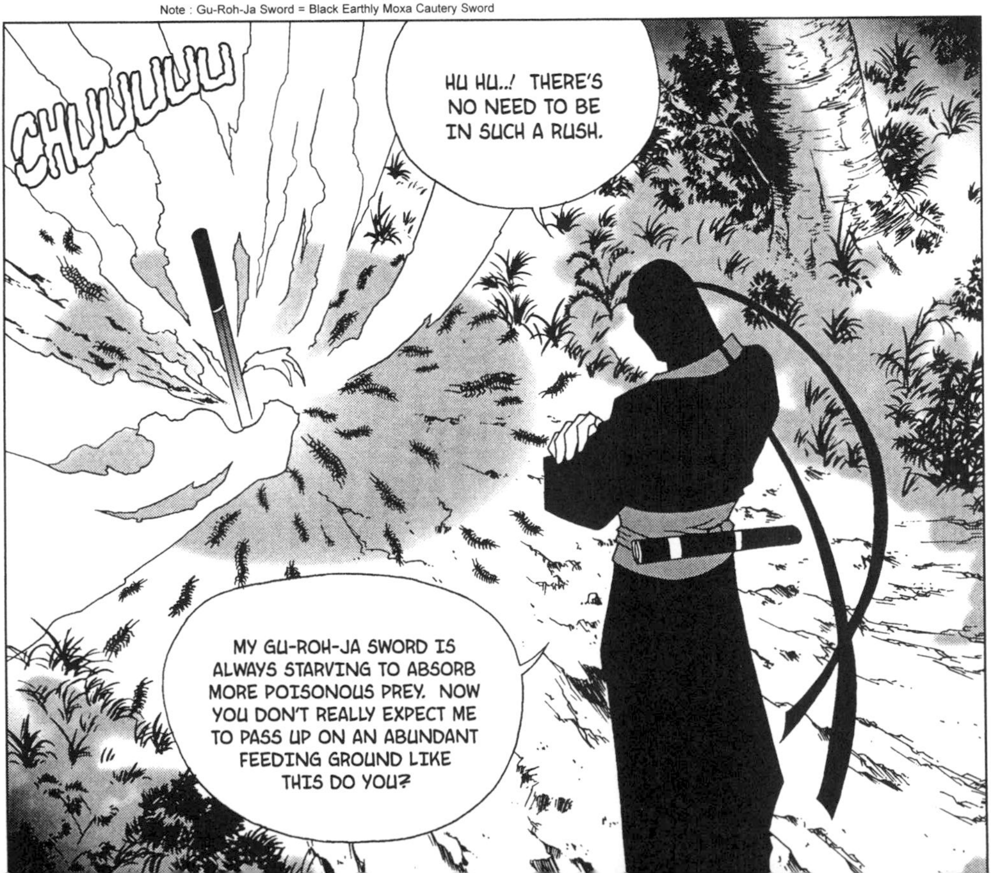
CHUUUUU
HU HU..! THERE'S NO NEED TO BE IN SUCH A RUSH.
MY GU-ROH-JA SWORD IS ALWAYS STARVING TO ABSORB MORE POISONOUS PREY. NOW YOU DON'T REALLY EXPECT ME TO PASS UP ON AN ABUNDANT FEEDING GROUND LIKE THIS DO YOU?

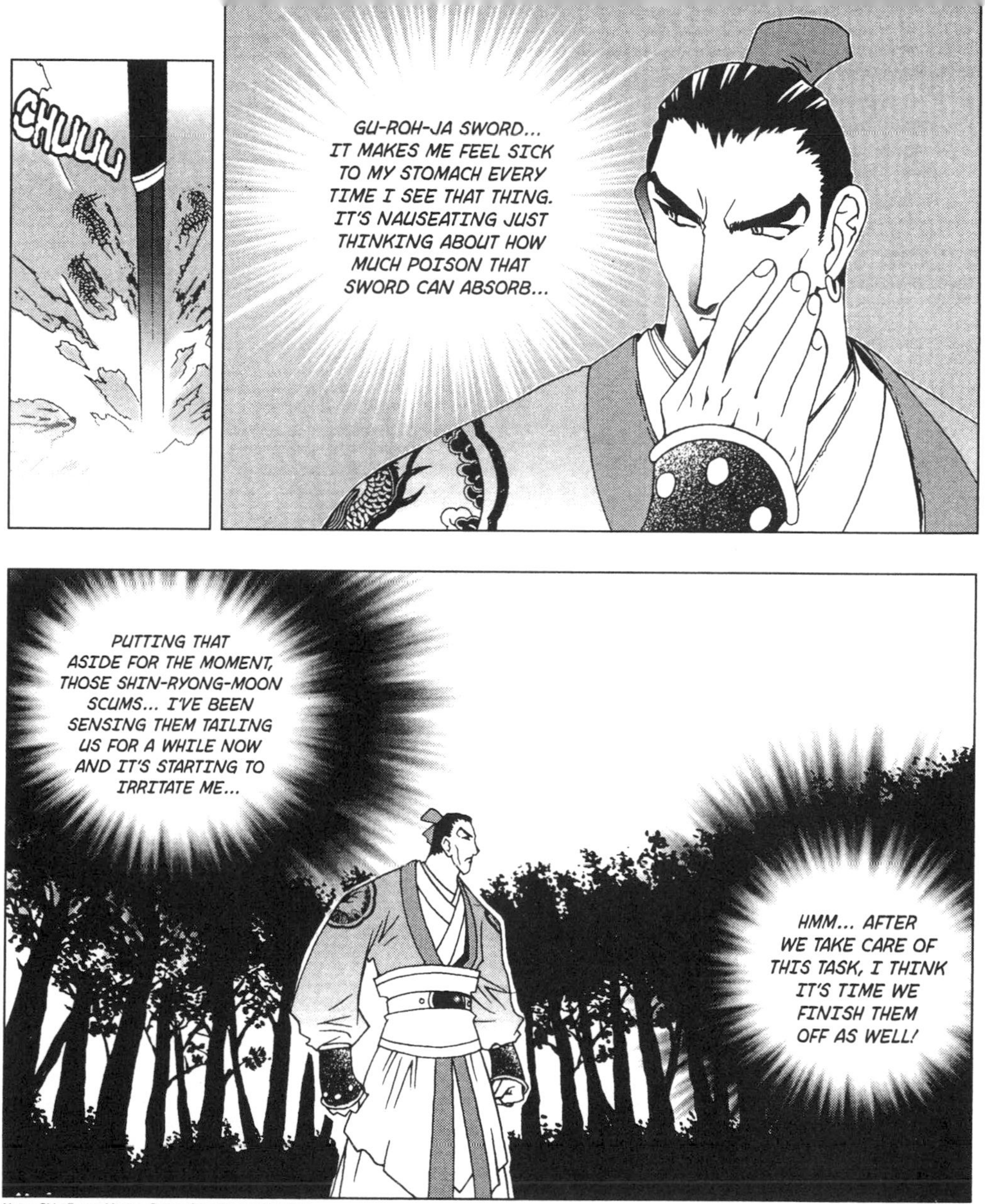
CHUUU
GU-ROH-JA SWORD... IT MAKES ME FEEL SICK TO MY STOMACH EVERY TIME I SEE THAT THING. IT'S NAUSEATING JUST THINKING ABOUT HOW MUCH POISON THAT SWORD CAN ABSORB...
PUTTING THAT ASIDE FOR THE MOMENT, THOSE SHIN-RYONG-MOON SCUMS... I'VE BEEN SENSING THEM TAILING US FOR A WHILE NOW AND IT'S STARTING TO IRRITATE ME...
HMM... AFTER WE TAKE CARE OF THIS TASK, I THINK IT'S TIME WE FINISH THEM OFF AS WELL!

Note : Shin-Ryong-Moon = Gates of the Dragon God Clan

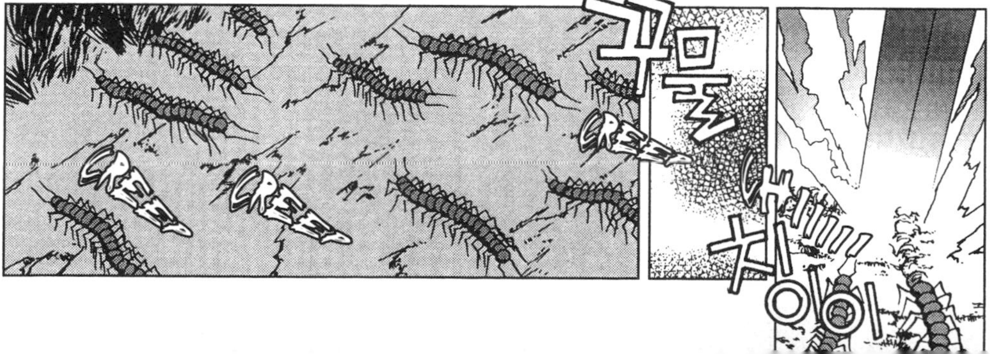
CRESS
CRESS
꾸물
CRESS

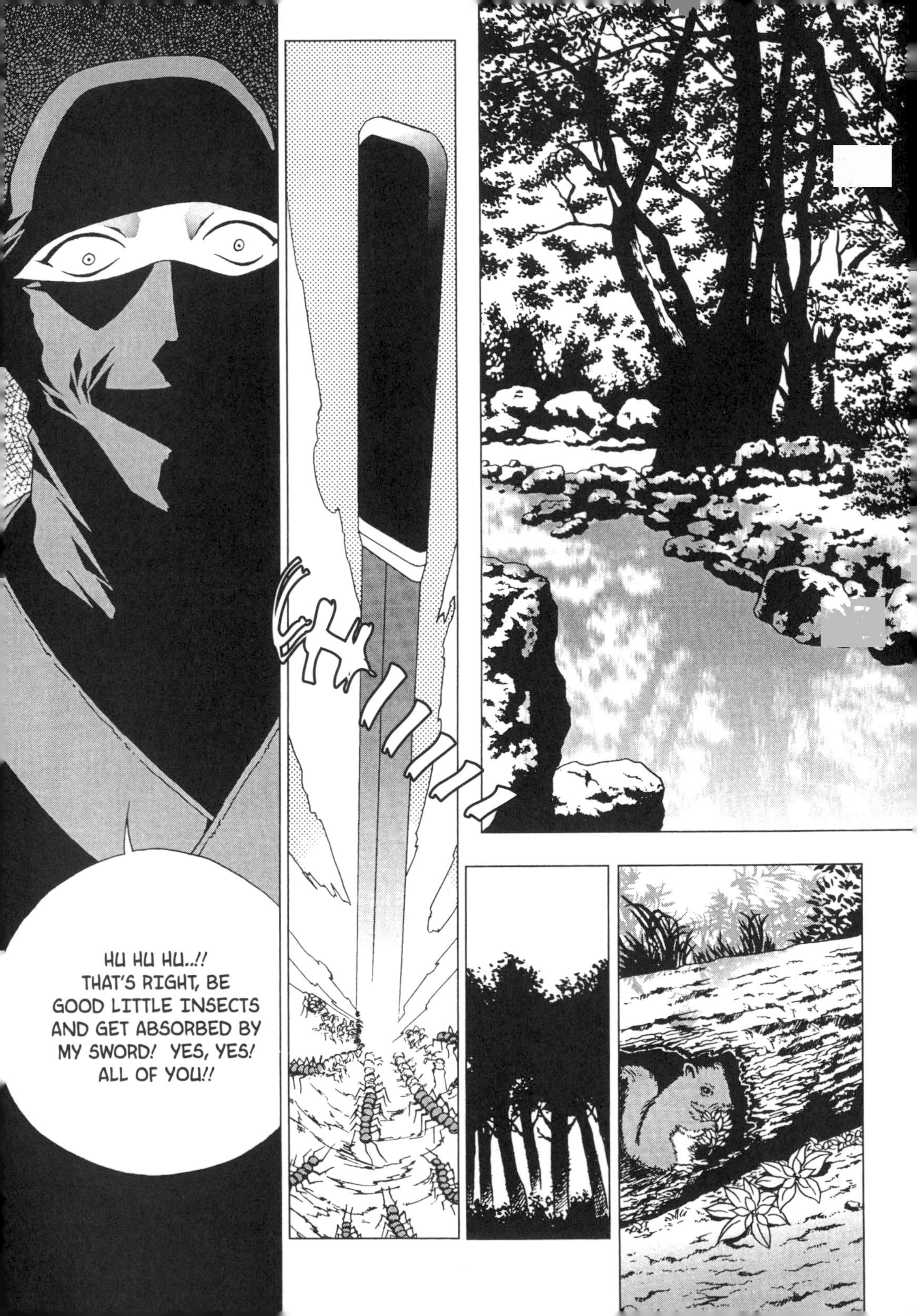
HU HU HU..!! THAT'S RIGHT, BE GOOD LITTLE INSECTS AND GET ABSORBED BY MY SWORD! YES, YES! ALL OF YOU!!

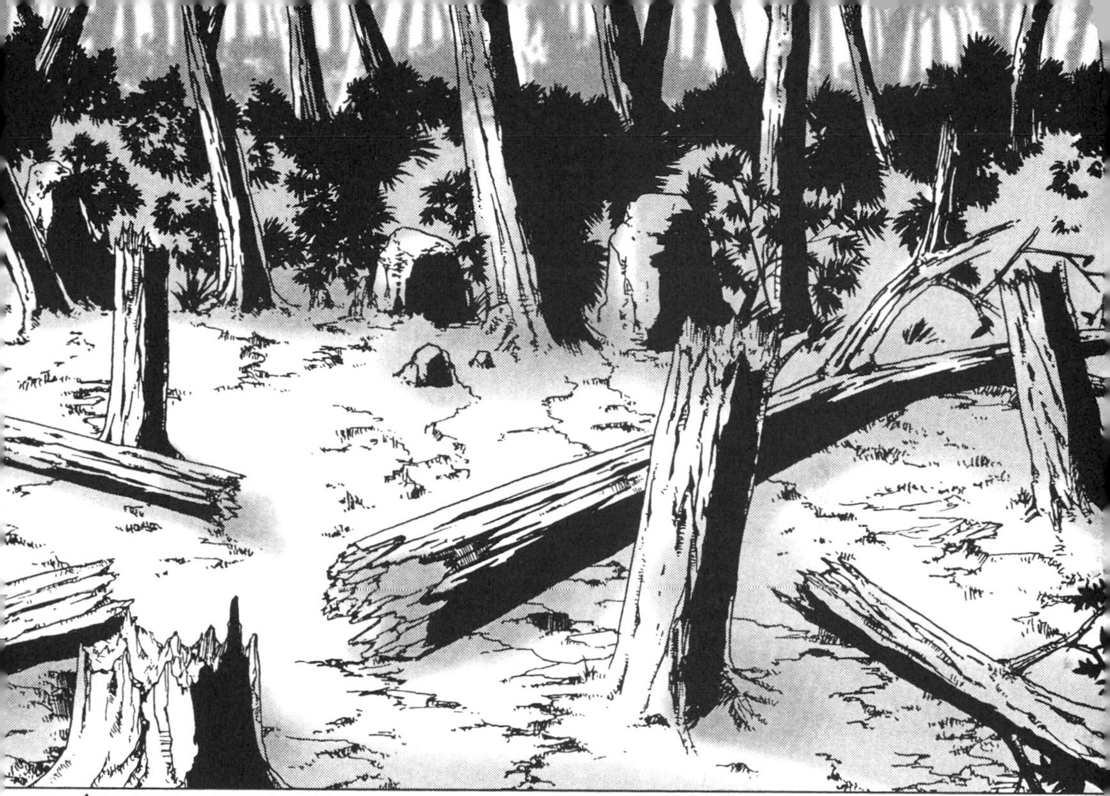

↑The place where O'Rhang Yhun's been practicing his Sa-Gook-Sung Yhunjoo-Boong-Gyuk (Combined Razing Attack of the 4 Directions)

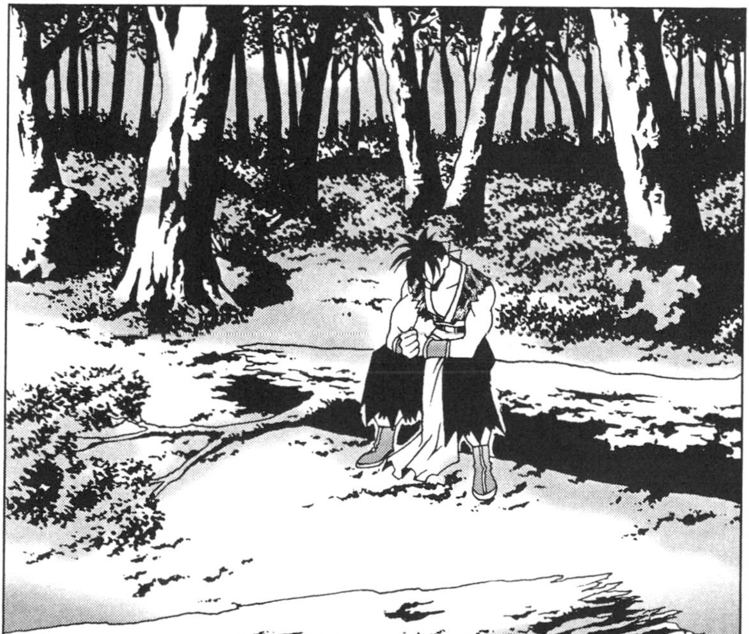

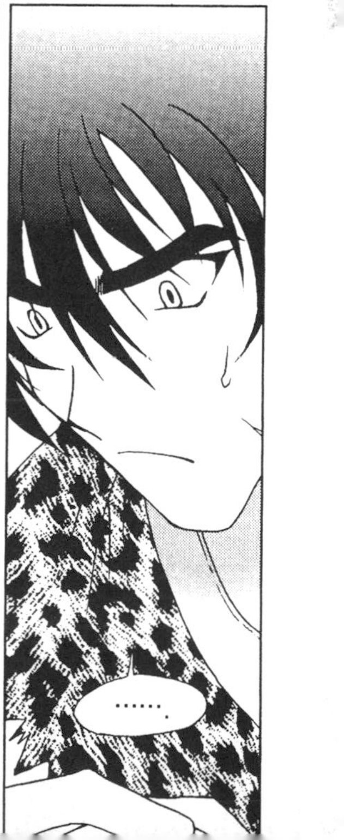
......

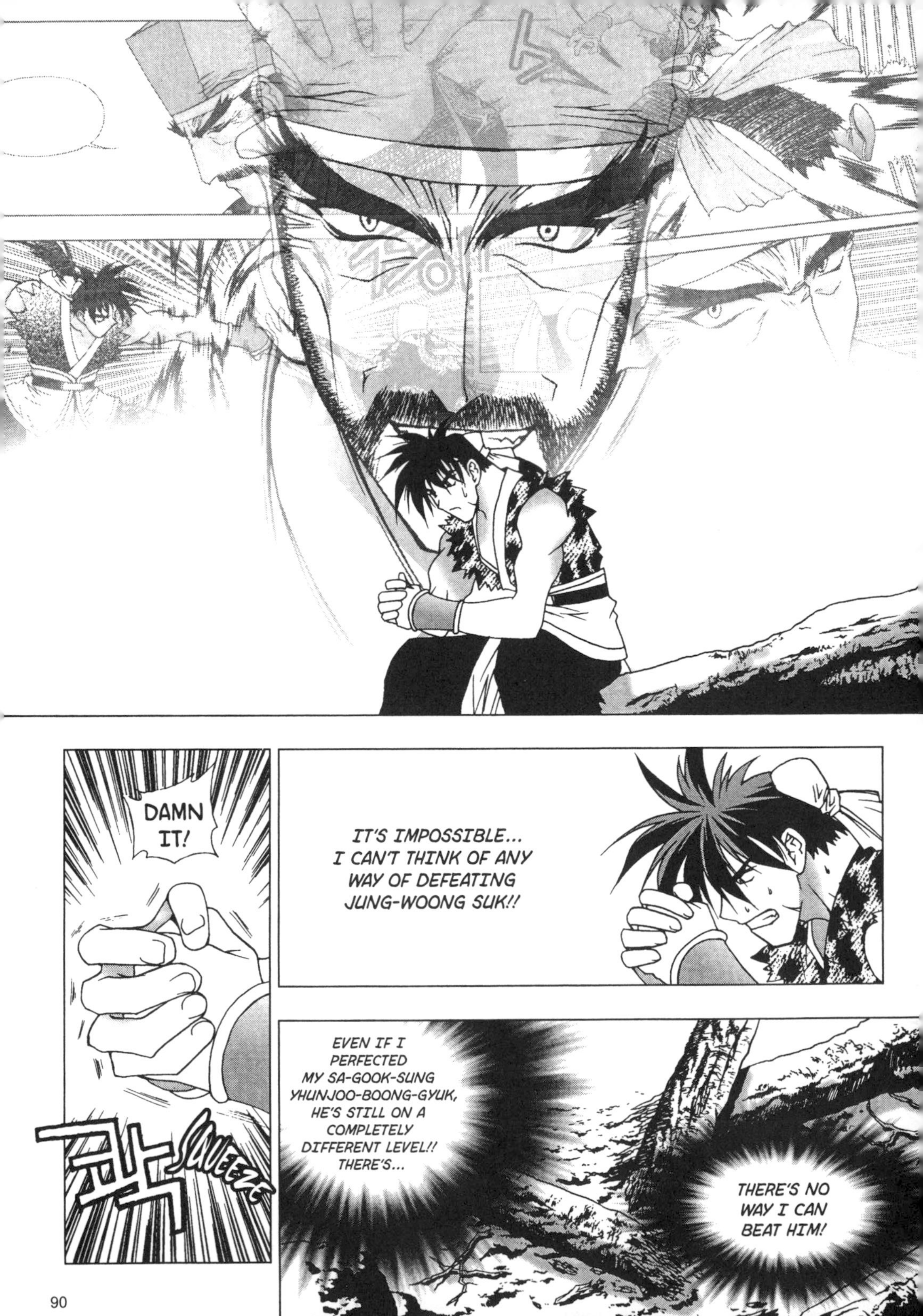
DAMN IT!
IT'S IMPOSSIBLE... I CAN'T THINK OF ANY WAY OF DEFEATING JUNG-WOONG SUK!!
SQUEEZE
EVEN IF I PERFECTED MY SA-GOOK-SUNG YHUNJOO-BOONG-GYUK, HE'S STILL ON A COMPLETELY DIFFERENT LEVEL!! THERE'S...
THERE'S NO WAY I CAN BEAT HIM!

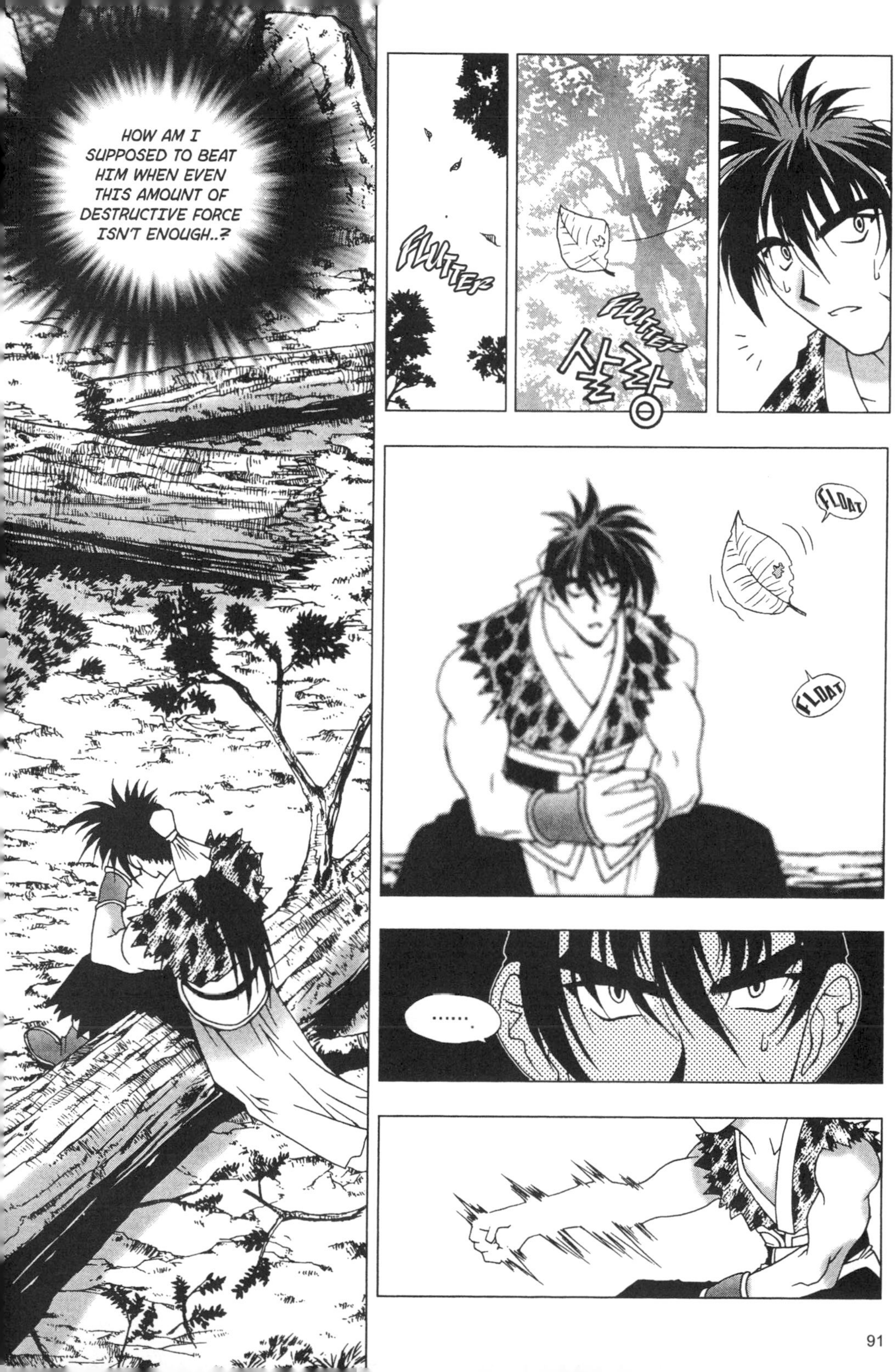
HOW AM I SUPPOSED TO BEAT HIM WHEN EVEN THIS AMOUNT OF DESTRUCTIVE FORCE ISN'T ENOUGH..?
FLUTTER
FLUTTER
살랑
FLOAT
FLOAT
......

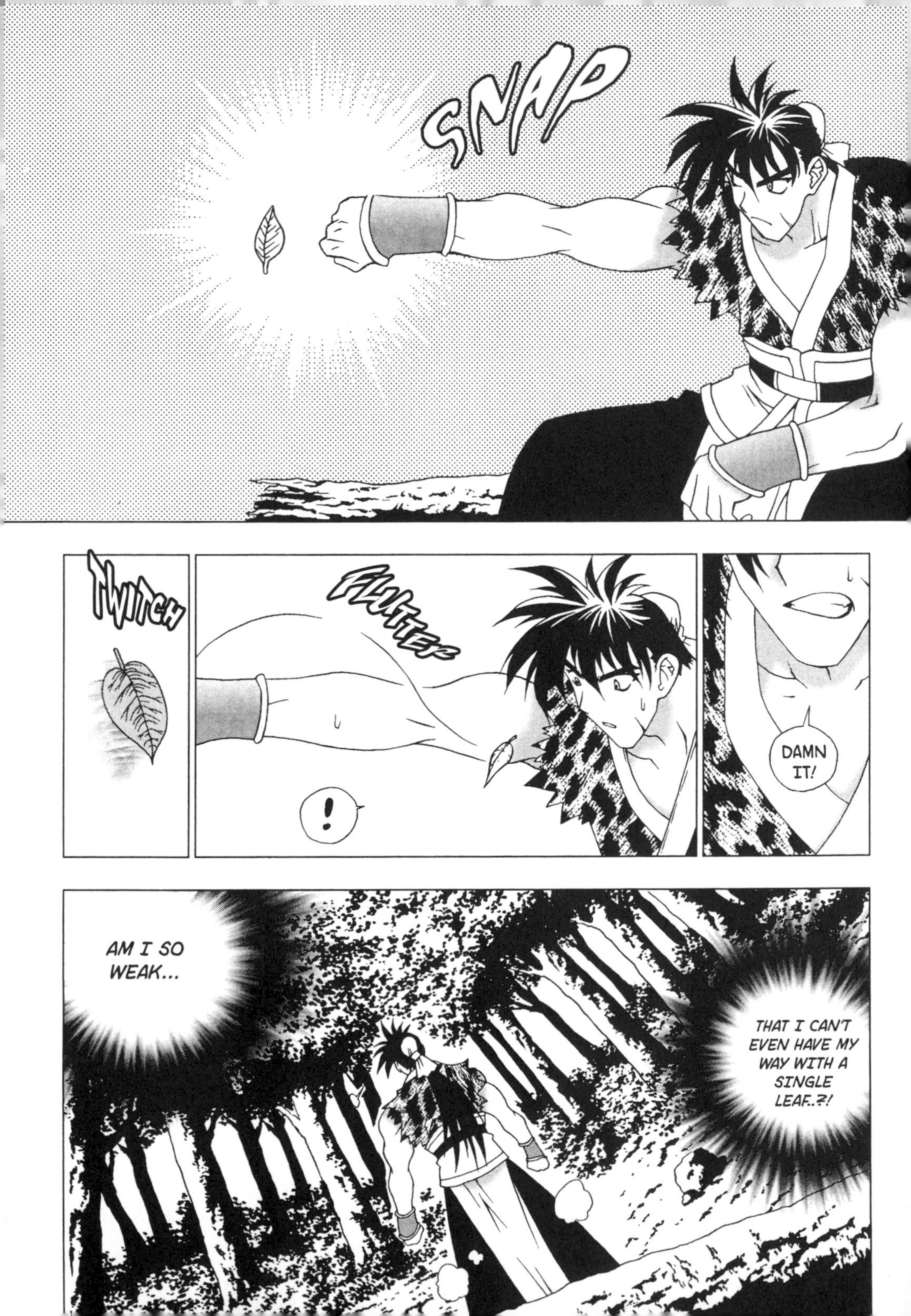
SNAP
TWITCH
FLUTTER
!
DAMN IT!
AM I SO WEAK...
THAT I CAN'T EVEN HAVE MY WAY WITH A SINGLE LEAF..?!

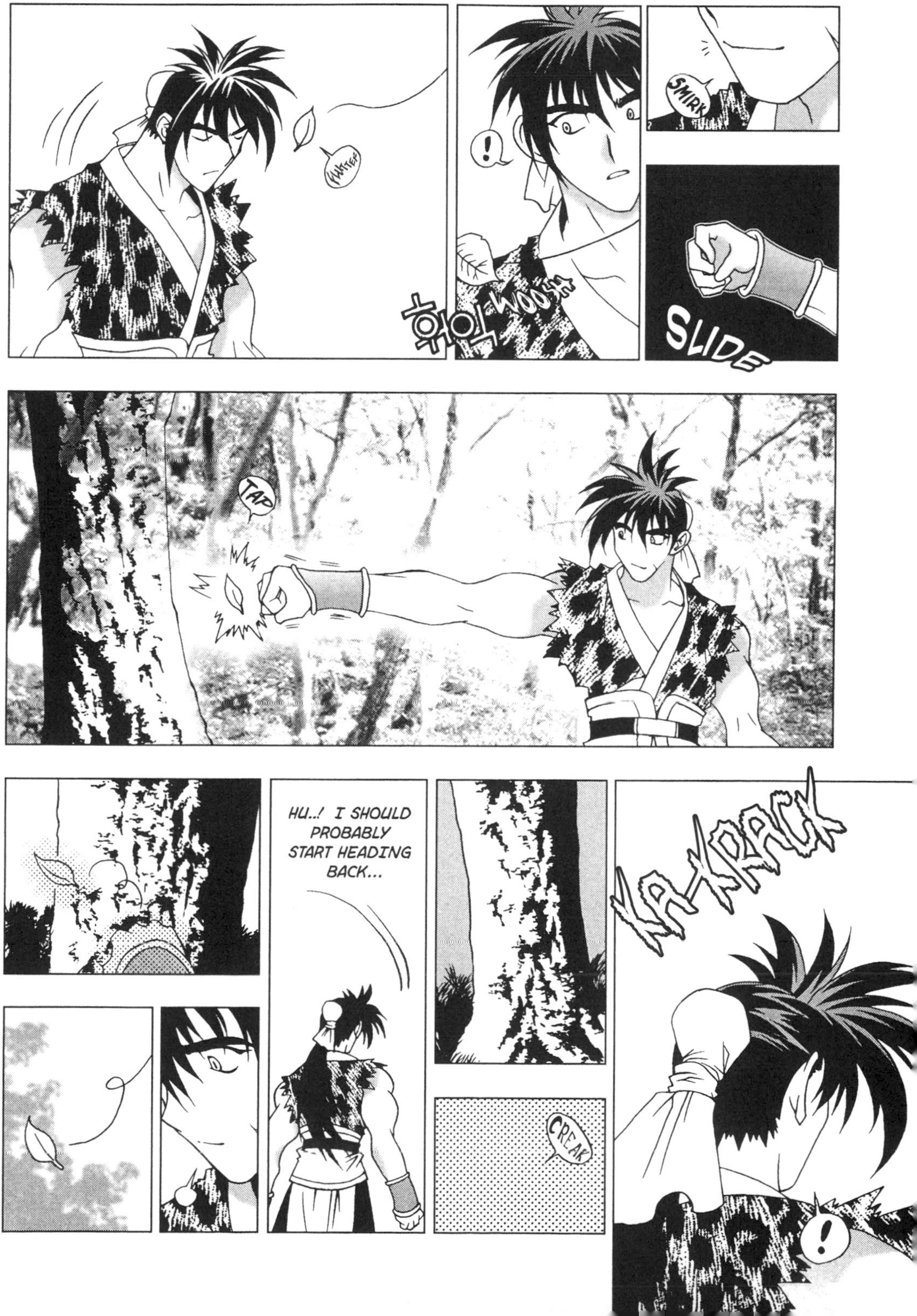
FLUTTER
!
WOOSH
SMIRK
SLIDE
TAP
HU..! I SHOULD PROBABLY START HEADING BACK...
CREAK
KA-KRACK
!

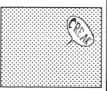

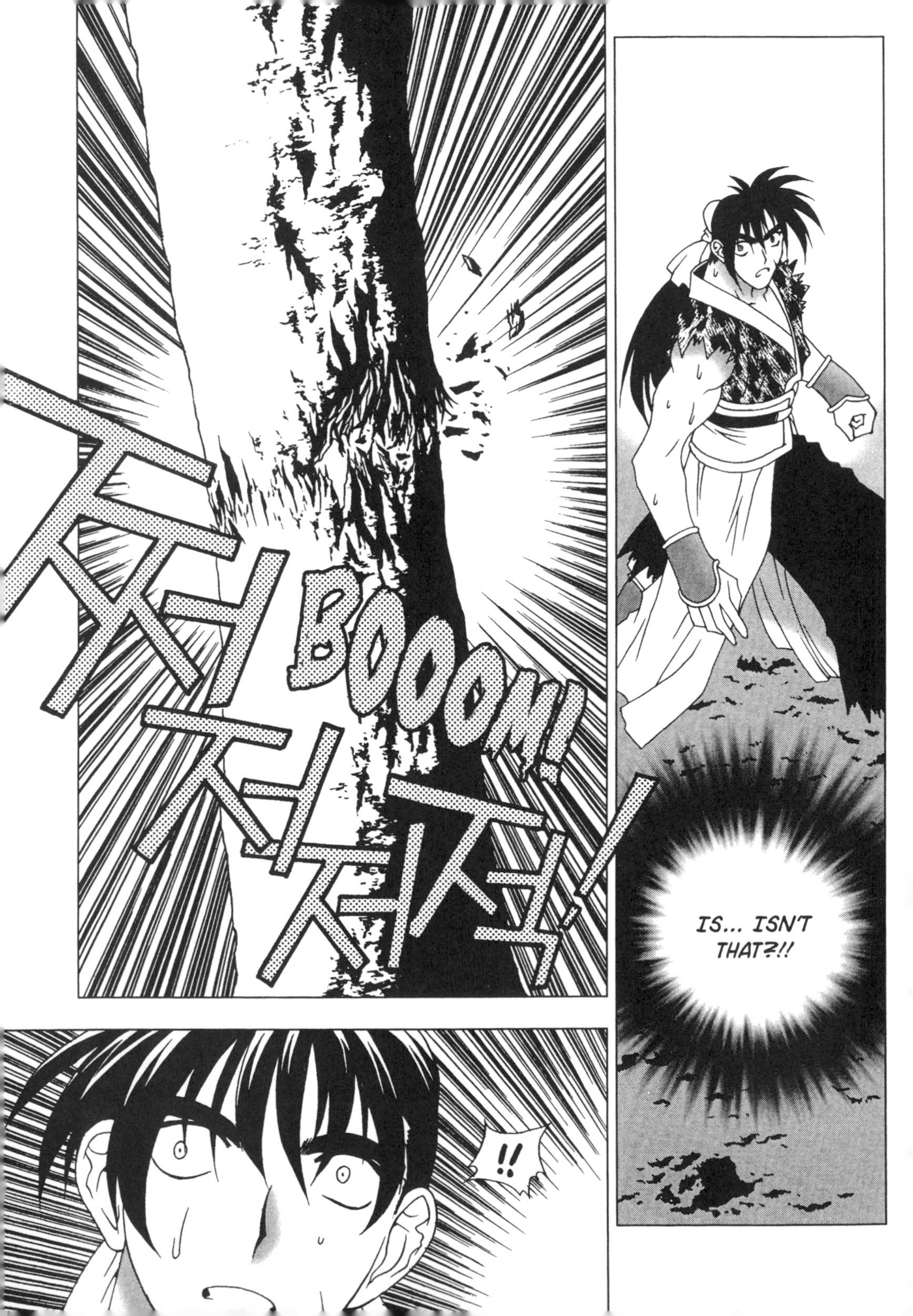

IS... ISN'T THAT?!!
BOOOM!
!!

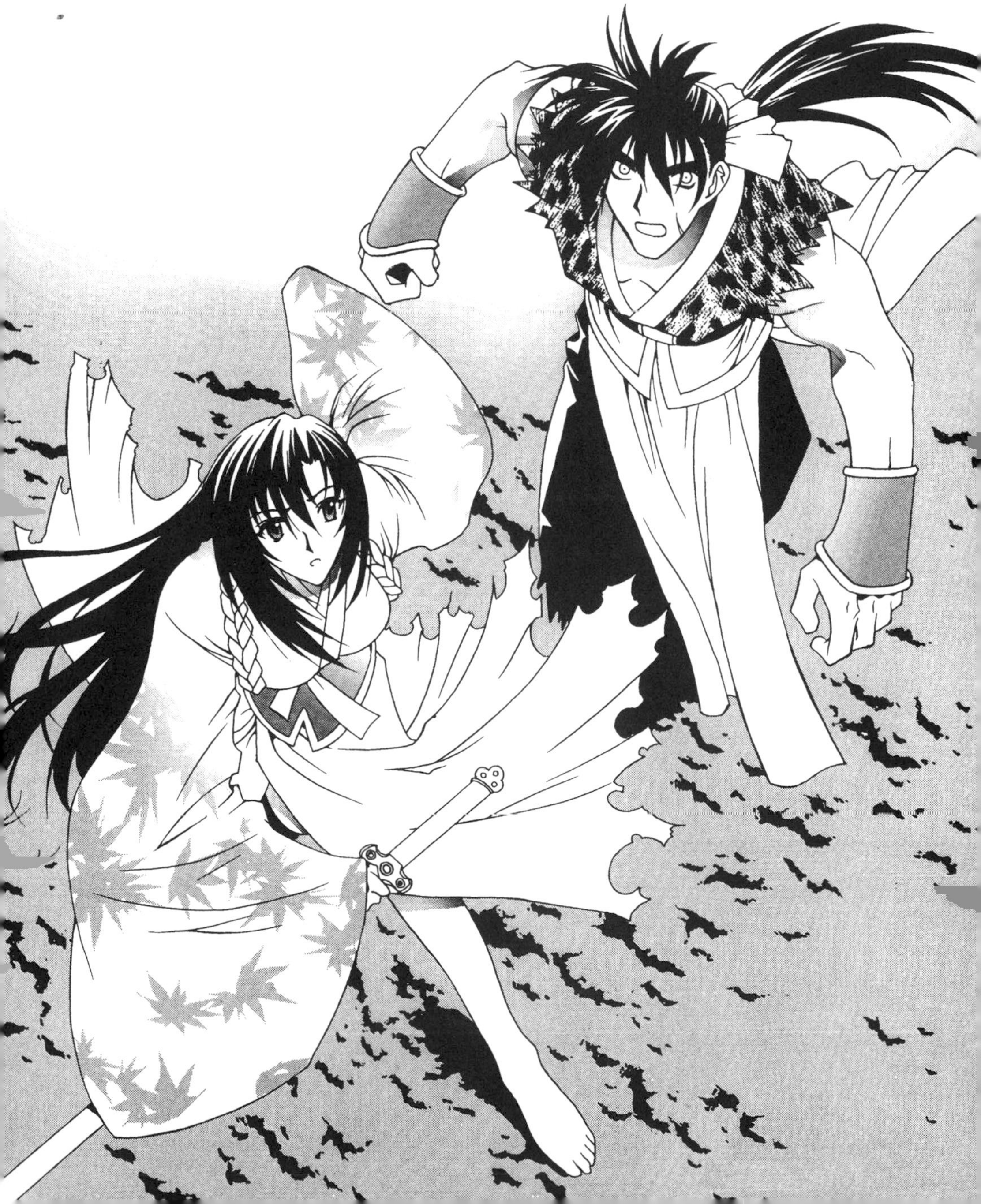

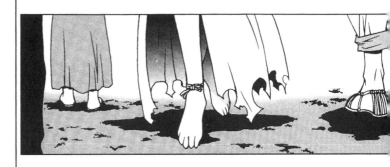

PHEW~!

MASTER YHUN HAS BEEN
SO QUIET SINCE HIS
ENCOUNTER WITH
JUNG-WOONG SUK...
BUT I'M CERTAIN OUR
ENEMIES WON'T LEAVE
US BE FOR MUCH LONGER...
I'D BETTER FIND A
WAY TO IMPROVE
MY OWN SKILLS
BEFORE THEN.

WELL, I WAS ABLE
TO GET ALL THE FOOD
WE NEED... SO THE
ONLY THING LEFT
IS TO ACQUIRE
SOME MEDICINE.

SIGH~
NOW THE ONLY PROBLEM LEFT IS TO FIGURE OUT WHAT TO DO ABOUT MY OWN TRAINING...

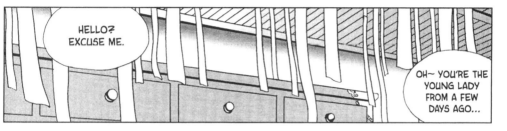

HELLO? EXCUSE ME.

OH~ YOU'RE THE YOUNG LADY FROM A FEW DAYS AGO...

SO, HOW IS YOUR HUSBAND DOING?

EH?

AHA~ UM, I THINK YOU MAY HAVE MISUNDERSTOOD, SIR... HE AND I AND AREN'T INVOLVED IN THAT MANNER~

COME NOW~! YOU CAN'T FOOL THE EYES ON THIS OLD MAN!

Really, we're not...

DOCTOR!

DOCTOR!!

STUMBLE CRASH

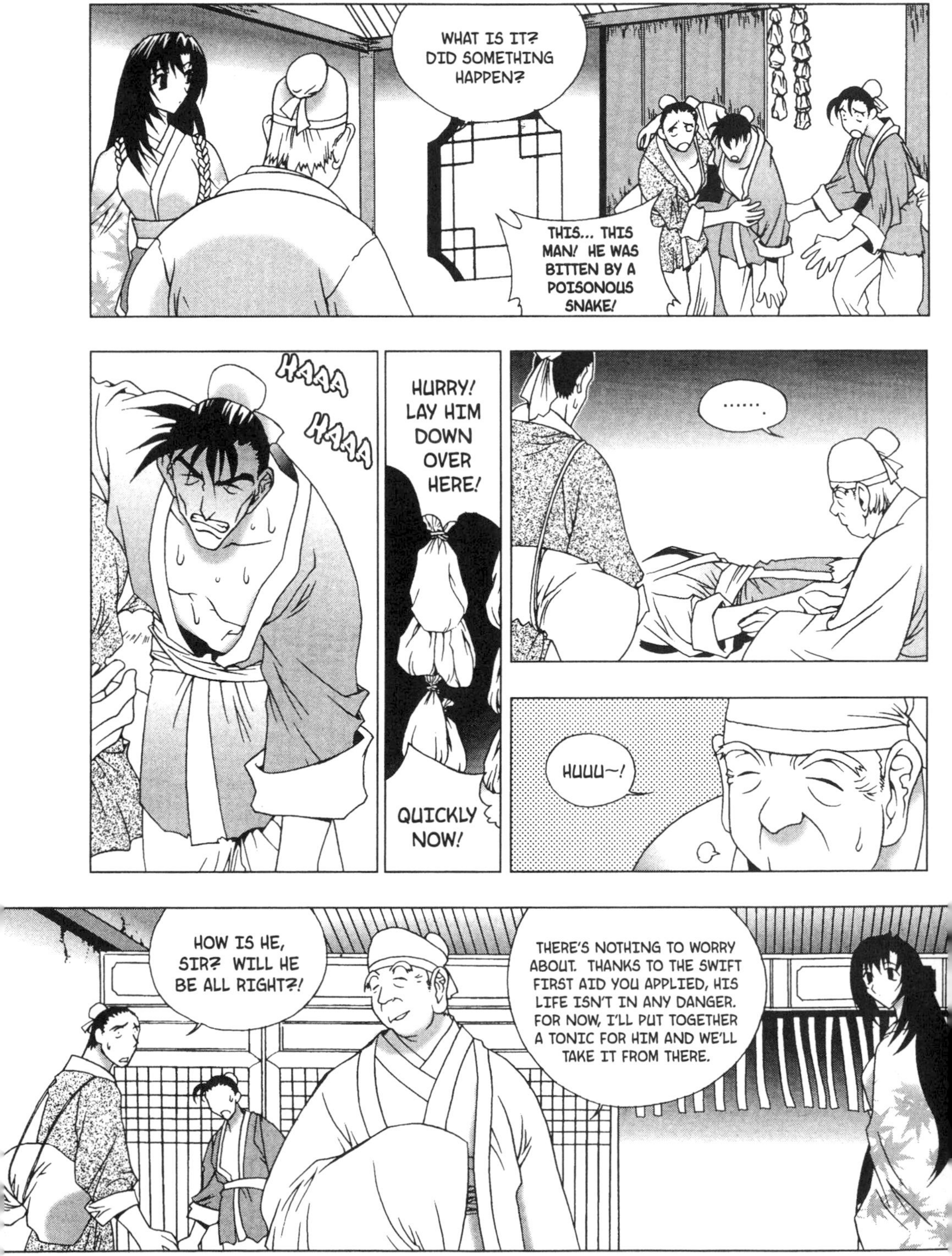
WHAT IS IT? DID SOMETHING HAPPEN?
THIS... THIS MAN! HE WAS BITTEN BY A POISONOUS SNAKE!
HAAA
HAAA
HURRY! LAY HIM DOWN OVER HERE!
QUICKLY NOW!
....
HUUU~!
HOW IS HE, SIR? WILL HE BE ALL RIGHT?!
THERE'S NOTHING TO WORRY ABOUT. THANKS TO THE SWIFT FIRST AID YOU APPLIED, HIS LIFE ISN'T IN ANY DANGER. FOR NOW, I'LL PUT TOGETHER A TONIC FOR HIM AND WE'LL TAKE IT FROM THERE.

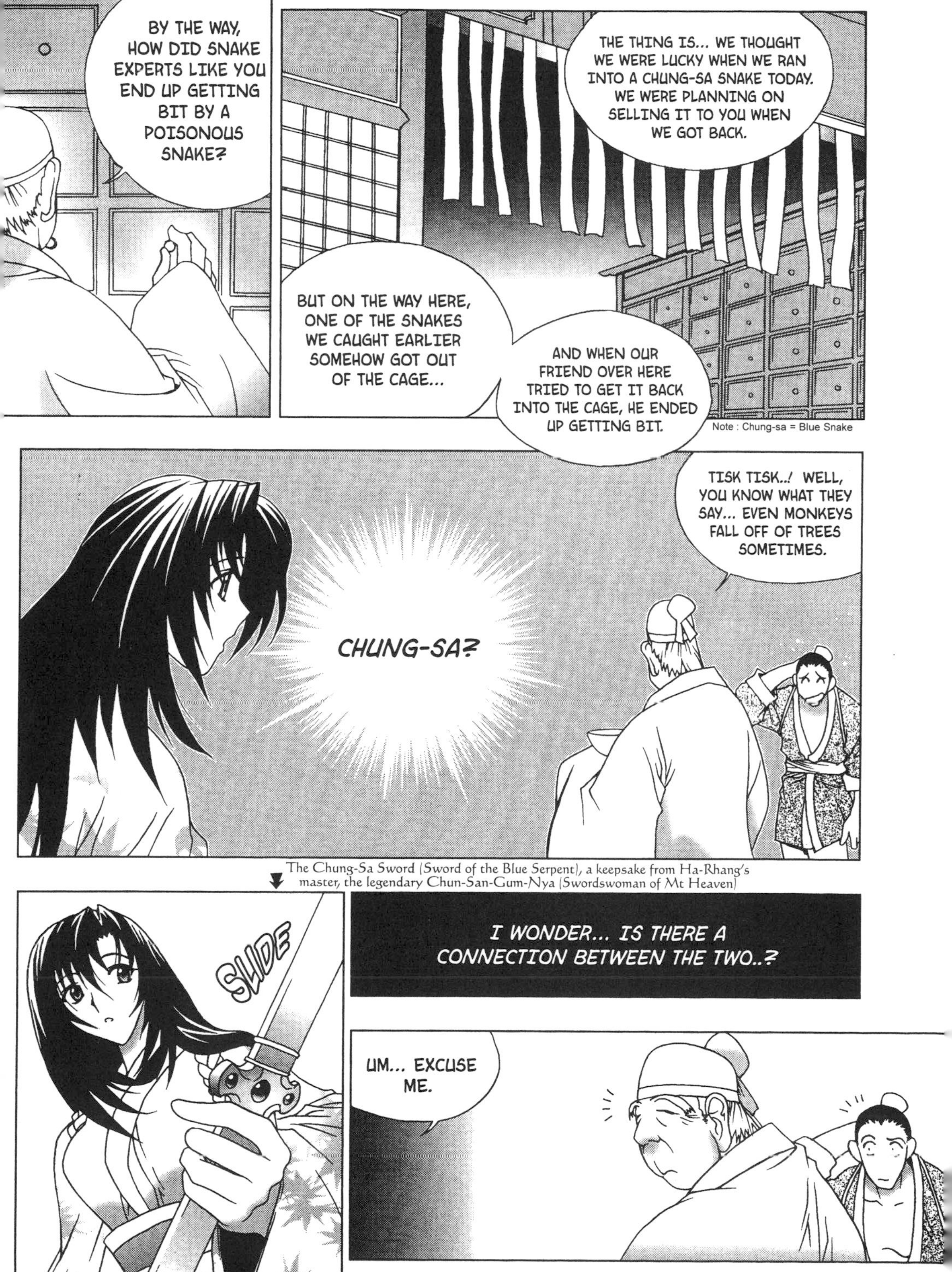

BY THE WAY, HOW DID SNAKE EXPERTS LIKE YOU END UP GETTING BIT BY A POISONOUS SNAKE?
THE THING IS... WE THOUGHT WE WERE LUCKY WHEN WE RAN INTO A CHUNG-SA SNAKE TODAY. WE WERE PLANNING ON SELLING IT TO YOU WHEN WE GOT BACK.
BUT ON THE WAY HERE, ONE OF THE SNAKES WE CAUGHT EARLIER SOMEHOW GOT OUT OF THE CAGE...
AND WHEN OUR FRIEND OVER HERE TRIED TO GET IT BACK INTO THE CAGE, HE ENDED UP GETTING BIT.
Note : Chung-sa = Blue Snake
TISK TISK..! WELL, YOU KNOW WHAT THEY SAY... EVEN MONKEYS FALL OFF OF TREES SOMETIMES.
CHUNG-SA?
The Chung-Sa Sword (Sword of the Blue Serpent), a keepsake from Ha-Rhang's master, the legendary Chun-San-Gum-Nya (Swordswoman of Mt Heaven)
SLIDE
I WONDER... IS THERE A CONNECTION BETWEEN THE TWO..?
UM... EXCUSE ME.

MAY I ASK ABOUT THE CHUNG-SA SNAKE YOU WERE JUST DISCUSSING? I WAS HOPING TO LEARN MORE ABOUT IT...

AH~!

Man~ she's hot...

THE CHUNG-SA SNAKE... IT'S A VERY RARE SNAKE SO THEY'RE ALMOST IMPOSSIBLE TO FIND.

NORMALLY WHEN SNAKES SHED THEIR SKIN THEY EITHER GET LARGER THAN BEFORE, OR AT THE VERY LEAST, REMAIN THE SAME SIZE. BUT IN THE CASE OF CHUNG-SA SNAKES, THEY ACTUALLY GET SMALLER. ON THE OTHER HAND, THEY BECOME MORE DANGEROUS AS THEIR VENOM BECOMES MUCH MORE POTENT. REGARDLESS THOUGH, CHUNG-SA SNAKES ARE SOUGHT AFTER BECAUSE OF THEIR MEDICINAL VALUE.

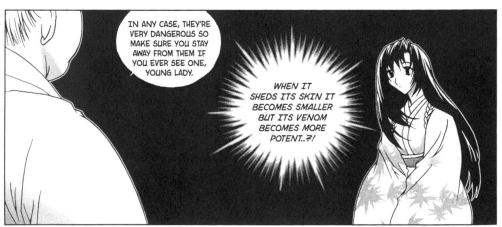

IN ANY CASE, THEY'RE VERY DANGEROUS SO MAKE SURE YOU STAY AWAY FROM THEM IF YOU EVER SEE ONE, YOUNG LADY.

WHEN IT SHEDS ITS SKIN IT BECOMES SMALLER BUT ITS VENOM BECOMES MORE POTENT..?!

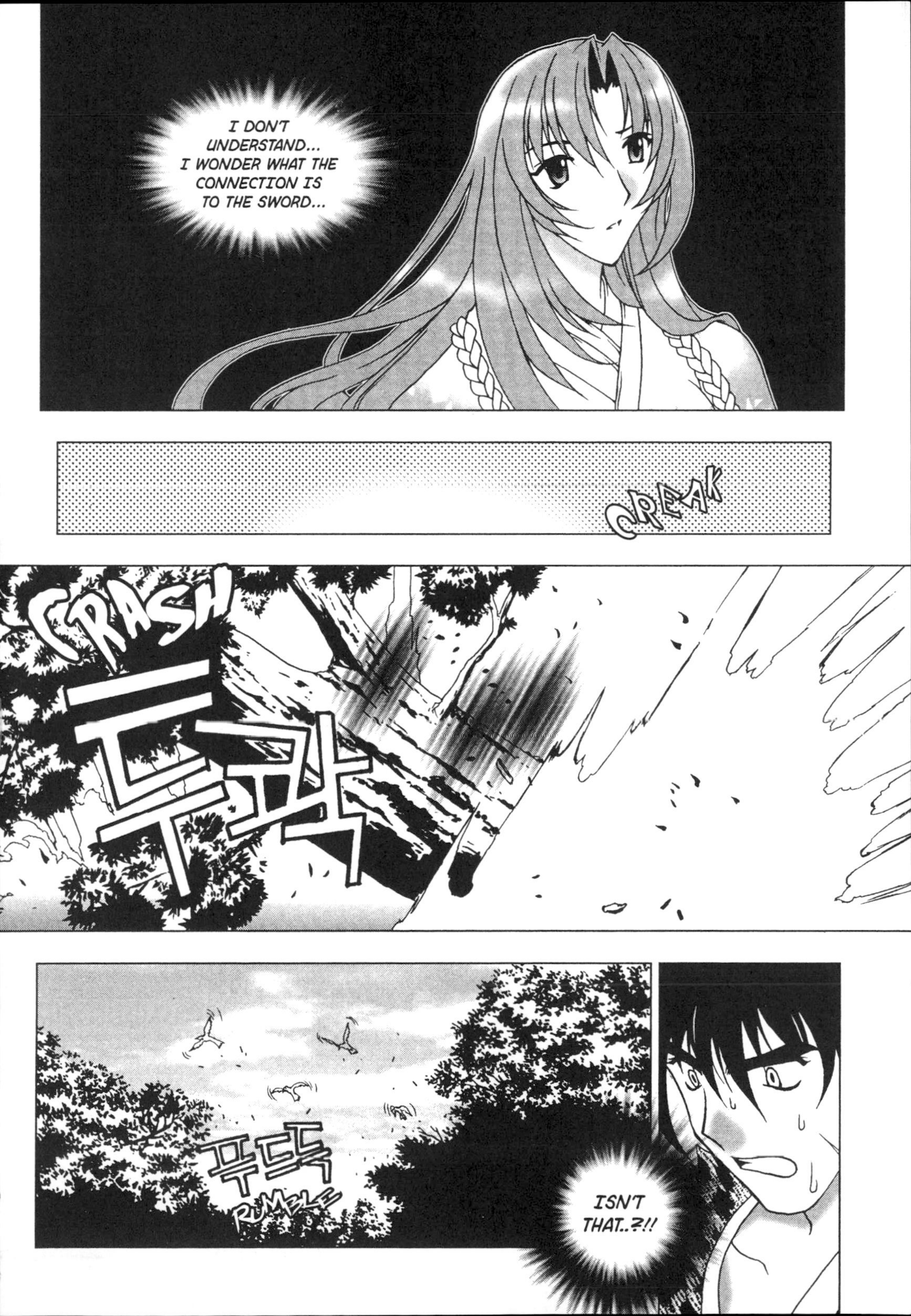
I DON'T UNDERSTAND... I WONDER WHAT THE CONNECTION IS TO THE SWORD...
CREAK
CRASH
RUMBLE
ISN'T THAT..?!!

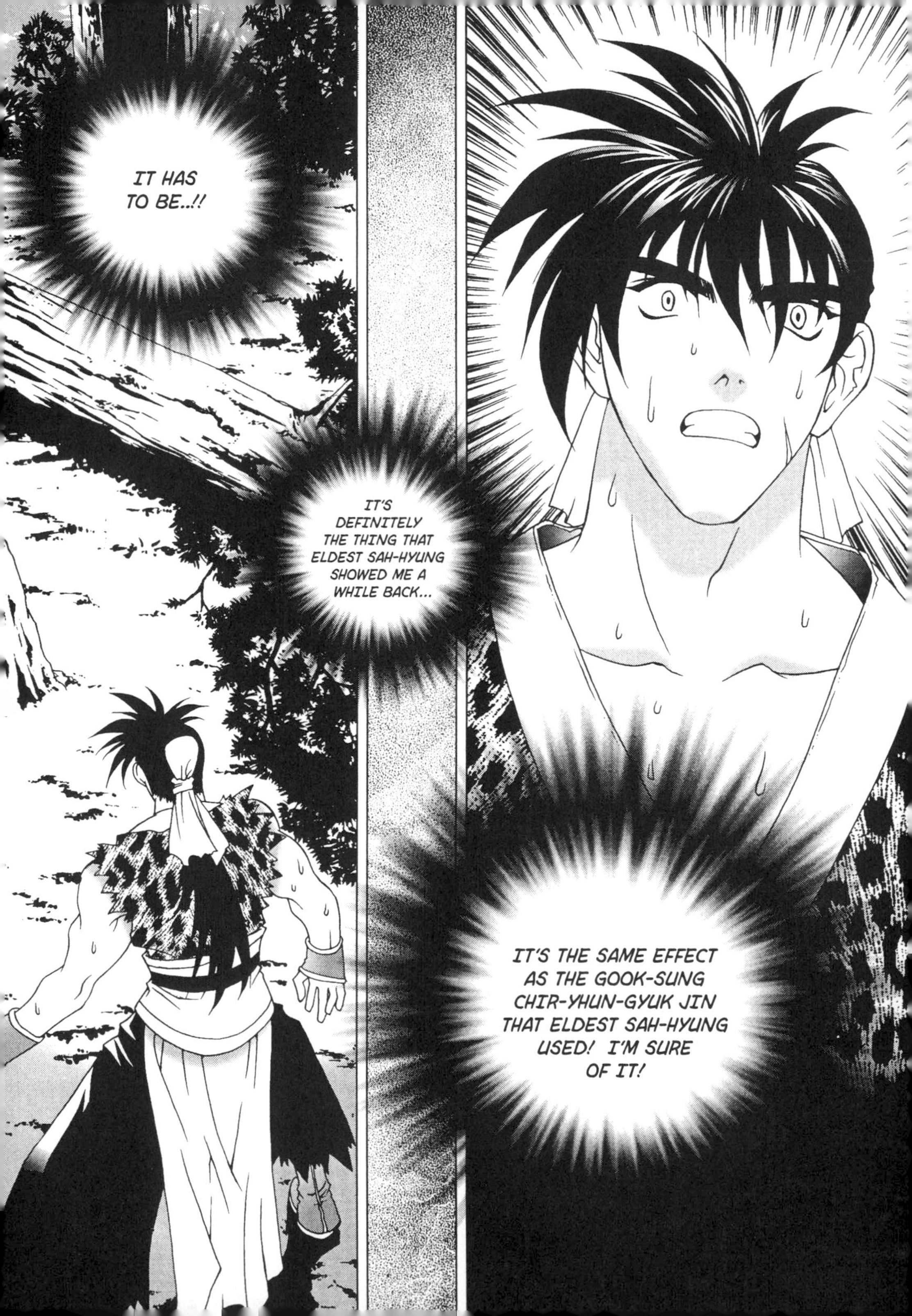
IT HAS TO BE..!!
IT'S DEFINITELY THE THING THAT ELDEST SAH-HYUNG SHOWED ME A WHILE BACK...
IT'S THE SAME EFFECT AS THE GOOK-SUNG CHIR-YHUN-GYUK JIN THAT ELDEST SAH-HYUNG USED! I'M SURE OF IT!

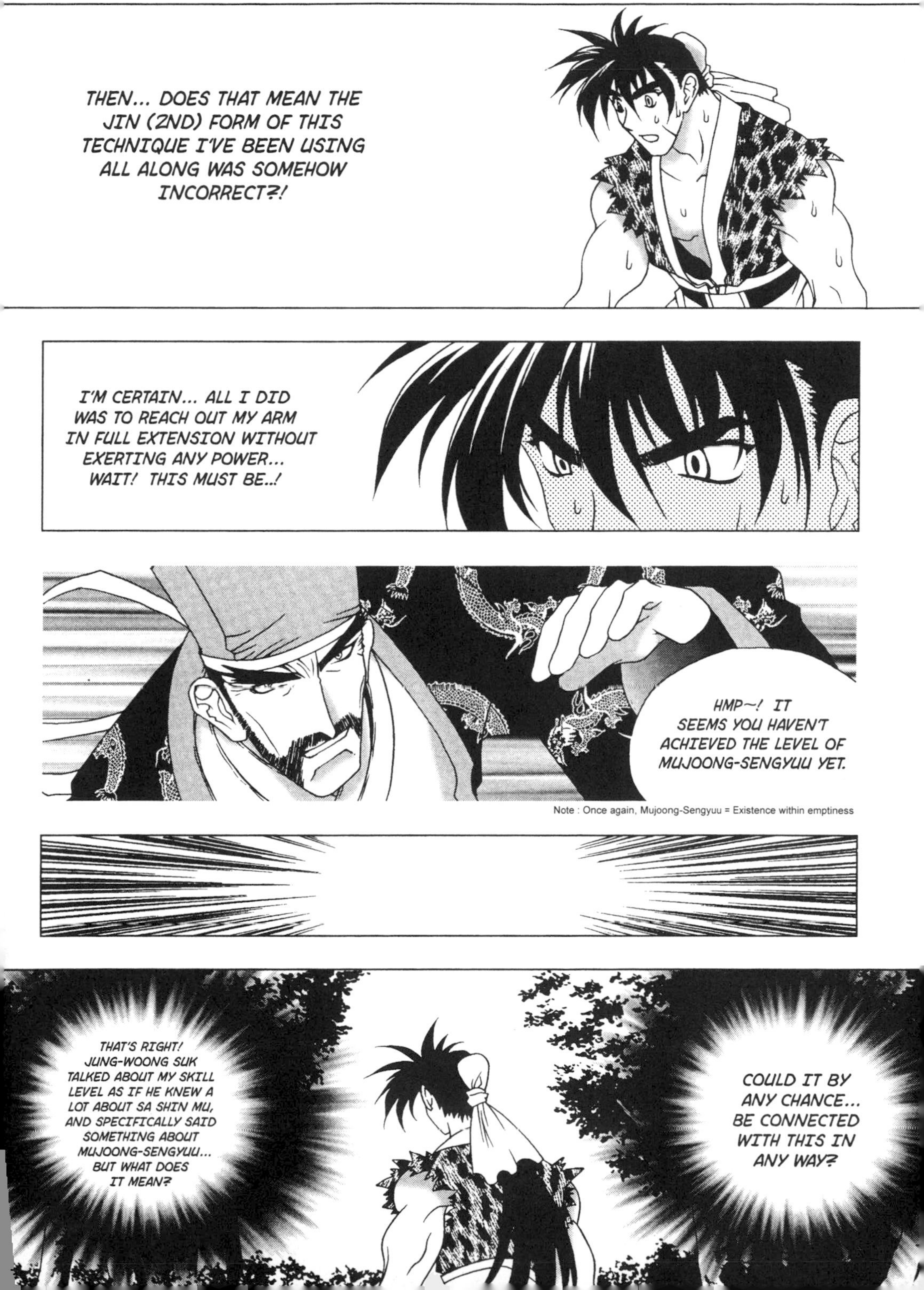
THEN... DOES THAT MEAN THE JIN (2ND) FORM OF THIS TECHNIQUE I'VE BEEN USING ALL ALONG WAS SOMEHOW INCORRECT?!
I'M CERTAIN... ALL I DID WAS TO REACH OUT MY ARM IN FULL EXTENSION WITHOUT EXERTING ANY POWER... WAIT! THIS MUST BE..!
HMP~! IT SEEMS YOU HAVEN'T ACHIEVED THE LEVEL OF MUJOONG-SENGYUU YET.
Note : Once again, Mujoong-Sengyuu = Existence within emptiness
THAT'S RIGHT! JUNG-WOONG SUK TALKED ABOUT MY SKILL LEVEL AS IF HE KNEW A LOT ABOUT SA SHIN MU, AND SPECIFICALLY SAID SOMETHING ABOUT MUJOONG-SENGYUU... BUT WHAT DOES IT MEAN?
COULD IT BY ANY CHANCE... BE CONNECTED WITH THIS IN ANY WAY?

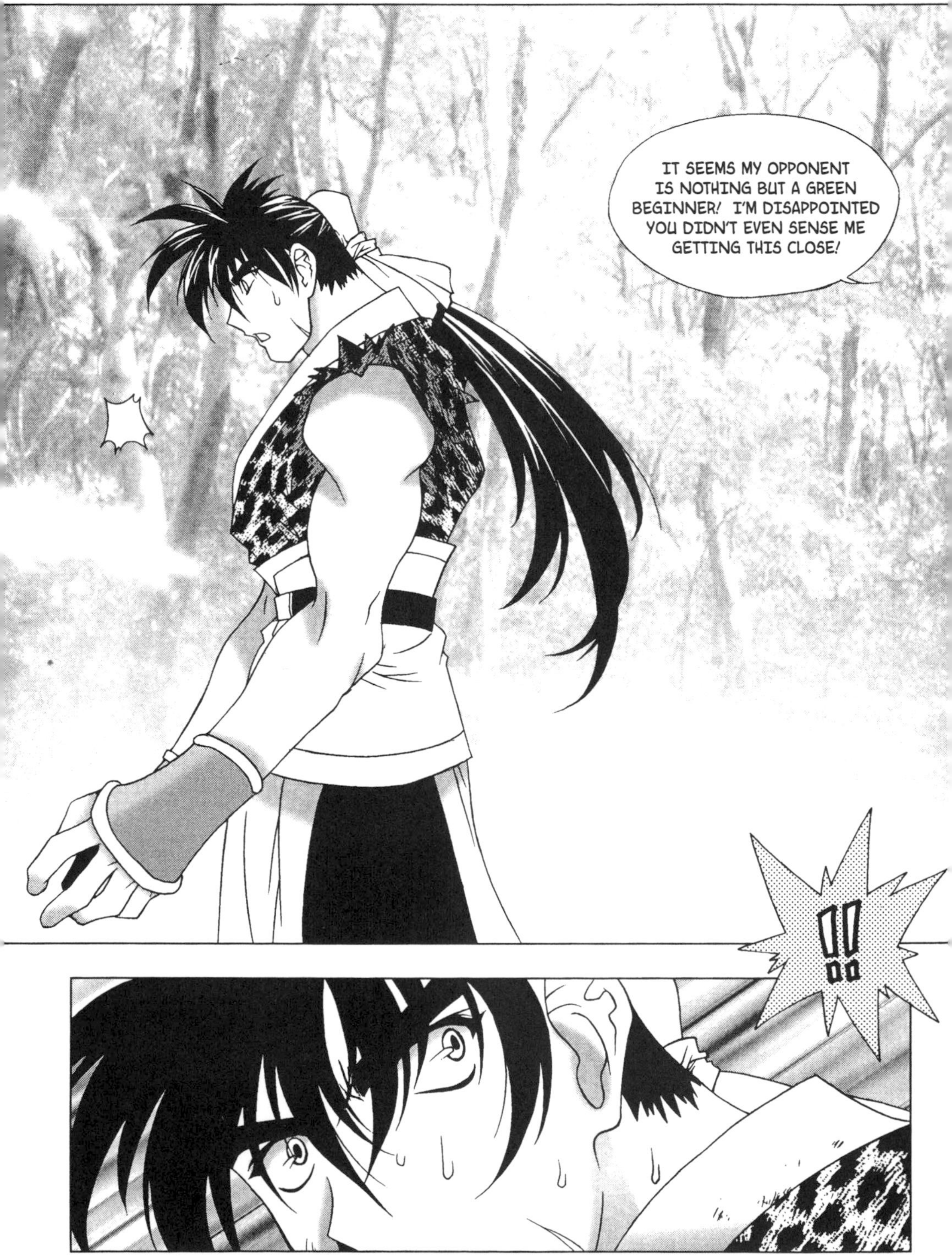
IT SEEMS MY OPPONENT IS NOTHING BUT A GREEN BEGINNER! I'M DISAPPOINTED YOU DIDN'T EVEN SENSE ME GETTING THIS CLOSE!
!!

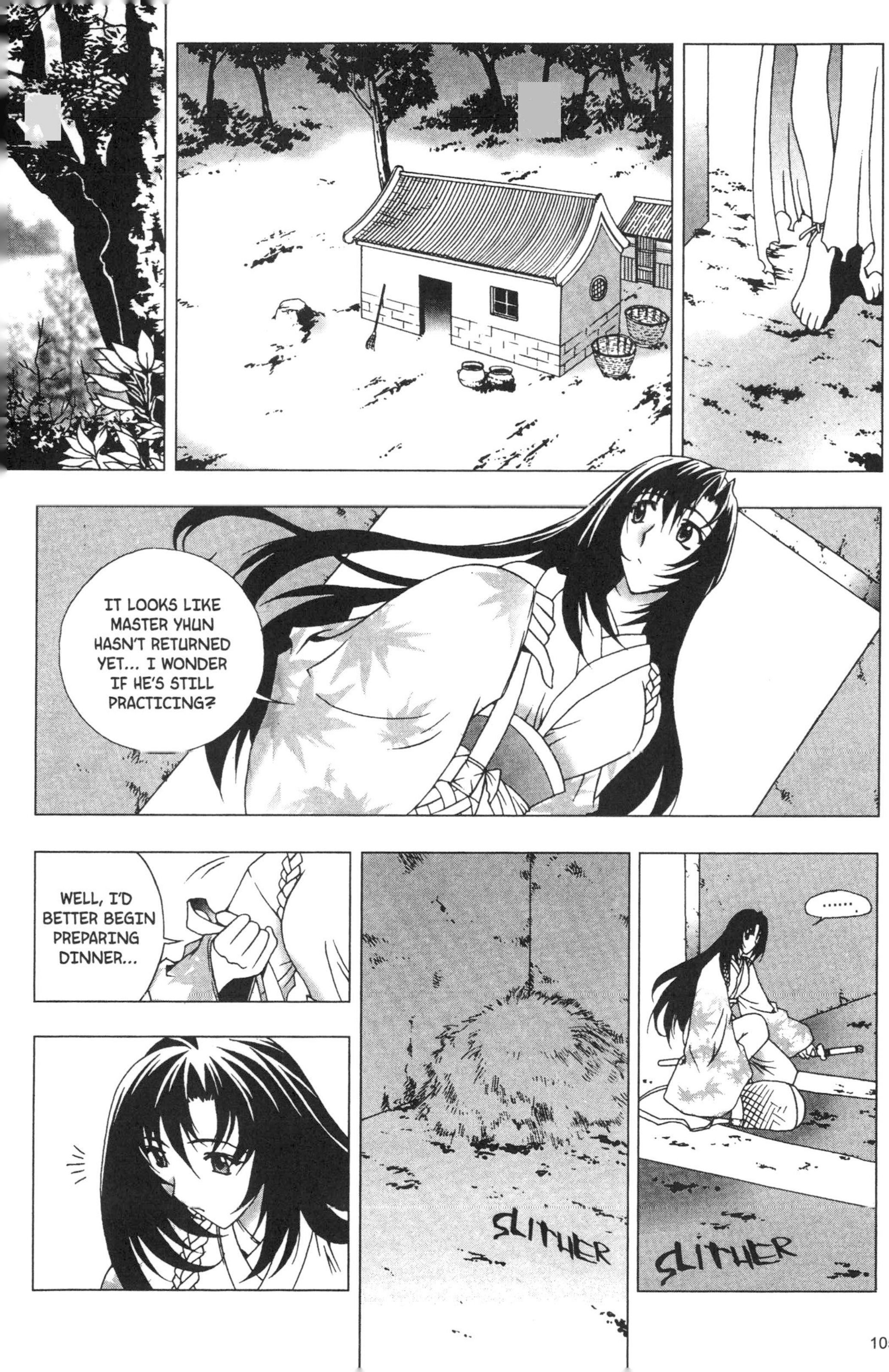
IT LOOKS LIKE MASTER YHUN HASN'T RETURNED YET... I WONDER IF HE'S STILL PRACTICING?
WELL, I'D BETTER BEGIN PREPARING DINNER...
......
SLITHER
SLITHER

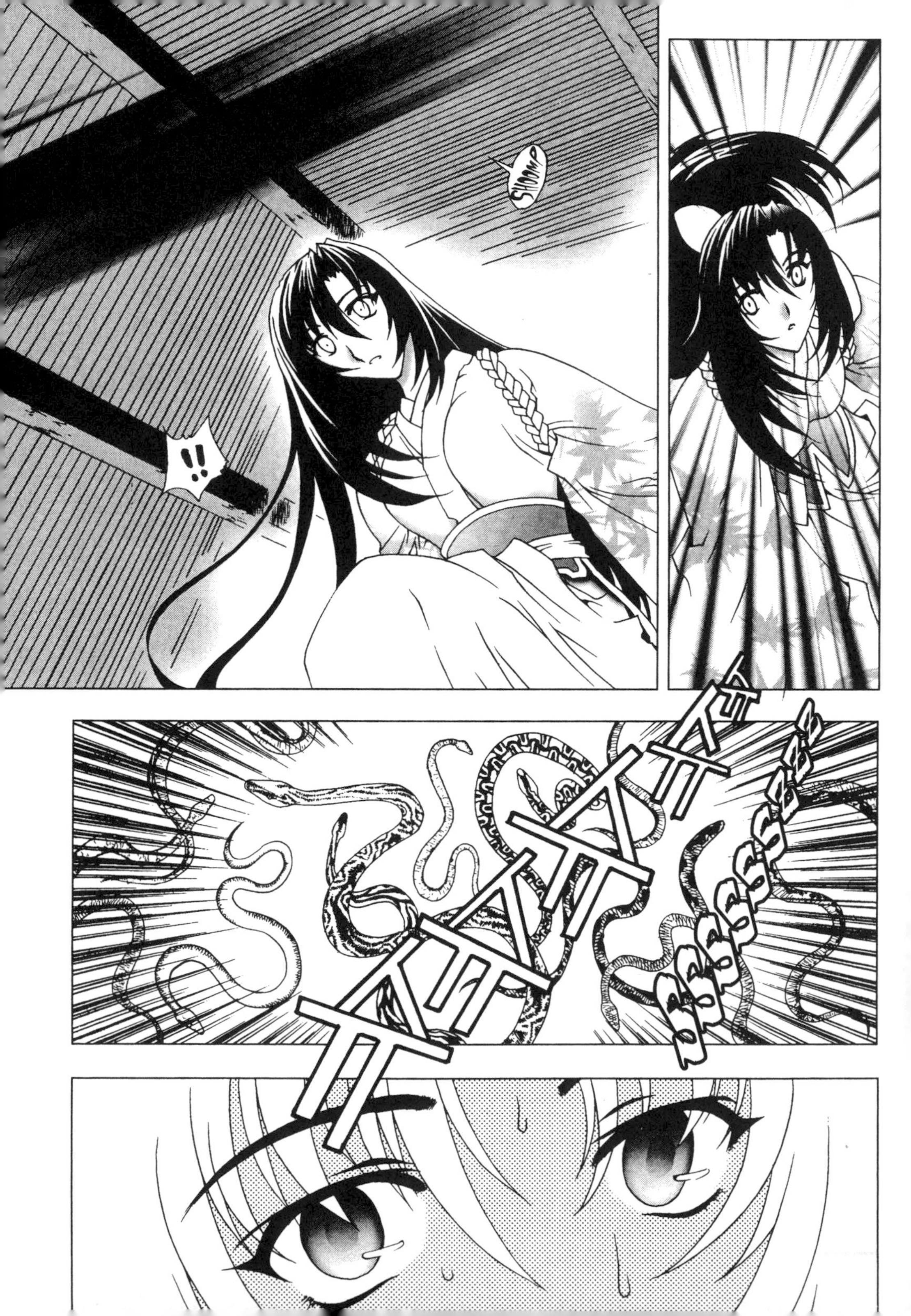

SHOOMP
!!
SSSSSSSSSZZZ

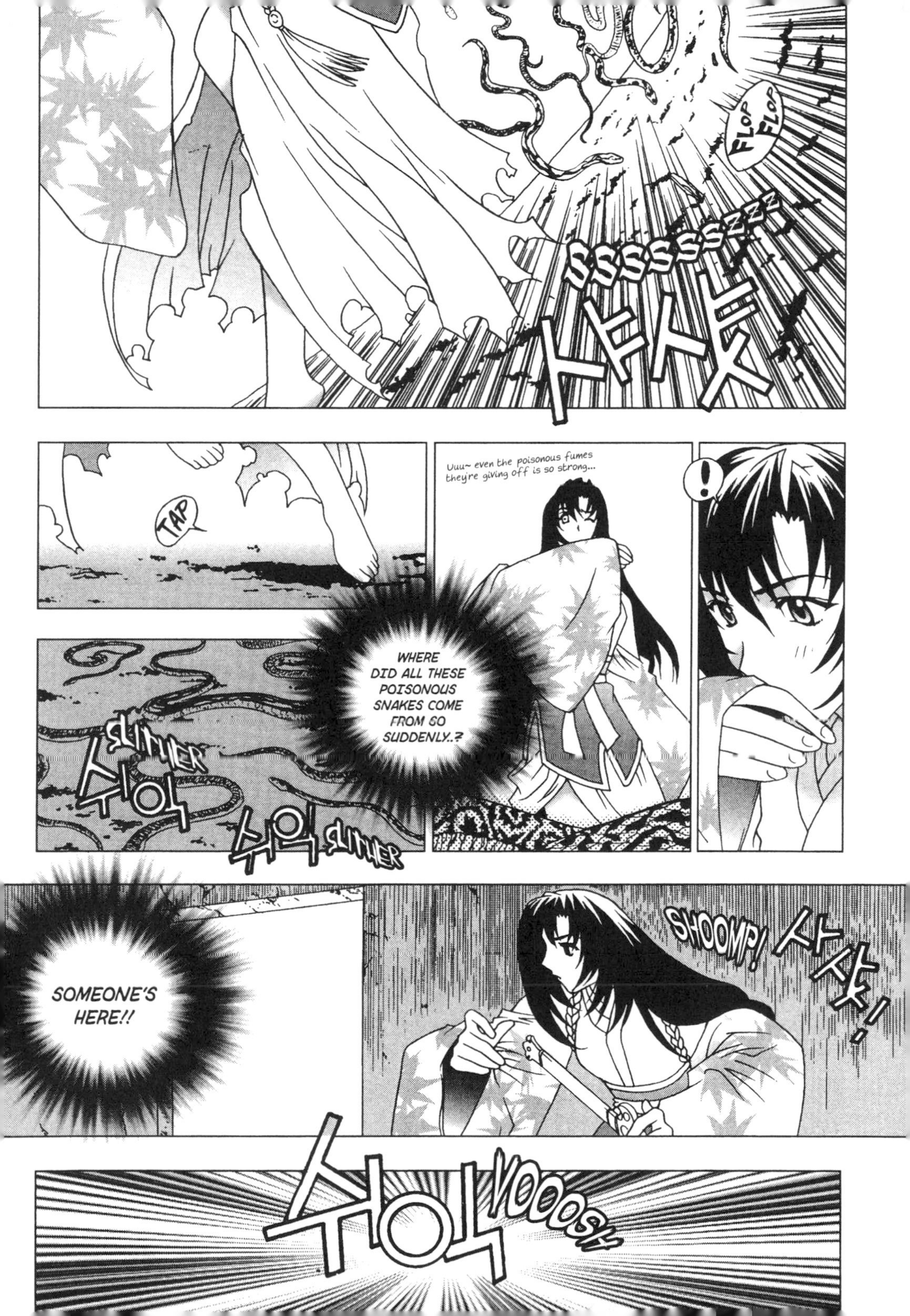
FLOP FLOP
SSSSSSSZZZ
TAP
Uuu~ even the poisonous fumes they're giving off is so strong...
!
WHERE DID ALL THESE POISONOUS SNAKES COME FROM SO SUDDENLY..?
SLITHER
SLITHER
SOMEONE'S HERE!!
SHOOMP!
VOOOOSH

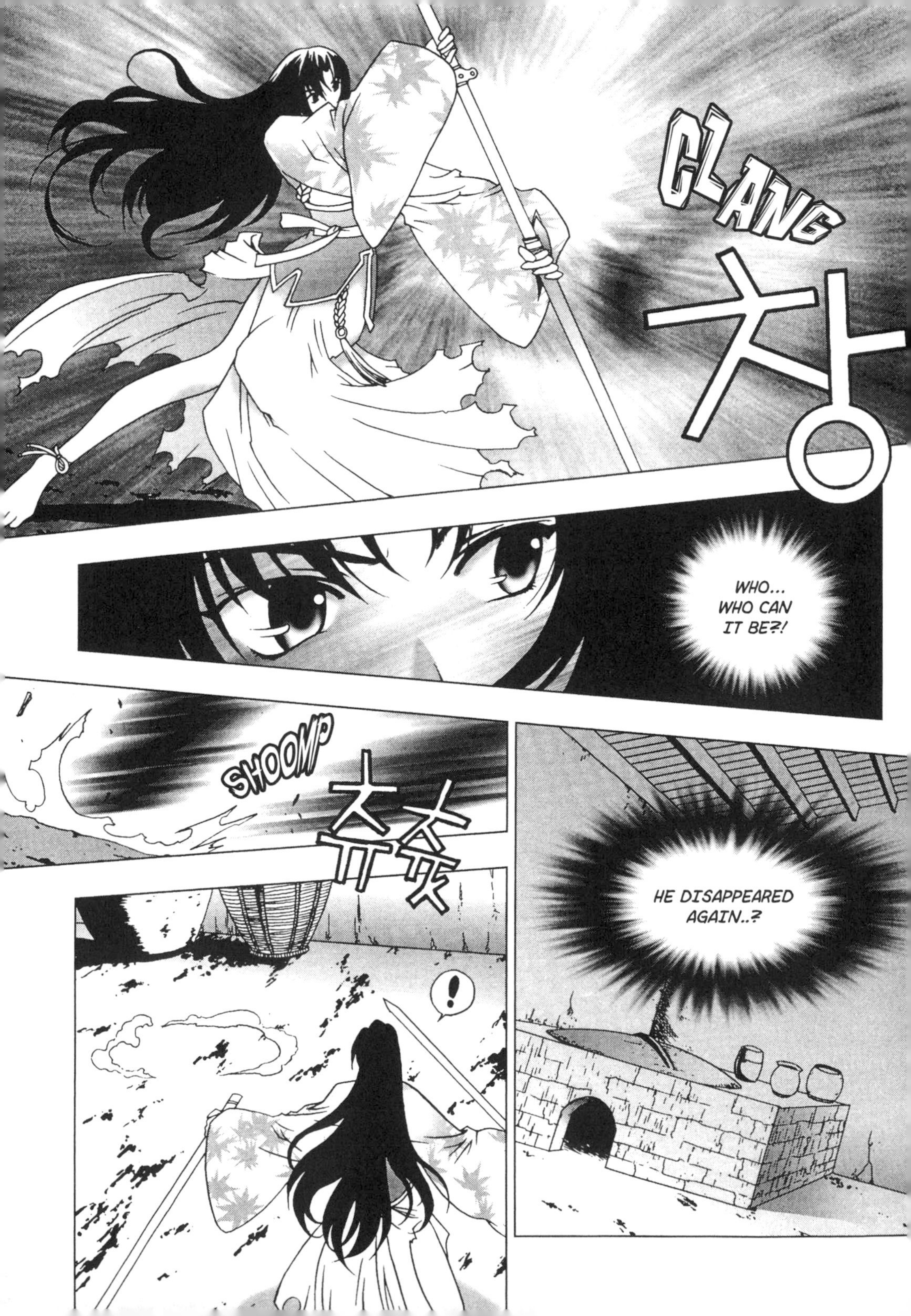

CLANG
WHO... WHO CAN IT BE?!
SHOOMP
HE DISAPPEARED AGAIN..?
!

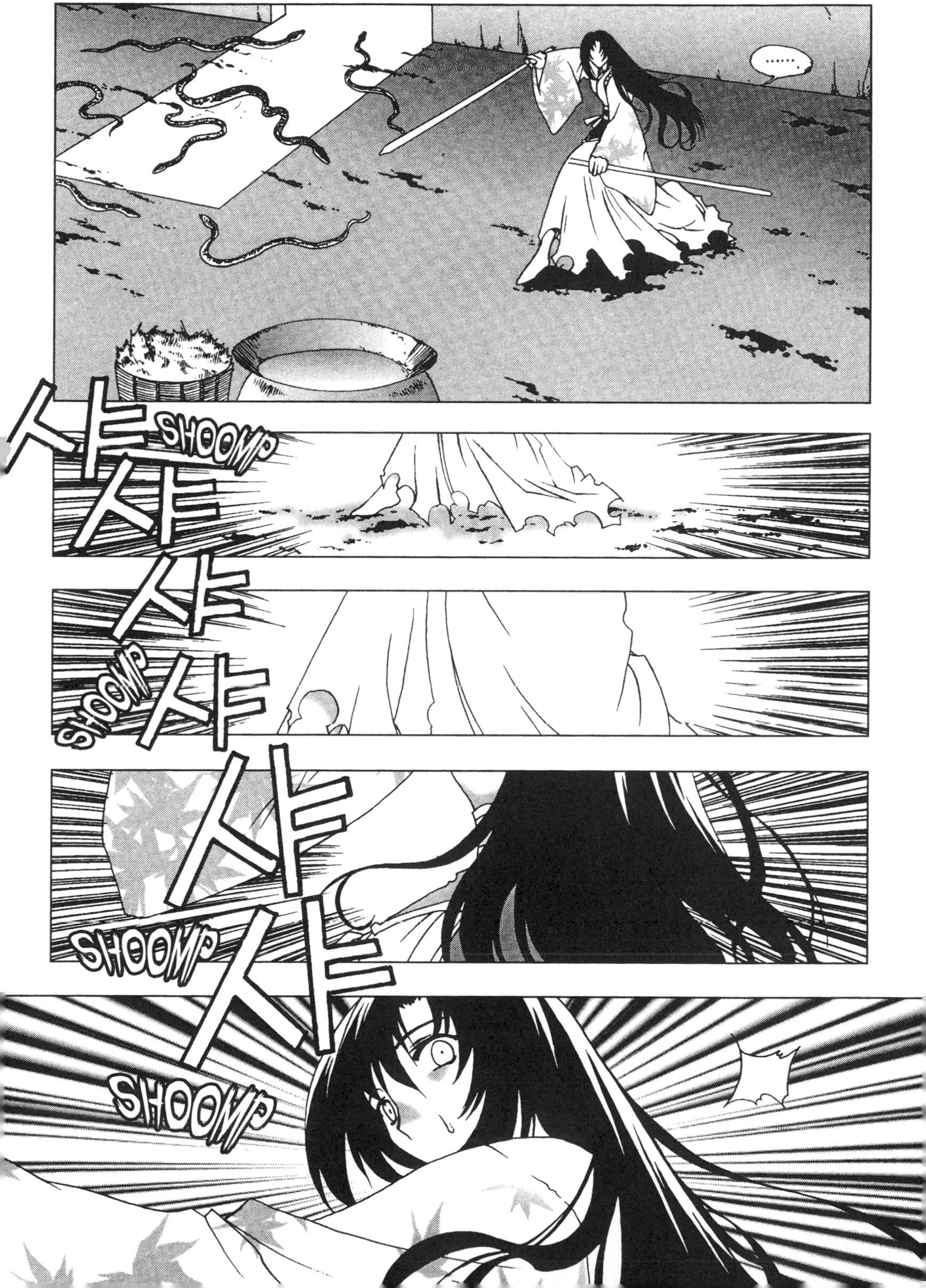

……
SHOOMP
SHOOMP
SHOOMP
SHOOMP

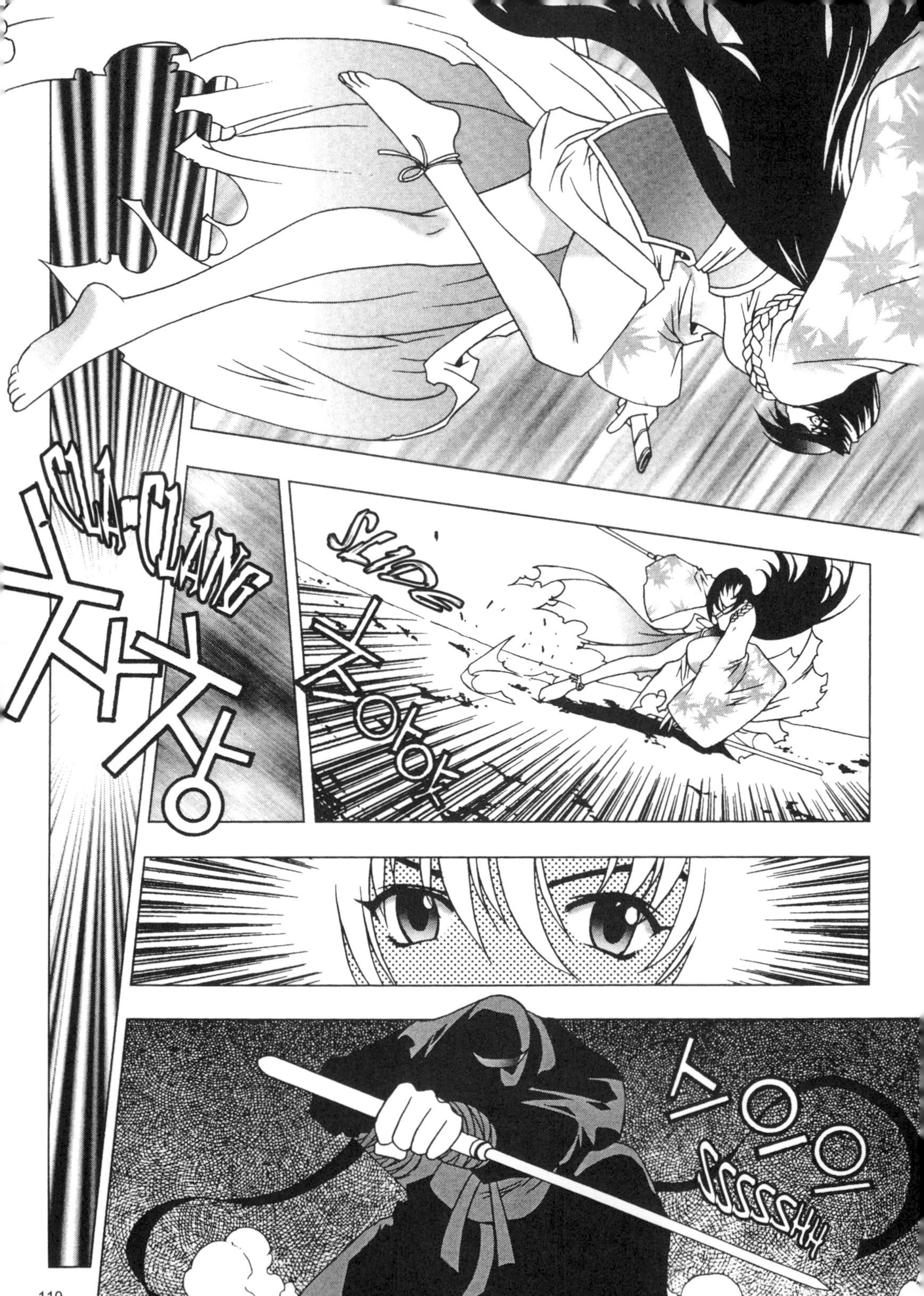
CLA-CLANG
SLIDE
SSSSSHH

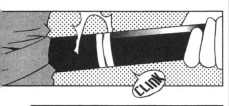

CLINK

KU HU..!

WHO ARE YOU?!

THE CHUNG-SA SWORD... I'VE ALWAYS WONDERED WHAT KIND OF SWORD IT WOULD BE SINCE IT WAS THE FAMOUS WEAPON OF CHOICE BY THE LEGENDARY CHUN-SAN-GUM-NYA... BUT IT SEEMS IT'S NO MATCH FOR MY GU-ROH-JA SWORD!

KU KU KU! INSTEAD OF ASKING QUESTIONS, LADY, WHY DON'T YOU TAKE A LOOK AT YOUR SWORD AND SEE THE CONDITION IT'S IN?

HOW... HOW CAN THIS BE?!! MY CHUNG-SA SWORD... THE BLADE HAS BEGUN TO SHATTER!!

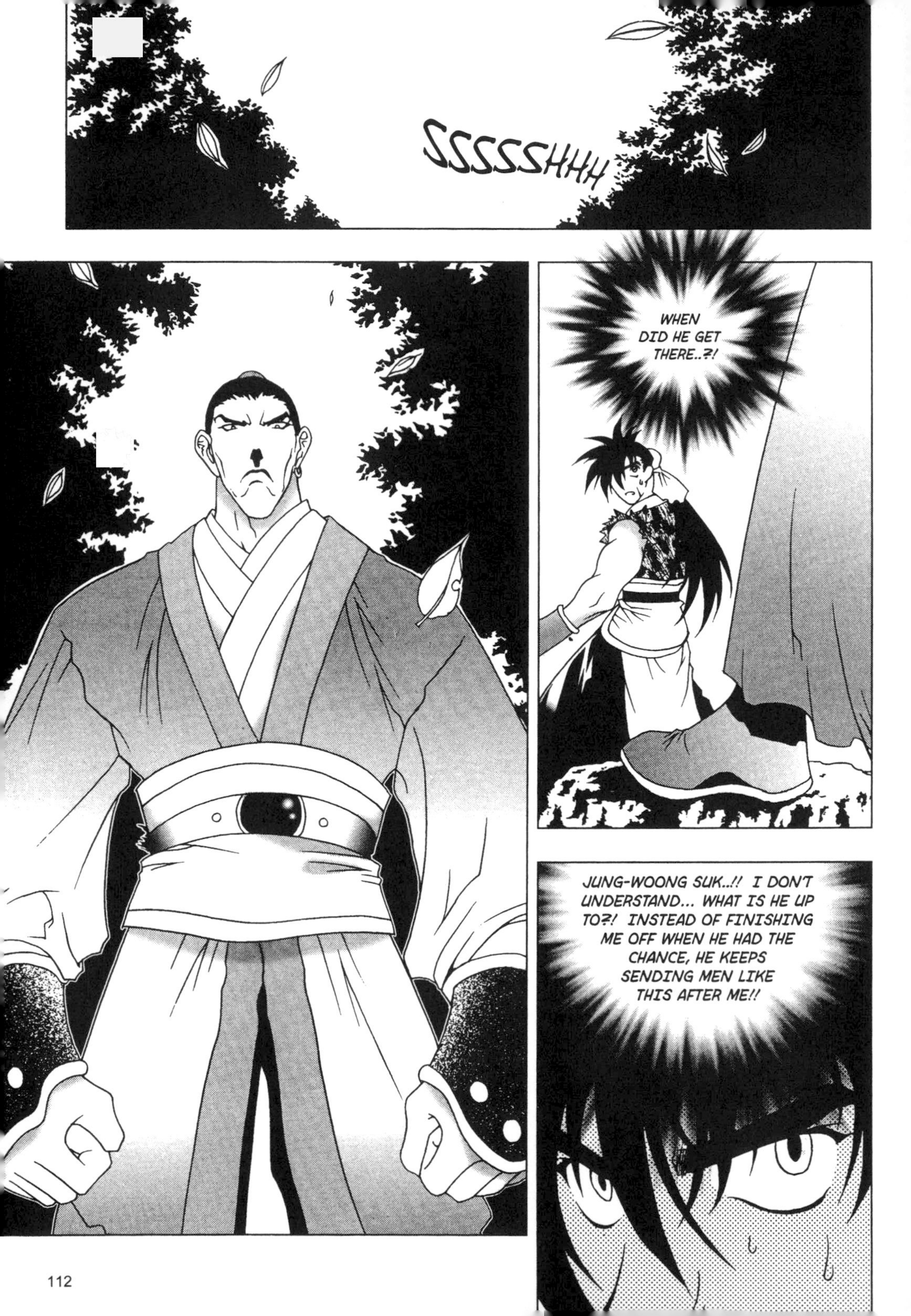
SSSSSHHH
WHEN DID HE GET THERE..?!
JUNG-WOONG SUK..!! I DON'T UNDERSTAND... WHAT IS HE UP TO?! INSTEAD OF FINISHING ME OFF WHEN HE HAD THE CHANCE, HE KEEPS SENDING MEN LIKE THIS AFTER ME!!

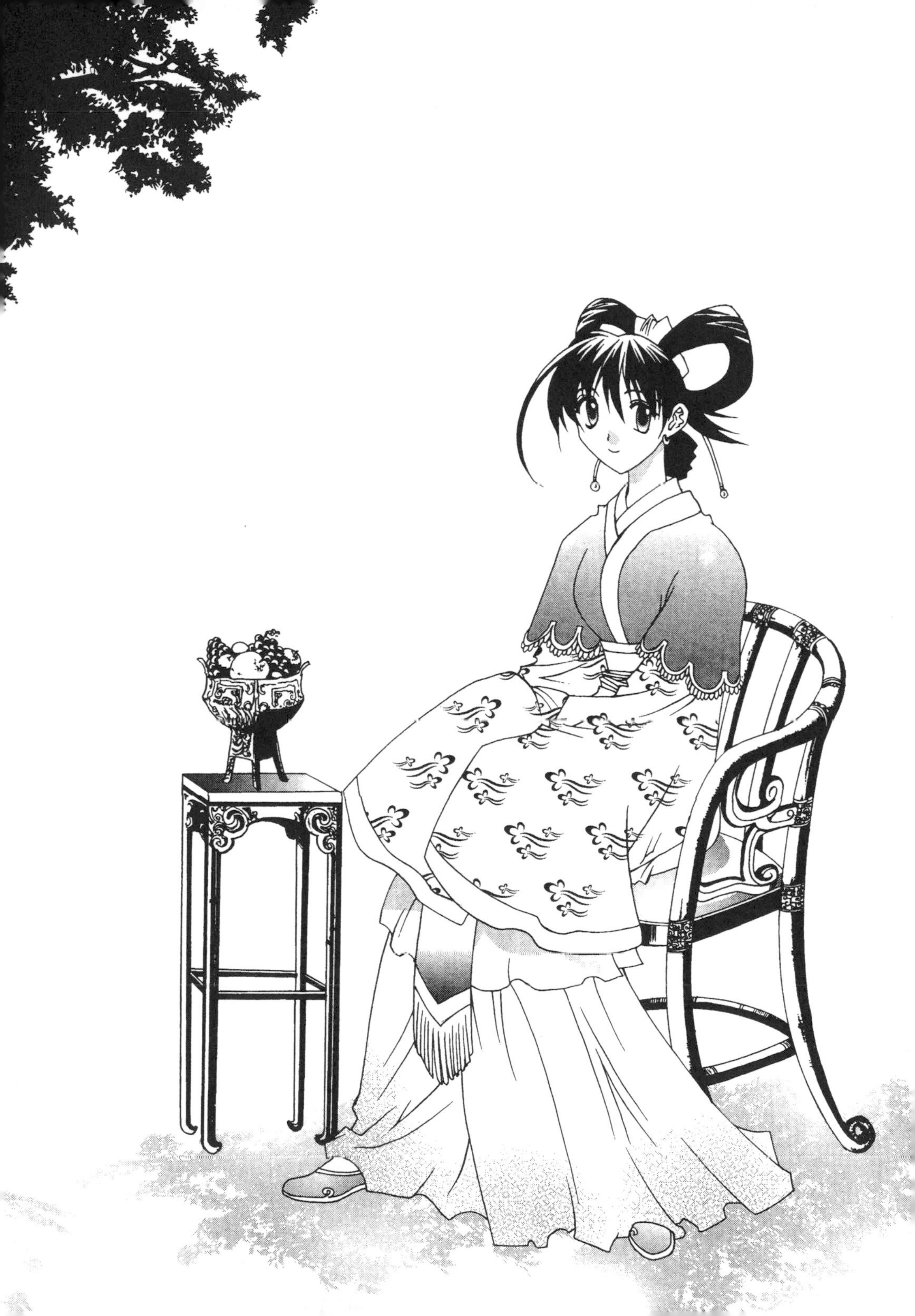

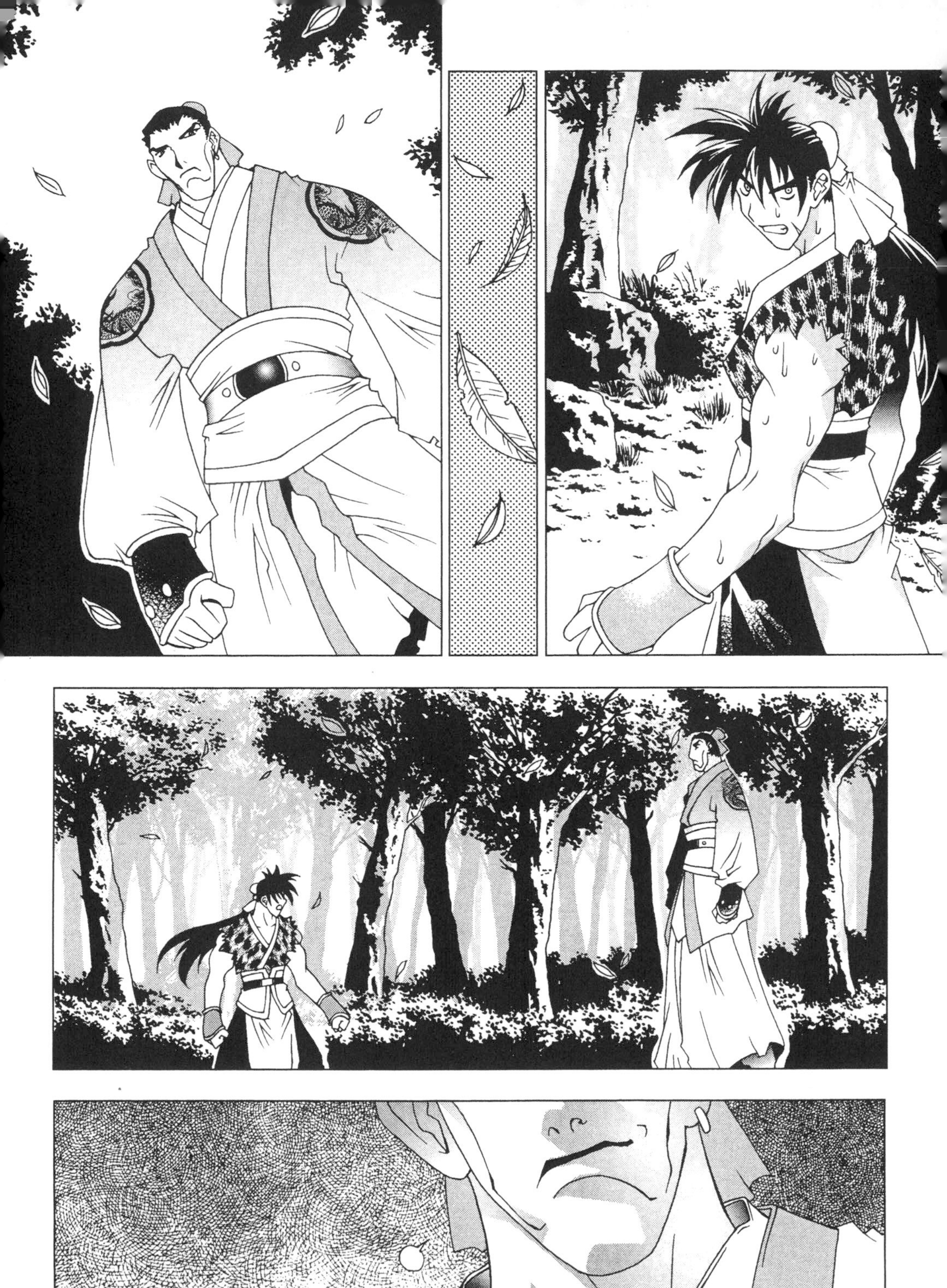

NO MATTER HOW I LOOK AT IT, IT SEEMS LIKE I CAME ALL THIS WAY FOR NOTHING.

I DIDN'T IMAGINE MY OPPONENT THIS TIME WOULD BE THIS PATHETIC!

ARE YOU ANOTHER ONE OF JUNG-WOONG SUK'S MEN?

YOU THINK I'M ONE OF HIS CRONIES? HMP! DON'T MAKE ME LAUGH!

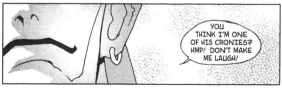

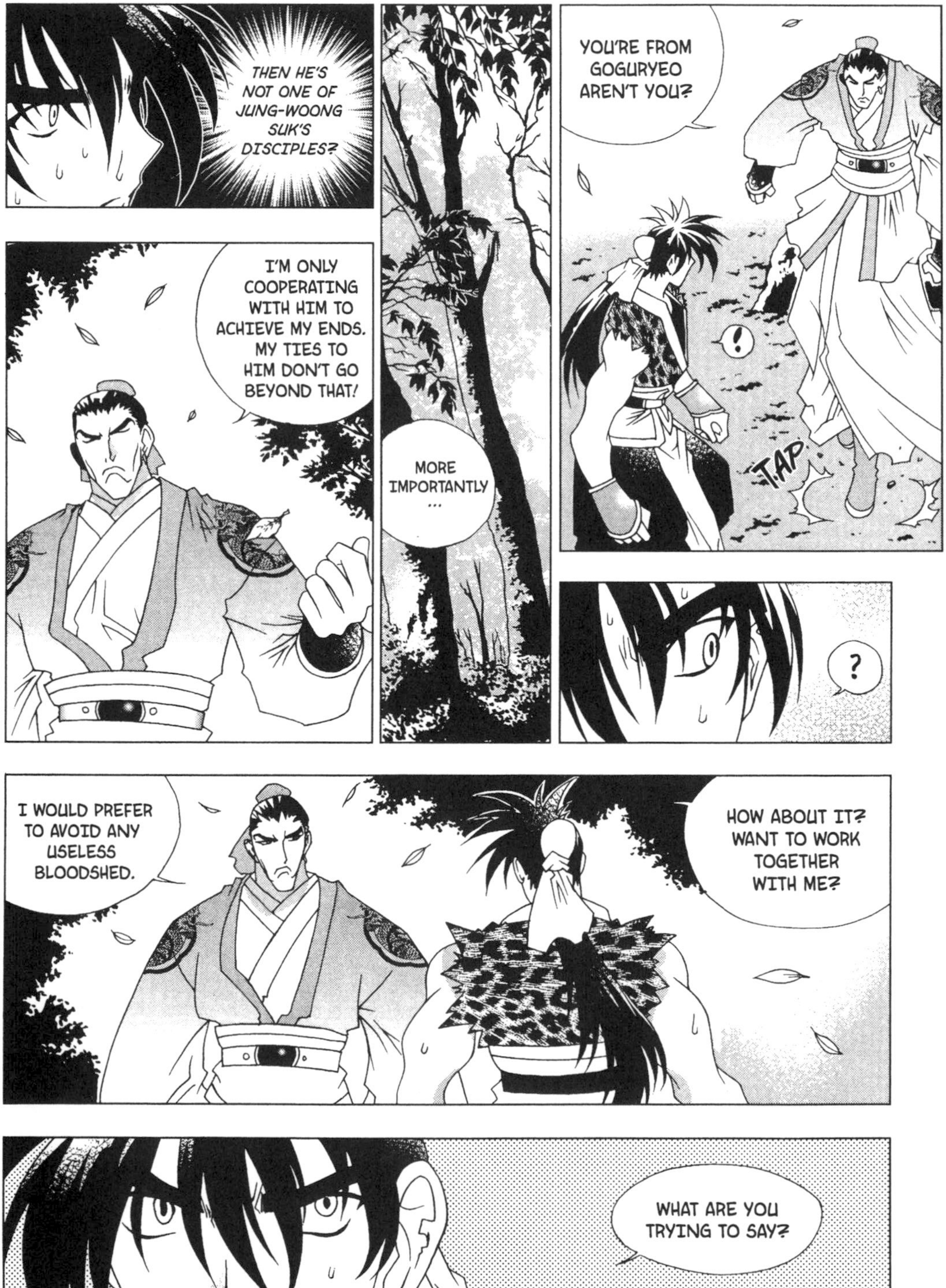
THEN HE'S NOT ONE OF JUNG-WOONG SUK'S DISCIPLES?
I'M ONLY COOPERATING WITH HIM TO ACHIEVE MY ENDS. MY TIES TO HIM DON'T GO BEYOND THAT!
MORE IMPORTANTLY ...
YOU'RE FROM GOGURYEO AREN'T YOU?
!
TAP
?
I WOULD PREFER TO AVOID ANY USELESS BLOODSHED.
HOW ABOUT IT? WANT TO WORK TOGETHER WITH ME?
WHAT ARE YOU TRYING TO SAY?

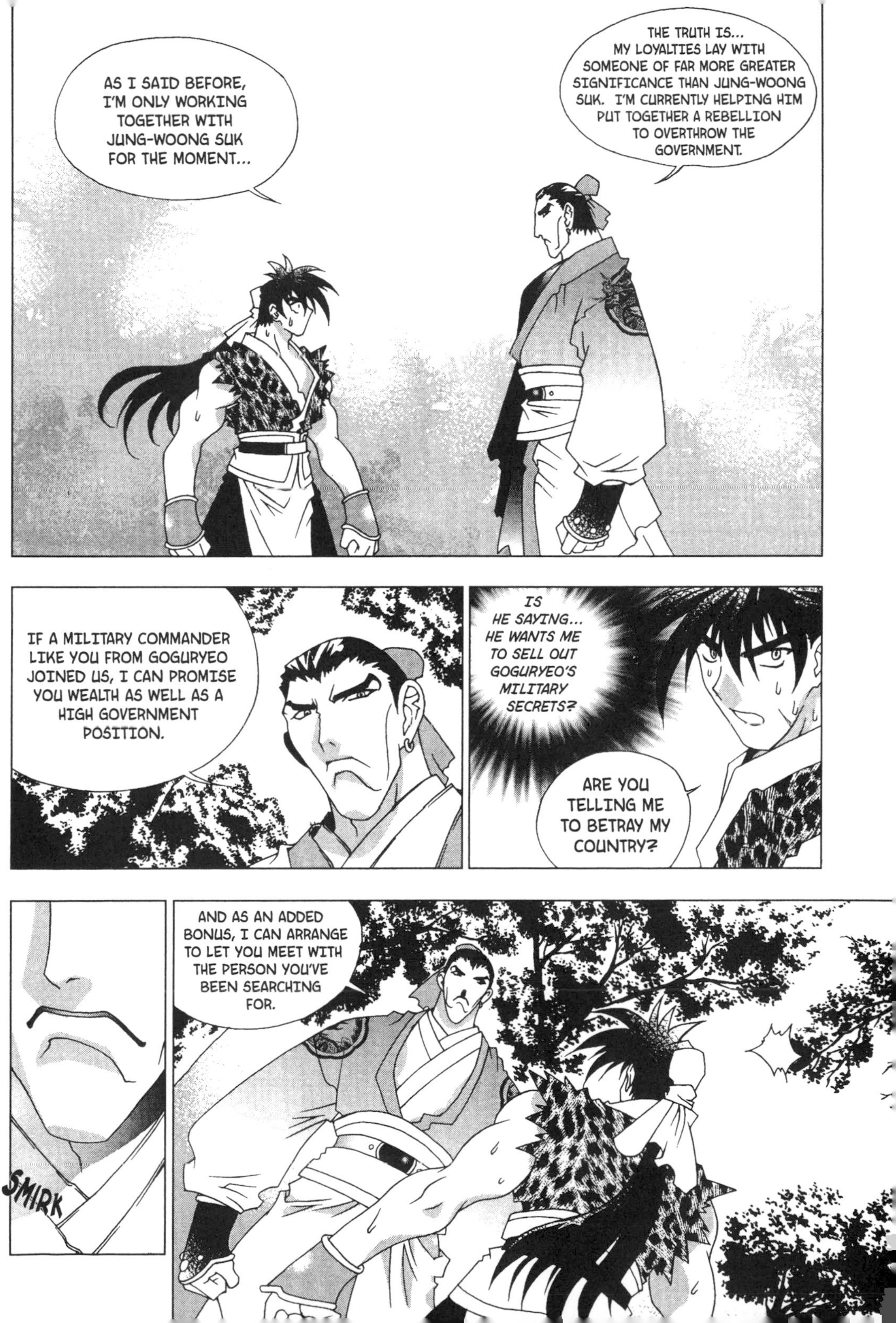

AS I SAID BEFORE, I'M ONLY WORKING TOGETHER WITH JUNG-WOONG SUK FOR THE MOMENT...
THE TRUTH IS... MY LOYALTIES LAY WITH SOMEONE OF FAR MORE GREATER SIGNIFICANCE THAN JUNG-WOONG SUK. I'M CURRENTLY HELPING HIM PUT TOGETHER A REBELLION TO OVERTHROW THE GOVERNMENT.
IF A MILITARY COMMANDER LIKE YOU FROM GOGURYEO JOINED US, I CAN PROMISE YOU WEALTH AS WELL AS A HIGH GOVERNMENT POSITION.
IS HE SAYING... HE WANTS ME TO SELL OUT GOGURYEO'S MILITARY SECRETS?
ARE YOU TELLING ME TO BETRAY MY COUNTRY?
SMIRK
AND AS AN ADDED BONUS, I CAN ARRANGE TO LET YOU MEET WITH THE PERSON YOU'VE BEEN SEARCHING FOR.

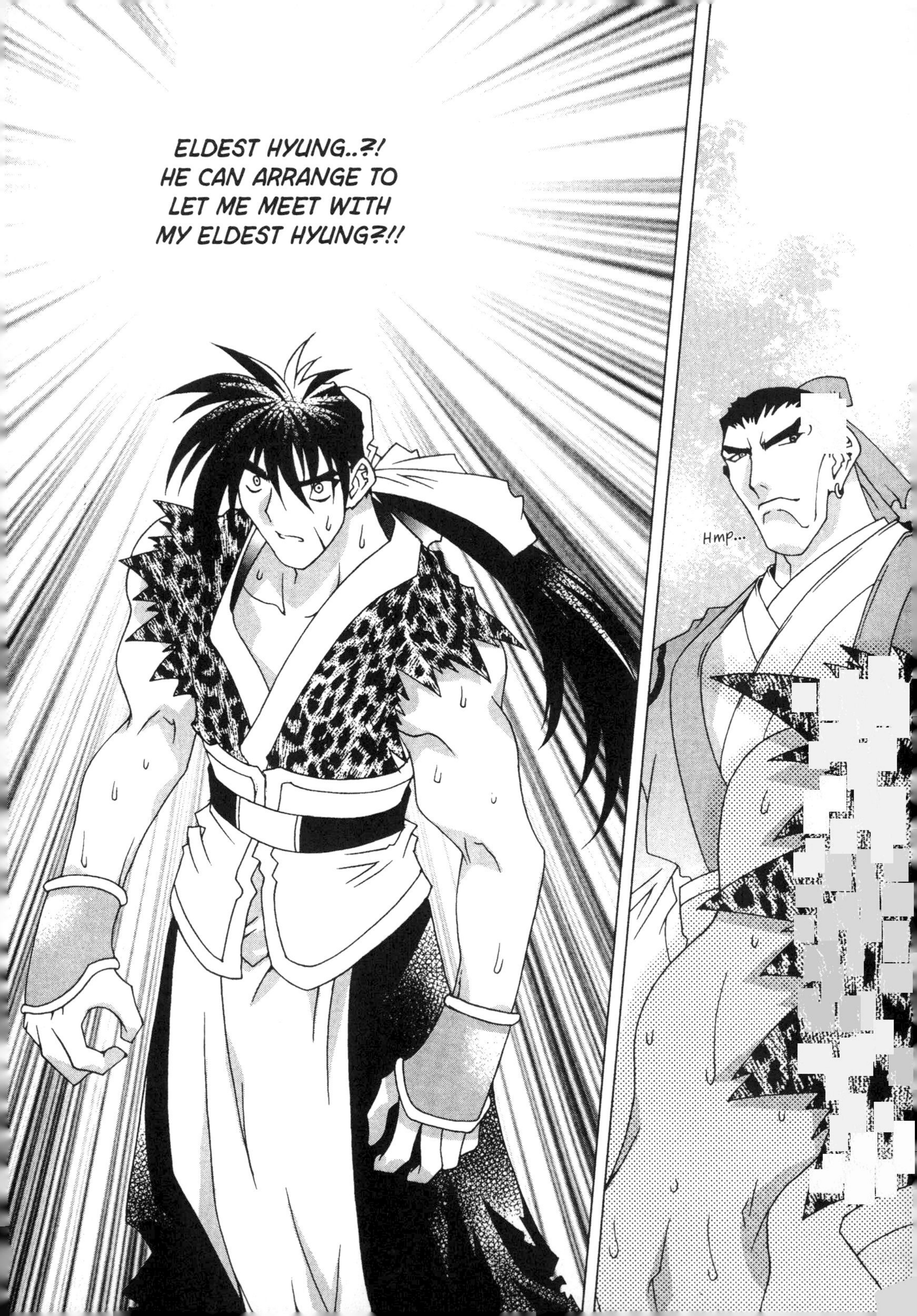
ELDEST HYUNG..?!
HE CAN ARRANGE TO
LET ME MEET WITH
MY ELDEST HYUNG?!!
Hmp...

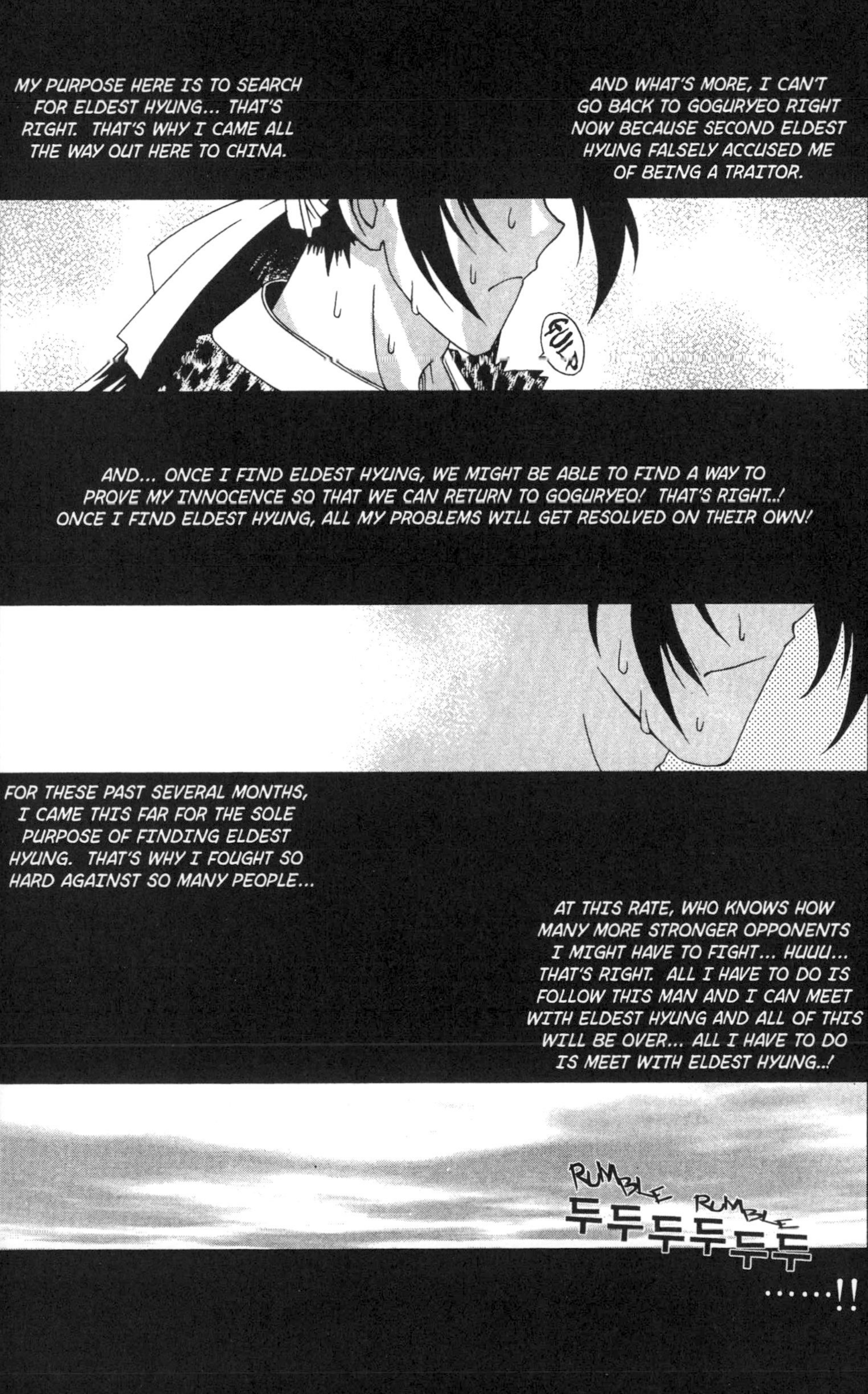

MY PURPOSE HERE IS TO SEARCH FOR ELDEST HYUNG... THAT'S RIGHT. THAT'S WHY I CAME ALL THE WAY OUT HERE TO CHINA.
AND WHAT'S MORE, I CAN'T GO BACK TO GOGURYEO RIGHT NOW BECAUSE SECOND ELDEST HYUNG FALSELY ACCUSED ME OF BEING A TRAITOR.
GULP
AND... ONCE I FIND ELDEST HYUNG, WE MIGHT BE ABLE TO FIND A WAY TO PROVE MY INNOCENCE SO THAT WE CAN RETURN TO GOGURYEO! THAT'S RIGHT..! ONCE I FIND ELDEST HYUNG, ALL MY PROBLEMS WILL GET RESOLVED ON THEIR OWN!
FOR THESE PAST SEVERAL MONTHS, I CAME THIS FAR FOR THE SOLE PURPOSE OF FINDING ELDEST HYUNG. THAT'S WHY I FOUGHT SO HARD AGAINST SO MANY PEOPLE...
AT THIS RATE, WHO KNOWS HOW MANY MORE STRONGER OPPONENTS I MIGHT HAVE TO FIGHT... HUUU... THAT'S RIGHT. ALL I HAVE TO DO IS FOLLOW THIS MAN AND I CAN MEET WITH ELDEST HYUNG AND ALL OF THIS WILL BE OVER... ALL I HAVE TO DO IS MEET WITH ELDEST HYUNG..!
RUMBLE RUMBLE
두두두두두두
.......!!

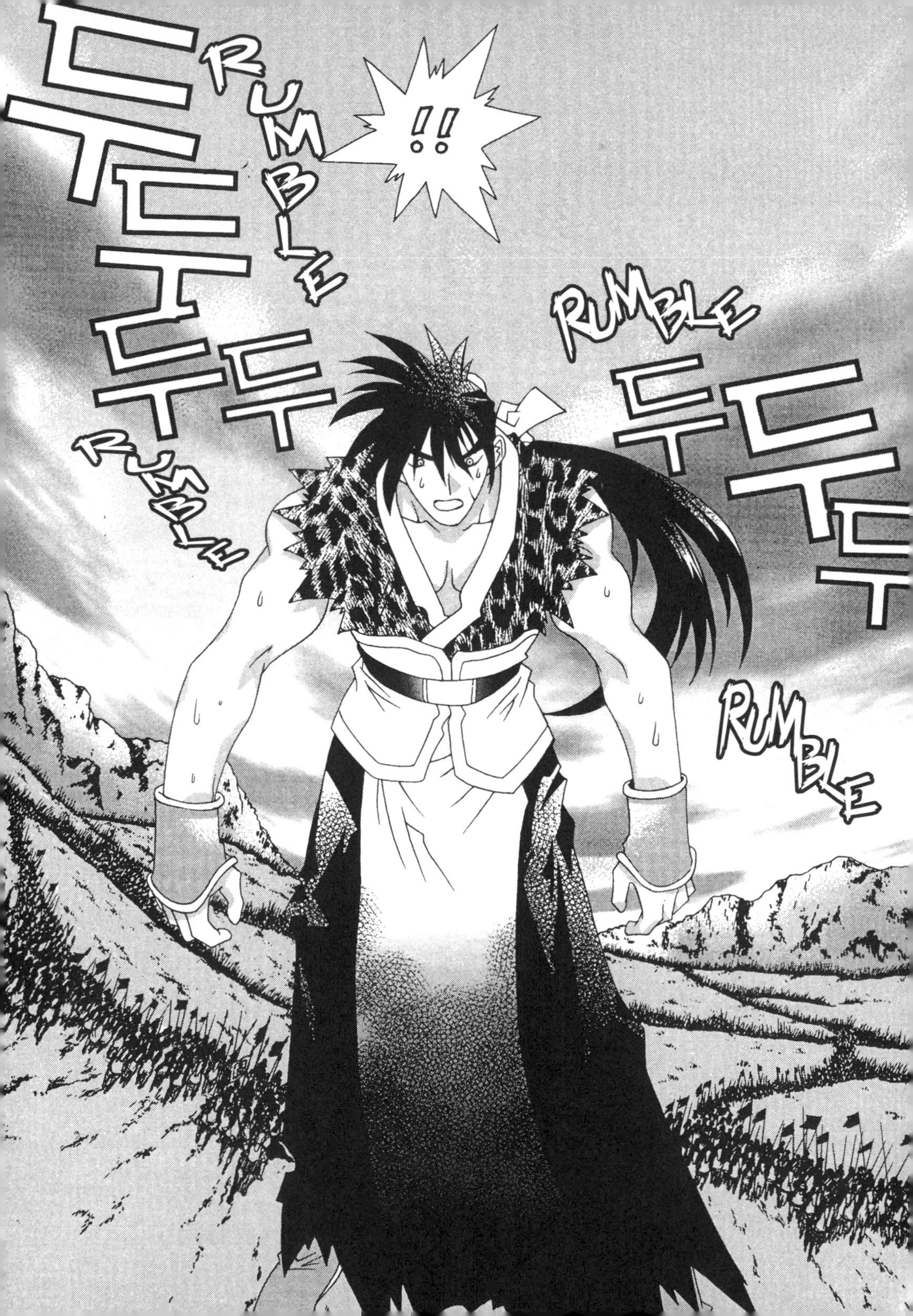
!!
RUMBLE
RUMBLE
RUMBLE
RUMBLE

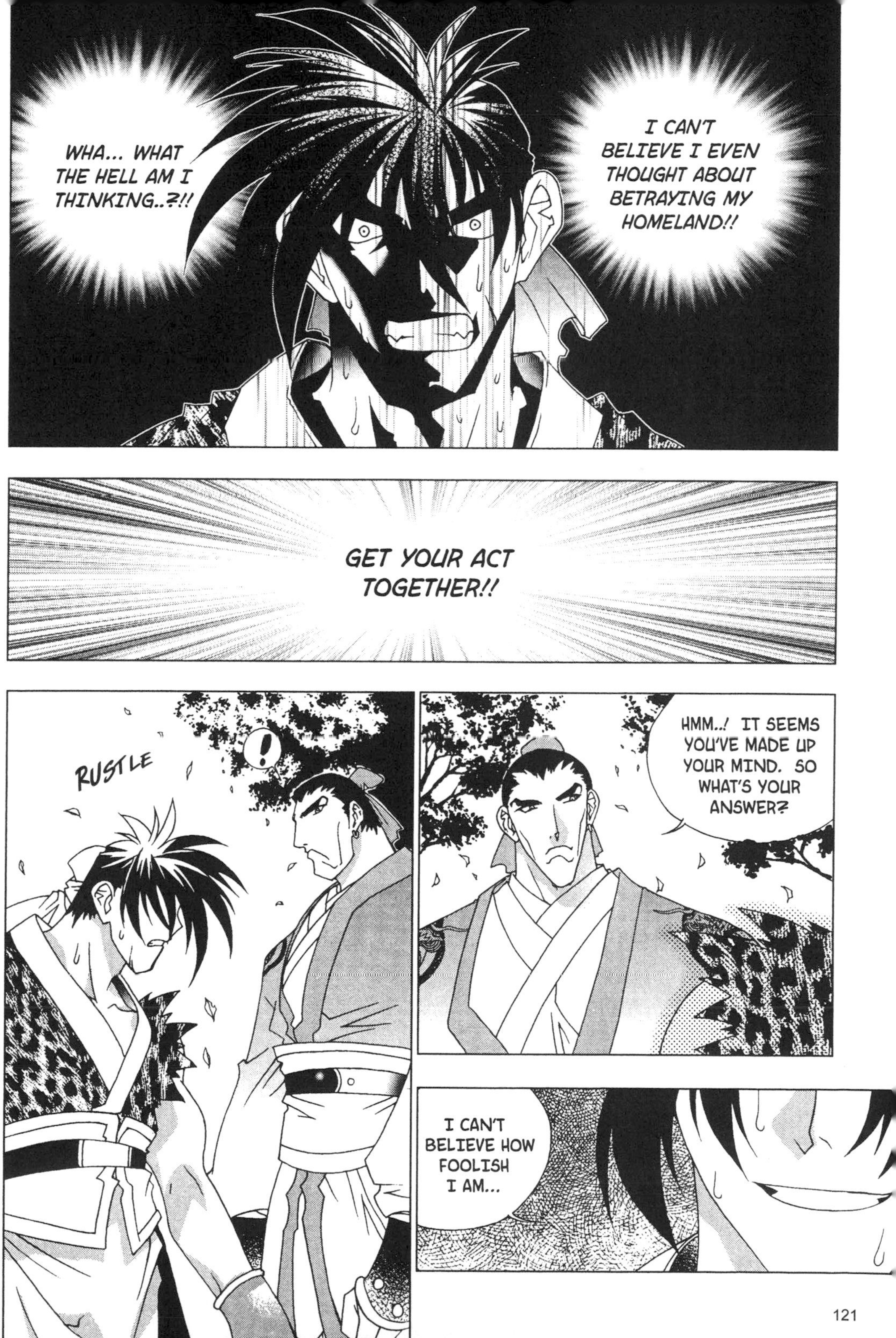
WHA... WHAT THE HELL AM I THINKING..?!!
I CAN'T BELIEVE I EVEN THOUGHT ABOUT BETRAYING MY HOMELAND!!
GET YOUR ACT TOGETHER!!
RUSTLE
!
HMM..! IT SEEMS YOU'VE MADE UP YOUR MIND. SO WHAT'S YOUR ANSWER?
I CAN'T BELIEVE HOW FOOLISH I AM...

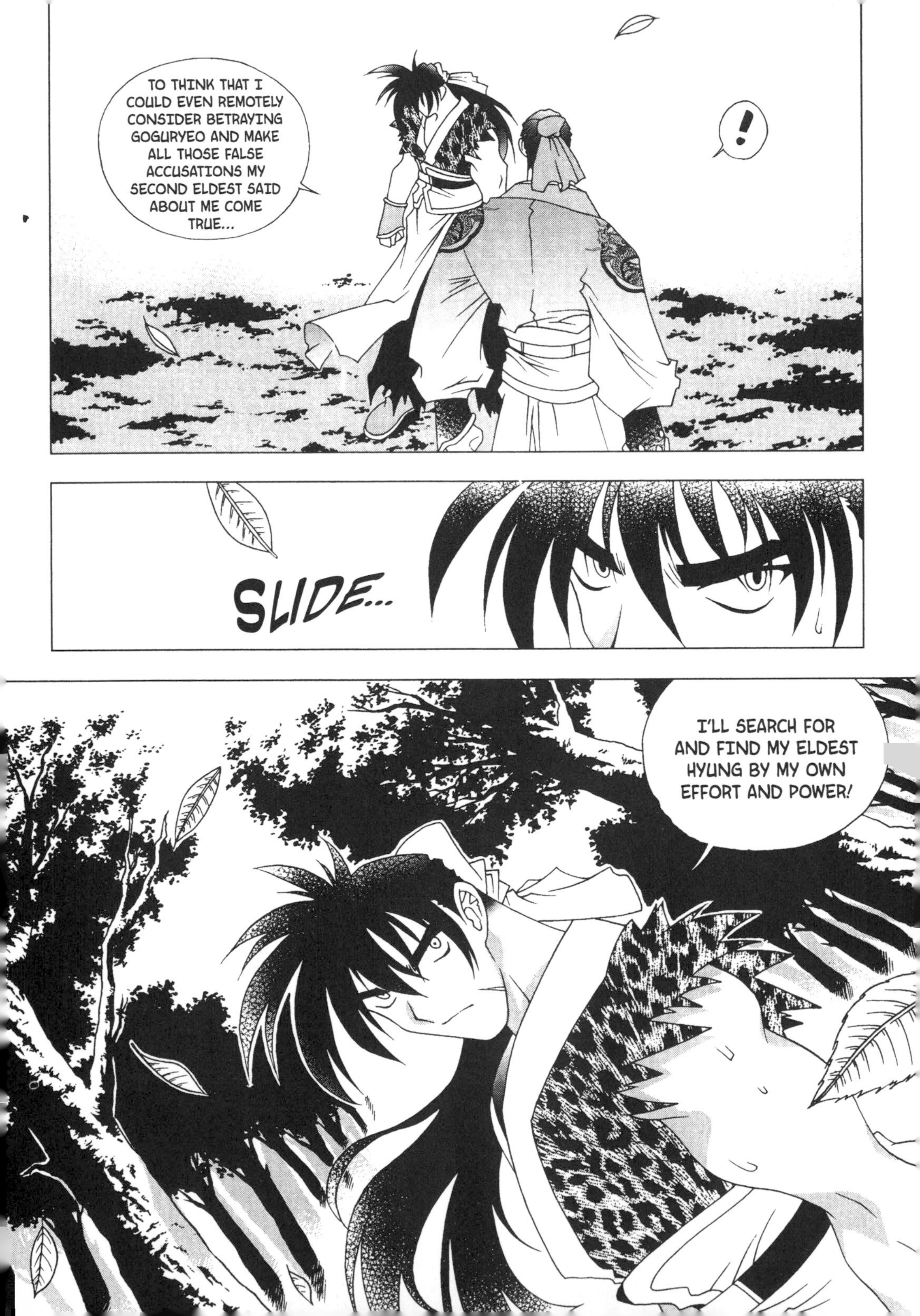
TO THINK THAT I COULD EVEN REMOTELY CONSIDER BETRAYING GOGURYEO AND MAKE ALL THOSE FALSE ACCUSATIONS MY SECOND ELDEST SAID ABOUT ME COME TRUE...
!
SLIDE...
I'LL SEARCH FOR AND FIND MY ELDEST HYUNG BY MY OWN EFFORT AND POWER!

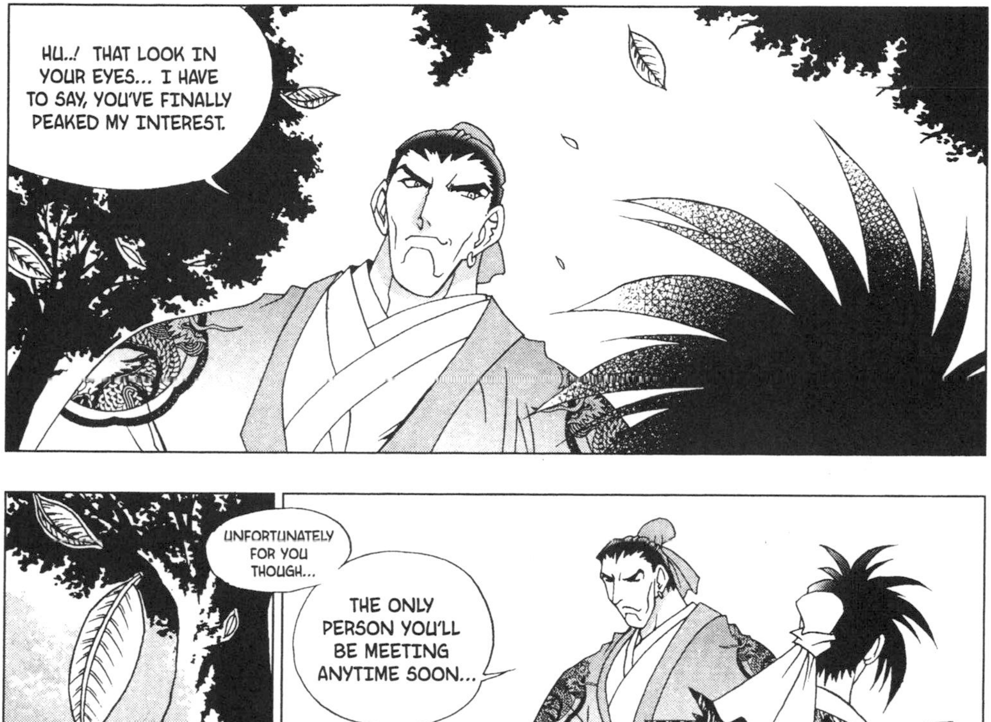
HU..! THAT LOOK IN YOUR EYES... I HAVE TO SAY, YOU'VE FINALLY PEAKED MY INTEREST.
UNFORTUNATELY FOR YOU THOUGH...
THE ONLY PERSON YOU'LL BE MEETING ANYTIME SOON...
IS KING YHUM-RA!!

Note : King Yhum-Ra is a mythical demon king who presides over the entrance to the netherworld in Asian cultures. He decides whether a person's soul goes to heaven or hell.

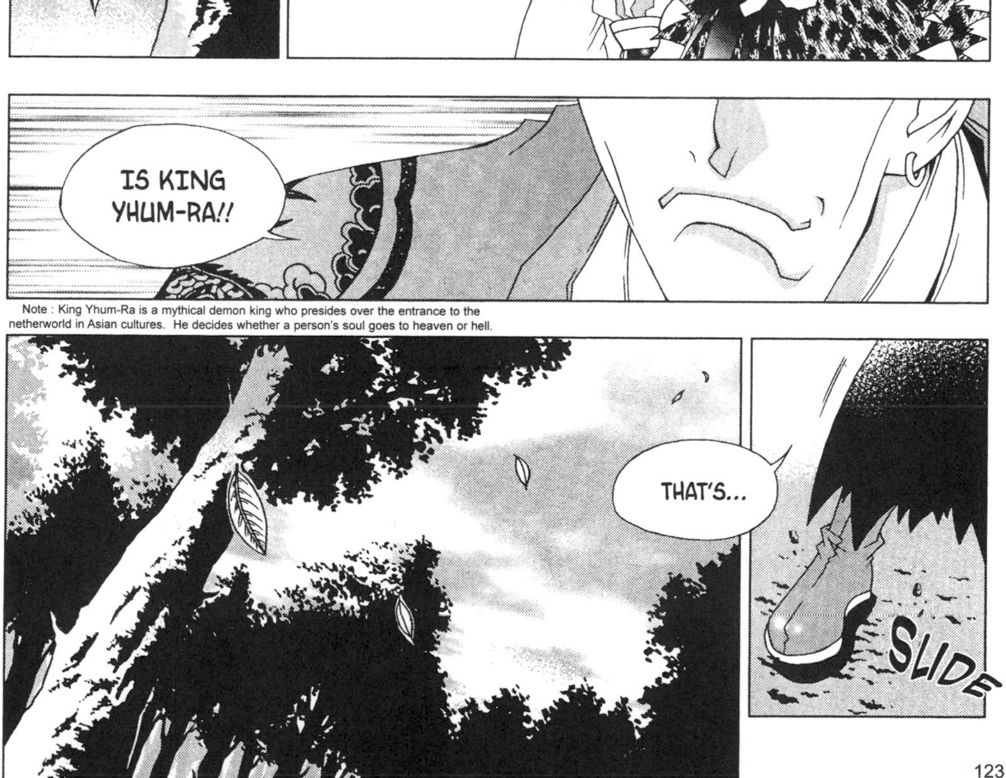
THAT'S...
SLIDE

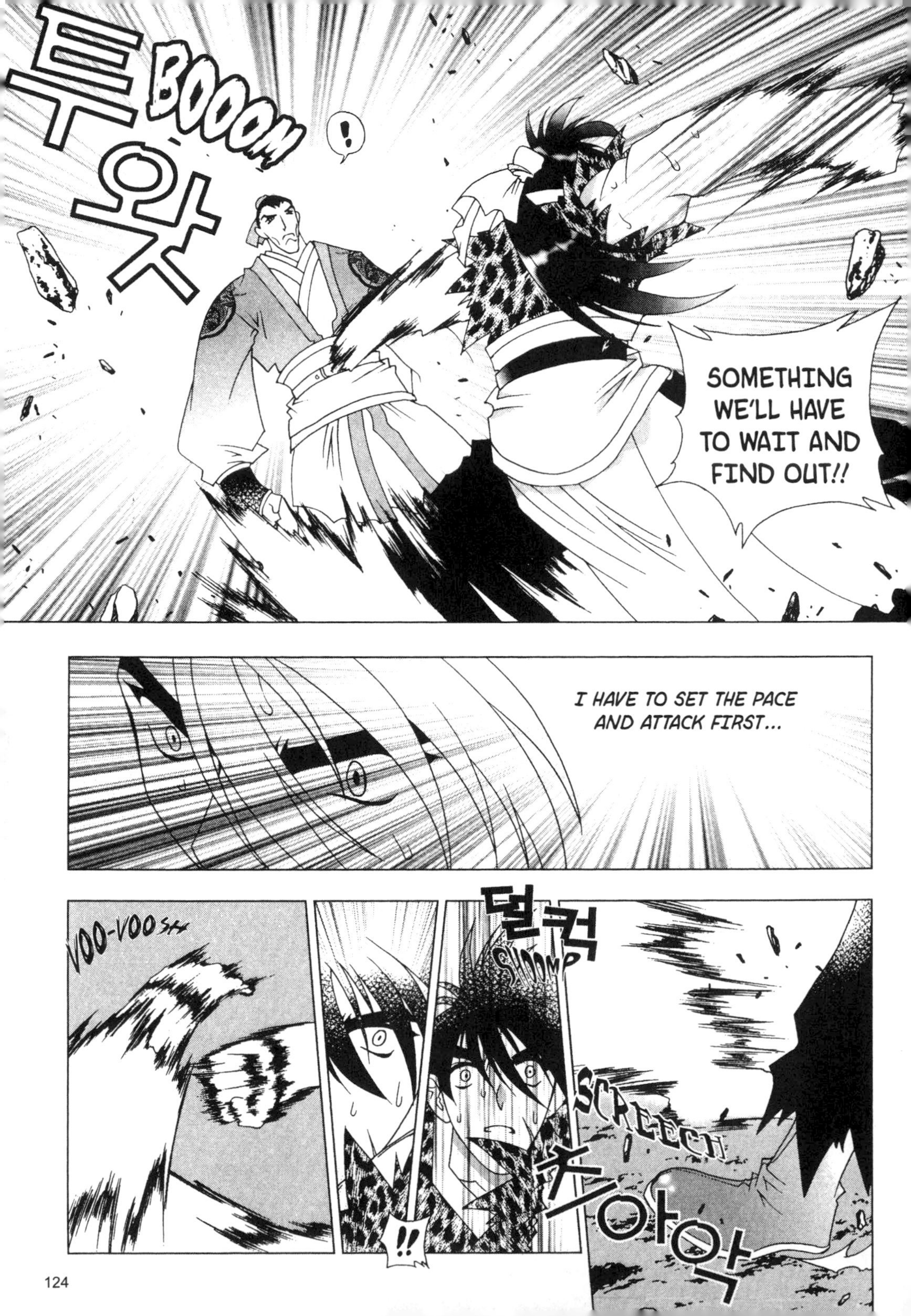
투왓
BOOOM
!
SOMETHING WE'LL HAVE TO WAIT AND FIND OUT!!
I HAVE TO SET THE PACE AND ATTACK FIRST...
VOO-VOOSH
덜컥
SHOOMP
!!
SCREECH
츠아악

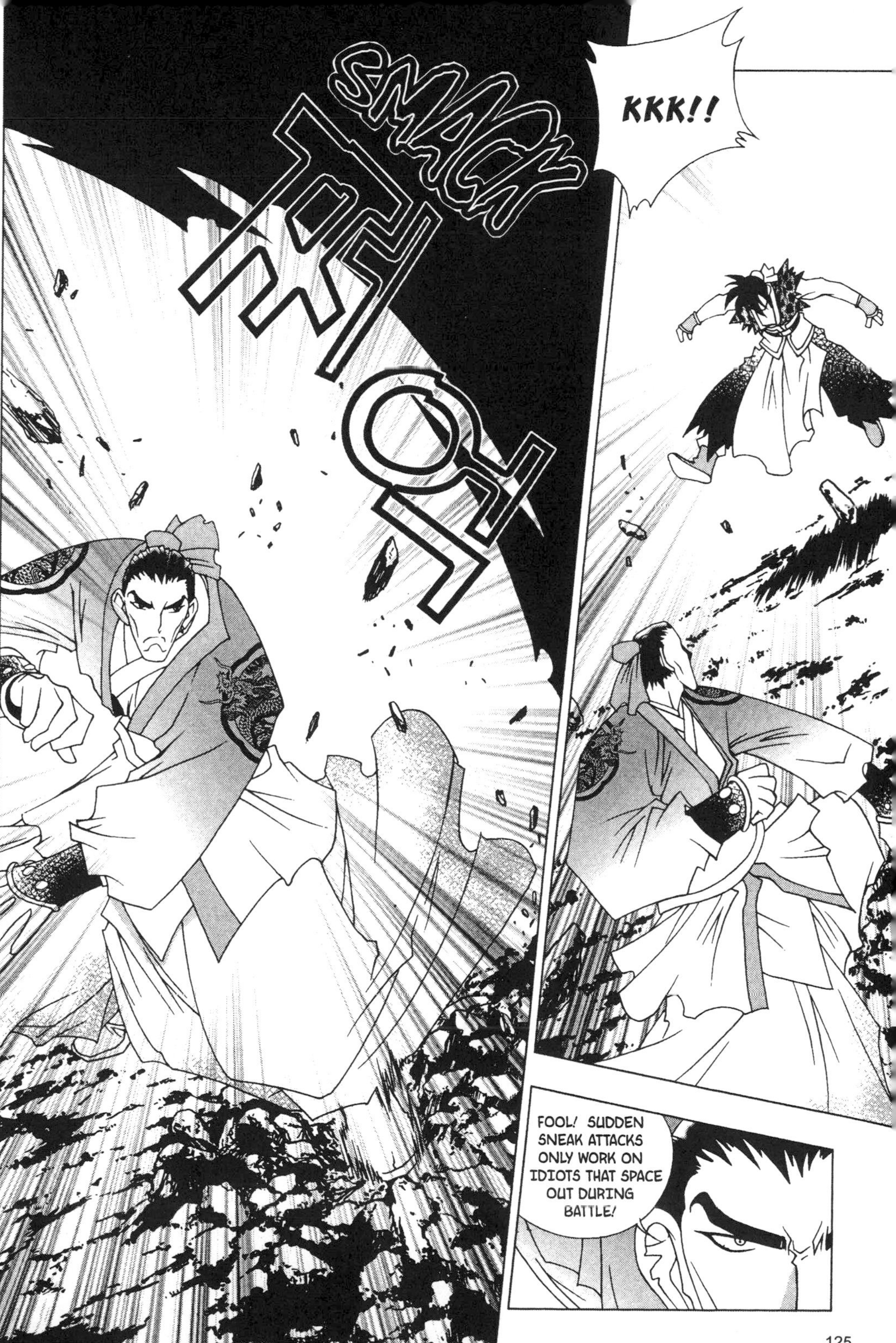
SMACK
KKK!!
FOOL! SUDDEN SNEAK ATTACKS ONLY WORK ON IDIOTS THAT SPACE OUT DURING BATTLE!

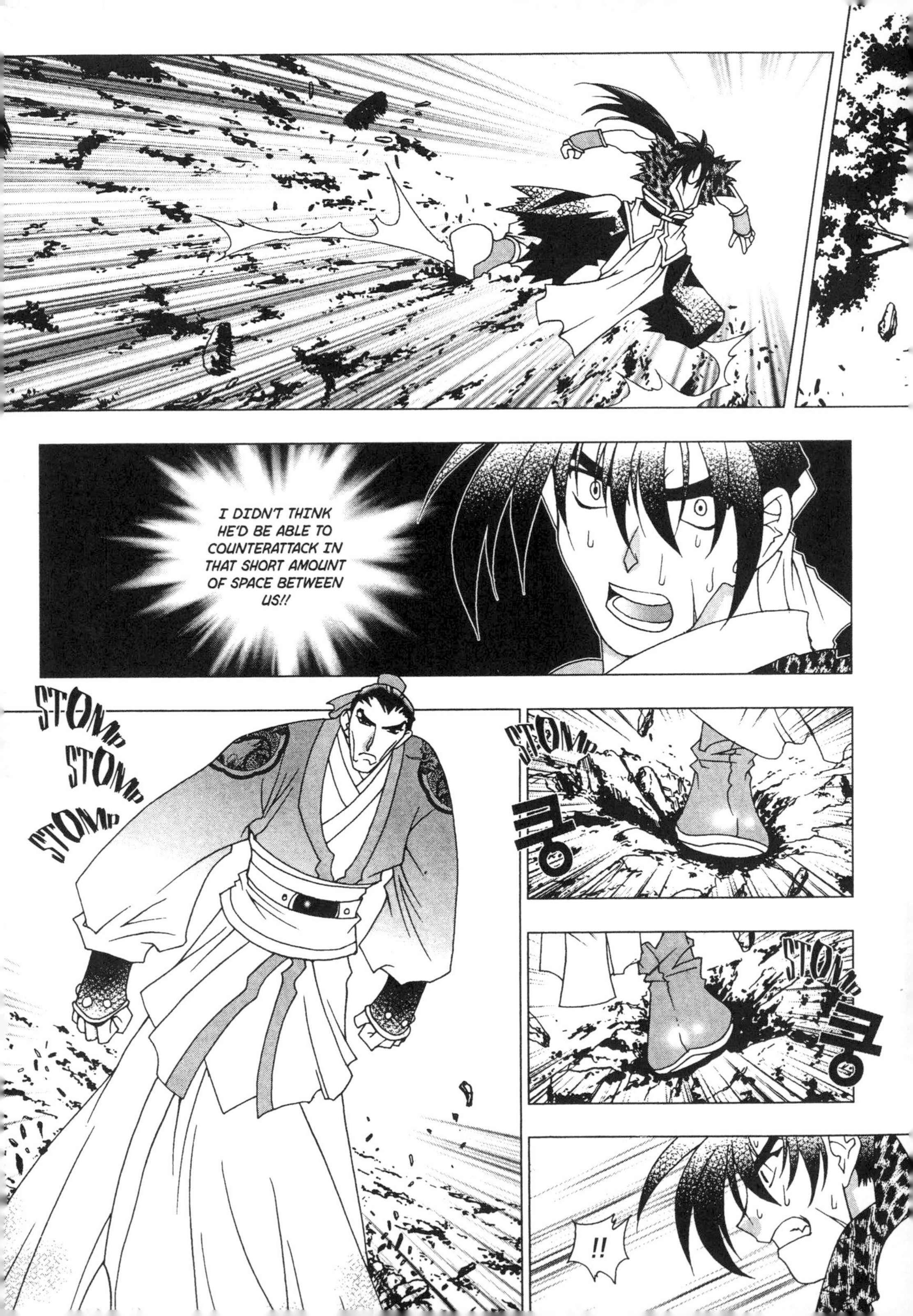
I DIDN'T THINK HE'D BE ABLE TO COUNTERATTACK IN THAT SHORT AMOUNT OF SPACE BETWEEN US!!
STOMP STOMP STOMP
STOMP
STOMP
!!

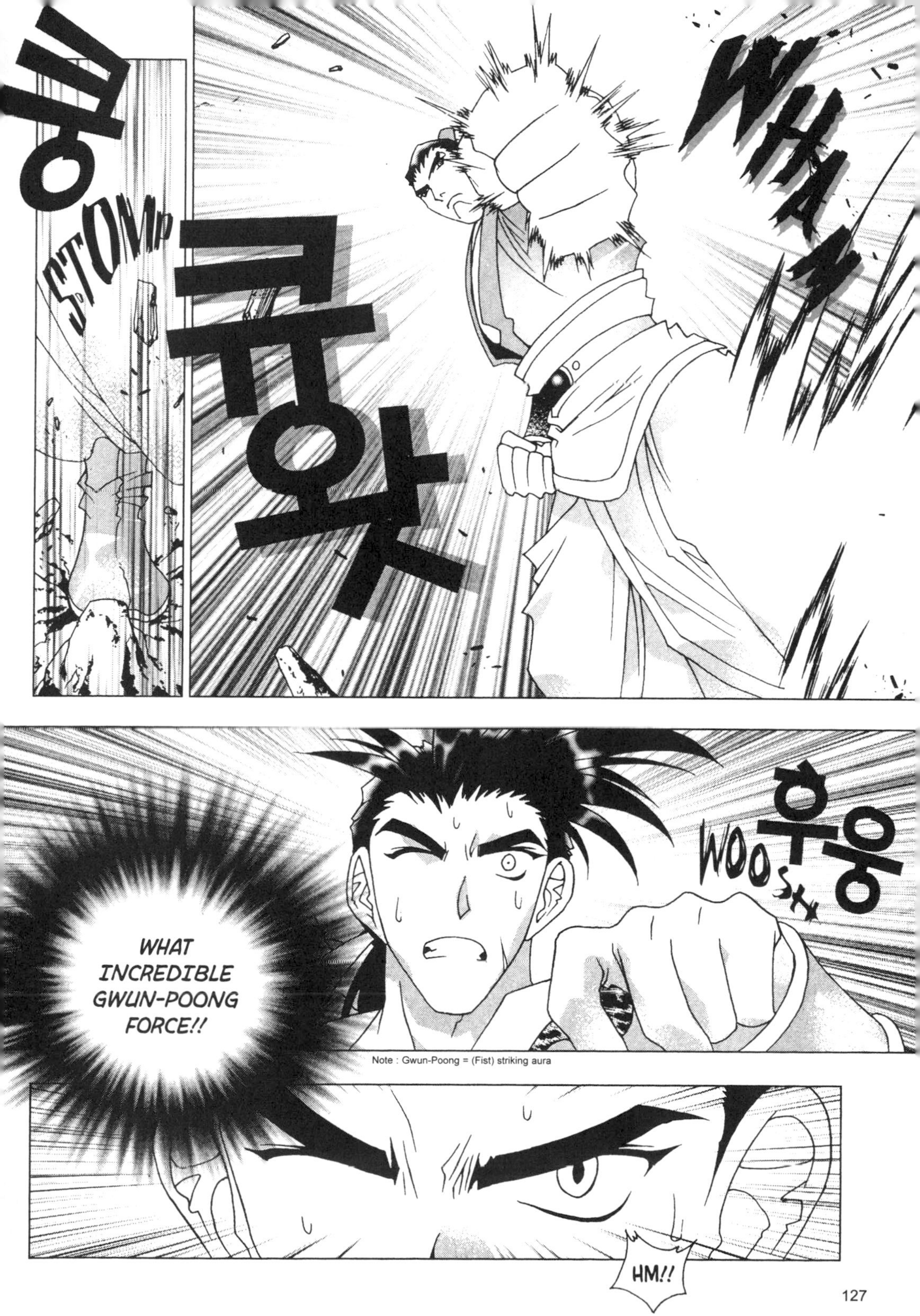

쿵
STOMP
콰앙
WHAM
후웅
WOOSH
WHAT INCREDIBLE GWUN-POONG FORCE!!
HM!!

Note : Gwun-Poong = (Fist) striking aura

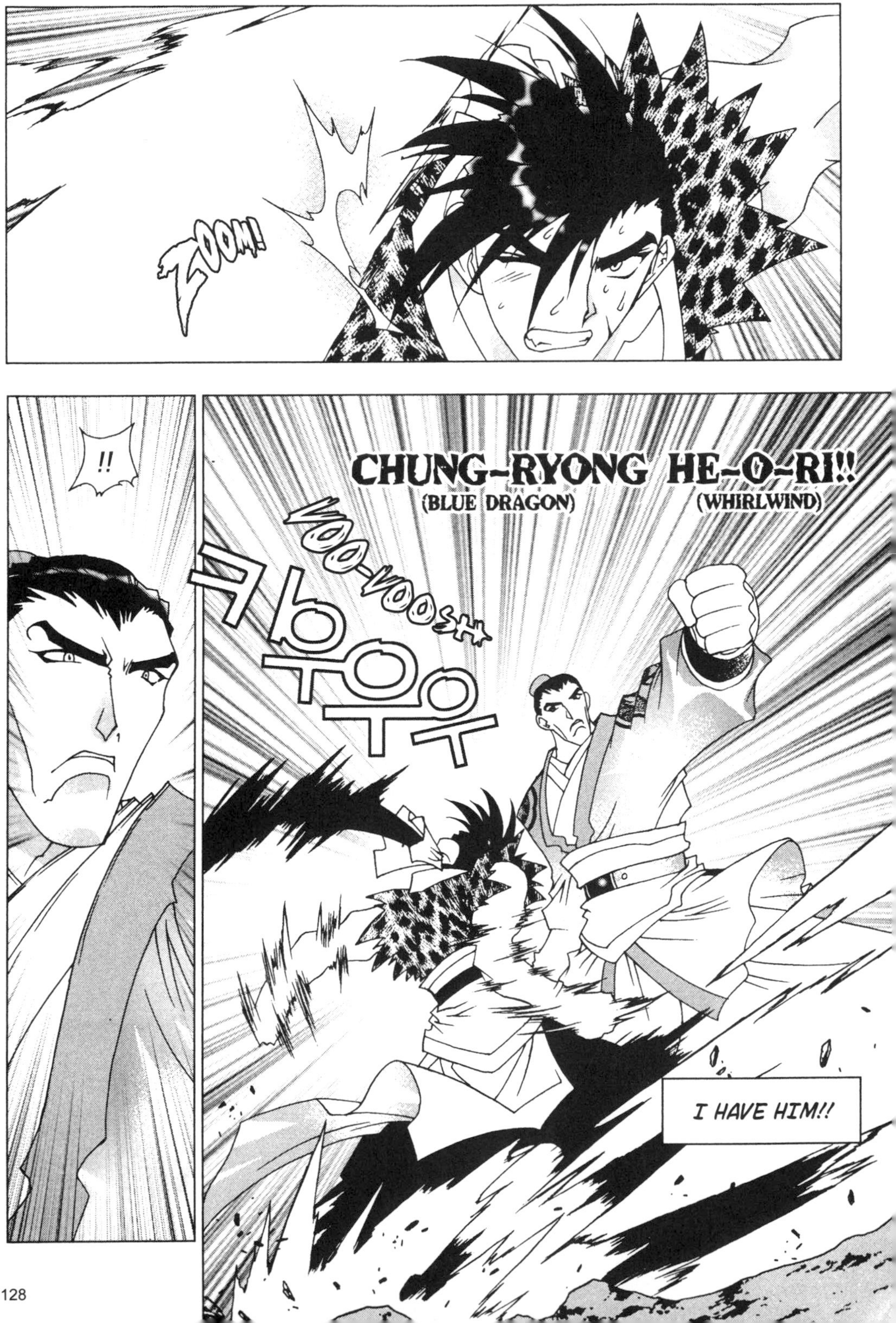

ZOOM!
!!
CHUNG-RYONG HE-O-RI!!
(BLUE DRAGON)
(WHIRLWIND)
VOO-VOOSH
I HAVE HIM!!

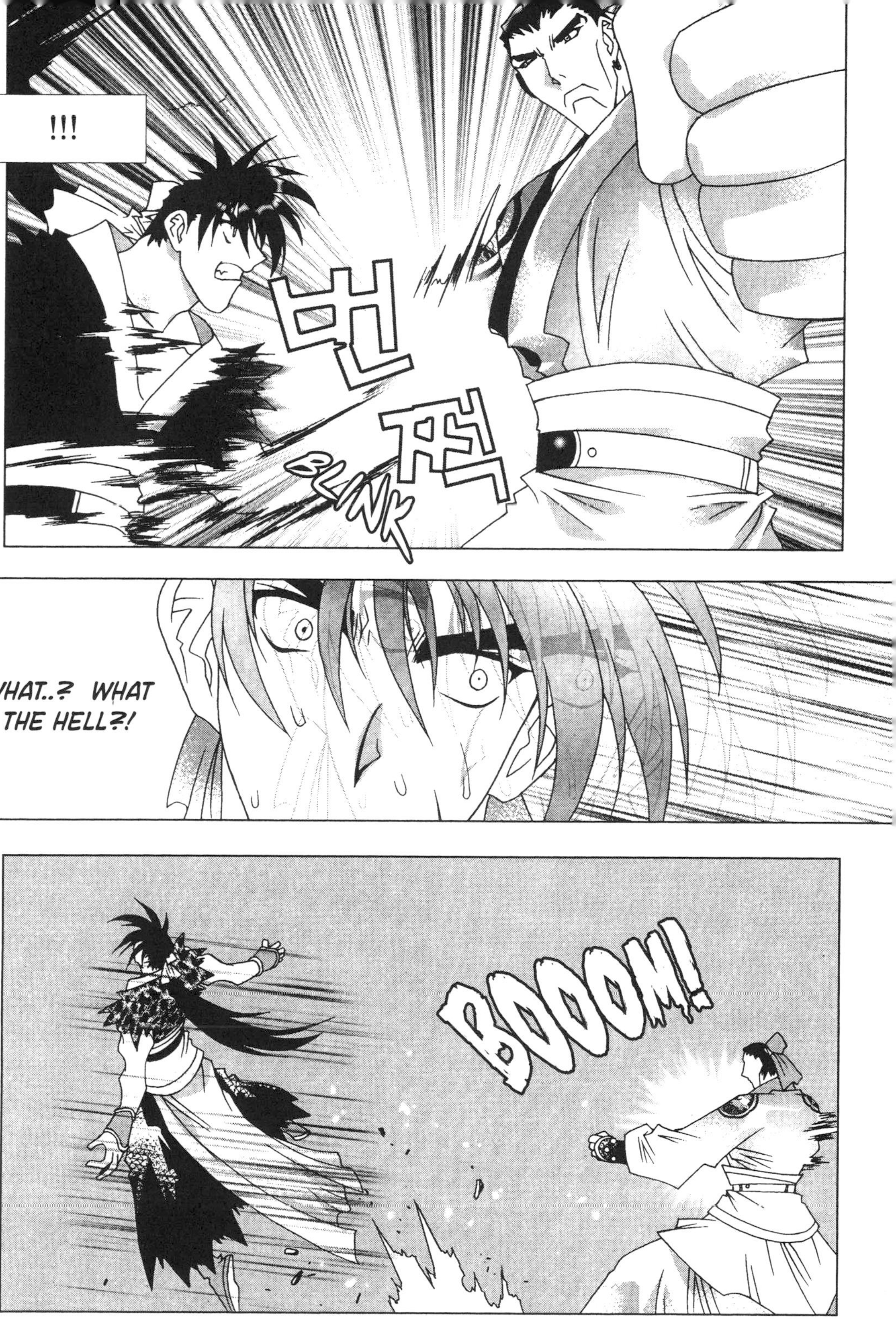
!!!
번쩍
BLINK
WHAT..? WHAT THE HELL?!
BOOOM!

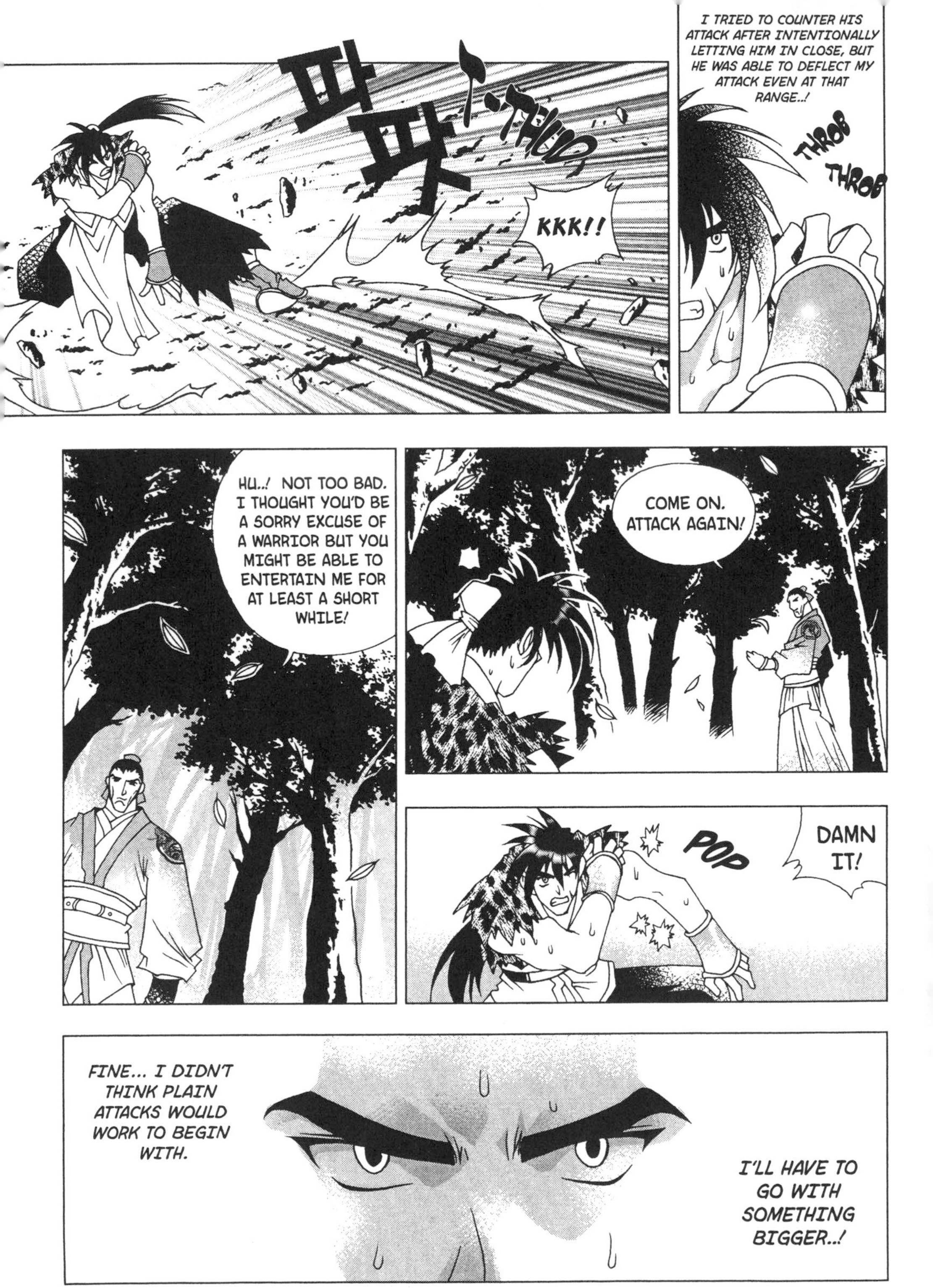
I TRIED TO COUNTER HIS ATTACK AFTER INTENTIONALLY LETTING HIM IN CLOSE, BUT HE WAS ABLE TO DEFLECT MY ATTACK EVEN AT THAT RANGE..!
THROB THROB
THUD
KKK!!
HU..! NOT TOO BAD. I THOUGHT YOU'D BE A SORRY EXCUSE OF A WARRIOR BUT YOU MIGHT BE ABLE TO ENTERTAIN ME FOR AT LEAST A SHORT WHILE!
COME ON. ATTACK AGAIN!
DAMN IT!
POP
FINE... I DIDN'T THINK PLAIN ATTACKS WOULD WORK TO BEGIN WITH.
I'LL HAVE TO GO WITH SOMETHING BIGGER..!

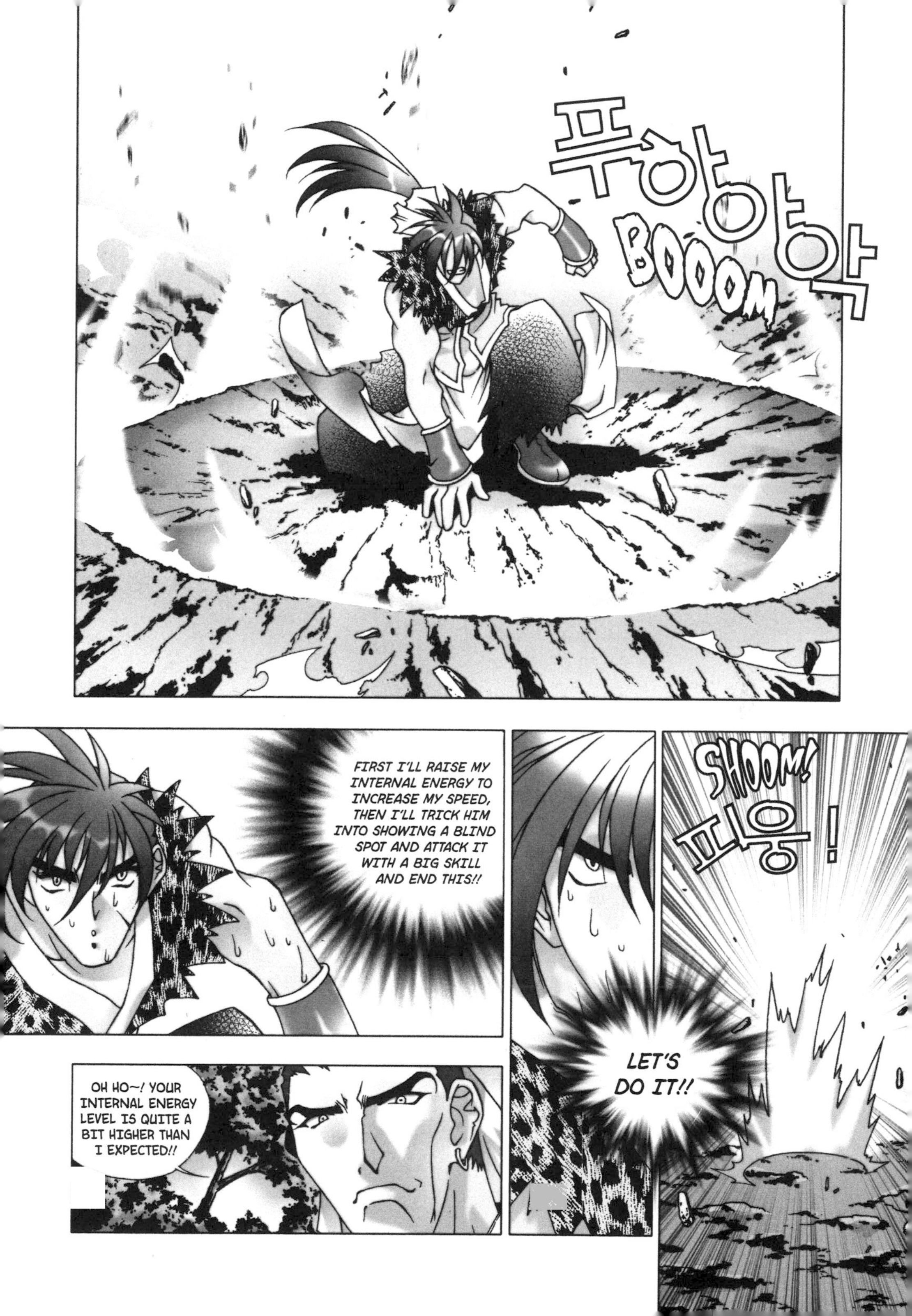

푸화앙악
BOOOM
FIRST I'LL RAISE MY INTERNAL ENERGY TO INCREASE MY SPEED, THEN I'LL TRICK HIM INTO SHOWING A BLIND SPOT AND ATTACK IT WITH A BIG SKILL AND END THIS!!
OH HO~! YOUR INTERNAL ENERGY LEVEL IS QUITE A BIT HIGHER THAN I EXPECTED!!
SHOOM!
피웅!
LET'S DO IT!!

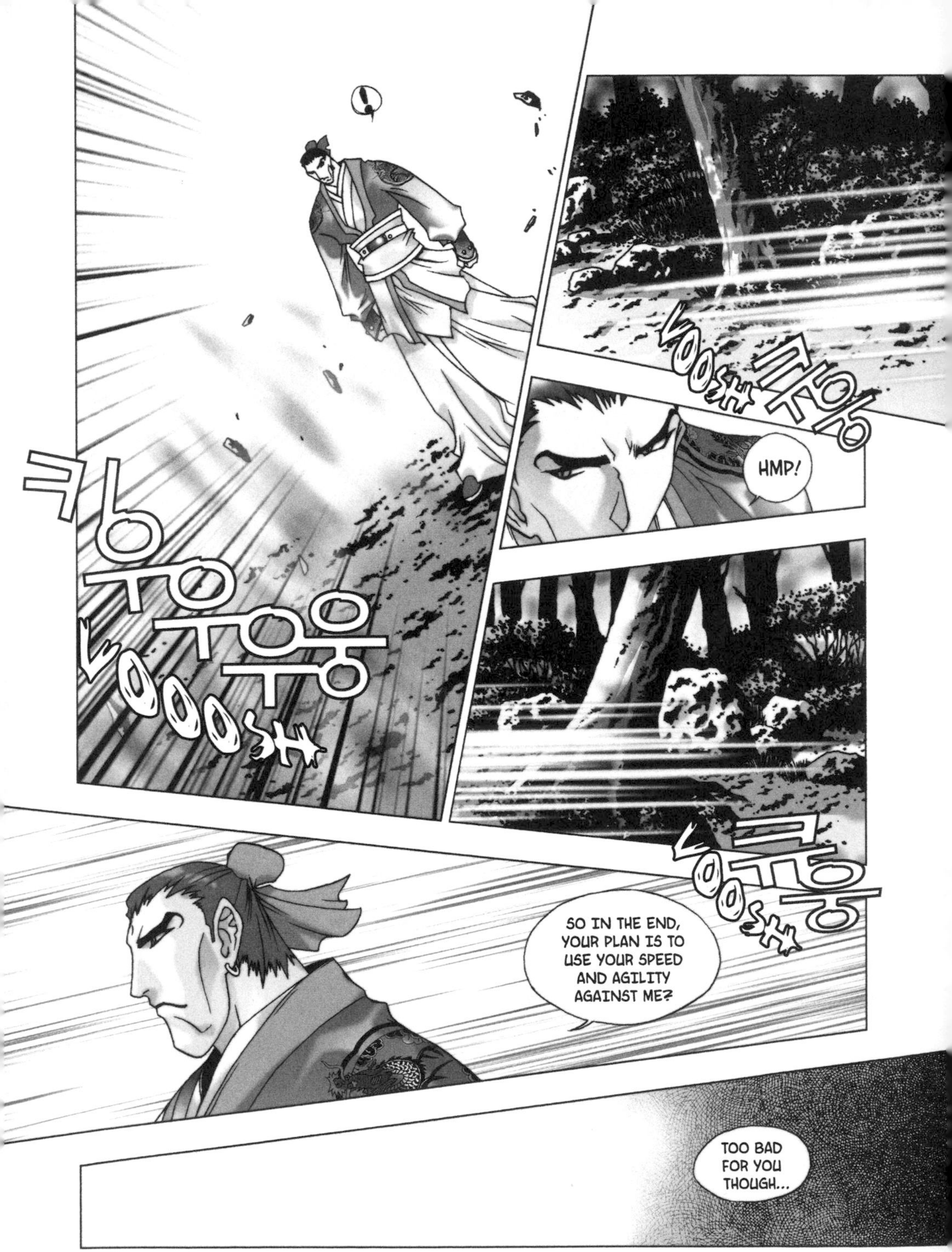
!
VOOOSH
VOOSH
HMP!
VOOSH
SO IN THE END, YOUR PLAN IS TO USE YOUR SPEED AND AGILITY AGAINST ME?
TOO BAD FOR YOU THOUGH...

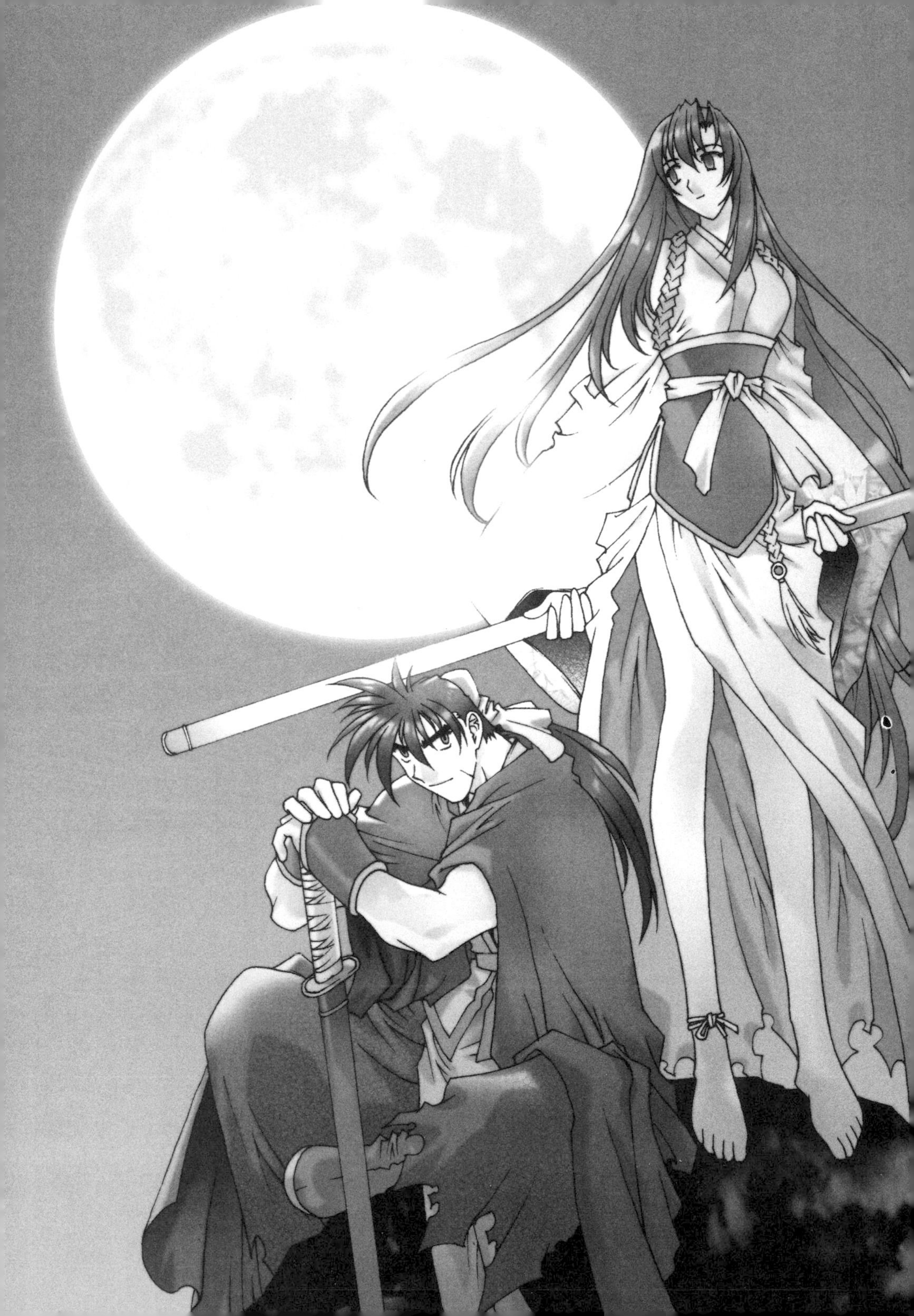

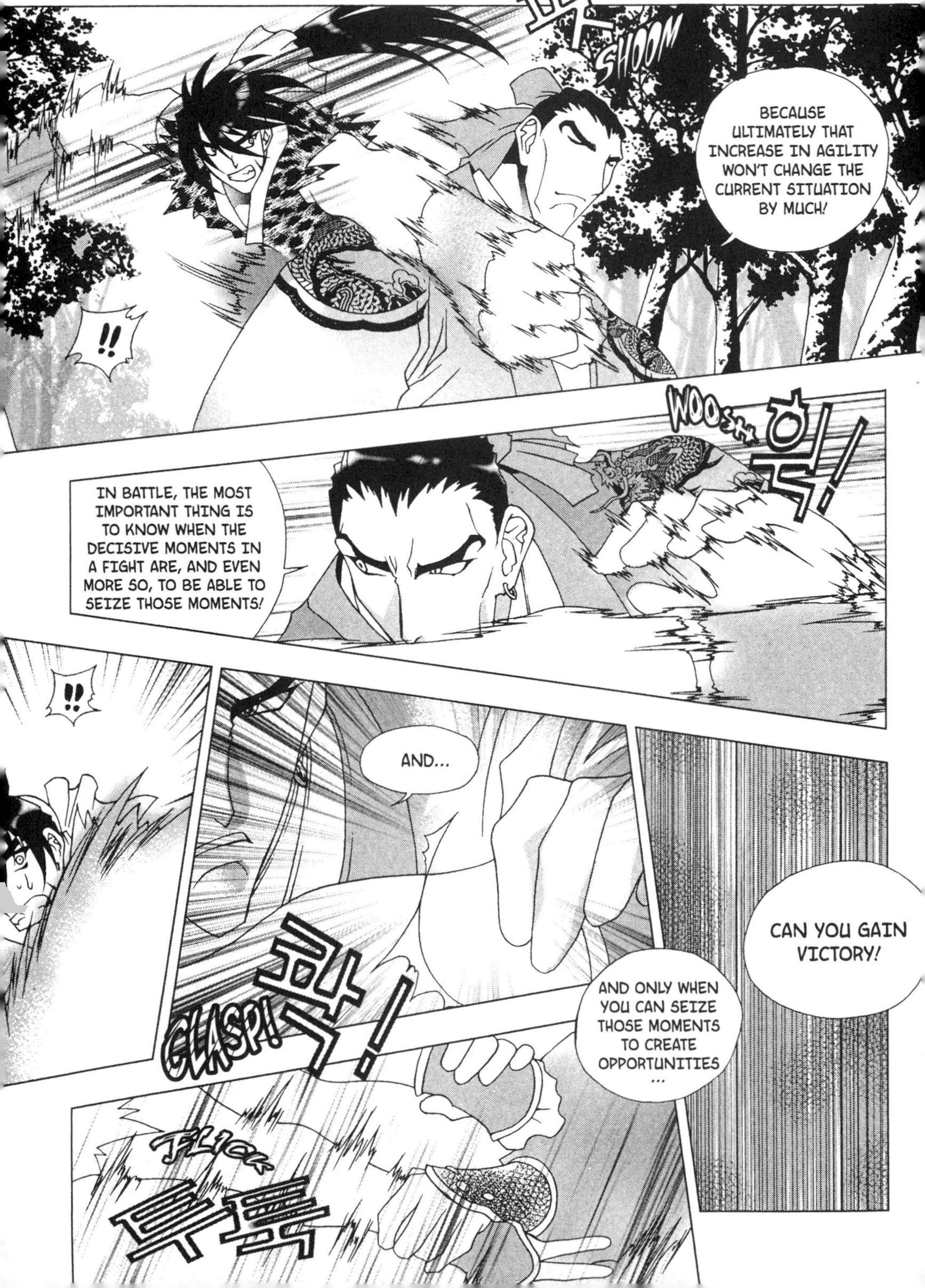
SHOOM
BECAUSE ULTIMATELY THAT INCREASE IN AGILITY WON'T CHANGE THE CURRENT SITUATION BY MUCH!
!!
WOOSH
IN BATTLE, THE MOST IMPORTANT THING IS TO KNOW WHEN THE DECISIVE MOMENTS IN A FIGHT ARE, AND EVEN MORE SO, TO BE ABLE TO SEIZE THOSE MOMENTS!
!!
AND...
CLASP!
AND ONLY WHEN YOU CAN SEIZE THOSE MOMENTS TO CREATE OPPORTUNITIES ...
CAN YOU GAIN VICTORY!
FLICK

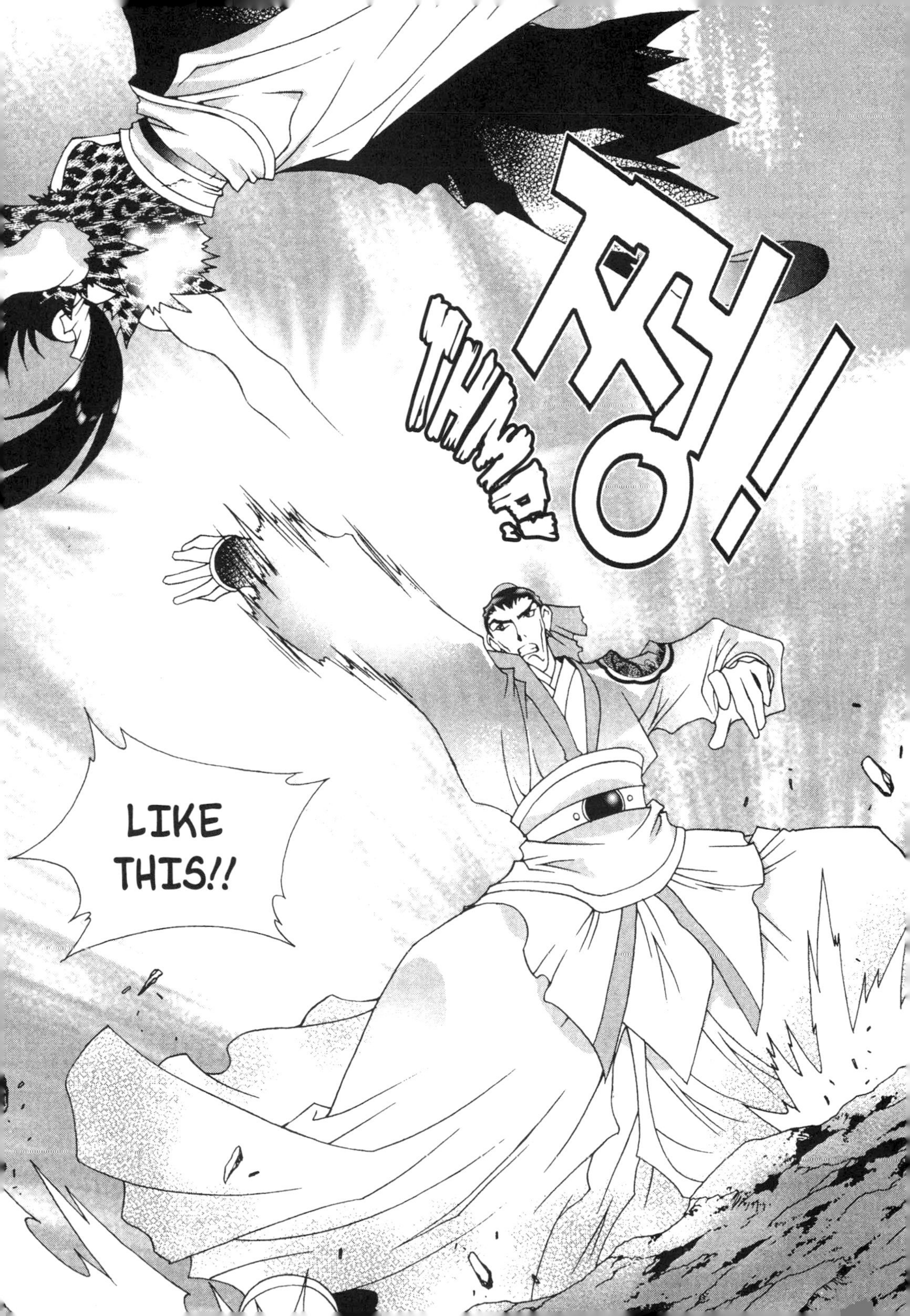
LIKE THIS!!

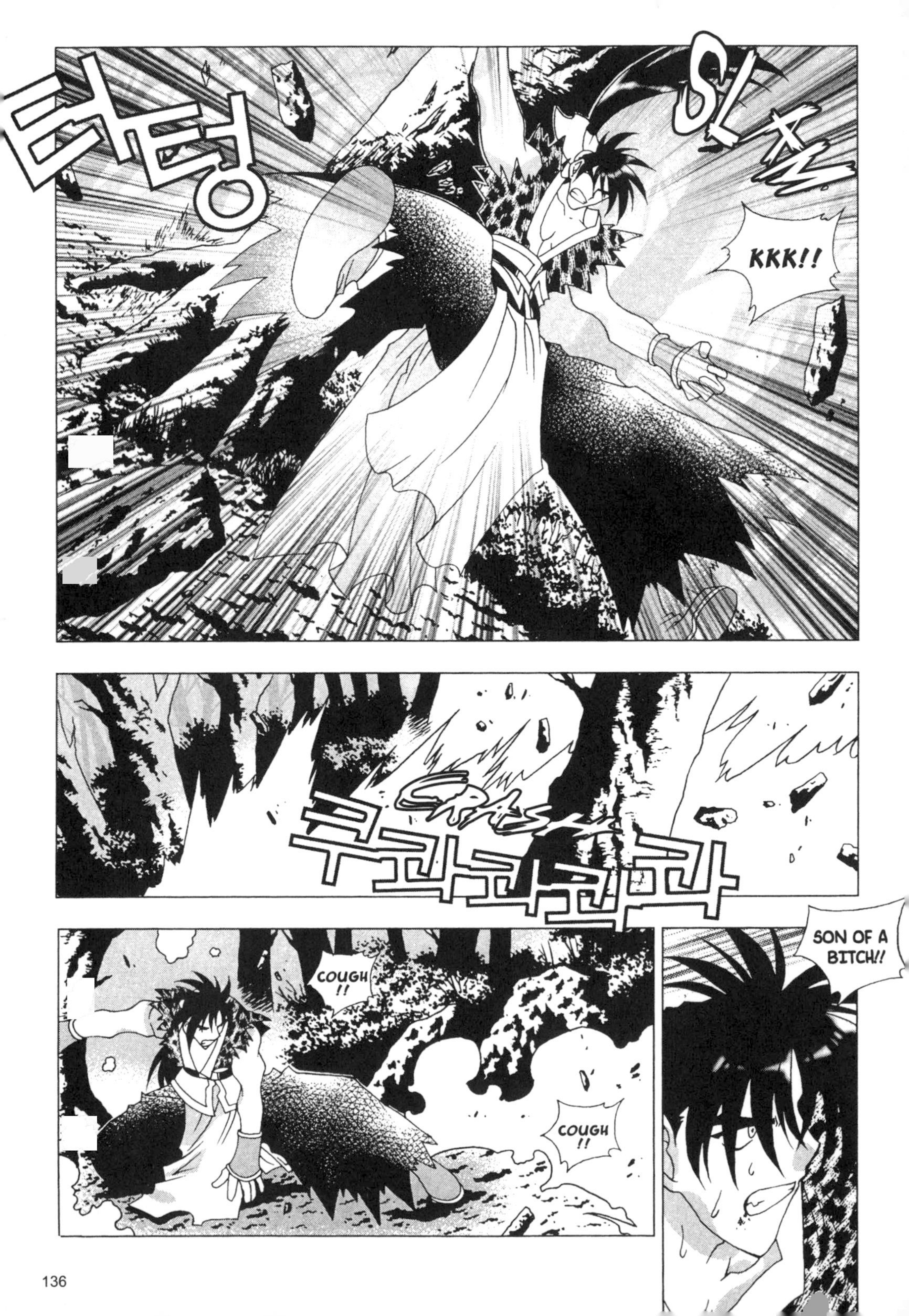
SLAM
KKK!!
CRASH
COUGH !!
COUGH !!
SON OF A BITCH!!

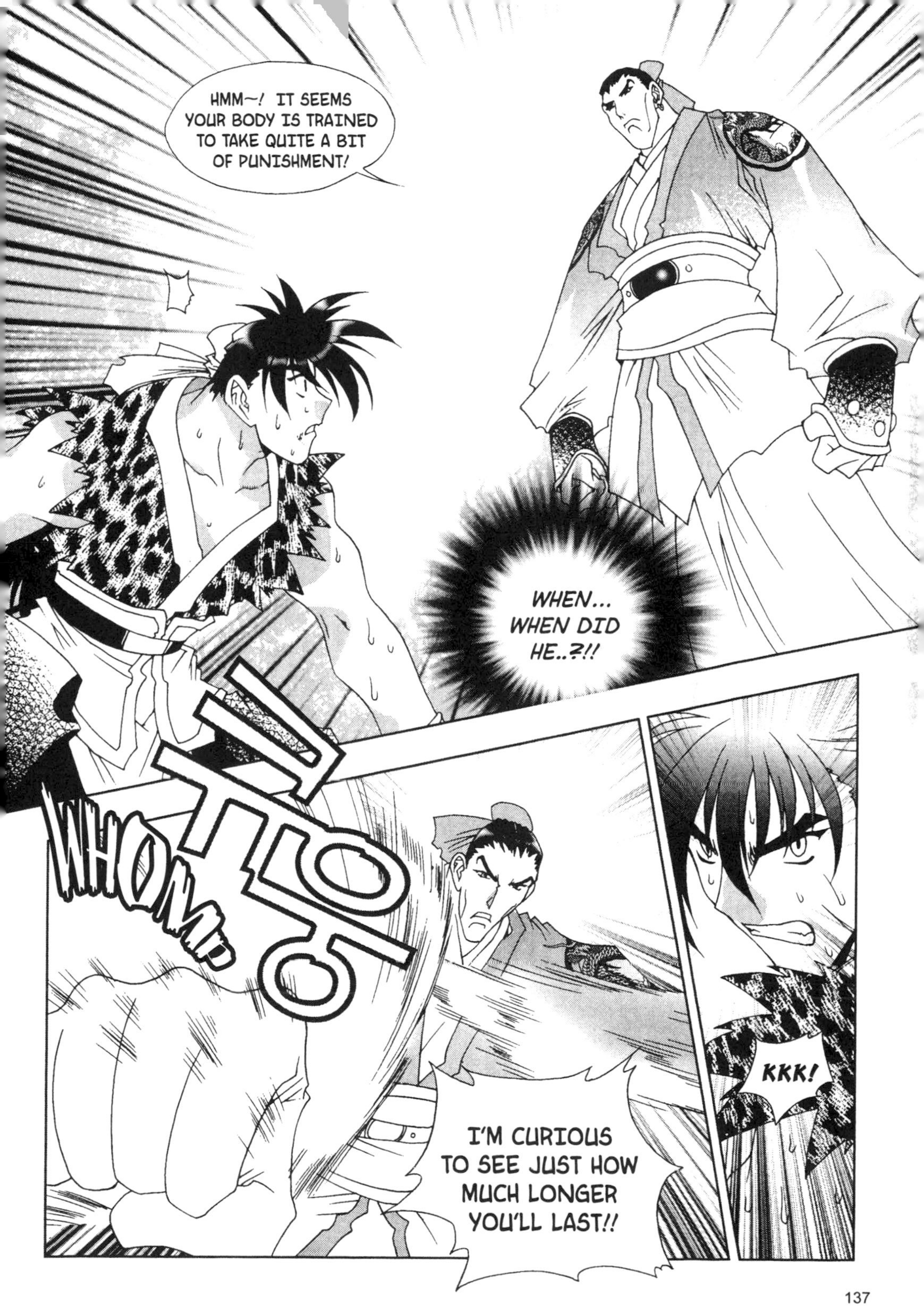
HMM~! IT SEEMS YOUR BODY IS TRAINED TO TAKE QUITE A BIT OF PUNISHMENT!
WHEN... WHEN DID HE..?!!
WHOMP
KKK!
I'M CURIOUS TO SEE JUST HOW MUCH LONGER YOU'LL LAST!!

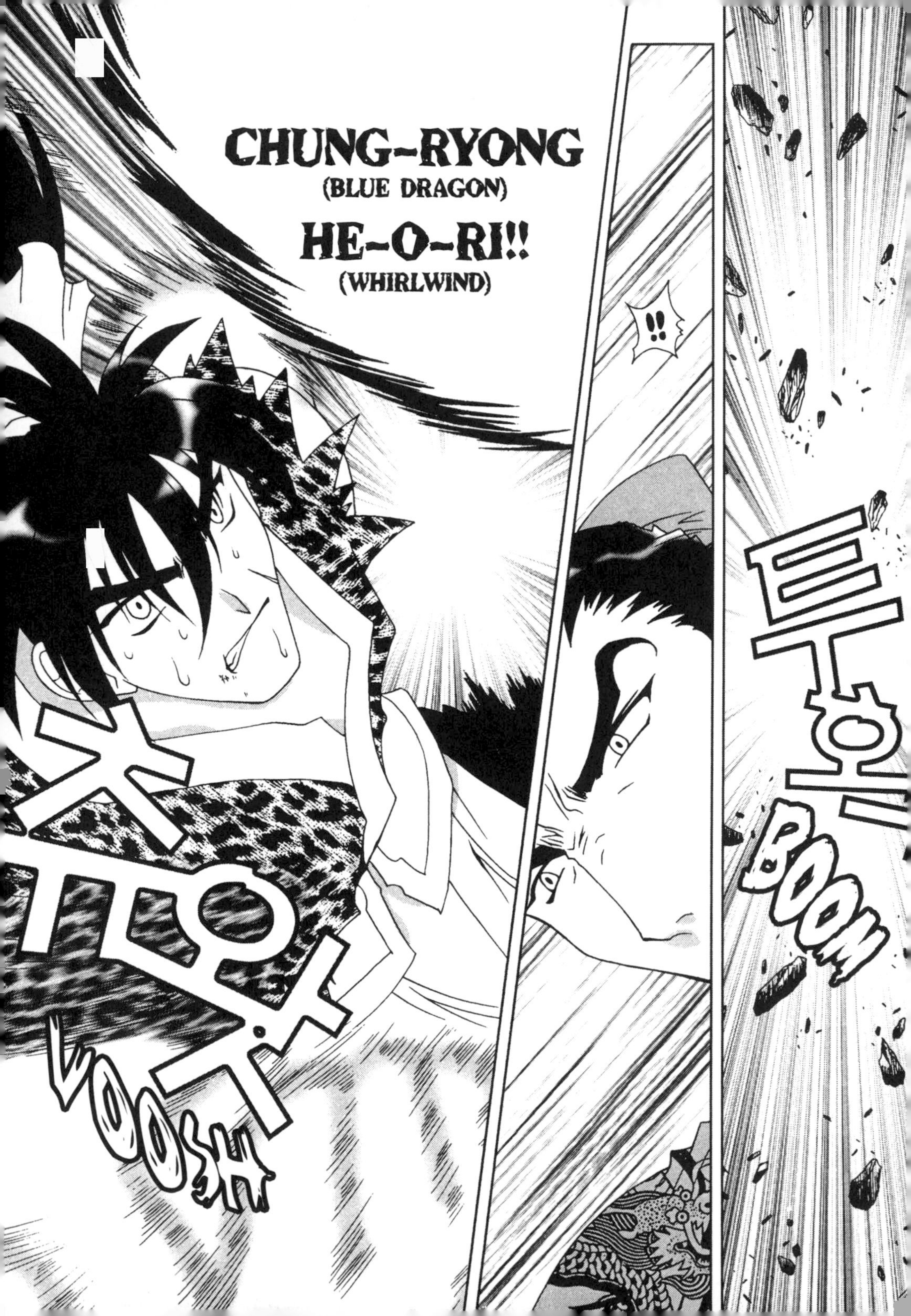
CHUNG-RYONG
(BLUE DRAGON)
HE-O-RI!!
(WHIRLWIND)
!!
BOOM
VOOSH

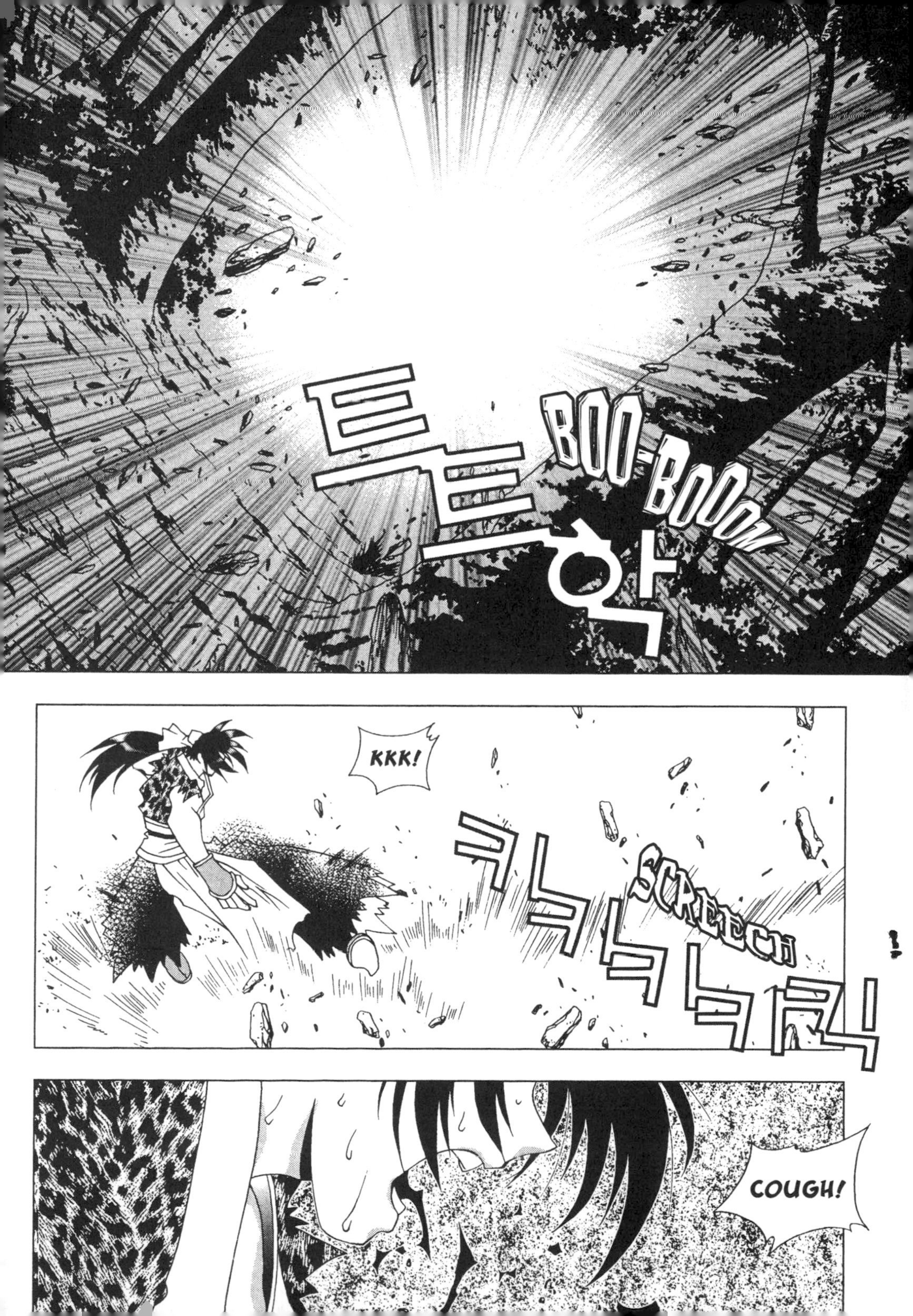

BOO-BOOOM
KKK!
SCREECH
COUGH!

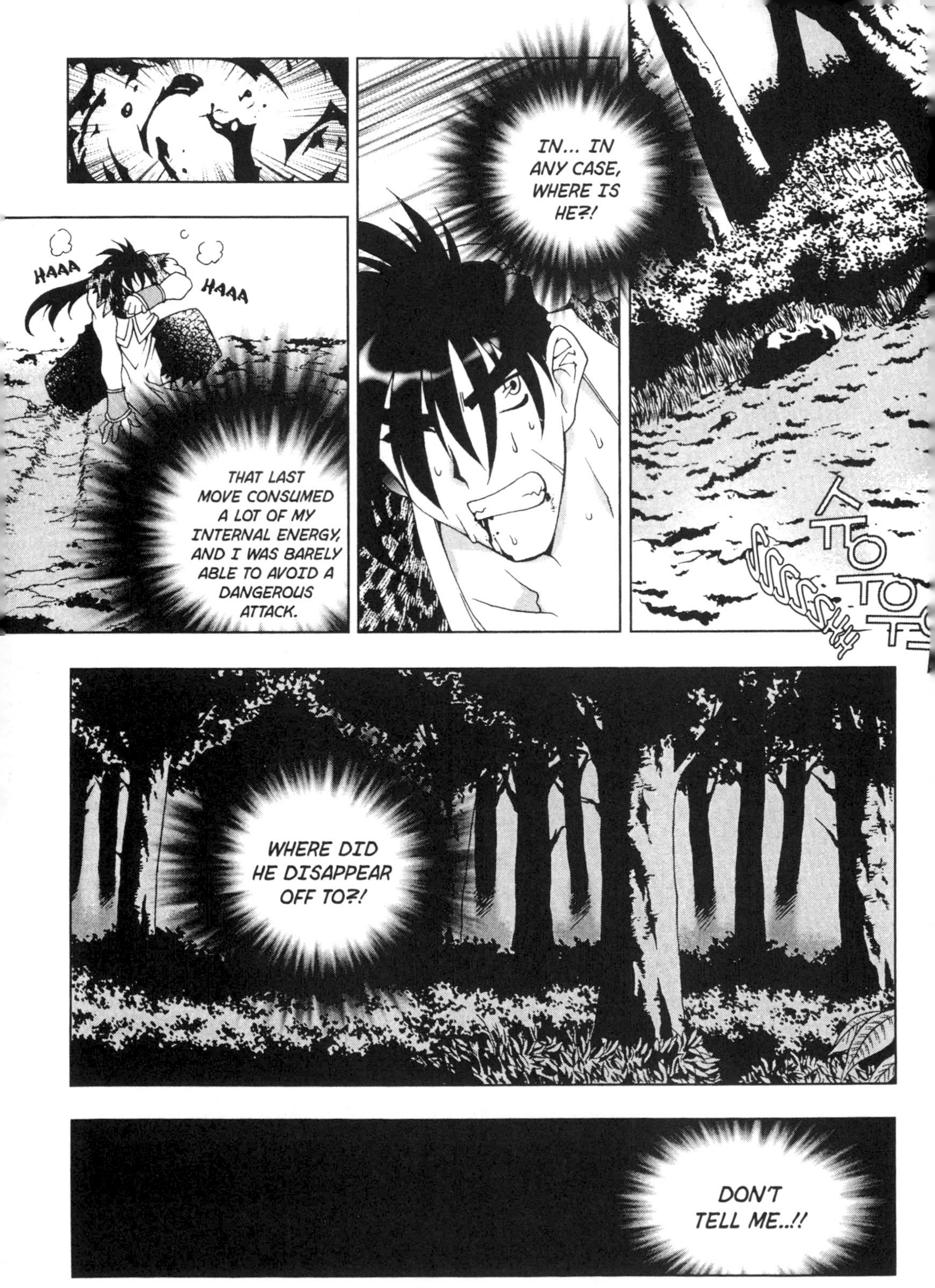
IN... IN ANY CASE, WHERE IS HE?!
HAAA
HAAA
THAT LAST MOVE CONSUMED A LOT OF MY INTERNAL ENERGY, AND I WAS BARELY ABLE TO AVOID A DANGEROUS ATTACK.
WHERE DID HE DISAPPEAR OFF TO?!
DON'T TELL ME..!!

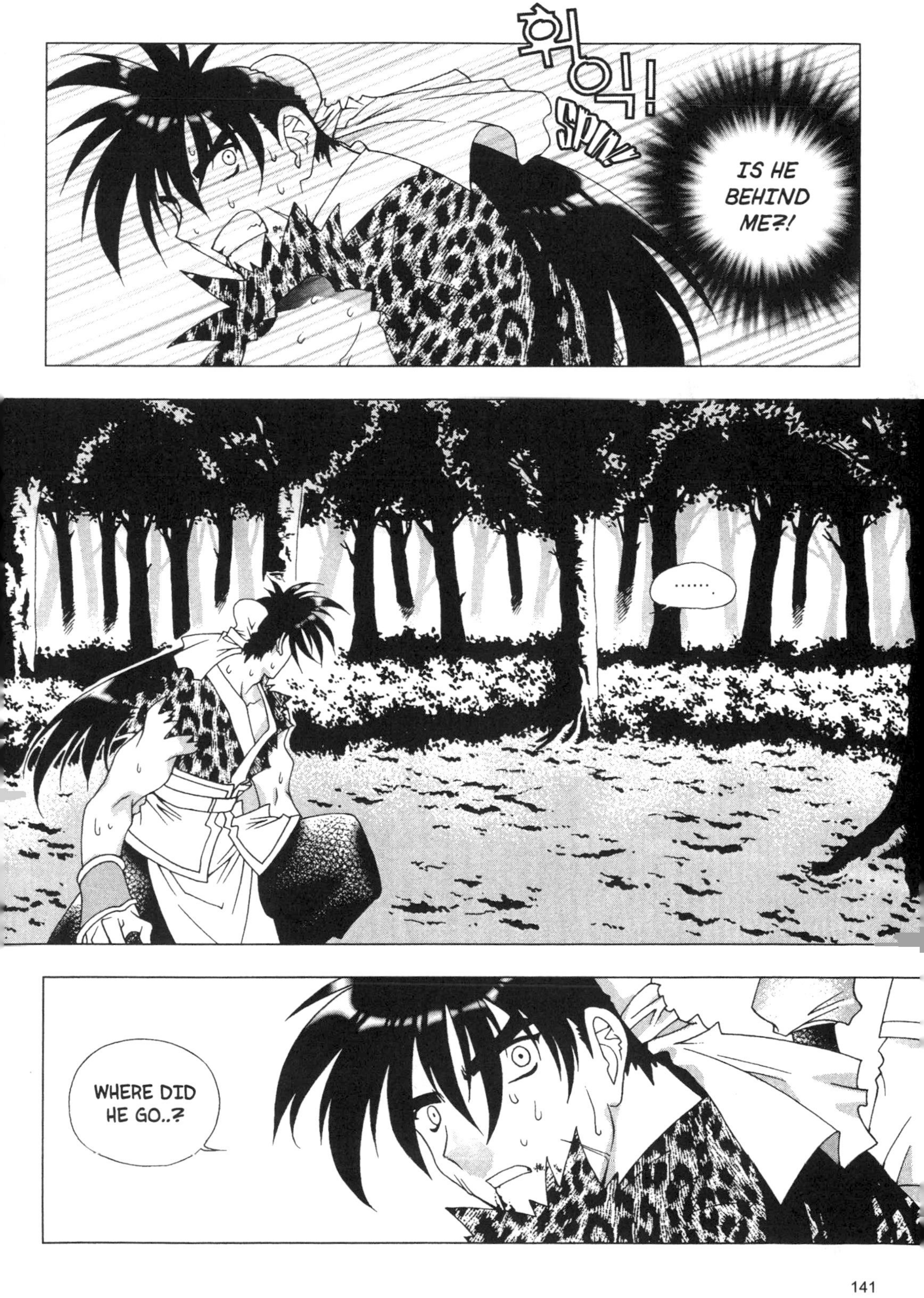
화악!
SPIN!
IS HE BEHIND ME?!
....
WHERE DID HE GO..?

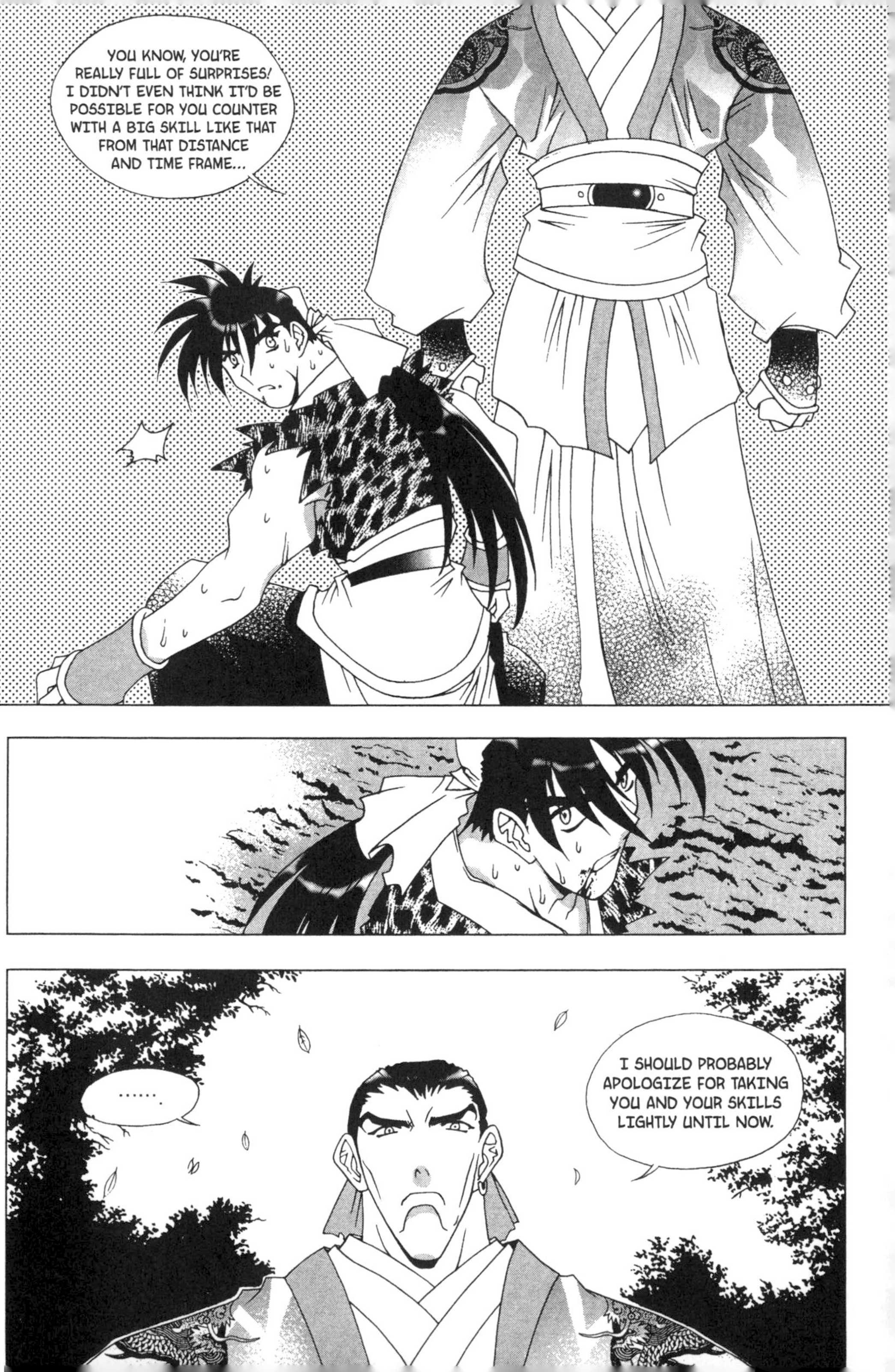

YOU KNOW, YOU'RE REALLY FULL OF SURPRISES! I DIDN'T EVEN THINK IT'D BE POSSIBLE FOR YOU COUNTER WITH A BIG SKILL LIKE THAT FROM THAT DISTANCE AND TIME FRAME...
....
I SHOULD PROBABLY APOLOGIZE FOR TAKING YOU AND YOUR SKILLS LIGHTLY UNTIL NOW.

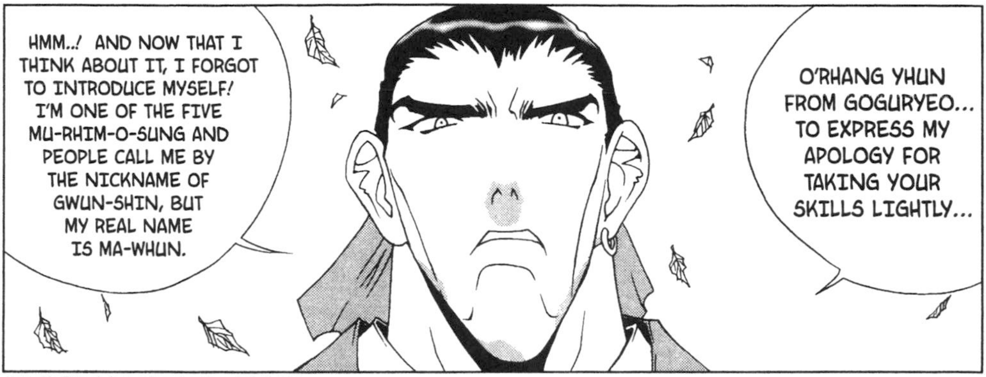
HMM..! AND NOW THAT I THINK ABOUT IT, I FORGOT TO INTRODUCE MYSELF! I'M ONE OF THE FIVE MU-RHIM-O-SUNG AND PEOPLE CALL ME BY THE NICKNAME OF GWUN-SHIN, BUT MY REAL NAME IS MA-WHUN.
O'RHANG YHUN FROM GOGURYEO... TO EXPRESS MY APOLOGY FOR TAKING YOUR SKILLS LIGHTLY...

Note : Mu-Rhim-O-Sung = The Five Stars of Martial Arts
Note : Gwun-Shin = Fighting God

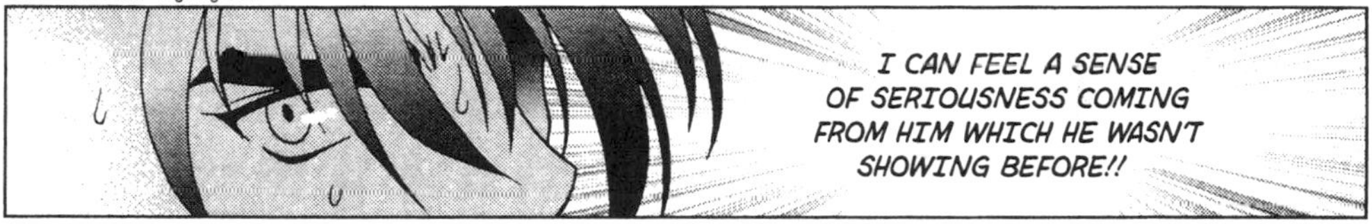
I CAN FEEL A SENSE OF SERIOUSNESS COMING FROM HIM WHICH HE WASN'T SHOWING BEFORE!!

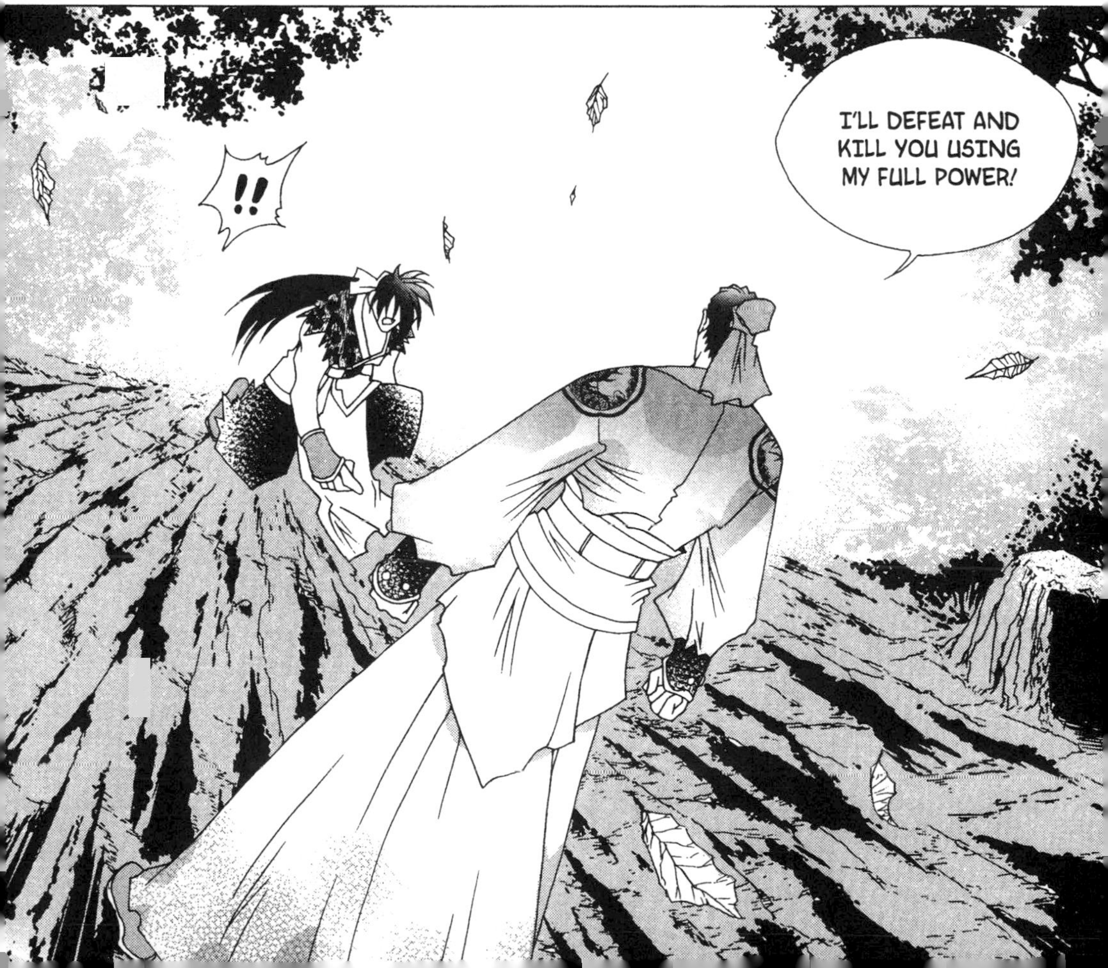
I'LL DEFEAT AND KILL YOU USING MY FULL POWER!
!!

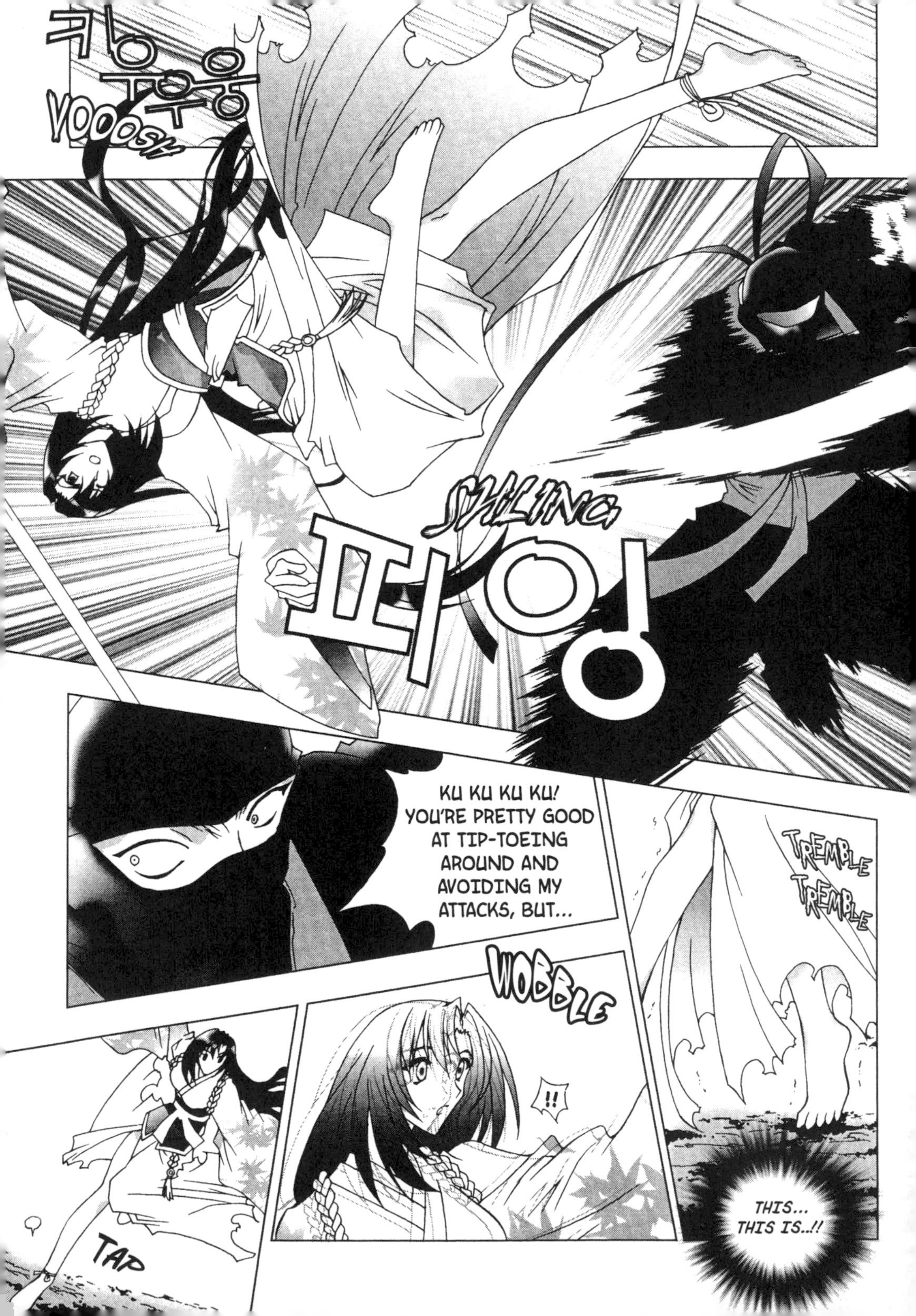

VOOOSH
SHLING
KU KU KU KU! YOU'RE PRETTY GOOD AT TIP-TOEING AROUND AND AVOIDING MY ATTACKS, BUT...
TREMBLE TREMBLE
WOBBLE
TAP
!!
THIS... THIS IS..!!

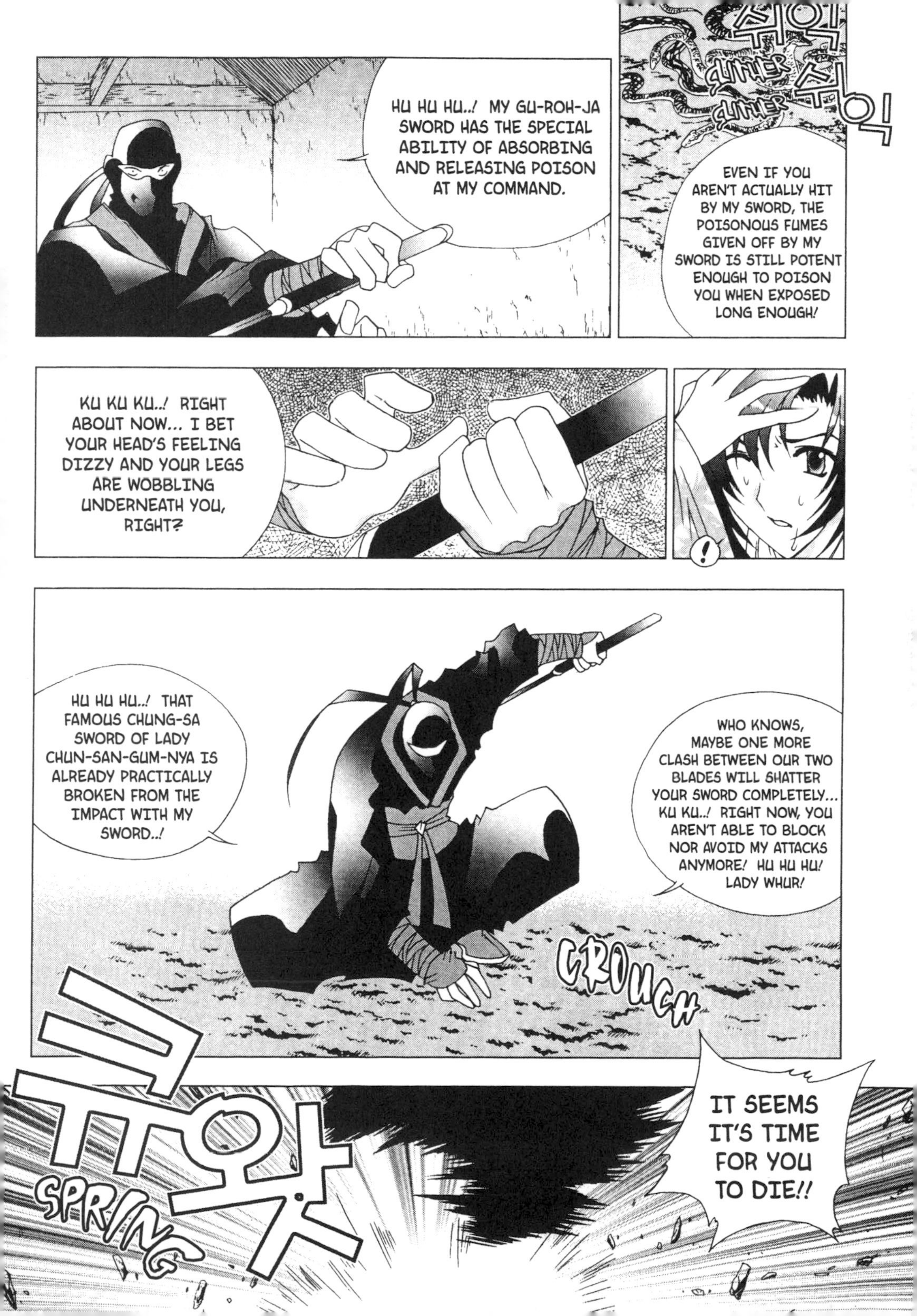
HU HU HU..! MY GU-ROH-JA SWORD HAS THE SPECIAL ABILITY OF ABSORBING AND RELEASING POISON AT MY COMMAND.
SLITHER
SLITHER
EVEN IF YOU AREN'T ACTUALLY HIT BY MY SWORD, THE POISONOUS FUMES GIVEN OFF BY MY SWORD IS STILL POTENT ENOUGH TO POISON YOU WHEN EXPOSED LONG ENOUGH!
KU KU KU..! RIGHT ABOUT NOW... I BET YOUR HEAD'S FEELING DIZZY AND YOUR LEGS ARE WOBBLING UNDERNEATH YOU, RIGHT?
!
HU HU HU..! THAT FAMOUS CHUNG-SA SWORD OF LADY CHUN-SAN-GUM-NYA IS ALREADY PRACTICALLY BROKEN FROM THE IMPACT WITH MY SWORD..!
WHO KNOWS, MAYBE ONE MORE CLASH BETWEEN OUR TWO BLADES WILL SHATTER YOUR SWORD COMPLETELY... KU KU..! RIGHT NOW, YOU AREN'T ABLE TO BLOCK NOR AVOID MY ATTACKS ANYMORE! HU HU HU! LADY WHUR!
CROUCH
SPRING
IT SEEMS IT'S TIME FOR YOU TO DIE!!

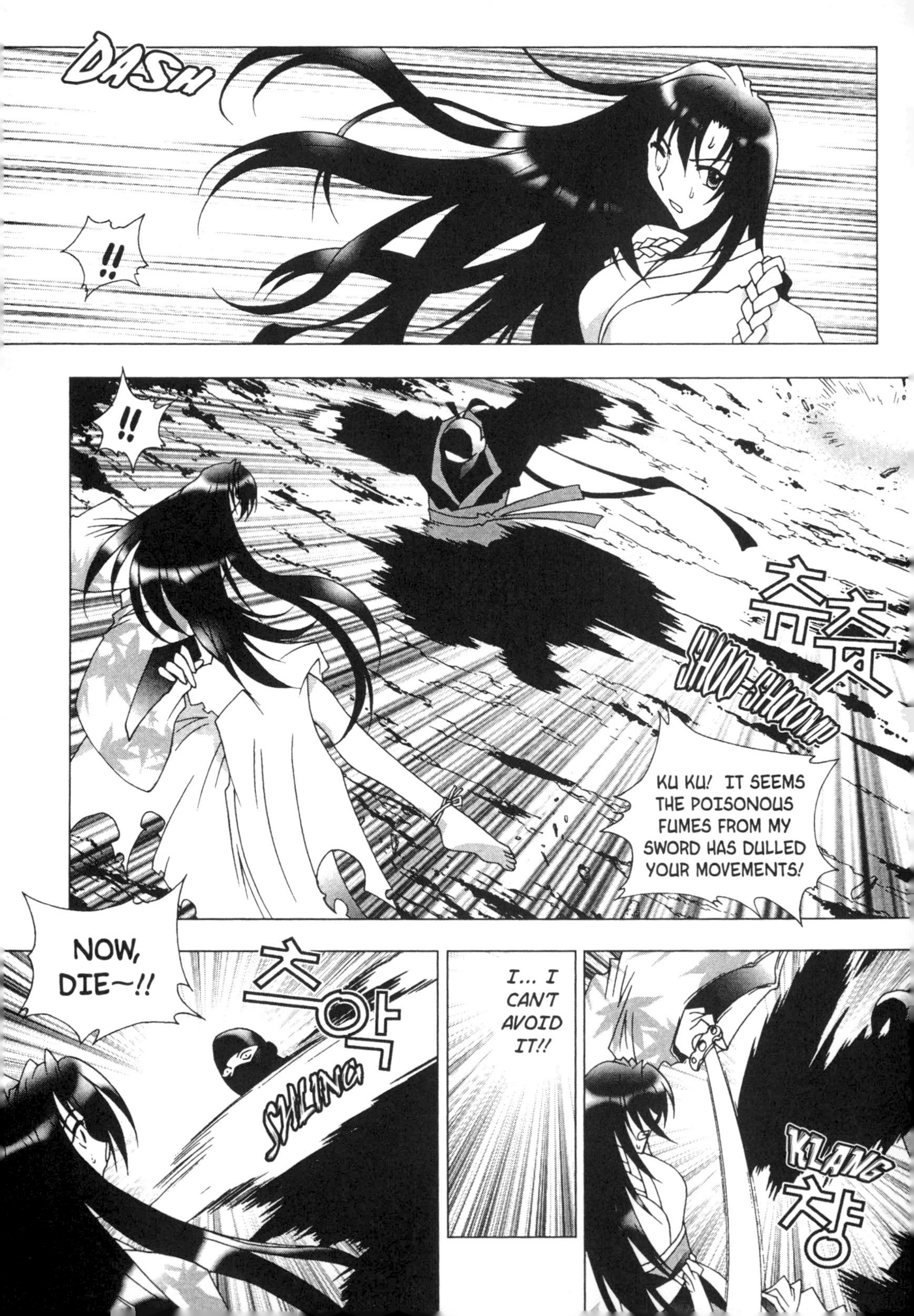
DASH
!!
!!
SHOO-SHOOW
KU KU! IT SEEMS THE POISONOUS FUMES FROM MY SWORD HAS DULLED YOUR MOVEMENTS!
NOW, DIE~!!
SHING
I... I CAN'T AVOID IT!!
KLANG

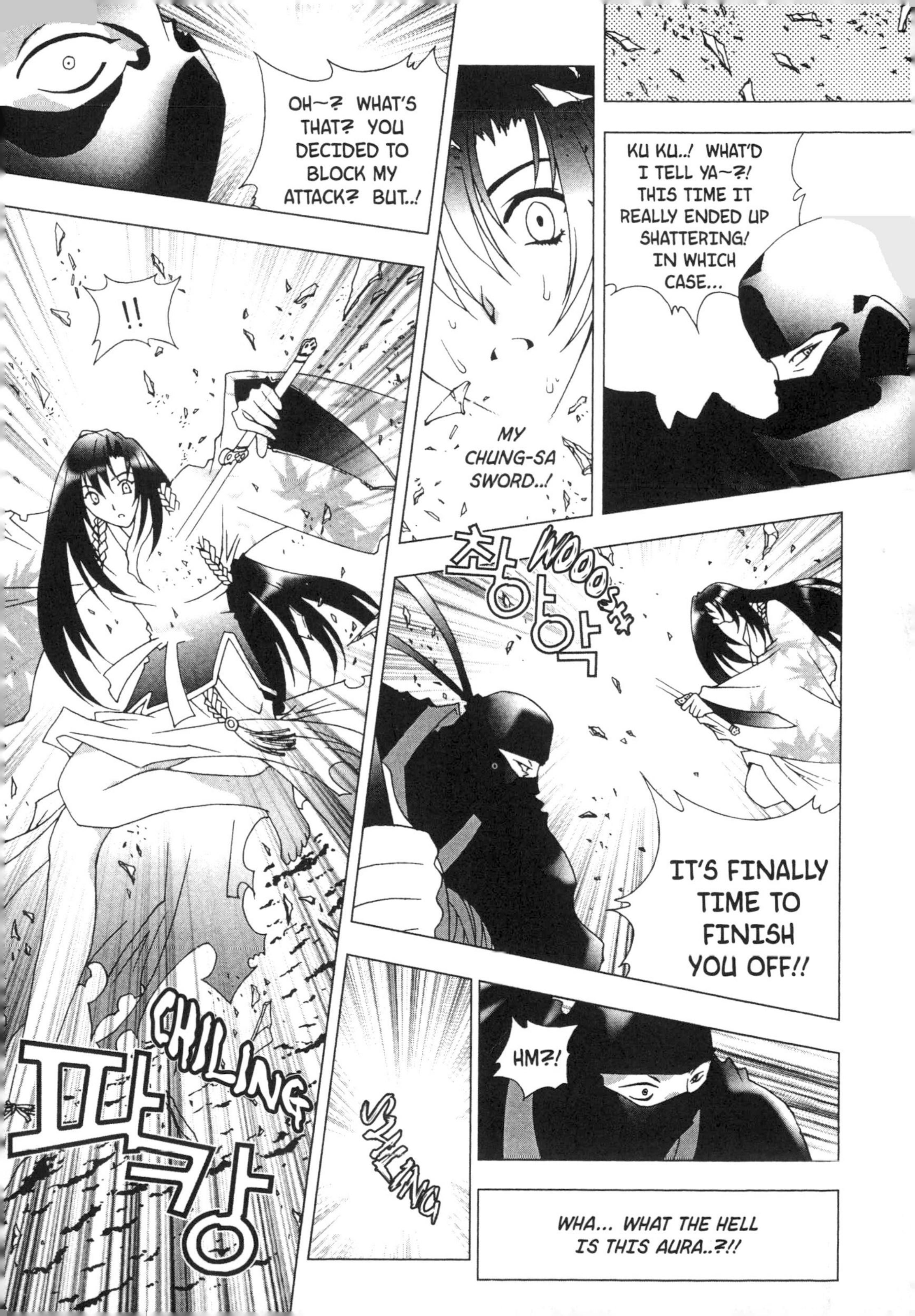
OH~? WHAT'S THAT? YOU DECIDED TO BLOCK MY ATTACK? BUT..!
MY CHUNG-SA SWORD..!
KU KU..! WHAT'D I TELL YA~?! THIS TIME IT REALLY ENDED UP SHATTERING! IN WHICH CASE...
!!
CHILING
파캉
WOOOSH
IT'S FINALLY TIME TO FINISH YOU OFF!!
SHING
HM?!
WHA... WHAT THE HELL IS THIS AURA..?!!

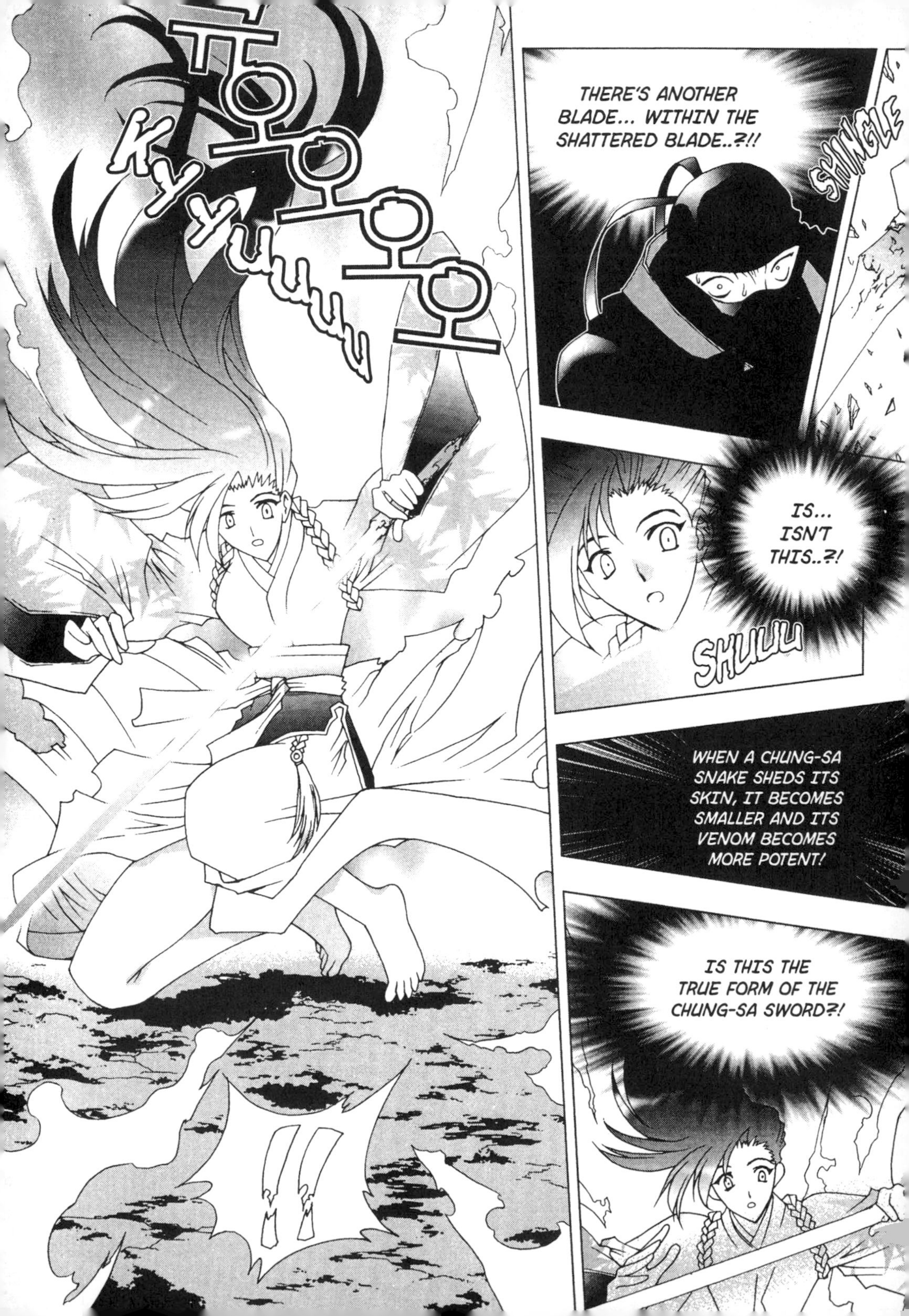
Kyyuuuu
THERE'S ANOTHER BLADE... WITHIN THE SHATTERED BLADE..?!!
SHINGLE
IS... ISN'T THIS..?!
SHUUU
WHEN A CHUNG-SA SNAKE SHEDS ITS SKIN, IT BECOMES SMALLER AND ITS VENOM BECOMES MORE POTENT!
IS THIS THE TRUE FORM OF THE CHUNG-SA SWORD?!

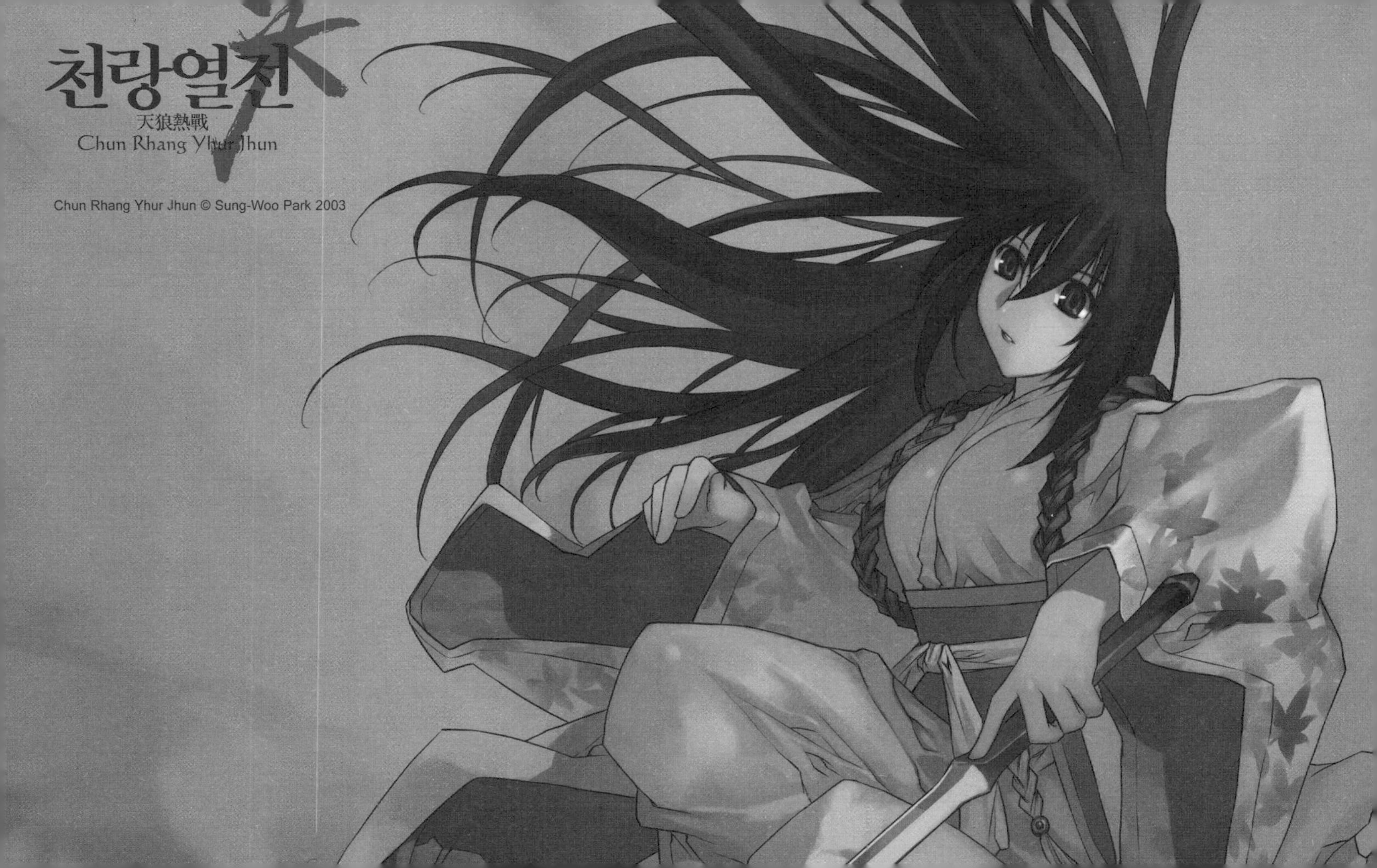
천랑열전
天狼熱戰
Chun Rhang Yhur Jhun
Chun Rhang Yhur Jhun © Sung-Woo Park 2003

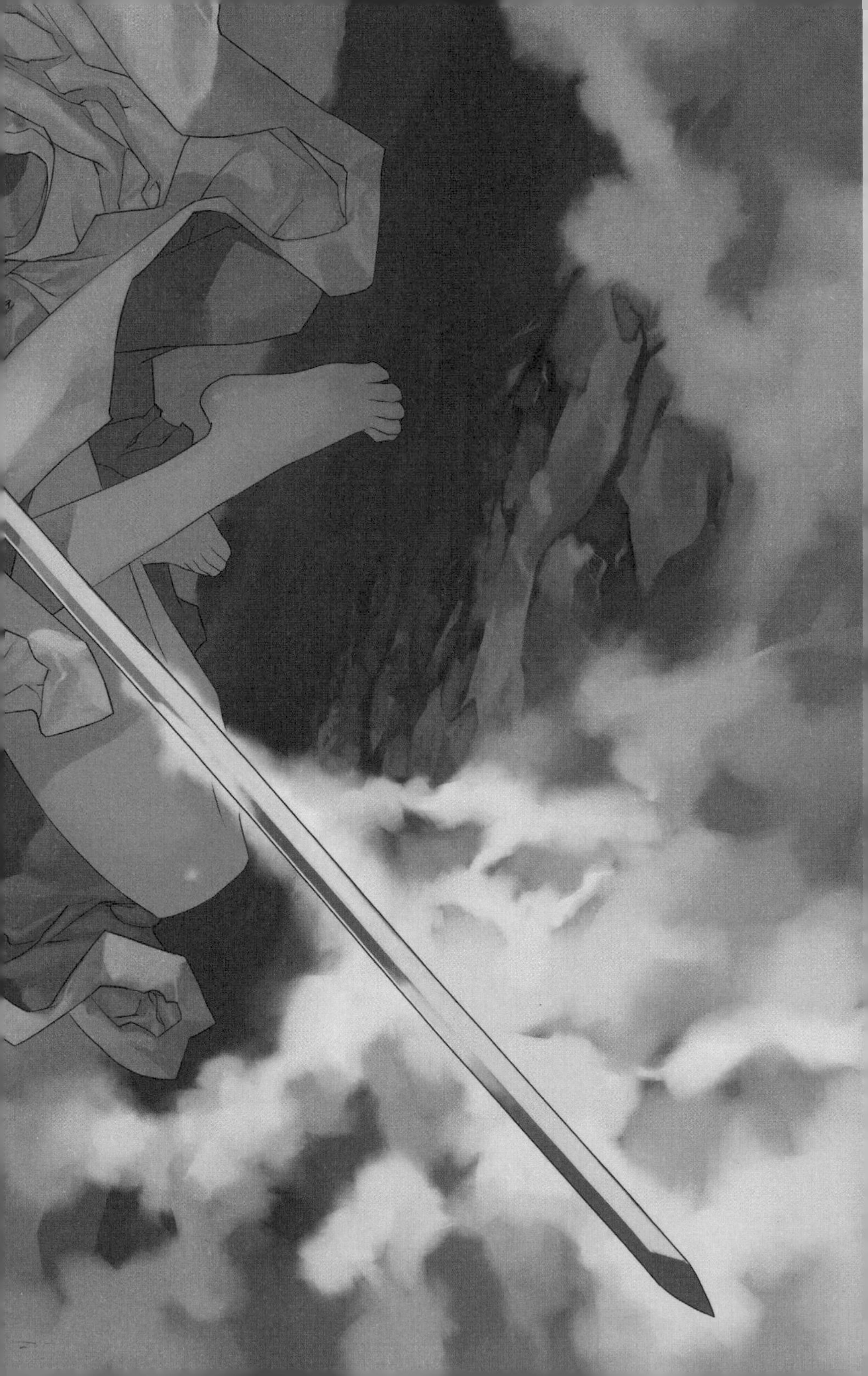

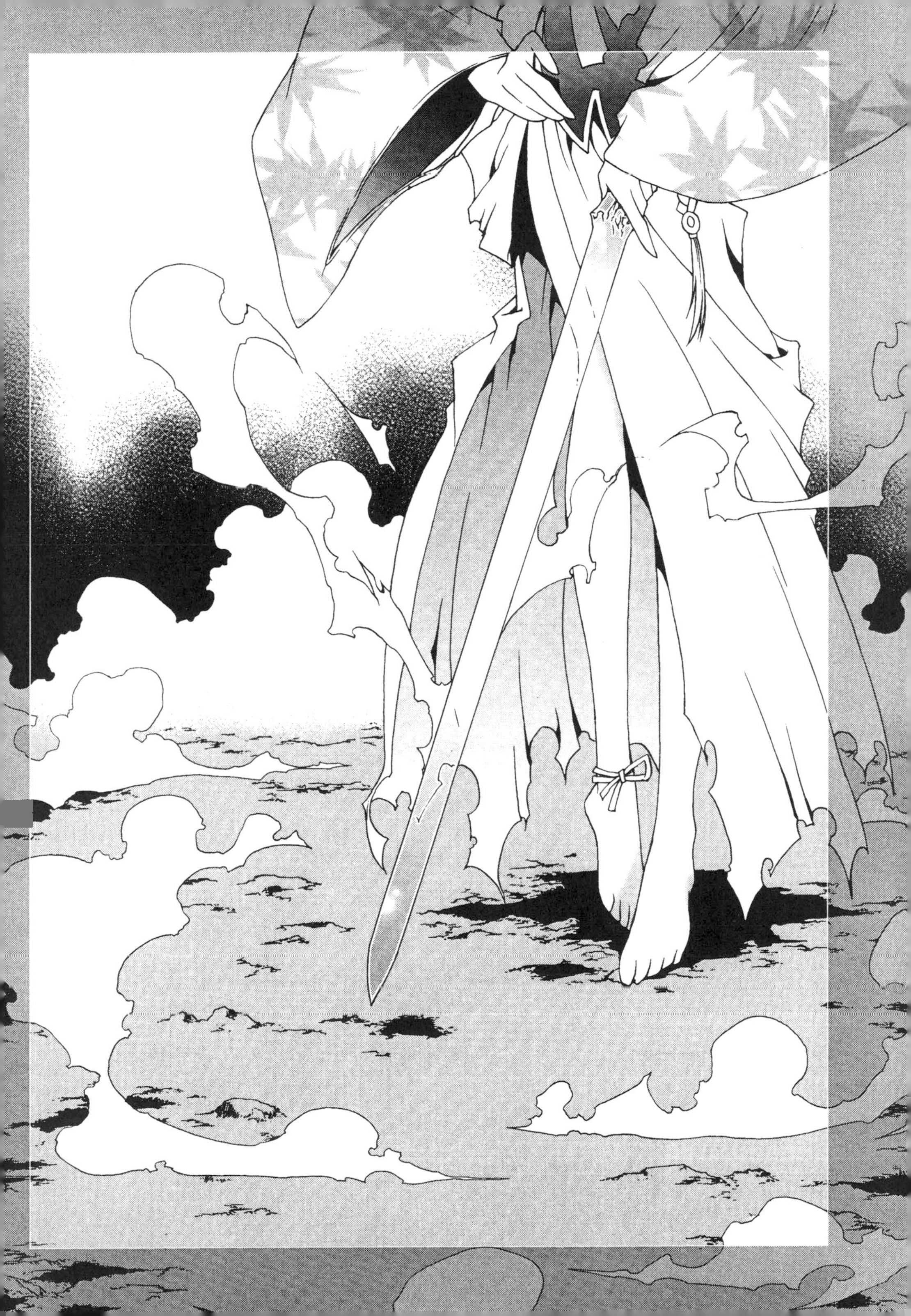

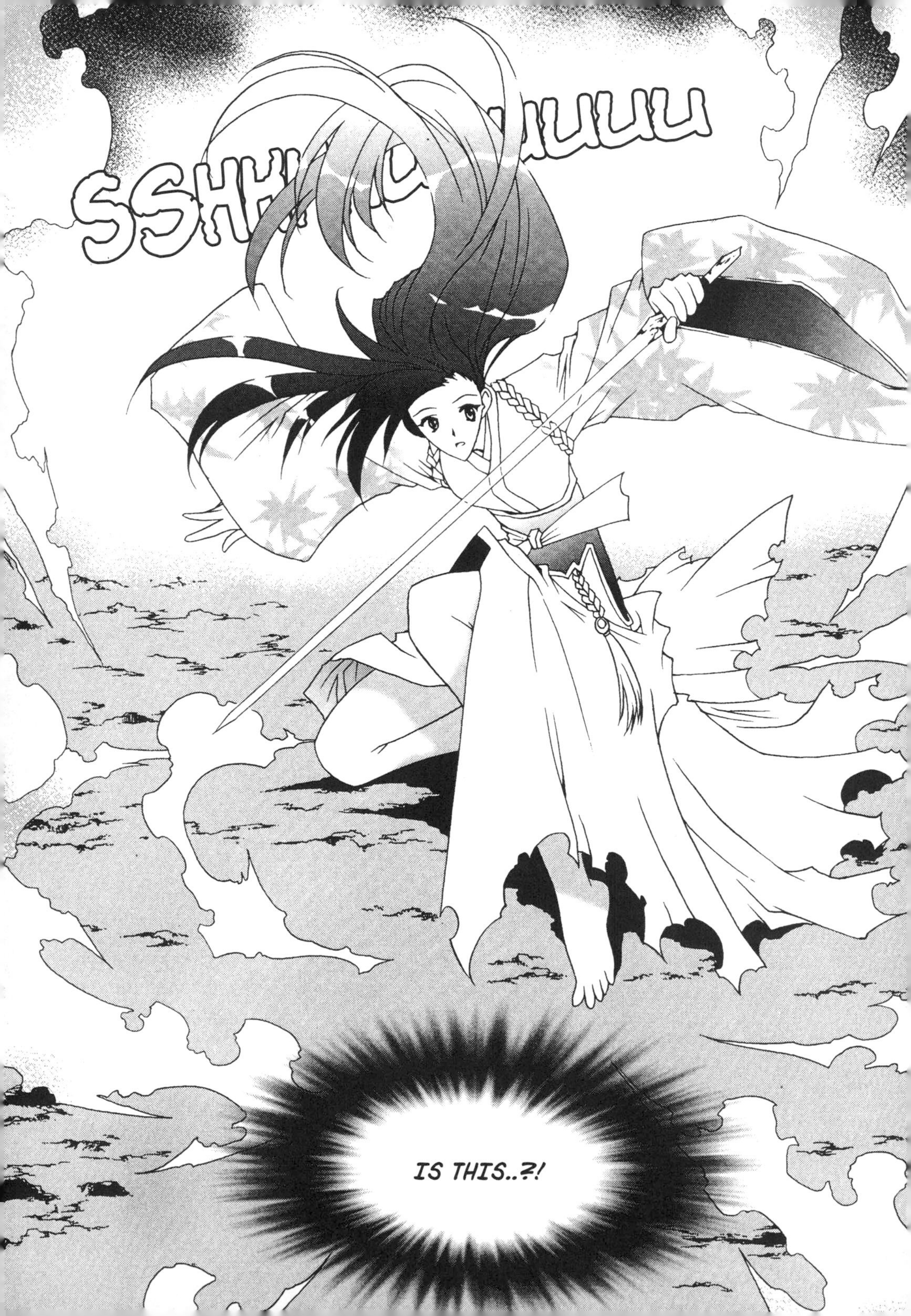
IS THIS..?!

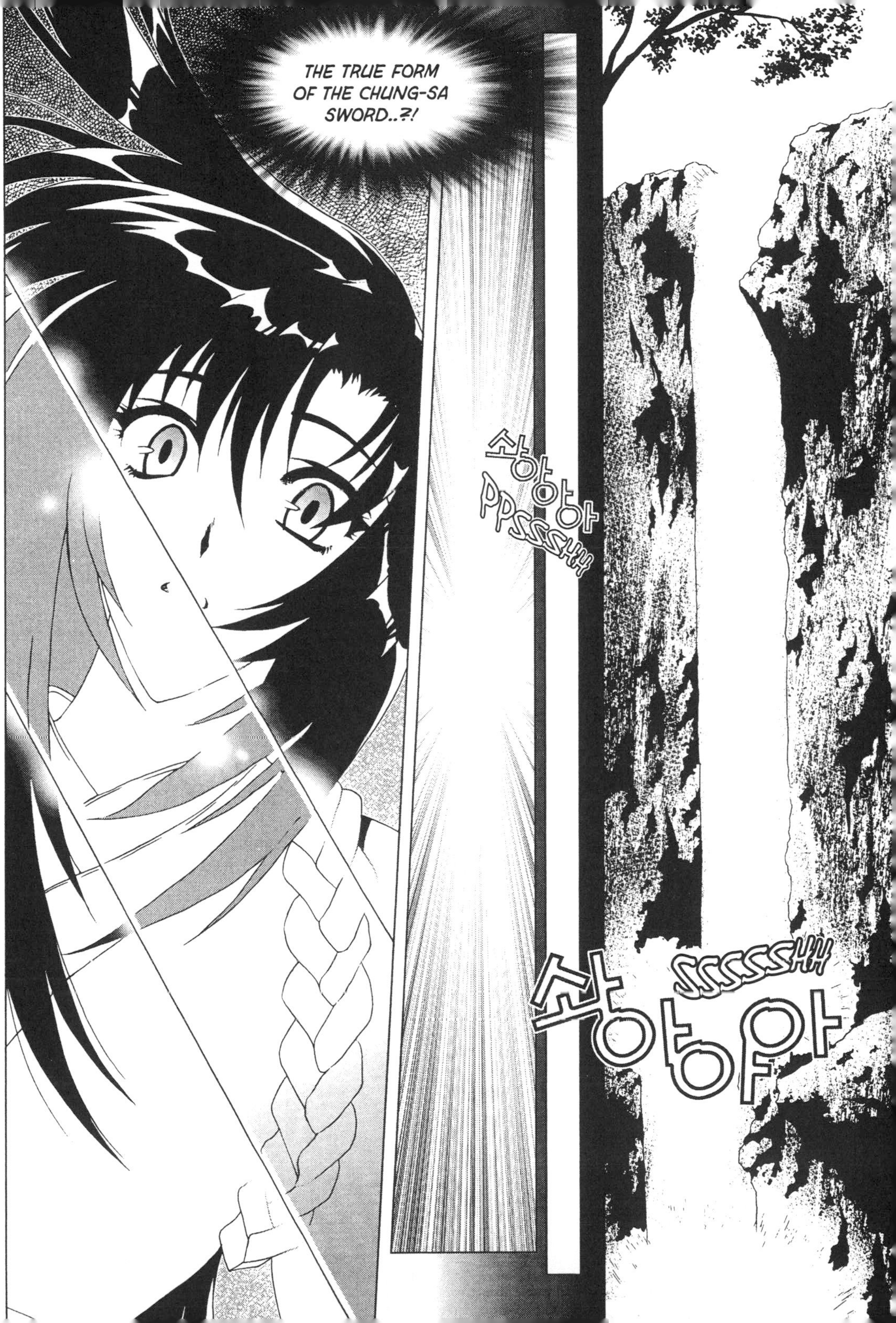
THE TRUE FORM OF THE CHUNG-SA SWORD..?!
솨아아
PPSSSSHH
솨아아아
SSSSSHH

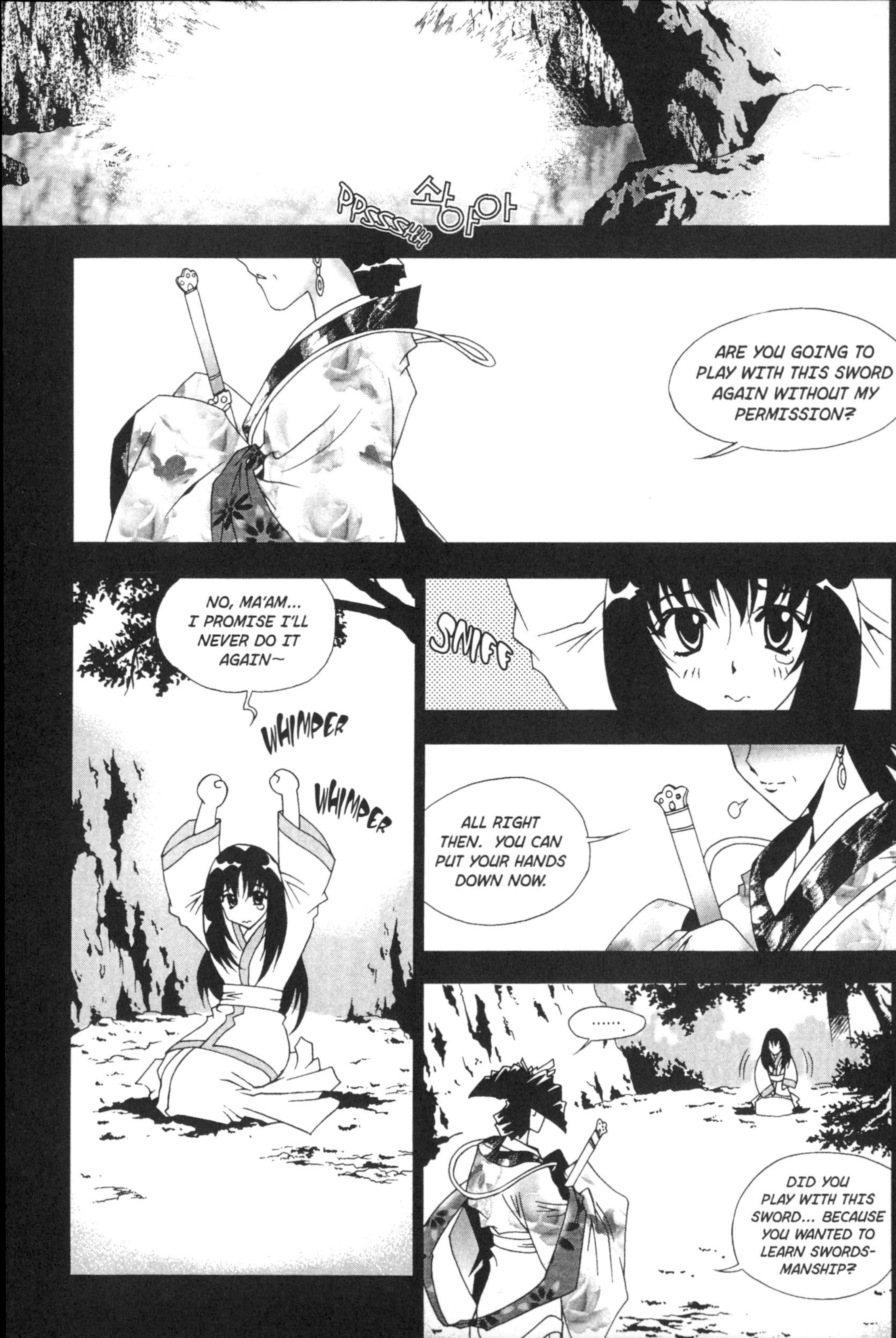
PPSSSHH
쏴아아
ARE YOU GOING TO PLAY WITH THIS SWORD AGAIN WITHOUT MY PERMISSION?
NO, MA'AM... I PROMISE I'LL NEVER DO IT AGAIN~
WHIMPER
WHIMPER
SNIFF
ALL RIGHT THEN. YOU CAN PUT YOUR HANDS DOWN NOW.
......
DID YOU PLAY WITH THIS SWORD... BECAUSE YOU WANTED TO LEARN SWORDS-MANSHIP?

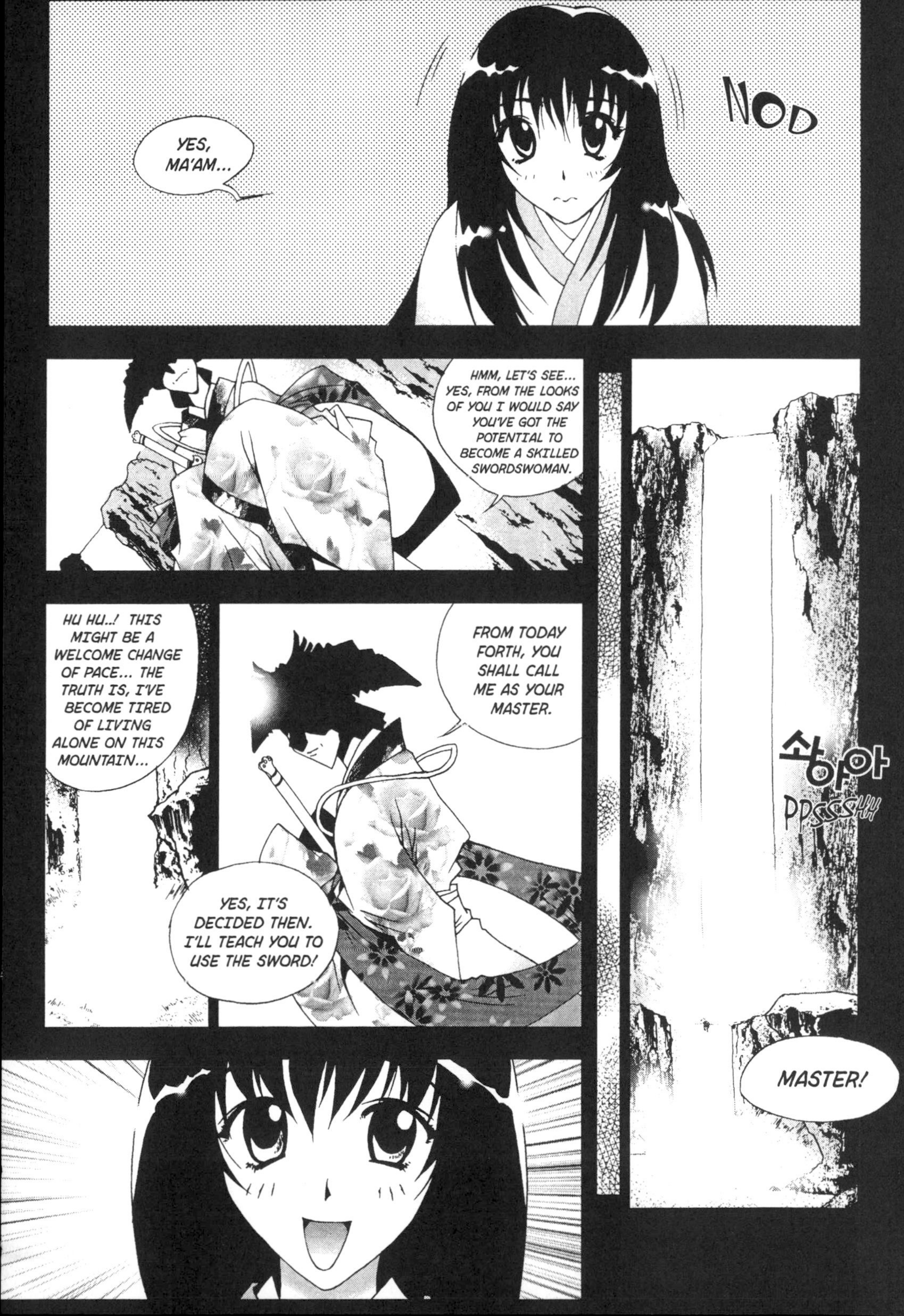
NOD
YES, MA'AM...
HMM, LET'S SEE... YES, FROM THE LOOKS OF YOU I WOULD SAY YOU'VE GOT THE POTENTIAL TO BECOME A SKILLED SWORDSWOMAN.
쏴아아
PPSSSSHH
FROM TODAY FORTH, YOU SHALL CALL ME AS YOUR MASTER.
HU HU..! THIS MIGHT BE A WELCOME CHANGE OF PACE... THE TRUTH IS, I'VE BECOME TIRED OF LIVING ALONE ON THIS MOUNTAIN...
YES, IT'S DECIDED THEN. I'LL TEACH YOU TO USE THE SWORD!
MASTER!

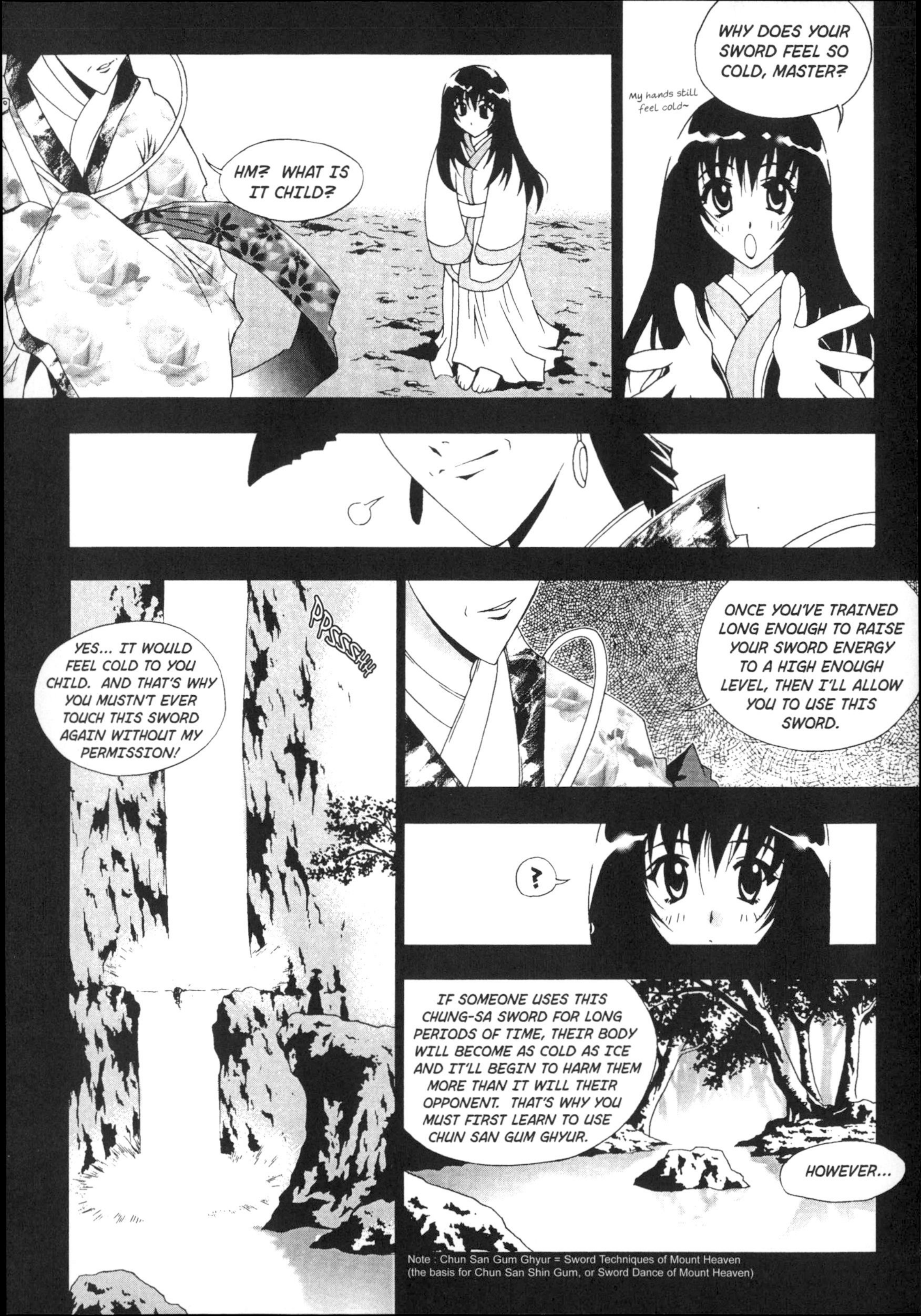
HM? WHAT IS IT CHILD?
WHY DOES YOUR SWORD FEEL SO COLD, MASTER?
My hands still feel cold~
YES... IT WOULD FEEL COLD TO YOU CHILD. AND THAT'S WHY YOU MUSTN'T EVER TOUCH THIS SWORD AGAIN WITHOUT MY PERMISSION!
PPSSSSH!!!
ONCE YOU'VE TRAINED LONG ENOUGH TO RAISE YOUR SWORD ENERGY TO A HIGH ENOUGH LEVEL, THEN I'LL ALLOW YOU TO USE THIS SWORD.
?
IF SOMEONE USES THIS CHUNG-SA SWORD FOR LONG PERIODS OF TIME, THEIR BODY WILL BECOME AS COLD AS ICE AND IT'LL BEGIN TO HARM THEM MORE THAN IT WILL THEIR OPPONENT. THAT'S WHY YOU MUST FIRST LEARN TO USE CHUN SAN GUM GHYUR.
HOWEVER...

Note : Chun San Gum Ghyur = Sword Techniques of Mount Heaven
(the basis for Chun San Shin Gum, or Sword Dance of Mount Heaven)

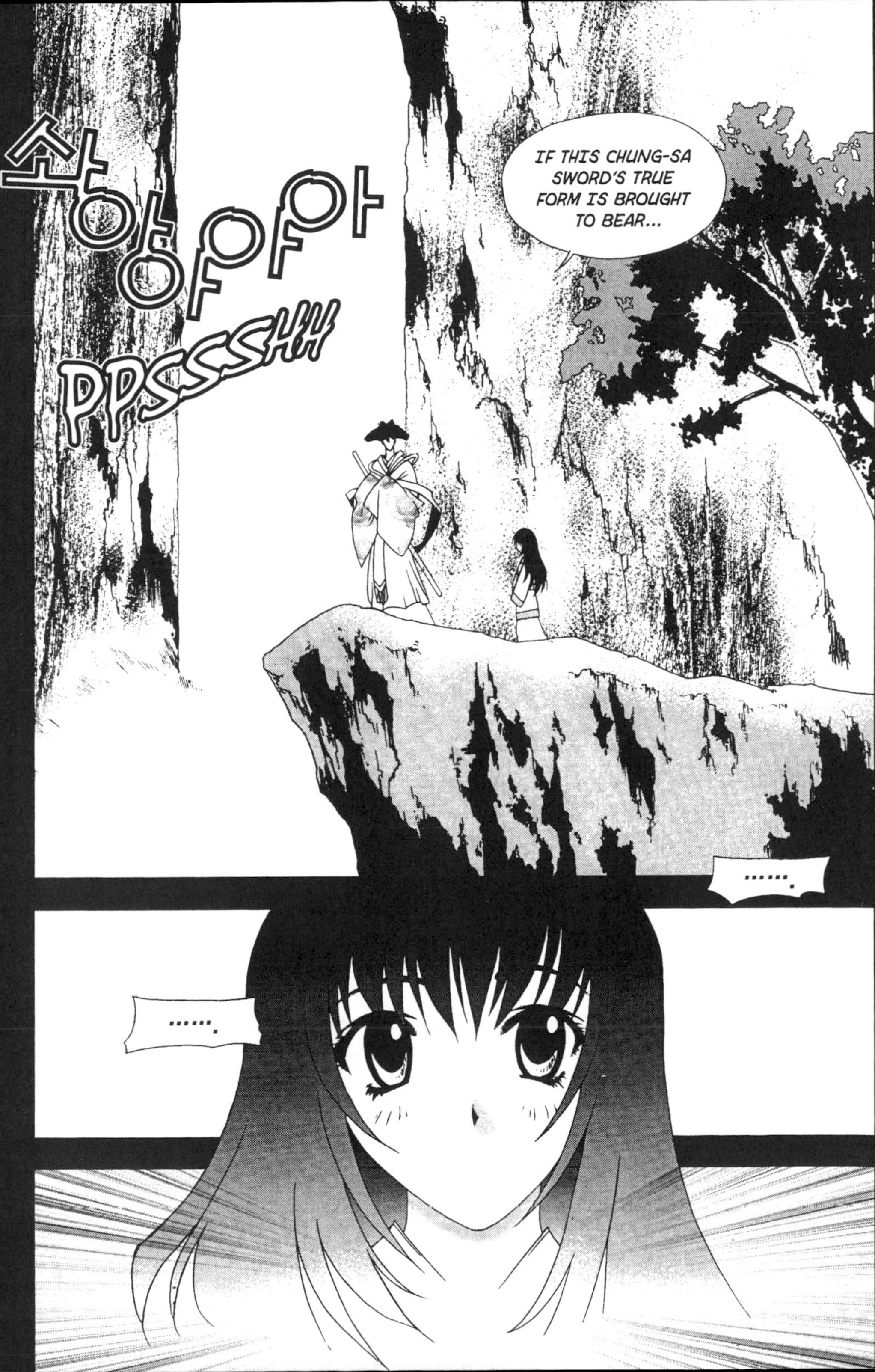
PPSSSHH
IF THIS CHUNG-SA SWORD'S TRUE FORM IS BROUGHT TO BEAR...
......
......

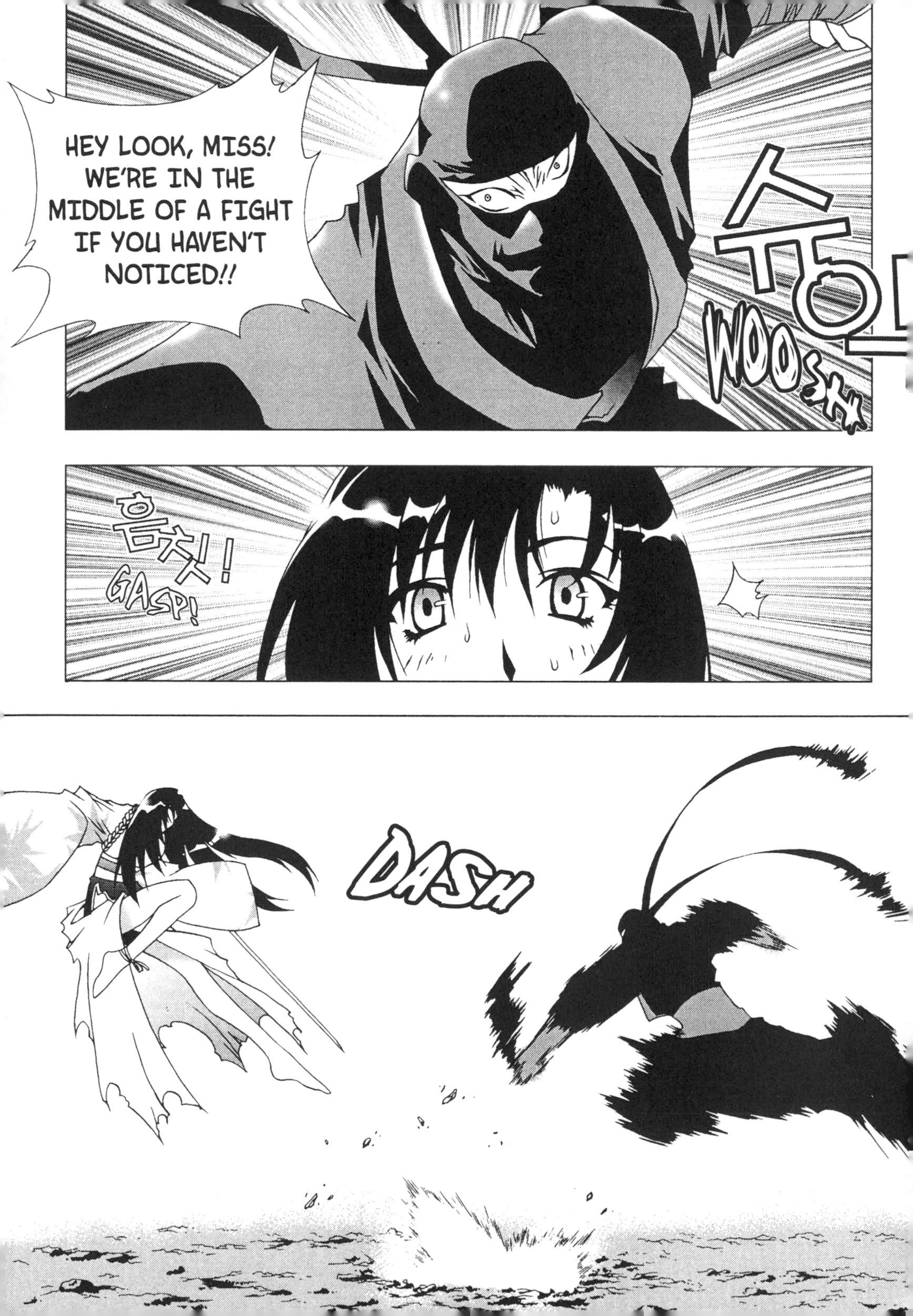
HEY LOOK, MISS! WE'RE IN THE MIDDLE OF A FIGHT IF YOU HAVEN'T NOTICED!!
WOOSH
흠칫!
GASP!
DASH

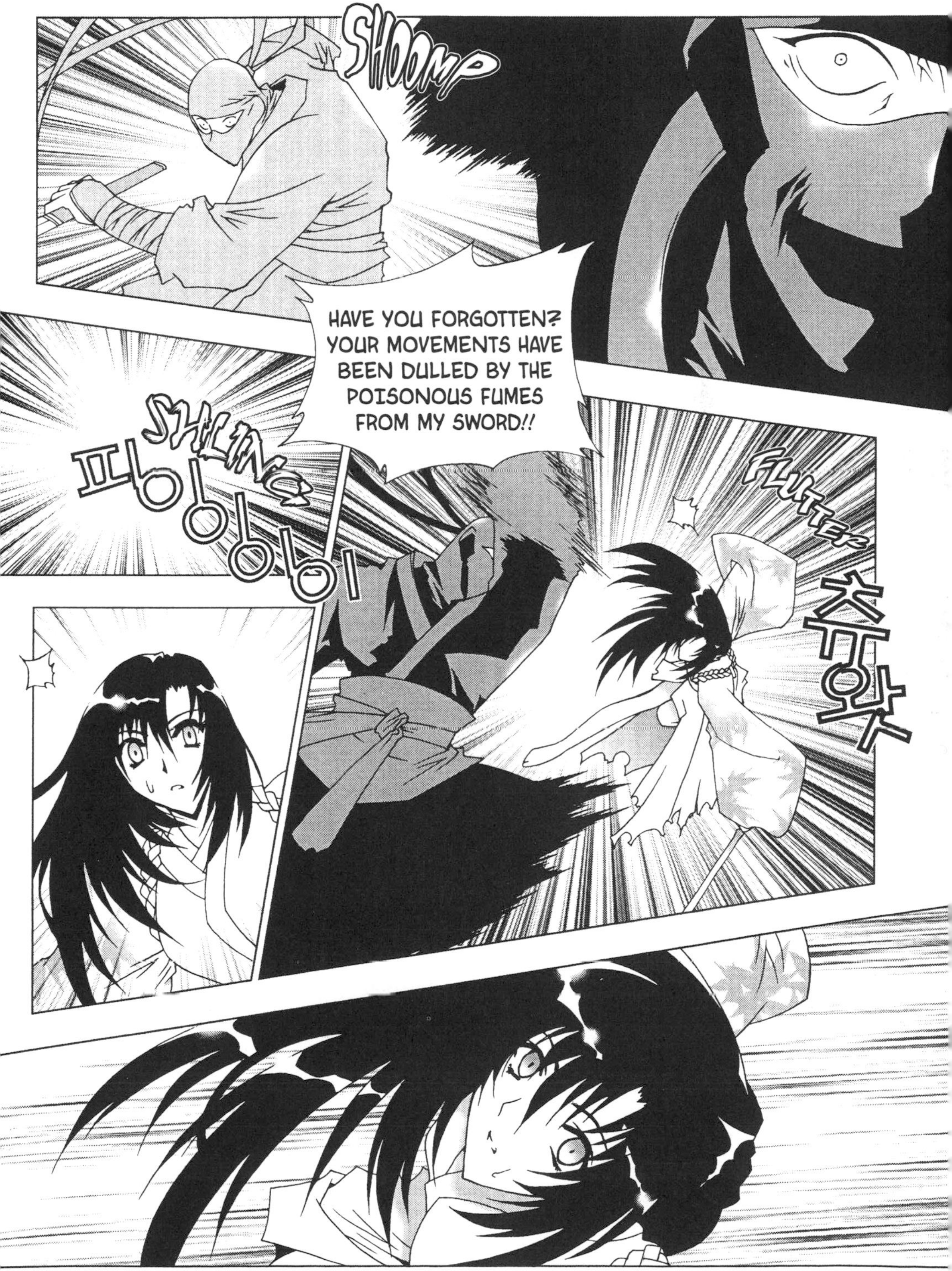
SHOOMP
HAVE YOU FORGOTTEN? YOUR MOVEMENTS HAVE BEEN DULLED BY THE POISONOUS FUMES FROM MY SWORD!!
SHLING
FLUTTER

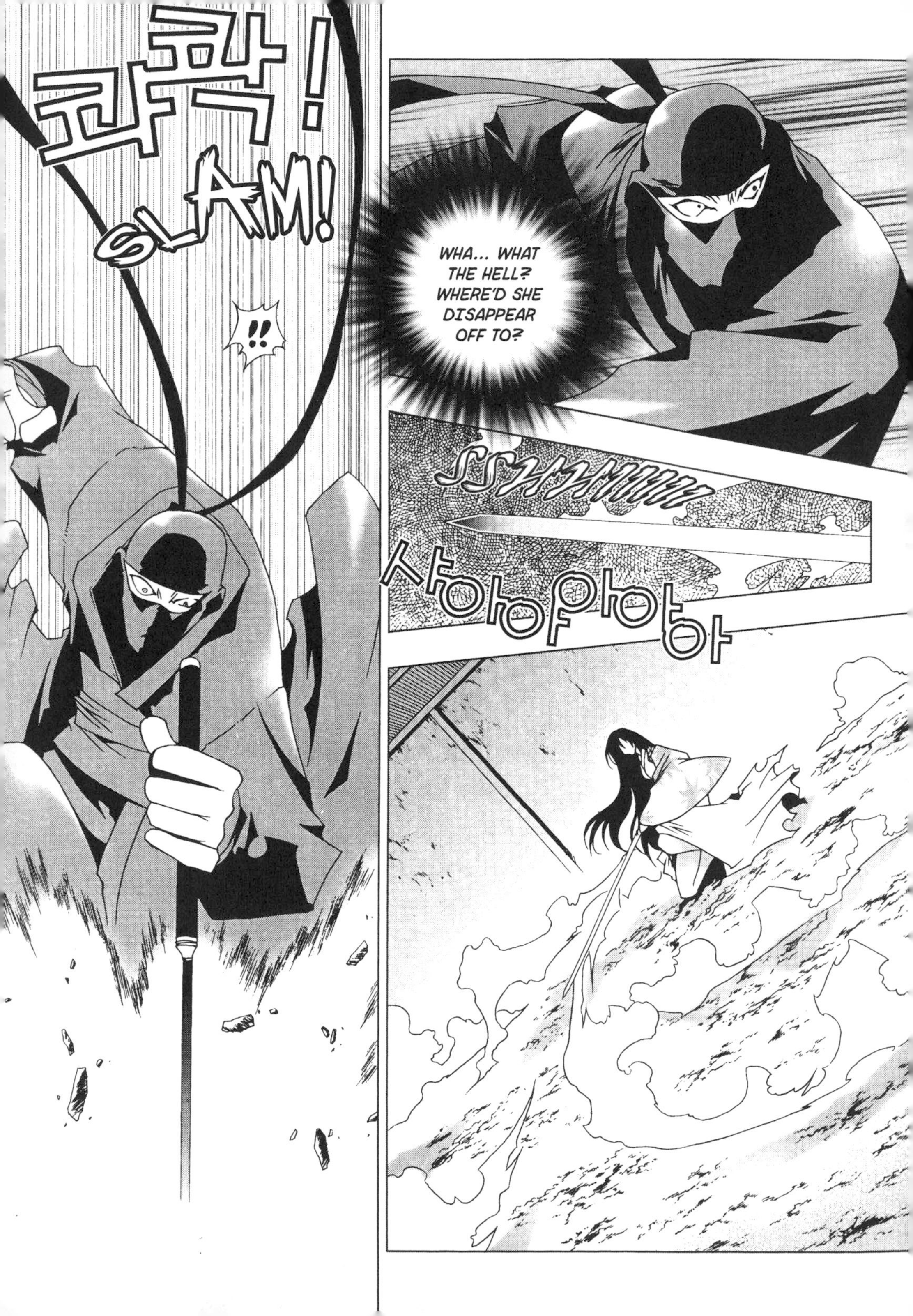
콰콱!
SLAM!
!!
WHA... WHAT THE HELL? WHERE'D SHE DISAPPEAR OFF TO?
SSHHHHHHH
사아아아아아

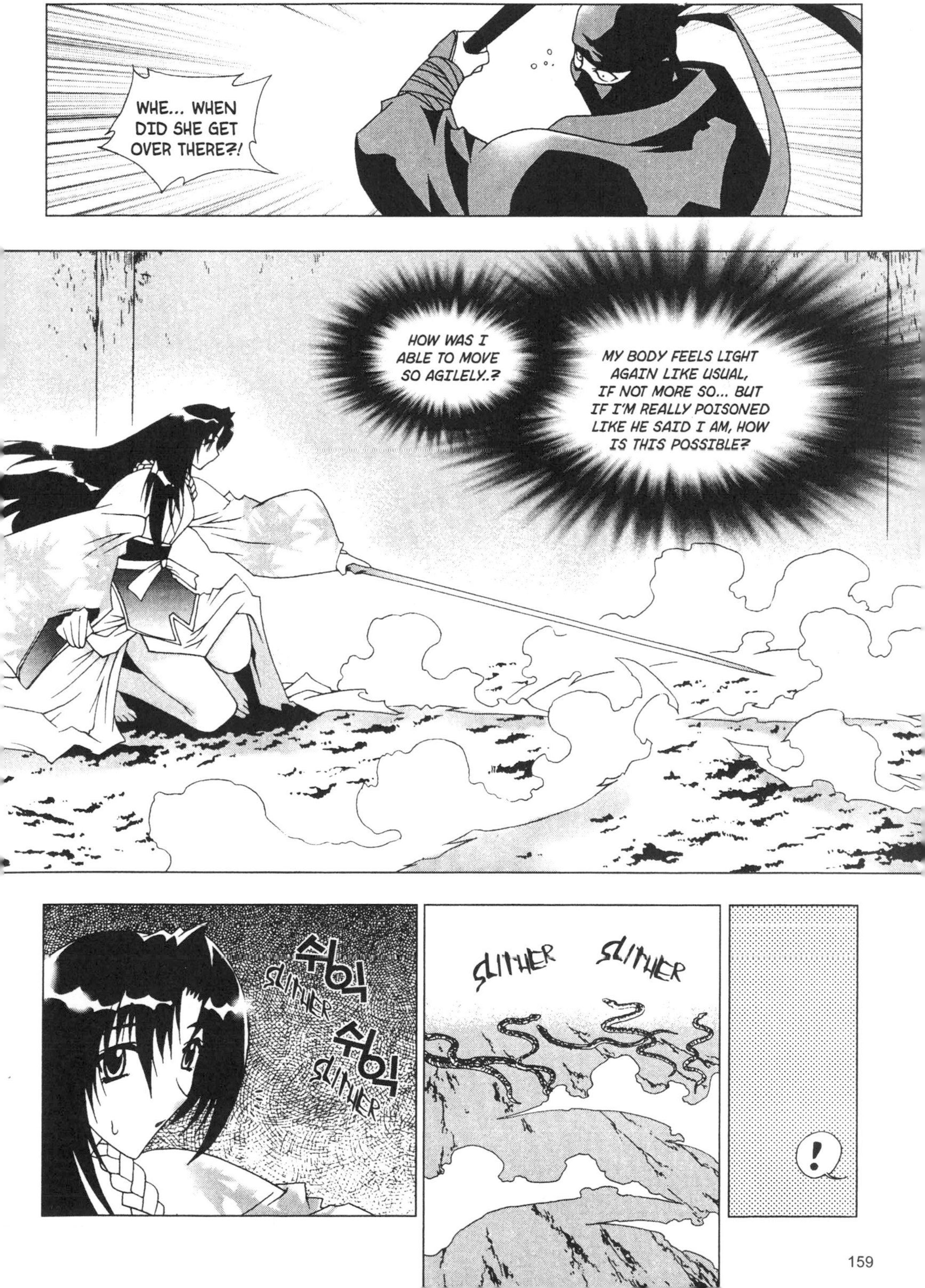
WHE... WHEN DID SHE GET OVER THERE?!
HOW WAS I ABLE TO MOVE SO AGILELY..?
MY BODY FEELS LIGHT AGAIN LIKE USUAL, IF NOT MORE SO... BUT IF I'M REALLY POISONED LIKE HE SAID I AM, HOW IS THIS POSSIBLE?
스윽 SLITHER
스윽 SLITHER
SLITHER
SLITHER
!

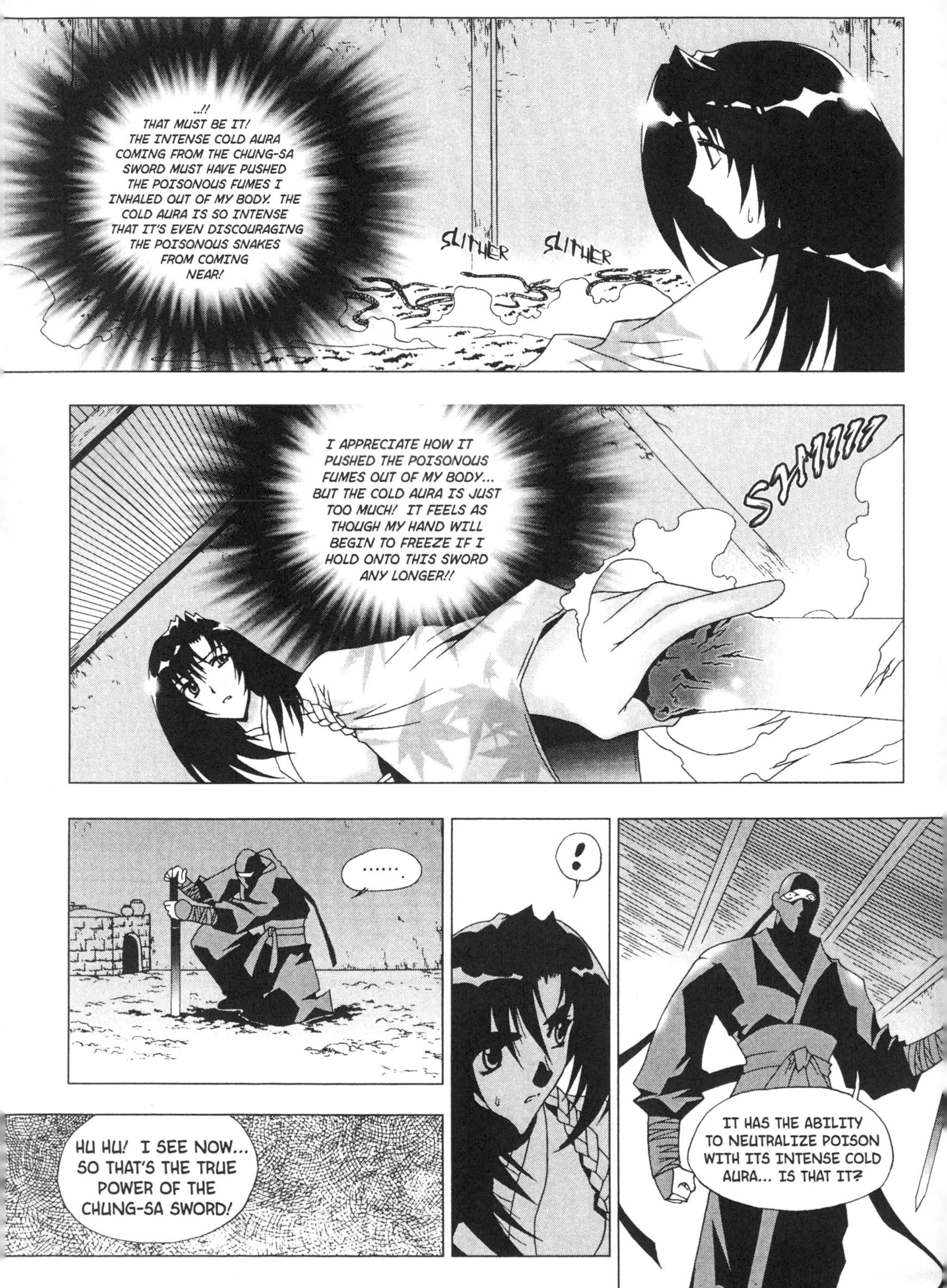
..!! THAT MUST BE IT! THE INTENSE COLD AURA COMING FROM THE CHUNG-SA SWORD MUST HAVE PUSHED THE POISONOUS FUMES I INHALED OUT OF MY BODY. THE COLD AURA IS SO INTENSE THAT IT'S EVEN DISCOURAGING THE POISONOUS SNAKES FROM COMING NEAR!
SLITHER SLITHER
I APPRECIATE HOW IT PUSHED THE POISONOUS FUMES OUT OF MY BODY... BUT THE COLD AURA IS JUST TOO MUCH! IT FEELS AS THOUGH MY HAND WILL BEGIN TO FREEZE IF I HOLD ONTO THIS SWORD ANY LONGER!!
SZZZZZZ
....
!
HU HU! I SEE NOW... SO THAT'S THE TRUE POWER OF THE CHUNG-SA SWORD!
IT HAS THE ABILITY TO NEUTRALIZE POISON WITH ITS INTENSE COLD AURA... IS THAT IT?

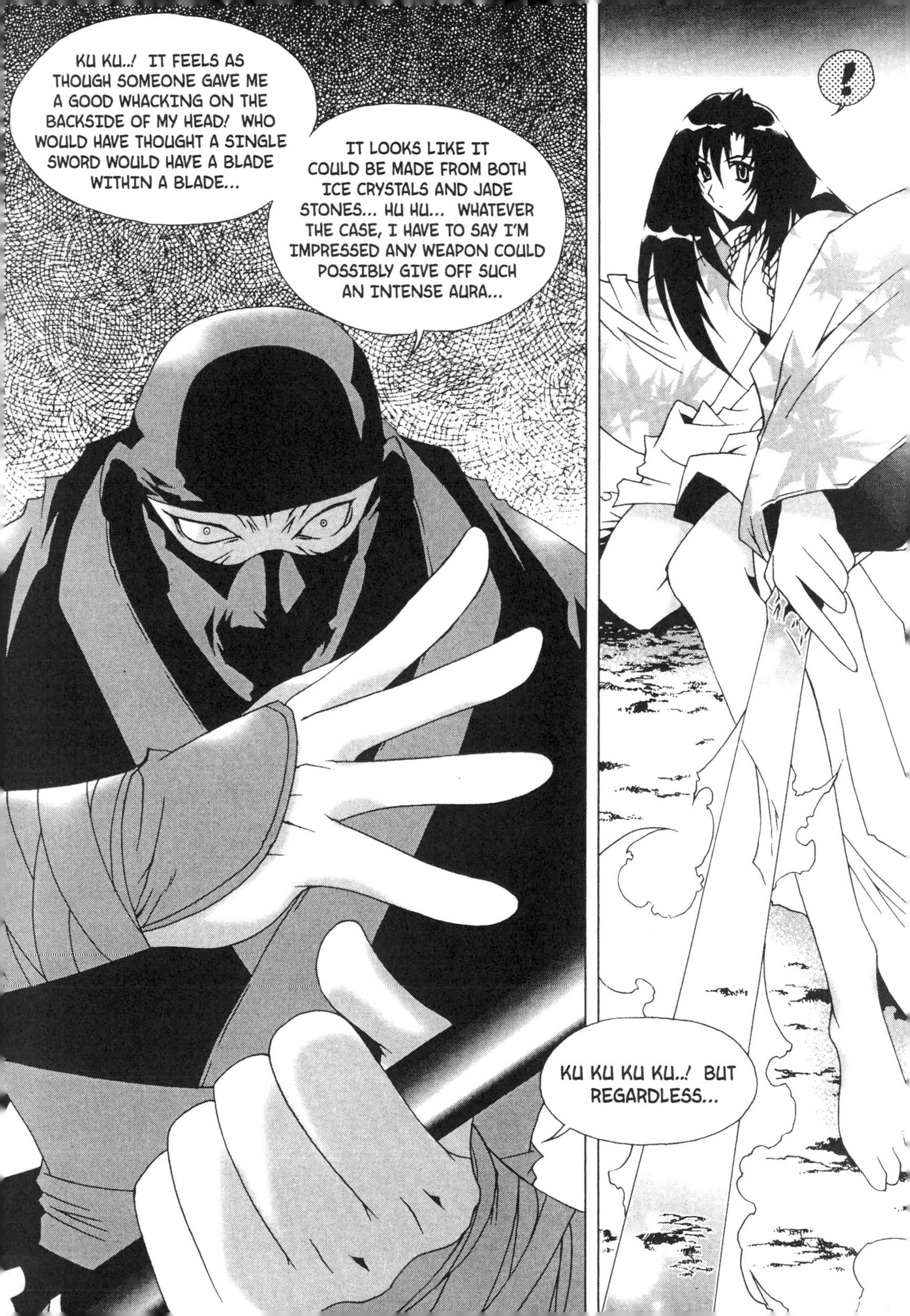
KU KU..! IT FEELS AS THOUGH SOMEONE GAVE ME A GOOD WHACKING ON THE BACKSIDE OF MY HEAD! WHO WOULD HAVE THOUGHT A SINGLE SWORD WOULD HAVE A BLADE WITHIN A BLADE...
IT LOOKS LIKE IT COULD BE MADE FROM BOTH ICE CRYSTALS AND JADE STONES... HU HU... WHATEVER THE CASE, I HAVE TO SAY I'M IMPRESSED ANY WEAPON COULD POSSIBLY GIVE OFF SUCH AN INTENSE AURA...
!
KU KU KU KU..! BUT REGARDLESS...

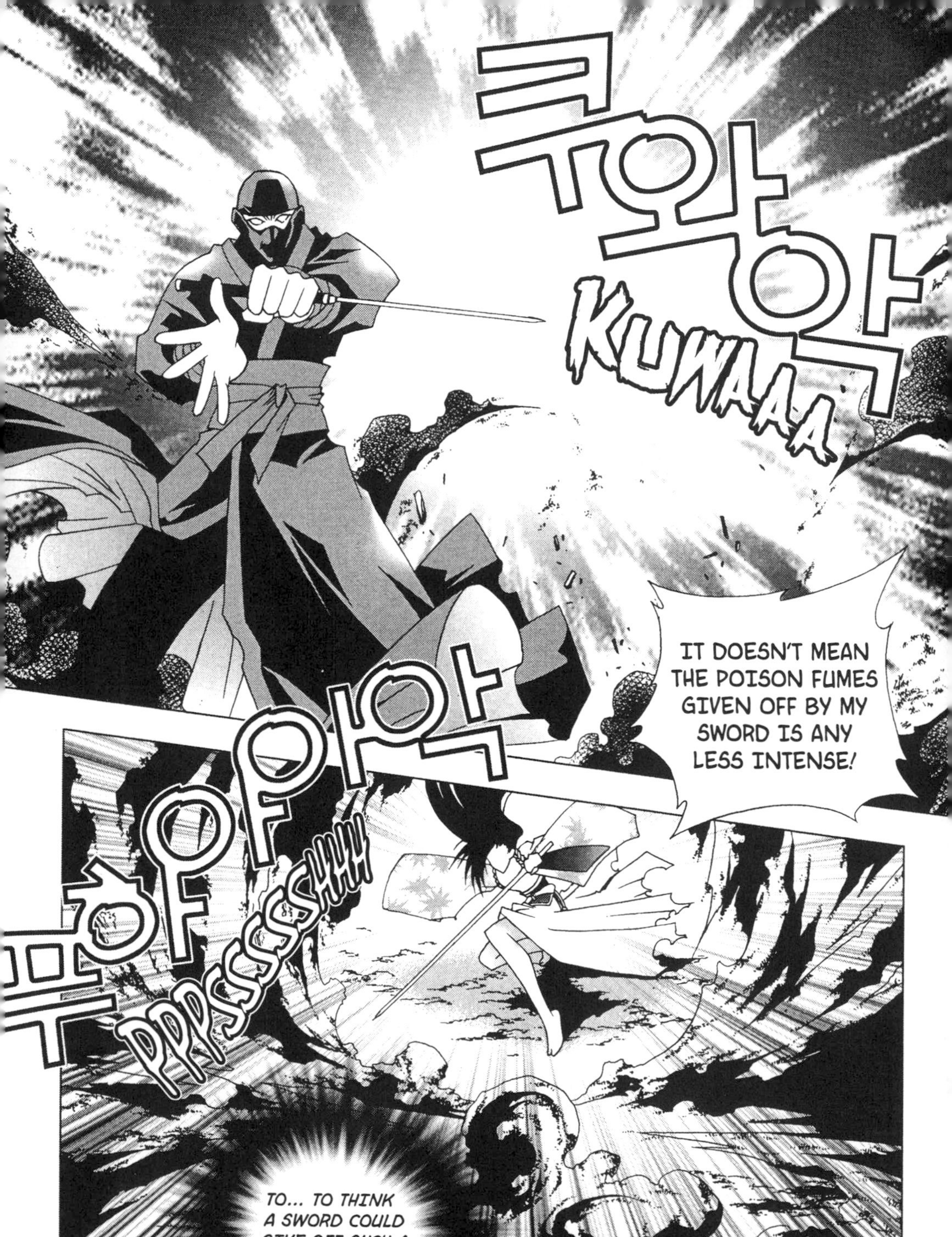
쿠와아
KUWAAA
IT DOESN'T MEAN THE POISON FUMES GIVEN OFF BY MY SWORD IS ANY LESS INTENSE!
푸쉬이악
PPPSSSSSHHH
TO... TO THINK A SWORD COULD GIVE OFF SUCH A GREAT AMOUNT OF POISON!!

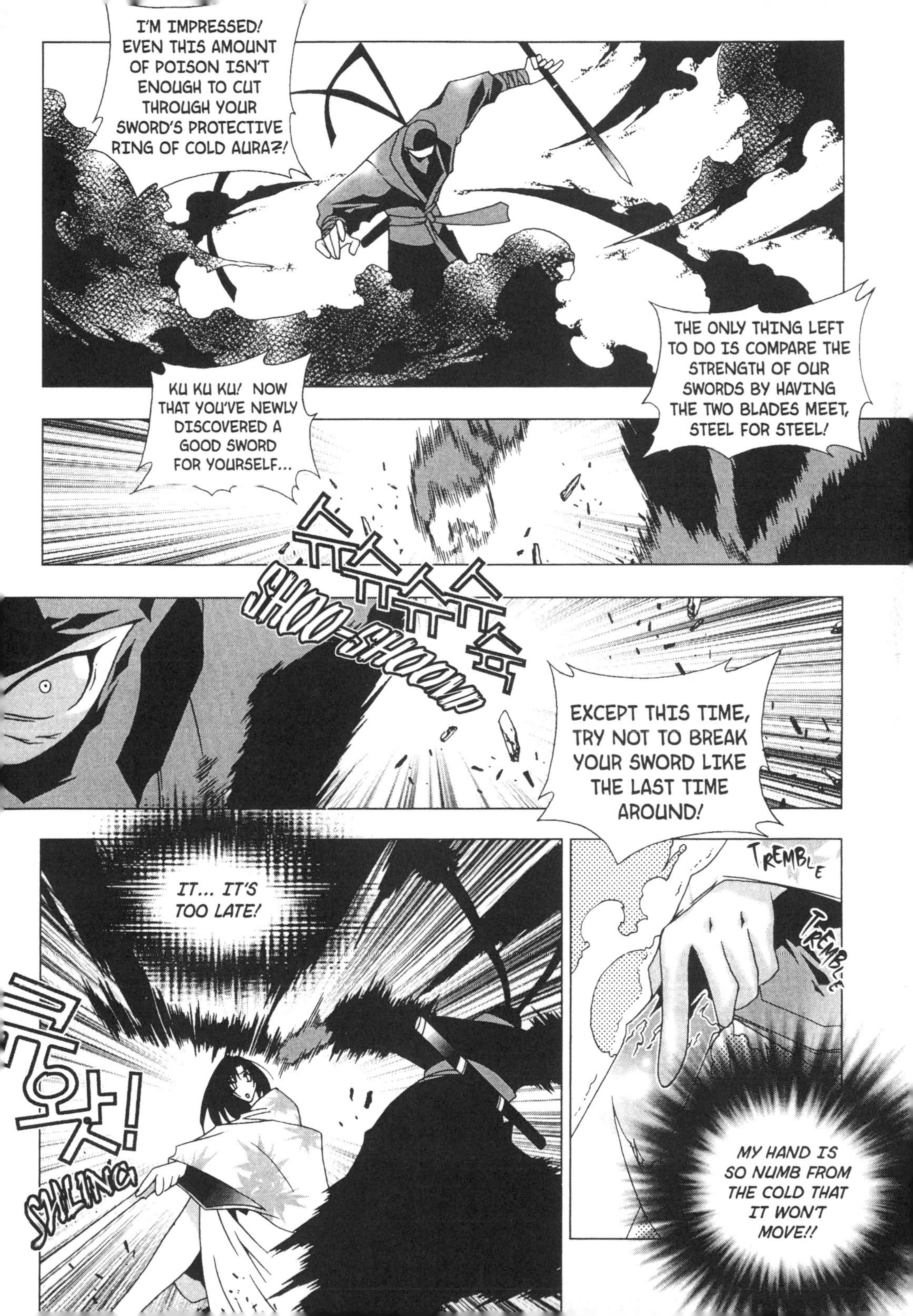
I'M IMPRESSED! EVEN THIS AMOUNT OF POISON ISN'T ENOUGH TO CUT THROUGH YOUR SWORD'S PROTECTIVE RING OF COLD AURA?!
KU KU KU! NOW THAT YOU'VE NEWLY DISCOVERED A GOOD SWORD FOR YOURSELF...
THE ONLY THING LEFT TO DO IS COMPARE THE STRENGTH OF OUR SWORDS BY HAVING THE TWO BLADES MEET, STEEL FOR STEEL!
SHOO-SHOOMP
EXCEPT THIS TIME, TRY NOT TO BREAK YOUR SWORD LIKE THE LAST TIME AROUND!
IT... IT'S TOO LATE!
SHLING
TREMBLE
TREMBLE
MY HAND IS SO NUMB FROM THE COLD THAT IT WON'T MOVE!!

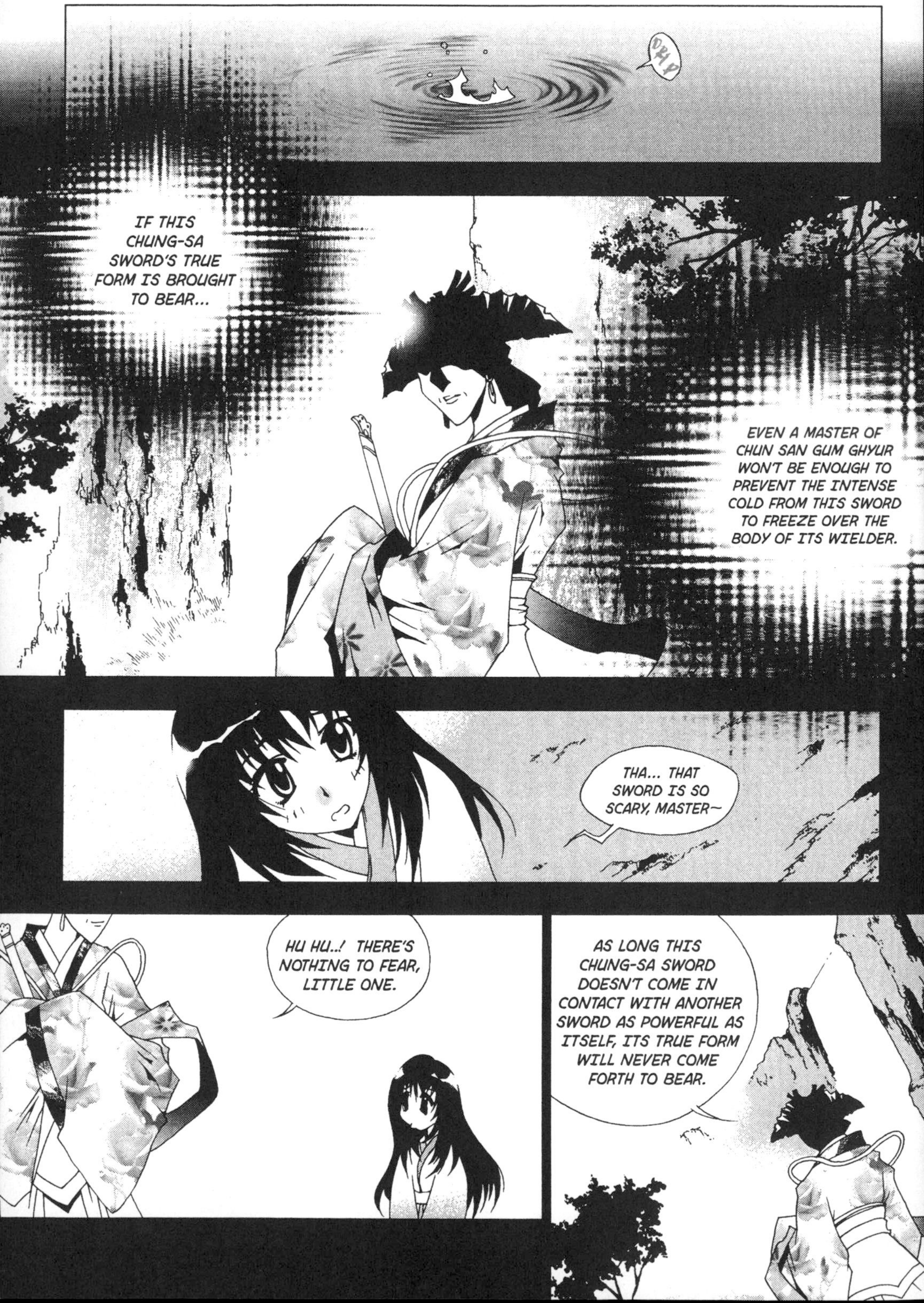
IF THIS CHUNG-SA SWORD'S TRUE FORM IS BROUGHT TO BEAR...
EVEN A MASTER OF CHUN SAN GUM GHYUR WON'T BE ENOUGH TO PREVENT THE INTENSE COLD FROM THIS SWORD TO FREEZE OVER THE BODY OF ITS WIELDER.
THA... THAT SWORD IS SO SCARY, MASTER~
HU HU..! THERE'S NOTHING TO FEAR, LITTLE ONE.
AS LONG THIS CHUNG-SA SWORD DOESN'T COME IN CONTACT WITH ANOTHER SWORD AS POWERFUL AS ITSELF, ITS TRUE FORM WILL NEVER COME FORTH TO BEAR.

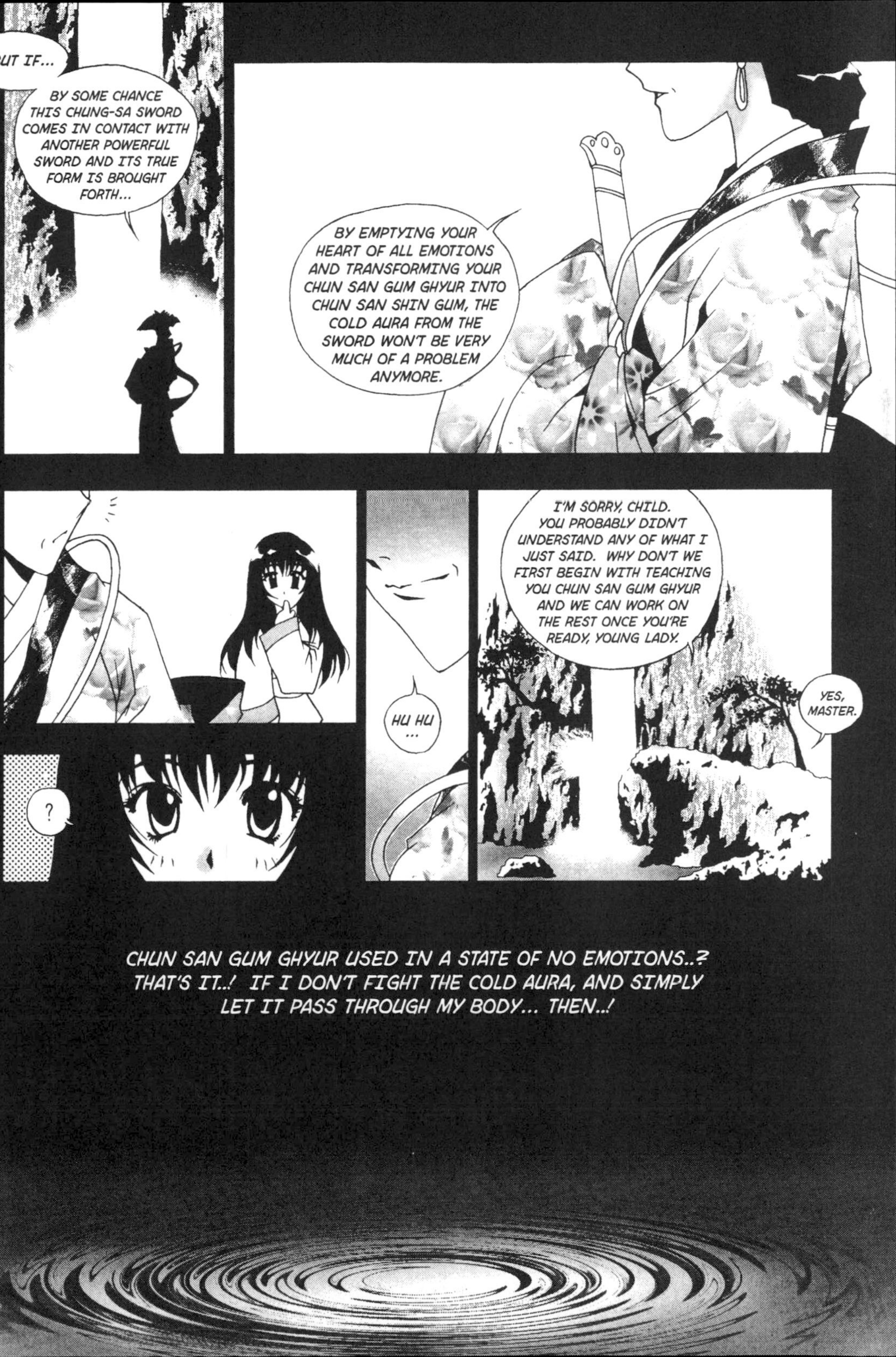
BUT IF...
BY SOME CHANCE THIS CHUNG-SA SWORD COMES IN CONTACT WITH ANOTHER POWERFUL SWORD AND ITS TRUE FORM IS BROUGHT FORTH...
BY EMPTYING YOUR HEART OF ALL EMOTIONS AND TRANSFORMING YOUR CHUN SAN GUM GHYUR INTO CHUN SAN SHIN GUM, THE COLD AURA FROM THE SWORD WON'T BE VERY MUCH OF A PROBLEM ANYMORE.
HU HU ...
I'M SORRY, CHILD. YOU PROBABLY DIDN'T UNDERSTAND ANY OF WHAT I JUST SAID. WHY DON'T WE FIRST BEGIN WITH TEACHING YOU CHUN SAN GUM GHYUR AND WE CAN WORK ON THE REST ONCE YOU'RE READY, YOUNG LADY.
YES, MASTER.
?
CHUN SAN GUM GHYUR USED IN A STATE OF NO EMOTIONS..?
THAT'S IT..! IF I DON'T FIGHT THE COLD AURA, AND SIMPLY LET IT PASS THROUGH MY BODY... THEN..!

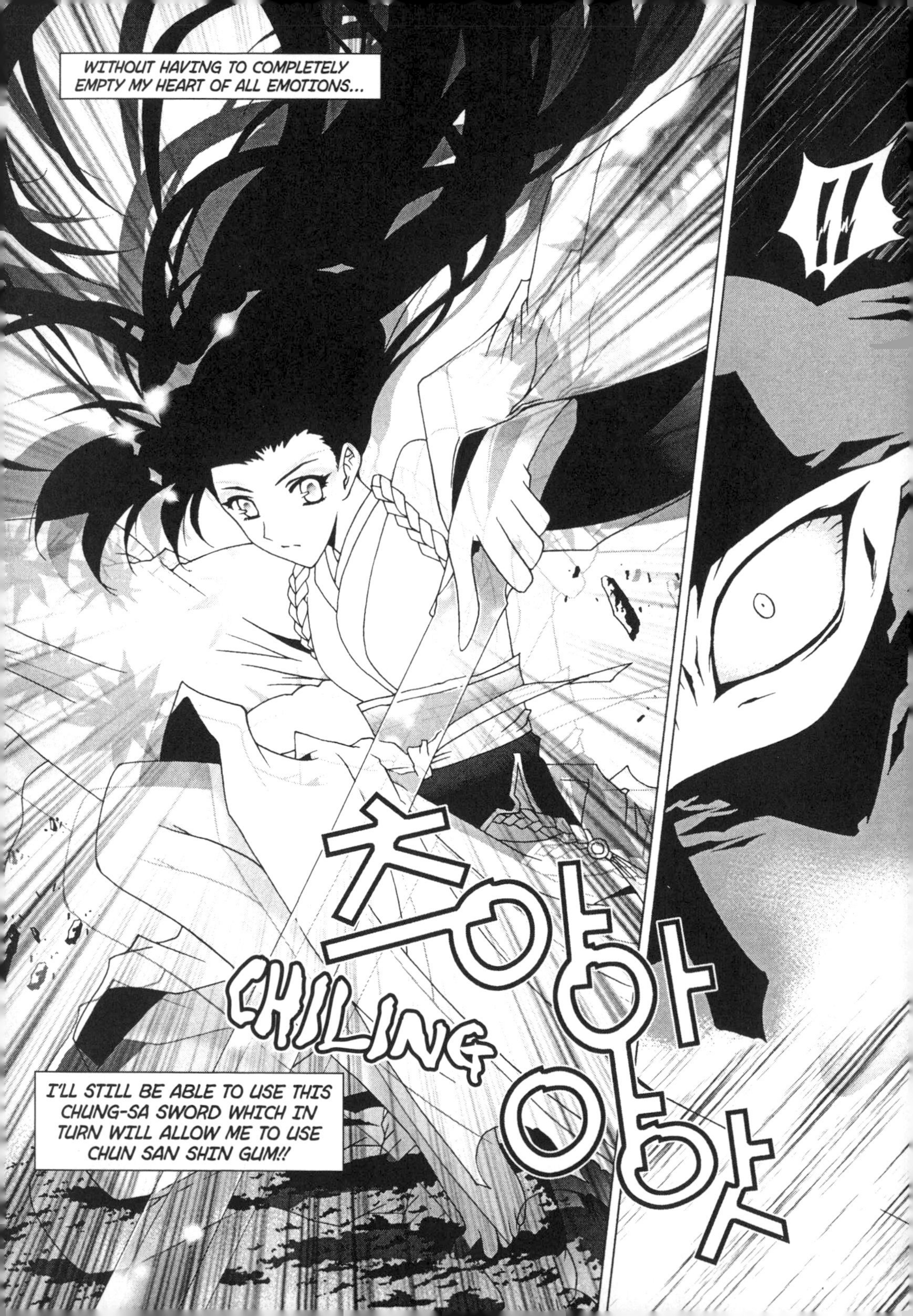
WITHOUT HAVING TO COMPLETELY EMPTY MY HEART OF ALL EMOTIONS...
!!
CHILING
I'LL STILL BE ABLE TO USE THIS CHUNG-SA SWORD WHICH IN TURN WILL ALLOW ME TO USE CHUN SAN SHIN GUM!!

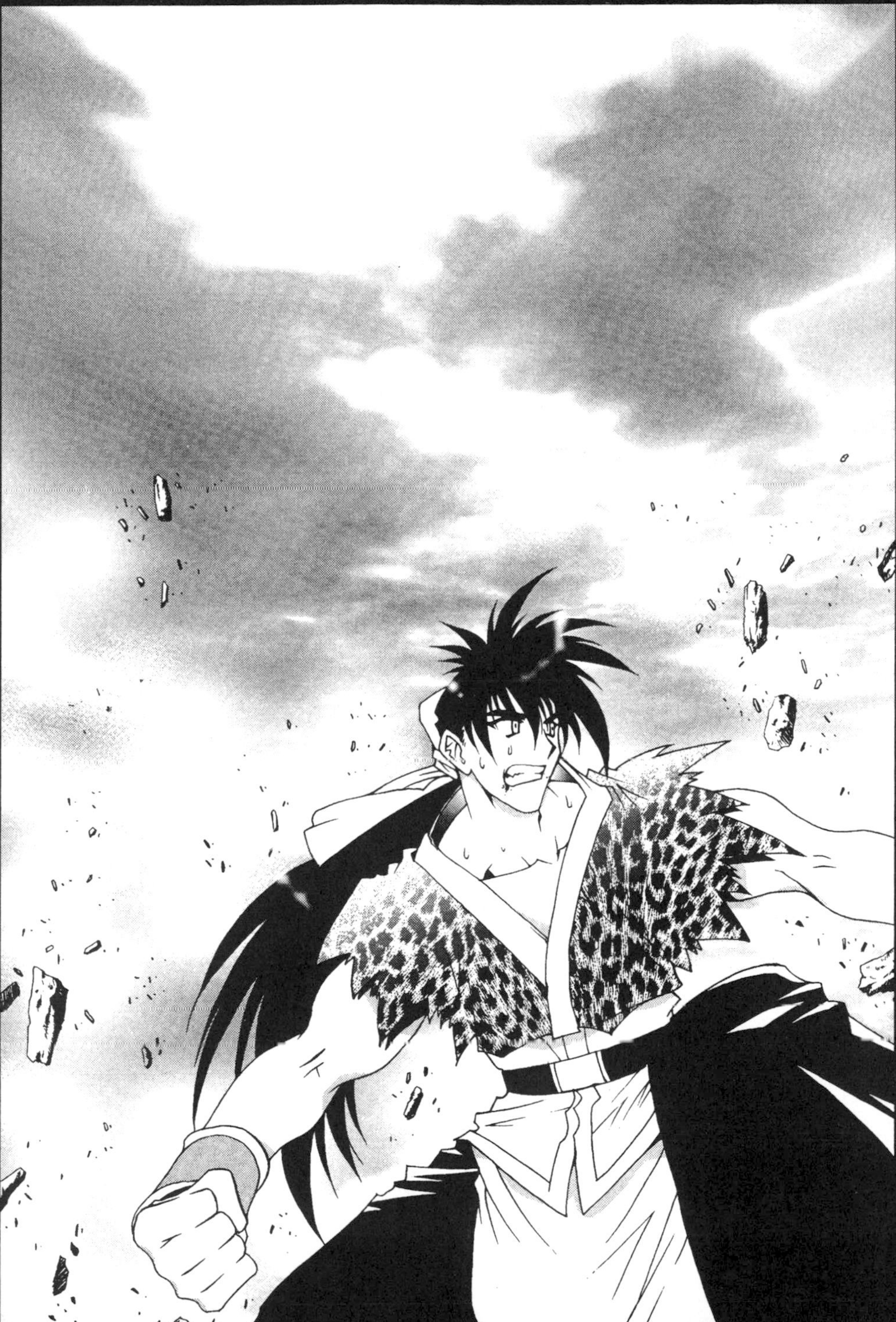

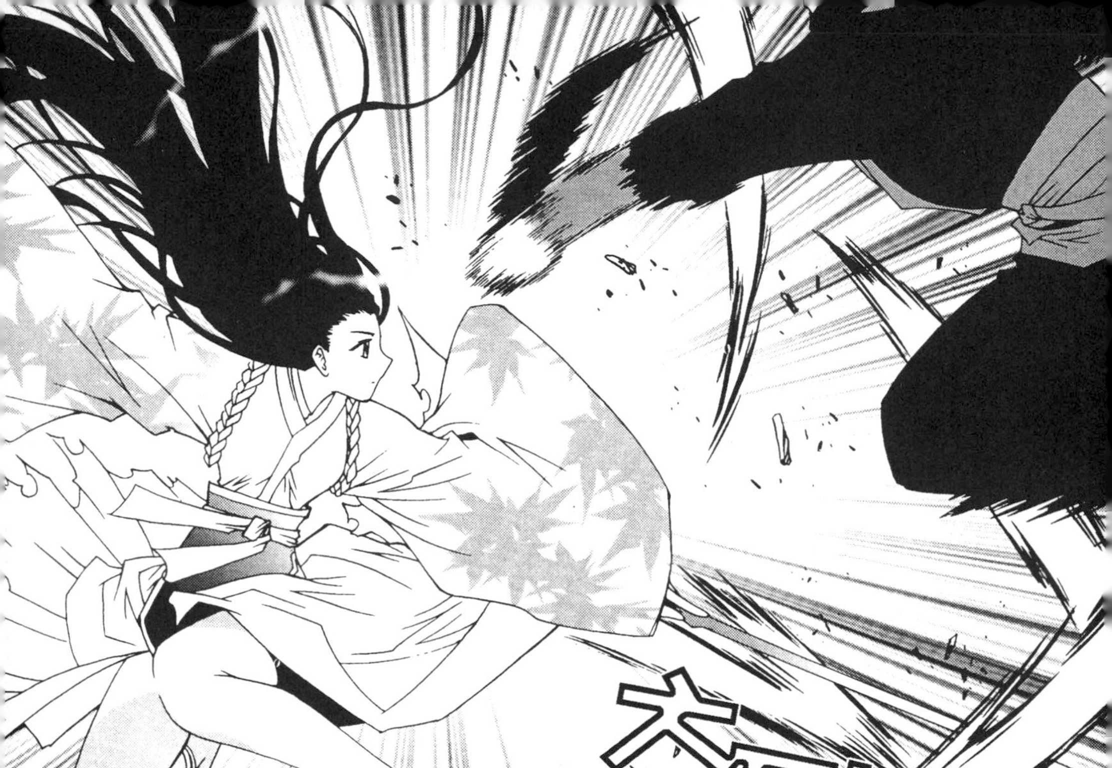
SHLING!

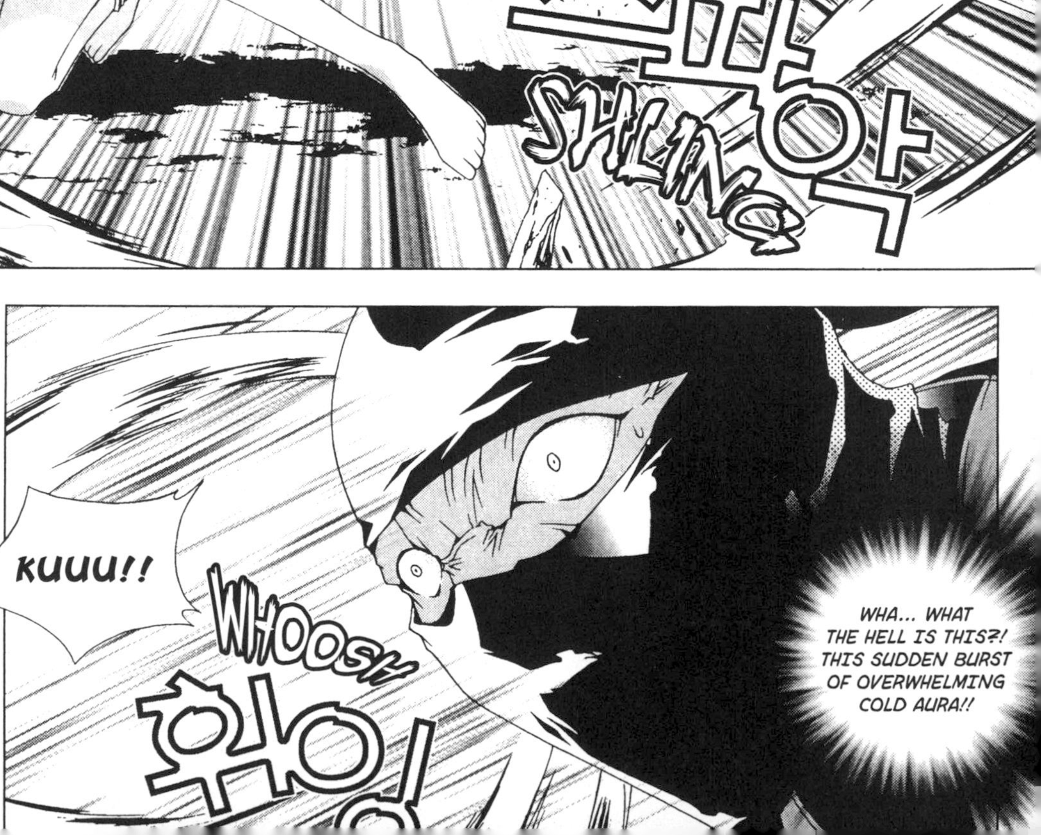
WHA... WHAT THE HELL IS THIS?! THIS SUDDEN BURST OF OVERWHELMING COLD AURA!!
WHOOSH
KUUU!!

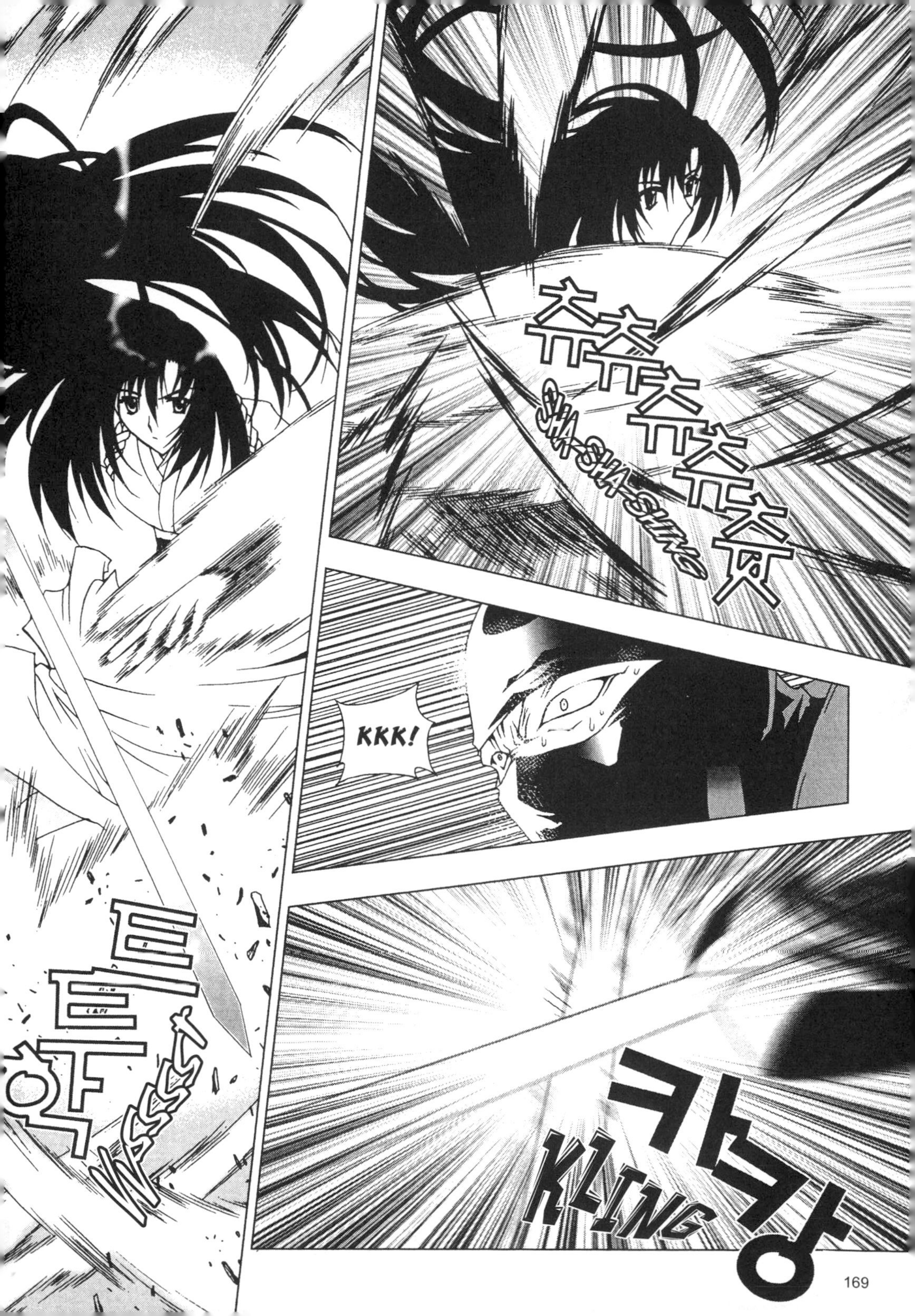
SHA-SHA-SHING
KKK!
KLING

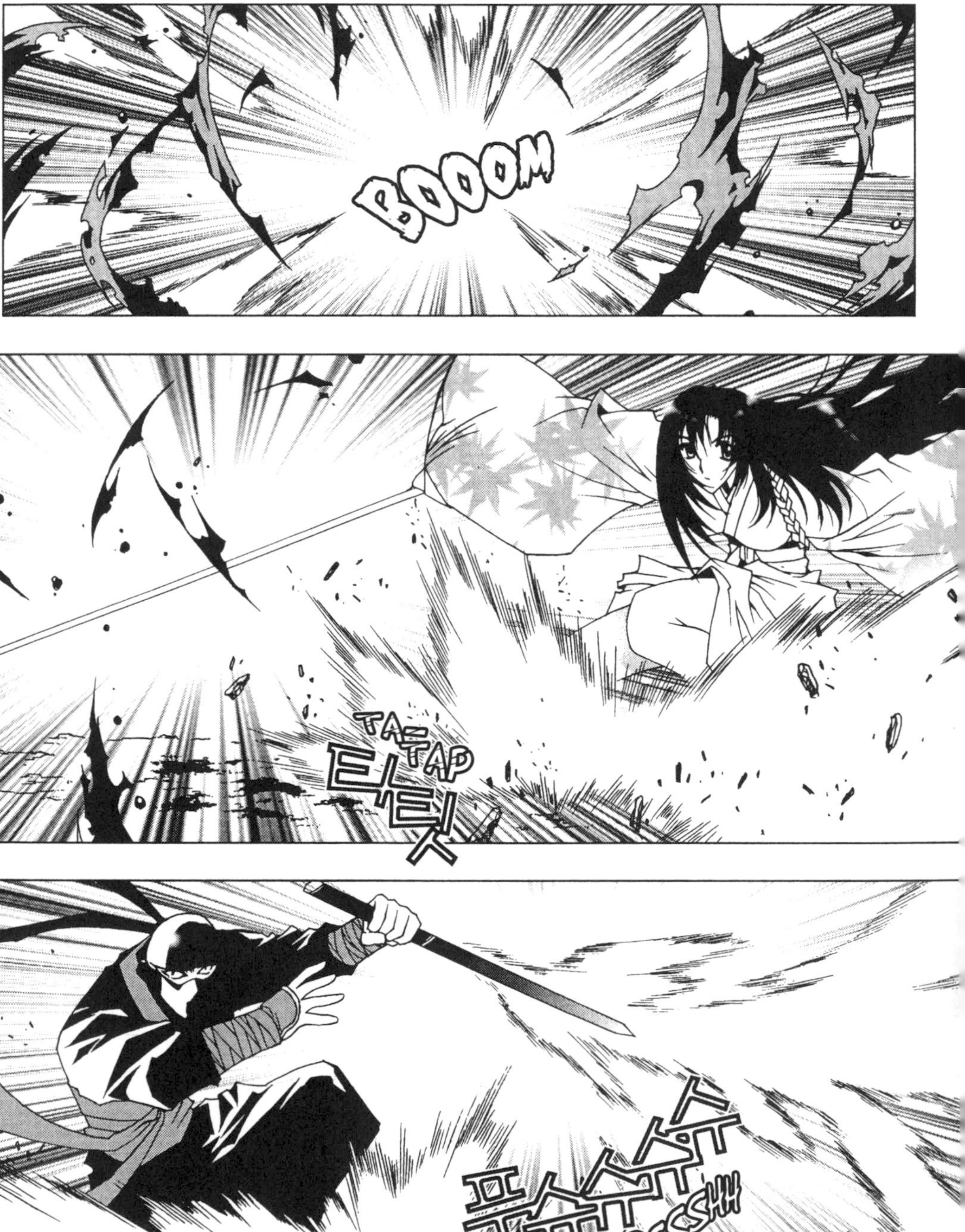
BOOOM
TA-TAP
PPSSSHH

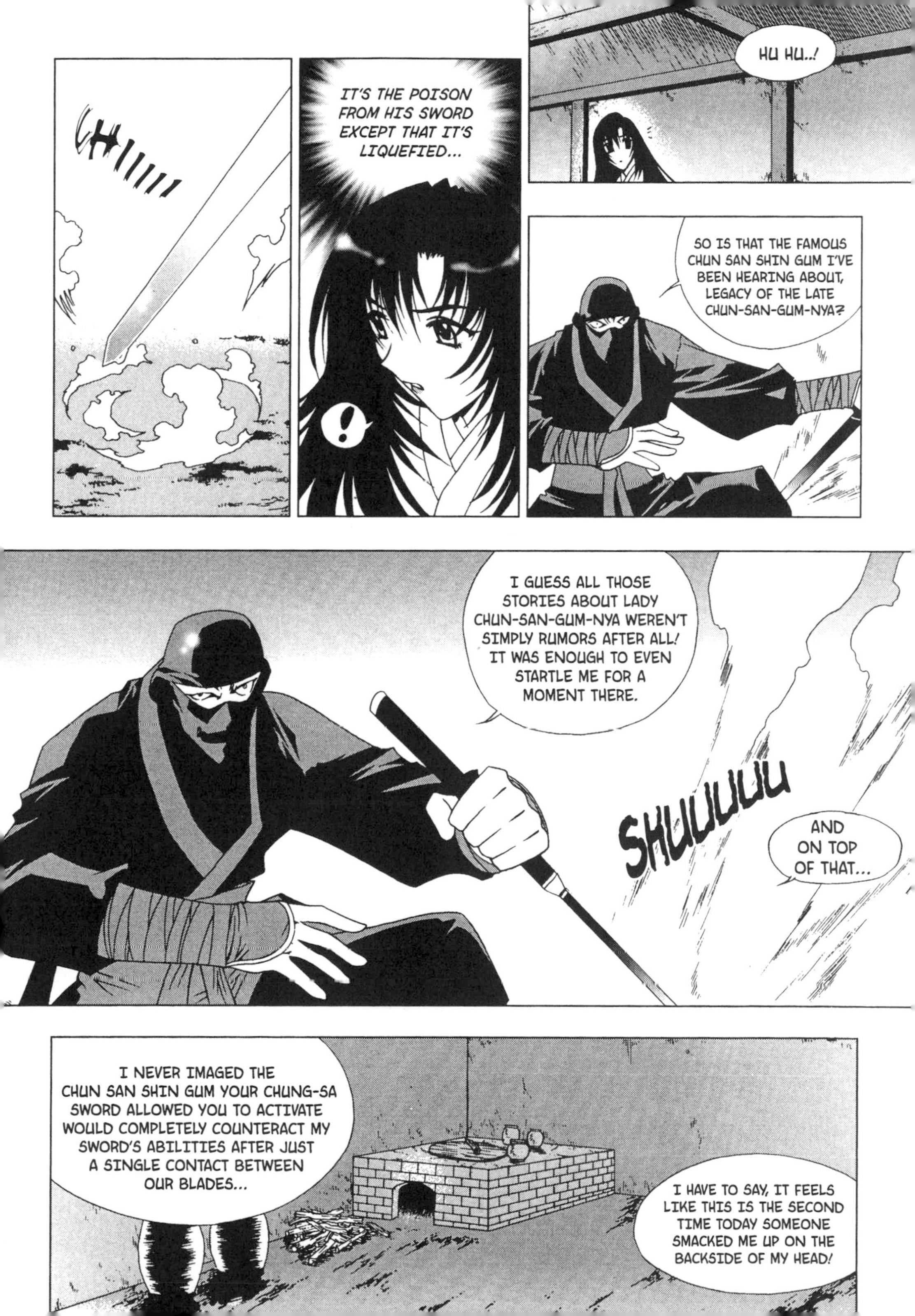
CHIIIIII
IT'S THE POISON FROM HIS SWORD EXCEPT THAT IT'S LIQUEFIED...
!
HU HU..!
SO IS THAT THE FAMOUS CHUN SAN SHIN GUM I'VE BEEN HEARING ABOUT, LEGACY OF THE LATE CHUN-SAN-GUM-NYA?
I GUESS ALL THOSE STORIES ABOUT LADY CHUN-SAN-GUM-NYA WEREN'T SIMPLY RUMORS AFTER ALL! IT WAS ENOUGH TO EVEN STARTLE ME FOR A MOMENT THERE.
SHUUUUU
AND ON TOP OF THAT...
I NEVER IMAGED THE CHUN SAN SHIN GUM YOUR CHUNG-SA SWORD ALLOWED YOU TO ACTIVATE WOULD COMPLETELY COUNTERACT MY SWORD'S ABILITIES AFTER JUST A SINGLE CONTACT BETWEEN OUR BLADES...
I HAVE TO SAY, IT FEELS LIKE THIS IS THE SECOND TIME TODAY SOMEONE SMACKED ME UP ON THE BACKSIDE OF MY HEAD!

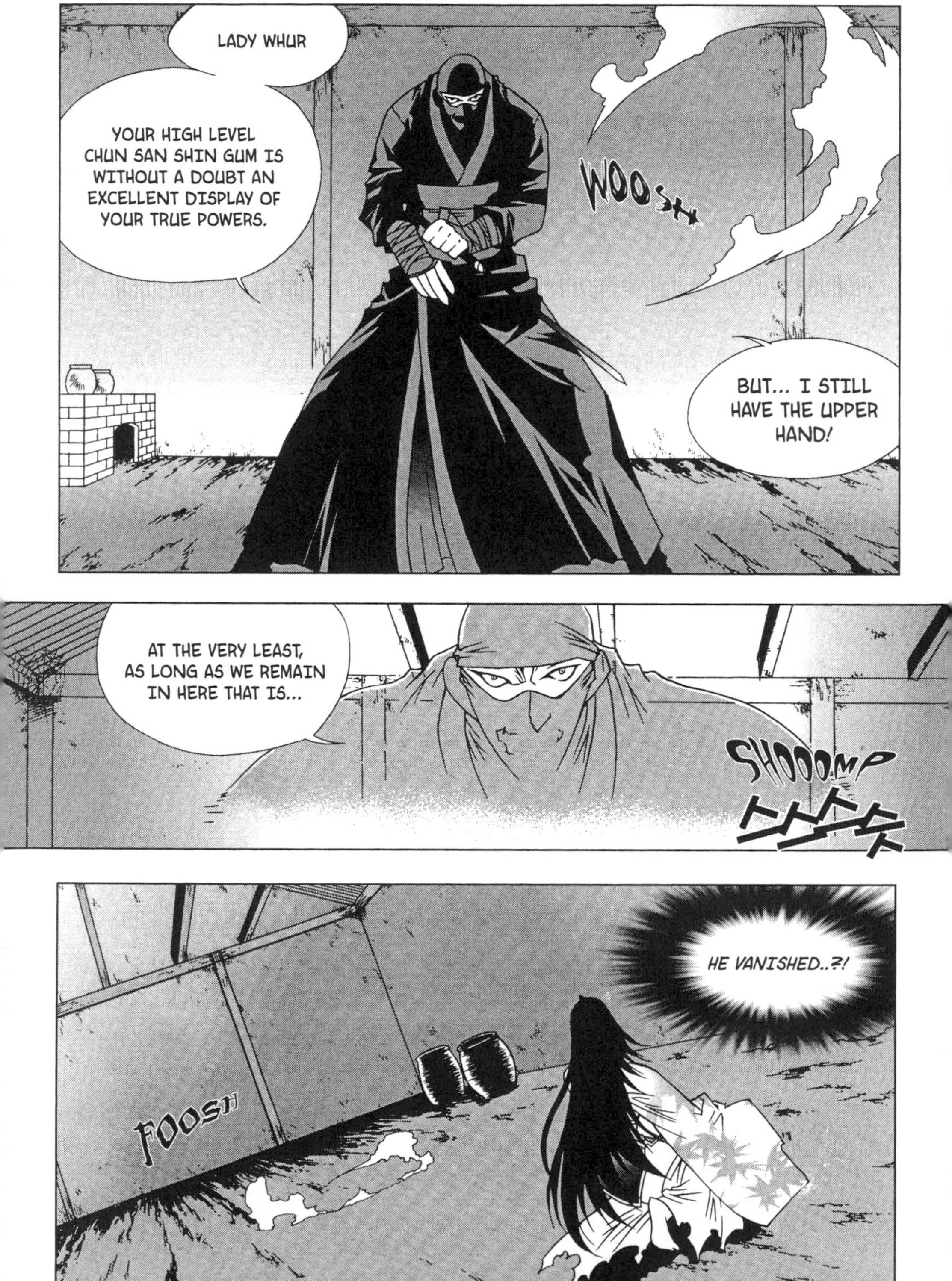
LADY WHUR
YOUR HIGH LEVEL CHUN SAN SHIN GUM IS WITHOUT A DOUBT AN EXCELLENT DISPLAY OF YOUR TRUE POWERS.
WOOSH
BUT... I STILL HAVE THE UPPER HAND!
AT THE VERY LEAST, AS LONG AS WE REMAIN IN HERE THAT IS...
SHOOOMP
HE VANISHED..?!
FOOSH

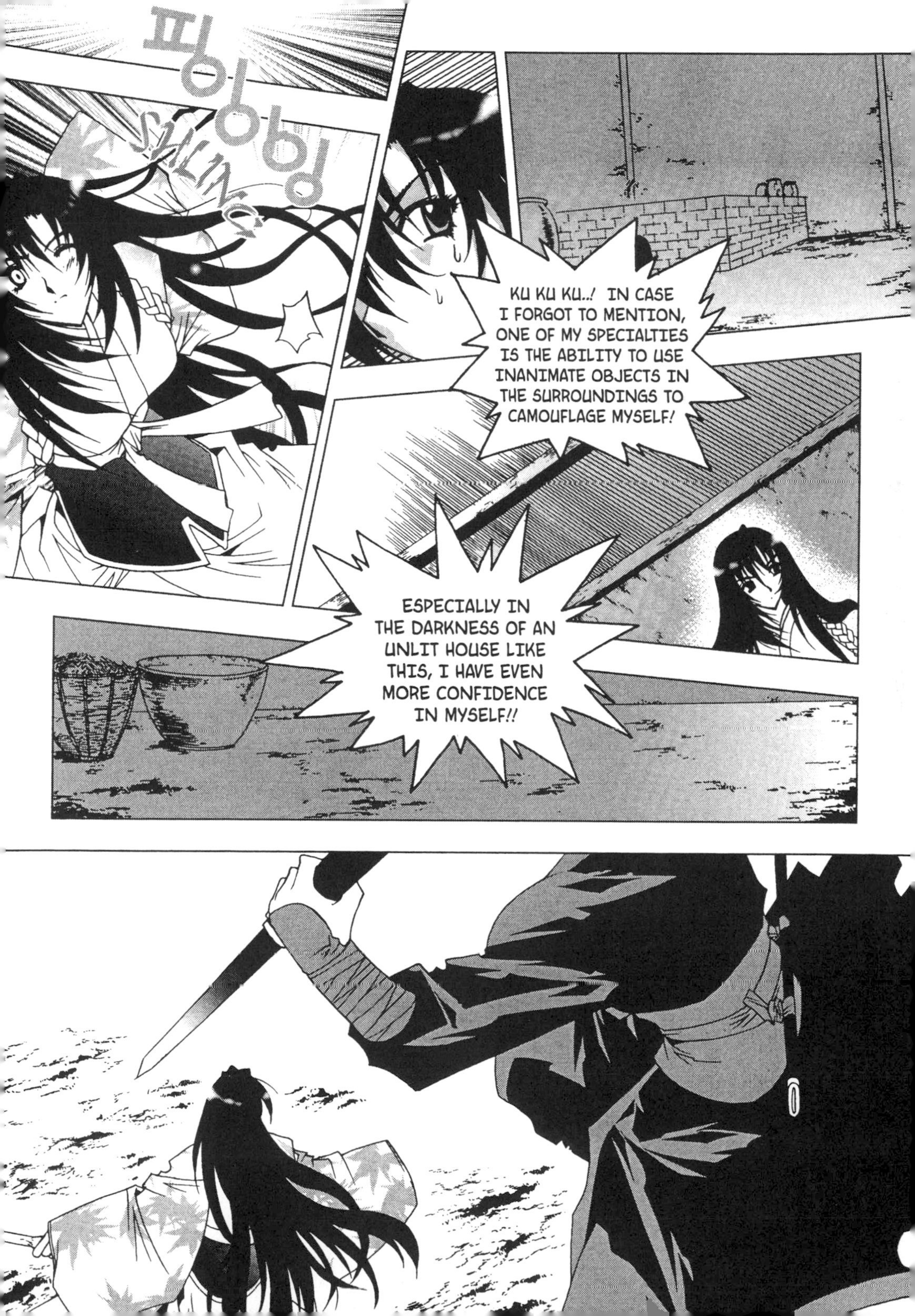
SWING
KU KU KU..! IN CASE I FORGOT TO MENTION, ONE OF MY SPECIALTIES IS THE ABILITY TO USE INANIMATE OBJECTS IN THE SURROUNDINGS TO CAMOUFLAGE MYSELF!
ESPECIALLY IN THE DARKNESS OF AN UNLIT HOUSE LIKE THIS, I HAVE EVEN MORE CONFIDENCE IN MYSELF!!

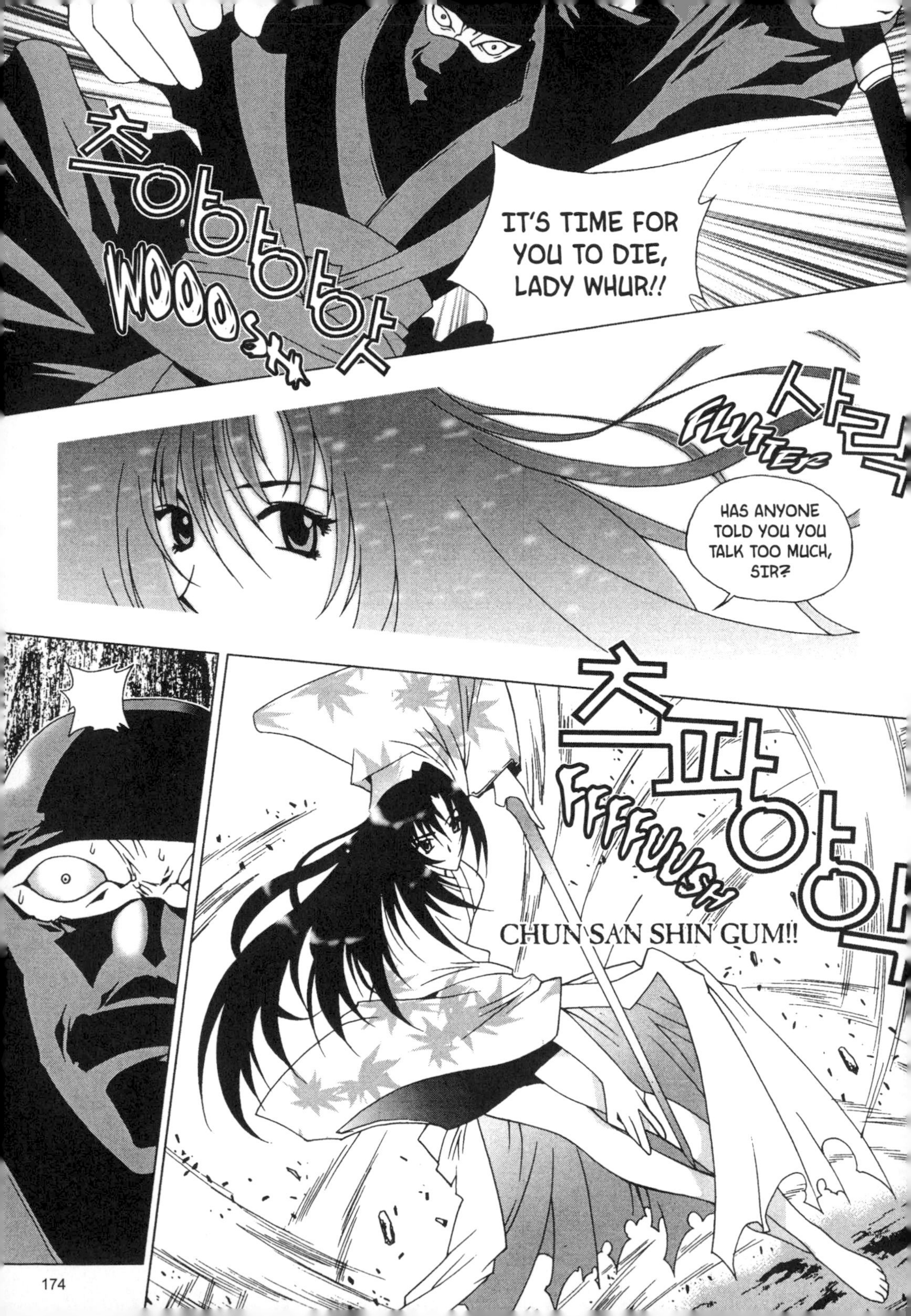
WOOOSH
IT'S TIME FOR YOU TO DIE, LADY WHUR!!
FLUTTER
HAS ANYONE TOLD YOU YOU TALK TOO MUCH, SIR?
FFFFUUSH
CHUN SAN SHIN GUM!!

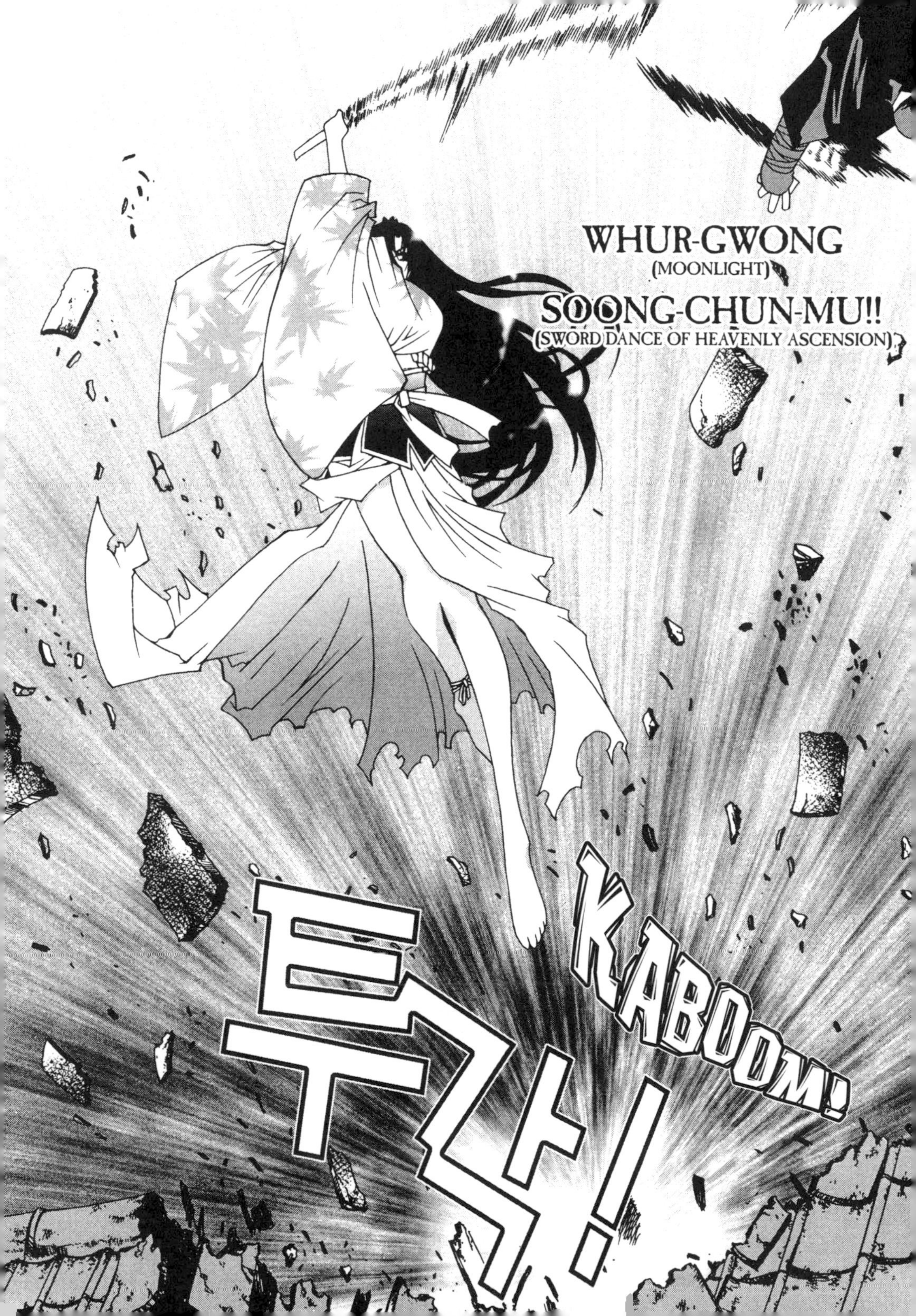
WHUR-GWONG
(MOONLIGHT)
SOONG-CHUN-MU!!
(SWORD DANCE OF HEAVENLY ASCENSION)
KABOOM!
콰앙!

TING

KKK!

SCREECH

DA...
DAMN
IT!

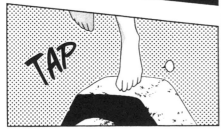

TAP

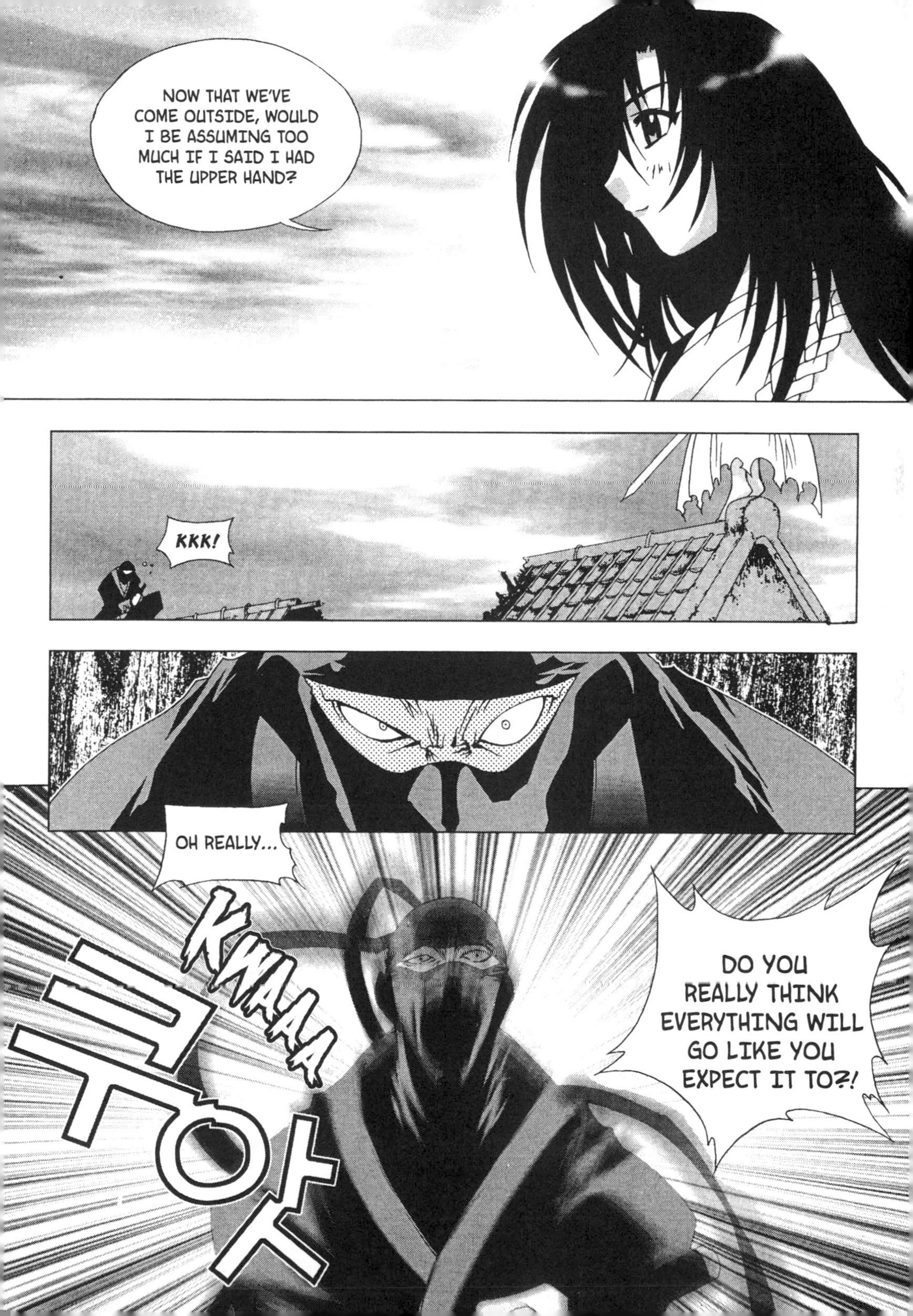
NOW THAT WE'VE COME OUTSIDE, WOULD I BE ASSUMING TOO MUCH IF I SAID I HAD THE UPPER HAND?
KKK!
OH REALLY...
KWAAAA
TTOT
DO YOU REALLY THINK EVERYTHING WILL GO LIKE YOU EXPECT IT TO?!

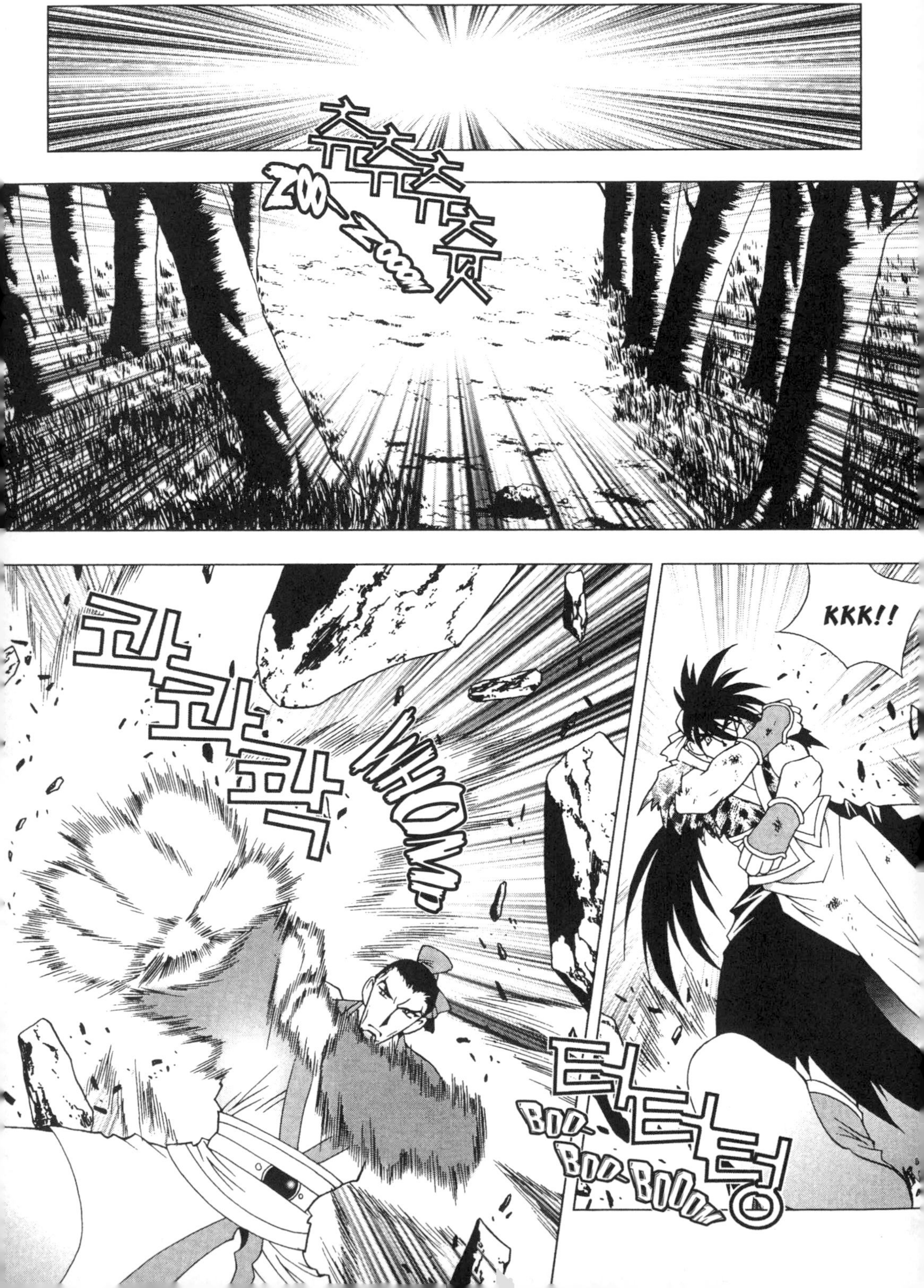
ZOO-ZOOOM
콰콰콰콱
WHOOMP
KKK!!
터터터텅
BOO-BOO-BOOOM

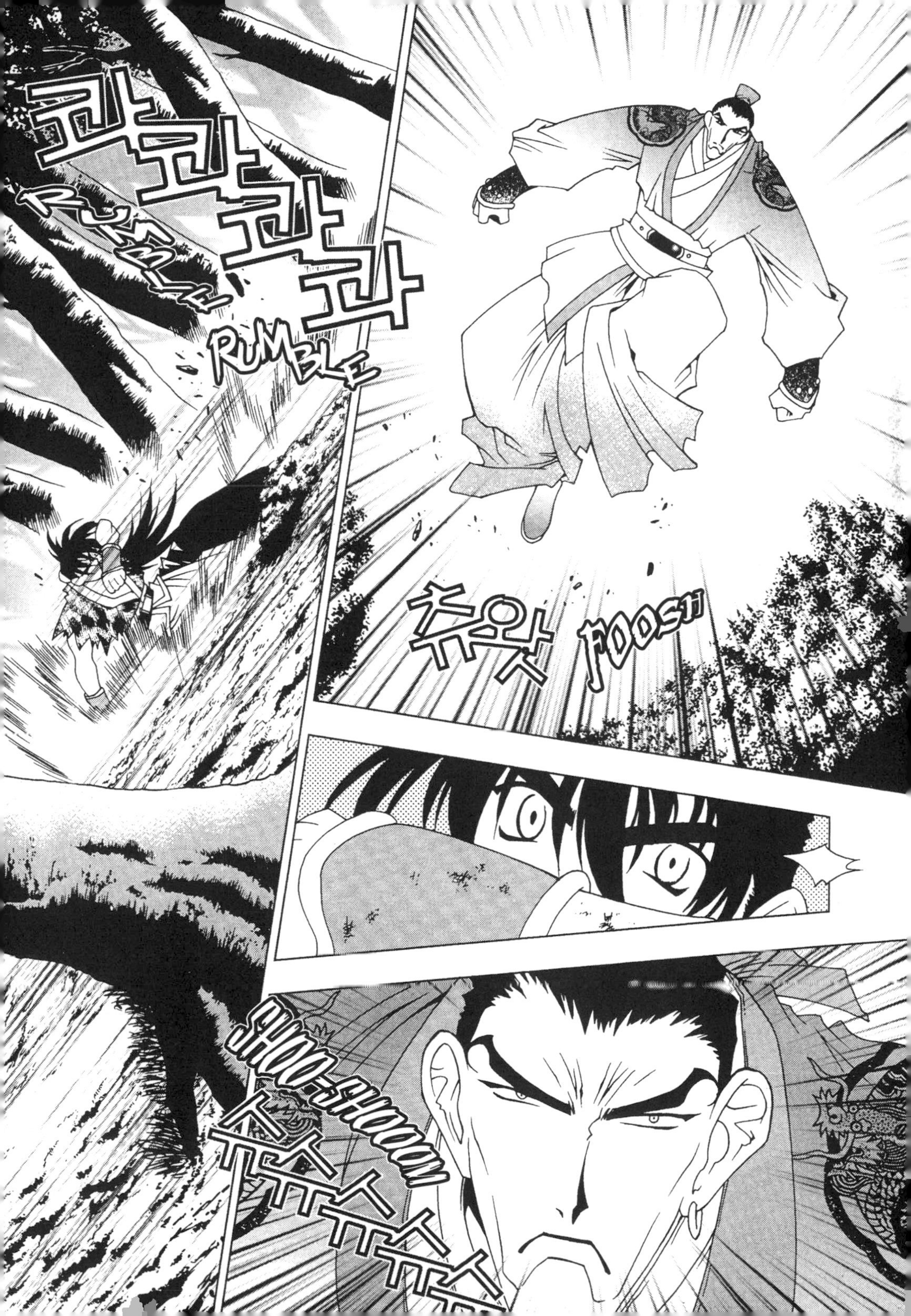
RUMBLE
RUMBLE
FOOSH
SHOOO-SHOOOOM

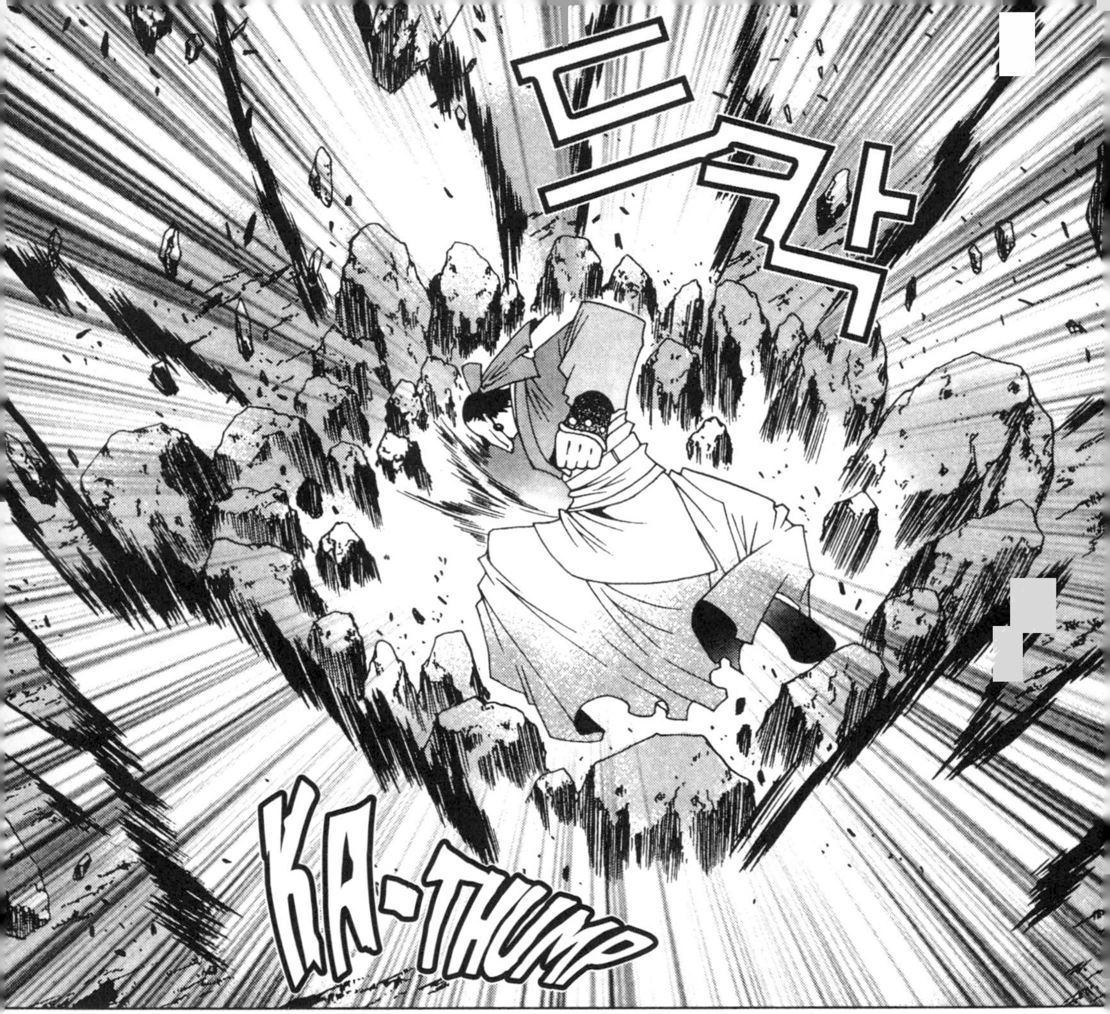
KA-THUMP

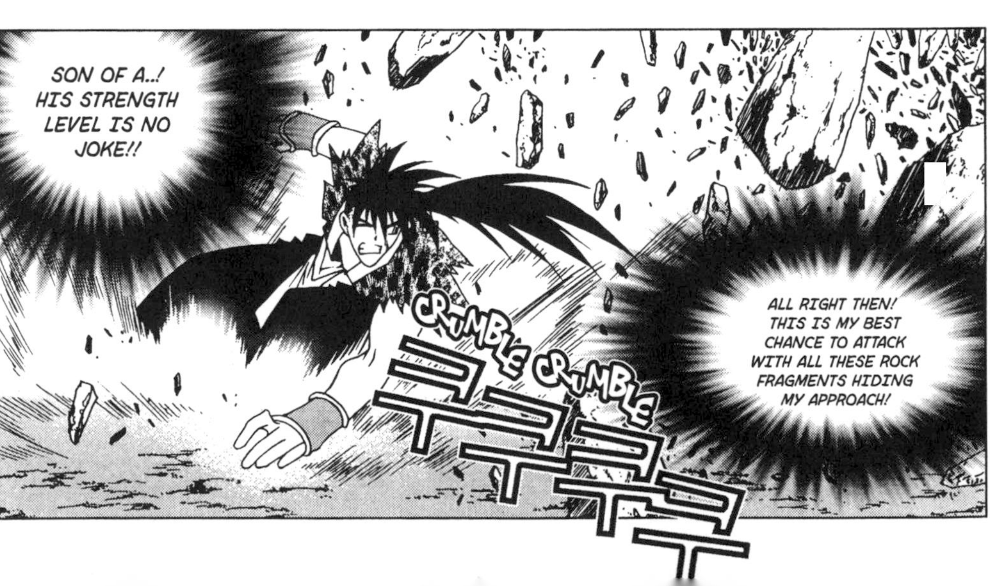
SON OF A..! HIS STRENGTH LEVEL IS NO JOKE!!
CRUMBLE CRUMBLE
ALL RIGHT THEN! THIS IS MY BEST CHANCE TO ATTACK WITH ALL THESE ROCK FRAGMENTS HIDING MY APPROACH!

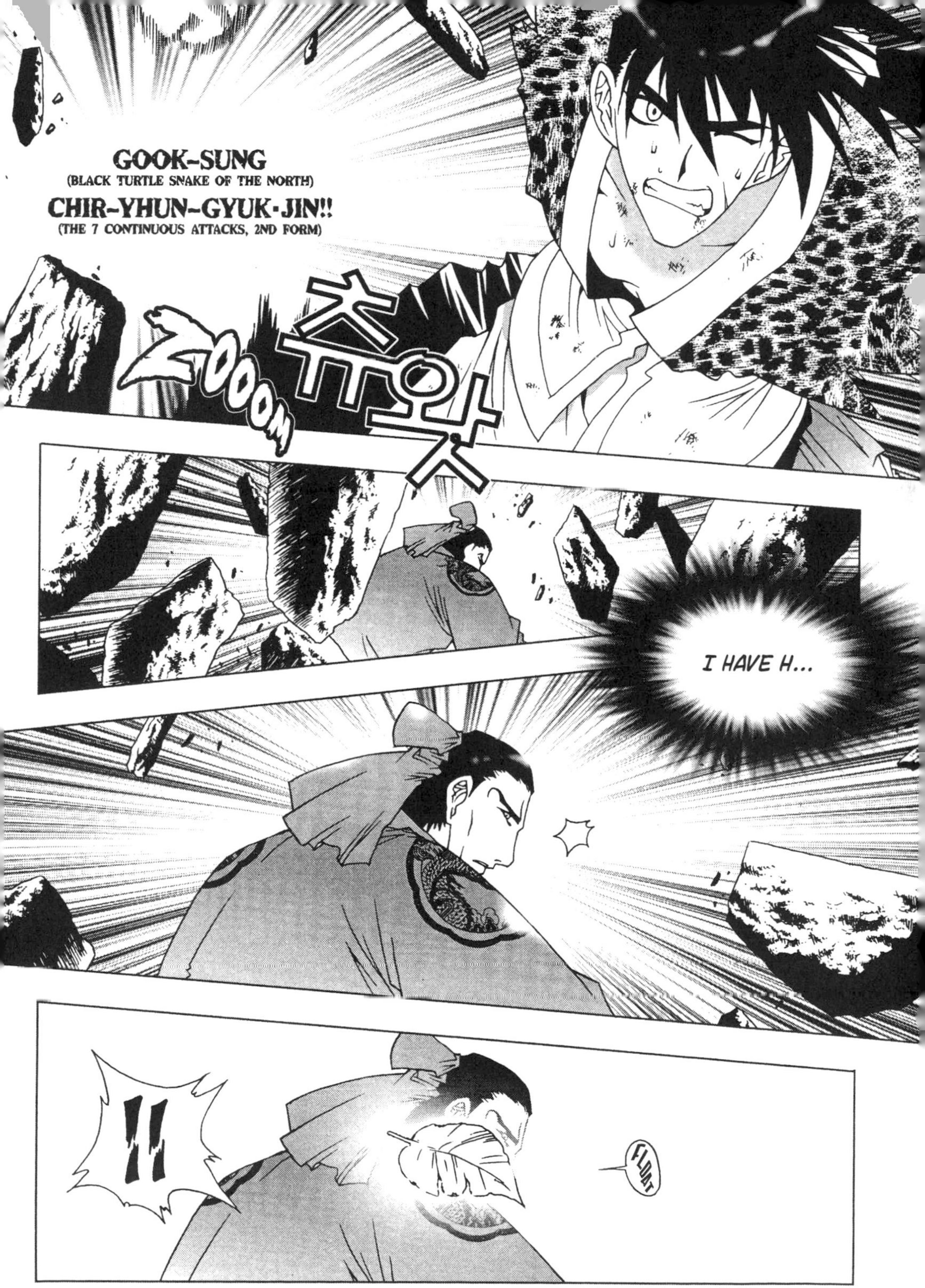
GOOK-SUNG
(BLACK TURTLE SNAKE OF THE NORTH)
CHIR-YHUN-GYUK-JIN!!
(THE 7 CONTINUOUS ATTACKS, 2ND FORM)
ZOOOOM
I HAVE H...
!!
FLOAT

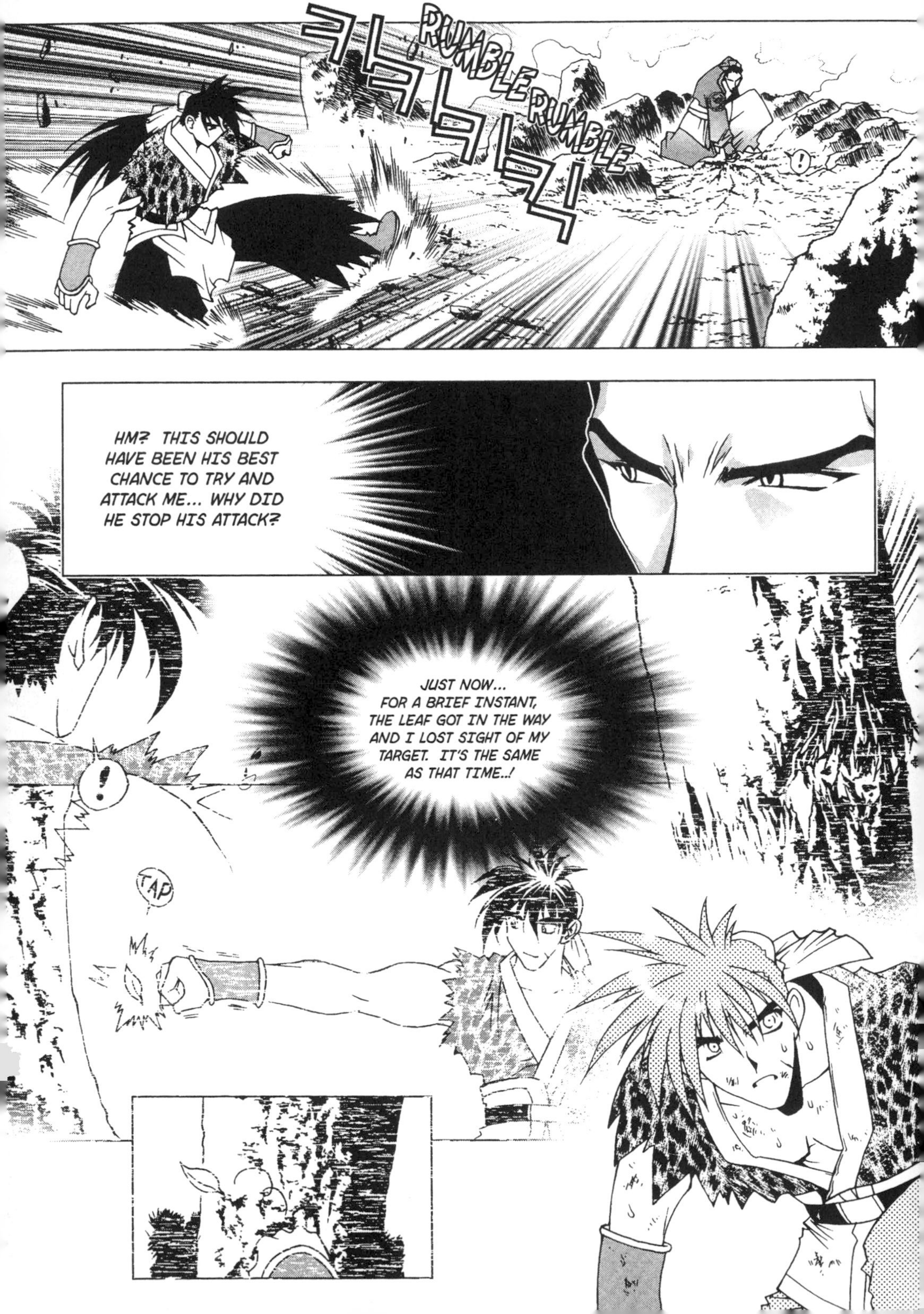
RUMBLE RUMBLE RUMBLE
!
HM? THIS SHOULD HAVE BEEN HIS BEST CHANCE TO TRY AND ATTACK ME... WHY DID HE STOP HIS ATTACK?
JUST NOW... FOR A BRIEF INSTANT, THE LEAF GOT IN THE WAY AND I LOST SIGHT OF MY TARGET. IT'S THE SAME AS THAT TIME...!
!
TAP

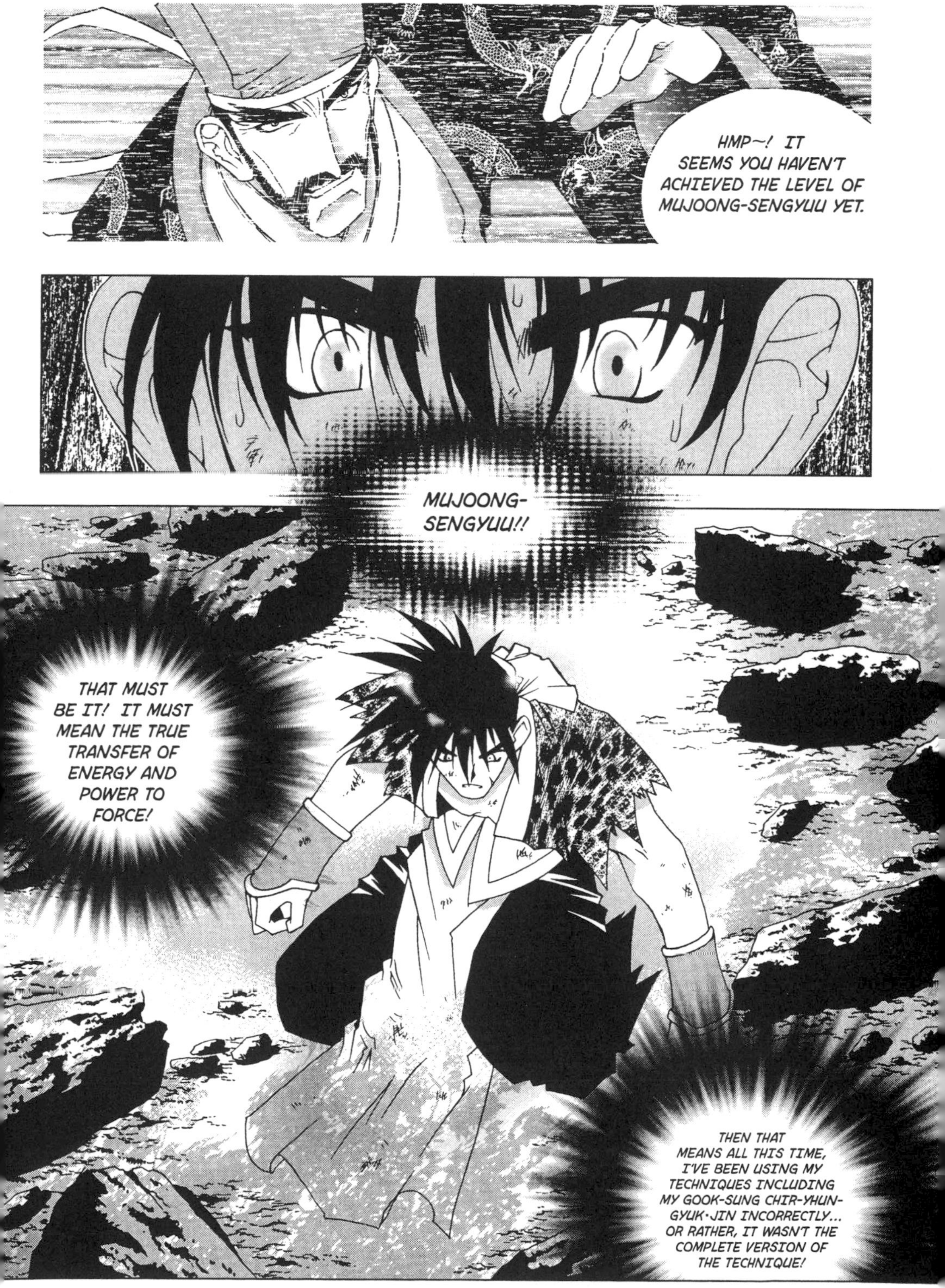
HMP~! IT SEEMS YOU HAVEN'T ACHIEVED THE LEVEL OF MUJOONG-SENGYUU YET.
MUJOONG-SENGYUU!!
THAT MUST BE IT! IT MUST MEAN THE TRUE TRANSFER OF ENERGY AND POWER TO FORCE!
THEN THAT MEANS ALL THIS TIME, I'VE BEEN USING MY TECHNIQUES INCLUDING MY GOOK-SUNG CHIR-YHUN-GYUK·JIN INCORRECTLY... OR RATHER, IT WASN'T THE COMPLETE VERSION OF THE TECHNIQUE!

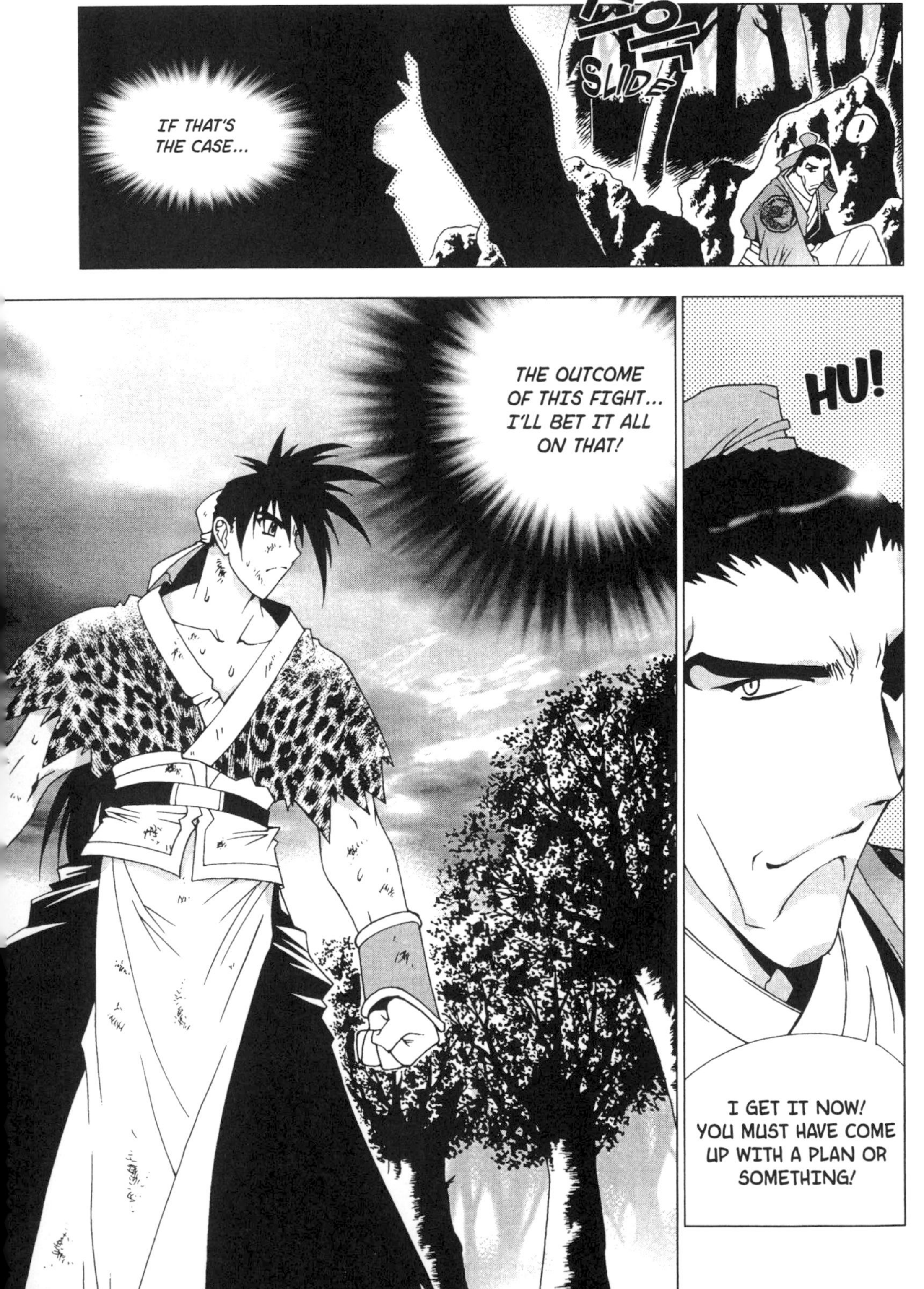
IF THAT'S THE CASE...
SLIDE
!
THE OUTCOME OF THIS FIGHT... I'LL BET IT ALL ON THAT!
HU!
I GET IT NOW! YOU MUST HAVE COME UP WITH A PLAN OR SOMETHING!

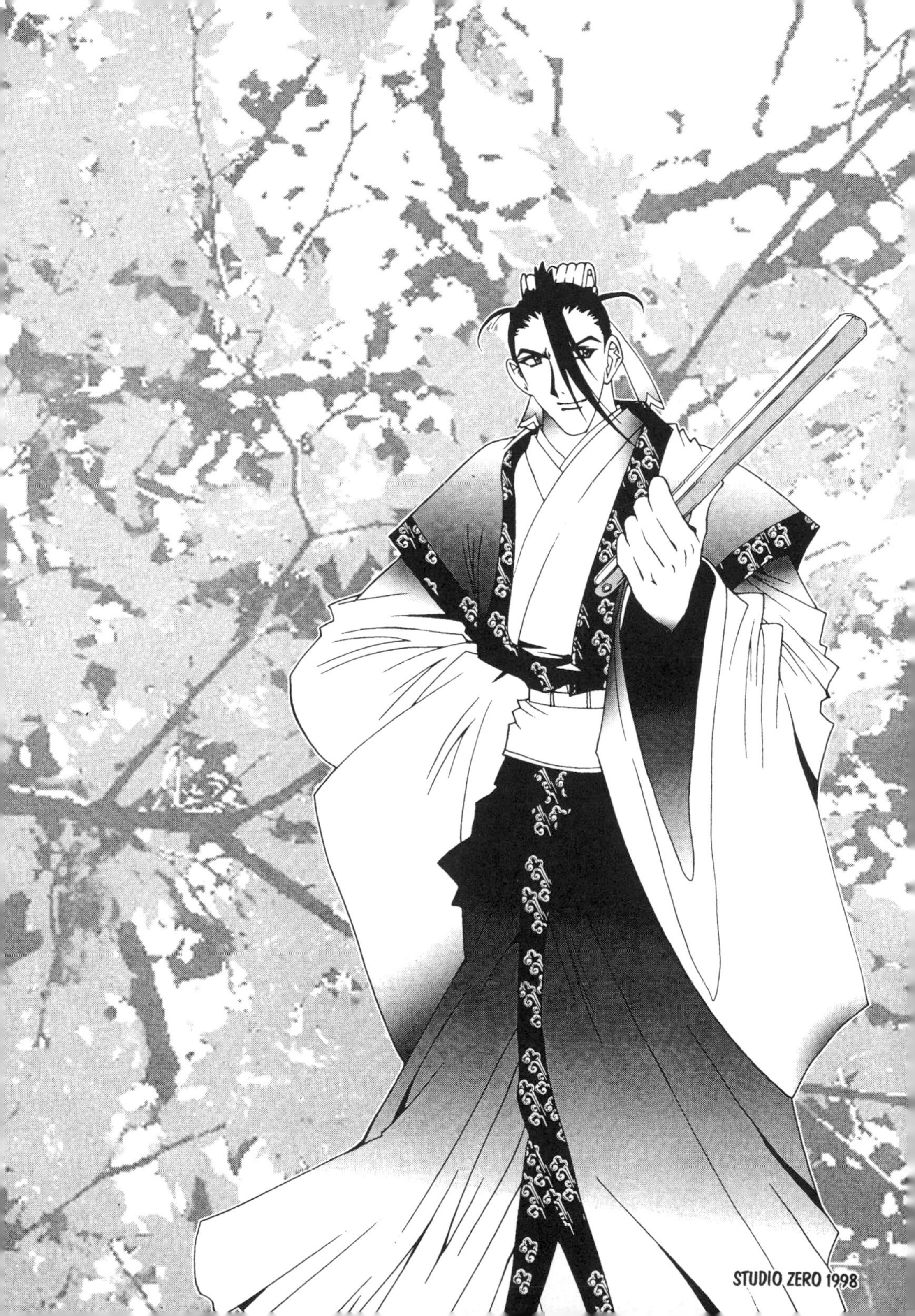
STUDIO ZERO 1998

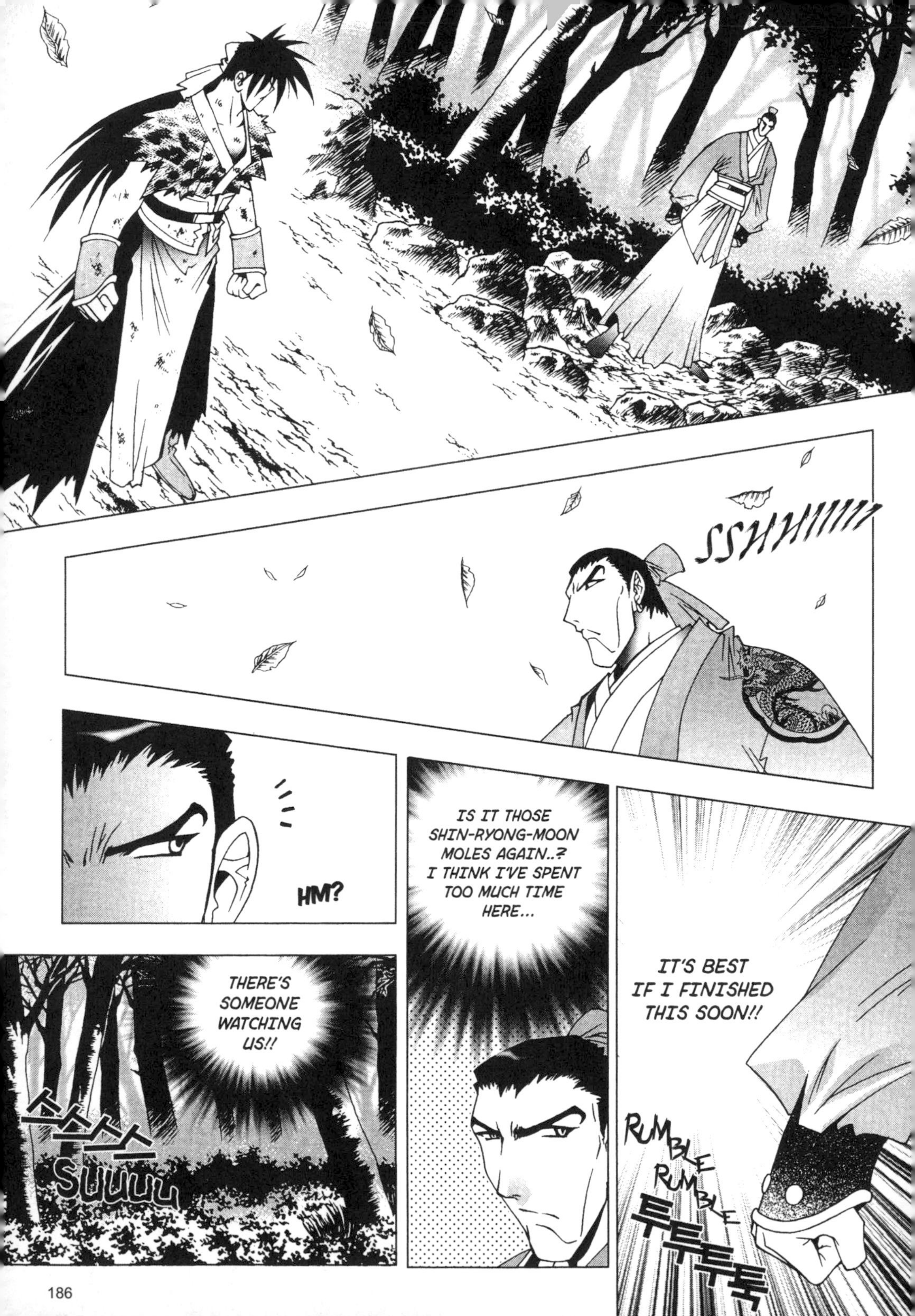
SSHHHH
HM?
IS IT THOSE SHIN-RYONG-MOON MOLES AGAIN..? I THINK I'VE SPENT TOO MUCH TIME HERE...
IT'S BEST IF I FINISHED THIS SOON!!
THERE'S SOMEONE WATCHING US!!
스스스
Suuuu
RUMBLE RUMBLE
투두두둑

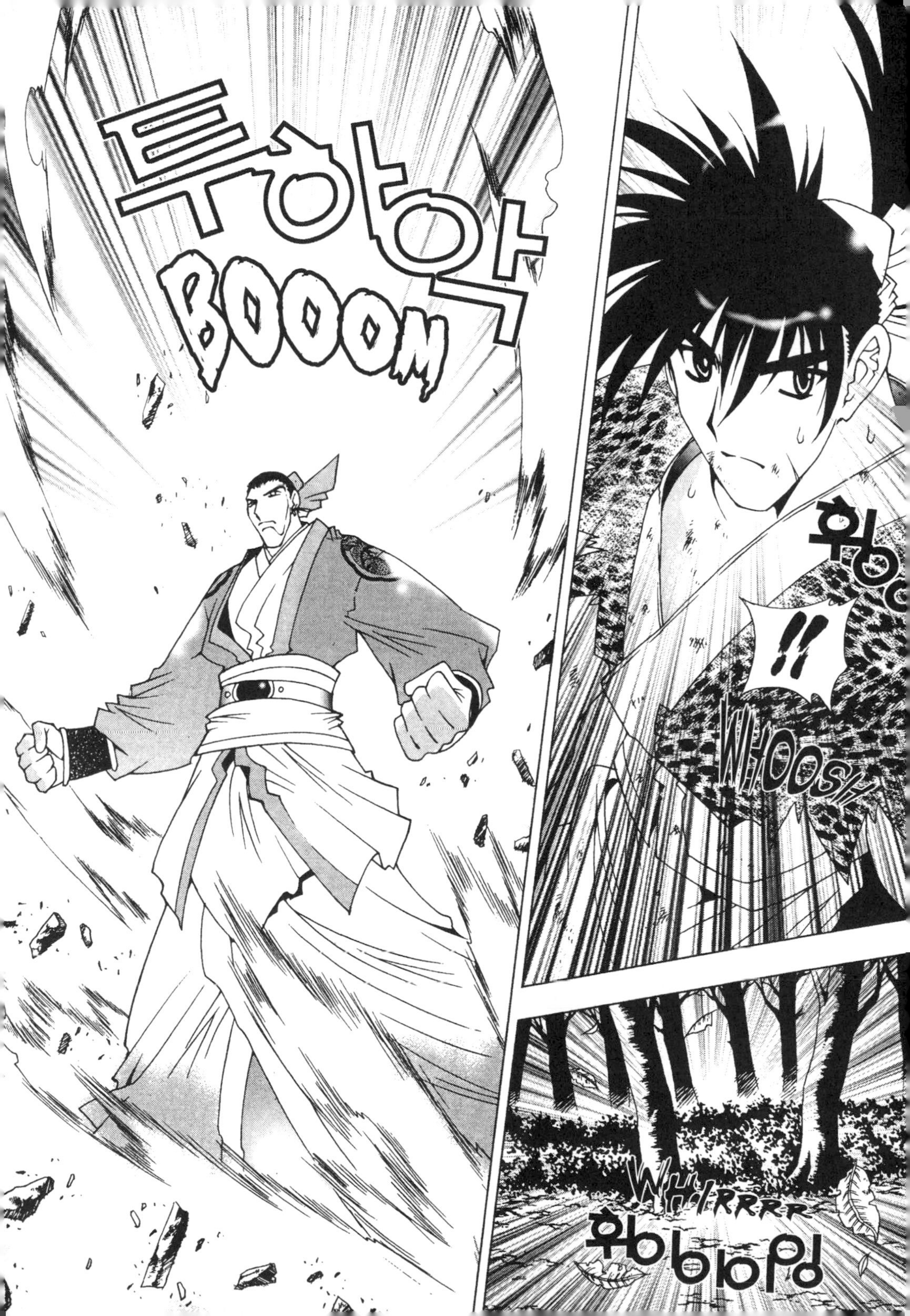
BOOOM
!!
WHOOSH
WHIRRRR

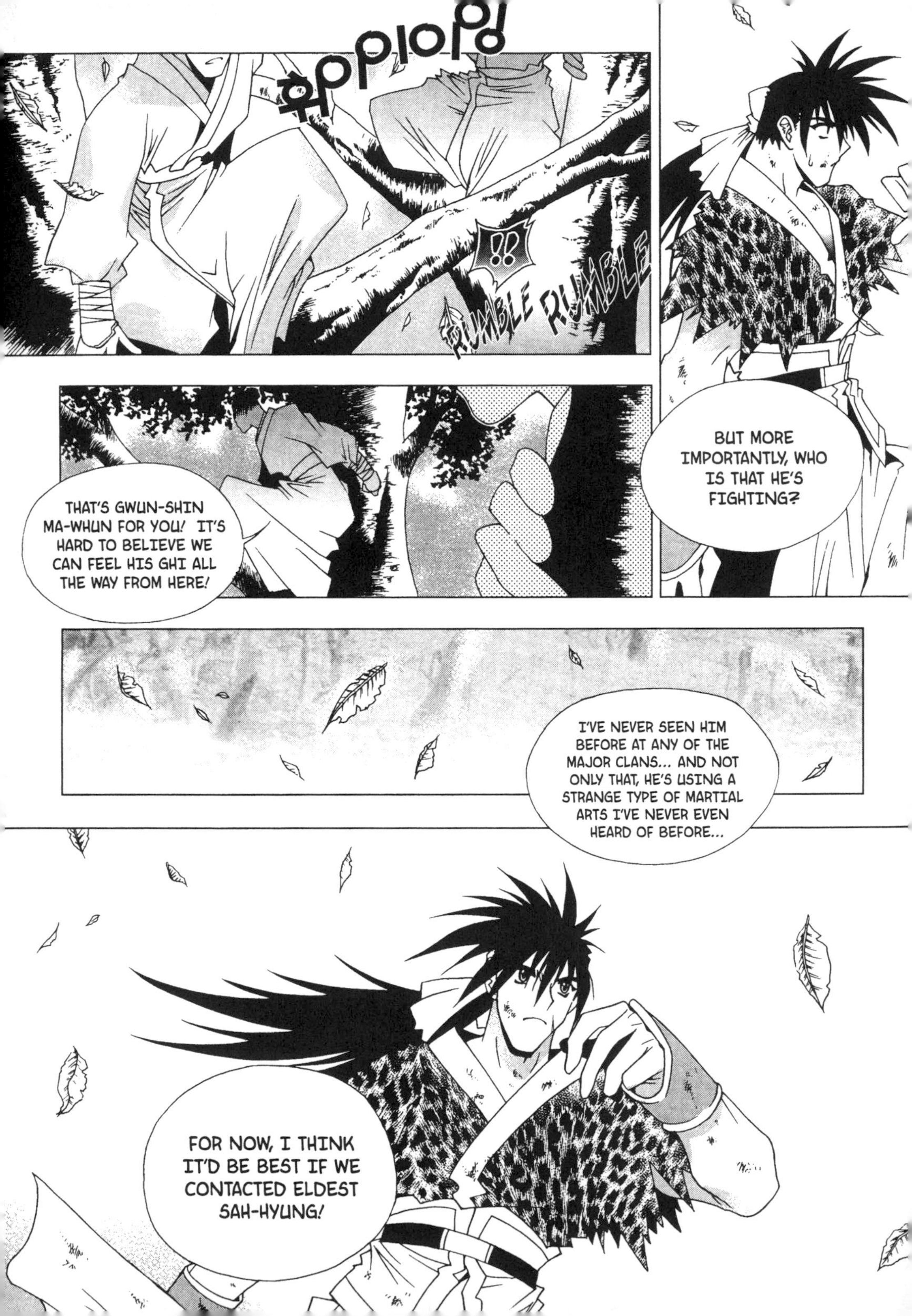

!!
RUMBLE RUMBLE
THAT'S GWUN-SHIN MA-WHUN FOR YOU! IT'S HARD TO BELIEVE WE CAN FEEL HIS GHI ALL THE WAY FROM HERE!
BUT MORE IMPORTANTLY, WHO IS THAT HE'S FIGHTING?
I'VE NEVER SEEN HIM BEFORE AT ANY OF THE MAJOR CLANS... AND NOT ONLY THAT, HE'S USING A STRANGE TYPE OF MARTIAL ARTS I'VE NEVER EVEN HEARD OF BEFORE...
FOR NOW, I THINK IT'D BE BEST IF WE CONTACTED ELDEST SAH-HYUNG!

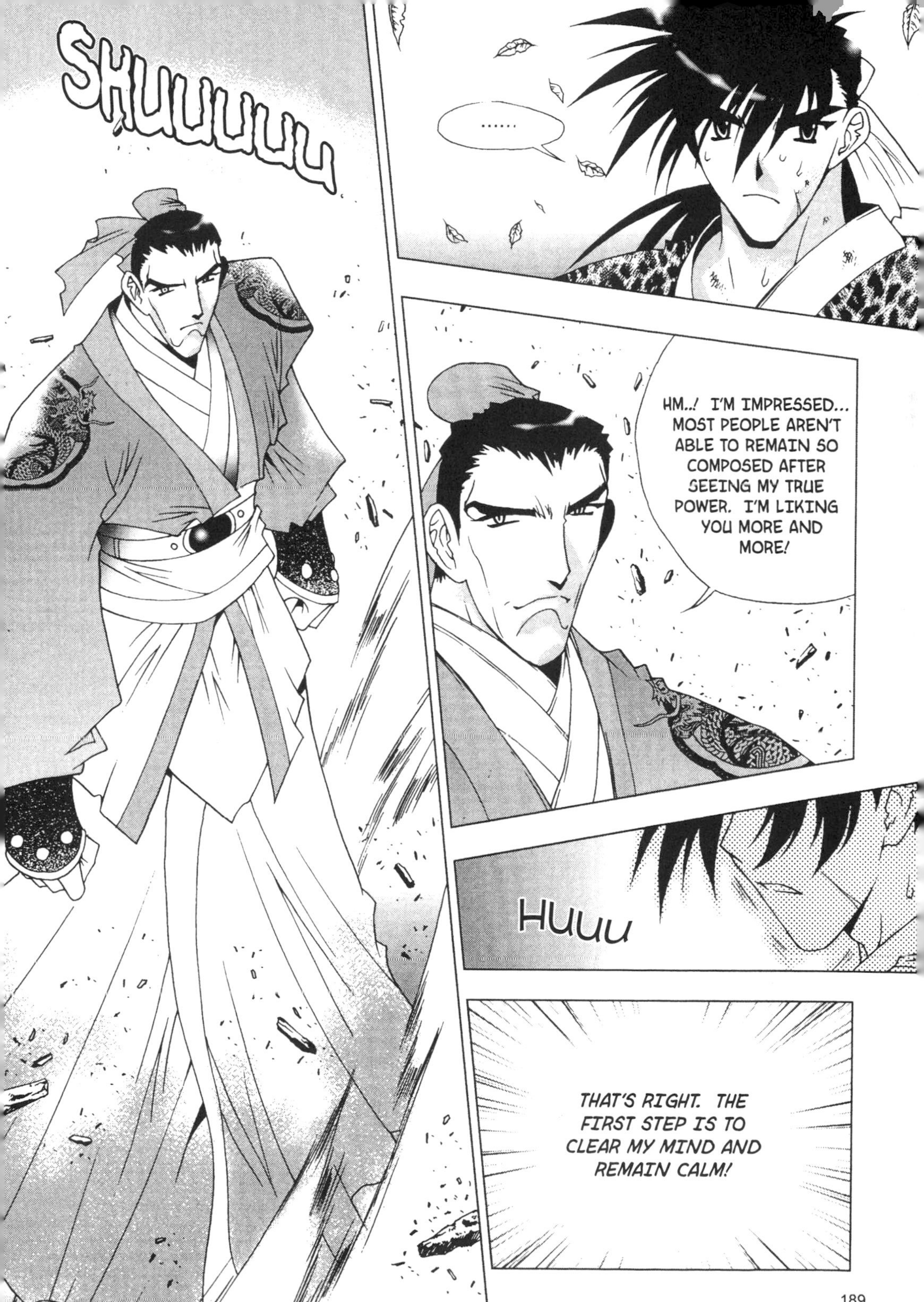
SHUUUUU
......
HM..! I'M IMPRESSED... MOST PEOPLE AREN'T ABLE TO REMAIN SO COMPOSED AFTER SEEING MY TRUE POWER. I'M LIKING YOU MORE AND MORE!
HUUU
THAT'S RIGHT. THE FIRST STEP IS TO CLEAR MY MIND AND REMAIN CALM!

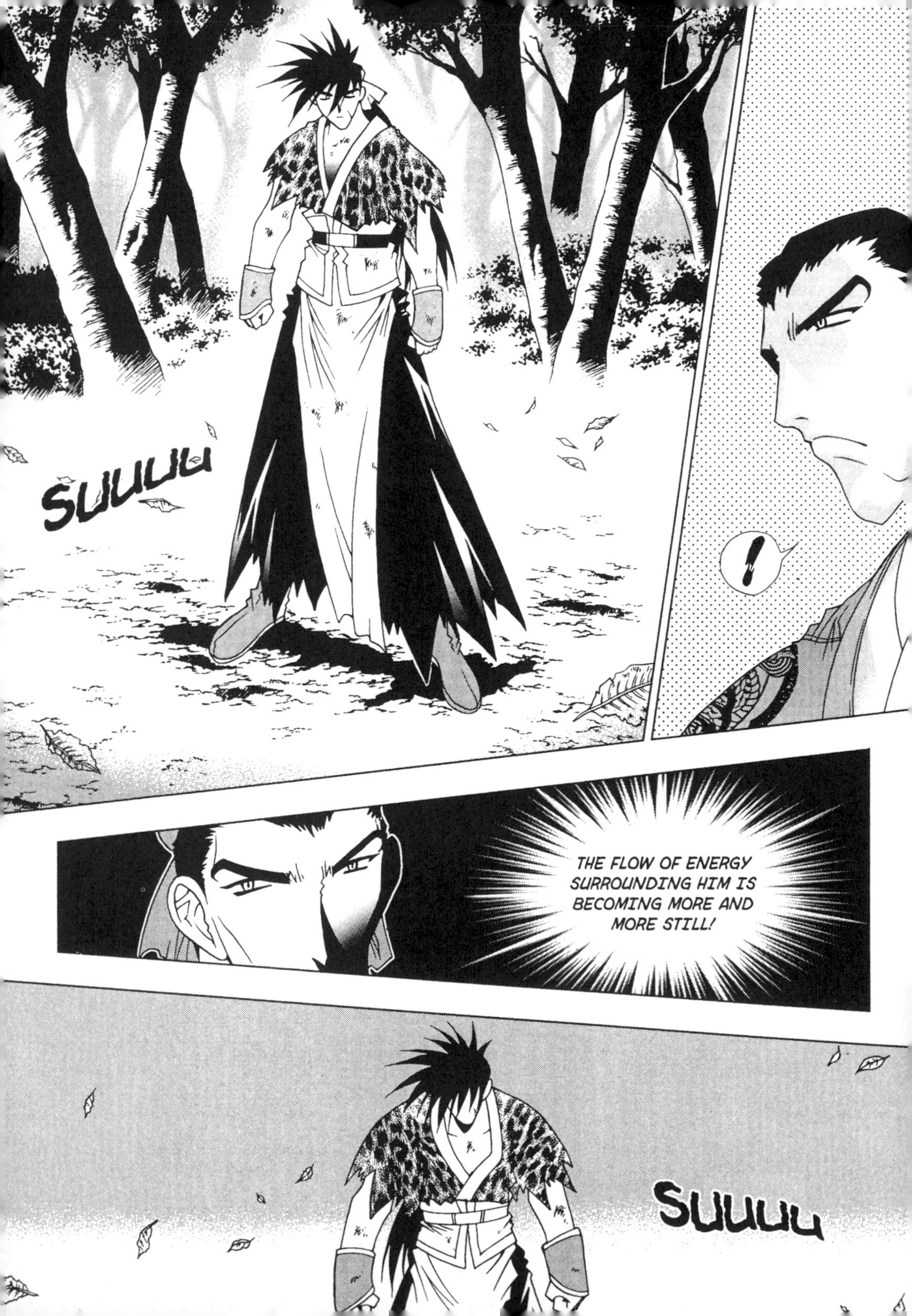

!
SUUUU
THE FLOW OF ENERGY SURROUNDING HIM IS BECOMING MORE AND MORE STILL!
SUUUU

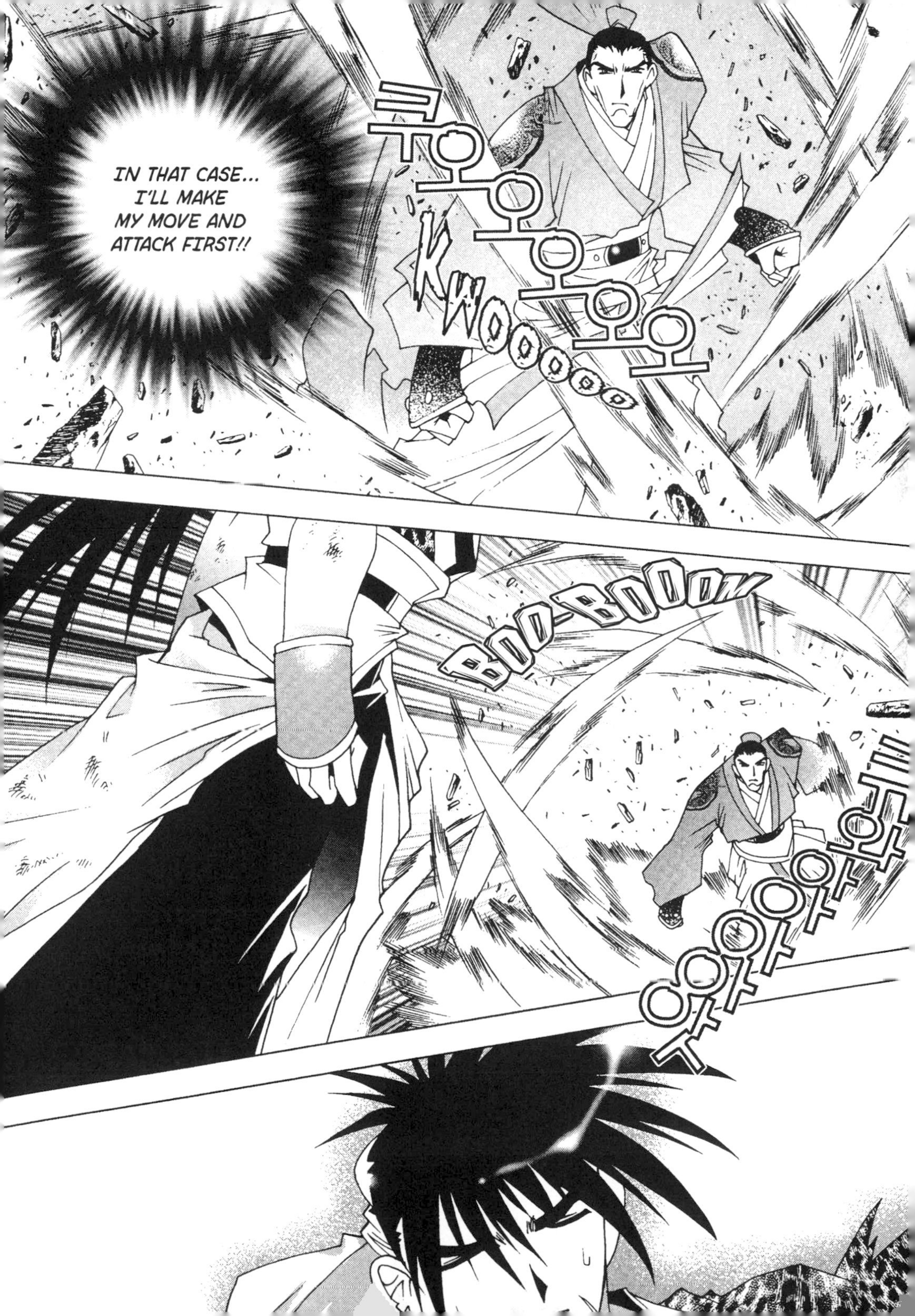

IN THAT CASE... I'LL MAKE MY MOVE AND ATTACK FIRST!!
KWOOOOOOO
BOO-BOOOOM

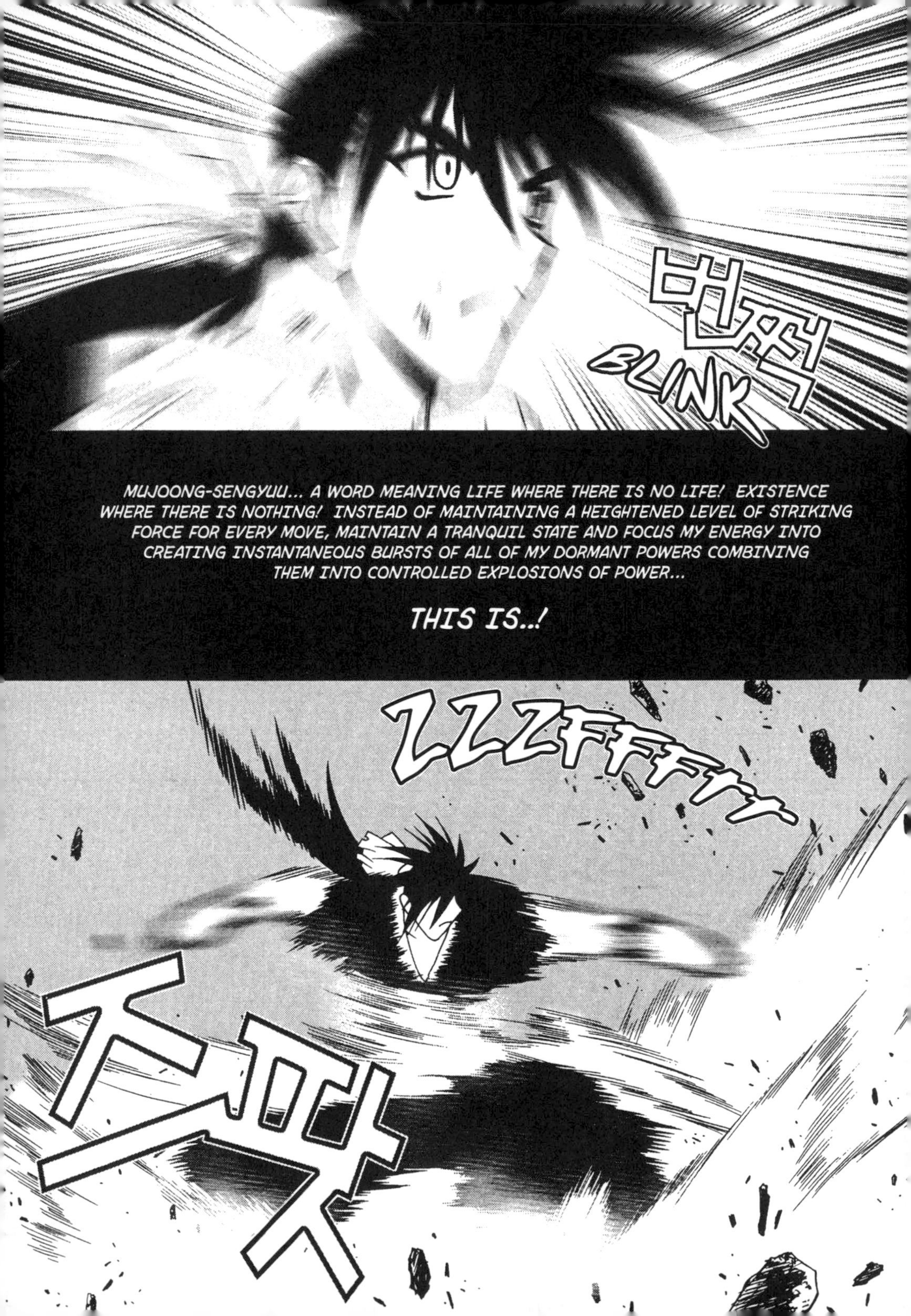
번쩍
BLINK
MUJOONG-SENGYUU... A WORD MEANING LIFE WHERE THERE IS NO LIFE! EXISTENCE WHERE THERE IS NOTHING! INSTEAD OF MAINTAINING A HEIGHTENED LEVEL OF STRIKING FORCE FOR EVERY MOVE, MAINTAIN A TRANQUIL STATE AND FOCUS MY ENERGY INTO CREATING INSTANTANEOUS BURSTS OF ALL OF MY DORMANT POWERS COMBINING THEM INTO CONTROLLED EXPLOSIONS OF POWER...
THIS IS..!
ZZZFFFFYY

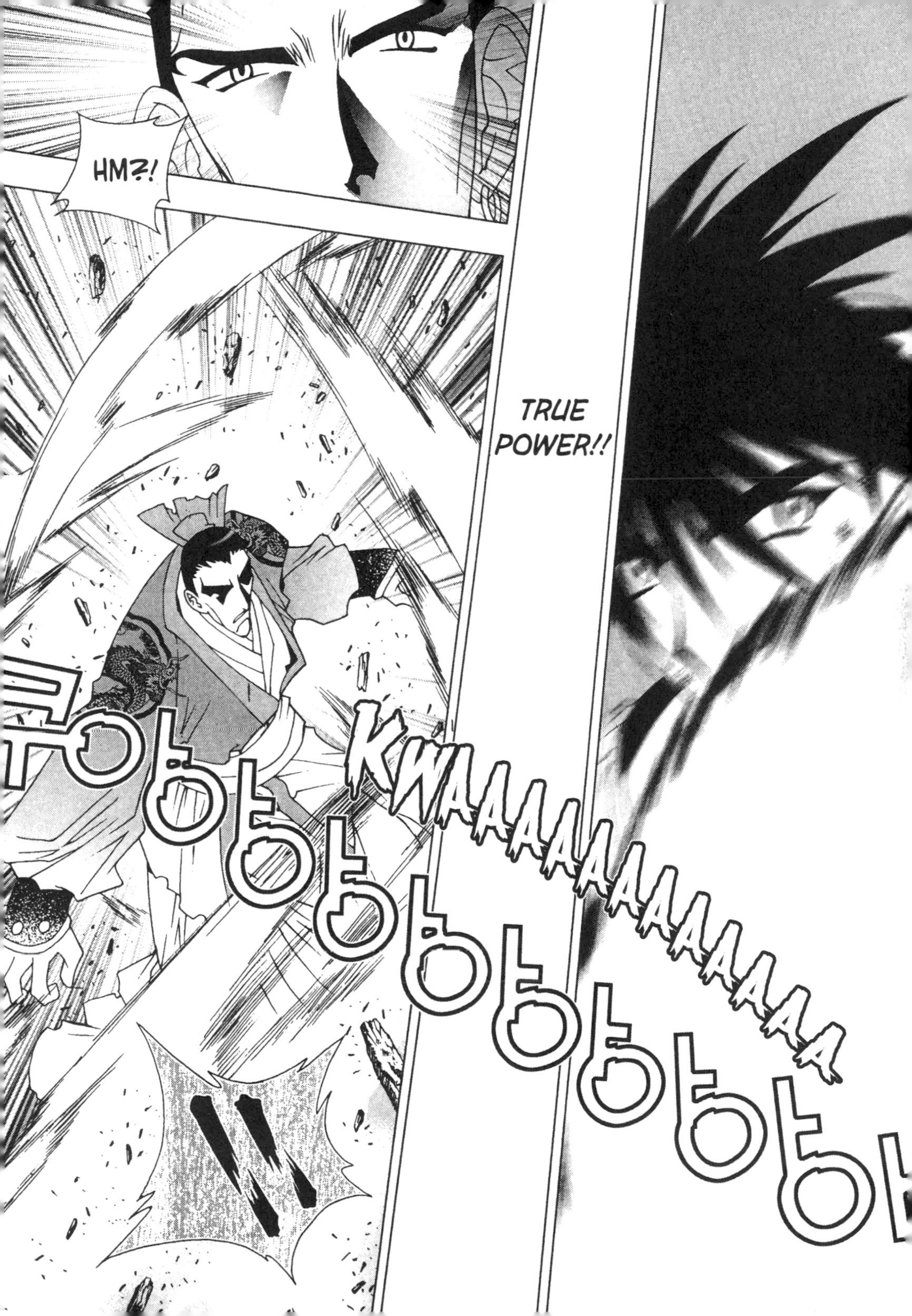
HM?!
TRUE POWER!!
KWAAAAAAAAAAAAA

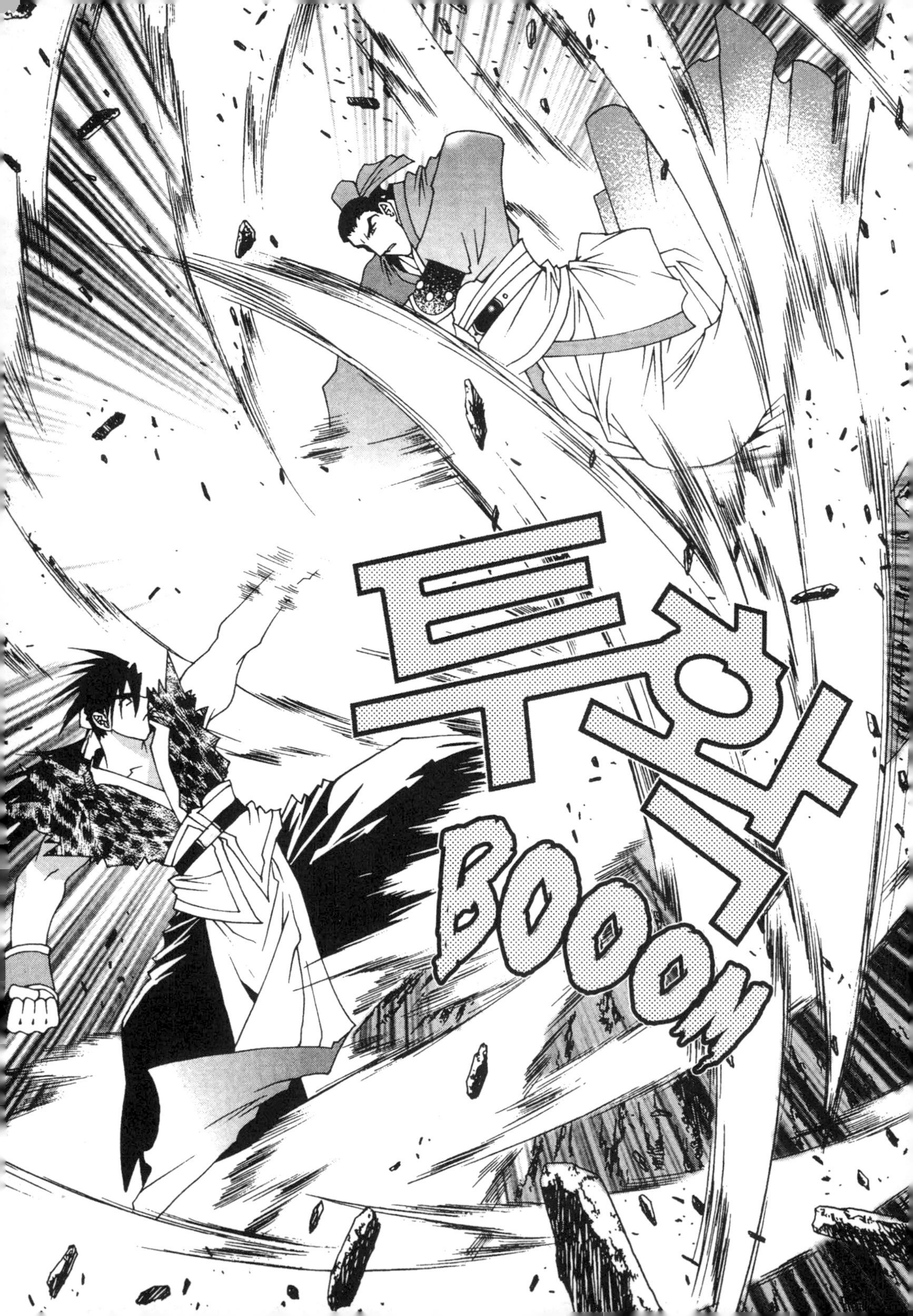
BOOOM

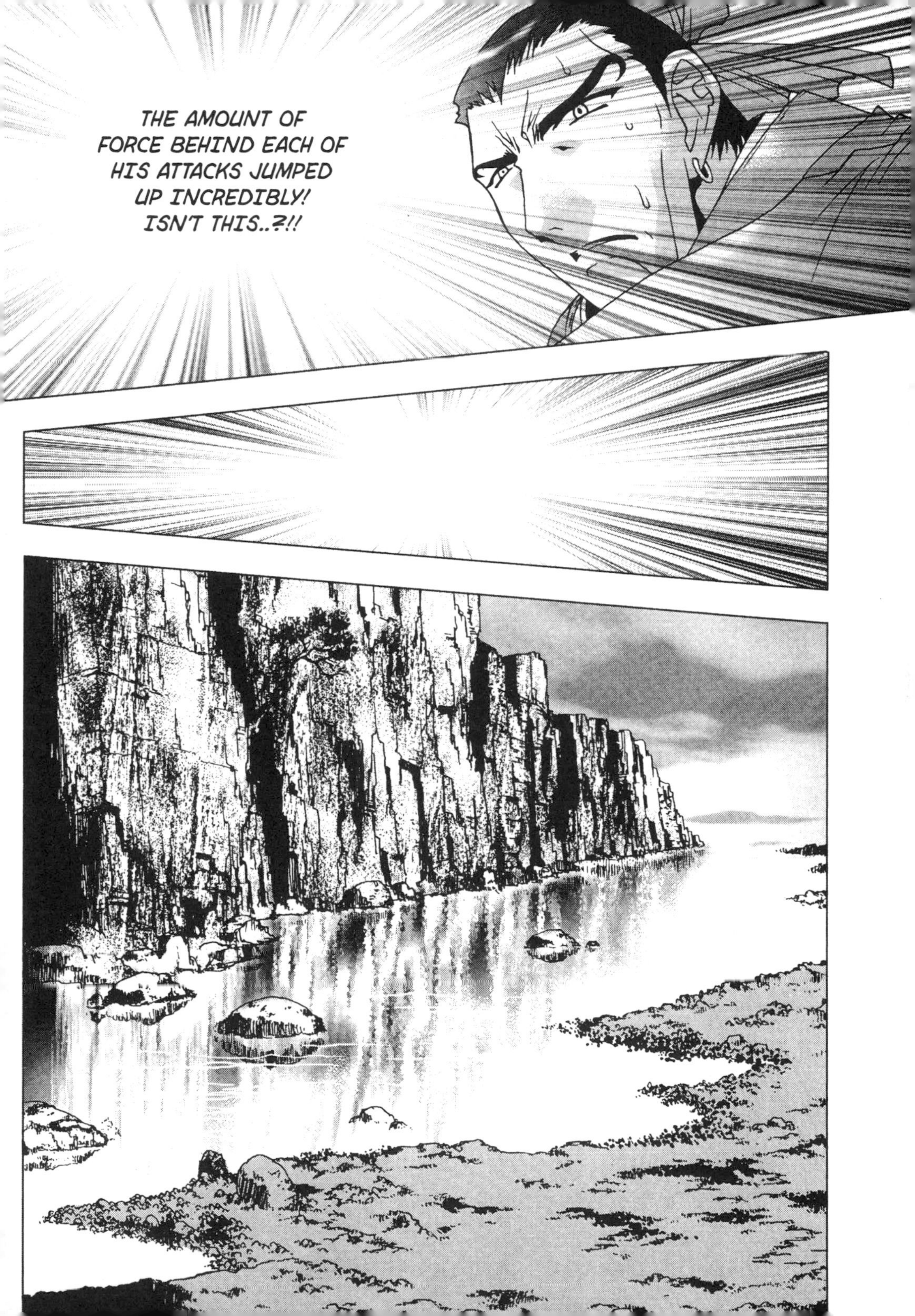
THE AMOUNT OF FORCE BEHIND EACH OF HIS ATTACKS JUMPED UP INCREDIBLY! ISN'T THIS..?!!

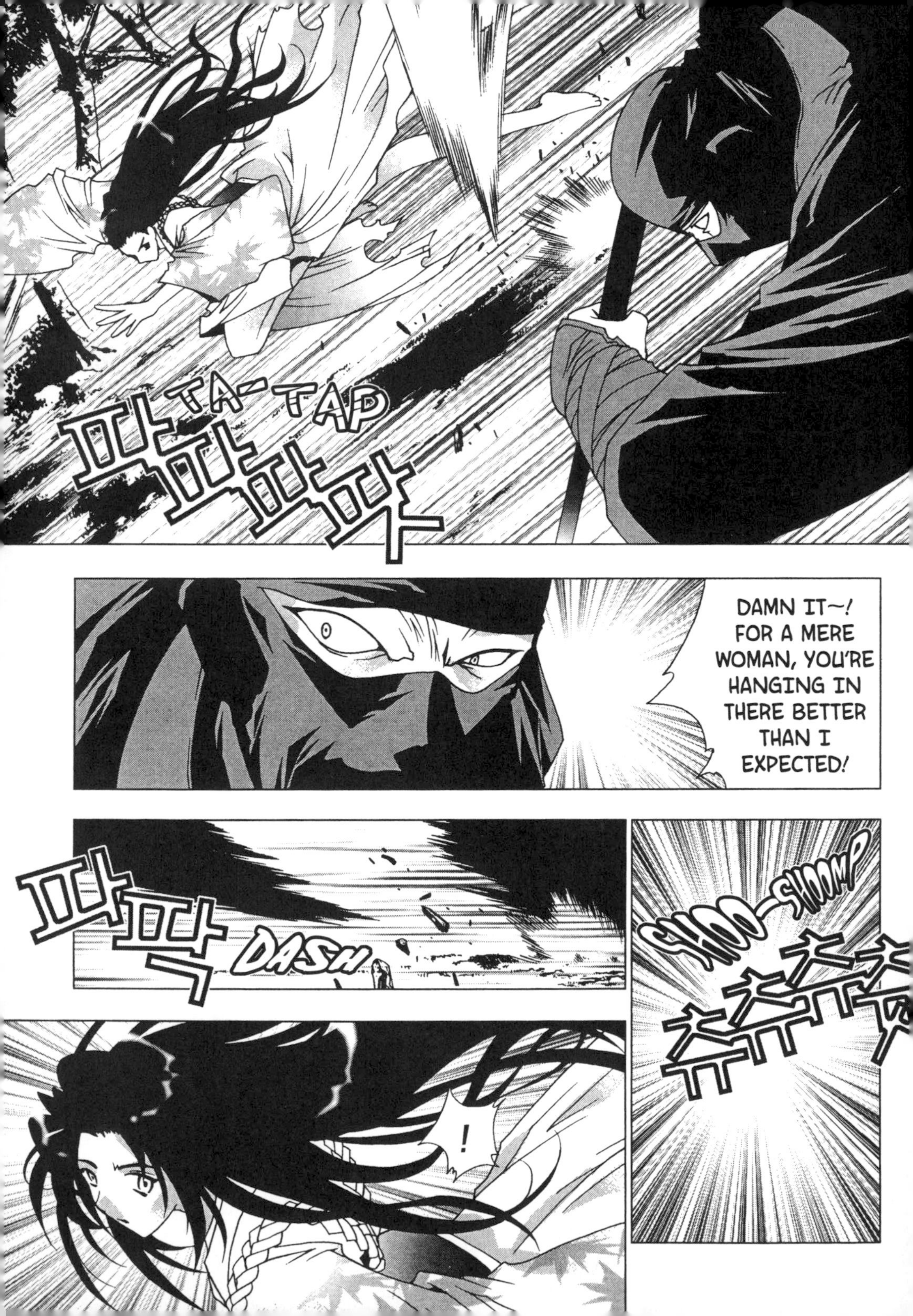
TA-TAP
DAMN IT~! FOR A MERE WOMAN, YOU'RE HANGING IN THERE BETTER THAN I EXPECTED!
DASH
SHOO-SHOOMP
!

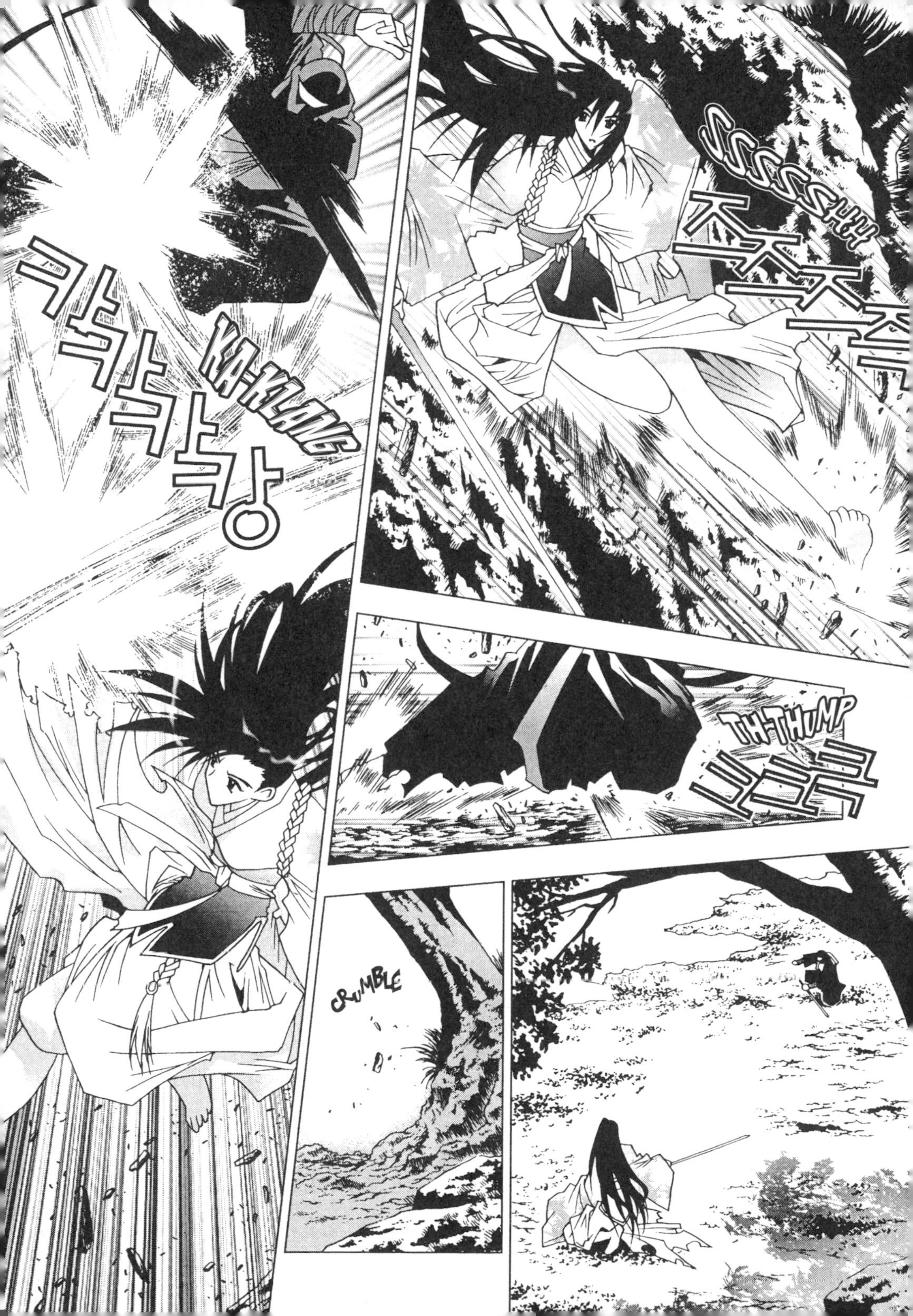
SSSSSHH
KA-KLANG
TH-THUMP
CRUMBLE

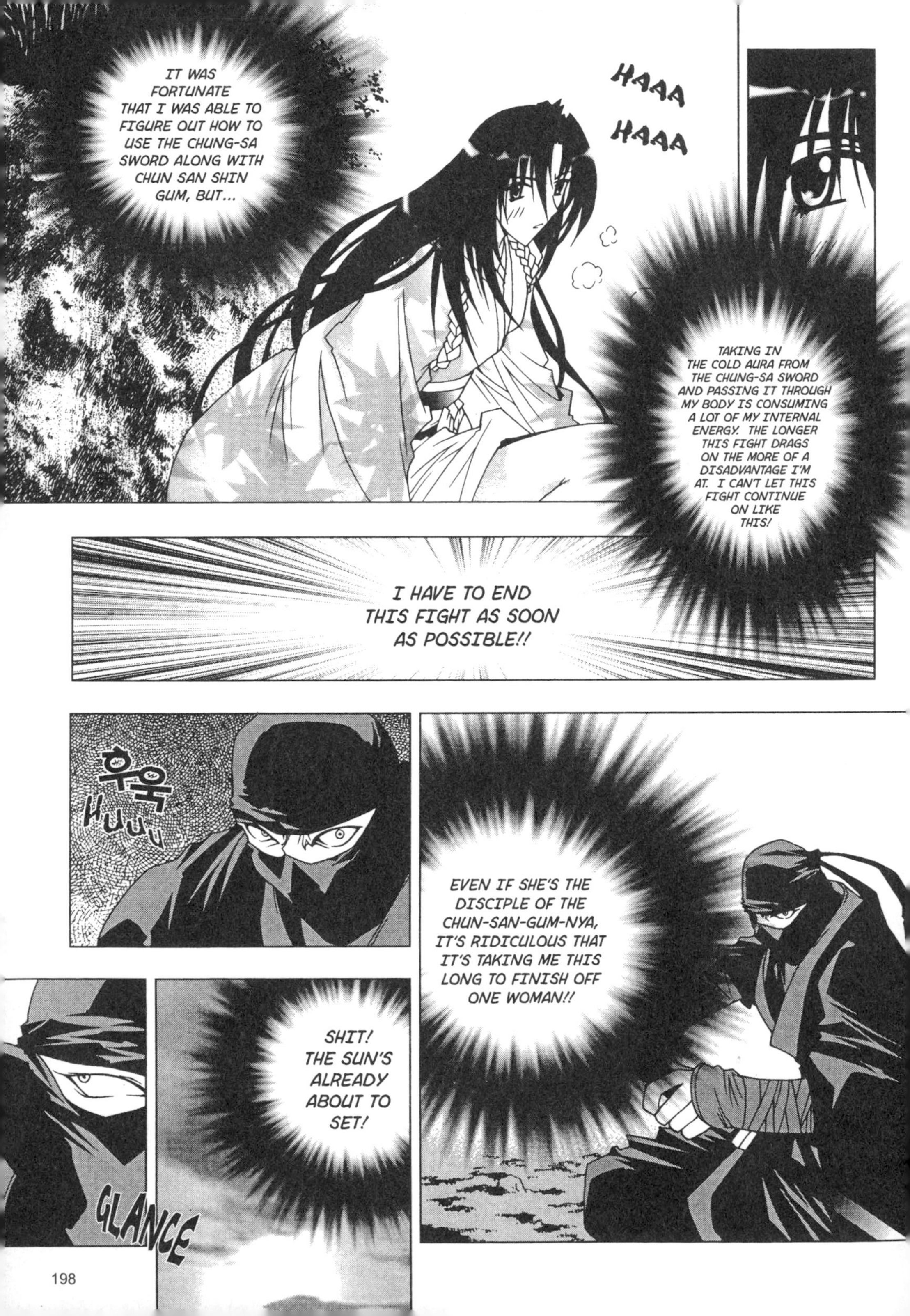
IT WAS FORTUNATE THAT I WAS ABLE TO FIGURE OUT HOW TO USE THE CHUNG-SA SWORD ALONG WITH CHUN SAN SHIN GUM, BUT...
HAAA HAAA
TAKING IN THE COLD AURA FROM THE CHUNG-SA SWORD AND PASSING IT THROUGH MY BODY IS CONSUMING A LOT OF MY INTERNAL ENERGY. THE LONGER THIS FIGHT DRAGS ON THE MORE OF A DISADVANTAGE I'M AT. I CAN'T LET THIS FIGHT CONTINUE ON LIKE THIS!
I HAVE TO END THIS FIGHT AS SOON AS POSSIBLE!!
EVEN IF SHE'S THE DISCIPLE OF THE CHUN-SAN-GUM-NYA, IT'S RIDICULOUS THAT IT'S TAKING ME THIS LONG TO FINISH OFF ONE WOMAN!!
후욱
HUUU
SHIT! THE SUN'S ALREADY ABOUT TO SET!
GLANCE

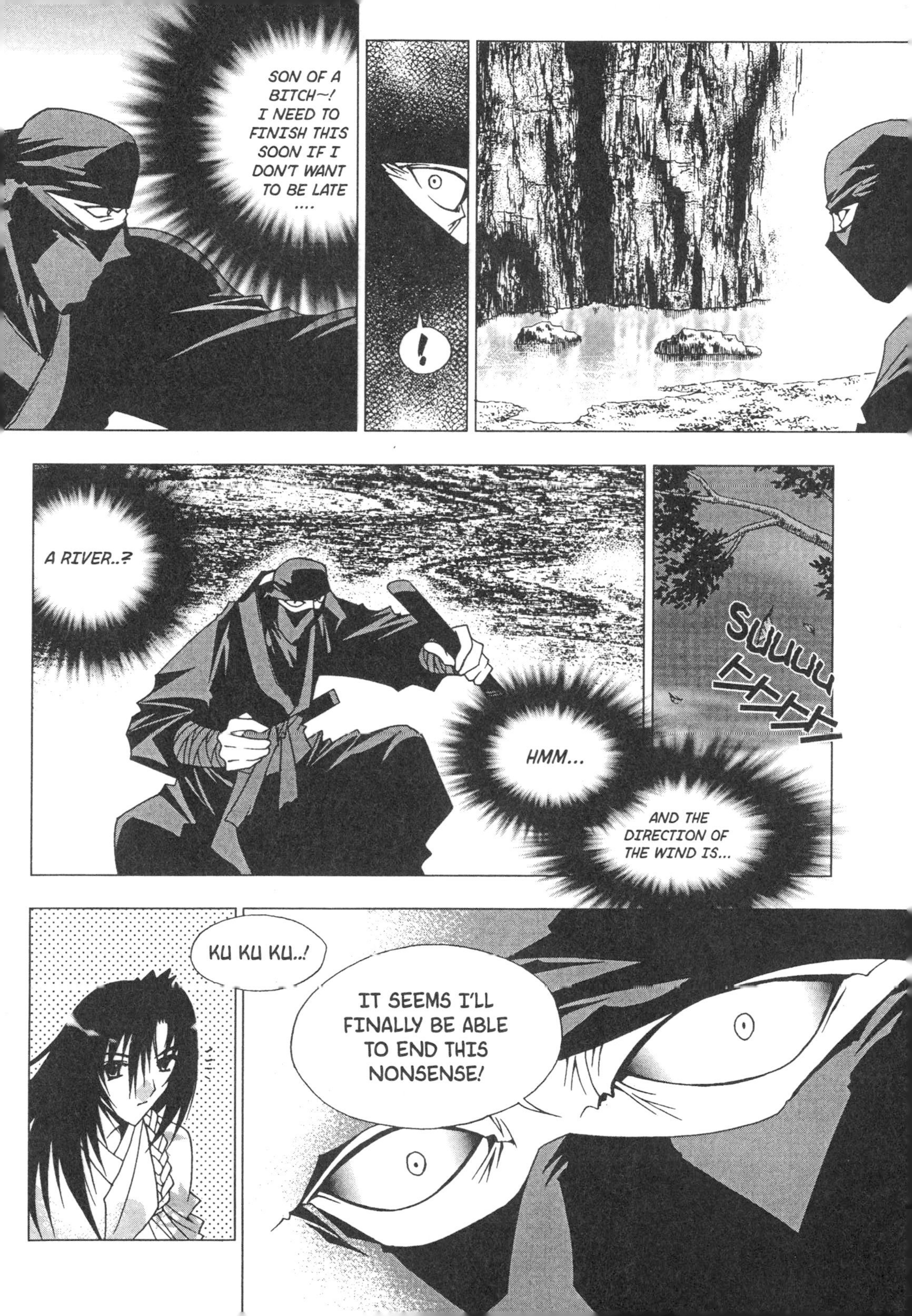
SON OF A BITCH~! I NEED TO FINISH THIS SOON IF I DON'T WANT TO BE LATE ....
!
A RIVER..?
SUUUU
HMM...
AND THE DIRECTION OF THE WIND IS...
KU KU KU..!
IT SEEMS I'LL FINALLY BE ABLE TO END THIS NONSENSE!

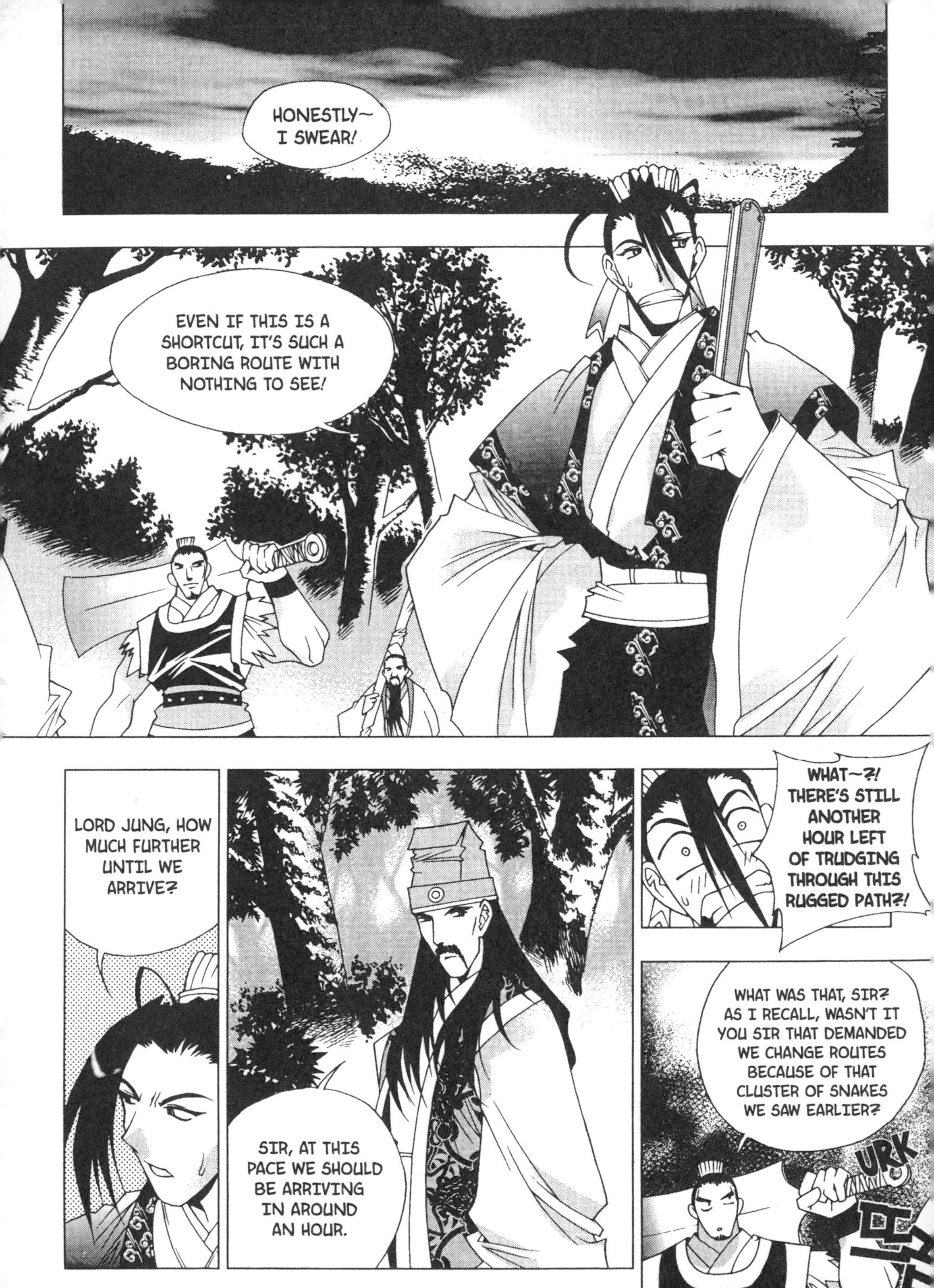
HONESTLY~ I SWEAR!
EVEN IF THIS IS A SHORTCUT, IT'S SUCH A BORING ROUTE WITH NOTHING TO SEE!
LORD JUNG, HOW MUCH FURTHER UNTIL WE ARRIVE?
SIR, AT THIS PACE WE SHOULD BE ARRIVING IN AROUND AN HOUR.
WHAT~?! THERE'S STILL ANOTHER HOUR LEFT OF TRUDGING THROUGH THIS RUGGED PATH?!
WHAT WAS THAT, SIR? AS I RECALL, WASN'T IT YOU SIR THAT DEMANDED WE CHANGE ROUTES BECAUSE OF THAT CLUSTER OF SNAKES WE SAW EARLIER?
URK

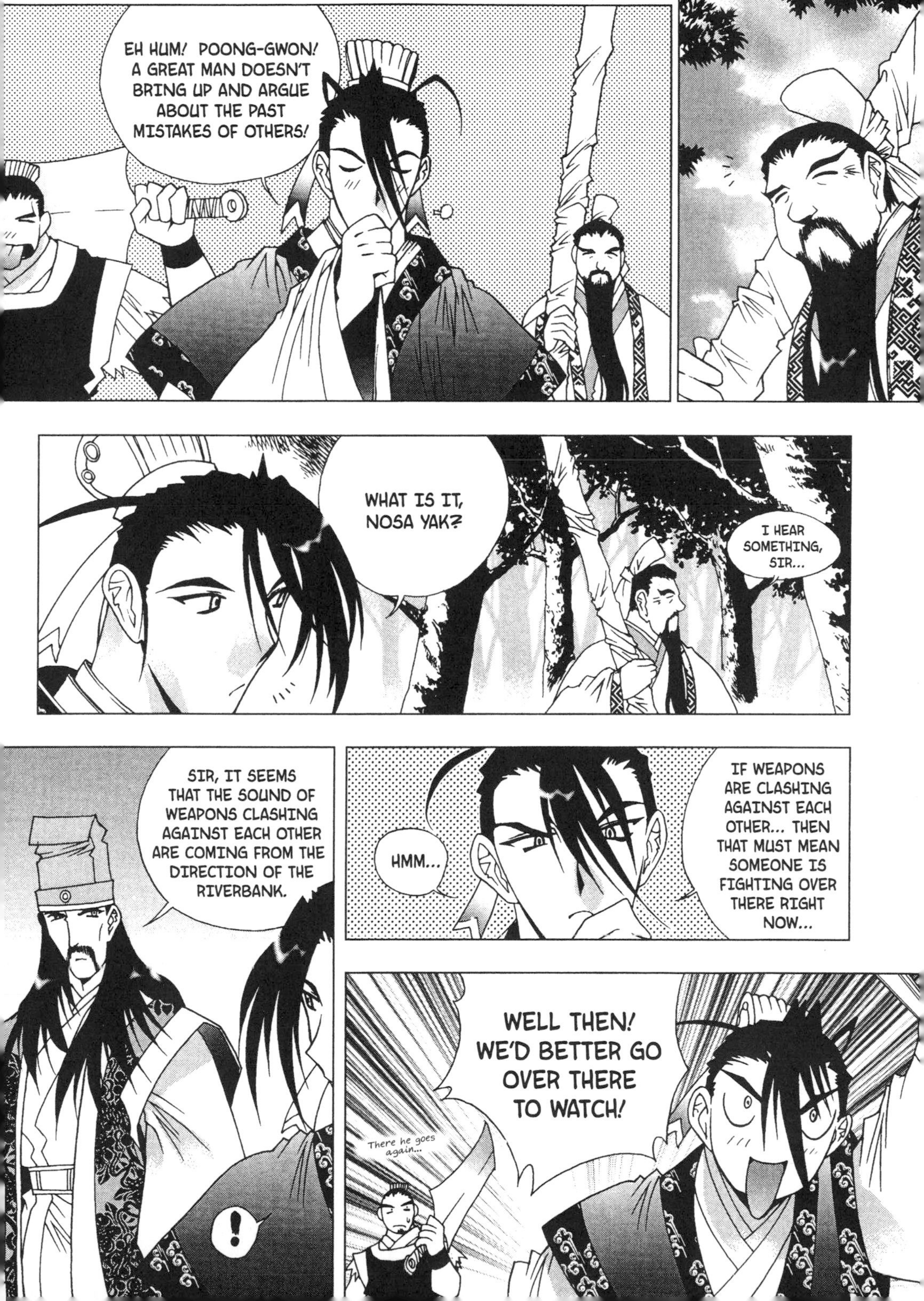
EH HUM! POONG-GWON! A GREAT MAN DOESN'T BRING UP AND ARGUE ABOUT THE PAST MISTAKES OF OTHERS!
WHAT IS IT, NOSA YAK?
I HEAR SOMETHING, SIR...
SIR, IT SEEMS THAT THE SOUND OF WEAPONS CLASHING AGAINST EACH OTHER ARE COMING FROM THE DIRECTION OF THE RIVERBANK.
HMM...
IF WEAPONS ARE CLASHING AGAINST EACH OTHER... THEN THAT MUST MEAN SOMEONE IS FIGHTING OVER THERE RIGHT NOW...
!
WELL THEN! WE'D BETTER GO OVER THERE TO WATCH!
There he goes again...

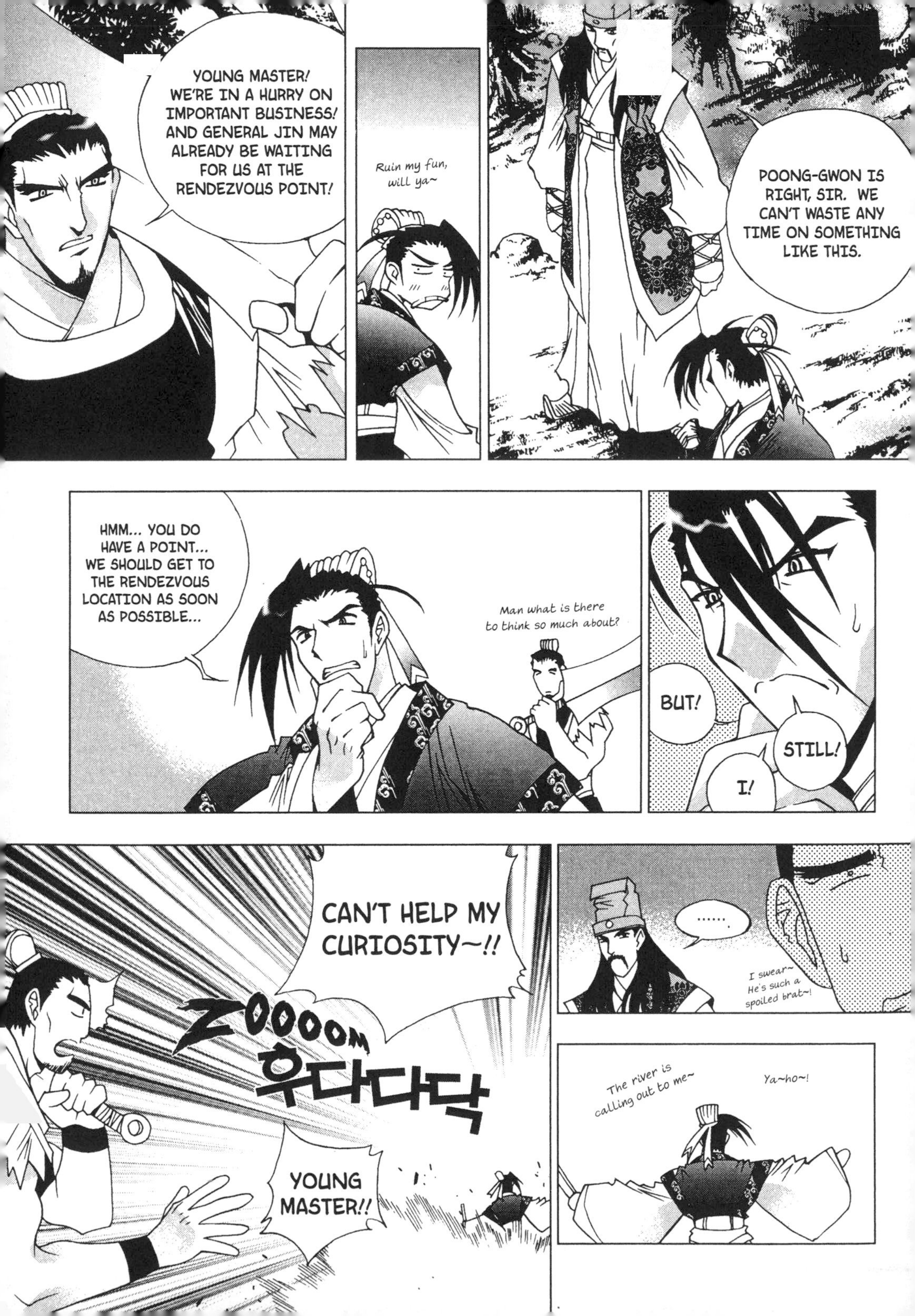
YOUNG MASTER! WE'RE IN A HURRY ON IMPORTANT BUSINESS! AND GENERAL JIN MAY ALREADY BE WAITING FOR US AT THE RENDEZVOUS POINT!
Ruin my fun, will ya~
POONG-GWON IS RIGHT, SIR. WE CAN'T WASTE ANY TIME ON SOMETHING LIKE THIS.
HMM... YOU DO HAVE A POINT... WE SHOULD GET TO THE RENDEZVOUS LOCATION AS SOON AS POSSIBLE...
Man what is there to think so much about?
BUT!
STILL!
I!
CAN'T HELP MY CURIOSITY~!!
ZOOOOM
우다다닥
YOUNG MASTER!!
......
I swear~ He's such a spoiled brat~!
The river is calling out to me~
Ya~ho~!

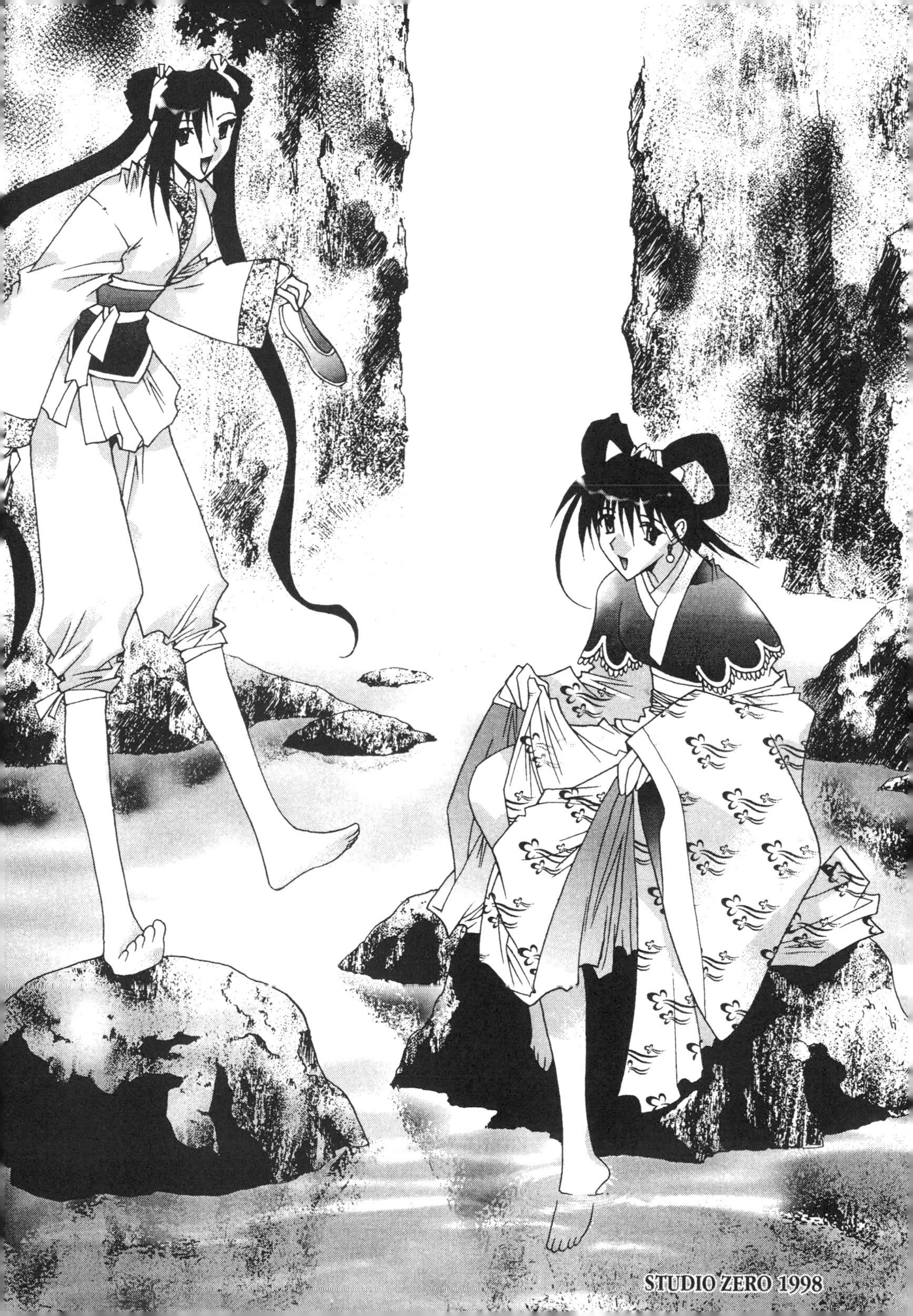
STUDIO ZERO 1998

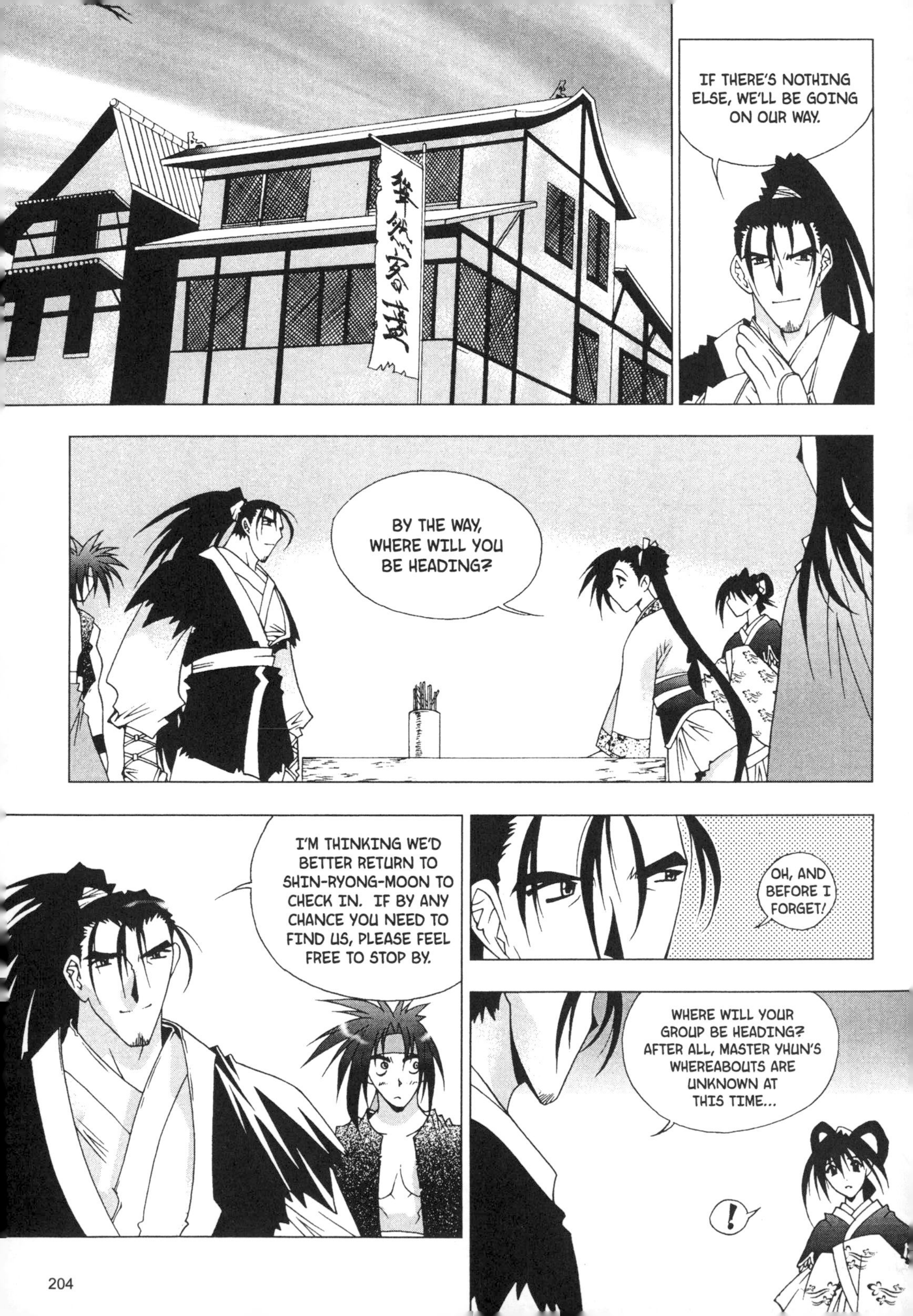

IF THERE'S NOTHING ELSE, WE'LL BE GOING ON OUR WAY.
BY THE WAY, WHERE WILL YOU BE HEADING?
I'M THINKING WE'D BETTER RETURN TO SHIN-RYONG-MOON TO CHECK IN. IF BY ANY CHANCE YOU NEED TO FIND US, PLEASE FEEL FREE TO STOP BY.
OH, AND BEFORE I FORGET!
WHERE WILL YOUR GROUP BE HEADING? AFTER ALL, MASTER YHUN'S WHEREABOUTS ARE UNKNOWN AT THIS TIME...
!

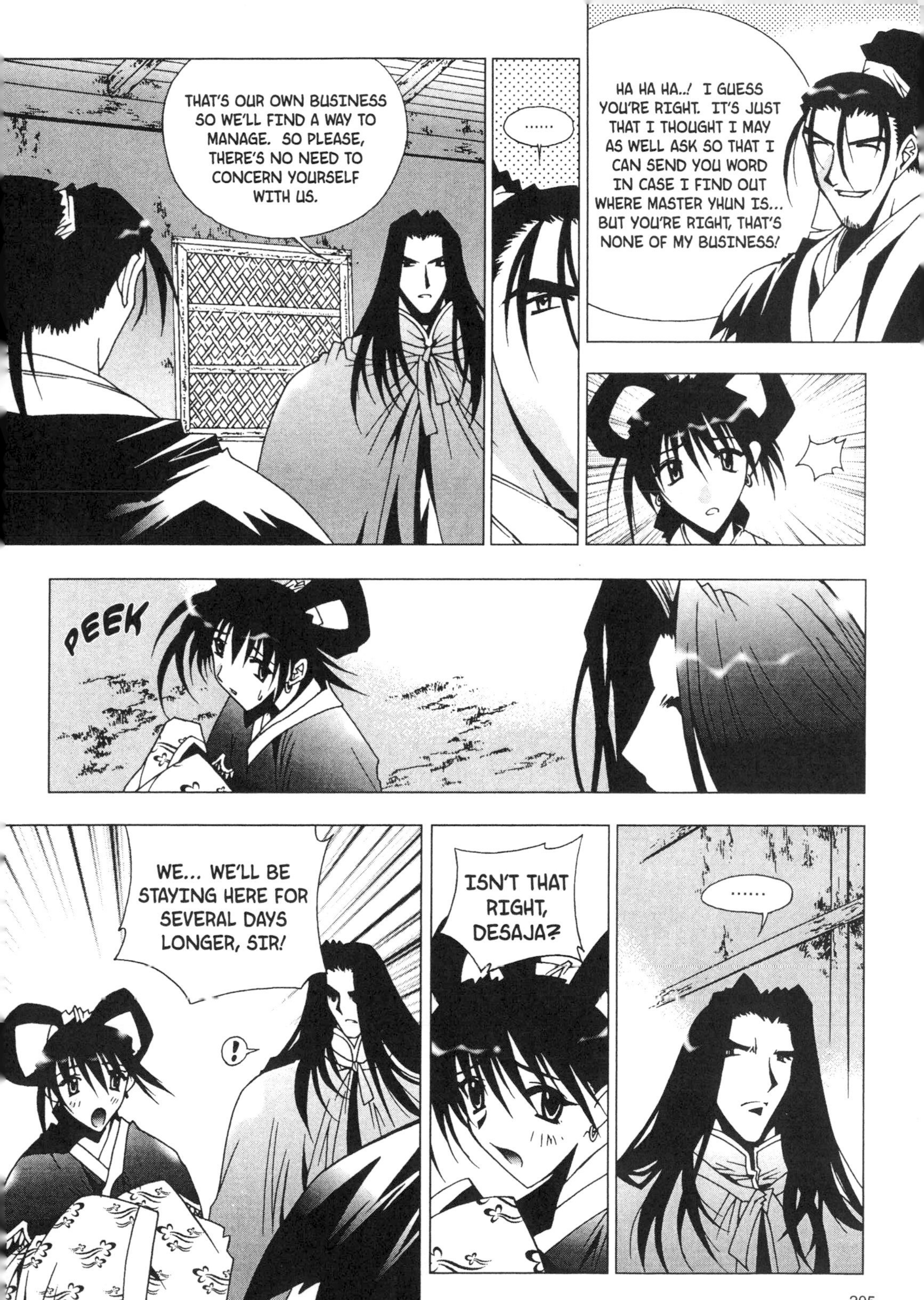

HA HA HA..! I GUESS YOU'RE RIGHT. IT'S JUST THAT I THOUGHT I MAY AS WELL ASK SO THAT I CAN SEND YOU WORD IN CASE I FIND OUT WHERE MASTER YHUN IS... BUT YOU'RE RIGHT, THAT'S NONE OF MY BUSINESS!
......
THAT'S OUR OWN BUSINESS SO WE'LL FIND A WAY TO MANAGE. SO PLEASE, THERE'S NO NEED TO CONCERN YOURSELF WITH US.
PEEK
WE... WE'LL BE STAYING HERE FOR SEVERAL DAYS LONGER, SIR!
!
ISN'T THAT RIGHT, DESAJA?
......

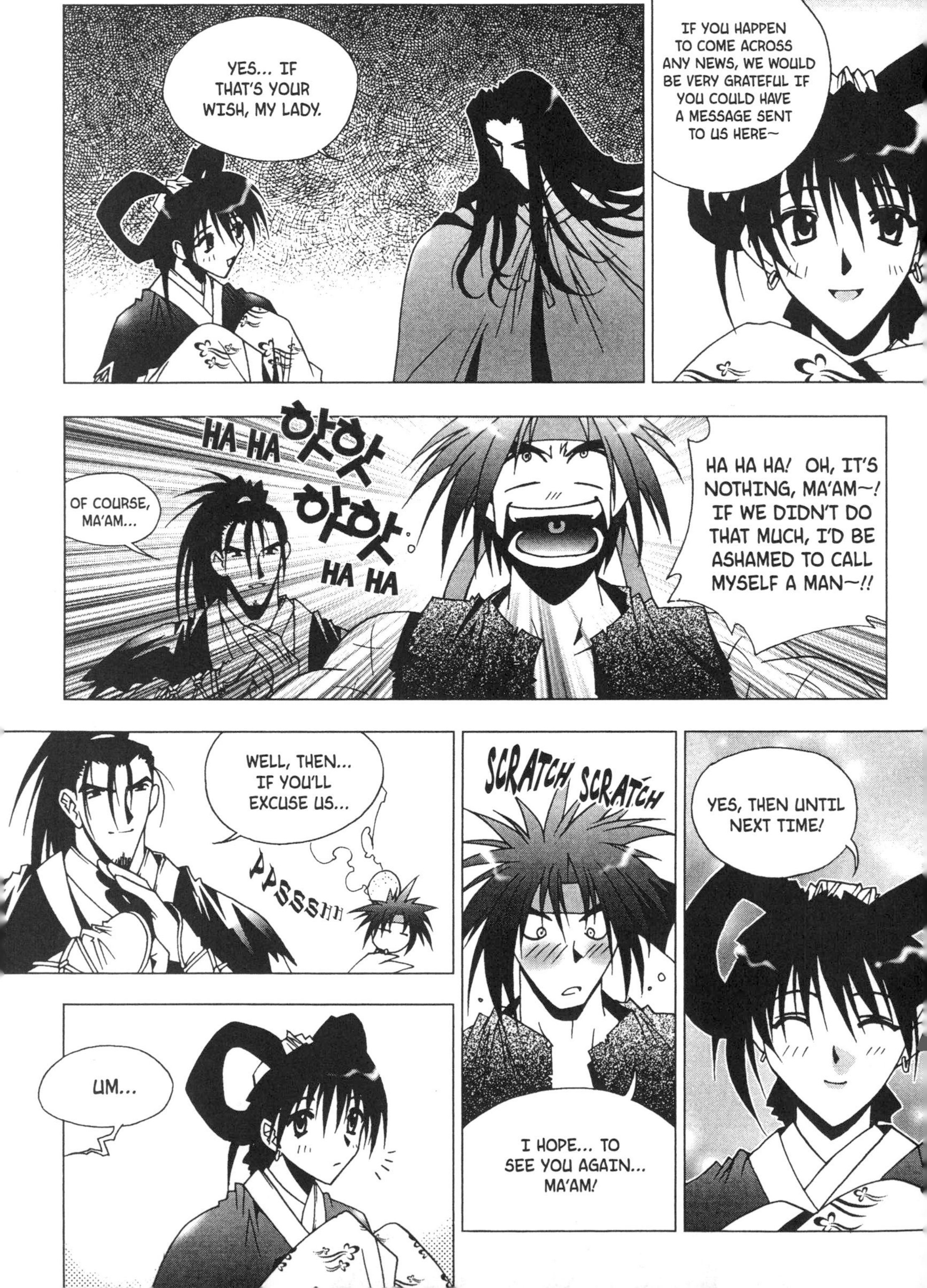
YES... IF THAT'S YOUR WISH, MY LADY.
IF YOU HAPPEN TO COME ACROSS ANY NEWS, WE WOULD BE VERY GRATEFUL IF YOU COULD HAVE A MESSAGE SENT TO US HERE~
OF COURSE, MA'AM...
HA HA
HA HA
HA HA HA! OH, IT'S NOTHING, MA'AM~! IF WE DIDN'T DO THAT MUCH, I'D BE ASHAMED TO CALL MYSELF A MAN~!!
WELL, THEN... IF YOU'LL EXCUSE US...
PPSSSH!!
UM...
SCRATCH SCRATCH
I HOPE... TO SEE YOU AGAIN... MA'AM!
YES, THEN UNTIL NEXT TIME!

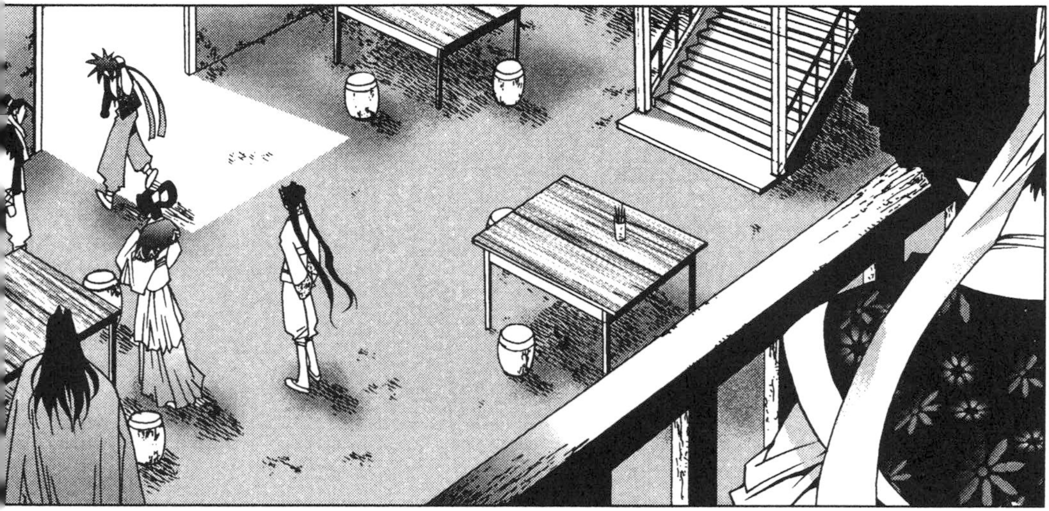

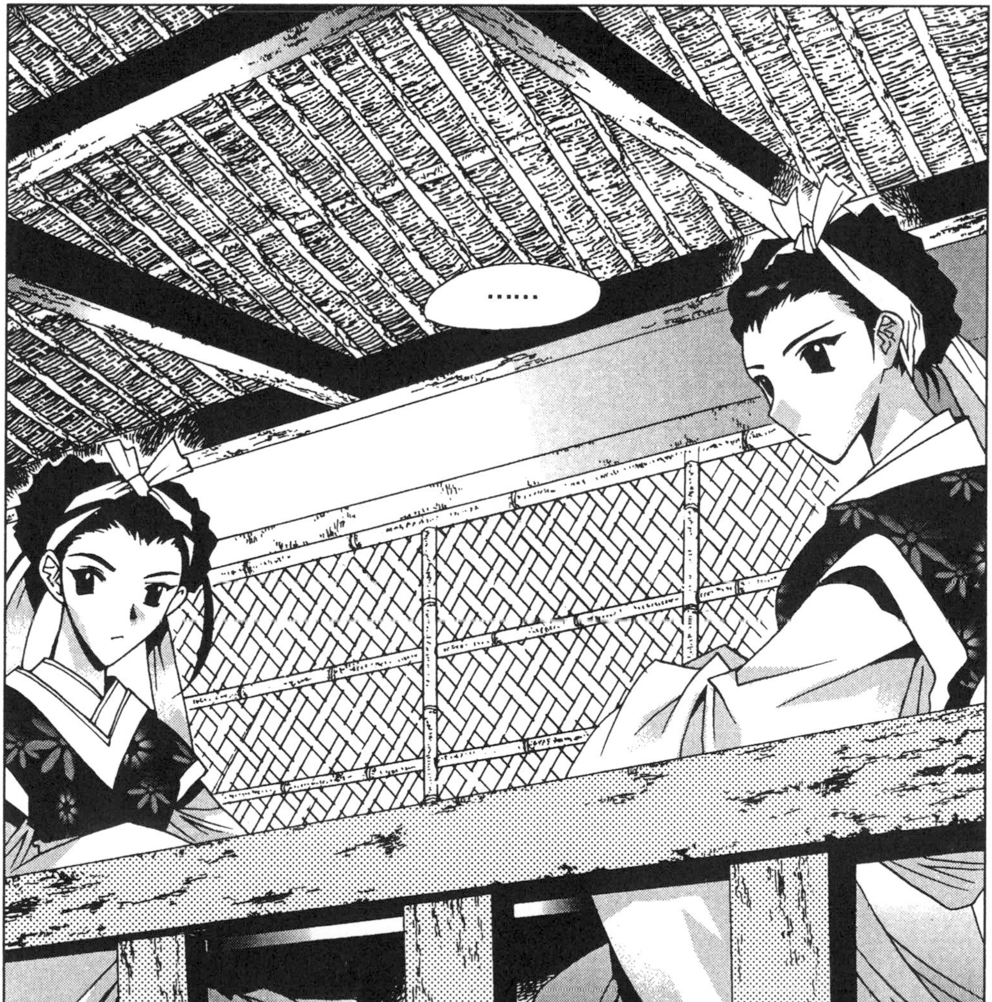
......

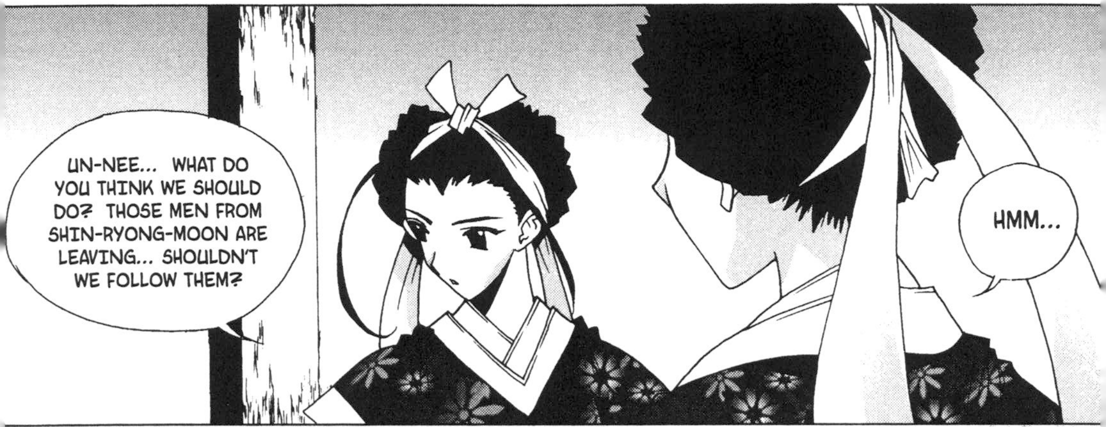
UN-NEE... WHAT DO YOU THINK WE SHOULD DO? THOSE MEN FROM SHIN-RYONG-MOON ARE LEAVING... SHOULDN'T WE FOLLOW THEM?
HMM...

Note : Un-nee is the Korean word that women use to address an older sister (men use a different word). The word un-nee can also be used to refer to any older female acquaintance but it implies a degree of affection and closeness.

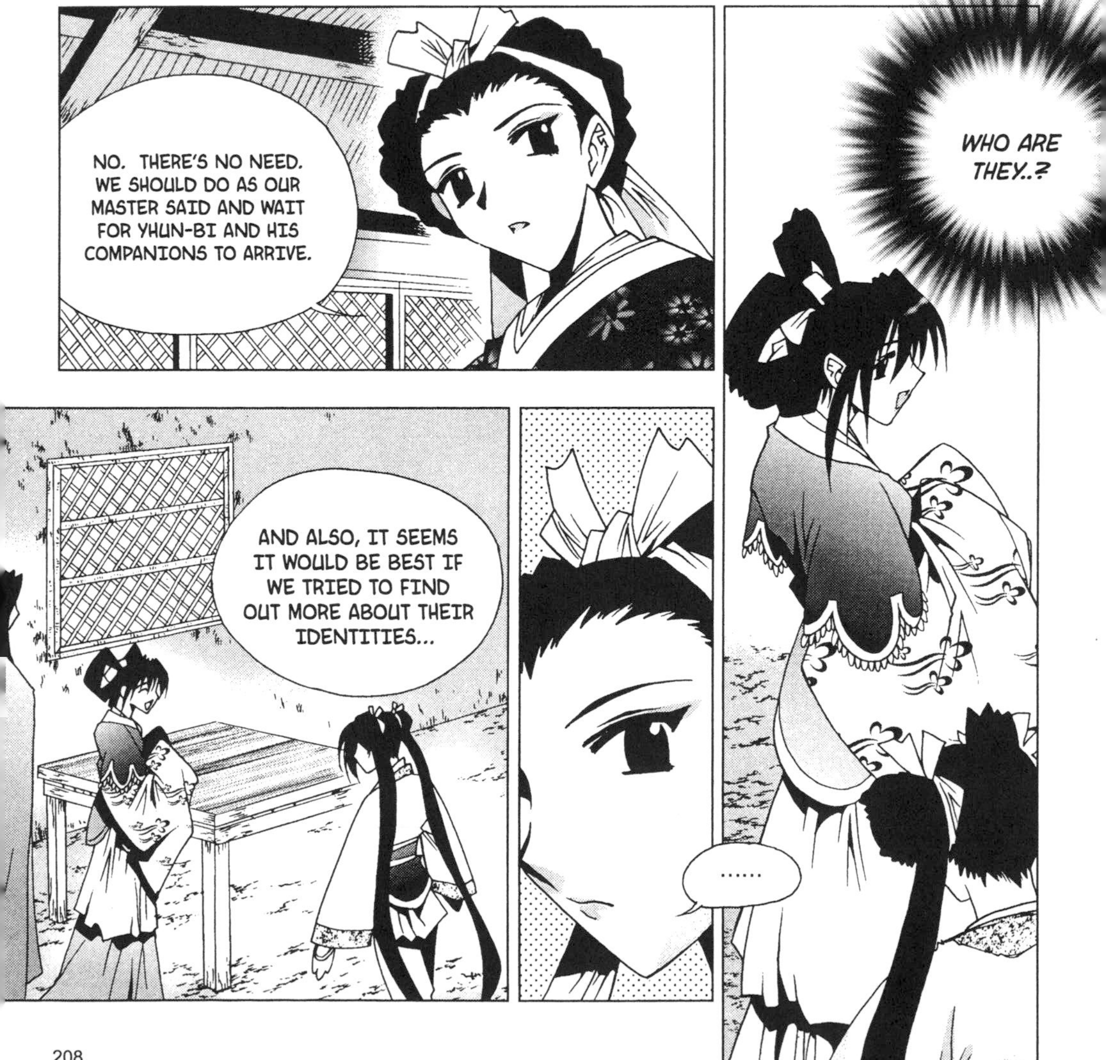
NO. THERE'S NO NEED. WE SHOULD DO AS OUR MASTER SAID AND WAIT FOR YHUN-BI AND HIS COMPANIONS TO ARRIVE.
WHO ARE THEY..?
AND ALSO, IT SEEMS IT WOULD BE BEST IF WE TRIED TO FIND OUT MORE ABOUT THEIR IDENTITIES...
......

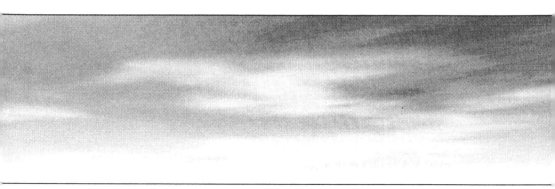

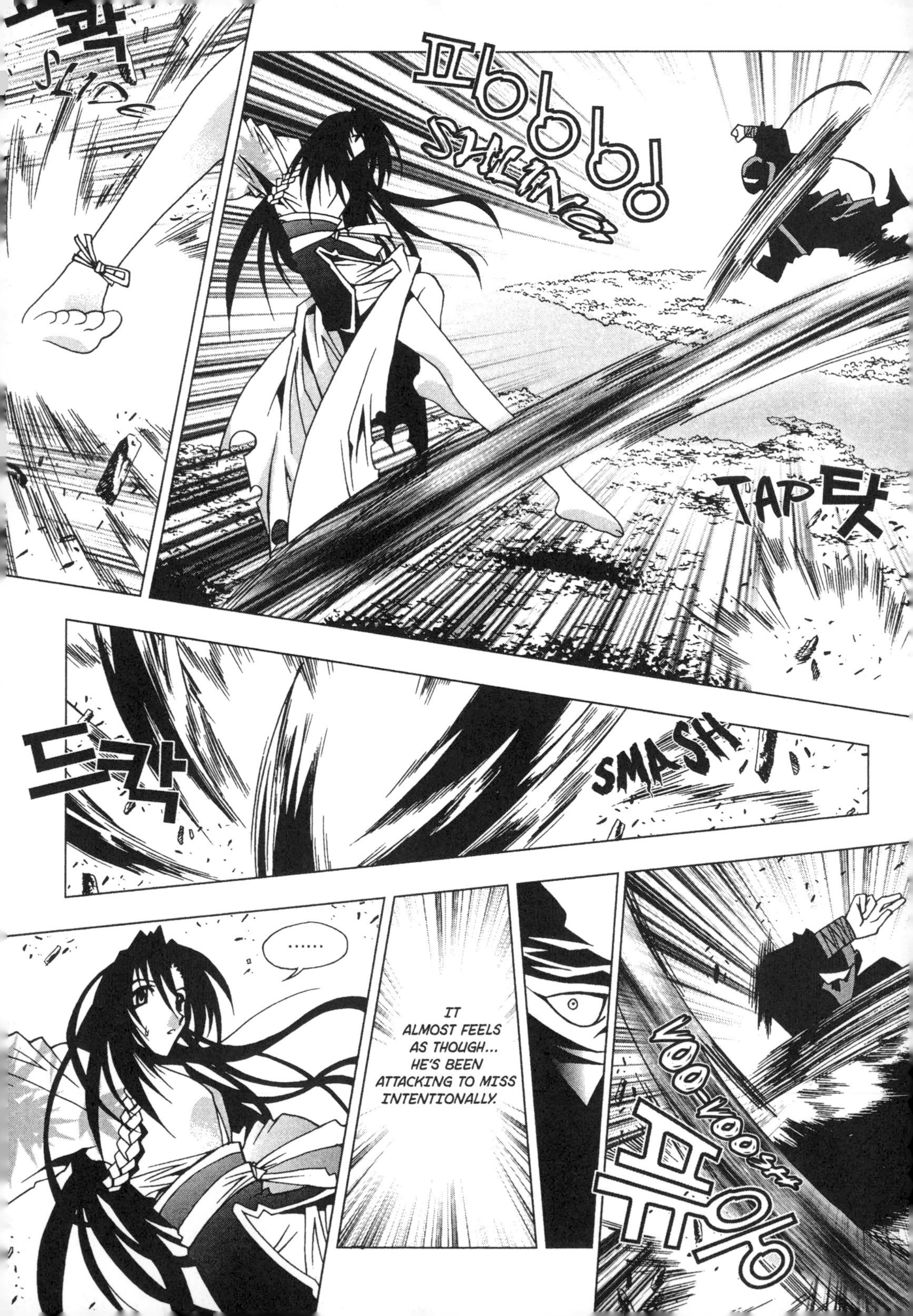
SLICE
SHLING
TAP
탓
SMASH
......
IT ALMOST FEELS AS THOUGH... HE'S BEEN ATTACKING TO MISS INTENTIONALLY.
VOO-VOOSH

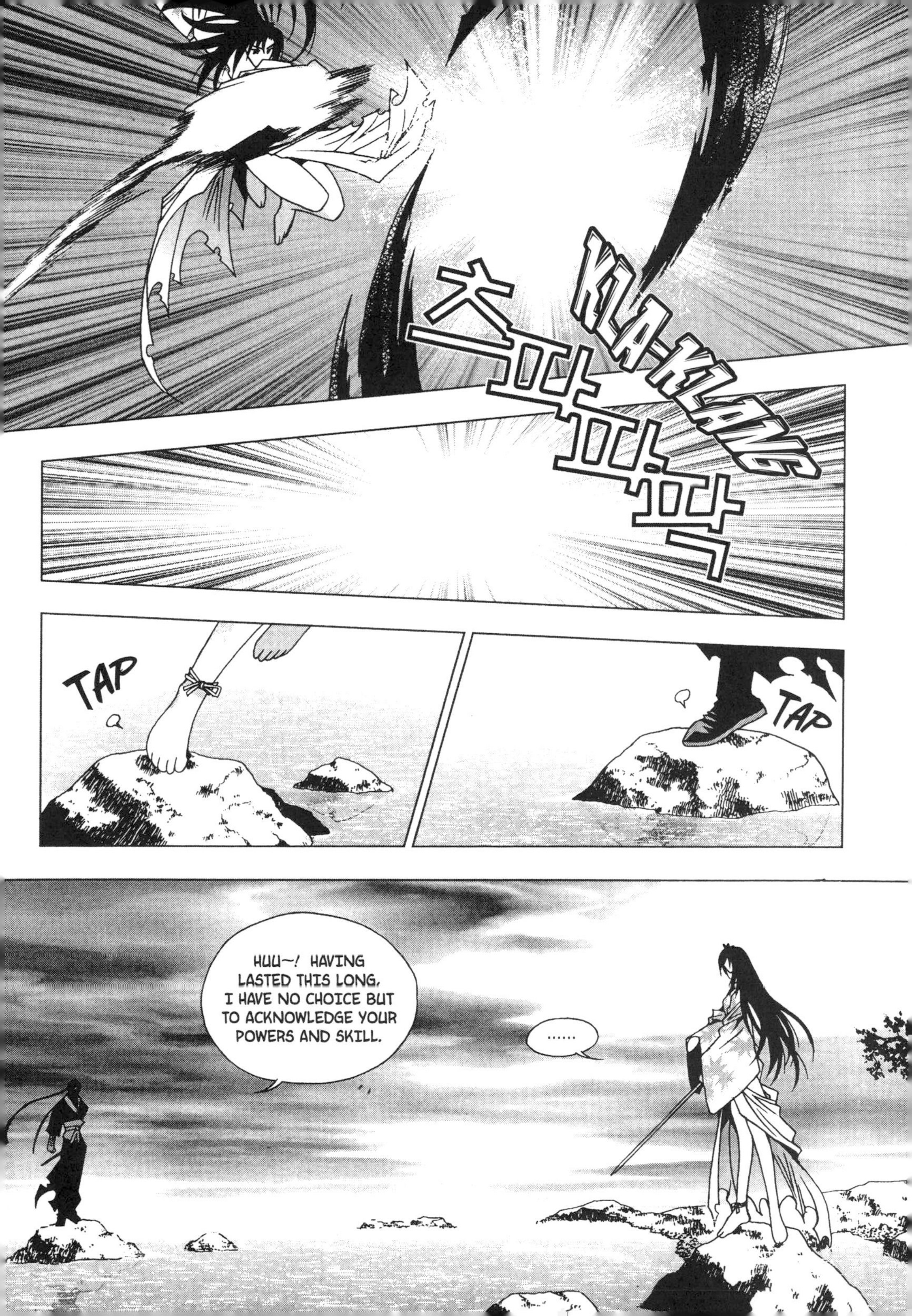

KLA-KLANG
챠파파팍
TAP
TAP
HUU~! HAVING LASTED THIS LONG, I HAVE NO CHOICE BUT TO ACKNOWLEDGE YOUR POWERS AND SKILL.
......

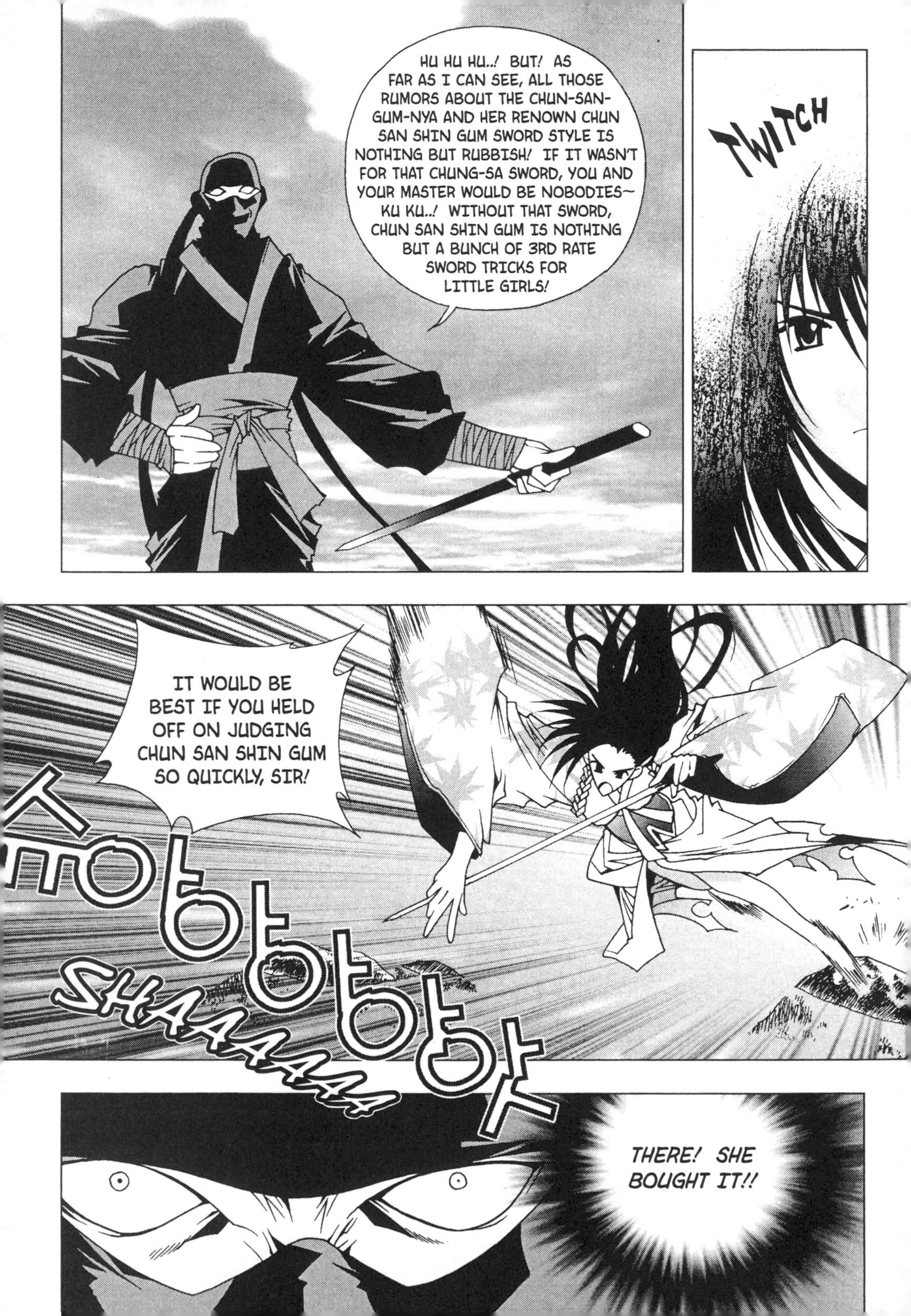

HU HU HU..! BUT! AS FAR AS I CAN SEE, ALL THOSE RUMORS ABOUT THE CHUN-SAN-GUM-NYA AND HER RENOWN CHUN SAN SHIN GUM SWORD STYLE IS NOTHING BUT RUBBISH! IF IT WASN'T FOR THAT CHUNG-SA SWORD, YOU AND YOUR MASTER WOULD BE NOBODIES~ KU KU..! WITHOUT THAT SWORD, CHUN SAN SHIN GUM IS NOTHING BUT A BUNCH OF 3RD RATE SWORD TRICKS FOR LITTLE GIRLS!
TWITCH
IT WOULD BE BEST IF YOU HELD OFF ON JUDGING CHUN SAN SHIN GUM SO QUICKLY, SIR!
TOTTTOT
SHAAAAAA
THERE! SHE BOUGHT IT!!

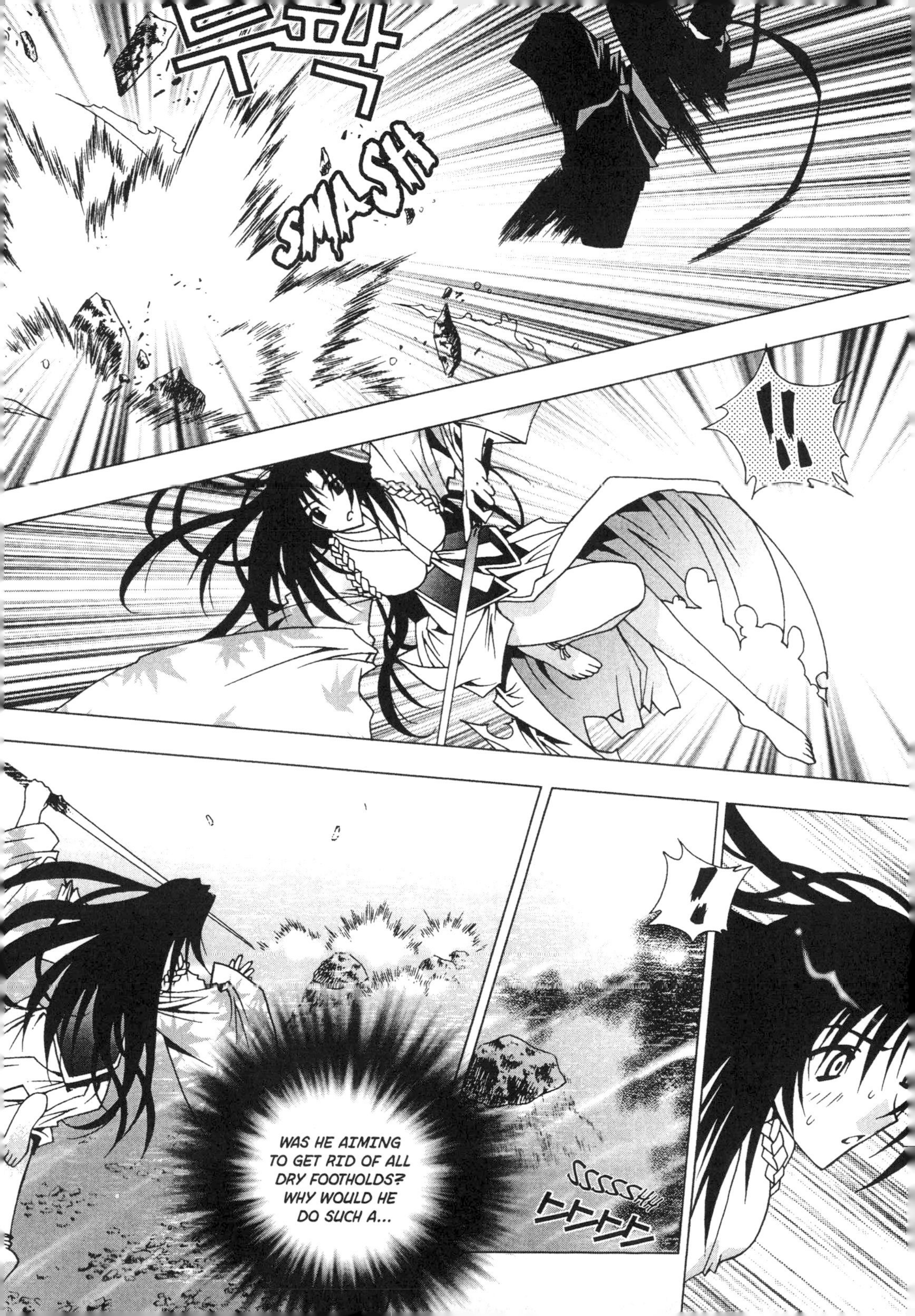
SMASH
!!
!
WAS HE AIMING TO GET RID OF ALL DRY FOOTHOLDS? WHY WOULD HE DO SUCH A...
SSSSSHH

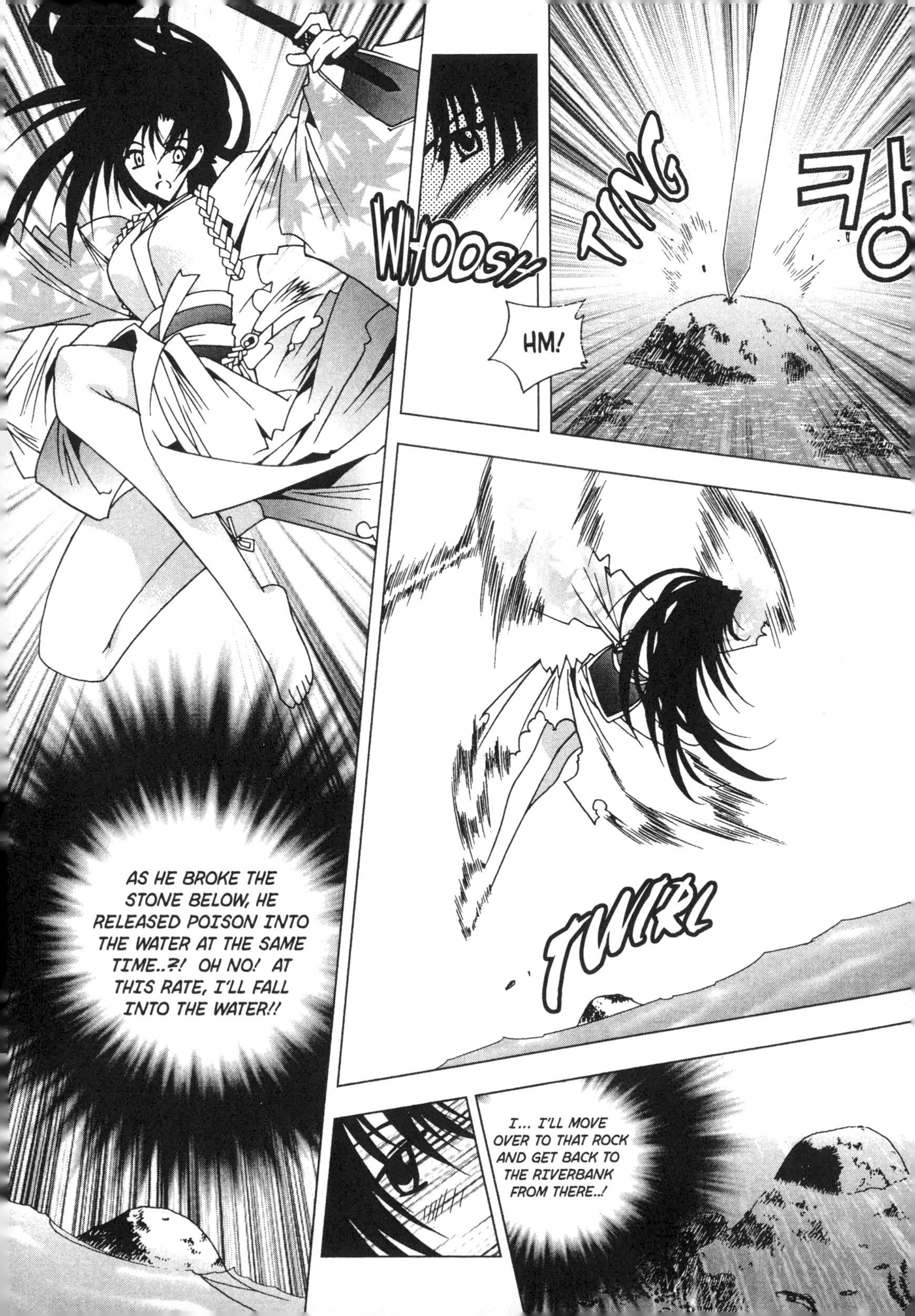

WHOOSH
HM!
TING
캉
TWIRL
AS HE BROKE THE STONE BELOW, HE RELEASED POISON INTO THE WATER AT THE SAME TIME..?! OH NO! AT THIS RATE, I'LL FALL INTO THE WATER!!
I... I'LL MOVE OVER TO THAT ROCK AND GET BACK TO THE RIVERBANK FROM THERE..!

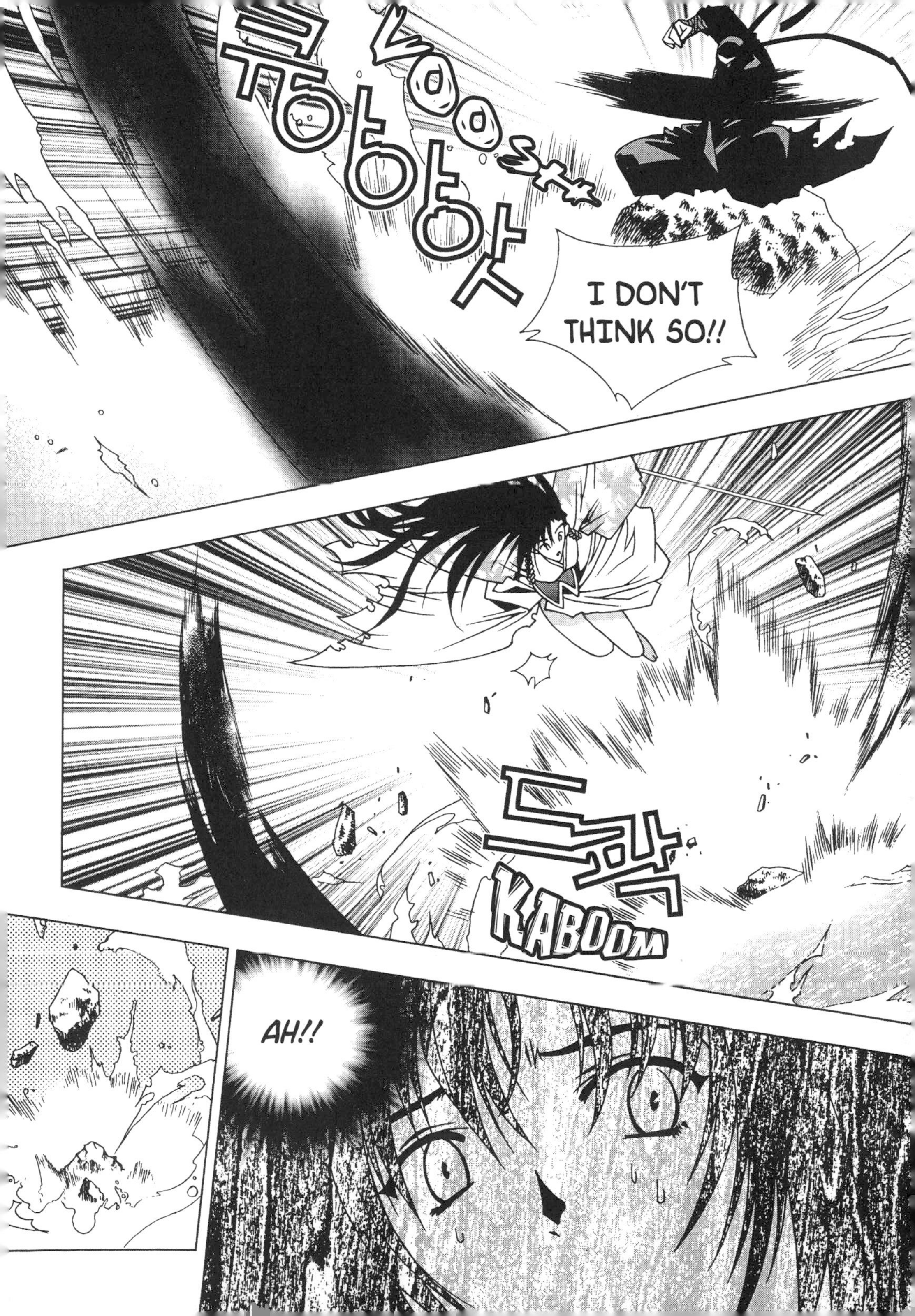
Vooosh
I DON'T THINK SO!!
KABOOM
AH!!

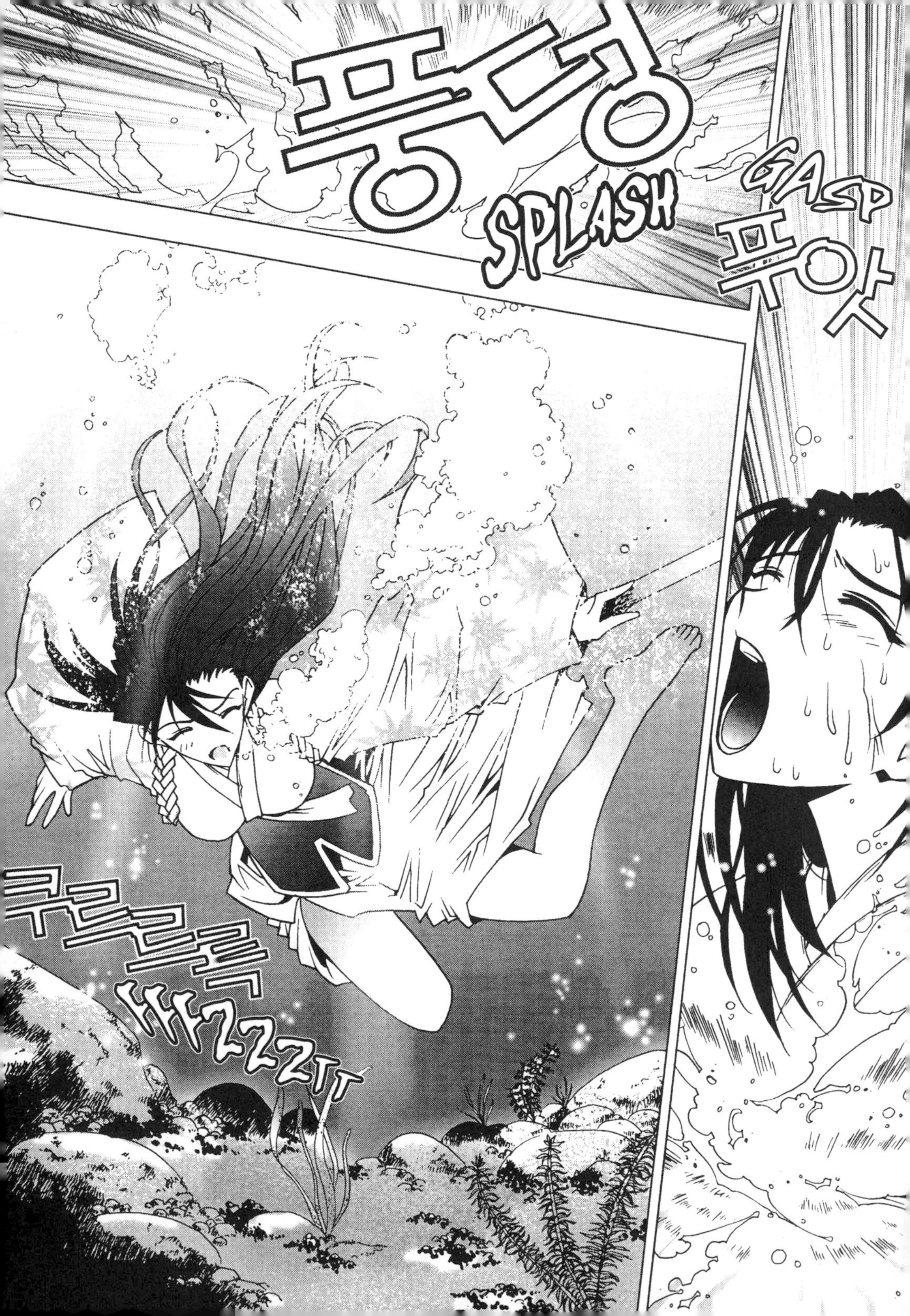
풍덩
SPLASH
GASP
푸앗
구르르륵

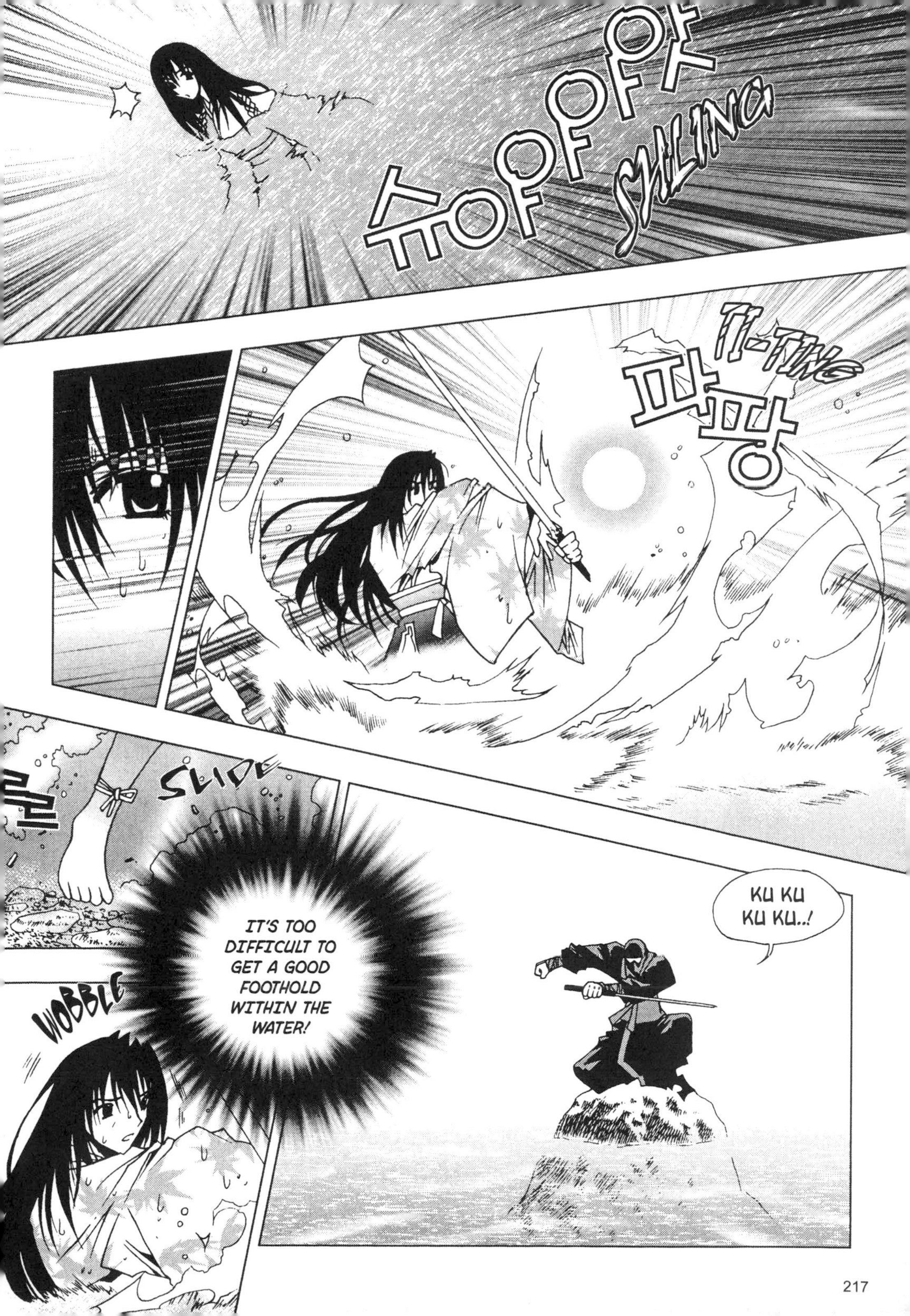
SHLING
TI-TING
파팡
SLIDE
KU KU KU KU..!
IT'S TOO DIFFICULT TO GET A GOOD FOOTHOLD WITHIN THE WATER!
WOBBLE

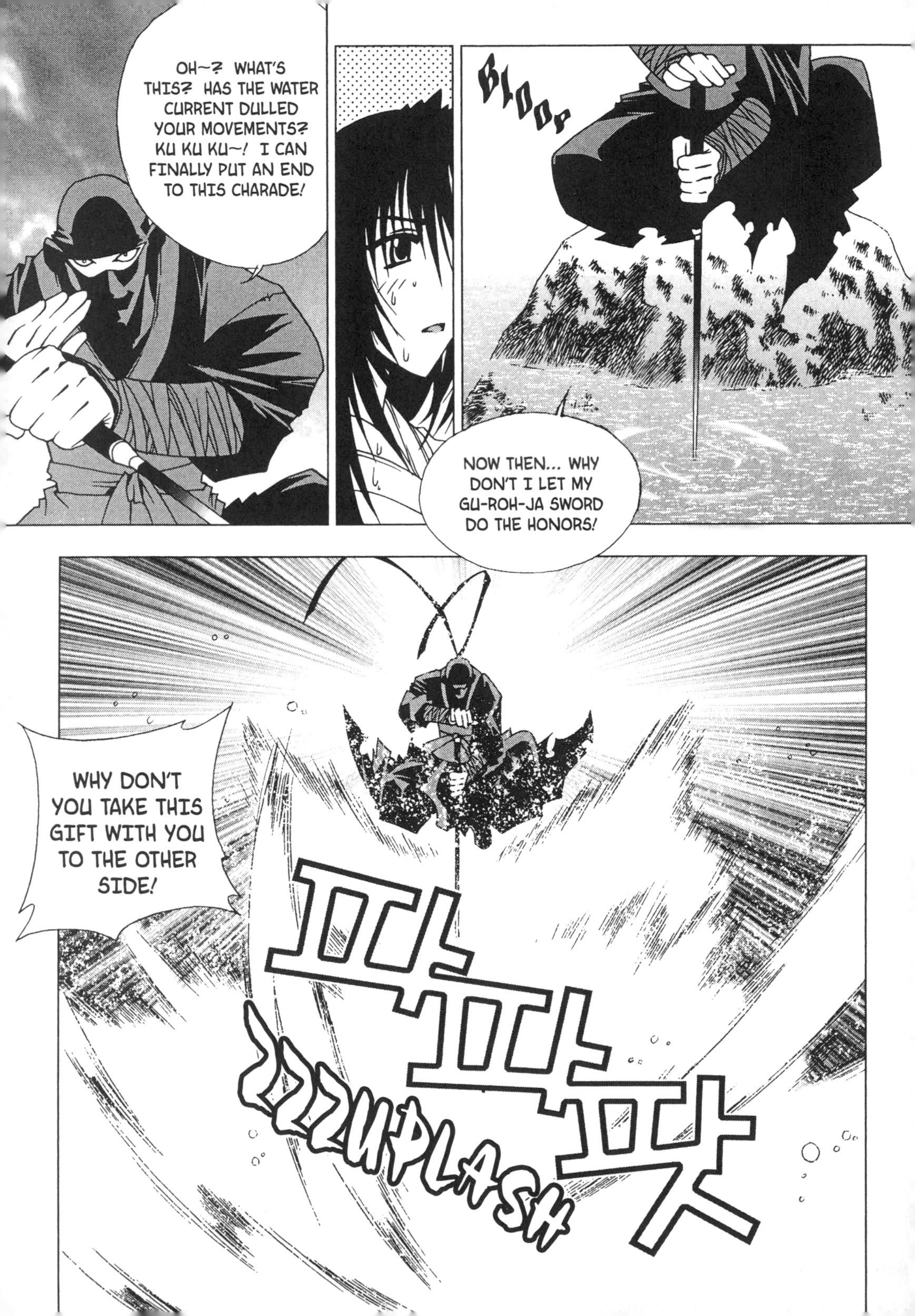
OH~? WHAT'S THIS? HAS THE WATER CURRENT DULLED YOUR MOVEMENTS? KU KU KU~! I CAN FINALLY PUT AN END TO THIS CHARADE!
BLOOP
NOW THEN... WHY DON'T I LET MY GU-ROH-JA SWORD DO THE HONORS!
WHY DON'T YOU TAKE THIS GIFT WITH YOU TO THE OTHER SIDE!
ZZZUPLASH

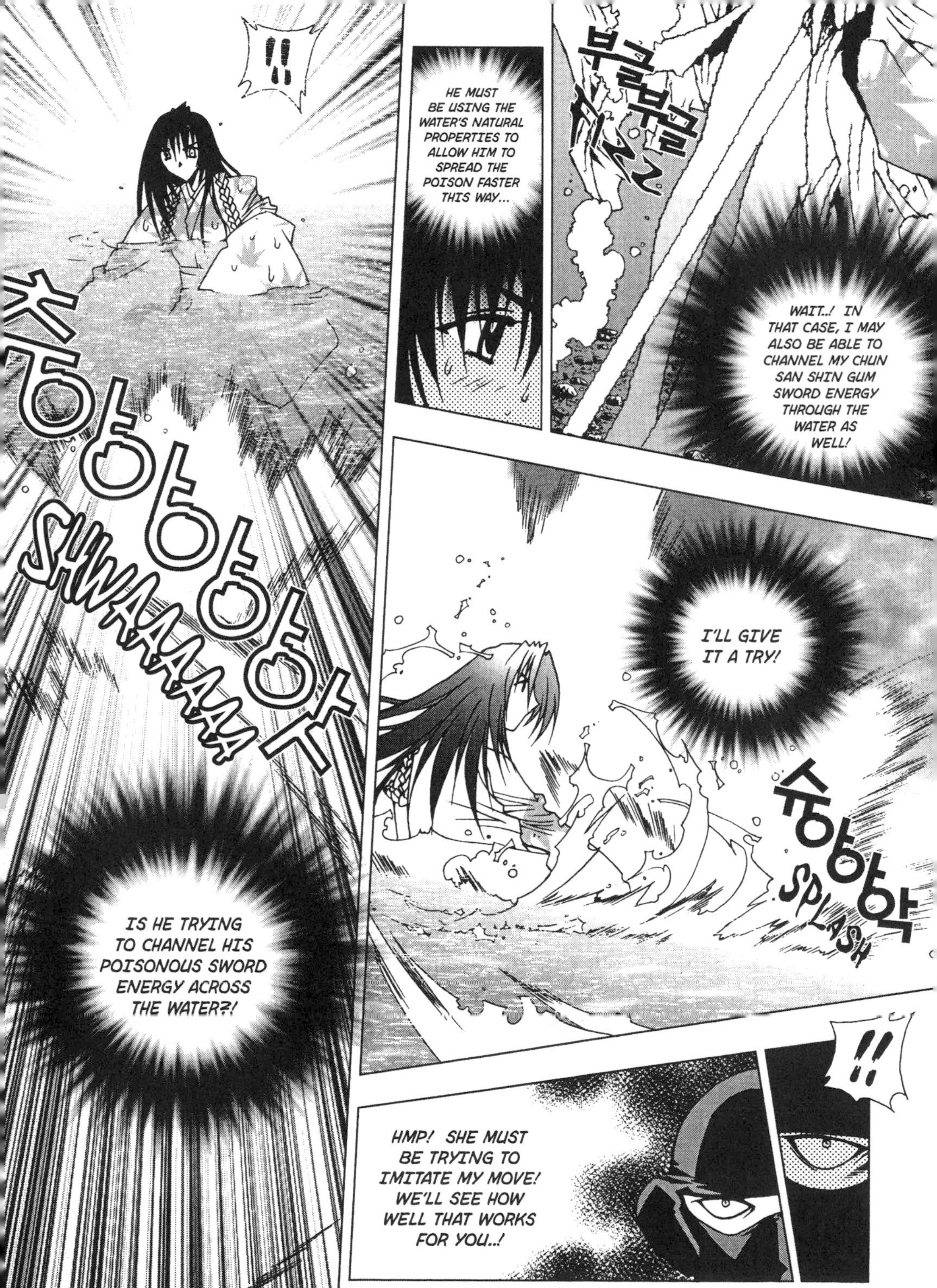

!!
SHWAAAAAAA
IS HE TRYING TO CHANNEL HIS POISONOUS SWORD ENERGY ACROSS THE WATER?!
HE MUST BE USING THE WATER'S NATURAL PROPERTIES TO ALLOW HIM TO SPREAD THE POISON FASTER THIS WAY...
부글부글
WAIT..! IN THAT CASE, I MAY ALSO BE ABLE TO CHANNEL MY CHUN SAN SHIN GUM SWORD ENERGY THROUGH THE WATER AS WELL!
I'LL GIVE IT A TRY!
SPLASH
!!
HMP! SHE MUST BE TRYING TO IMITATE MY MOVE! WE'LL SEE HOW WELL THAT WORKS FOR YOU..!

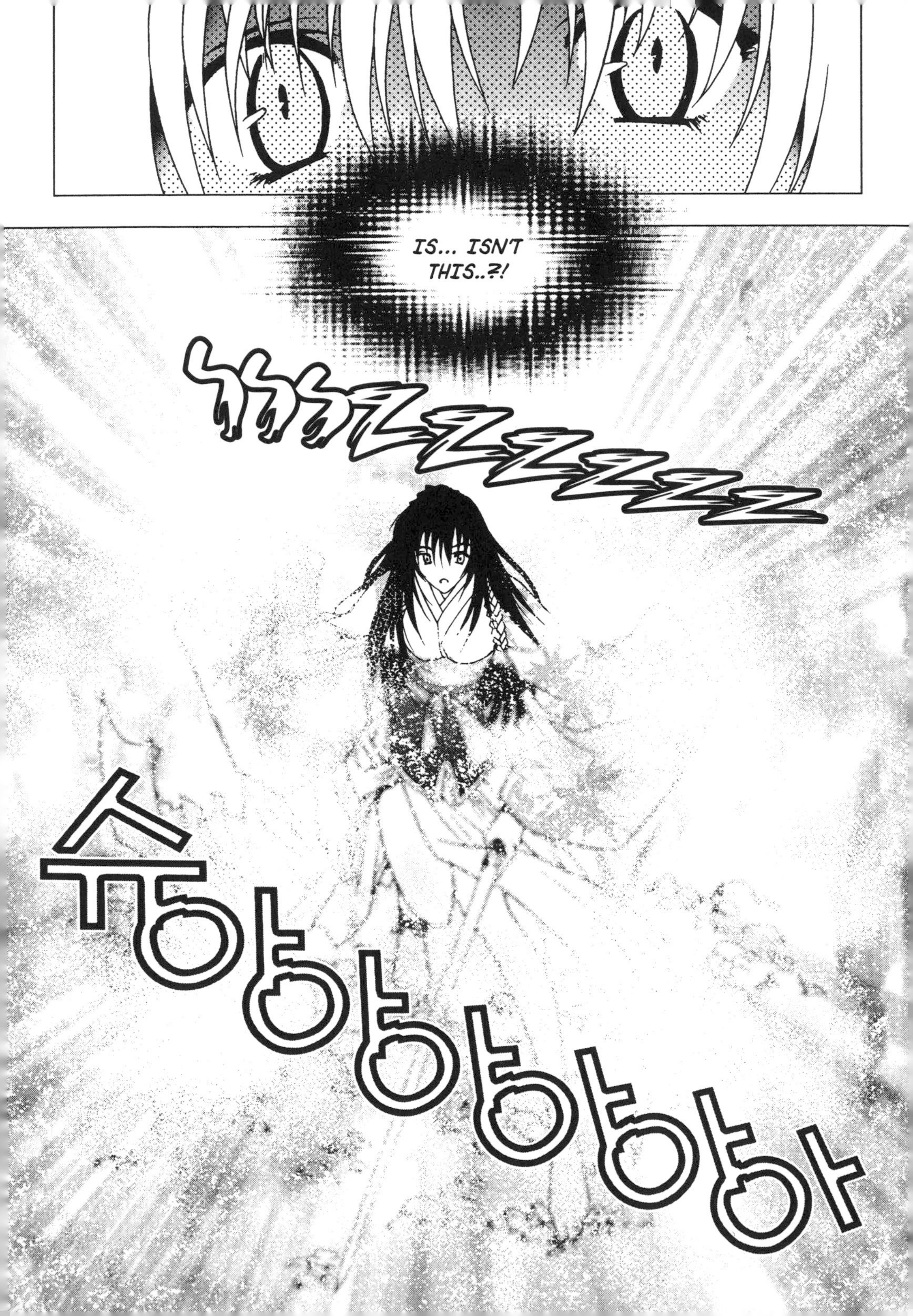
IS... ISN'T THIS..?!

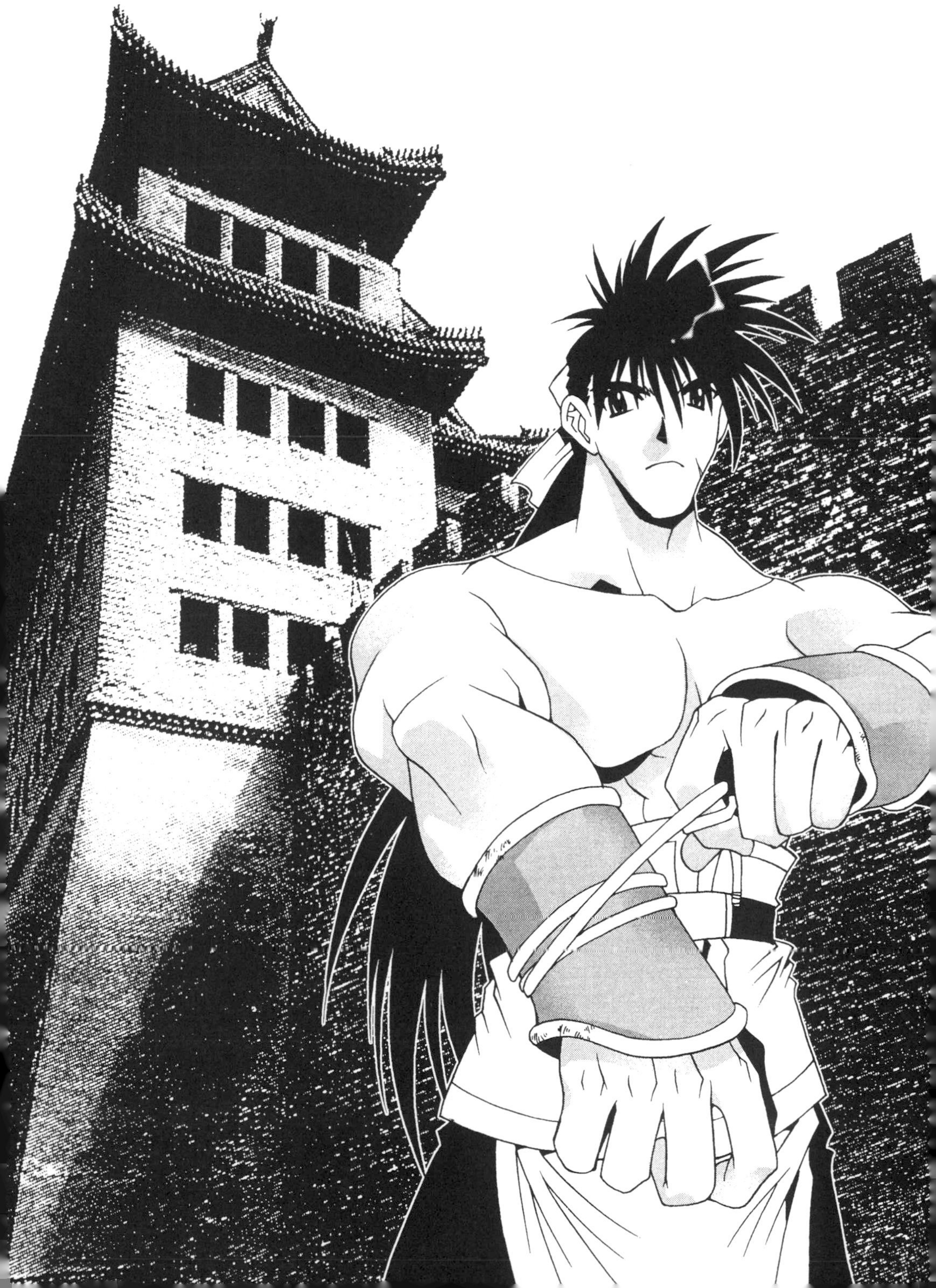

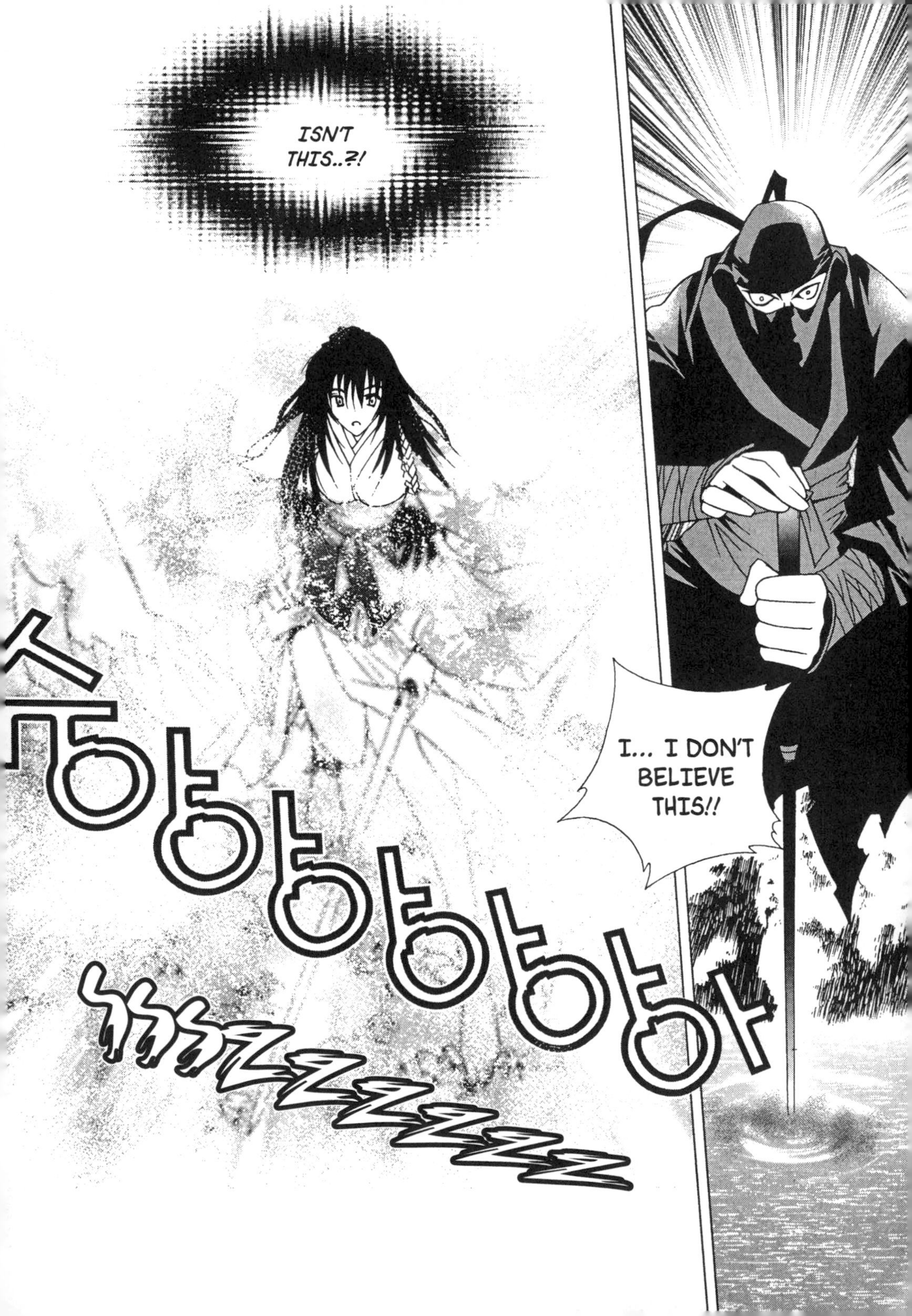
I... I DON'T BELIEVE THIS!!
ISN'T THIS..?!

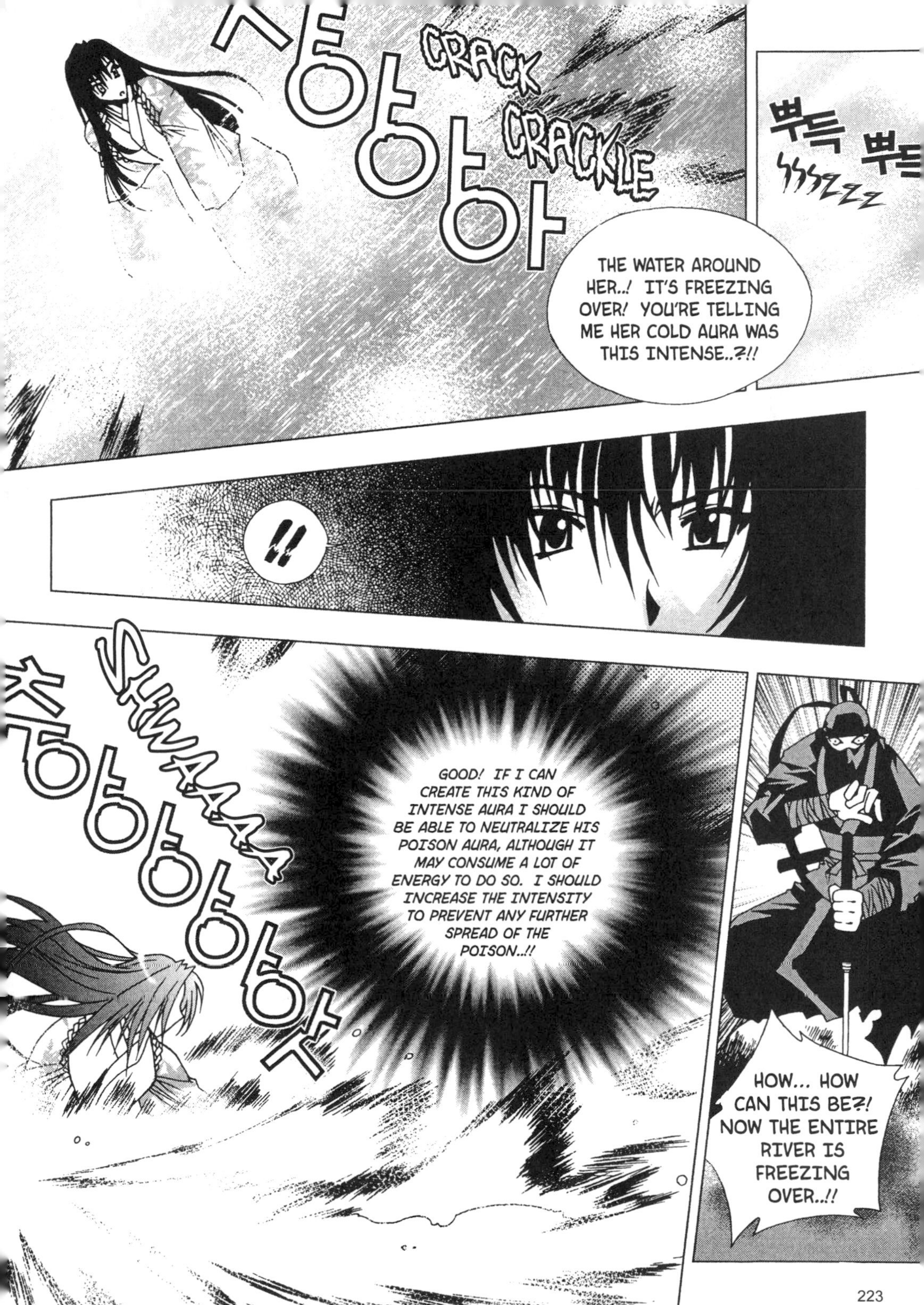

CRACK
CRACKLE
쩌저저적
뿌드득 뿌드
SSSSZZZ
THE WATER AROUND HER..! IT'S FREEZING OVER! YOU'RE TELLING ME HER COLD AURA WAS THIS INTENSE..?!!
!!
SHWAAAAA
촤아아아아아앗
GOOD! IF I CAN CREATE THIS KIND OF INTENSE AURA I SHOULD BE ABLE TO NEUTRALIZE HIS POISON AURA, ALTHOUGH IT MAY CONSUME A LOT OF ENERGY TO DO SO. I SHOULD INCREASE THE INTENSITY TO PREVENT ANY FURTHER SPREAD OF THE POISON..!!
HOW... HOW CAN THIS BE?! NOW THE ENTIRE RIVER IS FREEZING OVER..!!

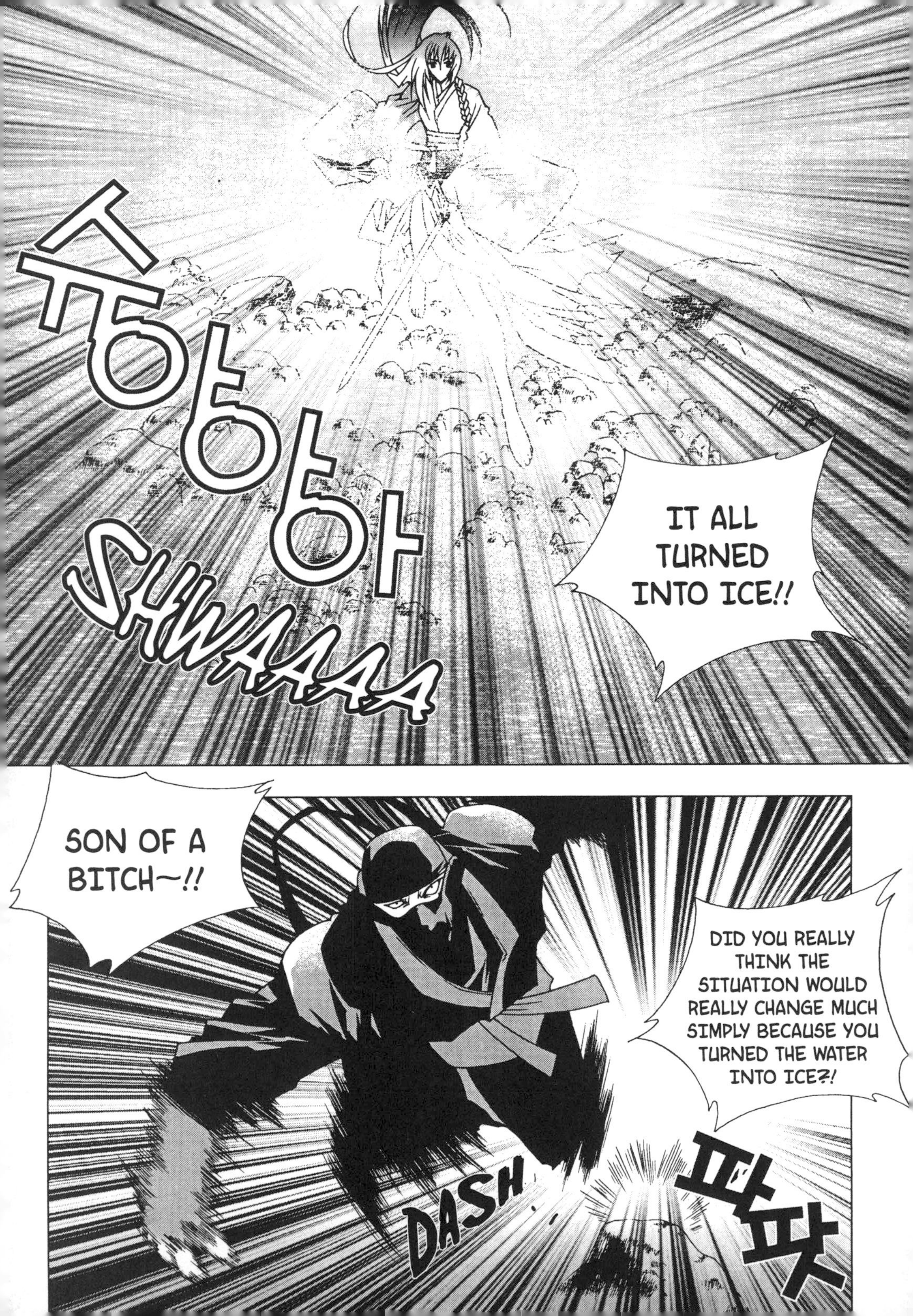
SHWAAAA
IT ALL TURNED INTO ICE!!
SON OF A BITCH~!!
DID YOU REALLY THINK THE SITUATION WOULD REALLY CHANGE MUCH SIMPLY BECAUSE YOU TURNED THE WATER INTO ICE?!
DASH

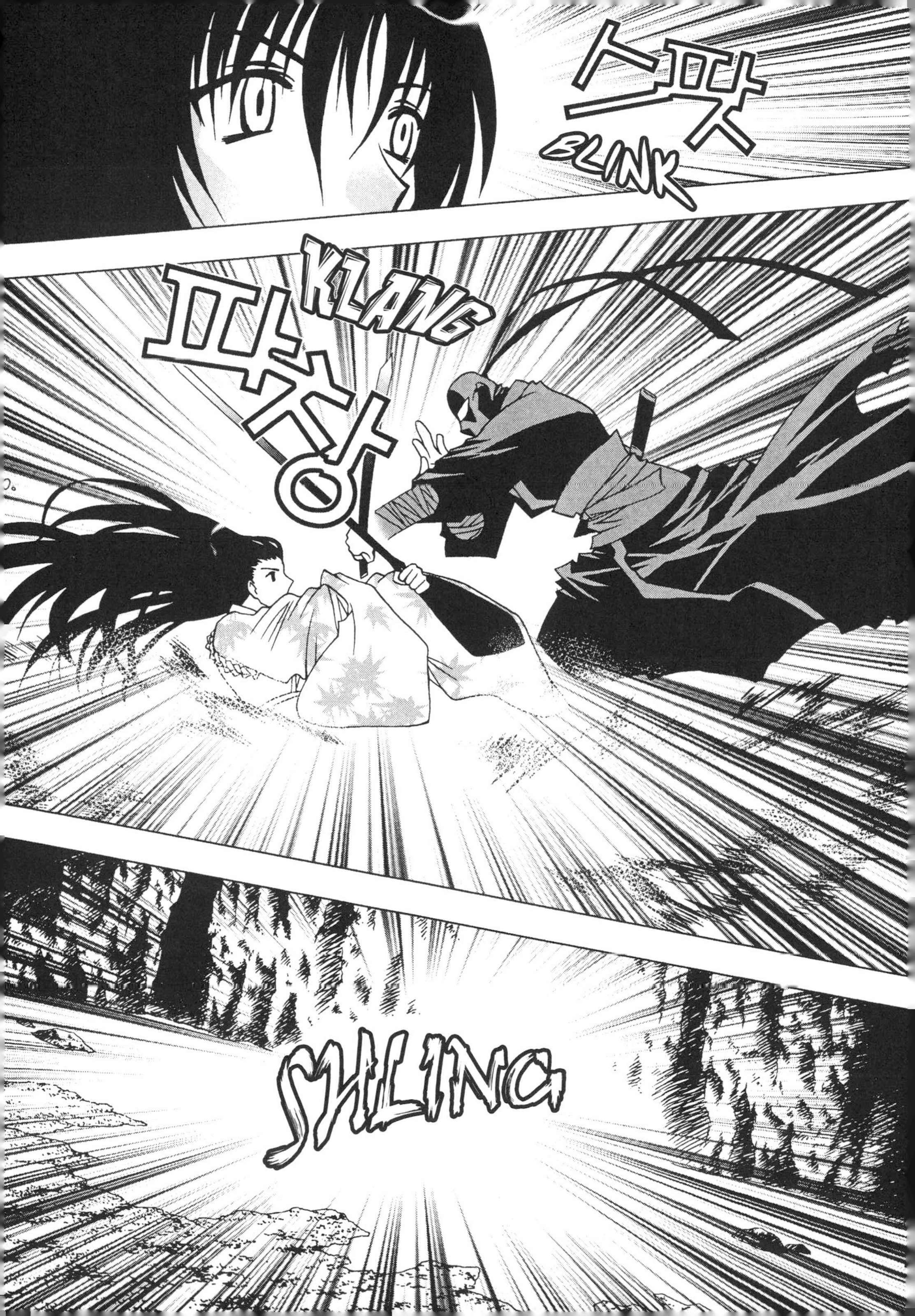
BLINK
KLANG
파창
SHLING

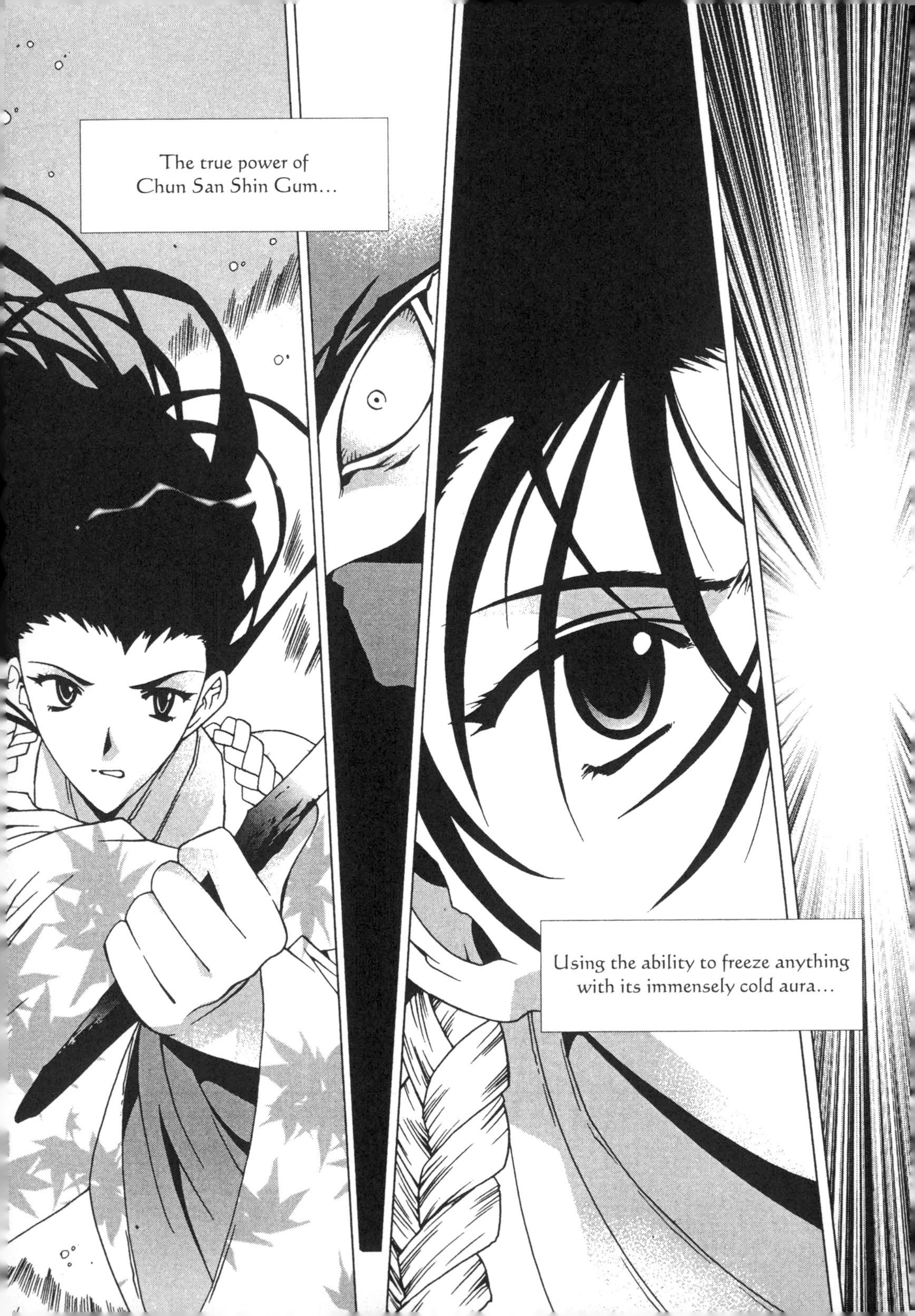
The true power of Chun San Shin Gum...
Using the ability to freeze anything with its immensely cold aura...

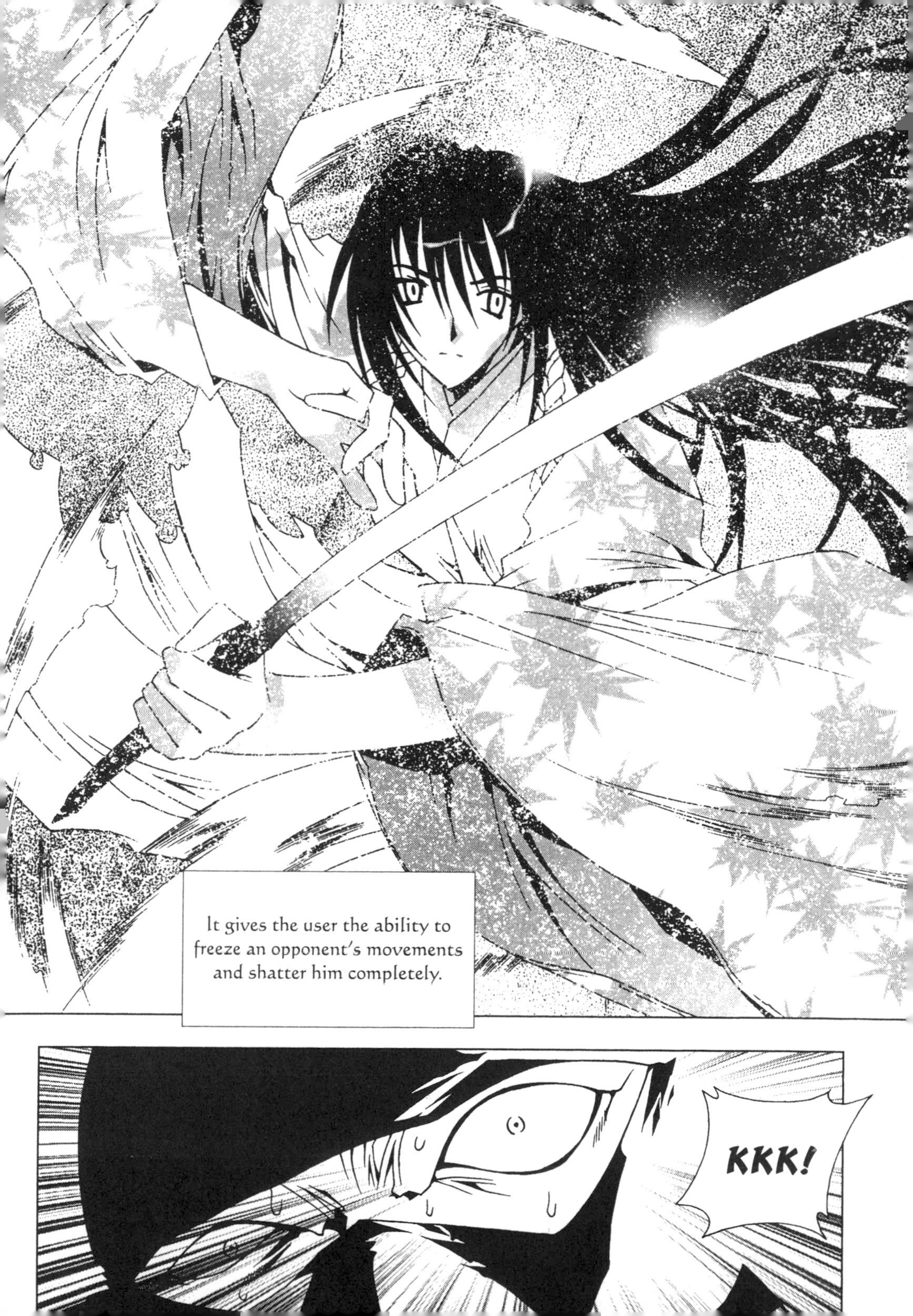
It gives the user the ability to freeze an opponent's movements and shatter him completely.
KKK!

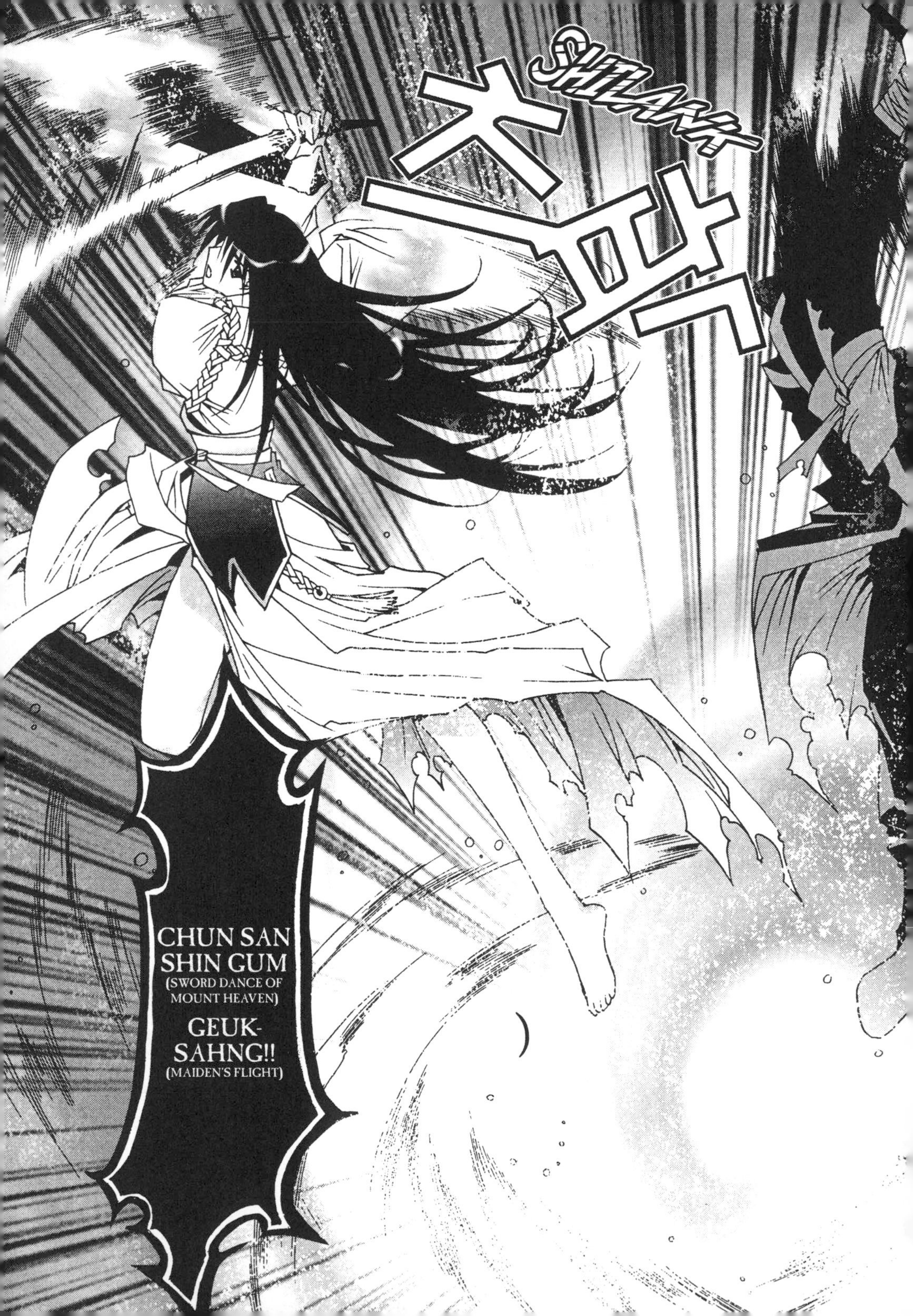
SHHLANK
CHUN SAN SHIN GUM (SWORD DANCE OF MOUNT HEAVEN)
GEUK-SAHNG!! (MAIDEN'S FLIGHT)

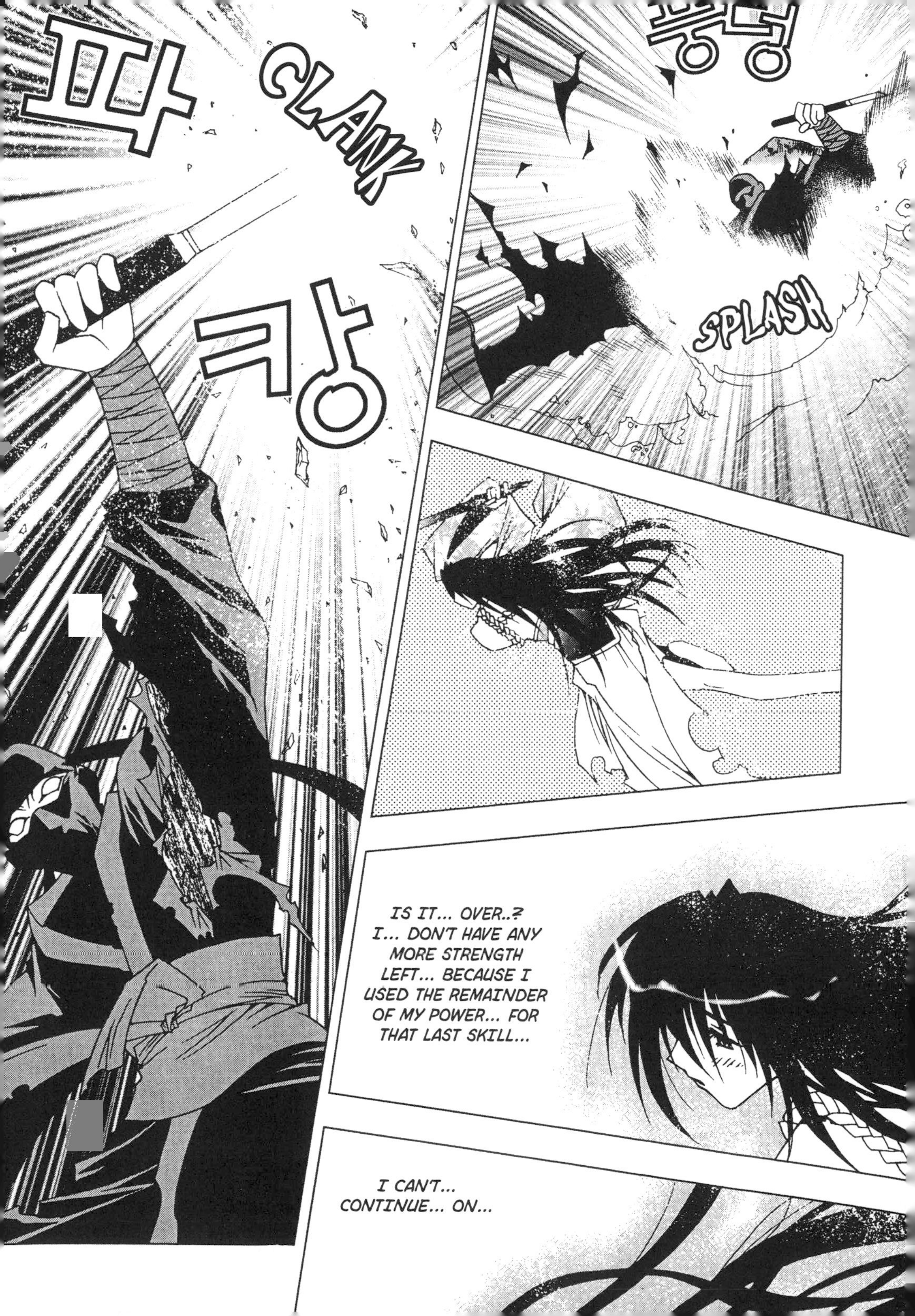

붕웅
SPLASH
파
CLANK
캉
IS IT... OVER..?
I... DON'T HAVE ANY MORE STRENGTH LEFT... BECAUSE I USED THE REMAINDER OF MY POWER... FOR THAT LAST SKILL...
I CAN'T... CONTINUE... ON...

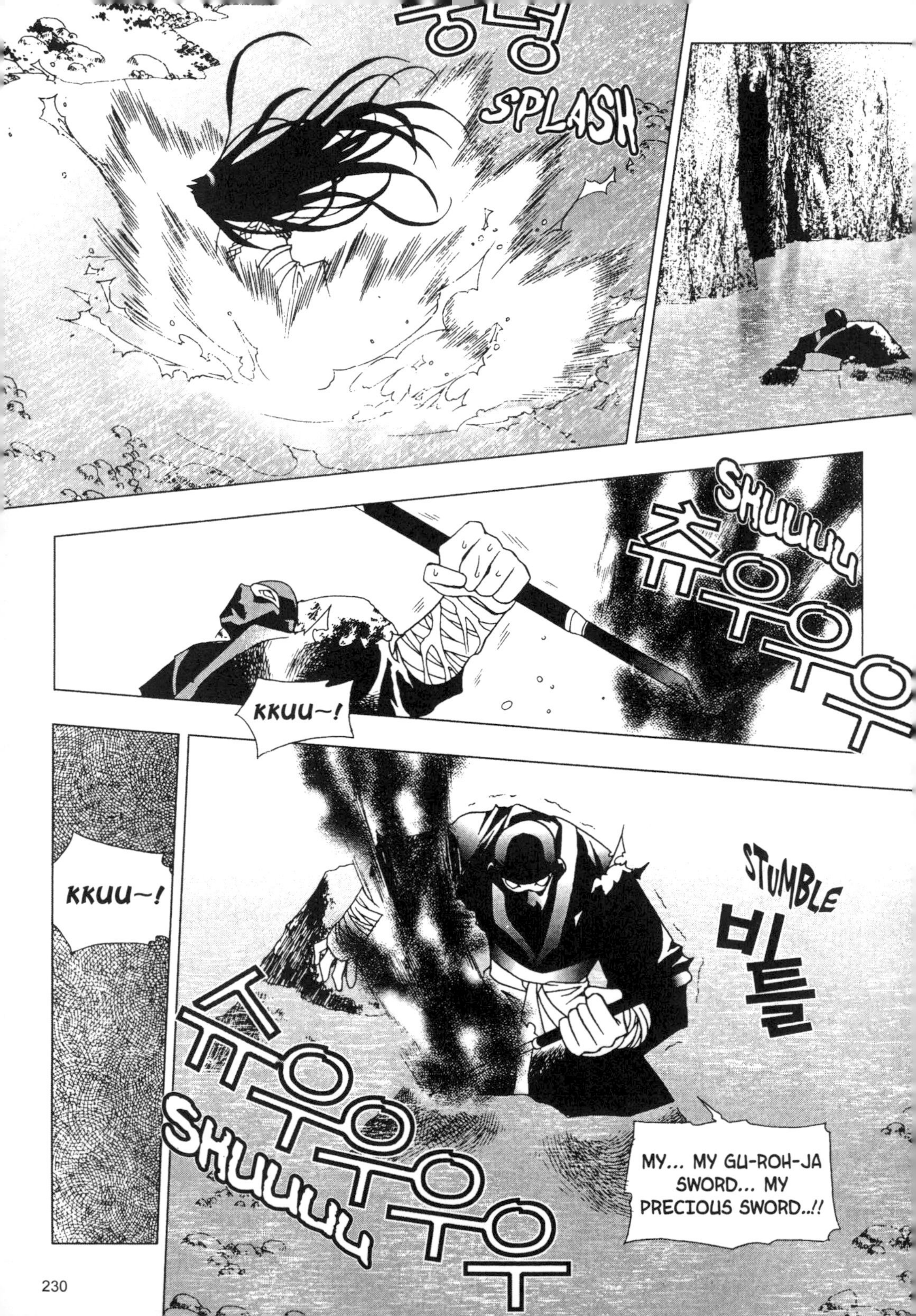
SPLASH
SHUUUU
KKUU~!
KKUU~!
STUMBLE
비틀
SHUUUU
MY... MY GU-ROH-JA SWORD... MY PRECIOUS SWORD..!!

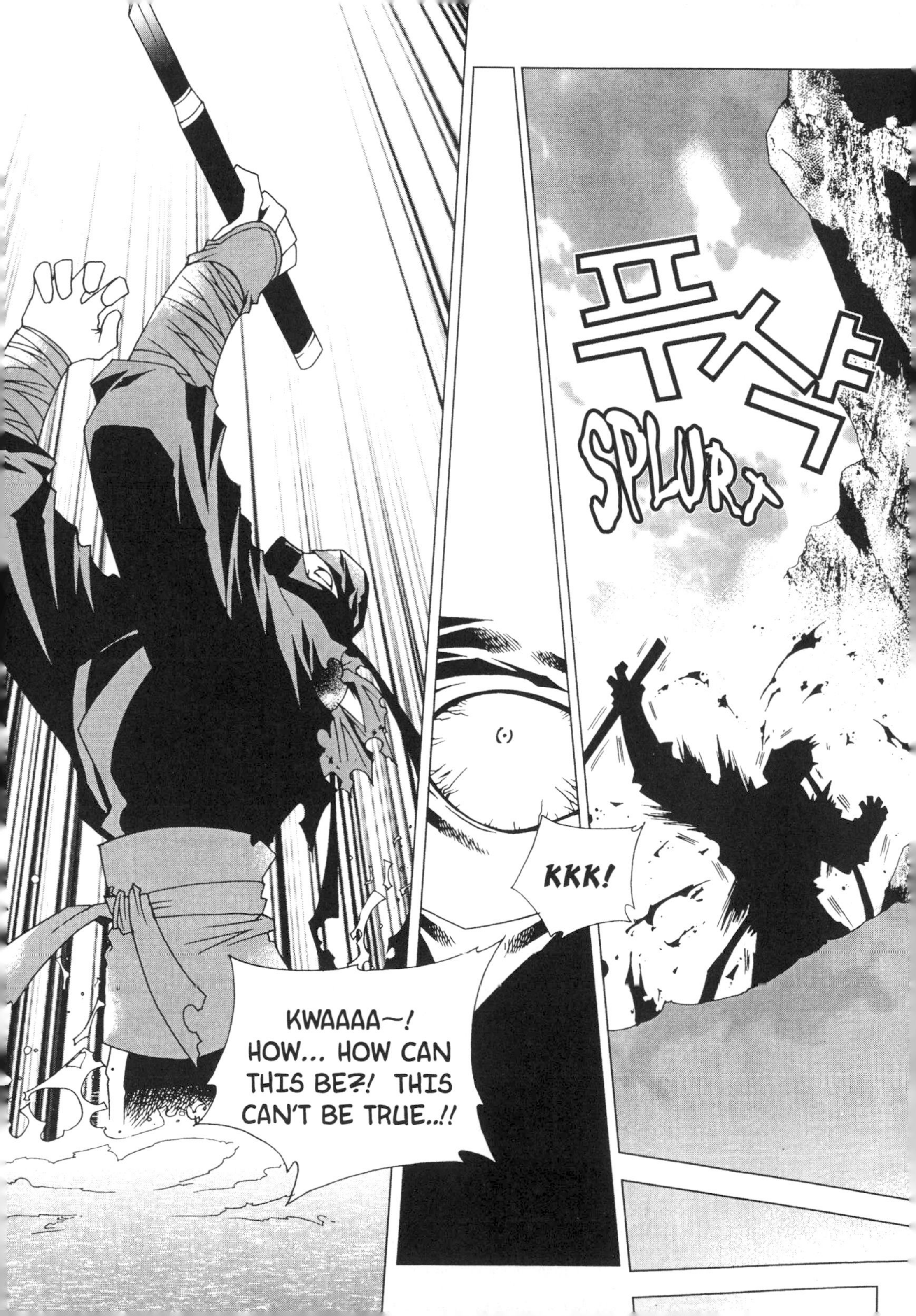

푸욱
SPLURT
KKK!
KWAAAA~! HOW... HOW CAN THIS BE?! THIS CAN'T BE TRUE..!!

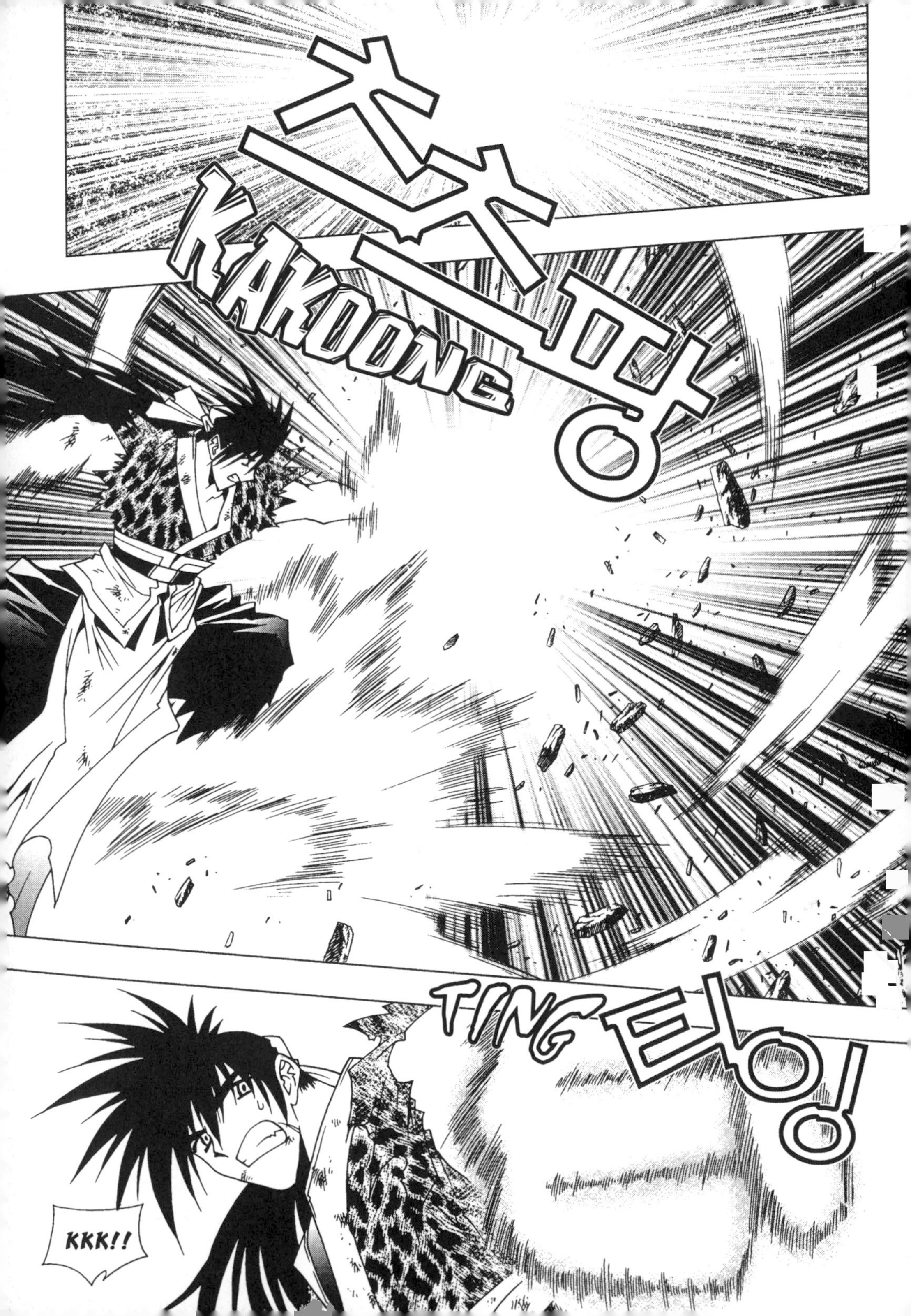

꽈
KAKOONG
땅
TING
팅
KKK!!

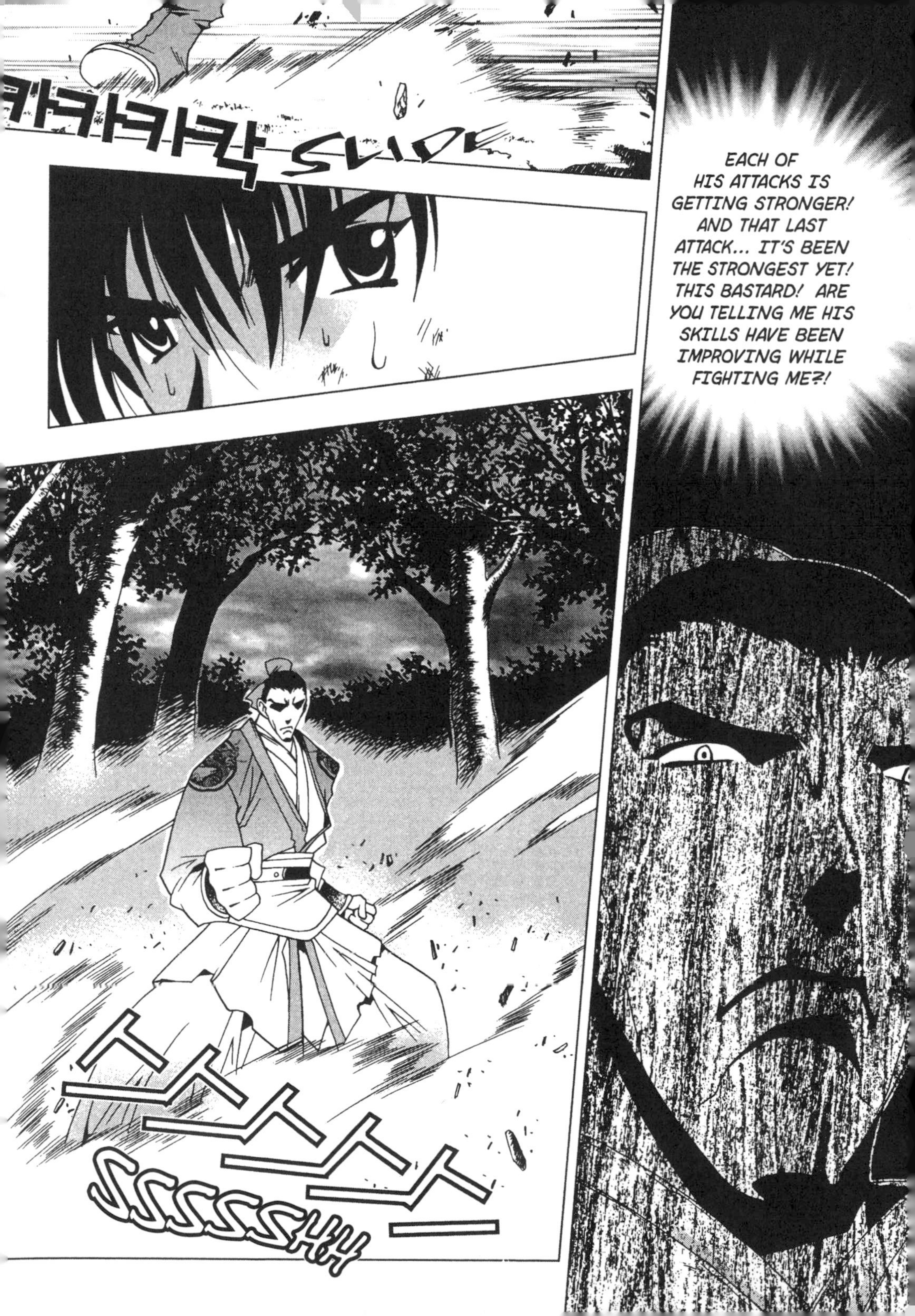
SLIDE
EACH OF HIS ATTACKS IS GETTING STRONGER! AND THAT LAST ATTACK... IT'S BEEN THE STRONGEST YET! THIS BASTARD! ARE YOU TELLING ME HIS SKILLS HAVE BEEN IMPROVING WHILE FIGHTING ME?!
SSSSSHH

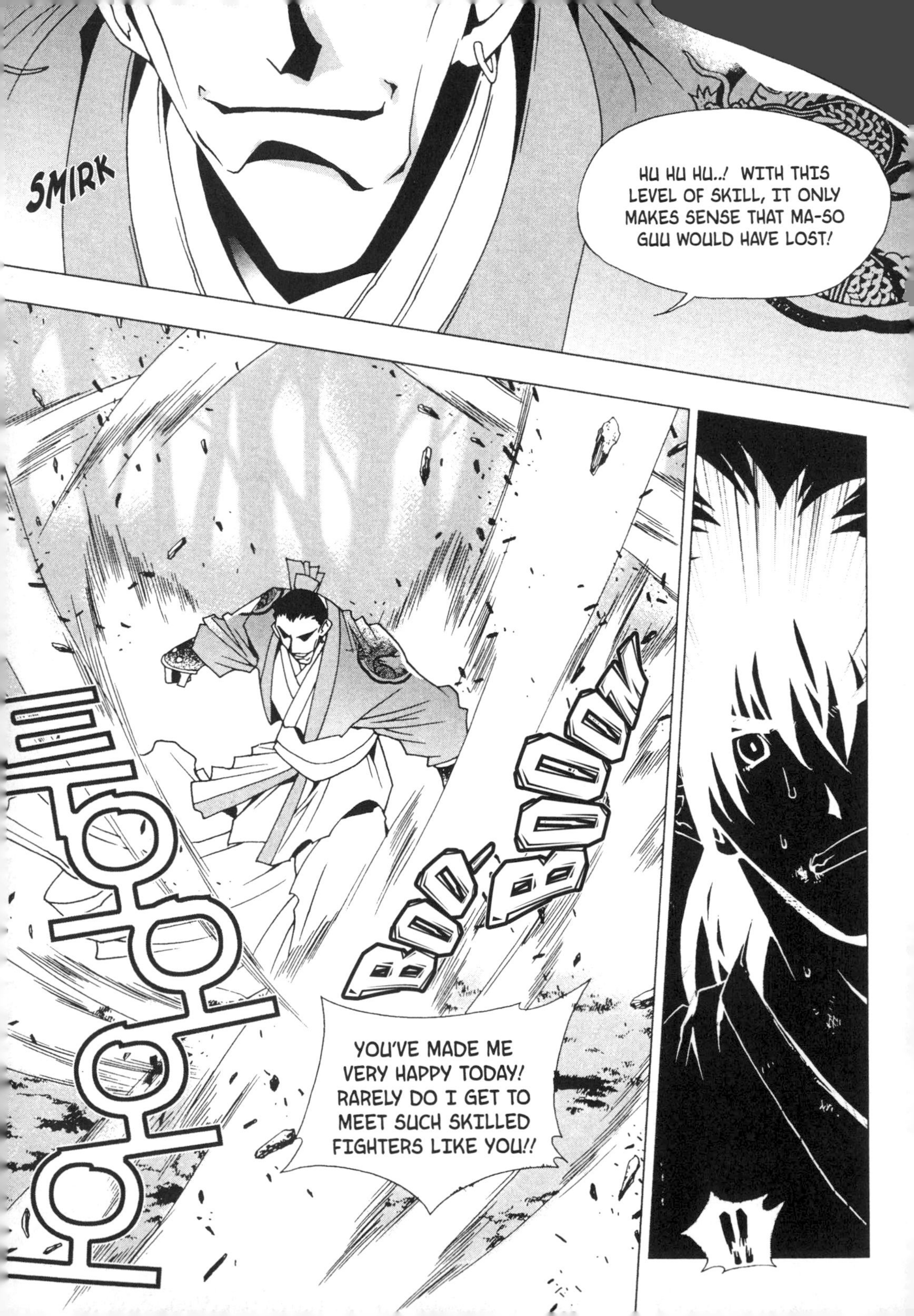
SMIRK
HU HU HU..! WITH THIS LEVEL OF SKILL, IT ONLY MAKES SENSE THAT MA-SO GUU WOULD HAVE LOST!
BOOOOOM
YOU'VE MADE ME VERY HAPPY TODAY! RARELY DO I GET TO MEET SUCH SKILLED FIGHTERS LIKE YOU!!
!!

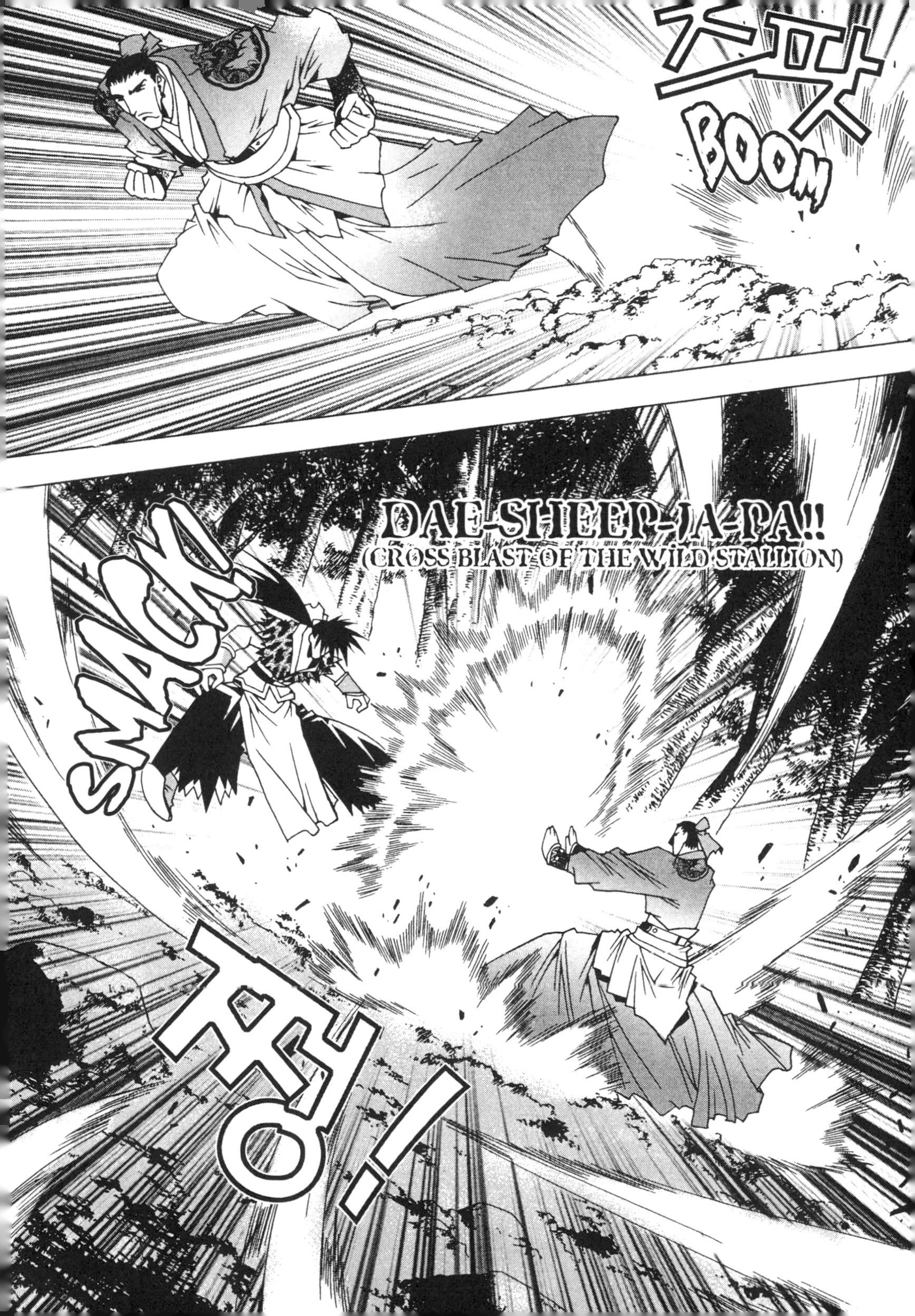
BOOM
DAE-SHEEP-JA-PA!!
(CROSS BLAST OF THE WILD STALLION)
SMACK!

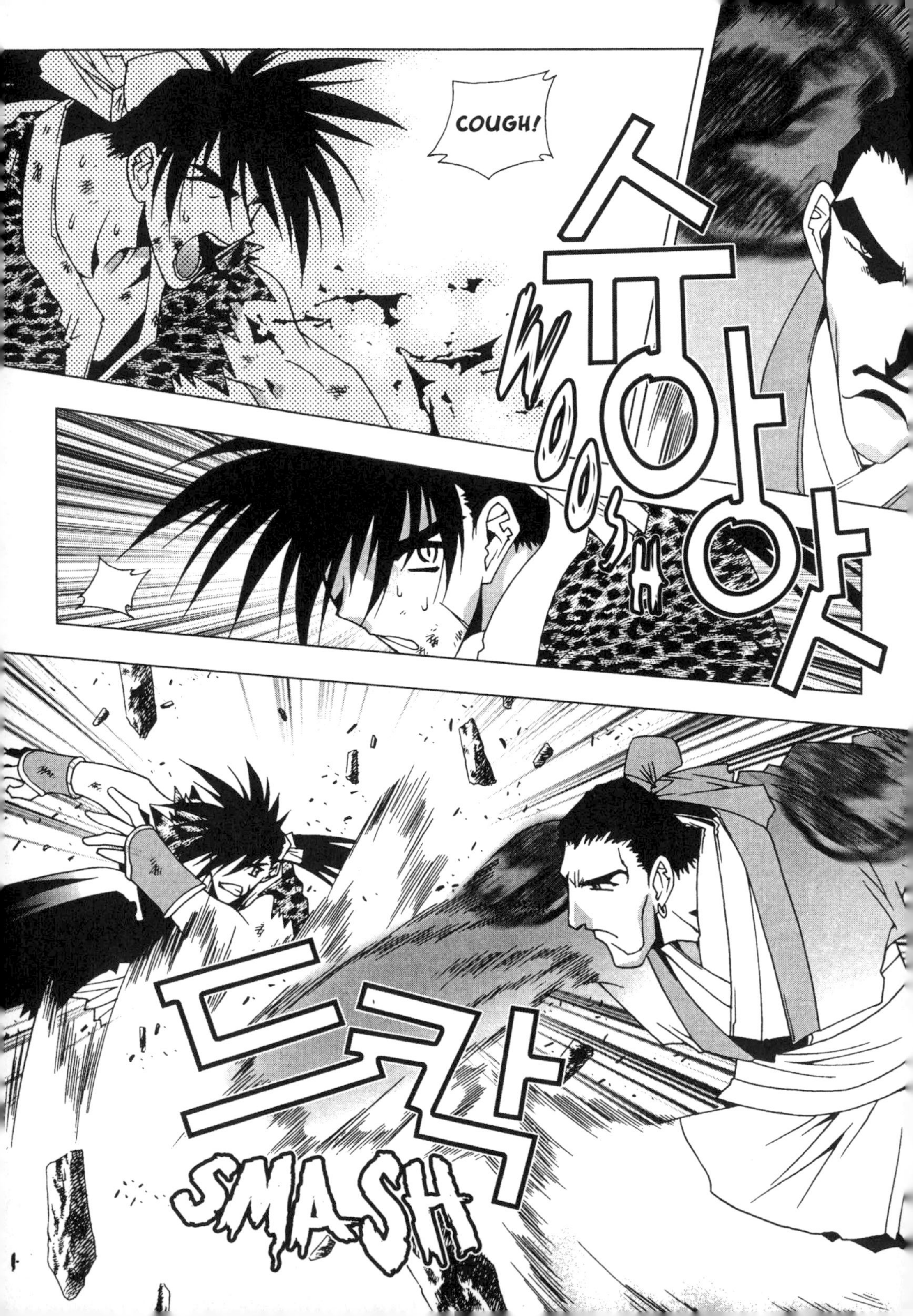
COUGH!
WOOOSH
SMASH

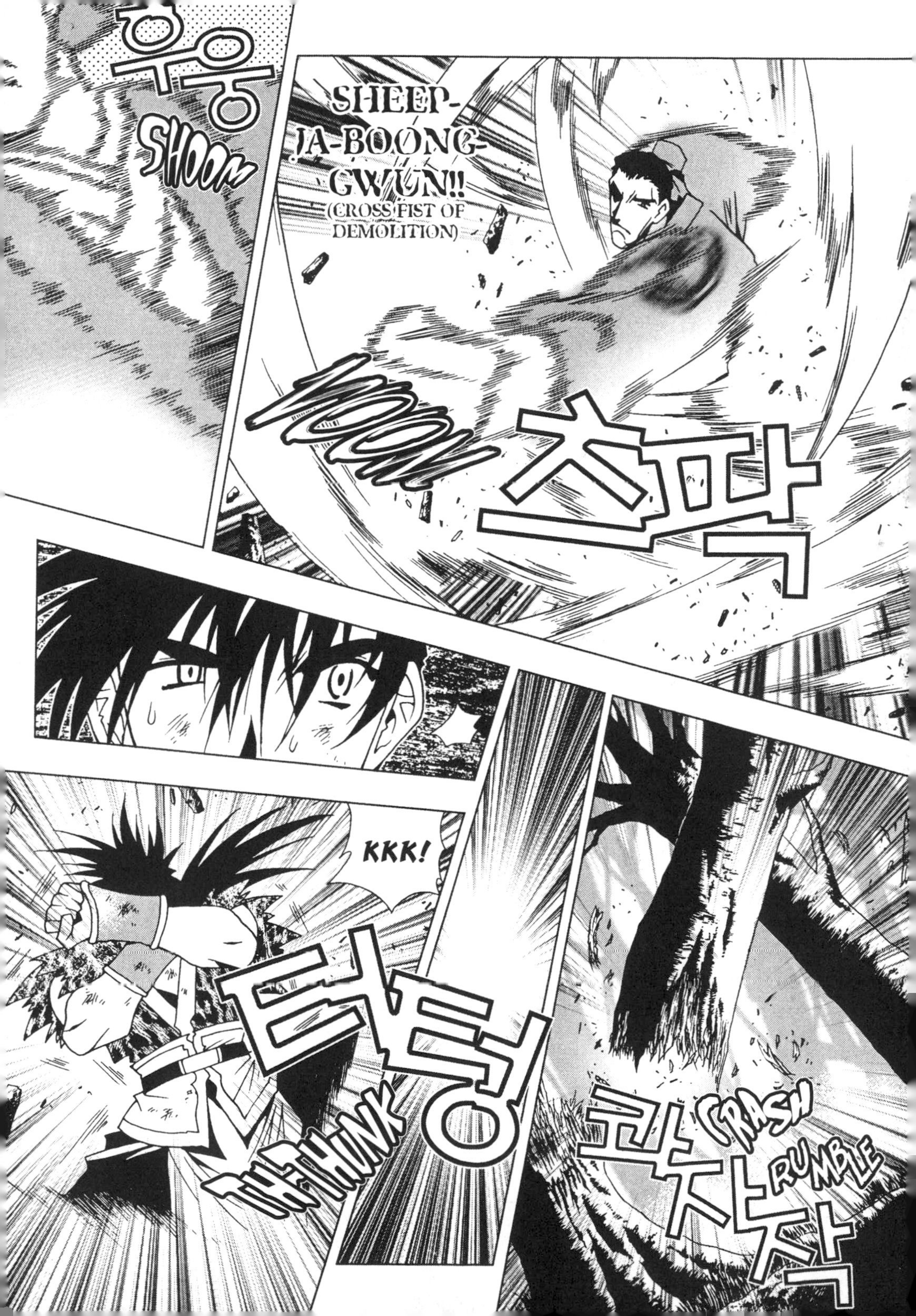

우웅
SHOOM
SHEEP-JA-BOONG-GWUN!!
(CROSS FIST OF DEMOLITION)
KKK!
CRASH
RUMBLE

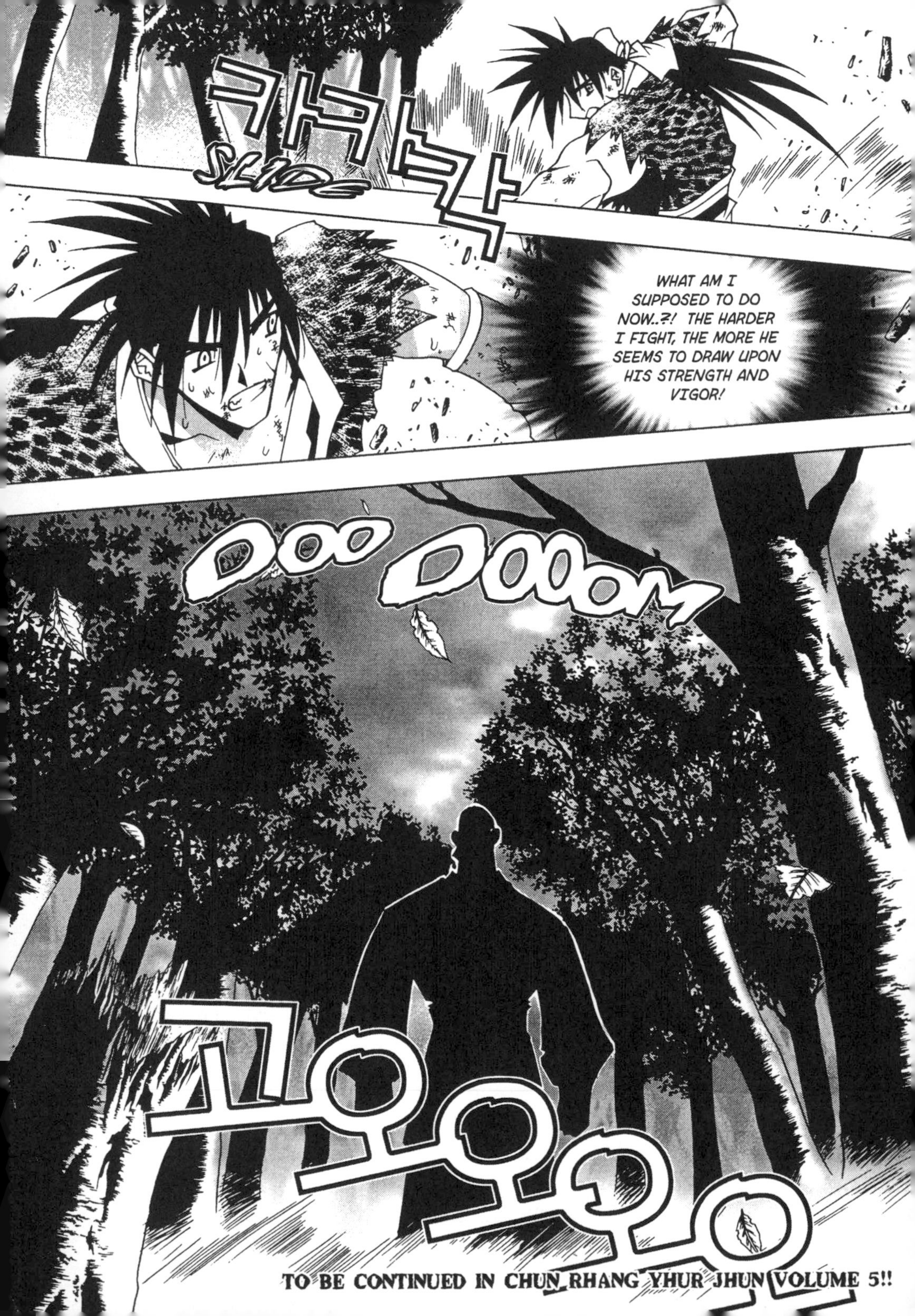

SLIDE
WHAT AM I SUPPOSED TO DO NOW..?! THE HARDER I FIGHT, THE MORE HE SEEMS TO DRAW UPON HIS STRENGTH AND VIGOR!
DOO DOOOOM
TO BE CONTINUED IN CHUN RHANG YHUR JHUN VOLUME 5!!

Translator Notes :

Disciple Rank Levels - Rank levels are more or less a determination of when a master took in a particular disciple. For example, 1st rank level disciples are merely an honorary title meaning that they were the first group of people to have been taken in by their master as disciples. While it doesn't correlate directly with skill level, the general idea is that a disciple who has been training longer under a master will be more skilled than disciples who were taken in later.

Desaja - O'Rang Yhun's 2nd eldest sah-hyung, Ghyur-Mahro, has the official title of "Desaja." While the literal meaning of that word is "Champion of Champions," it is also the title of a very high government position during the Goguryeo period of Korean history. During this time, there were between 7 and 10 highest level cabinet members directly under the king. The position of Desaja is within the highest ranks of this royal cabinet.

Assassins - It was common for assassins, spies, and soldiers laying an ambush to dress in all black. While they dressed very similar to Japanese ninjas, please do not mistake them for ninjas. In addition, while there were "specialists" who took up the assassin trade during this time period, Korea does not have an equivalent to ninjas. Assassins were mostly average soldiers or mercenaries who were highly skilled with weapons such as poisoned needles, throwing daggers, and disguises.

Name Etymology

Ha-Rhang Whur - Her name means "The cold beauty under the moon." In Asian mythology, the moon was a representation of feminine beauty as well as yin energy (whereas the sun represented masculinity and yang energy). Out of the numerous folktales involving the moon and beautiful maidens, the primary derivation of Ha-Rhang's name comes from the Chinese legend of Chang E. Cutting out a lot of the details, Chang E was a beautiful palace maiden residing in the Jade Emporer's palace within the heavens. She was sent to Earth as punishment for breaking a valuable porcelain jar. On Earth, the beautiful Chang E eventually marries a celebrated hero who later turns into a tyrant king. When he demands that Chang E use her celestial powers to create an elixir of immortality for him, she creates the elixir but doesn't hand it over to her husband. Instead, she drinks it herself and leaps off from the top of the King's palace. However, instead of falling to her death, she flies through the heavens and escapes to the moon where her immortal beauty lives on forever. The implication of this story to Ha-Rhang's name is that she's a "cold" and "emotionless" beauty. This explains why the swordstyle she uses (Chun San Shin Gum) requires her to be emotionless. In addition, it explains why the sword used by her gives off such a cold aura. On a side note, please note that there are several different variations of the Chang E legend. Some have a rather cynical ending for the beautiful Chang E, and in other versions, her husband is a woodcutter instead of a celebrated hero / king.

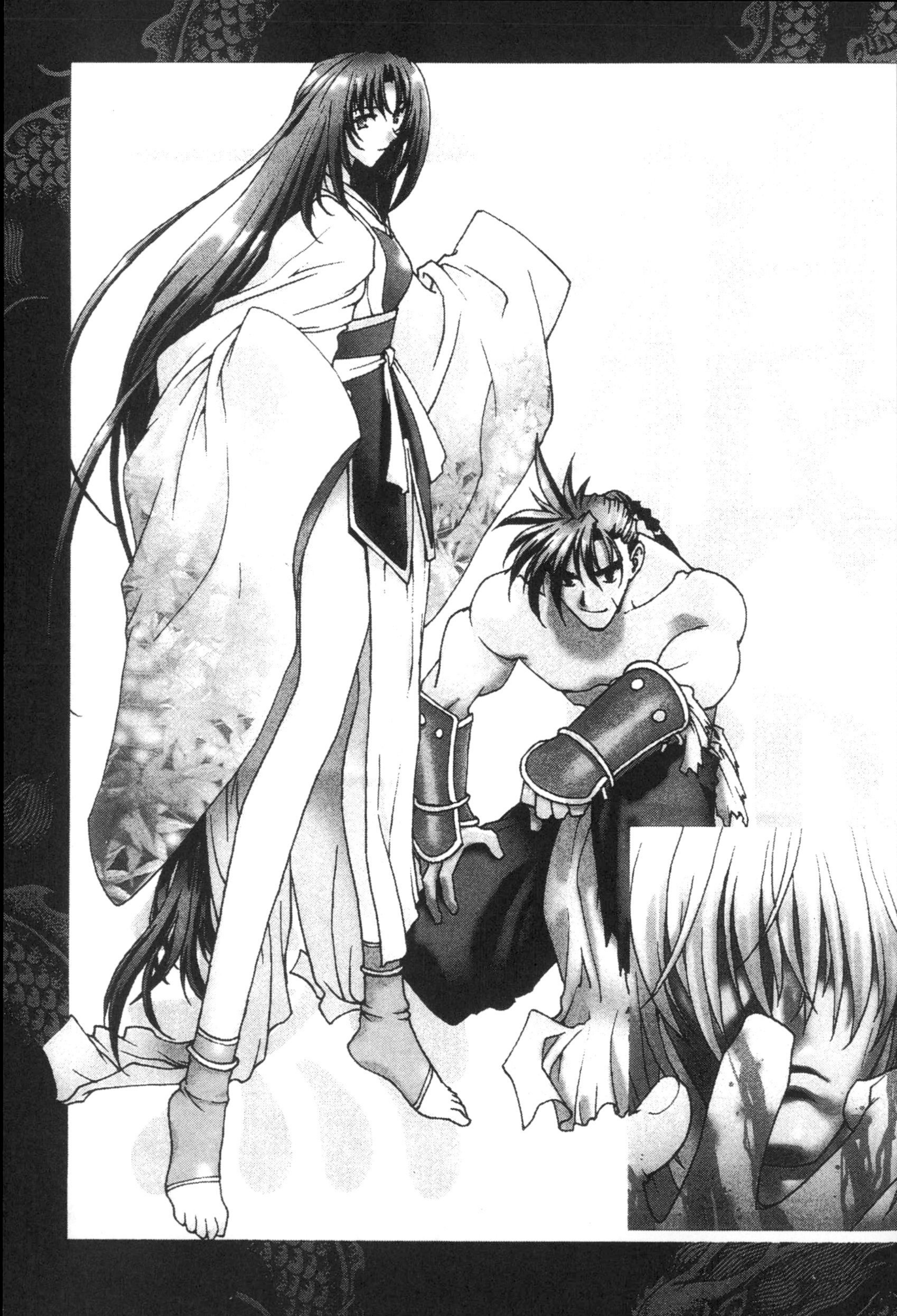

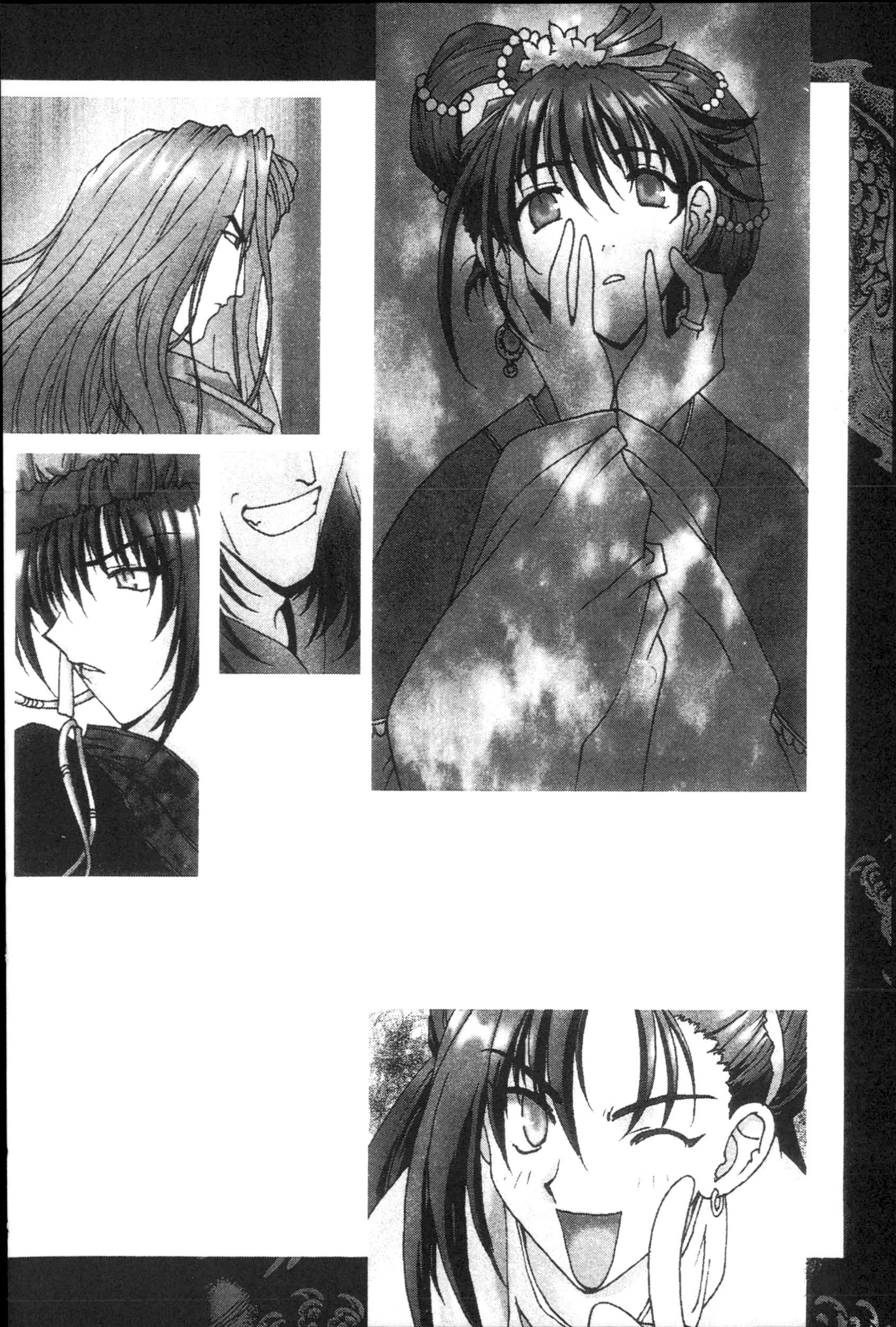

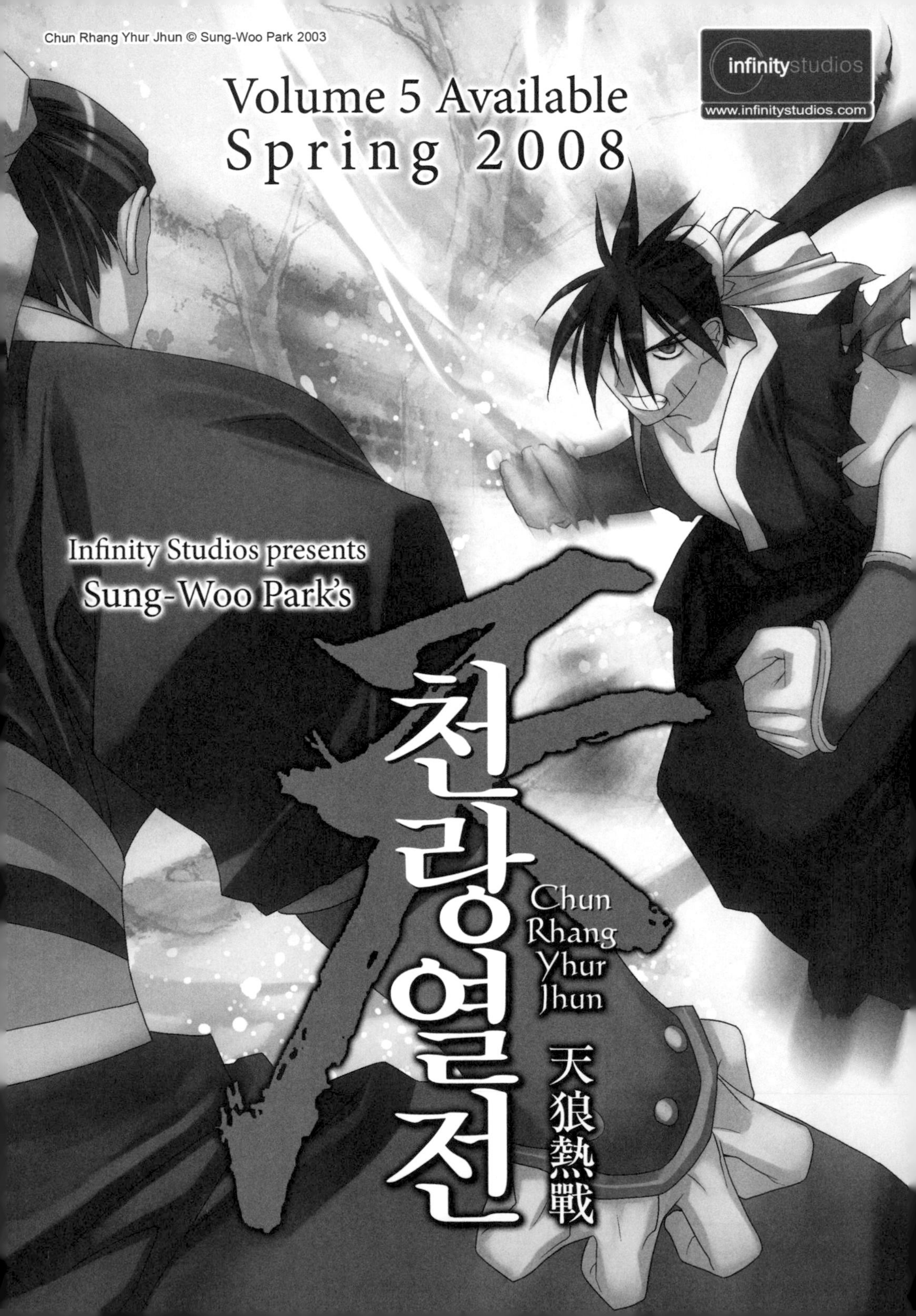
Chun Rhang Yhur Jhun © Sung-Woo Park 2003
infinitystudios
www.infinitystudios.com
Volume 5 Available
Spring 2008
Infinity Studios presents
Sung-Woo Park's
천랑열전
Chun
Rhang
Yhur
Jhun
天狼熱戰

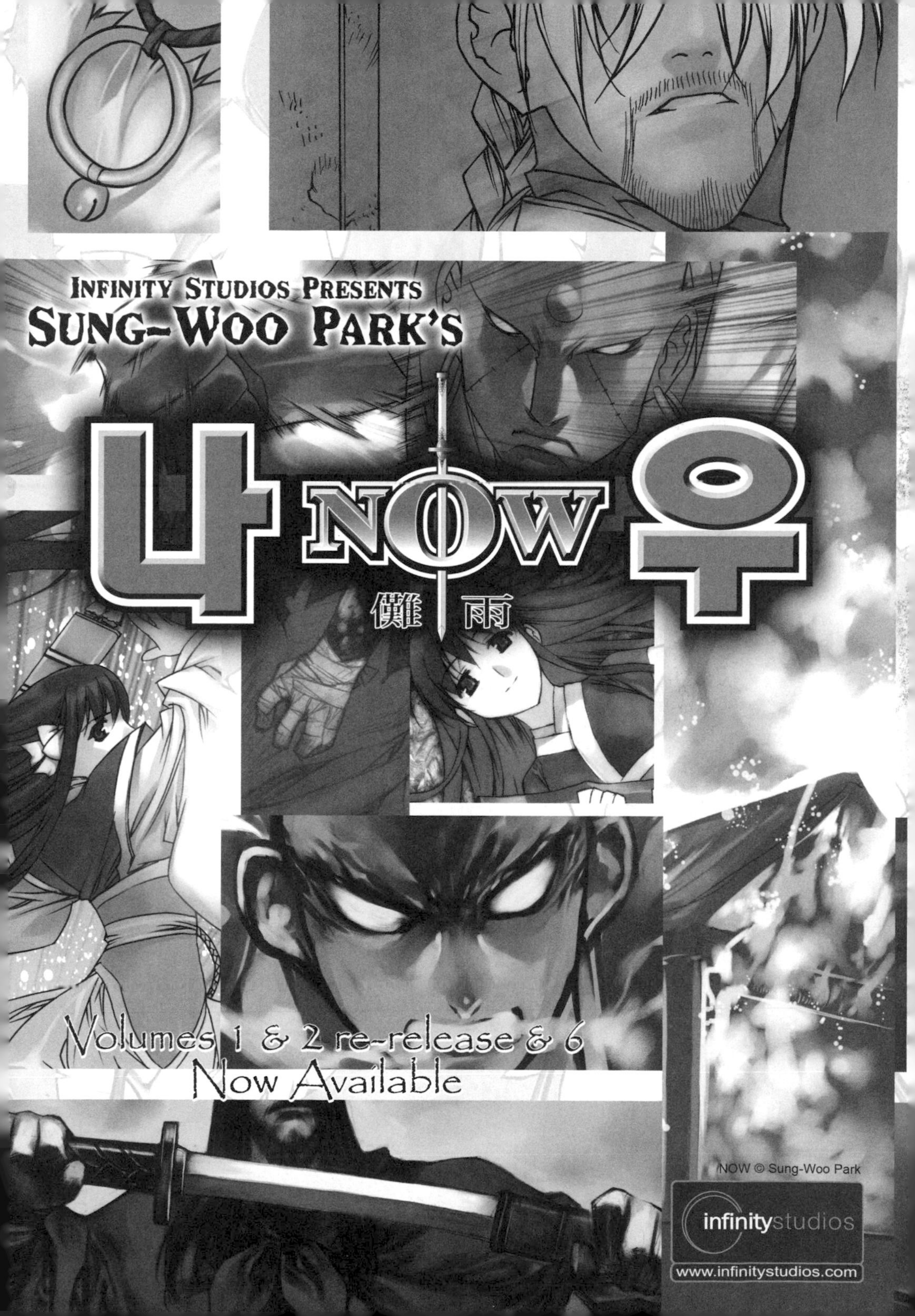

INFINITY STUDIOS PRESENTS
SUNG-WOO PARK'S
나 NOW 우
儺 雨
Volumes 1 & 2 re-release & 6
Now Available
NOW © Sung-Woo Park
infinitystudios
www.infinitystudios.com

Art : Sung-Woo Park
Story : Dall-Young Lim

ZERO
THE BEGINNING OF THE COFFIN

Volumes 1~3
Now Available

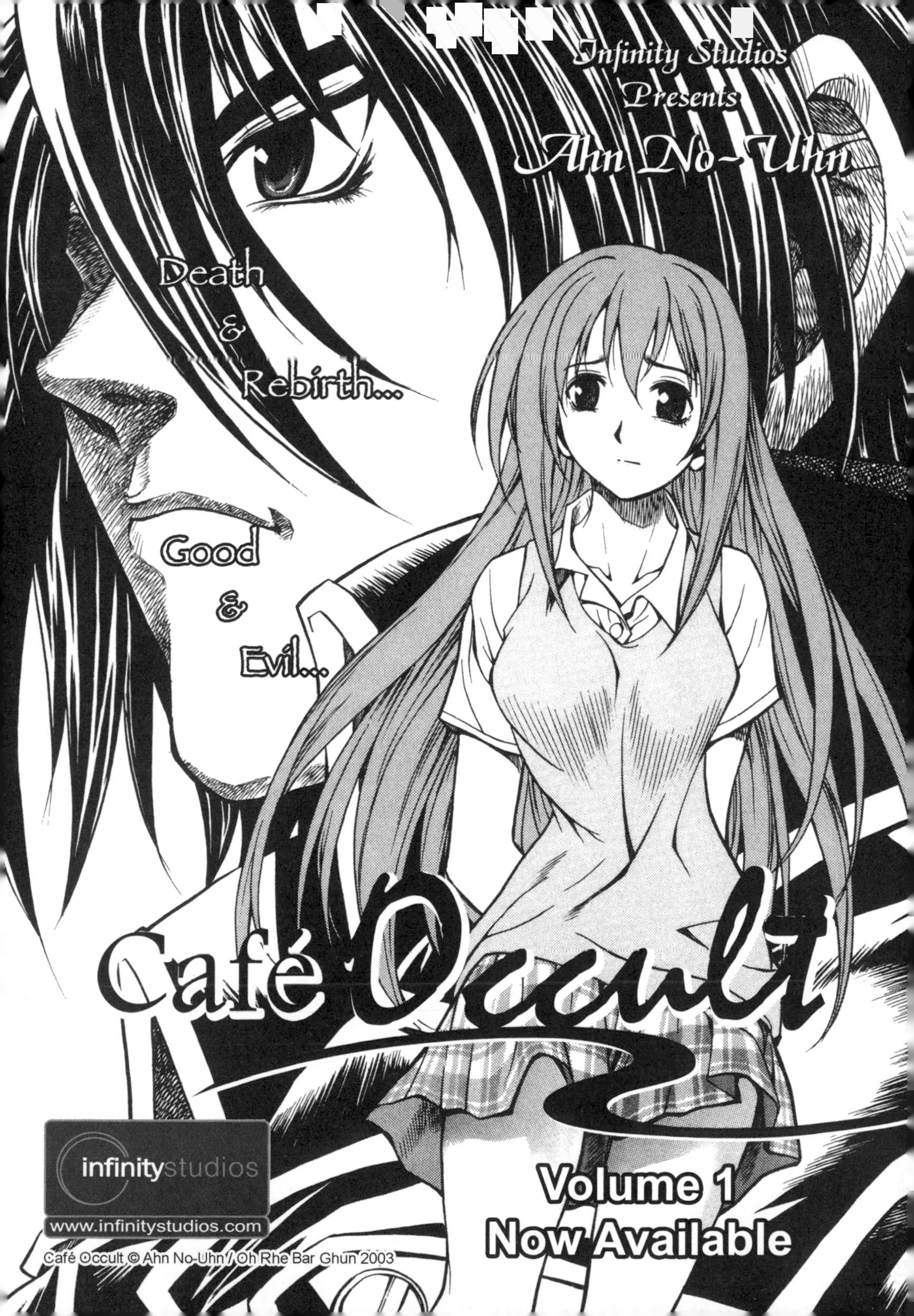

Infinity Studios
Presents
Ahn No-Uhn
Death
&
Rebirth...
Good
&
Evil...
Café Occult
infinitystudios
www.infinitystudios.com
Volume 1
Now Available
Café Occult © Ahn No-Uhn / Oh Rhe Bar Ghun 2003

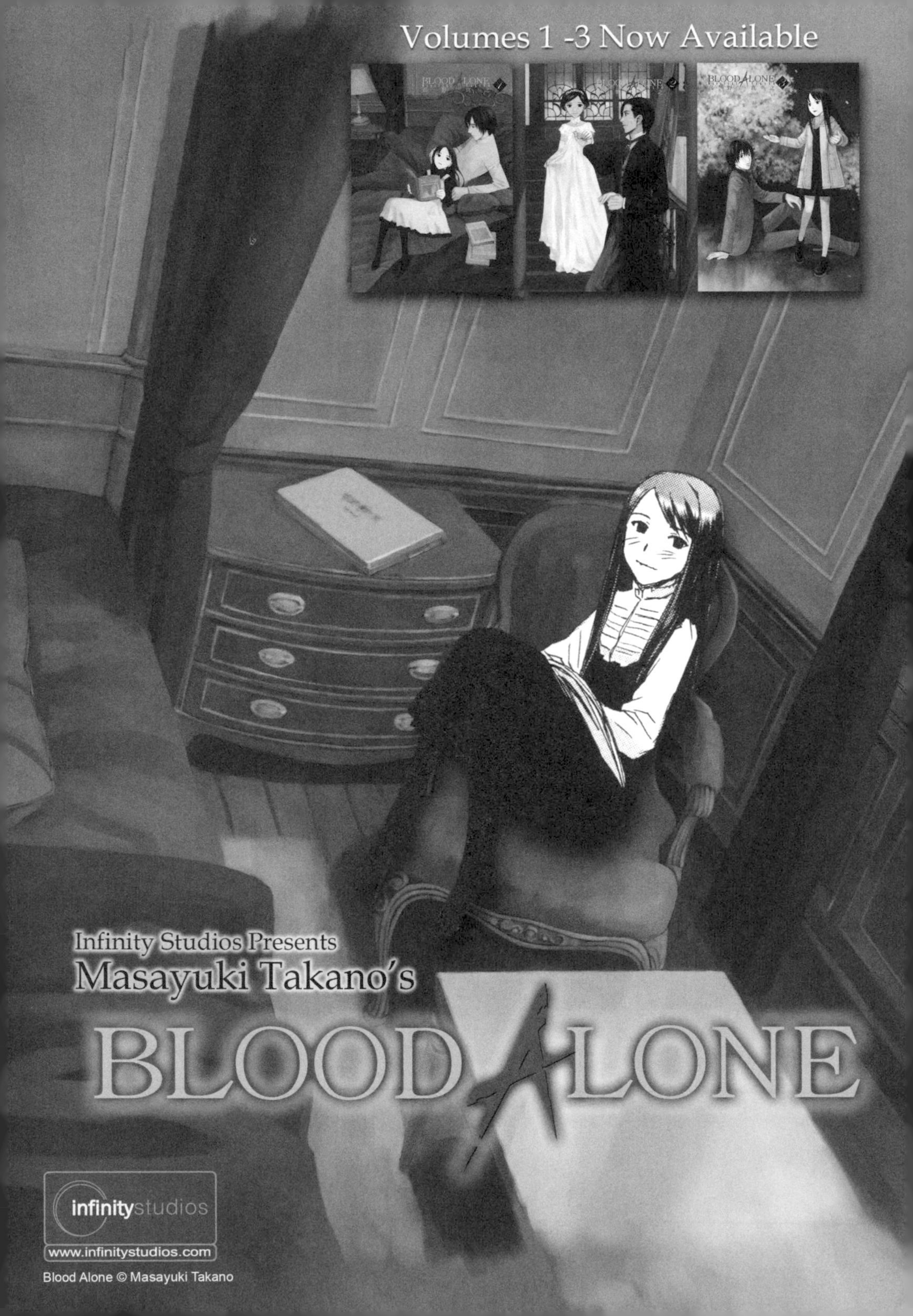

Volumes 1 -3 Now Available
Infinity Studios Presents
Masayuki Takano's
BLOOD ALONE
infinitystudios
www.infinitystudios.com
Blood Alone © Masayuki Takano

O'Rhang Yhun

The third and youngest disciple of a famous warrior who has developed a new form of martial arts called Sa Shin Mu. He has come to China in search of his oldest sa-hyung.

Ha-Rhang Whur

A mysterious young woman who is the lone disciple of the legendary Lady Chun-San-Gum-Nya (Swordswoman of Mt Heaven)

Ghyur-Mahro

He is the 2nd disciple of O'Rhang Yhun's master. But instead of teaching him Sa Shin Mu, their master had taught him Bi Hong Gum Soor, a powerful sword style.

Yu-Hwa

Daughter of Goguryeo's supreme commanding general, she travels to China in search of O'Rhang Yhun with Ghyur-Mahro who acts as her bodyguard.

Dahn-Ryoung

After her bothers were murdered, she joined O'Rhang's party to get revenge for her brothers' deaths. She's currently travelling with Yu-Hwa after being separated from O'Rhang's party.

천랑열전
天狼熱戰
Chun Rhang Yhun Jhun

Chun-Mu Goom

He is the eldest disciple of one of the largest and most respected clans in China. He is currently assigned to gathering intelligence on Chung-Sue-Moon.

The story so far...

After an intense battle with 2 of the Mu-Rhim-O-Sung, both O'Rhang and Ha-Rhang were seriously injured. And if it wasn't for the intervention of a mysterious old man, they may not have survived the battle. The old man turned out to be a martial arts master who once had traveled with both O-Rhang and Ha-Rhang's masters.

Juhk-Woon

Unlike his sa-hyung, Chun-Mu Goom, he is short tempered and fairly hot headed. He was disowned from his clan after seeking revenge for the slaughtering of his family.

Meanwhile, So-Gwong Bi was sent out to investigate the death of his fellow comrads only to run into Yu-Hwa and Dahn-Ryoung who were still searching for O'Rhang. And in the battle with Ghyur-Mahro, So-Gwong is not only easily defeated, he also learns that his master, Jung-Woong Suk, has somehow learned Sa Shin Mu techniques and called them his own.

So-Gwong Bi

An ambitious young man who is a member of the Mu-Rhim-O-Sung. He's ruthless and will do anything to achieve his goals.

Upon recovering from his wounds, O'Rhang has a chance encounter with Jung-Woong Suk.

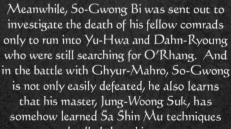

Jung-Woong Suk

He is the leader of one of China's largest and most famous clans known as Chung-Sue-Moon (The Gates of Blue Water). While he appears to be composed and respectable, he's actually a cruel villain.

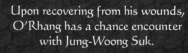

Pa Goon Sung

He is the 1st and eldest disciple of O'Rhang Yhun's master. While on a training journey to China, he went missing. Rumor has it that he went berserk and he ended up murdering hundreds of people.

천랑열전
Chun Rhang Yhur Jhun
天狼熱戰

Translator : Je-Wa Jeong
Editor : Je-Wa Jeong / Miho Koto / Soung Lee / Kentaro Abe
Layout : Kentaro Abe
Touch-Up Artist : Miho Koto
Art Director : Soung Lee
Licensing : Masayoshi Kojima
Vice President : Steve Chung
C.E.O. : Jay Chung

This translated edition is published
by arrangement with Seoul Cultural Publishers, Inc.
through Shinwon Agency Co. in Korea

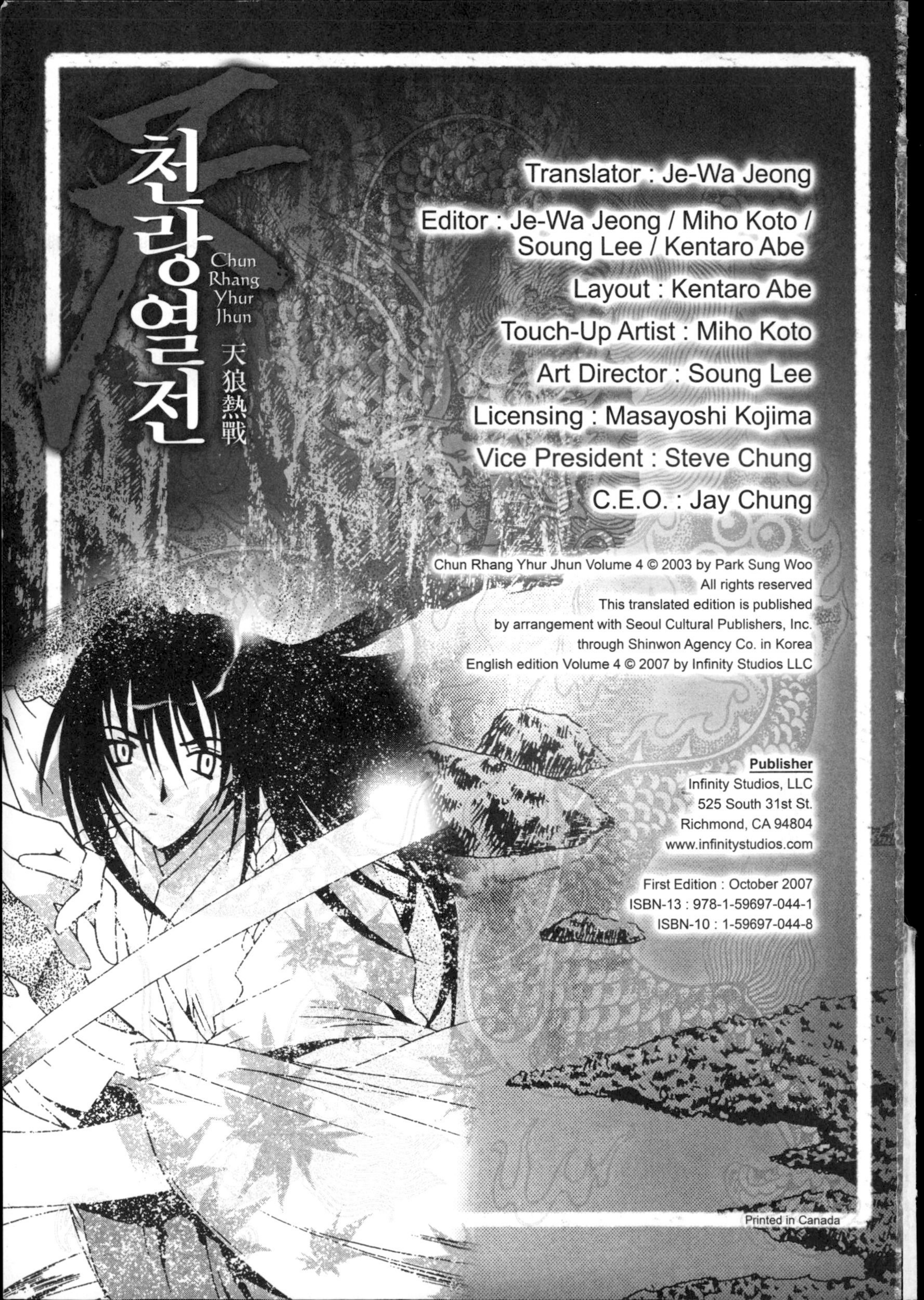

Publisher
Infinity Studios, LLC
525 South 31st St.
Richmond, CA 94804
www.infinitystudios.com

First Edition : October 2007
ISBN-13 : 978-1-59697-044-1
ISBN-10 : 1-59697-044-8

Printed in Canada